P9-APW-989

It's a Crime

It's a Crime

Women and Justice

Second Edition

❖

ROSLYN MURASKIN
Long Island University

Prentice Hall
Upper Saddle River, NJ 07458

177914

Library of Congress Cataloging-in-Publication Data

It's a crime : women and justice / [edited by] Roslyn Muraskin. -- 2nd
  ed.
      p.   cm.
  Includes bibliographical references.
  ISBN 0-13-011389-1
  1. Female offenders--United States. 2. Women criminal justice
personnel--United States.   I. Muraskin, Roslyn.
  HV6046.I86 2000
  364.3'74'0973--dc21

99-26309
CIP

Acquisitions Editor: *Neil Marquardt*
Editorial Assistant: *Susan Kegler*
Editorial/Production Supervision,
  Interior Design, and Electronic Paging: *Naomi Sysak*
Cover Art: *Jane Sterrett*
Cover Design: *Wanda España*
Manufacturing Buyer: *Ed O'Dougherty*
Managing Editor: *Mary Carnis*
Marketing Manager: *Shannon Simonsen*
Director of Production: *Bruce Johnson*

©2000 by Prentice-Hall, Inc.
Upper Saddle River, New Jersey 07458

All rights reserved. No part of this book may be
reproduced, in any form or by any means,
without permission in writing from the publisher.

Printed in the United States of America

10 9 8 7 6 5 4 3 2 1

ISBN 0-13-011389-1

Prentice-Hall International (UK) Limited, *London*
Prentice-Hall of Australia Pty. Limited, *Sydney*
Prentice-Hall Canada Inc., *Toronto*
Prentice-Hall Hispanoamericana, S.A., *Mexico*
Prentice-Hall of India Private Limited, *New Delhi*
Prentice-Hall of Japan, Inc., *Tokyo*
Simon & Schuster Asia Pte. Ltd., *Singapore*
Editora Prentice-Hall do Brasil, Ltda., *Rio de Janeiro*

Dedication

Dedicated to the memory of my grandmother,
Henrietta Kroll, a woman before her time,
and to my daughter, Tracy, a woman of our time.

—Roslyn Muraskin

Contents

❖

177914

Foreword

The era of modern scholarship may be assumed to coincide with the existence of universities. The first of these was the University of Bologna, a daughter of the Renaissance, founded in 1119. Eight hundred and seventy-nine years have passed since then, and during most of these years, scholarship produced no insight whatsoever on any aspect of the role of women in crime and justice. It was less than a century ago that the first scholarly book on female offenders appeared: Cesare Lombroso's *La Donna Delinquente* (1893). The following half-century produced only three additional works on the topic: W. I. Thomas's *Unadjusted Girl* (1923), Sheldon and Eleanor Glueck's *Five Hundred Delinquent Women* (1934), and Otto Pollack's *Criminality of Women* (1952). By contrast, over the last generation we have witnessed a flowering of interest, of concern, and of dedicated scholarship focused on women as offenders, as victims, as justice officials, and as change agents. The books, essays, and dissertations on this topic, in many languages, and for many cultures, number in the thousands.

Rita Simon and I did not anticipate this avalanche of interest and response when, in 1975, we independently sought to make a contribution to criminological scholarship focused on what we perceived to be a subject that was consciously or unconsciously suppressed. Since then, the subject of women in crime and justice has undergone a rapid and significant metamorphosis. Initially, much of what was written on women in crime—and later, in criminal justice—was viewed by some as subjective. Indeed, it had to be anticipated that the abuses and discrimination uncovered by scholars in the field would cause the disapproval and condemnation of those who learned of them. Thus the literature of the 1970s reflected a fervor born out of frustration over apparent or perceived biases and neglect in the system. In this sense, all scholars are conditioned by the *Zeitgeist* of their era. Indeed, was not Lombroso a captive of the prejudices of his time, as much as he wanted to escape them by addressing a subject that had been taboo until then?

It was not until the 1980s that the subject of women and justice became a recognized area of concern in the increasing body of empirical research dealing with contemporary problems. Questions for researchers rose faster than they could be answered. How does current female criminality relate to historical stereotypes, to the present criminal justice system, and to future patterns of behavior? What are the effects of economic marginalization? How does the criminal justice system discriminate against women offenders, victims, and functionaries? What accounts for the differential treatment of male and female delinquents? Empirical research flourished. So, also, did feminist theoretical explanations.

At the American Society of Criminology meeting in 1975 (Toronto, Canada), one lone panel represented women and justice. Through the 1980s the number of papers presented grew above all expectation. At major scientific meetings convened in all parts of the world, women's issues were debated—and manuscripts began to make their way into major journals. By now the subject was fully "arrived."

The history of this book well demonstrates the evolution of scholarship on the role of women in crime and justice. The first edition was startling in its portrayal of the breadth and depth of research. But now, six years later, research on women in crime and justice has expanded beyond expectations. The developments, in fact, have been so vast that the second edition of *It's a Crime: Women and Justice* is, in fact, a new book, reflective of the advances of just a few years of scholarship within this ever-broadening field. At the same time, it must be noted with some concern that the scholars in the field still express considerable frustration with the lack of impact of their labors on the criminal justice system and its processes. That alone justifies this new book as it challenges the system itself.

Indeed, with this second edition, Roslyn Muraskin has developed a new book on women in crime and justice that is entirely novel, challenging, and scholarly. It comes at a time when nearly every university or college offers, or even mandates, courses on women's issues, including those on crime and justice. This volume brings into the classroom an exciting, new-era assembly of contributions by some of the country's most respected researchers in the field. I anticipate that the readers will derive as much pleasure and insight from the twenty-nine creative contributions as I have. This book is bound to find an honored place in the scholarly literature on the role of women in crime and criminal justice. May this book advance us all on the road to achieving an approach to crime and justice that is based on justice rather than bias in the third millennium.

Freda Adler
Distinguished Professor
Rutgers University

Preface

It's a Crime: Women and Justice (second edition) continues to be a comprehensive text with readings on the subject of women and their involvement in the criminal justice system. This new work takes us from the "Historical Development of Women's Issues," to our "Legal System," to "Women, Drugs, and AIDS," to a discussion of "Women in Prison," "Women: Victims of Violence," to rights of privacy as they affect the issue of "Abortion," to issues that deal with "Women and Policing," then to "Women and Crime," and finally to "Girls and Delinquency." This work provides a means of studying and integrating the diversity of perspectives that exist in this very contemporary and provocative field of study. The focus of this second edition is on gender-based differences related to law and justice.

The potential for progress in the realm of women's issues and the criminal justice system is possible because of the continuous battles that women have continued to fight in striving for something called equality or parity of treatment. The history of women indicates that sex should not be a factor in determining the legal rights of women and men, but it has been. Dating back to 1776, when this country was being formed and the laws were being written by *men*, it was Abigail Adams, in a letter to her husband, John, who insisted that if in the new American Constitution, "care and attention are not paid to the ladies," they will foment a rebellion. Women have been fomenting that rebellion ever since. The reader will find that although the struggle is not over, women have a voice and are being heard.

In this work we talk about slave women, women on the bench, affirmative action, disparate treatment by the legal system, sexual harassment, women and their use/abuse of drugs and the HIV factor, women in prison and their disparate treatment, their gains and losses, women as continued victims of violence, rights of privacy, women in policing, women being trained for careers in organized crime, as well as women who are serial killers. And finally, we deal with the very young, juvenile women who turn to crime.

The chapters that follow are written by scholars and practitioners in the field. This second edition, as the first edition, deals with issues pertaining to women as well as those basic rights that are believed fundamental to all of us. The material and topics as presented provide the most up-to-date and relevant materials concerning the gender-based problems we face in society as we move into the twenty-first century.

In the words of the late Ted Alleman (with whom I worked on the first edition of this book), "[t]hose who see the world entirely from a man's perspective and are simply blind to the existence and influence of women are said to be androcentric in their thinking." Traditional literature ignores the role of women. There are those who will deprecate and/or ignore a woman's point of view entirely. For women public denigration is not to be socially acceptable. Personal attacks should be a thing of the past.

It is my fervent hope that this work will result in more meaningful and thought-provoking dialogue concerning the important problems we face regarding women and justice. It's a crime if we do not realize the importance of the role that women play. Basic human rights are fundamental to all, women and men alike. The raw material is presented—hopefully, you will make it come alive.

Roslyn Muraskin

Acknowledgments

I wish to thank all the contributors to this second edition of *It's a Crime: Women and Justice*—indeed a work of love. All of the contributors have written in their areas of expertise demonstrating the struggles of women within the criminal justice system. There is so much more to do, yet together we will endure.

Special thanks to Neil Marquardt of Prentice Hall for all his encouragement and help in putting together this second edition. Thanks also to my university, Long Island University, C.W. Post Campus, for their encouragement to work on research projects such as this.

And a BIG THANK YOU to my loving husband, Matthew, who understood my need to get this project done.

Roslyn Muraskin

It's a Crime

Women and Justice

Roslyn Muraskin

Justice means fairness. No one can make you feel inferior without your consent. This is a work about women and issues of justice that have faced them over time. As written, this work brings to the reader a clear understanding of the issues that affect women today.

There exists a continuing debate among feminist legal scholars about whether equality under the law is good for women. Do we push for continued equalization and champion equal rights for women and oppose legislation that treats women and men differently? Does equality with men hurt women, or is it the only way to guarantee that women will be considered as equal partners?

Are women and men the same, thereby requiring equal treatment? Or do we recognize the "special" needs of women and treat each gender differently? What does it mean to be equal? Do we mean that women have to be like men in order to gain equal rights? Is parity enough?

This book introduces us to the issues of equality, or lack of it, between the sexes. Women and men may not be the same, but both are entitled to equal justice (fairness) under the law. Both deserve equal protection of the law as well as enjoyment and protection of their constitutional rights.

This book is divided into ten sections, each introduced to generate thought and spark debate. Although women's issues infuse every aspect of social and political thought, in this book the focus is in the areas of crime and criminal justice because our basic human rights in society are inextricably linked to our treatment by and our participation in the criminal justice system.

Historically, women have not enjoyed equal protection under the law as afforded by the Fourteenth Amendment to the Constitution. Nor have they enjoyed many of those rights fully enunciated in the Bill of Rights. We speak of the twenty-first century, yet we are still concerned with the treatment of women by the criminal justice system. There is no automatic way to allow both sexes to enjoy equal protection under the law unless there is a commitment to the elimination of all sexual discrimination, something that we have been striving for since the early beginnings of this country.

Gender has never been declared a "suspect classification" under the law, although we have come close. As pointed out by Justice Brennan in *Frontiero v. Richardson* (1973):

Traditionally, [sex] discrimination was rationalized by an attitude of romantic paternalism which in practical effect put women not on a pedestal, but in a cage.

Or as pointed by Justice Miller in *Bradwell v. Illinois* (1872):

Man is or should be, women's protector and defender. The natural and proper timidity and delicacy which belongs to the female sex evidently unfits it for many of the occupations of civil life.

The paramount destiny and mission of woman are to fulfill the noble and benign offices of wife and mother. This is the law of the Creator.

Women have yet to achieve all they want. They still struggle. They are still victimized by our criminal justice system. They are still discriminated against and they are still harassed.

Theoretically, the law has attempted to end discrimination. What has not ended is the practice of discrimination. Discrepancy of treatment based on sex is what is under discussion in this book. The criminal justice system is a microcosm of the turbulence in society as a whole. Thus, a study of women's issues as they operate in the criminal justice system can provide a solid basis from which to explore ourselves and the society of which we are a part.

In the words of Dr. Martin Luther King, Jr.:

we ain't what we oughta be,
we ain't what we wanta be,
we ain't what we gonna be,
but Thank God we ain't what we was.

Adjustment to the world in which we live may not be as easy as we presume, but it is something that all women and men must do. Enjoy this work.

C A S E S

Bradwell v. Illinois, 83 U.S. 130 (1872).
Frontiero v. Richardson, 411 U.S. 677 (1973).

SECTION I

Historical Development of Women's Issues

The study of history is important because it discloses the underlying pulse of existence. To demonstrate regularity in social affairs is to uncover the fundamental structure of society. The study of history and its treatment of women reveals a long chain of events that binds generation after generation of women to the control of men.

That women have historically been discriminated against by law is a fact. In the United States no constitutional obligation exists for all persons to be treated alike. In the opening chapter of this section, Roslyn Muraskin traces the history of litigation and its connection to patriarchal control. She succinctly states that "women have historically been victimized by policies designed to protect them." A study of women's inequality before the law is of utmost importance because it is clear that in a democracy, without the force of law behind them, women have been and will continue to be civilly dead. Because changes in the criminal justice system are fundamental to the advancement of women in society, a clear understanding of the specific ways in which the criminal justice system has reinforced and intensified patriarchal control of women is of utmost importance.

Nanci Koser Wilson presents for us a fascinating account of the witch hunts that occurred in Puritan Salem Village in the year 1692, demonstrating that casting out demons was not simply an anomaly of life that occurred in early America. As made clear by Wilson's insightful historical analysis, the need to tame women and nature is one of those persistent themes that ties the cosmos of Western culture to a system of male patriarchal control and persists to this day. Casting out devils by the Puritan community, according to this account, is no different from today's efforts by the criminal justice system to criminalize drug use by pregnant mothers. This engaging account of how the motivation to destroy female witches is really an account of how men continue to act to preserve the privileged position they hold in what they define to be "the natural order of things."

Laura T. Fishman's chapter, "'Mule-Headed Slave Women Refusing to Take Foolishness from Anybody': A Prelude to Future Accommodation, Resistance, and Criminality," describes how the slavery system legitimized and facilitated the sexual exploitation of black women. As blacks, both sexes experienced harsh and inhumane consequences of racism and economic exploitation. Her chapter sets the tone showing how the slave system shaped some of the black slave women's accommodations and resistance to the institution and, in turn, set the stage for black women's participation in criminal activities characteristic of today. Being black, women, and of a lower class, the kinds of crimes engaged in during the times of slavery and the twentieth century are indeed similar yet different from men's crimes.

1

Remember the Ladies

Roslyn Muraskin

Women have had to take their cases to court to argue for equality. The history of women's struggles has taught us that litigation is but a catalyst for change. Much has been accomplished, but more has yet to be accomplished. Discrimination and harassment exist today. This chapter highlights what women have sought since the early days of the constitutional history of our country. Equality and parity, the right to be treated equally or similarly.

Controversy abounds. Women of today, admittedly, are involved in professions where once they were not allowed. The classification by gender evident in the early days is slowly being eroded. But sexual inequality still exists. The decision makers are still primarily men. The women's movement has been the most integrated and populist force in this country. More than 200 years have passed since the Declaration of Independence was accepted. We still await the day when both women and men can be defined as persons; then equality will abound for all.

HISTORICAL OVERVIEW

The search by women for equality is not a recent phenomenon. In 1776, Abigail Adams admonished her husband, John, to "remember the ladies" in the drafting of the Constitution. She insisted that

> ...in the new code of laws which I suppose it will be necessary for you to make, I desire you would remember the ladies and be more generous and favorable to them than your ancestors. Do not put such unlimited power into the hands of the husbands. Remember, all

men would be tyrants if they could. If particular care and attention is not paid to the ladies, we are determined to foment a rebellion, and will not hold ourselves bound by any laws in which we have no voice or representation.

Adams replied back to his wife:

As to your extraordinary code of laws, I cannot but laugh. We have been told that our struggle has loosened the bonds of government everywhere; that children and apprentices were disobedient; that schools and colleges were grown turbulent; that Indians slighted their guardians, and Negroes grew insolent to their masters. But your letter was the first intimation that another tribe, more numerous and powerful than all the rest, were grown discontented.

The wife, Abigail responded:

I cannot say that I think you are very generous to the ladies; for, whilst you are proclaiming peace and good-will to men, emancipating all nations, you insist upon retaining an absolute power over wives. But you must remember that arbitrary power is like most other things which are very hard, very liable to be broken; and, notwithstanding all your wise laws and maxims, we have it in our power, not only to free ourselves, but to subdue our masters, and, without violence, throw both your natural and legal authority at our feet.

Nowhere in the Constitution of the United States is the word *woman* used. The battle had begun.

The Declaration of Independence as signed in 1776 stated that *all men are created equal* and that *governments derive their power from the consent of the governed.* Women were not included in either concept. The only time the word *sex* is referred to is in the Nineteenth Amendment to the Constitution, signed in 1920, giving women the right to vote.

The original American Constitution of 1787 was founded on English law and did not recognize women as citizens or as individuals with legal rights. A woman was expected to obey her husband or nearest male kin—the power of the ballot having been denied to her. Women were not considered persons under the Fourteenth Amendment to the Constitution, which guaranteed that no state shall deny to "any person within its jurisdiction the equal protection of the laws." Women have historically been victimized by policies designed to protect them (Muraskin & Alleman, 1993).

SENECA FALLS

Constitutionally, no obligation exists for the government to provide any benefits beyond basic requirements. In 1848, a convention was held in Seneca Falls, New York to mark the beginnings of the first organized feminist movement of the nineteenth century. The convention, attended by some 300 women, demonstrated a collective effort to achieve equal rights for women. Their focus was property and suffrage. They went so far as to adopt their own Declaration of Independence:

We hold these truths to be self-evident: that all men and women are created equal; that they are endowed by their creator with certain inalienable rights; that among these are life, liberty, and the pursuit of happiness; that to secure these rights governments are instituted, deriving their just powers from the consent of the governed.

Whenever any form of government becomes destructive of these ends, it is the right of those who suffer from it to refuse allegiance to it, and to insist upon the institution of new government....The history of mankind is a history of repeated injuries and usurpation on the part of men toward women, having in direct object the establishment of an absolute tyranny over her. To prove this, let the facts be submitted to a candid world.

He has never permitted her to exercise her inalienable right to the elective franchise.

He has compelled her to submit to laws in the formation of which she has no voice.

He has withheld from her rights which are given to the most ignorant and degraded men—both natives and foreigners.

Having deprived her of this first right of a citizen, the elective franchise, thereby leaving her without representation in the halls of legislation, he has oppressed her on all sides.

He has made her, if married, in the eyes of the law, civilly dead.

He has taken from her all rights in property, even to the wages she earns.

He has made her, morally, an irresponsible being, as she can commit crimes with impunity, provided they be done in the presence of her husband. In the covenant of marriage, she is compelled to promise obedience to her husband, he becoming, to all intents and purposes, her master—the law giving him power to deprive her of her liberty, and to administer chastisement.

He has so framed the laws of divorces, as to what shall be the proper cause, and in cases of separation, to whom the guardianship of the children shall be given, as to be wholly regardless of the happiness of women—the law, in all cases, going upon a false supposition of the supremacy of man, and giving all power into his hands.

After depriving her of all rights as a married woman, if single, and the owner of property, he has taxed her to support a government which recognizes her only when her property can be made profitable to it.

He has denied her the facilities for obtaining a thorough education, all colleges being closed against her.

He allows her in church, as well as State, but in a subordinate position.

He has endeavored, in every way that he could, to destroy her confidence in her own powers, to lessen her self-respect, and make her willing to lead a dependent and abject life. (Schneir, 1972, pp. 77–82)

So 300 women declared. They therefore resolved the following at Seneca Falls:

That all laws which prevent women from occupying such a station in society as her conscience shall dictate, or which place her in a position inferior to that of man, are contrary to the great precept of nature, and therefore of no force or authority.

That the women of this country ought to be enlightened in regard to laws under which they live, that they may no longer publish their degradation by declaring themselves satisfied with their present position....

That the same amount of virtue, delicacy, and refinement of behavior that is required of women in the social state, should be required of men, and the same transgression should be visited with equal severity on both man and woman.

And that it be further resolved

[t]hat the speedy success of our cause depends upon the zealous and untiring efforts of both men and women, for the overthrow of the monopoly of the pulpit, and for the security to women an equal participation with men in the various trades, professions, and commerce. (Schneir, 1972)

LEGAL SYSTEM

This was the year 1848. The property rights of American women in the nineteenth century as truly reflected in the declaration at Seneca Falls was set forth earlier by the legal scholar Blackstone, who wrote that by marriage, the husband and wife are one person in law. The very being of all women at this time was suspended during marriage. Laws were passed that give the husband the right to give his wife "moderate correction"; he could hit her to *restrain her* but with nothing larger than his thumb.

A federal equal rights amendment was first introduced to Congress in 1923, and was submitted to the states continuously over a period of time for ratification until it finally failed in the year 1972. Stated simply:

Section 1.   Equality of rights under the law shall not be denied or abridged by the United States or by any other State on account of sex.

Section 2.   The Congress shall have the power to enforce, by appropriate legislation, the provisions of this Article.

Section 3.   This Amendment shall take effect two years after the date of ratification.

It never happened.

Jean-Jacques Rousseau, an eighteenth-century French philosopher, wrote in his work *Émile*:

Men and women are made for each other, but their mutual dependence is not equal....We could survive without them better than they could without us....Thus women's entire education should be planned in relation to men. To please men, to be useful to them, to win their love and respect, to raise them as children, care for them as adults, counsel and console them, make their lives sweet and pleasant; these are women's duties in all ages and these are what they should be taught from childhood. (Deckard, 1979, p. 217)

Oberlin College was the first college to admit women, in 1833. Until 1841, women could only take a shortened literary course, on the theory that the education of women had a different purpose than that for men. For many years women were not permitted to speak in class and were required to wait on male students. It was believed that women's high calling was to be the mothers of the race and that they should stay within that special sphere in order that future generations should not suffer from the want of devoted and undistracted mother care. If women were to enter the areas of law, religion, medicine, academics, government, or any sort of public character, the home would suffer from neglect. Washing men's clothes, caring for their rooms, serving the men at dining tables, remaining respectfully silent in public assemblages, the Oberlin coeds were being prepared for motherhood and to serve their men.

Elizabeth Blackwell was the first woman in the United States to get a medical degree, in 1849. She applied to twenty-nine medical schools until one finally accepted her. She had to fight for the right to be present at the dissection of human organs, part of the training for any doctor.

In 1873, the U.S. Supreme Court upheld an Illinois state law prohibiting female lawyers from practicing in state courts (*Bradwell v. Illinois*, 1972). The court *in its wisdom* (emphasis mine) noted that the civil war as well as nature herself, has always recognized a wide difference in the respective spheres and destinies of man and woman. Man is or should be woman's protector and defender. The natural and proper timidity and delicacy which belong to the female sex evidently unfits it for many of the occupations of civil life. The constitution of the family organization, which is founded in the divine ordinance, as well as in the nature of things indicates the domestic sphere as that which belongs to the domain and functions of woman-hood. The harmony of interests and views which belong or should belong to the family institution, is repugnant to the idea of a woman adopting a distinct and independent career from that of her husband.

The court continued by declaring that

[t]he paramount destiny and mission of woman are to fulfill the noble and benign offices of wife and mother. This is the law of the Creator. And the rules of civil society must be adopted to the general constitution of things, and cannot be based upon exception cases.

Justice Miller summed it up when he stated:

I am not prepared to say that it is one of her fundamental rights and privileges to be admitted into every office and position, including those which require highly special qualifications and demanding social responsibilities. In the nature of things it is not every citizen of every age, sex, and condition that is qualified for every calling and position.

It took until 1860 in New York to pass the Married Women's Property Act, an attempt to give to women property that she owned as her sole and private property. Until this time a married woman was not entitled to own or keep property after marriage. This act stated "that which a woman married in this state owns at the time of her marriage, and the rents, issues and proceeds of all such property, shall notwithstanding marriage, be and remain her sole and separate property."

The right to vote, which was not won until 1920, with the passage of the Nineteenth Amendment to the Constitution, was a struggle for women. In the case of *Minor v. Happersett* (1874) the U.S. Supreme Court denied women the right to vote. The argument then was "that as a woman born or naturalized in the United States is a citizen of the United States and of the State in which she resides, she has therefore the right to vote." The Court stated that there is no doubt that women may be citizens. The direct question as presented was whether all citizens are necessarily qualified to be voters. "The Constitution has not added the right of suffrage to the privileges and immunities of citizenship as they existed at the time it was adopted" (*Minor*). In no state constitution was suffrage conferred upon women. It took the Nineteenth Amendment to the Constitution to grant women the right to vote. Neither John Adams or those following him were willing to "remember the ladies."

Federal and state legislation prohibiting sex discrimination in selected areas does not fill the absence of a constitutional prohibition of discrimination on the basis of sex. Under the federal constitution and most state constitutions, women have not yet been raised to the status of constitutional protection enjoyed by males. (Thomas, 1991, p. 95)

Even the language of the law refers to such terms as a *reasonable man*, *he*, and *his*. When a question about this is raised, the answer given is usually that the male terms used generically include females. Gender-neutral language does not solve the problem either. Such gender-neutral language "serves only to reward the employers ingenious enough to cloak their acts of discrimination in a facially neutral guise, identical though the effects of [a facially neutral seniority] system may be to those of a facially discriminatory one" (Thomas, 1991).

RIGHT TO WORK

During the nineteenth century differential treatment of women and men was challenged. A most striking incident was that of the protective state labor laws. During the early days of the twentieth century, protective labor laws were allegedly enacted to protect both sexes from inhuman conditions. However, it was the women who suffered. In the case of *Muller v. Oregon* (1908), a challenge was made to the Oregon statute prohibiting the employment of women in mechanical establishments, factories, or laundries for more than 10 hours a day. This law was upheld by the U.S. Supreme Court using a reasoning that was to haunt the advocates of women's rights for years to come.

Justice Brenner delivered the majority opinion of the Court:

> [W]omen's physical structure and the performance of maternal functions places her at a disadvantage in the struggle for subsistence....This is especially true when the burdens of motherhood are upon her. [And] even when they are not, by abundant testimony of the medical fraternity continuance for a long time on her feet at work, repeating this from day to day, tends to injurious effects upon the body...the physical well-being of woman becomes an object of public interest and care in order to preserve the strength and vigor of the race. [As dictated by history] women has always been dependent upon man. He established his control at the outset by *superior physical strength* (emphasis mine), and this control in various forms, with diminishing intensity has continued to the present....She is properly placed in a class by herself, and legislation designed for her protection may be sustained, even when legislation is not necessary for men, and could be sustained.

RIGHT TO SERVE ON JURIES

And so it continued. Struggles ensued, with women bringing to court their case to serve on juries. In the case of *Hoyt v. Florida* (1961), Justice Harlan delivered the opinion of the Supreme Court. The issue was whether exclusion of women from jury service discriminated against a defendant's right to a fair trial. Justice Harlan stated:

> Manifestly Florida's [law] does not purport to exclude women from state jury service. Rather, the statute "gives to women the privilege to serve but does not impose service as a duty." It accords women an absolute exemption from jury service unless they expressly waive that privilege.
>
> It has given women an absolute exemption from jury based solely on their sex, no similar exemption obtaining as to men.
>
> Despite the enlightened emancipation of women from the restrictions and protections of bygone years, and their entry into many parts of community life formerly considered to be reserved to men, *women is still regarded as the center of home and family life* [italics added].

This was 1961.

In 1975 in the *Taylor* case (*Taylor v. Louisiana*, 1975), a male criminal defendant challenged his conviction on the ground that his jury had not been drawn from a fair cross section of the community. Women had been systematically excluded from jury lists. Using statistics to demonstrate that 54.2 percent of all women between 18 and 64 years of age were in the labor force, that 45.7 percent of women with children under the age of 18 were working, that 67.3 percent of mothers who were either widowed, divorced, or separated were in the workforce, and that 51.2 percent of the mothers whose husbands were gainfully employed were also working, the court declared:

> [I]f it was ever the case that women were unqualified to sit on juries or were so situated that none of them should be required to perform jury services that time has long past.

A victory had been won.

GENDER AS A SUSPECT CLASSIFICATION

What has not been declared is that gender is a suspect classification. It was not until 1971 that the U.S. Supreme Court considered that many of the laws and official practices at all levels of government as practiced were in violation of the equal protection clause (Fourteenth Amendment to the Constitution). "No state shall deny equal protection of the laws to any person," according to the Fourteenth Amendment. But what does that mean?

A rational relationship test was developed indicating that any classification "must be reasonable, not arbitrary, and must rest upon some ground of difference having a fair and substantial relation to the object of the legislation, so that all persons similarly situated shall be treated alike" (*Reed v. Reed*, 1971). There can exist no discrimination against women unless it is demonstrated that reasonable grounds exist for such discrimination.

Throughout the history of the courts, several classifications, including gender, religion, and national origin, have been labeled "suspect" classifications. What this means is that any time a law is passed that discriminates in its language or is found to have a discriminatory effect on a suspect class of persons, the state has the burden not simply of showing that the law is rational, but must prove additionally that such a law serves a compelling governmental interest and that no other discriminatory law could accomplish the same or similar purpose. This is the principle referred to as a *compelling state interest test*. We came close with the case of *Frontiero v. Richardson* (1973), but because there was a 4–4 plurality vote of the justices of the Supreme Court, such a decision of gender as a suspect classification never came about. With gender not being labeled a suspect classification, the government has the power to justify any type of discrimination as not being arbitrary and irrational. In the words of Justice Brennan:

> There can be no doubt that our Nation has had a long and unfortunate history of sex discrimination. Traditionally, such discrimination was rationalized by an attitude of 'romantic paternalism' which in practical effect, put women, not on a pedestal, but in a cage.

If there had been just one more vote, the courts would have been obliged to treat gender classifications as race classifications. It was not meant to be. The rational basis for classifications is still based on the factor of women being dependent on their spouses, girls being dependent on parents for support, and men having more and better business experience than women. If the courts can determine that discrimination serves the purpose of the rational relationship test, it can and will stand. To this day there remains confusion regarding the standard of review in cases of gender discrimination. The issue remains whether gender and race classifications are ever constitutionally permissible. Are there instances in which it is proper to afford preferential treatment to one group above another? Clear answers do not exist. Each case is considered on an individual basis and on individual merit.

Even the Equal Rights Amendment (ERA) could not be passed. Concerns about family law, protective labor laws, the military, and the establishment of unisex bathrooms were enough to vote down the ERA. If ever there were stereotypical attitudes about women, one is found in the "wisdom" of many of the justices of the Supreme Court.

GENDER NEUTRAL

Admittedly, some progress has been demonstrated, as, for example, in the changing roles of women and men that have led to gender-neutral, functional family laws. Today, the obligation of supporting a spouse is predicated on who can afford it and not simply on who needs it.

Women are not inferior to men. Nevertheless, there is much evidence of sexual discrimination, even with all the history and struggles of women to gain equality and similarity of treatment under the law. We have not yet reached the day when we can say honestly that women have been raised to the status of full constitutional protections as enjoyed by the male sex.

"Remember the ladies," said Abigail Adams. We are constantly reminded of her statement as we are of the statement in *Glover v. Johnson* (1975):

Keep it simple, they are only women.

REFERENCES

DECKARD, B. S. (1979). *The women's movement: Political, socioeconomic, and psychological issues.* New York: Harper & Row.
MURASKIN, R., & ALLEMAN, T. (1993). *It's a crime: Women and justice.* Englewood Cliffs, NJ: Regents/Prentice Hall.
SCHNEIR, M. (ED.) . (1972). *Feminism: The essential historical writings.* New York: Vintage Press.
THOMAS, C. S. (1991). *Sex discrimination.* St. Paul, MN: West Publishing.

CASES

Bradwell v. Illinois, 83 U.S. 130 (1972).
Frontiero v. Richardson, 411 U.S. 677 (1973).
Glover v. Johnson, 478 F. Supp. 1075 (1975).
Hoyt v. Florida, 368 U.S. 57 (1961).
Minor v. Happersett, 88 U.S. 162 (1874).
Muller v. Oregon, 208 U.S. 412 (1908).
Reed v. Reed, 404 U.S. 71 (1971).
Taylor v. Louisiana, 419 U.S. 522 (1975).

2

Taming Women and Nature

The Criminal Justice System
and the Creation of Crime in Salem Village

Nanci Koser Wilson

Female-on-female violent crime is a rarity. Yet in 1692, in Puritan Salem Village, Massachusetts, hundreds of women were accused, and fourteen executed, for violent crimes, many of whose victims were female. Contemporary Americans view witchcraft as an imaginary offense, so this episode has been seen by most scholars as an aberration, atypical of U.S. criminal justice. But a careful examination of charges against these women reveals an offense that was not so imaginary after all—one for which women are still being brought to account. The Salem witches were persecuted because they were seen as wild women, in need of taming, just as was the rest of "nature." For the patriarchal mind, wild women and wild nature still pose a significant threat to orderly male-controlled production and reproduction, and are still sometimes met with a criminal justice response.

American women, like most women, are infrequent criminal offenders, especially as against one another and especially in violent crime. The rarest criminal event is female-on-female violent crime. Yet in 1692, in Puritan Salem Village, Massachusetts, hundreds of women were accused, and fourteen executed, for violent crimes, many of whose victims were female.

The Salem witch hysteria has been seen by most historians as an aberration, a bump in our history, completely atypical of U.S. criminal justice. No longer believers in witchcraft, modern Americans are horrified that such an injustice could have occurred in relatively modern times. It is assumed that the witches were innocent of any crime, and [(with the exception of Chadwick Hansen (1968)] scholars have sought explanations outside the phenomenon of witchcraft itself to account for the persecutions.

Yet if we examine carefully the charges against these women, we discover an offense that was not so imaginary after all, and one for which women are still being brought to account. The witches of Salem Village were thought to be disruptive of a natural hierarchy established by men at the behest of a male god. The image of divinely ordained masculine control of nature was captured for Puritans in the metaphor of the Great Chain of Being. This metaphor is still powerful today, with the exception that contemporary Americans have replaced the top rung in the hierarchy. How, scientific technology reigns as God, and the only telos, or design, in nature is the continued unfolding of evolutionary process. The new divinity is as thoroughly masculinist as Yahweh, and is capable of directing evolution by itself. A masculinist science embodies, as complete as did the old God, the American Dream of conquering wilderness, in its vision of total control over nature. In this vision, what counts is not so much more and more productivity (although this is certainly important) but *human control* of natural productivity.

This is well illustrated in modern agricultural practices. Bovine growth hormone does not produce more milk per cow over the entire span of the cow's life. Similarly, chemical fertilizers do not make the soil more fertile in the long run. Nor do dams create water, nor does experimentally induced laboratory growth replicate natural growth. At the core of all these ways of growing and knowing is the farmer's and the scientist's total control over (what are deemed to be) relevant conditions. It is apparent that this control is desired more than fertility itself. In the 1990s, this can be seen clearly in plans to "develop" wetlands as farms and shopping malls. Although the necessity to the hydrological cycle of these wetlands is now recognized, legislators and environmental agencies in state after state are permitting the development of wetlands upon the agreement by developers to create man-made substitute wetlands as "replacement parts."

But as Lewis (1943/1988, p. 449) has noted, control over nature is really "a power exercised by some men over other men with nature as its instrument." Many feminist scholars believe that control over women was exerted to exploit their labor and was the first form of exploitation man invented, upon which he then modeled other forms of exploitation. Ecofeminists hold that the exploitation of nature and of women developed coterminously, nourishing one another. And many scholars have noted the centrality of conquest, especially the conquest of wilderness, to the development of the American character (Turner, 1920).

In the Salem witchcraft hysteria we see the convergence of all of these themes, as the Puritan criminal justice system created in the Bay Colony a frightful specter to contain their fears of wild nature—both in human females and in the nonhuman nature around them. In tracing witch-beliefs within the context of Puritan technology and examining the evidence brought against the witches, we see a strong device for social control of natural forces—as Lewis stated, the control of some men over other men (and all women), using nature as the tool. The relevance of Puritan cosmology and its use of criminal justice to achieve the ends of control and domination to contemporary gendered criminal justice can be seen as evidence for a consistent theme running through Western and American history.

PURITAN METAPHYSICS

According to a contemporary witch (Starhawk, 1989, p. 18), "witchcraft takes its teaching from nature." Further, witches understand nature as cyclical, spiral. "There is nothing to be saved *from*, no struggle of life *against* the universe, no God outside the world to be feared and obeyed; only the Goddess, the Mother, the turning spiral that whirls us in and out of existence, whose winking eye is the pulse of being" (p. 29).

Whether any Salem women understood themselves to be practicing an ancient religion centered on the immanence of divinity in the natural world [as Murray (1921) asserted of the European witches], or whether any of the accused believed themselves to be malefic witches [as Hansen (1968) maintains], it is clear that at one time such religions were strong competitors for Christianity. In Europe, that part of earlier nature-centered religion that could not be absorbed effectively into Christianity was vigorously suppressed. The struggle with these heretics left a legacy of witch-beliefs among European Christians, which, imported to the American continent with the Puritans, formed the basis for the Salem female crime wave of 1692.

Puritan metaphysics (like all such patriarchal systems) presented a markedly different view of nature to that embodied in nature-centered religions. Puritan cosmology was strongly hierarchical, and within its metaphysics, the ultimate source of life existed beyond it. Puritans saw the cosmos as a

> Vast chain of being! which from God began,
> Natures aethereal, human, angel, man,
> Beast, bird, fish, insect, what no eye can see,
> No glass can reach; from Infinite to thee,
> From thee to nothing.—On Superior pow'rs
> Were we to press, inferior might on ours;
> Or in the full creation leave a void,
> Where, one step broken the great scale's destroy'd;
> From Nature's chain whatever link you strike,
> Tenth, or thousandth, breaks the chain alike.
>
> *(Pope, 1733)*

These lines from Pope, although written in the eighteenth century, reflect a "conception of the plan and structure of the world which, through the Middle Ages and down to the late 18th century, many philosophers, most men of science, and indeed, most educated men, were to accept without question" (Lovejoy, 1936/1953, p. 59). The universe was seen as a Great Chain of Being, "composed of an immense...number of links ranging in hierarchical order from the meagerest kind of existence, which barely escape non-existence, through 'every possible' grade up to...the Absolute Being."

For Puritans, each link in the chain fulfilled its nature and purpose partly by obeying the next highest link in the chain. Among human beings, a similar hierarchy had been ordained with "husbands superior to wives, parents to children, masters to servants, ministers to congregants, and magistrates to subjects....In each of these relations, inferiors served God by serving their superiors. Men promised to ensure obedience in all their dependents, in return for God's promise of prosperity" (Karlsen, 1987, p. 164).

Although the Puritan God existed prior to his creation, and Puritan theology embraced a deity whose transcendence outshone his immanence, their theology was also strongly incarnational. Elements of the natural world reflected and sometimes revealed to humans a supernatural plan, and, on occasion, a struggle between supernatural forces. Both God and Satan, his fallen angel, took an intense interest in the created world.

Created below God in the hierarchy, but above all other things, angels were required to fulfill their place in the Chain through obedience. Satan's obedience consisted precisely in his rebellion against his place. His desire to be "as God" included a struggle with the deity *within nature itself.* Satan not only attempted to seduce humans but also caused various natural disasters lower on the chain.

Long before Puritanism arose, European Christians had begun to understand Genesis 1:28[1] as a mandate to exploit all of nature below man in the hierarchical chain (White, 1967); and this exploitation, of course, required the taming of wild nature—both human and nonhuman. Puritan theology thus fit neatly with the colonization of an uncivilized territory. The new immigrants found a land peopled by hunting and gathering groups who, for the most part, did not have established cities, agriculture, or a settled existence. Puritans viewed this land as a wilderness in need of taming, which would order it to God.

Part of this impulse was surely secular; but it had a sacred stamp and warrant. Strong strains in Judeo-Christian mythology emphasize the wilderness experience. The wilderness is a setting for man's struggle with his lower nature, a place of suffering and purification, from which he emerges dedicated completely to God and to His divine plan.

> [T]he desert wilderness…where the very existence of man is constantly threatened, is also the place specially chosen by God to manifest Himself as His "mighty acts" of mercy and salvation. Obedience to a divine call brings into this dreadful wilderness those whom God has chosen to form as His own people….Failure to trust Yahweh in the wilderness is not simply an act of weakness: it is disobedience and idolatry. (Merton, 1978, p. 190)

This theme of wilderness was "taken over in the theology of radical Protestantism in the seventeenth century and hence entered into the formation of the Christian ideal of North American culture that grew up out of the Puritan colonies of New England" (Merton, 1978, p. 195).

The wilderness, once tamed, would become the orderly paradise the Puritan God commanded man to create. Importantly, a failure to conquer the wilderness was also a failure at individual salvation. If the Bay Colonists failed to establish the paradise of the "City on the Hill," this might be a sign that each Puritan was damned. Fearful for their own souls, frightened of wild nature both on its own terms and for the damnation that failure to tame it portended, Puritans attempted to contain their fears by sacrificing some of their middle-aged women. These women became the very emblem of their fears—of wilderness, of failure, and ultimately of eternal damnation.

THE WITCHES AS WILD WOMEN

Although it has been suggested that "a genuine coven was meeting in the woods of Salem before the trials" (Starhawk, 1989, p. 21), evidence from the Salem trials does not support such a conclusion. What is more important are the witch-beliefs Puritans held which allowed for the persecutions.

Nature-focused religions had been of concern to the Judeo-Christian tradition since its inception. In the fifth century B.C., tempted to desert his patriarchal God during a time of great personal suffering, Job had proclaimed:

> If I beheld the sun when it shined, or the moon walking in brightness; and my heart hath seen secretly enticed…this also were an iniquity to be punished by the judge; for I should have denied the God that is above. (Job 31:27–28)

Steeped in a tradition that had shaped its theology in direct contrast to animistic, nature-centered rival religions, the Puritans inherited a linear, hierarchical monotheism. While ancient religions had long since ceased to pose a genuine threat to the newer, patriarchal religion, during time of stress, the fear of heresy arose with new vigor.

Christianity met the challenge in two ways. It absorbed prior religions by building churches on the old sacred sites and by changing names of festivals while keeping their dates. It directly challenged such religions by turning its gods and goddesses into the Christian devil (Adler, 1986, p. 45). The witch persecutions were part of that transformation. What came to be called witchcraft included some elements of pagan belief systems, but "these survivals only became an organized system when the Church took the older beliefs and fragments and created an organized, systematic demonology, complete with new elements including the pact with the devil, the coven and the sabat" (Adler, 1986, p. 53; Trevor-Roper, 1970).

But witch persecutions were useful beyond the purposes of the Church in validating the new patriarchal religion. As Trevor-Roper (1970) notes, in the sixteenth and seventeenth centuries this new demonology acquired momentum. These were the centuries during which modern science was born and the Western world-view became more and more human-control oriented. The massive witch persecutions of the period also validated an increasingly centralized secular and male hierarchy in medicine, politics, and agriculture. The specter of possible resistance to this project of taming all of nature produced intense witch fears, culminating in the deaths of perhaps nine million persons (Daly, 1978, p. 183).

The struggle against wild nature as seen in untamed women produced important tracts whose dissemination was abided by the invention of printing. In *Malleus Malificarum* of Institoris (Kramer and Sprenger, 1948; o.d. 1486), readers would learn precisely what to fear from women presumed to be in league with the devil. In books such as this and in the teachings of the clergy, witchcraft was invented.

The *Malleus Maleficarum* "explained and justified the Church's view that most witches were women" (Karlsen, 1987, p. 155). Women, the authors instructed, were more evil than men by nature, and because they were created inferior to men, were more susceptible to deception. Witches were also seen as dissatisfied with their place in the natural hierarchy. This made them angry and vengeful. Specific sorts of crimes were likely to be performed by witches, according to this tract. They were responsible for generative problems—they could cause men to be impotent, they could prevent conceptions and procure abortions in women. They also might kill newborns. They frequently attempted to dominate their husbands, which was a "natural vice" in women (Karlsen 1987).

The witch-beliefs that the Puritans imported thus were strongly marked by fears of disruption of the Chain of Being, particularly of rebellion among women and damage caused to domesticated nature. The fear was that of tamed nature "going wild." Theologically and legally, the crime of witchcraft consisted in making a pact with the devil, whose supernatural power he lent to humans. With this power, a person could perform *maleficium*, that is, harm various parts of the natural order. She could cause disease, injury, or even death among humans and other animals. She could interfere with domestic processes such as dairying, brewing beer, and making cloth. Witches were also thought capable of causing disturbances in weather patterns—they could create droughts and storms at sea, for instance. Maleficium could be performed by look, by touch, and specifically, *by curse*.

Although invested with supernatural power, witches apparently refrained from certain kinds of harm, and specialized in others. They were not suspected of financial offenses such as theft, fraud, or embezzlement. In fact, they appeared unable to bring about good outcomes for themselves. It was not said that they increased the productivity of their own fields or domestic stocks; that they could weave superior fabrics or make finer butter, produce more food, or enhance the health of children, adults, or stock.

Rather, witches specifically engaged in actions that threatened to upset a natural hierarchy, to wreak havoc in domesticated nature—to unleash wild forces. The New England witch "was frequently suspected of causing illnesses or death, particularly to spouses or infants and young children." She also was likely to direct her malice toward domesticated animals—she could bewitch cows, horses, and swine—they would sicken and die, or simply wander off. She was often accused of "obstructing reproductive processes, either by preventing conceptions or by causing miscarriages, childbirth fatalities or 'monstrous' (deformed) births." She could procure abortions and cause impotence among men. She harmed domestic processes by spoiling beer in the brewing or making it disappear altogether. She could cause cows to stop giving milk and hens to lay fewer eggs. She could make spinning and weaving impossible (Karlsen, 1987).

If the Salem hysteria can be explained by Puritan uneasiness and fears during a period of political upheaval, as some have suggested (see, e.g., Erikson, 1966), it is clear from the nature of the accusations that these fears were of a specific sort. And if the high concentration of women among the accused can be explained in terms of misogyny and the desire to control women, as most feminist students of witchcraft have maintained (Daly, 1978; Ehrenreich & English, 1973; Karlsen, 1987), it is similarly clear from the nature of the accusations that women were thought to pose a particular kind of danger.

The Puritans had reserved an important and specific role for their women; and it is likely that female failure to fulfill their function was seen as extremely dangerous, in that one link in the Chain of Being broken, all else would disintegrate. Women were a part of wild nature that needed taming; once tamed, their role was to nurture. Men apparently realized that the creation of an inherently unfair and exploitative system carried within it the seeds of dissatisfaction and rebellion among the tamed. They expected women to rebel, and in their cosmology created an explanation for female dissatisfaction. Just as Eve had succumbed to the devil's wiles, so might other women. But Puritans did not fear self-aggrandizement on the part of the witches. Rather, they feared the vengeance of dissatisfied women. Insufficiently tamed women, it would appear, were the cause of fear. Untamed themselves, in league with the disruptive forces of wild nature, witches might unhook the carefully constructed Chain of Being.

ACCUSATIONS AGAINST THE SALEM WITCHES[2]

The Salem hysteria began in the early months of 1692 when a number of young women were stricken with fits. Reverend Samuel Parris' household contained a prepubescent daughter and a household servant, Tituba, from the West Indies. Elizabeth Parris, age 9, a number of preteen and teenage friends, and often, three older women gossiped and chatted in the Parris kitchen. Tituba, who knew the witchcraft of her native island, helped the girls to forecast their futures, focusing on the occupations of their future husbands. Later, Jonathan Hale was to blame the entire event on these seemingly innocent actions. He maintained that the girls in their "vain curiosity" had "tampered with the devil's tools" (cited in Boyer & Nissenbaum, 1974, p. 23).

The most immediate result of this tampering was that the young girls became possessed. Their symptoms ranged from feelings of being pinched, pricked, and choked, to full-scale seizures. Two of the "circle girls" were epileptics (Gemmill, 1924, p. 48); the fits of the other girls were perhaps caused by ergot poisoning (Caporael, 1976) or the power of suggestion (Caulfield, 1943). Taken to the local doctor, they could neither be diagnosed nor cured by his arts, and he then declared that the cause was outside his profession. The appropriate jurisdiction was theological and legal.

Witchcraft was more than crime, although it was that—it was treason and heresy as well. And it was the most threatening offense in the Puritan world, because it was contagious. The authorities reacted promptly and predictably—they asked the girls to indicate who was bewitching them. Guided perhaps by the mother of one of the girls (Ann Putnam), who held grudges against some of her neighbors (Boyer & Nissenbaum, 1974; Gemmill, 1924), and by their own beliefs about just who a witch might be, the girls identified several local women—including, of course, Tituba, who confessed immediately. The hunt began.

In the pattern of the accusations, in the kinds of victims and offenders, and in the nature of the harm done, we begin to see what the Puritans feared. The power of maleficium was given by Satan himself, so Puritan officials were at pains to ascertain if the accused had actually made a pact with the devil. They looked for evidence of such a pact in confessions and in the testimony of witnesses that an accused had "signed the devil's book," had attended a witches' sabbat, or taken the devil's communion. Further, if a witness testified that an accused witch had urged her to engage in any of these actions, this testimony was evidence that the accused had attempted to seduce another human, drawing her, too, into the devil's snare, and therefore had obviously made a pact herself. Such evidence was produced for 77 percent of the accused women in our sample (see Table 1).

Entering in such a pact with the devil meant that a Puritan was in league with profane forces, unsanctioned authority. As a being who himself had rebelled against established authority, Satan was wild. Satan's fight with God was a rebellion against authority which was carried out in the world—that is, within created nature. Thus, at the heart of the witches' crime was rebellion against hierarchical order and allegiance to an alternative force whose main purpose and power appeared to be the creation of chaos.

Maleficium directed at human beings was the most common charge in Salem, as it had been in England (Macfarlane, 1970, p. 154; Thomas, 1971, p. 539, who estimates that 70 to 80 percent of the victims were other humans). In our sample, 97 percent of the women accused were charged with assaulting or murdering humans (see Table 2).

TABLE 1   Evidence of Pact

	Number	Percent
Confession	7	20
Signing the devil's book	2	6
Attending the witch's sabbath	13	37
Taking the devil's communion	2	6
Seducing others	17	49
Total[a]	27	77

[a]In this and the following tables, totals will add to more than 100% because more than one form of evidence was brought for several of the witches.

Evidence for human harm began with and most usually involved evidence that the circle girls had been tortured by the accused. These girls were present in court and frequently went into fits when an accused entered the room. Eighty-nine percent of the accused women were charged with tormenting these girls. Since the medical profession had not been able to find a natural cause, these fits were continually attributed to supernatural actions by witches. Obviously, for Salem Villagers, unexplained events were also uncontrollable events—and it was this lack of control which they feared. The first, and always the central, victims were the circle girls. They were the reliable indicators that an

TABLE 2   Evidence of Maleficium

	Number	Percent
Harming human beings	34	97
Assault upon circle girls	31	89
Assault upon others	20	57
Murder	8	23
Harming domesticated nature	9	26
Damaging domestic production	1	3
Stopping domestic production	3	8.5
Damaging domesticated stock	9	26
Possessing supernatural powers	18	51
Flying through the air	6	17
Performing "impossible" physical feats	1	3
Predicting the future	2	6
Possessing poppets	7	20
Possessing familiars	10	29
Suckling familiars, having witch's teats	5	14

accused was actually a witch. In this regard, the age and gender of the victims and offenders is important.

There were ten circle girls; their ages ranged from 9 to 20, with a mean of 15.9 years (see Table 3). One of the oldest, Mary Warren, who was 20, was later accused of witchcraft herself, as were two of the older women present (Sarah Biber and Goody Pope). The accused were, for the most part, middle-aged women who were unmarried. Although the girls themselves could logically be accused, except for Warren (who confessed spontaneously, then later retracted her statements) they were not. Thus the pattern is that young, fertile, nulliparous women were assaulted by postfertile and/or unmarried women. Women who were past the stage when their tamed fertility could be useful, apparently deliberately made fertile young women useless by making them wild.

The witches were thought to harm other humans as well, and 57 percent of them were accused of doing so, some (23 percent) to the point of death (see Table 2). These middle-aged women were also accused of harming domesticated nature. They were thought to be able to damage domestic processes. As Table 2 shows, 3 percent of our sample were accused of doing so. Mary Bradbury, for example, caused butter to go bad. They were also thought to stop production altogether, as when Elizabeth How caused the Perley's cow to stop giving milk. Altogether, 8.5 percent of the samples were so accused. They could damage or bewitch domestic stock, as 26 percent of them did. Sometimes the cattle, pigs, or draft animals sickened or died, and sometimes they went wild. One witch in our sample was accused of damaging an artifact—but, tellingly, one which kept tamed nature "inside"—she was accused of using supernatural means to break a fence.

Evidence of maleficium also frequently took the form of testimony that the accused possessed superhuman powers. As can be seen from Table 2, such evidence was brought for 51 percent of the accused women. These women were thought to raise storms at sea, thus casting away vessels, as was thought of Mary Bradbury. They were believed to make hogs chase men, as Mary Parker was accused of doing. They were thought to create a light

TABLE 3　　The Circle Girls[a]

	Age
Elizabeth Parris	9
Abigail Williams	11
Ann Putnam	12
Mercy Lewis	17
Mary Walcott	17
Elizabeth Hubbard	17
Elizabeth Booth	18
Susan Sheldon	18
Mary Warren	20
Sarah Churchill	20

[a]In addition, three older women were often present: Sarah Bibber, Goodwife Pope, and Mrs. Ann Putnam (Gemmill, 1924).

in a field that caused human accidents. Some of them, it was thought, could perform seemingly impossible feats, such as walking through the rain without becoming wet. Or, they could fly through the air or ride airborne on a broom. They could predict the future.

Some of the witches were believed to have worked their evil through a medium. They were accused of possessing "poppets"—small rag dolls in the image of an enemy, which when pricked with pins would cause the victim himself to suffer pain. Thirty-five percent of the women were accused of possessing "familiars," or suckling them. Familiars were small animals (dogs, cats, birds) which the devil sent to witches to aid them in doing their evil work. The familiar was believed to suckle the witch from a prenatural teat located somewhere on her body. Thus, when a witch was accused, a jury of same-gender townspeople was appointed to conduct a physical examination to determine if the witch possessed such a teat. The Salem Villager who had a wart, mole, or hemorrhoid was in grave danger.

The role of the familiar was somewhat different from that of the poppet. Poppets were inert—the supernatural force somehow transferred itself from this image of the victim's body to the victim. Familiars had the added advantage that they could be sent on malefic missions—a small blue bird, a black puppy, or usually, a cat—would suddenly appear in the victim's home to torment him.

The witch's possession and use of natural and supernatural forces was threatening because it was assumed to be evil. Puritans were able to conceive of nature as saturated with supernatural forces only when such forces were evil. Why was this so?

The Puritan God was not within nature. He had made it, and existed outside and above it. As created, it was chaos and could only fulfill its telos when ordered into a Great Chain of Being, tamed and controlled from above, by man. In this manner all being was ordered to the Supreme Being in hierarchical fashion, through many layers of command and obedience. For the Puritans, there was thus only one appropriate relation to nature—to tame wild nature, order it to God, and nurture it in its tamed state. They could not conceive of working with nature, respecting its boundaries and limits, its right to be *for* itself. A careful observation of wild nature might allow one to predict its course. A respect for nature's own nature, for her limits and necessities, a capacity to "let grow and to make grow" (Meis 1986) might yield human good by creating a harmonious relationship. Instead, for the Puritans, all of nature was first, wild: uncontrollable, unpredictable, unyielding, profane. Unless it was controlled and tamed, it was not only unfruitful, it was dangerous.

In possessing supernatural powers, it was thought that the witch used life forces to pervert the Chain of Being. She did not work against nature to control it. Rather than working to tame animals, she worked with wild animals to do evil. Rather than staying in her place, she flew through the air. Rather than contending herself to whatever fate God ordained for her, calmly waiting for it to unfold, she attempted to discern the future.

Susanna Martin's case[3] is quite typical. This 72-year-old widow was accused by the circle girls, who ratified their accusations by falling into fits at her preliminary hearing. She did not help her case by laughing at their antics and declaring a lack of sympathy for them.

Martin was charged with assaulting the circle girls, and she was accused of harming others as well. Bernard Peach testified that she (or her spectral shape) entered his bedroom one Sunday night, took hold of his feet, and "drew my body into a whoope and lay upon me about an hour and one-half or two hours all of which time I could not stir or speak."

He finally managed to bite three of her fingers. The next day he found her footprints and blood outside in the snow. She also apparently assaulted Elizabeth Brown, who when in her presence experienced a sensation "like birds pecking her leggs or picking her with the motion of their wings and…it would rise up into her stomach like a pricking payne as nayls and pinns…and it would rise up in her throat like a pullet's egg." She appeared in Jarvis Ring's bedchamber, lay upon him and bit his finger so hard that the mark "is still to be seen on the little finger on my right hand."

She was thought not only to have harmed humans, but to have harmed domesticated nature as well. In testimony against her, John Pressey claimed that she had bewitched his milk cattle and was capable of directing supernatural forces against him. On one occasion, he had become lost after dark and kept sighting a strange light. Frightened, he tried to strike the light with his stick, but after he gave it about "forty smart blows," he fell into a deep pit, yet "I do not know any such pit to be in the place where I was sliding into." Shortly thereafter, Susanna Martin appeared in exactly the place where the light had been. A few years later, she reviled him and his wife and claimed that he should never prosper. Specifically, she told them they would "never have but two cows" and "from that day to this we have never exceeded that number for something or other has prevented it."

John Kimball testified that he and the Martins had had a quibble about appropriate payment for a piece of land Kimball had bought from him. Kimball had offered them their choice of two cows and some other cattle but "did reserve two cows which I was not desirous to part with they being the first I ever had." Susanna threatened him in this way: "You had better [pay with those particular cows] for those will never do you no good." Kimball testified, "and so it came to pass that the next April following that very cow lay in the fair dry yard with her head to her side but starc dead; and a little while after another cow died and then an ox and then other cattle to the value of thirty pounds." In the same year Kimball desired to buy a puppy from her, but she would not let him have his choice from the litter, so he didn't agree to buy any. Upon hearing this, she said, "If I live, I'll give him puppies enough." A few days later he stumbled unaccountably upon some stumps in the woods. But soon he perceived the source of his difficulty—he was being attacked by several dark puppies, who were not hurt even when he cut them with his ax.

John Atkinson testified that Martin was angry with him because her son had traded one of their cows to him. When he went to the Martin place to receive the cow, she muttered and was unwilling that he should have the cow. When he took possession of it "notwith-standing the homstringing and halting of her she was so mad that we could scarce get her but she broke all ropes fastened to her and we put the rope two or three times around a tree but she broke it and ran away and when she came down to the ferry we were forced to run up to our arms in water she was so fierce but after much adieu we got her into the boat and she was so tame as any creature whatever."

On another occasion, William Osgood turned down the Martins when they asked him for a gift of beef. The next day one of his best cows went wild. And when Joseph Knight encountered her in the woods, his horses suddenly refused to cross a causeway—instead, they simply ran wild.

Other testimony suggested that she was a woman who could fly, walk in the rain without getting wet, and could change herself into the shape of a hog or a cat. And clearly she had made a pact with the devil because otherwise she would not possess such super-natural powers, nor would she have urged Mercy Lewis to sign the devil's book.

What did Puritans believe was the motive for such damage? The witches were asked repeatedly why they had bewitched the girls, but no satisfactory answer ever emerged. For other harms, a motive was sought and found. Usually, a witch who had harmed someone or someone's domestic production was seen to be displeased with that person. Just as Puritans believed that Satan was dissatisfied with his place, they believed some of their middle-aged women were similarly dissatisfied. Apparently, they were really frightened of this rebellion against authority and of the disruption in the Great Chain it signified.

This may be explain why the officials were also interested in eliciting two other types of evidence. Table 4 shows that 34 percent of the women were accused of muttering after being refused some item for which they had begged, and 23 percent of possessing bad language or manners. Altogether, 43 percent of the women in the sample were accused of "unseemly behavior." Why were the Puritans interested in this type of evidence?

Muttering after begging might mean that the woman had actually placed a curse on the one who gave her offense. Some scholars have suggested that the real offense was not malefic witchcraft but abrasive behavior to the one who had refused, following on the heels of the refusal of neighborly aid. Thomas (1971) argues that in the most common situation, "the victim had been guilty of a breach of charity or neighborliness, by turning away an old woman who had come to the door to beg or borrow some food or drink, or the loan of some household utensil." Witch-beliefs implied that a neighborly obligation left unfulfilled might result in malefic witchcraft directed against the unneighborly person. Thomas suggests that the high percentage of women is most "plausibly explained by economic and social considerations, for it was the women who were the most dependent members of the community, and thus the most vulnerable to accusation" (Thomas, 1971, p. 553). Macfarlane's argument is similar, although he maintains that women predominated in the accusations because they were the most resistant to change, and their social position and power led to mounting hatred against them (Macfarlane, 1970).

These scholars refer to English witchcraft, but Boyer and Nissenbaum (1974) have made the same argument for Salem. They believe the accused were "on the move, socially and economically"; they were independent of the old social order. In their lack of willingness to accept their given station in life, they were typical of the emergent personality of citizens in a capitalist economy. The accusers represented the old order. "The social order was being profoundly shaken by a superhuman force which had lured all too many into active complicity with it. We have chosen to construe this force as emergent mercantile capitalism. Mather and Salem Village called it witchcraft" (Boyer and Nissenbaum, 1974, p. 209).

TABLE 4   Evidence of Unseemly Behavior

	Number	Percent
Muttering after begging	12	34
Bad language/ill manners	8	23
Total	15	43

But this theory fails to explain why none of the men in our sample were accused of unseemly behavior and yet were accused of witchcraft. Nor does it explain why fewer than half of the accused female witches were accused of possessing bad manners, or why they were also accused of other depredations.

Rather, it seems the explanation may lie in the *meaning* of such behavior. Bad language or manners was evidence for rebellion against authority, the sign of a possible break in the Great Chain of Being. Six of the eight women accused of unmannerly behavior had been rude to a direct superior—a husband or a parent. The others were simply generally rude—but such testimony was always brought by a man.

The centrality of bad manners is demonstrated also by the evidence offered in *defense* of accused women. Testimony for Elizabeth How thus indicated that she was "neighborly," that she "carried it very well," that she never reviled anyone, that she had a courteous and peaceable disposition (Woodward, 1864/1969, p. 78). Wild women were dangerous. Just by looking, touching, or cursing, just by being in the same room with domesticated pubescents, they were thought to be able to make tamed nature go wild.

The males in this sample are quite different from the women who were accused. For all thirteen, evidence was brought that they had afflicted the circle girls, and five of them were accused of harming other humans. But only one of them harmed domestic nature in any way, and none was accused of unseemly, unmannerly, or unruly behavior. The most striking thing about the male witches is their atypicality. Apart from George Burroughs, a former Puritan minister who was believed to be the Satanic priest officiating at the sabbats (where, of course, a priest was necessary) and a deputy sheriff (John Willard), who was probably accused because he was publicly sympathetic to those he was forced to jail, 72 percent (eight of eleven) of the accused men were relatives of accused female witches. Thus, as John Demos has suggested (1970, p. 1311), they "belonged to a kind of derivative category."

The only truly typical witch among the men was Samuel Wardwell. About 55 years of age at the time of the hysteria, Wardwell owned a little farm and "for many years had been a fortune teller, strolling about, reading palms and solving life's mysteries from the broken tea leaves in the bottom of the cup" (Gemmill, 1924, p. 185). His rather high success rate at this enterprise was part of his undoing. Accused and jailed, he promptly confessed. He claimed that he was able to control animal nature—he could banish wild creatures from his fields by "bidding the devil to take" them, and he could make domesticated stock "come round about and follow me." Wardwell later retracted his confession, whereupon he was tried, convicted, and hanged (Gemmill, 1924; Woodward, 1969).

Reflection on the patterns formed by the evidence brought against witches and by their age and sex leads us to select as symbol and metaphor of witch fears the unfortunate Sarah Biber. A middle-aged woman who gossiped in the Parris kitchen with the circle girls, perhaps participating in their fortune telling, Biber was never accused of maleficium, or indeed of having made a pact with the devil. She *was* accused of "often quarreling with her husband," during which quarrels she "would call him very bad names," and of behaving in an unnurturing manner toward her children. "She wished that when her child fell into the river she had never pulled it out." Three of the four men who testified against her cited her "unruly, turbulent spirit" (Woodward, 1864/1969, pp. 203–205). Apparently Sarah Biber's sole crime was her wildness.

WILDERNESS AND CRIMINAL JUSTICE

At its birth, philosophers justified the modern criminal justice system as a device to tame the naturally wild instincts of human beings. Its necessity was recognized when men became "weary of living in a continual state of war," as Beccaria wrote (1963, p. 11), following Hobbes's (1651/1947, p. 31) assumption that all mankind possessed "a perpetual and restless desire for power after power, that ceaseth only in death."

Contemporary criminologists often retain this frightening vision of nature as wildly dangerous. Travis Hirschi (1969, p. 31) finds no need to search for motivations to crime because "we are all animals and thus all naturally capable of committing criminal acts."

Our modern criminal justice system is permeated with this view—that only when nature is controlled is it safe. Erickson (1966) says of it that we have inherited from the Puritans an assumption that "the convict's soul is permanently depraved and that sin is an inevitable part of his personal endowment." In light of this model of the convicted criminal as inherently wild, it "makes very little sense to…reform him…The best one can do for him is to contain his reprobate spirit, in much the same way that one tames the wilder instincts of animals…The object [of criminal justice] is not to improve his nature but to harness it so completely that it cannot assert itself" (p. 203).

What legacy then, did the witch hysteria of 1692 and the Puritan criminal justice system's handling of it bequeath to us? What did Puritans think their purpose was? How successful were they in achieving it? How successful is the contemporary criminal justice system in achieving this same purpose?

Puritans were intensely frightened by two kinds of wilderness—that in the forests surrounding them at the edges of their carefully cultivated fields and neat towns, and that which was within human nature (and especially female human nature). Both kinds of wilderness were evil precisely because they were wild.

"Seventeenth century writing is permeated with the idea of wild country as the environment of evil," Nash (1982, p. 36) tells us. "The new world wilderness was linked with a host of monsters, witches and similar supernatural beings" (p. 29). The wilderness was evil because it had not been ordered to the patriarchal God; it was seen not only as uncontrolled, but as the location of rival religion. A "dark wilderness cave" was believed to be the site of pagan rites, and the native Americans were "not merely heathens but active disciples of the devil" (pp. 33–36). For Puritans, "the untamed forests and the Indians that lurked in their shadows represented fallen nature inhabited by the powers of darkness" (Ruether 1983, p. 81). The wild evil of nature outside the village and farm was echoed in human nature as well. The Puritan mission thus involved both "an inner battle over that 'desolate and outgrowne wildernesse of humain nature' and on the New England frontier it also meant conquering wild nature" (Nash, 1982, p. 36). In the crime of witchcraft, these two wildernesses came together in wild women who used their evil power to make tamed nature wild, too. The Puritan "errand into the wilderness" (Miller, 1956) was a mission that would bring Godly order out of a natural chaotic fecundity. Only through a project of taming could they bring fertility under control.

The criminal justice response to witchcraft focused on women apparently because it was precisely among women that the relationship to nature was wrong. Fearful of the wild in nature and in human beings, knowing no way to deal with these fears other than by creating an orderliness based upon hierarchical control, Puritan justice announced in the witch trials that which it absolutely would not tolerate. The idea of women embodied, and some of their own middle-aged widows exemplified, what Puritans feared most. Where in the natural world there is harmony based upon each creature's capacity to be for-itself and simultaneously for-the-whole, the Puritan mind saw chaos. They sought to replace the "for-itself" and "for-the-whole" of nature with a system of nature-for-man and man-for-God, ordered in hierarchical neatness through a Great Chain of (Patriarchal) Being.

In the witches, Puritans saw wild creatures independent of the Great Chain, immersed in untamed natural processes: pure chaos, pure evil. What they tried to kill in Puritan women, all Puritan women, when they hanged the witches, was a particular relationship to the created world and its fertility—a metaphysic and an epistemology diametrically opposed to their own. Were they successful?

As a boundary maintenance device (Erikson, 1966), the witch trials were certainly successful. The Puritans sacrificed a few middle-aged widows, who were not particularly useful to them in any case. But the effect of trying, imprisoning, and hanging the witches was to send a message to all the Puritans, especially to the women. Henceforward, gossiping in a group of women, having a close or familiar relationship with animals, and observing nature's ways in a respectful manner that would allow prediction of the future would be dangerous. Henceforth, fertility in women and in nature would be subjected to strict masculine design and control—and where it went wild, it would be criminally punished. Were the Puritans successful in bequeathing to their descendants a metaphysic, or epistemology, and a criminal justice system that would continue to control unruly feminine nature?

CONTEMPORARY WITCHCRAFT: THE CRIMINAL JUSTICE SYSTEM RESPONSE

> The…Great Chain of Being has been converted into a Becoming…[and] God himself is…identified with this Becoming. But the inversion…while it converts the Scale of Being into an abstract ideal schema, does not alter its essential character.
>
> *Lovejoy (1936/1953, p. 326)*

Americans no longer hunt witches in the fashion of their Puritan ancestors. But the fear of wild nature and the intense desire to tame it for man's benefit (the source of the hysteria in Salem) is still strong. Having lopped off the top of the Great Chain of Being, postmoderns have neither God nor telos to guide and restrain their interactions with nature. Instead, a "neutral" scientific technology informs our actions. Nature now tends toward no other end than to be molded by men in power to their current benefit. For while the notion of the Great Chain of Being is now identified with evolution itself and inverted so that the tendency toward diversity and fullness is seen to arise from the bottom of the hierarchy, spontaneously rather than as a deliberate plan from the top, its danger to women and nature is not lessened, but perhaps increased. If there is a God in these waning years of the second millennium, He is science, now seen as capable of altering evolution itself, to the special benefit of those men currently in power. For the patriarchal mind, wild women and wild nature still pose a significant threat to orderly, male-controlled production and reproduction. Sometimes this threat is met with a criminal justice system response as it was in Salem Village.

Human reproduction was a significant concern of the Puritan witch hunters, who blamed female witches for abortions (both spontaneous and induced), "monstrous births," and untimely deaths from disease in young children. Exertion of male control over human reproduction is still a vital concern, as evidenced by newly enacted abortion laws which require male consent, by strict hedges on surrogacy requiring contracts to protect the rights of fathers in their unborn children, denial of child custody to lesbian mothers (and to many heterosexual mothers where custody is challenged by fathers), restrictive laws on midwife-attended birthing, and the increasing criminalization of pregnancy, which prescribes a criminal justice system response of imprisonment for addicted mothers.

Concerns regarding domestic production plagued the Puritans as well. Witches were blamed for infertile fields, dairying problems, diseases among domesticated stock. Late twentieth-century Americans believe they have solved the problems of unruly nature through chemical control, vast water diversion projects, and an agriculture that has become agribusiness featuring vast monocultures. With agriculture almost completely under control of the patriarchal mind, contemporary Americans are satisfied that endless orderly production will prevail.

The newest wrinkles in control over nature with regard to domestic production are hormonal control of production and genetic engineering. Agricultural technologists invent methods to splice bean genes onto corn, frost-resistant genes onto strawberries. They feed BGH to dairy cattle to increase milk production, with the result that cows suffer mastitis and die untimely deaths after living what must be a very unpleasant existence.

While conservationists and animal rights activists deplore these devices and warn of impeding disaster from soil depletion, deforestation, and a host of other possible ecocata-strophes, the desire to seek total control over natural processes and the belief that this is possible guide American policy in food production, as in human reproduction. The desire is total control—an orderly hierarchical arrangement of fecundity.

The Puritans sacrificed some of their middle-aged women to further their project of taming. Similarly, in the 1990s, the addicted women who give birth to crack babies are being sacrificed. Again, it is powerless women who are of very little use to the social system who are subjected to a criminal justice system response. And again, the effect is boundary maintenance—a deterrence that affects all fertile women. Now al! women are put on warning that what they ingest during pregnancy will be carefully monitored. Posters in liquor stores and labels on bottles warn us, as do a plethora of articles in women's magazines, that any misbehavior during pregnancy is dangerous not only to the fetus but also to the mother. Only a few women need be imprisoned for the most serious violations in order that all women receive the message. A chaotic fertility, a careless pregnancy, a selling of one's self "body and soul to the devil" (whether Satan or cocaine) will not meet with caring, with medical treatment—but with a punishment response.

Perhaps twentieth-century Americans have no more need than did our seventeenth-century ancestors to punish wild women for its immediate effect. Perhaps, now as then, the crucial effect of the criminal justice process is a boundary maintenance that tames all women, bringing their fertility under control, ordering it into a neat hierarchical Great Chain of (patriarchal) Being.

NOTES

1. "And God said [to man], Be fruitful, and multiply, and replenish the earth, and subdue it: and have dominion over every living thing that moveth upon the earth."
2. Information on the specific charges leveled at the witches comes from Woodward's (1864/1969) *Records of Salem Witchcraft*. Woodward collected and compiled material from preliminary hearings which includes testimony of witnesses, victims, and the accused. Woodward's records are incomplete but provide us with a sample of forty-eight accused persons, thirteen men and thirty-five women. The tables in this section are based only on the women. Later, there is a separate discussion of the accused men.
3. Evidence on Susanna Martin's case comes from Woodward (1864/1969, pp. 193ff.) and Gemmill (1924, pp. 114ff.).

REFERENCES

ADLER, M. (1986). *Drawing down the moon*. Boston: Beacon Press.

BECCARIA, C. (1963). *On crimes and punishment*. New York: Macmillan.

BOYER, P., & NISSENBAUM, S. (1974). *Salem possessed*. Cambridge, MA: Harvard University Press.

CAPORAEL, L. R. (1976, April 2). Ergotism: The satan loosed in salem? *Science, 192*.

CAULFIELD, E. (1943, May). Pediatric aspects of the Salem witchcraft tragedy. *American Journal of Diseases of Children, 65*.

DALY, M. (1978). *Gyn/ecoolgy* Boston: Beacon Press.

DEMOS, J. (1970, June). Underlying themes in the witchcraft of 17th century New England. *American Historical Review, 75*.

EHRENREICH, B., & ENGLISH D. (1973). *Witches, midwives and nurses: A history of women healers*. New York: Feminist Press.

ERIKSON, K. (1966). *Wayward Puritans*. Wiley.

GEMMILL, W. N. (1924). *The Salem witch trials*. Chicago, IL: A.C. McClurg.

HANSEN, C. (1968, April). Salem witches and DeForest's *Witching Times. Essex Institute Historical Collections, 104*.

HIRSCHI, T. (1969). *Causes of delinquency*. Berkeley, CA: University of California Press.

HOBBES, T. (1947). *Leviathan*. New York: Macmillan. (Original work published 1651)

KARLSEN, C. F. (1987). *The devil in the shape of a woman: Witchcraft in colonial New England*. New York: W.W. Norton.

KRAMER, H., & SPRENGER J. (1948). *Malleus maleficarum* (Montague Summers, Trans.). Magnolia, MA: Peter Smith Publishing. (Original work published 1486)

LEWIS, C. S. (1988). The abolition of man. In L. W. Dorset (Ed.), *The essential C. S. Lewis*. New York: Collier. (Original work published 1943)

LOVEJOY, A. O. (1953). *The great chain of being*. Cambridge, MA: Harvard University Press. (Original work published 1936)

MACFARLANE, A. (1970). *Witchcraft in Tudor and Stuart England*. London: Routledge & Kegan Paul.

MERTON, T. (1978). Wilderness and paradise. In *The Monastic Journey*. New York: Image Books.

MIES, M. (1986). *Patriarchy and accumulation on a world scale*. London: Zed Books.

MILLER, P. (1956). *Errand into the wilderness*. Cambridge, MA: Harvard University Press.

MURRAY, M. A. (1921). *The witch cult in western Europe*. New York: Oxford University Press.

NASH, R. (1982). *Wilderness and the American mind*. New Haven, CT: Yale University Press.

POPE, A. (1733). *Essay on man*.

RUETHER, R. R. (1983). Woman, body and nature. In *Sexism and God talk: Toward a feminist theology*. Boston: Beacon Press.

STARHAWK (1989). *The spiral dance: A rebirth of the ancient religion of the great goddess*. San Francisco: Harper & Row.

THOMAS, K. (1971). *Religion and the decline of magic*. London: Weidenfield and Nicoesen.

TREVOR-ROPER, H. R. (1970). The European witchcraze and social change. In M. Marwick (Ed.), *Witchcraft and sorcery*. New York: Penguin.

TURNER, F. J. (1920). *The frontier in American history*. New York: Krieger.

WHITE, L. JR. (1967, March 10). The historical roots of our ecological crisis. *Science, 155,* 1203–1207.

WOODWARD, W. E. (1969). *Records of Salem witchcraft*. New York: DeCapo Press. (Original work published 1864)

3

"Mule-Headed Slave Women Refusing to Take Foolishness from Anybody"

A Prelude to Future Accommodation, Resistance, and Criminality[1]

Laura T. Fishman

The system of slavery, a reflection of a patriarchal and racist social order, legitimized and facilitated not only the economic and racist oppression but the sexual exploitation of black slave women. An extensive review of the literature on slavery was used to address how slave women accommodated and resisted these multiple forms of oppression. The findings presented here indicated that as blacks, both sexes experienced the harsh and inhuman consequences of racism and economic exploitation. In response, there was a significant convergence in male and female involvement in such forms of "criminal" resistance as murder, assault, theft, and arson. These actions were employed to improve the slaves' lot in life and to express opposition to the slave system. "Criminal" resistance therefore set the stage for black women's participation in the criminal activities characteristic of today. Findings also suggested that in response to sexual exploitation, gender-specific forms of accommodation (e.g., acting as breeders and sex workers) were utilized to make slave women's lives bearable. It is concluded that these forms of accommodation served as a preface to black women's vulnerability to sex-oriented crimes within the context of twentieth-century American society.

The American slave system involved the forcible importation of black Africans for the express purpose of economic exploitation of their labor and bodies. Slavery was a form of involuntary servitude in which slaves were owned by others and were legal chattel. Thus slaves were a privately owned commodity to be bought and sold and disposed of at the slave owner's will. As property, slaves were deprived of most human rights and freedom, while slave owners established for themselves the rights to the services of the slaves.

Given this, black slave women were obliged to submit to their masters' orders and prohibitions and therefore to submit to whatever economic and sexual exploitation was imposed upon them. Not all women reacted to the events and demands that they encountered as stoic women who accepted their life conditions passively and helplessly. Instead, slave narratives documented how black slave women actively manipulated their environment while continuously attempting to survive the inhumane conditions of slavery. In this chapter I examine how the slave system, patriarchal in its culture and structure, by legitimizing and facilitating economic and sexual exploitation, shaped some of the black women's accommodations and resistance to the institution and, in turn, set the stage for black women's participation in criminal activities characteristic of today.

Within recent years, the literature on African-American women had begun to look at the intersection of multiple structures of domination. A consistent theme in this literature (see, e.g., Dill, 1979, 1990; Lewis, 1990) suggested that the term *double jeopardy* described the dual discrimination of racism and sexism that subjugate black women. Beale (1979) contended that as blacks, they suffer all the burdens of prejudice and mistreatment that fall on anyone with dark skin. However, as women, they carry the extra burden of coping with both white and black men. King (1988, 1990) elaborated on this observation by suggesting that the reality of dual discrimination often entailed economic disadvantage. She contended that black women encountered multiple jeopardy; the simultaneous oppression of race, gender, and class. Under a system of slavery, therefore, black women were exposed simultaneously to the multiple oppressions of race, gender, and caste.

As a *total institution*[2] (Goffman, 1961), the slave system regulated every aspect of the slaves' lives from sunup to sundown (e.g., the types of work they performed, the quality and amount of food, shelter and clothing which they received; the reproductive rights of slave women). In her examination of the Auschwitz concentration camp, Pawelcznska (1979) offered some important insights into the resistance of prisoners. She observed that the formal norms and goals of the concentration camp were rendered dysfunctional to the survival of prisoners. For instance, she reported that if the prisoners abided by the rule "Thou shalt not steal" within the Ten Commandments, survival was questionable. In the face of scarce food and inadequate clothing and shelter, prisoners who did not steal would be most vulnerable to death by starvation and/or by exposure to harsh weather conditions. To steal, therefore, meant to survive. She also noted that a deeply internalized value system enabled many prisoners to survive biologically and morally, that is, to resist surrender and total submission.

Several recent research findings on the mechanisms of individual slave resistance to coercion complemented her findings. From the existing literature on slave narratives, we learned that resistance was made within the context of the slave women's particular social milieu.[3] Slave women were not only responding to their masters' values and norms, which were not, in many instances, suited to black survival, but also to stresses and strains that stemmed from their status as slaves, blacks, and women.

A number of studies reported that since black slave women shared in all aspects of the oppression of slaves in general, they participated in forms of resistance similar to those of black men. Knowing that they could not make themselves free, many investigators (e.g., Blassingame, 1972; Escott, 1979; Fox-Genovese, 1988, 1990; Genovese, 1974) reported that the vast majority of slaves struggled instead to lessen the extent of their enslavement by attempting to restrict abuses and improve their treatment. Resistance was expressed in many ways. For instance, these works indicated that such resistance was carried off both overtly in the form of slave rebellions and covertly in indirect attacks on the system, through resistance to the whip, feigning illness, conscious laziness, and other means of avoiding work and impeding production. The slave narratives also suggested that there were more extreme forms of resistance, such as murder, infanticide, assault, arson, theft, and abortion.

Within this context, then, Pawelcznska (1979) observed that not every situation in the concentration camps afforded prisoners the chance to give open battle or even to make a passive protest. Under the circumstances of the concentration camp, accommodations had to be achieved to make life more bearable and to survive. Recent research on the slave narratives (Beale, 1981; Blassingame, 1972; Rawick, 1972) has reported that slave women and slave men both accommodated to most aspects of the slave system. But as women, black slaves made some gender-specific forms of adaptation in order to improve their lot and/or to survive. Slave women outwardly accommodated to such forms of sexual oppression as breeding and prostitution. I will elaborate on these findings by describing how these forms of accommodation, functional for the perpetuation of slavery, served as a preface to black women's participation in sex-oriented crimes within the context of twentieth-century American society.

Almost no work has dealt explicitly with the more extreme forms of resistance as a precursor of current black female criminality. In the present study I examine these extreme forms of resistance as forms of "criminal resistance" that were utilized by black slave women as a means to express opposition to the slave system as well as to undermine the system that oppressed and exploited the slaves. I therefore use the concept *crimes of resistance* to broaden our analysis of crime, and I posit that crime itself can be a form of resistance insofar as it can be committed to improve one's social condition or to protest the existing social order.

However, it remains difficult to draw conclusions about the full range of patterns of accommodation and resistance employed by slave women. The literature can only provide a window on some of the kinds of accommodations and resistance strategies described by a unique population of black women and men. Information gathered here is derived primarily from the narratives of slaves who escaped to freedom through the underground railroad or by other means and from the oral history of slaves emancipated by the Civil War and whose testimonies were recorded at the end of the last century and the beginning of the twentieth century. There was consensus that these were the richest sources as to the very significant ways in which black female slaves accommodated to and resisted their condition (see, e.g., Escott, 1979; Hine, 1990; Lerner, 1972; Obitko, 1990; White, 1985). The reportings on these narratives provided an in-depth picture of the mechanisms of black slave women's accommodation and resistance, which laid the foundation for the criminal behavior of black women today.

THE SLAVE SYSTEM AND MULTIPLE OPPRESSION

As mentioned earlier, as a total institution, the slave system oppressed black women on the basis of their status as members of a degraded caste and on the basis of their race and gender. The slave and plantation system were patriarchal in structure and in culture. These systems were created by white men to benefit their monetary and personal needs. To a considerable extent, the types of jobs slaves did and the amount and regularity of labor they were forced to devote to such jobs—whether in the fields or in the masters' homes—were all dictated by the slaveholders. Given this, Fox-Genovese (1988) observed that black slave women, as workers in the fields or the Big House, were able to assume independent roles as working members of their households. As a consequence of their independence, they were able to obtain a modicum of freedom from domination of their men. It should be noted here, however, that slave women belonged to households that were not governed by their own husbands, brothers, and fathers but by their masters, and as the property of their masters, they belonged to a lower caste in which the members had no relational rights.

The treatment of slaves in terms of food, clothing, and housing was oppressive for men and women equally. Slave narratives were quite explicit about the poor quality of food, clothing, and housing that slaves were given. According to Burnham (1990), a slave woman's heavy workload, inadequate diet, and poor housing conditions constituted a serious threat to her health and life expectancy. Nevertheless, some slaves described the necessities of life as simple but supplied in adequate quantity. Others reported that food from the plantation was basically the same: cornmeal, fat pork, molasses, sometimes coffee, and depending on the master, greens and vegetables from a garden or animals hunted in the woods. As one woman said, "It warn't nothin' fine, but it was good plain eatin' what filled you up" (Blassingame, 1972). Several investigators (e.g., Blassingame, 1972; Burnham, 1990; Genovese, 1974) found that slaves resided in cramped and crowded living quarters. Shacks given to the slaves were likely to be 10 or 12 feet square with mud chimneys and no floors, doors, or windows. Because the majority of the huts contained no furniture, slaves had to sit on boxes or planks and slept on straw or dirty blankets. In addition, only enough clothing was issued for the barest level of survival. Women generally received one garment for summer and one for winter and a single pair of shoes.

Another aspect of slavery that made life onerous for male and female slaves were the harsh rules that constricted the bounds of daily life and the punishments meted out for any deviations from the rules. Most masters enforced the law strictly, rarely taking gender differences into consideration. A variety of punishments were inaugurated by slave owners, ranging from mutilation and extreme physical cruelty, to removing the slave from a work position, to selling the slave. Both Escott (1979) and Stevenson (1996) reported that the whipping of slaves was common practice, used almost universally for punishment of both female and male slaves. Punishment was meted to female slaves regardless of motherhood, pregnancy, or physical injury.

Physical coercion was not the primary territory of the male slaveholder. Jones (1985) and Fox-Genovese (1988) both observed that mistresses, in their role as labor managers, lashed out at slave women not only to punish them but also to vent their anger on slave women, who were even more oppressed than themselves. When punishing black women for minor offenses, mistresses were likely to use any readily available weapon: for example, forks, knives, or knitting needles (see, e.g., Blassingame, 1972; Burnham, 1990; Fox-Genovese, 1988; Genovese, 1974; White, 1985). According to Jones (1990): "Some of the most barbaric forms of punishment resulting in the mutilation and permanent scarring of female servants were devised by white mistresses in the heat of passion. As a group they received well-deserved notoriety for the 'veritable terror' they unleashed upon black women in the Big House" (p. 750). The slave narratives led to the conclusion that the poverty of living conditions and white violence aimed at slaves simply because of caste and race, cut across gender differences.

Economic Exploitation as One Form of Oppression

They worked, in a manner of speaking, from can to can't, from the time they could see until the time they couldn't.

Abbie Lindsay, ex-slave from Louisiana (Lerner, 1972, p. 15)

From the earliest moments of African slavery in the United States, the economic exploitation of black women became a permanent feature of the white patriarchal and capitalist society. A brutal kind of equality was thrust upon both sexes, a process dictated by the conditions of production. The plantation system did not differentiate between the sexes in exploiting slave labor. As noted by Higgenbotham (1990), slave women were first considered to be full-time laborers and then only incidentally, wives, mothers, and homemakers. As was the case with their male counterparts, slave women labored from sunup to sundown and sometimes beyond. Unremitting toil was the cultural birth right of slave women. Jones (1985) recorded an interview by a Federal Writers Project (FWP) worker in 1937 with Hanna Davidson, who spoke of her experiences as a slave in Kentucky: "'Work, work, work,' she said; it had consumed all her days (from dawn until midnight) and all her years (she was only eight when she began minding her master's children and helping the older women with their spinning). 'I been so exhausted working, I was like an inchworm crawling along a roof. I worked till I thought another lick would kill me'" (p. 13).

Slave women generally performed the same types of labor performed by men. Fox-Genovese 91988) observed that masters commonly assigned slave women to perform labor that was considered to be inappropriate work for white women. Slaveholders did not refrain, out of respect for female delicacy, from letting a slave woman exercise her full strength. The notion of a distinctive "women's work" disappeared as slaveholders realized that "women can do the plowing very well"; slave narratives reported that a great many women did plow. To harness a double team of mules or oxen and steer a heavy wooden plow was no easy feat, yet a substantial minority of slave women endured these rigorous activities.

Although black women generally worked "like men" in the fields, researchers (Fox-Genovese, 1988; Genovese, 1974; Higginbotham, 1992; Jones, 1985, 1990) contended that masters commonly differentiated the kinds and quantities of work that slave men and women were expected to perform. Some slave narratives reported that out in the field the men each had to pick 300 pounds of cotton, while the women were each responsible for picking 250 pounds per day. Work assignments for women and men also differed according to the size of the plantation and its degree of specialization. Often, the tasks that demanded sheer muscle power were reserved exclusively for men (clearing the land of trees, rolling logs, and chopping and hauling wood). However, plantation exigencies sometimes mandated women's labor in this area, too; in general, the smaller the farm, the more arduous and varied was women's fieldwork. For instance, Jones (1990) noted: "Lizzie Atkins, who lived on a twenty-five acre Texas plantation with only three other slaves, remembered working 'until slam dark every day'; she helped to clear land, cut wood, and tend the livestock in addition to her other duties of hoeing corn, spinning thread, sewing clothes, cooking, washing dishes, and grinding corn" (p. 743).

Black women also worked under the close supervision of whites (the master, overseer, or mistress) at a forced pace in the Big House. A division of labor based on gender and age was more apparent, reflecting slave owners' attitudes about the nature of domestic service.

Women predominated as household workers and were assigned to such tasks as cleaning, laundering, caring for the master's children, cooking, ironing, spinning wool, sewing, and other numerous tasks. Although the household servants may have eaten better food and worn better clothes than the field slaves, their labor was an unbearable load. It was unending toil and trouble. They were at the constant beck and call of the owner or his wife, who demanded service from the time the slaves were awakened early in the morning until the household was ready for retirement. The master's house offered no shelter from the brutality of slavery, so it is not surprising that many black women preferred fieldwork to housework.

A consistent theme in the literature suggested that the sexual division of labor under slavery actually assumed two forms: one system of work forced upon slaves by masters who valued women only as work-oxen and brood-sows, and the other initiated by the slaves themselves in the quarters. But as Jones (1985) pointed out:

> However, slave women also worked on behalf of their own families, and herein lies a central irony in the history of their labor. Under slavery, blacks' attempts to sustain their family life amounted to a political act of protest against the callousness of owners, mistresses, and overseers. In defiance of the slaveholders' tendencies to ignore gender differences in making assignments in the fields, the slaves whenever possible adhered to a strict division of labor within their own households and communities. (p. 14)

According to some researchers (see Davis, 1971, 1981; Farnham, 1990; Fox-Genovese, 1988; White, 1985), after working in the field or in the master's house all day, black women returned to their cabins to care for their children, cook, wash, sew, knit, weave, or do other kinds of work before retiring for the evening. Thus Jones (1985) and Farnham (1990) contended that the slave narratives were at odds with some historians' observations that relations between the sexes approximated domestic sexual equality. Instead, slave narratives showed that the reverse situation occurred (i.e., men working in the home was but a "sometime" activity). For example, there was no evidence that men engaged in spinning, a job that occupied much of the women's time in the evenings, nor were husbands "equally" willing to wash clothes. Men were more likely to be involved in what has been termed "traditional men's work," collecting firewood, hunting, gardening, and constructing beds, tables, and chairs. In the absence of their men, women also performed male duties, such as gathering firewood.

Sexual Oppression as Gender-Specific Oppression

In addition to economic exploitation, women under slavery were oppressed sexually. As stated by Marable (1990): "Sexual oppression and exploitation refer not only to the obvious and well-documented fact of forced sexual intercourse with white masters, but also to those forms of exploitation resulting from the very fact of her female biological system" (p. 408). Controlling black women's reproduction was essential to the perpetuation of the slave system (see, e.g., Clinton, 1990; Collins, 1990; Davis, 1971, 1981; Hine, 1990; Marable, 1990). During the decades preceding the Civil War, black women came to be valued increasingly for their fertility. Those who conceived ten or more children became a coveted treasure. Davis (1971, 1981) noted that the ideological exaltation of motherhood did not apply to slave women. In fact, in the eyes of slaveholders, slave women were not mothers at all. Instead, as "breeders," they were simply instruments ensuring the growth of the slave labor force. They were considered animals whose monetary value could be accurately calculated in terms of their ability to bear children. Finally, as "breeders" as opposed to "mothers," their children could be sold away from them like calves from cows.

Thus it was expected that slave women would bear children as frequently as possible and if they failed to give birth, they would be sold. Barren women were avoided by their communities and punished by their owners. Some slave owners voided blacks' marriages if they suspected that the men or women were sterile. Many masters did not wait for the slaves themselves to reproduce in sufficient numbers and took matters into their own hands (Clinton, 1990; Escott, 1979). Slaves reported that one way forced breeding occurred was by masters attempting to control mating by matching up couples. In addition to manipulating pair bonding, some masters rented or borrowed men for stud service, subjecting their female slaves to forced breeding or rape. These men were referred to in slave narratives as "stock men," "travelin' niggers," or "breedin' niggers." According to Sterling (1984): "On the Blackshear place, they took all the fine looking boys and girls that was thirteen years old or older and put them in a big barn. They used to strip them naked and put them in a big barn every Sunday and leave them there until Monday morning. Out of that came sixty babies" (pp. 31–32). And Escott (1979) noted that for a much smaller number of planters, intervention took more direct forms. Some masters supervised the pairing among their slaves and encouraged or even required a "fine and stout" man to marry a similarly built woman.

Many slaveholders also took control of reproduction by constantly subjecting black slave women to violent rape. As Angela Davis (1971, 1981) observed, the slave owner, like a feudal lord, manifested and reinforced his authority to have intercourse with all the females. Many women were severely punished or threatened with being sold South if they resisted this particular terrorization. White (1985) and Farnham (1990) reported that recourse to punitive measures was not the only method employed to encourage women to reproduce. As part of their manipulation of reproduction, some slave owners adopted the practice of rewarding prolific women. For example, each time a baby was born, the slave owners might reward the mother with bonuses. Sterling (1984) further elaborated: "The majority of planters utilized the carrot rather than the stick to increase their stock. A 'good breeder' was given a pig, a calico dress, or better rations. One planter ruled that 'women with six children alive are allowed Saturday to themselves'; another promised his house servant her freedom after she bore five children, one for each of his sons and daughters. Lulu Wilson was persuaded by a white dress" (p. 32). Other subtle, or perhaps not-so-subtle, inducements were to ensure that pregnant women did less work and received more attention and rations than did nonpregnant women. This technique was employed not only to ensure the good health of mother and fetus alike, but also served as a reward for overworked slave women to have children. On plantations where the workload was exhausting and backbreaking, a lighter work assignment could be enough of an incentive to get pregnant as often as possible.

Another form that sexual exploitation assumed with the institution of slavery was prostitution. Most frequently, prostitution assumed such forms as (1) regularly providing sexual services to enhance the profit of a master, (2) concubinage, and (3) acceptance of a trinket upon acquiescing to forced sex with white overseers and planters.

However, although brothels abounded in southern cities, most of the prostitutes were not black. White (1985) provided some evidence that there existed the "fancy trade," the sale of light-skinned black women for the exclusive purpose of prostitution and concubinage.

Slaves selected for their grace, beauty, and light skin were shipped to the "fancy-girl markets" of New Orleans and other cities. Thus, whereas some women worked in bordellos, the majority became the mistresses of wealthy planters, gamblers, or businessmen. Generally speaking, reported Blassingame (1972), black slave women were literally forced to offer themselves "willingly" and sometimes received a trinket for their compliance rather than a flogging for their refusal and resistance.

Expediency governed the slaveholders' posture toward female slaves. When it was profitable for the masters to exploit them as if they were men, black women were regarded, in effect as genderless, but when they could be exploited and punished in ways suited only for women, they were locked into their exclusively female roles (Davis, 1971, 1981). Slave women, therefore, could hardly shape their ways of acting according to the normative structure inherent in the model of white womanhood.

ACCOMMODATIONS AND BLACK FEMALE CRIMINALITY

The findings presented here remind us about the cruelty of bondage for slave women. Like their black brothers, black women were abused physically, exploited economically, denied physical comforts and rewards, separated at times from their loved ones, denied education, and deprived of basic freedoms. But black women suffered from the anguish of sexual subjection as well. They were used as sexual objects by their masters and became victims of forced "breeding." In the face of these difficult circumstances, black slave women engaged in overt compliance to their masters' demands and conformed to the norms imposed on them in order to mollify whites, avoid trouble, or gain some benefit.

Such accommodations helped to ease the pains of their existence and to make their lives bearable. Of particular interest is that these women not only accommodated to their economic exploitation (by complying with their masters' work ethics, by working long hours in the field or in the Big House, and then returned to their homes to do domestic chores), they also coped with their sexual exploitation by becoming what their masters desired ("breeders," sexual objects to be sexually abused, prostitutes, and concubines). However, there were rewards for their compliance. Thus many slave women did not resist these exploitations because it was futile, could offer them prestige and protection, or provide them with material advantages. Clinton (1990) reported that "'[a] woman's being a slave, don't stop her from having genteel ideas; that is, according to their way, and as far as they can. They know they must submit to their masters; besides, their masters, maybe, dress 'em up, and make 'em little presents, and give 'em more privileges, while the whim lasts.' The divorce records and wills of slaveowners provide testimony of the power and influence many black concubines possessed" (p. 233).

Many slave women, especially concubines and "yeller gals," who otherwise had limited opportunities within the severely circumscribed sphere of slavery, improved their status and that of their offspring through liaisons with their owners (see Blassingame, 1972; Clinton, 1990; Frazier, 1968; White, 1985). Within this context, subjecting slave women to sexual exploitation was "naturally" done by slaveholders and overseers. This form of exploitation was justified by the common belief that unlike the sexually virtuous white woman, black women were promiscuous Jezebels. On the other hand, any kind of sexual exploitation of mistresses, who were perceived as the embodiment of various otherwordly virtues, would be sacrilegious.

An important component of black womanhood is a strong work orientation and independence. Fox-Genovese (1988) contended that black women acted autonomously and self-reliantly in response to the circumstances of slavery, in order to effectively survive the system of slavery; black women took care of themselves because the circumstances of slavery forced them to do so. She argued further that the strongest case for the autonomy of slave women lay in their freedom from the domestic domination of their black men. However, slave women were not completely free of male domination. They were under the political and economic domination of their white owners. The power of the master constituted the fundamental condition of slave women's lives, however much it was hedged in by the direct and subtle resistance of the women themselves.

CRIMINAL RESISTANCE

Although black slave women accommodated to the harsh conditions of slavery, they did not passively accept the treatment dictated by their masters. Several investigators noted the significant role played by black female slaves in obstructing and thwarting the wishes and plans of their slave holders as well as the role they played resisting the slave system. This section is concerned with uncovering the more extreme forms of "criminal resistance"—murder, infanticide, theft, arson, assault—which female slaves employed to express their opposition to the slave system.

Within the more recent literature on slave women, there is consensus that since black women were equal to their men in the oppression they suffered, in some instances they asserted their equality aggressively by challenging the inhumane slave system (see Davis, 1971, 1981). Some researchers (Fox-Genovese, 1988; Genovese, 1974; White, 1985) contended that their forms of individual resistance differed somewhat from those of men, in part because of their childbearing and child care responsibilities. These responsibilities affected the female slaves' patterns of resistance. Differences in these forms of resistance also occurred as a consequence of slave owners' attitudes and beliefs about the significance of gender roles. For instance, slave narratives revealed that many slaveholders' notions of womanhood led them to reserve domestic tasks exclusively for women and specialized crafts—such as blacksmiths and carpenters—for slave men. Since these specialized crafts frequently required the men to move around the countryside, they were afforded greater opportunities to escape. In turn, as house servants, female slaves' proper "place" was in their masters' houses. Under these circumstances, they enjoyed far fewer opportunities for successful escape. Thus female and male slaves experienced some gender-specific opportunities for various forms of resistance which will be examined.

Characteristics of Female Slaves Who Resisted

In his extensive examination of slave narratives, Escott (1979) provided some important insights into characteristics of slaves who utilized some form of resistance. Escott noted that although field slaves engaged in more frequent forms of resistance, house servants also performed resistance activities. The differing roles of the sexes may account for a greater frequency of resistance performed by males. Escott's (1979) evidence showed that men were more likely to participate in those areas of resistance that required strength and endurance, such as joining in fatal confrontations with a white man. Women, on the other hand, were less likely to take part in this kind of action and approached parity with men in the area of theft. However, in two categories—verbal confrontations and striking the master—the women's resistance activities outnumbered that of the men. Most of the women who dared to strike the master were fieldhands and not house servants.

Theft: Emergence of Hustling as a Way of Life

The literature on slavery reported that stealing was commonplace among field and house slaves. Escott (1979) contended that theft was the most widespread practice of resistance and might better be called the appropriation or reappropriation of forbidden goods. Genovese (1974) reported that masters perceived theft as a normal feature of plantation life. To the slaveholders and whites generally, all blacks stole by nature. They convinced themselves that because slaves steal, they, as good fathers and mothers, merely had to take this in stride. They defined "a thieving Negro" simply as one who stole more than the average. He further stated: "Even on the best-managed plantations, which boasted well-fed slaves, the plundering of the hogpen, the smokehouse, the chicken coop, and the corncrib constituted a normal feature of plantation life" (p. 599). Acts of thievery generally were tolerated among masters and mistresses as long as the thief consumed her loot, but they were less tolerant when goods were used for trading purposes.

It was widely documented that cooks and house servants—mainly women—benefited from their position to supplement the diets of their families and friends from the storerooms of their masters (see, e.g., Burnham, 1990; Genovese, 1974). For instance, many female cooks smuggled extra rolls or meat to their homes in the slave quarters. This stolen food generally fed their families, runaways, or short-term fugitives hiding in nearby forests or swamps (Holt, 1994). Many former slaves described the pleasures of eating almost every kind of plantation produce: watermelons, eggs, chickens, sweet potatoes, hams, pig, cattle, and corn (Escott, 1979).

According to Genovese (1974), the main excuse given for stealing rested on the charge of underfeeding. Some, in fact, did not get enough to eat. Others said that even when they had no complaint about the amount of food issued, they resented the lack of variety and the assumption that they did not care about anything other than a full dinner pail of pork and cornmeal. "We had some good eats," remarked Walter Rimm of Texas "but had to steal de best things from de white folks."

Some slaves justified thievery by arguing that they stole from each other but merely took from their masters. As reported by Genovese (1974), slave women figured that if they belonged to their masters, they could not steal from him. The act of "theft" in their view only transferred the masters' property from one form to another and the slave owner lost nothing in the process. In addition, they reasoned that if it was so wrong to steal, then why had their masters stolen the black people from their homeland in the first place? There was satisfaction to be gained from outwitting and outfoxing "Old Massa" in this fashion. Other slave narratives documented another satisfaction to be gained from theft. According to Lichtenstein (1988), some slaves perceived theft as the expression of the rights of parents to provide extra food for their children. Theft then functioned not only to feed the slave children but to undermine the control of slave diets as dictated by their slave owners. Finally, a few slaves explained that theft occurred at the instigation of their masters, who encouraged them to steal from neighboring farms and plantations (see Genovese, 1974).

For the many female slaves, stealing became a science and an art employed as much for the satisfaction of outwitting the slave owner as anything else (see Lichtenstein, 1988). To prevent detection, female slaves devised many strategies from putting pepper in the dog's eyes, to striking a single blow to silence their prey, to burying all the chicken feathers in the ground (Escott, 1979; Genovese, 1974). Genovese (1974) noted that:

> Lewis Clarke told a particularly adept woman whose overseer once almost caught her boiling a pig. Upon hearing his approach, she placed the pot on the floor, covered it with a board, and sat her young daughter upon it. It seemed the poor child had a terrible cold that just had to be sweated out of her. Quick thinking, but not so quick. Like many other slaves this woman had done her thinking in advance and tried to have a contingency plan for every emergency. (p. 606)

It is clear from slave accounts that one component of the hustling strategy emerged during slavery as a response to the harsh physical deprivations as well as the inhumane treatment of masters. For example, a female ex-slave's account revealed that the slaves' food allowance was not considered a gift to them from their masters and mistresses. Instead, she argued that this food allowance was given in exchange for the slaves' labor. Upon making this observation, she then came to the conclusion that, "if a slave did steal, he never take nothin' but what been belong to him" (see Lictenstein, 1988, p. 259). Theft therefore became part of a slave's survival package, as income from theft had become an integral part of lower-income blacks' females' survival package within twentieth-century American society. Several authors who studied the more current black lower-class community (Brooks, 1980; Fields & Walters, 1985; Glasgow, 1981; Valentine, 1978) suggested that most black males and females, being offered little from the community in the way of resources or controls, developed some knowledge of hustling in order to survive. They needed to combine income from intermittent employment, welfare, and hustling to maintain even a low standard of living. According to Fields and Walters (1985) and Valentine (1978), hustling referred to a wide variety of conventional, sometimes extralegal or illegal activities, designed to produce economic gain and was widely accepted and practiced in the slums and ghettos of larger cities. The findings presented here indicated that slavery was a precursor to hustling, which not only ensured survival but served as an active form of resistance to the slave system.

Homicide and Assault as Criminal Resistance

> "Fight, and if you can't fight, kick; if you can't kick, then bite," one slave advised her daughter. A sizable minority of "fighting, mule-headed" women refused to "take foolishness" from anybody.
>
> *Sterling (1984, p. 56)*

Insolence to the masters and overseers comprised only one aspect of slave resistance to slavery. Overt resistance in the form of assaultive and homicidal behavior made up another form of slaves' reactions to the system. This form of resistance strongly suggested that female slaves took their multiple oppression personally.

Frequently, violent confrontations that led to assault and homicide were spontaneous and unplanned when they occurred in the fields and in the Big House. The most common types of violent confrontations occurred as an outcome of vigorous altercations with the slave owners or overseers. Fights were often vigorous. Disagreements could escalate into physical battles. Any spark could set off the reaction (e.g., criticism for work the slave women knew had been done). A slave woman might submit to any and all abuse for years, then, suddenly fed up, fight any owner or overseer who attempted to criticize her. The slave women who struck back did not suffer a paralysis of fear; it was not unthinkable to stand up and fight (Escott, 1979; Jones, 1985; Lerner, 1972; Sterling, 1984).

Violence also frequently grew out of confrontations in the field over the amount and pace of work. According to Fox-Genovese (1988) and Stevenson (1996), field women fiercely defended their sense of acceptable workloads and violently resisted abuse of power, which for many meant any discipline at all. In some instances, reported Fox-Genovese (1988), some overseers rashly sought confrontations:

> Irene Coates remembered that one day when a group of women were hoeing, the overseer rode by and struck one of them across the back with a whip. A woman nearby said "that if he ever struck her like that, it would be the day he or she would die." The overseer overheard her and took the first opportunity to strike her with his whip. As he started to ride off, the woman whirled around, struck him on the head with her hoe, knocking him from his horse, and then "pounced upon him and chopped his head off." Then, going temporarily mad, she "proceeded to chop and mutilate his body; that done to her satisfaction, she then killed his horse." Her work completed, she "calmly went to tell the master of the murder." (p. 317)

Some women resorted to assault and/or murder in response to threats of whippings and actual brutal assaults perpetuated by masters, mistresses, and overseers. The following account revealed several incidents in which black women reacted violently (Obitko, 1990):

> There was Crecie, for example, who pulled up a stump and whipped an overseer with it when he tried to lash her; or Aunt Susie Ann, who pretended to faint while she was being whipped and then tripped the overseer so that he couldn't stand up; or Lucy, who knocked an overseer over and tore his face up so that the doctor had to tend to him; or the mammy who nursed a child but later, when he tormented her, did not hesitate to beat him until he wasn't able to walk; or Aunt Adeline, who committed suicide rather than submit to another whipping; or Cousin Sally, who hit her master over the head with a poker and put his head in the fireplace. (p. 988)

Not only did women attempt to protect themselves but also resisted their slaveholders' meting out lashings to their children. These mothers considered protection of their children as an important obligation, and occasionally they were willing to risk death by trying to terminate these whippings by physically attacking the slaveholders (Holt, 1994). Slave women also sometimes violently resisted sexual exploitation. Since southern law did not recognize the rape of black women as a crime, often the only recourse slave women had was to fight off their assailants (Weiner, 1998). The following incident is from the life of Bishop Loguen's mother, who was the mistress of a white man near Nashville, Tennessee (Frazier, 1968):

> When she was about the age of twenty-four or five, a neighboring planter finding her alone at the distillery, and presuming upon privileges of his position, made insulting advances, which she promptly repelled. He pursued her with gentle force, and was still repelled. He

then resorted to a slaveholder's violence and threats. These stirred all the tiger's blood in her veins. She broke from his embrace, and stood before him in bold defiance. He attempted again to lay hold of her—and careless of caste and slave laws, she grasped the heavy stick used to stir the malt, and dealt him a blow which made him reel and retire. But he retired only to recover and return with the fatal knife, and threats of vengeance and death. Again she aimed the club with unmeasured force at him, and hit the hand which held the weapon, and dashed it to a distance from him. Again he rushed upon her with the fury of a madman, and she then plied a blow upon his temple, which laid him, as was supposed, dead at her feet. (p. 56)

Fox-Genovese (1988) noted that some women reacted in a violent manner when they believed their masters had overstepped the limits of their authority that they could accept as legitimate. Finding themselves in an untenable situation, they frequently turned to violent resistance. Fox-Genovese (1988) recorded how one of Nancy Bean's aunts "was a mean, fighting woman": "Her master, presumably because he could not master her, determined to sell her. 'When the bidding started she grabbed a hatchet, laid her hand on a log and chopped it off. Then she throwed the bleeding right hand in her master's face'" (p. 329).

Specialization of skills according to gender offered female slaves some gender-specific opportunities to engage in homicide. For instance, gender conventions that assigned slave women to kitchens, to child care, and to nursing resulted in poisoning becoming an increasingly female activity. In the case of cooks and house servants, they had the greatest accessibility to the necessary ingredients for poisoning. Arsenic and other similar compounds were most frequently used. When they were not accessible, slaves were known to have resorted to mixing ground glass in the gravy for their master's table. Black slave women proved especially skilled at poisoning their masters, a skill that must have been transmitted down through the generations. Generally, these acts were calculated and initiated on an individual basis (Fox-Genovese, 1988, 1990; Genovese, 1974; White, 1985).

Periodically, the slaves on a plantation conspired to murder a master or overseer; such a murder reflected the collective judgment of the quarters. According to Genovese (1974), these actions struck at especially brutal whites, but in some cases slaves claimed the lives of reputedly kind masters and thereby suggested intense hostility toward slavery itself. In the face of the kinds of physical and sexual abuse that slaves encountered, it was not surprising to find that throughout slavery there was a persistence in the hostility of slaves and violence against slave owners and overseers as immediate oppressors.

Men and women conspiring together to kill overseers and their masters was not out of the ordinary. The literature on slave revolts occasionally mentioned that a woman was part of a conspiracy, but no documentation of the specific contribution of black women in these plots had been made. Obitko (1990) contended that if more males than females participated in rebellions, perhaps such a form of resistance presented the only successful manner in which the males could resist the forces of slavery. Black women, on the other hand, were constantly in a day-to-day manner resisting the conditions of slavery. Therefore, it could not be said that females did not participate in slave insurrections but that they simply found other means of resistance more effective.

Brutal resistance therefore was not the sole preserve of slave men. As documented here, slave women also physically fought their masters, mistresses, and overseers as well as rebelled and ran away. In many instances, these women refused to be broken no matter how many floggings they received. Instead, they continued to fight back in an uncompromising manner. Black slave women earned reputations as fighters. According to Obitko

(1990), they were tough, powerful, and spirited. As pointed out, the black female directed most of her resistance against physical cruelty; some women would not submit to the whip, while others endured it until they reached a point when they would no longer tolerate their oppression.

Fox-Genovese (1988) contended that black women had to rely on themselves for protection against the attacks of masters and overseers. It was they who most likely had to defend themselves and their families since their men—brothers, fathers, and husbands—could offer them neither protection nor security. It therefore was expected that slave women would learn to defend themselves against abusive masters or mistresses, against attacks on their integrity or work ethics, and finally, against sexual violation of their bodies. In addition, women who knew that they were their masters' children had special reason to resent the orders of his overseers and drivers and to test the limits of their enslavement.

Arson as a Form of Criminal Resistance

Arson was another favored form of violent resistance. For the slaves, arson had much to recommend it as a way of settling scores. Arson required no great physical strength or financial resources and could easily be concealed. Genovese (1974) noted that next to theft, arson was the most common slave "crime," one that slaveholders dreaded almost constantly. All too frequently, slaveholders saw their gin houses, barns, or homes burned down, and in some cases, slaveholders saw the better part of a year's harvest go up in smoke.

From the literature we gleaned that women, to a lesser extent than men, did participate in arson (Escott, 197; Giddings, 1984). As arsonists, women usually worked alone or at most in groups of two or three (Giddings, 1984): "In 1766 a slave woman in Maryland was executed for setting fire to her master's home, tobacco house, and outhouse, burning them all to the ground. The prosecutor in the case noted that there had been two other houses full of tobacco burnt 'in the country this winter'" (p. 39). As reported by Genovese (1974), an arsonist's display of resistance did not always win support or encouragement in the slave quarters. If the slave, for instance, burned down the master's house, the carriage-house, or some other building with little economic significance, the slaves might protect the arsonist. However, when a corncrib, smokehouse, or gin house was burned down, other slaves were not likely to feel any sympathy for the arsonist. Destruction of food stores meant that they would have less to eat. Destruction of cotton meant severe losses to their master and the potential sale of one or more members of the slave community, or even worse, bankruptcy and the breakup of the community together.

GENDER-SPECIFIC FORMS OF CRIMINAL RESISTANCE

As mentioned earlier, slave women performed a reproductive function vital to slave owners' financial interests and to the growth of the slave system in general. Yet slave women resisted slaveholders and overseers' attempts to exploit them sexually. As women, female slaves engaged in such forms of resistance associated with their sexuality and reproductive capacities as (1) infanticide, and (2) abortion.

Possibly the most devastating means for undermining the slave system that slave women had at their disposal was infanticide. The frequency with which this occurred is by no means clear. Several historians contended that infanticide was quite rare and did not become a major problem for the slaveholders. It is important to note that the relatively small number of documented cases is not as significant as the fact that infanticide occurred at all (Genovese, 1974; Hine, 1990; White, 1985).

There was some consensus in the literature that the major motivation behind infanticide was that slave women preferred to end their children's lives rather than allow the children to grow up enslaved. Fox-Genovese (1988, pp. 315–316) observed that some women who could live with their own situation but could not accept what was done to their children, took some drastic measures. For instance:

> Lou Smith's mother told her of a woman who had borne several children, only to see her master sell them when they were one or two years old. "It would break her heart. She never got to keep them." After the birth of her fourth baby, "she just studied all the time about how she would have to give it up," and one day she decided that she just was not going to let her master sell that baby. "She got up and give it something out of a bottle and purty soon it was dead. 'Course didn't nobody tell on her or he'd of beat her nearly to death."

Hine (1990) contended that slave women did not perceive infanticide as murder but as an act that expressed a higher form of love and a clear understanding of the "living death" that awaited children under slavery. These acts also occurred in response to the slave owners abusing their children. Thus, reported White (1985): "An Alabama woman killed her child because her mistress continually abused it. In confessing her guilt, she claimed that her master was the father of the child, and that her mistress knew it and treated it so cruelly that she had to kill it to save it from further suffering" (p. 88).

Another motivation behind infanticide was that it was a response to the slave owners' threats to sell slave children. Many times, owners used the sale or the threat of sale of slave children as a means of manipulating their troublesome slaves. In turn, many slave women used their children to manipulate their masters. According to White (1985, p. 88), there was one documented instance in which a female slave was told that she must be sold following an incident in which she physically attacked her mistress. To maximize the harshness of the punishment, she was informed by her master that her infant would remain on the plantation. One of her older daughters recalled her mother's response: "At this, Ma took the baby by its feet, a foot in each hand, and with the Baby's head swinging downward, she vowed to smash its brains out before she'd leave it. Tears were streaming down her face....It was seldom that Ma cried and everyone knew that she meant every word. Ma took her baby with her...." And finally, infanticide occurred as a response to rape or forced pregnancy.

A second method of female resistance to slavery in general and to sexual exploitation in particular took the form of abortion. It was, however, almost impossible to determine whether slave women practiced abortion. These matters were exclusive to the female world of the slave quarters, and when the women needed abortions performed, they were attended to in secret. In a recent study of the black family, Gutman (1976) observed that the slave woman's decision to terminate her pregnancy was one act that was totally beyond the control of the master of the plantation. Gutman offered evidence of several southern physicians who commented upon abortion and the use of contraceptive methods among the slave population:

> The Hancock County, Georgia, physician E. M. Pendleton reported in 1849 that among his patients "abortion and miscarriage" occurred more frequently among slave than white free

women. The cause was either "slave labor" (exposure, violent exercise, etc.) or "as the planters believe, that the Blacks are possessed of a secret by which they destroy the fetus at an early stage of gestation." All county practitioners, he added, "are aware of the frequent complaints of planters about the unnatural tendency in the African female population to destroy her offspring. Whole families of women…fail to have any children. (pp. 80–81)

Gutman also recounted a situation in which a planter had kept between four and six slave women "of the proper age to breed" for twenty-five years and that "only two children had been born on the place." When the slave owner brought new slaves, every pregnancy miscarried by the fourth month. Finally, it was discovered that the women were taking "medicine" supplied by an old slave woman to induce abortions. Hine (1990) suggested that if those women did not resist slavery by actually having an abortion, they resisted even more covertly by aiding those who desired them. It was possible that a sort of female conspiracy existed on the southern plantation.

White (1985) indicated some reasons why slave women might have practiced abortion. Certainly, they had reason not to want to bear and nurture children who could be sold from them at a slave master's whim. They had ample cause to deny whites the satis-faction of realizing a profit on the birth of their children. They may also have sought, as might any white or free black women, to avoid pregnancy and childbirth. Since obstetrics had not yet evolved into a science, childbirth was dangerous.

In these instances, contended Hine (1990), infanticide and abortion provided slave women with an effective means for gaining power over their masters and control over at least part of their lives. Slave women knew that if their infanticide and abortions were dis-covered, it was a crime against their masters' property. According to Giddings (1984), as documented in a slave narrative, the women understood the significance of their act. "If all bond women had been of the same mind," wrote the slave Jane Blake, "how soon the institution could have vanished from the earth" (p. 46).

In conclusion, slave narratives indicated that mothers cared dearly for their children and that infanticide and abortion constituted costly forms of resistance. Those who employed these forms of resistance did so at considerable pain to themselves, resisting from the very core of their experiences as women. Moreover, noted Giddings (1984), they were implicitly challenging their masters, who protected the sexuality and revered the motherhood of white women while denying these attributes of black women.

DISCUSSION

The findings presented here tell us that slave women were not sheltered from life's ugliness or dependent on their men for subsistence goods and service. Their society did not dis-courage them from taking initiatives in their quest for survival. The dehumanizing forces and the conditions of the slave system, as a total institution, warranted the rebelliousness and resistance that black women displayed. Coupled with the deplorable conditions created by the system was the unique position of women among the slaves—that is, they were valued as economic assets and exploited as sexual objects. By virtue of their participation in the slave economy and in reproduction, these women would not act the part of the passive female but could experience the need to challenge the conditions of their subjugation. They came to be active in such criminal forms of resistance as theft, murder, assault, and arson because of their social position, a position that encouraged women to be as assertive, independent, and risk taking as men. Within this context, the findings pointed out that slave women employed such forms of resistance as hustling and fighting in order to survive within the slave system as well as to undermine the system.

The findings presented here strongly suggested that some female offending could be interpreted as challenging patriarchal control and asserting independence, but much could be attributed to both economic necessity and rebellion. As suggested by King's (1988, 1990) observations, female participation in violent crimes as well as theft may stem from the frustration, alienation, and anger that was associated with gender and race. But it was through looking at the broader issues of multiple structures—in this case, caste, race, and gender as forms of oppression—that the resistance of black women had a more complex meaning.

It was important to note here that slave women's employment of resistance strategies was effective insofar as these strategies undermined the authority of slaveholders, gained the respect of their fellow slaves, and empowered the women themselves. In turn, these acts of resistance served as a mirror image of the slave system itself. Violence was a major dimension of slavery. Most white violence, directed at slaves, assumed the form of homicide, beatings, tortures, and rape. In turn, it was not surprising that black women responded to the pervasive violence by committing violent acts themselves. Theft was another major dimension of slavery. The form it assumed was the forcible kidnapping of African women and men in order to enslave them for the purposes of slaveholders. In turn, the findings indicated that slave women's reactions to the theft of their bodies included extended participation in theft from the masters' property.

From slave narratives, we also learned that black slave women had to perform socially and biologically determined gender-role-stereotyped work. Not only did they constitute an important and necessary part of the workforce but through their childbearing function, they became the one group responsible for the perpetuation of slavery. In turn, they were also utilized to satisfy the sexual needs of slaveholders and wealthy planters (i.e., they were sexually violated and forced into prostitution and concubinage). These accounts also revealed that in many instances, the accommodations women made to sexual exploitation could also be considered acts of resistance. To survive was to resist; and in order to survive, slave women complied to their masters' sexual violations. To participate in prostitution and rape meant nothing more than to survive, to try to adapt to conditions as they were. In this sense they may well have a great deal in common with inmates in concentration camps and other forms of total institutions.

Hooks (1981) broadened the analysis by pointing out that black slave women, engaged in various forms of accommodation and resistance associated with their sexuality and reproductive capacities, were reacting to the process of defeminization. She contended that slavery, a reflection of a patriarchal and racist social order, not only oppressed black men but oppressed and defeminized slave women. Black women were not permitted to conform to the dominant culture's model of "true womanhood," just as black men were unable to conform to the dominant culture's definition of "true manhood." The slave owners attempted to reestablish black women's femaleness by reducing them to the level of their biological being. Thus whites' sexual violations, enforced breeding, and other forms of sexual exploitation established black women as female animals. Slave women's resistance to the various forms of sexual exploitation posed an undermined threat to accept their defeminized status. They attacked the very assumption upon which the slave system was constructed and maintained.

Finally, the literature on slave narratives led to the conclusion that black women historically exhibited criminal behavior in response to the multiple oppressions they encountered. And in response to being black, women, and lower class, the kinds of crimes they engaged in during slavery and the twentieth century were both similar, yet different from black men's crimes. They might participate in aggressive crime, grand larceny, and sex crimes, but they tended to bring to these activities their gender identities as women. It is this identity that created a divergence from the kinds and manner in which black men committed crimes. Thus the findings here provide some important insights into how the "criminal" response of black women to slavery had persisted through the twentieth century.

N O T E S

1. This chapter is adapted from the author's article, "Slave women, resistance and criminality: A prelude to future accommodations," *Women and Criminal Justice, 7,* 35–65 (1995).
2. A total institution is one that completely absorbs and structures the identities and behavior of actors within it (see Goffman, 1961).
3. Fredrickson and Lasch (1989) corroborated the contention presented here that the social milieu in which slave resistance occurred typically was the plantation system, a total institution which for the most part resembled the prison system.

R E F E R E N C E S

BEALE, F. M. (1979). Double jeopardy: To be black and female. In T. Cade (Ed.), *The black woman: An anthology* (pp. 90–100). New York: New American Library.

BLASSINGAME, J. W. (1972). *The slave community: Plantation life in the antebellum South.* New York: Oxford University Press.

BROOKS, A. B. (1980). The black woman within the program and service delivery systems for battered women: A cultural response. In *Battered women: An effective response* (Chapter 2). St. Paul, MN: Minnesota Department of Corrections.

BURNHAM, D. (1990). The life of the Afro-African woman in slavery. In D. C. Hine (Ed.), *Black women in American history: From colonial times through the nineteenth century* (Vol. 1, pp. 197–211). Brooklyn, NY: Carlson Publishing.

CLINTON, C. (1990). Caught in the web of the Big House: Women and slavery. In D. C. Hine (Ed.), *Black women in American history: From colonial times through the nineteenth century* (Vol. 1, pp. 225–239). Brooklyn, NY: Carlson Publishing.

COLLINS, P. H. (1990). *Black feminist thought: Knowledge, consciousness, and the politics of empowerment.* Boston: Unwin Hyman.

DAVIS, A. Y. (1971). Reflections on the black women's role in the community of slaves. *The Black Scholar, 3,* 2–15.

DAVIS, A. Y. (1981). *Women, race and class.* New York: Random House.

DILL, B. T. (1979). The dialectics of black womanhood. *Signs: Journal of Women in Culture and Society, 4,* 543–555.

DILL, B. T. (1990). Race, class, and gender: Prospects for an all-inclusive sisterhood. In D. C. Hine (Ed.), *Black women's history: Theory and practice* (Vol. 1, pp. 121–140). Brooklyn, NY: Carlson Publishing.

ESCOTT, P. D. (1979). *Slavery remembered: A record of twentieth-century slave narratives.* Chapel Hill, NC: University of North Carolina Press.

FARNHAM, C. (1990). Sapphire? The issue of dominance in the slave family, 1830–1865. In D. C. Hine (Ed.), *Black women in American history: From colonial times through the nineteenth century* (Vol. 2, pp. 369–384). Brooklyn, NY: Carlson Publishing.

FIELDS, A., & WALTERS, J. M. (1985). Hustling: Supporting a heroin habit. In B. Hanson, G. Beschner, J. M. Walters, & E. Bouvelle (Eds.), *Life with heroin: Voices from the inner city* (pp. 49–73). Lexington, MA: Lexington Books.

FOX-GENOVESE, E. (1988). *Within the plantation household: Black and white women in the old South.* Chapel Hill, NC: University of North Carolina Press.

FOX-GENOVESE, E. (1990). Strategies and forms of resistance: Focus on slave women in the United States. In D. C. Hine (Ed.), *Black women in American history: From colonial times through the nineteenth century* (Vol. 2, pp. 409–431). Brooklyn, NY: Carlson Publishing.

FRAZIER, E. F. (1968). *The Negro family in the United States.* New York: Macmillan.

FREDRICKSON, G. M., & LASCH, C. (1989). Resistance to slavery. In P. Finkelman (Ed.), *Rebellions, resistance, and runaways within the slave South* (pp. 141–156). New York: Garland Publishing.

GENOVESE, E. D. (1974). *Roll, Jordan, roll: The world the slaves made.* New York: Pantheon Books.

GIDDINGS, P. (1984). *When and where I enter: The impact of black women on race and sex in America.* New York: William C. Morrow.

GLASGOW, D. G. (1981). *The black underclass: Poverty, unemployment and entrapment of ghetto youth.* New York: Vintage Books.

GOFFMAN, E. (1961). *Asylums: Essays on the social situation of mental patients and other inmates.* Garden City, NY: Doubleday.

GUTMAN, H. (1976). *The black family in slavery and freedom, 1750–1925.* New York: Pantheon Books.

HIGGINBOTHAM, E. B. (1990). Beyond the sound of silence: Afro-American women in history. In D. C. Hine (Ed.), *Black women's history: Theory and practice* (Vol. 1, pp. 175–191). Brooklyn, NY: Carlson Publishing.

HIGGINBOTHAM, E. (1992). We were never on a pedestal: Women of color continue to struggle with poverty, racism, and sexism. In M. L. Andersen & P. H. Collins (Eds.), *Race, class, and gender* (pp. 183–191). Belmont, CA: Wadsworth.

HINE, D. C. (1990). Female slave resistance: The economics of sex. In D. C. Hine (Ed.), *Black women in American history: From colonial times through the nineteenth century* (Vol. 2, pp. 657–666). Brooklyn, NY: Carlson Publishing.

HOLT, S. A. (1994). Symbols, memory, and service: Resistance and family formation in nineteenth century African America. In L. E. Hudson, Jr. (Ed.), *Working toward freedom: Slave society and domestic economy in the American South* (pp. 192–210). Rochester, NY: University of Rochester Press.

HOOKS, B. (1981). *Ain't I a woman: Black women and feminism.* Boston: South End Press.

JONES, J. (1985). *Labor of love, labor of sorrow: Black women, work, and the family from slavery to the present.* New York: Basic Books.

JONES, J. (1990). "My mother was much of a woman": Black women, work, and the family under slavery. In D. C. Hine (Ed.), *Black women in American history: From colonial times through the nineteenth century* (Vol. 3, pp. 737–772). Brooklyn, NY: Carlson Publishing.

KING, D. K. (1988). Multiple jeopardy, multiple consciousness: The context of a black feminist ideology. *Signs: Journal of Women in Culture and Society, 14,* 43–72.

KING, D. K. (1990). Multiple jeopardy, multiple consciousness: The context of a black feminist ideology. In D. C. Hine (Ed.), *Black women's history: Theory and practice* (Vol. 1, pp. 331–361). Brooklyn, NY: Carlson Publishing.

LERNER, G. (ED.). (1972). *Black women in white America. A documentary history*. New York: Pantheon Books.

LEWIS, D. K. (1990). A response to inequality: Black women, racism and sexism. In D. C. Hine (Ed.), *Black women's history: Theory and practice* (Vol. 2, pp. 383–405). Brooklyn, NY: Carlson Publishing.

LICHTENSTEIN, A. (1988). "That disposition to theft, with which they have been branded": Moral economy, slave management and the law. *Journal of Social History, 21*, 413–440.

MARABLE, M. (1990). Groundings with my sisters: Patriarchy and the exploitation of black women. In D. C. Hine (Ed.), *Black women's history: Theory and practice* (Vol. 2, pp. 407–445). Brooklyn, NY: Carlson Publishing.

OBITKO, M. E. (1990). "Custodians of a house of resistance": Black women respond to slavery. In D. C. Hine (ed.), *Black women in American history: From colonial times through the nineteenth century* (Vol. 3, pp. 985–998). Brooklyn, NY: Carlson Publishing.

PAWELCZNSKA, A. (1979). *Values and violence in Auschwitz: A sociological analysis*. Berkeley, CA: University of California Press.

RAWICK, G. P. (1972). *From sundown to sunup: The making of the black community*. Westport, CT: Greenwood Publishing.

STERLING, D. (1984). *We are your sisters: Black women in the nineteenth century*. New York: W.W. Norton.

STEVENSON, B. E. (1996). *Life in black and white: Family and community in the slave south*. New York: Oxford University Press.

VALENTINE, B. L. (1978). *Hustling and other hard work: Life styles in the ghetto*. New York: Free Press.

WEINER, M. F. (1998). *Mistresses and slaves: Plantation women in South Carolina, 1830–80*. Urbana, IL: University of Illinois Press.

WHITE, D. G. (1985). *Art'n't I a woman? Female slaves in the plantation South*. New York: W.W. Norton.

The Legal System

We explore in this section the status of women and gender bias in the courts. In a chapter by Susan L. Miller and Michelle L. Meloy, "Women on the Bench: Mavericks, Peacemakers, or Something Else? Research Questions, Issues, and Suggestions," the authors explore the experiences and perceptions of female judges based on a study conducted in one jurisdiction. One question raised is whether or not male and female judges bring different perspectives and methods of case resolution to the bench. Women on the bench remain a token percentage of the sitting judiciary. Among other issues, they examine gender bias and the perceptions of and about women and their effect on women's experience in the courtroom as well as the legal outcome.

Alida Merlo, Kate Bagley, and Michele C. Bafuma talk about the need for affirmative action "In Defense of Affirmative Action for Women in the Criminal Justice Professions." Affirmative action must continue if women are to be fairly represented in the field of criminal justice. After a review of the laws and policies regarding affirmative action, the authors present examples of the progress of women working in areas related to criminal justice: attorneys, judges, women in policing, women in corrections, and in areas of probation and parole. Even today we note that women have made gains over the past quarter of a century, yet more is still needed. Attitudes still persist regarding "allowing" women to work in what has traditionally been considered male dominated-professions. As progress is demonstrated but is slow, the authors conclude that within the legal system, affirmative action programs cannot end.

In the chapter, "Postpartum Syndromes: Disparate Treatment in the Legal System," by Cheryl L. Meyer, Tara C. Proano, and James R. Franz, the authors point out that sexism permeates every aspect of society and has many supporters. Those in power are reluctant to equalize power between men and women, because it would mean giving up some of their power. Postpartum syndromes are rarely acknowledged by the psychological and medical communities. Although postpartum syndromes are considered mitigating factors in criminal responsibility in other countries, postpartum syndromes can be and are admitted into custody proceedings. The authors outline for us the medical and psychological ambiguities regarding postpartum syndromes and the legal inconsistencies created by such ambiguities.

Despite the increased sensitivity to the problem of sexual harassment following the Thomas–Hill hearings, working women are still faced with cases of sexual harassment. "The Legal System and Sexual Harassment" by Roslyn Muraskin explores the cases that have been decided by the courts and the principles of law as they affect such cases. Sexual harassment is not something that employers can wholly prevent. It is expected that employers will act in a reasonable and proper manner. Sexual harassment from a legal perspective is still part of a continuum of violence against women. Should women's rights be written into the Constitution? Without such an amendment, what constitutional protections for women are there? The legal question is whether the bodily integrity of women is protected by law.

4

Women on the Bench: Mavericks, Peacemakers, or Something Else?

Research Questions, Issues, and Suggestions

Susan L. Miller and Michelle L. Meloy

This chapter begins by providing an overview of the findings of the state and federal task forces commissioned to explore the status of women and gender bias in the courts. In a more specific context, the experiences and perceptions of female judges, as revealed in a case study of one state, are explored next. Using qualitative data from in-depth interviews, three areas are examined: women judges' contemporary working environments; the dynamics of balancing private and professional conflicts, and the manner in which judges think about gender-related issues. The results demonstrate the enduring effects of a gendered judiciary, exposing women's distinct perspectives when presented with structural and philosophical issues. Future research questions are identified that extend beyond the women's voices in this study to a larger consideration of gender and justice issues across a variety of samples, methods, and substantive issues.

Judicial sentencing is the outcome of a cumulative process reflecting many earlier decisions and stages. One question raised by researchers is whether or not male and female judges bring different perspectives and methods of case resolution to the bench. Most of the research conducted on sentencing outcomes thus far has been quantitative, and as such, may mask subtle distinctions between how male and female judges operate. What may be needed in studying gender and judicial decision making, then, is a *deeper*, qualitative examination of the social context of the judiciary through the exploration of individual attitudes of female judges and their role orientations, as well as the organizational/social factors that affect them. There are two related parts to this chapter. First, we examine what we know about women judges in general according to studies conducted by state and federal

53

gender task forces and related literature; and second, we explore what a "woman judge" means and what this experience implies as described by a sample of women judges.

Despite the unprecedented numbers of women judges at the local, state, and federal level today, including two U.S. Supreme Court Justices, women on the bench remain very much a token percentage of the judiciary. In 1990, 6 to 8 percent of state appellate and trial judges and 9 percent of federal appellate and trial judges were women ("Different voices," 1990); less than 8 percent of the circuit bench and 14 percent of district bench judgeships are held by women (Merlo & Pollock, 1995). For most elective state judgeships, women had to wait until after the passage of the Nineteenth Amendment to be eligible (Cook, 1978; Feinman, 1986). The first attorney-trained woman in the United States was elected to a state trial court (Ohio) in 1920, and the first woman was appointed to the federal bench in 1934. Even after that, the numbers remained small and it was not until 1979 that all states had at least one attorney-trained woman on their courts (Berkson, 1982). For the state in which our sample of female judges was selected, the number of female attorney-judges increased from eight in 1980 to twenty in 1990.

The chapter begins with an overview of the state and federal gender task force findings and an examination of factors and circumstances that have shaped many of the contemporary beliefs, behaviors, and working environments of women judges. In particular, we explore the ramifications of a male-dominated justice profession for women who join, the dynamics of personal and professional conflicts, and gender-related issues in judicial decision making. Within this broader framework, we also specifically examine women's own words about their judicial experiences and actions.

GENDER TASK FORCES

Fighting the war against gender bias is nothing new for women, and the battles won have afforded them the right to vote, to enter traditionally male-dominated occupations, and lifted legal prohibitions against gender-based discrimination. Although progress has been made on many fronts, the courts and the legal profession remain "one of the most durable fortresses of patriarchy and bias…[thus]…as long as women do not receive fair and equal treatment under the law and in the halls of justice, their struggle remains bittersweet and incomplete" (Kearney & Sellers, 1996, p. 586).

Beginning in 1983, under the urging of the National Organization for Women's Judicial Educational Program, the publication of the first gender task force (New Jersey Task Force on Women and the Courts) was released. To date, more than forty states and nine of the thirteen federal circuits have established task forces to study the degree to which gender bias exists within the court system and propose ways of eliminating it. The primary questions the task forces sought to answer include: Is justice really "blind"? In other words, is equal justice afforded to all players? Who is left out? Does the context in which women fight against injustices ironically engage in its own discriminatory practices?

Generally, the task force findings can be categorized into two groups. The first dealt with gender bias as a constant factor in the daily operations of the courtroom and in the judicial decision-making process. In other words, the gender task forces of the state and federal judiciary closely examined how the perceptions *of* and *about* women (i.e., as jurors, witnesses, attorneys, judges, plaintiffs, defendants, etc.) affect not only the women's experience in the courtroom but potentially its legal outcome as well. The second category looked at how gender bias affected the *occupational positions* available to women within the legal profession and court administration. Stated differently, the gender task forces investigated the extent to which professions within judicial circles remained segregated by gender (Kearney & Sellers, 1997, p. 8).

Time and again, the reports cited the "pervasiveness" of gender bias in the judiciary specifically, in regard to issues of domestic violence, divorce economics, child custody, courtroom dynamics (Riger, Foster-Fishman, Nelson-Kuna, & Curran, 1995, p. 466), sexual harassment and discrimination, occupational and pay range segregation, haphazard commitment to affirmative action principles, and employee benefit packages that are insensitive to the needs of women (Kearney & Sellers, 1997, p. 8). Therefore, rather than being a repository of justice and fairness, the courts, at times, engage in their own form of discrimination (Resnik, 1996, p. 957).

Traditionally, the courts have viewed women in stereotypical fashion. For instance, according to the task force findings, many courts continue to believe that women are partially, if not primarily, responsible for their own domestic violence and sexual harassment victimization and also prejudge the type of juror or witness a woman will be based solely upon her gender. Additionally, women's performance as mothers and wives is critiqued by the courts according to conventional expectations. These images remain apparent today, in that "sex of females showhow defines their role and nature" (Kearney & Sellers, 1996, p. 9).

Gender stereotypes may help explain the courtroom insensitivity that male professionals exhibit toward female professionals. The task force reports revealed a consistent pattern: Women employed by the court, including those sitting on the bench, stated that men addressed them by terms of endearment (i.e., *honey, sweetheart* and *dear*) and subjected women to jokes, at their own expense, emphasizing gender and sexuality (Rosenberg, Pearlstadt, & Phillips, 1993, p. 422). Female lawyers and judges were often referred to by their first name, while men of equal or lower stature were called "your honor" or "counselor" (Kearney & Sellers, 1997, p. 10). Therefore, women are seen as women, first and foremost, regardless of their formal and actual powers. "That women judges and lawyers who possess the privilege of formal authority can still be subjected to minor and major harassment bears testament to the pervasive modes by which [male] domination continues" (Resnik, 1996, p. 972).

Gender bias and sexism in the courts is enduring despite the fact that women enter law school at nearly the same rate as their male counterparts, come from similar backgrounds, attend the same law programs, and perform equally well in their academic endeavors. However, the similarities between female and male lawyers end after graduation. Female lawyers are overrepresented in lower-prestige ranks (government, legal aid, and public defender work), while males are overrepresented in the higher-prestige positions (large law firms and the judiciary) (Coontz, 1995, p. 2). The higher "echelons" of the court remain dominated by white men (Resnik, 1996, p. 957). Unfortunately, this trend does not appear to be dissipating and law as an occupation remains highly stratified by gender. For instance, one study found that as more women enter the profession, the "career gap" between women and men deepened (Tiedna, Smith, & Ortiz, 1987, p. 197).

This career gap is not only true for attorneys but is also the case for other female court employees. Court personnel systems are plagued by rampant gender bias, with some states (Rhode Island, Connecticut, Utah, Colorado, and Massachusetts) reporting upward of 95 percent of female court personnel sharing in the lowest seven pay grades and none in the top seven. Men dominate key administrative positions throughout the court system, while the low-paying "clerical ghetto" is reserved, almost exclusively, for women (Kearney & Sellers, 1996, p. 590).

The task force reports have made a significant impact on the administration of justice at the state and federal level and offer many recommendations to eliminate gender bias in the courts. Several states have published follow-up reports that track the court's progress in implementing change.[1] Some examples of these "judicial revisions" are education and training highlighting gender bias, new sexual harassment policies, revamped personnel procedures designed to include family-sensitive measures for court employees and witnesses, increased emphasis on affirmative action procedures to encourage the recruitment of minorities and women, and the elimination of gender-bias terminology in legal statutes and court documents. Some jurisdictions have also initiated "court watching programs" to serve as overseers of gender bias in courtrooms (Kearney & Sellers, 1996, p. 562). However, perhaps the single greatest achievement of the task force movement has been its ability to make women's voices heard and to illustrate that women suffer from gender bias in courts and the legal system differently than men (Resnik, 1996, p. 963). We turn now to an overview of the organizational and professional barriers that women face when entering the legal and judicial professions.

BREAKING INTO ALL-MALE DOMAINS: WOMEN'S ENTRANCE INTO THE CRIMINAL JUSTICE PROFESSION

The far-reaching influence of "separate spheres" mentality (which divided the world into the public sphere of economic and intellectual pursuits for men, and the private sphere of [supposedly] tranquil domesticity for women) confined women—both perceptually and structurally—to differential utilization in the labor market (Flynn, 1982). Rigid gender-role expectations, socialization practices, and institutionalized exclusionary practices operate to perpetuate the dearth of job opportunities for women in the criminal justice and legal fields, with the notable exception of supportive roles such as staff positions. These practices were eventually challenged by women, who sought entrance into policing, corrections, and the courts in the 1970s (see Belknap, 1991; S. E. Martin, 1980; Price & Sokoloff, 1995; Zimmer, 1986).

Even when successful, as in the past twenty years, women often have found that once inside, their roles and advancement opportunities are severely curtailed because of stereotypes, differently applied performances and evaluation standards, and lack of access to the "old boys' network" (see Epstein, Saute, Oglensky, & Gever, 1995; Schafran, 1987). "Although these problems are not peculiar to criminal justice, they are keenly felt among women in this area, perhaps because crime and crime control are so closely associated with traditionally 'masculine' values" (Flynn, 1982, p. 344). "Masculine" traits, such as power, force, authority, and aggressiveness, are seen as belonging only to men and as the central qualifications for professions such as police officers, lawyers, judges, and correctional officers, and therefore are used to justify maintaining them as male-only domains: "the link between masculinity and criminal justice is so tightly bound that we may say it is true not merely that only men can be crime fighters, but even that to be a crime fighter means to be a man" (Wilson, 1982, p. 361). Some scholars suggest, however, that the *most* resistance to admitting women to positions of traditional male power has been by the courts due to the law degree requirement (Baunach & Rafter, 1982). Mandating additional educational credentials—when structural access to law schools have not been equal for men and women until recently—exacerbates an already lopsided gatekeeping process. Nowhere is women's underrepresentation more glaring than in the courts (Githens, 1995, p. 2).

ACCESS TO THE OLD BOYS' NETWORK AND GATEKEEPING OF POLITICAL POWER

There is an inclination on the part of [male] gatekeepers to maintain judicial selection criteria that favor men. For instance, the American Bar Association embraces career paths that are typically male dominated. Older, wealthy, corporate attorneys are awarded high judicial selection ratings at the expense of women, who are less likely to share similar background characteristics, career patterns, and political activism (Githens, 1995, p. 3).

> No doubt the key to judicial selection lies in the political system. Since federal and state bar associations exert substantial influence over judicial appointments, it is significant that women are largely excluded from the boards of governors of bar associations and from executive positions within these organizations. Rather, political party leaders who slate judicial candidates tend to follow value systems that invariably favor the selection of male candidates. (Flynn, 1982, p. 319)

Criminal justice agencies generally are are regarded as "bastions of classical male chauvinism which operate in a variety of unspoken ways to effectively exclude women" (Lamber & Streibe, 1974; see also S. E. Martin & Jurik, 1996). One way that antiwomen attitudes emerge is through the operating stereotypical assumption that the "male" characteristics of brute force, physical prowess, and toughness are the desirable characteristics of the job. These stereotypical characteristics are emphasized in the courts as well: Women are viewed as not being tough, analytical, or unemotional enough to function successfully as attorneys or to make the hard decisions that judges face (Merlo & Pollock, 1995).

Another way that such attitudes emerge is through the development of the "all-male clubhouse" where "[i]n such work environments, participants often value the exclusivity of totally male companionship as a desirable goal in itself" (Wilson, 1982, p. 366). The process is informal, with old boys' networks established through which favors are exchanged, barriers to inclusion are constructed, and bonding among the dominant (male) players is facilitated (Farr, 1988). Socializing and other informal interactions with colleagues contribute to a more satisfying working environment. Women are typically more isolated than men in the criminal justice profession, given the scarcity of female colleagues. This isolation is exacerbated for women occupying high positions in their professions, such as judgeships (Merlo & Pollock, 1995). Apart from the job morale/satisfaction issue, informal exchanges with colleagues also offer opportunities to learn important job-related information. Women become disadvantaged if they are excluded from these: "[I]f you don't sit down and talk with your colleagues, you miss an awful lot of information: What's going on? What bills are pending in the legislature? Who's going to be the next director or something or other? If you just go about your business, you'll be the only one who doesn't know that something critical is about to happen and you'll look foolish because you ask stupid questions.

It's a big dilemma" (Baunach & Rafter, 1982, pp. 351–352). Unfortunately, despite growth in the numbers of women entering criminal justice professions today, in the decade and a half since these early studies were conducted, not much has changed in the restructuring of gendered patterns in male-dominated organizations (S. E. Martin & Jurik, 1996; Belknap, 1996; Messerschmidt, 1993; Moyer, 1992).

LISTENING TO THE WORDS OF FEMALE JUDGES

In this section we explore the perceptions and experiences of a small sample of female judges. A total of twenty active female judges were identified in 1990 using state bar association information on all attorney–judgeships in any capacity (civil, criminal, administrative, appellate, etc.) in the state under investigation.[2]

These twenty female judges represent 8.4 percent of the available attorney–judgeships in the state. Although all twenty judges were invited to participate by responding to a written survey and to in-depth interviews, only five judges comprised the final sample.[3] The sample of judges who participated include an illustrious group: an appellate court judge, two district court judges, and two circuit court judges, some of whom hold high-ranking positions in the state bar association. We explored judges' demographic characteristics, educational experiences, aspects of their private lives, political and legal philosophies, and other attitudes concerning the intersection of their personal and professional lives.

The judges are all white, range in age from 41 to 68, represent various religious orientations, all are either currently married or were married, and all have children. In addition, the judges come from families steeped in the legal professions, which may play a role in facilitating the women's interest in law. This type of familial influence may be typical of the women who headed for higher education before the great changes of the 1970s.

Parents, teachers, and Eleanor Roosevelt were most often cited as people who served as role models for the participants as they were growing up. However, when asked specifically about whom the role models were who encouraged and supported their decision to enter law school, those most often mentioned were *male* family members, *male* bosses, and *male* lawyers and judges. Despite current statistics indicating that 40 to 50 percent of all students enrolled in law schools are women, the judges in this sample remember the numbers of women in their graduating law school class (between the years 1951 and 1975) never exceeding more than 10 percent. Survey responses indicate that none of these judges encountered a female law professor or advisor. Male classmates and male professors gave no support or only moderate support. For instance, one respondent was asked while in law school why she was taking up a chair that "rightly" belonged to a male.

All of the judges self-identified as feminists, Democrats, and liberal in philosophy. The political or social causes in which they indicated the most interest include women's rights, domestic violence, gender bias in the courts, women in the law, and financial problems experienced by economically despondent spouses. We focus on three areas revealed as significant to the judges: first, we examine the women's entrance process into the judiciary. Next, we explore the intricacies involved in balancing public and private lives and the isolating effects of the bench.

Finally, we examine the judges' own perceptions of how being female might affect judicial decision making as well as their opinion on criminal justice and legal issues.

Impressions of the Gatekeeping Process

The judges were asked if they faced any gender-related difficulties in becoming a judge (including earlier phases of their legal careers) and whether or not their access to the bench was limited in any way.[4] All judges indicated that they faced discrimination; actions addressing these instances of discrimination, however, were rarely taken because of the possibility of jeopardizing one's future. Several also were unwilling to risk financial security by challenging such discrimination. One judge said she took no action "…although I could have. I knew it would ruin my reputation if I did." Another judge said, "Depending on the circumstances, I would ignore it or respond with humor or challenge the treatment." Still another judge said that her strategy was to find a different job. These discriminatory experiences are confirmed by the findings of the state committee formed to study gender bias in the courts. Specifically, the committee found that 13 percent of the male attorneys, 20 percent of the female attorneys, 15 percent of the male judges, and 69 percent of the female judges responded that they were aware of gender bias in the selection process.[5]

In contrast to the obstacles identified that curtailed or discouraged women from pursuing the bench, judges were also asked to identify the specific factors that *helped* them to become judges and what kinds of support or reactions they received from their male colleagues:

> First, a plan. The plan was to cultivate the Judicial Nominating Committee, place myself in a position of prominence, in continuing legal education and in Bar Association and cultivate the person best known to have the Governor's ear. (Judge A)
>
> Motherhood! Of course, being a Master because it was a courtroom situation; Also, being the first woman Bar President, having worked around the judges for years, political activities, affiliations with individuals and groups. (Judge E)
>
> I always knew that they did not want the women getting, you know, these positions. But, they were always very cordial….I find that the younger lawyers (when I say younger I mean in their 40s and younger) don't have, I don't think, the hang-ups as much. You know, they went through law school together, accept women, and are just used to women being in everything they do and it's just a very normal things. But [the older men] are falling back and re-grouping. In other words, the women have a very tough time….Every time a woman tried to get on the Circuit Court, they kind of close forces and really resist because you're getting to the top of the pinnacle, see, and they're very afraid that they're going to lose their strong-hold. Gender bias is still there. We're breaking down the barriers, you know, it takes time. I see these young women coming on, 35, 38 years old, you know, it's going to be a different world for them as they go through, I think. (Judge C)

These statements demonstrate that the women are savvy to the political networking process even if their access to this network is more restricted than members of the (male) political in-group. Overall, three of the judges believed their gender played a role to get them on the bench because "those in power" finally agreed to consider women and began deliberately to search for qualified female candidates. In fact, the state committee explicitly recognized the harm created when the number of female appointments were limited: It "reinforces the discriminatory environment women face" (based on the state's Special Joint Committee, 1989) and this recognition may have stimulated judicial nominations of female candidates.[6]

Reconciliation of Personal and Public Lives and the Isolating Effects of the Bench

The judges discussed at length the difficulties in juggling and combining career and family roles. Without prompting, the judges indicated that motherhood was one of the best preparatory jobs they could have experienced before becoming a judge. The judges repeatedly stressed that motherhood prepared them best for the bench, for it taught them "to be patient, to listen, to be firm, and to be fair." One judge said:

> I think that being a mother has got to be a good background for being a judge. You do a lot of decision-making when you're raising a family—all the time. I raised a family from a desk. Also, at the dinner table, when you're trying to find out something, you learn never to act surprised. You learn skills that are very, very useful on the bench. (Judge C)

Similarly, being a working mother helped the following judges to appreciate the dilemmas many women face when balancing family and professional responsibilities.

> Child care problems. I am certainly very sympathetic to child care problems. And I've had women write to me thanking me for understanding that they have to go, for example, at 5:00 pm because they have to have their kids picked up by 5:30 pm and they've gone in front of other judges who don't understand. And I understand that, and I would never make a lawyer who couldn't stay for those reasons really stay. I'm almost shocked, this is almost the 21st century, I mean, we've got to get in line here. Not everybody can afford care in the house and they don't choose that method and kids need to be dealt with and it's a societal issue. So, in that respect, I certainly think my gender and experience as a working mother have played a big role....I've had people thank me profusely and I think other magistrates they wouldn't even ask, but they somehow know they can ask me. (Judge C)

The judges were also queried about whether they found their positions socially isolating as well as the reaction they received from strangers upon discovering their occupation. The judges responded as follows:

> The black robe is isolating....Reactions I received from others? Surprise. You go into a group with a man and someone will say do you know Judge _____. They will invariably look at the man and shake his hand. (Judge A)
>
> I feel less isolated because there is fairly good representation of women and blacks. But I do feel isolated from my former lawyer friends and bar associate friends. People are standoffish and reserved about what they say in my presence. Some men are disrespectful or don't show deference. They are usually litigants....Some lawyers make inappropriate jokes to ingratiate themselves. (Judge B)
>
> Isolated? Yes. Appearance of impropriety rules mandate isolation; only lawyers you *know* have no chance of appearing before you can you see socially on a court day (e.g., lunch!). Reaction from others? Surprise, dismay, respect....What I enjoy least about being a judge is the isolation from other lawyers; isolation from my friends, particularly lawyers. (Judge D)

This isolation may be related to *both* professional position and gender. Increased professional envy of female judges by their male colleagues may also be a factor related to women's isolation.

Gender-Related Attitudes and Justice-Based Philosophies

The judges were asked to discuss a variety of topics related to gender, such as: Does being a woman play a role in decision making? Do women judges impose harsher sentences to overcompensate for any stereotype that women are more lenient? The judges explicitly acknowledged that being a woman did play a positive role in how they responded to some cases. The judges generally felt that *they* behaved more patiently, more humanely, and possessed the ability to admit when *they* don't always have all the answers. These traits were not perceived as weaknesses, however, but as positive skills and strengths women judges bring to the bench to complement their legal knowledge and professional experience.

> We're all a product of who we are, and I think there's a difference somehow in the way we do our jobs as judges. I'm not unhappy, as being perceived to be reasonable, I think it's what I really am. I am quite willing to admit when I don't know the answer. I don't feel hung up on not being able to admit that. I don't feel I have to pretend that I know everything. (Judge C)
>
> I think any woman has an empathy for a woman that comes before her who has been beaten. I think that we can relate to what this woman is going through; how embarrassed she is to stand up in front of the world and talk about being beaten by her husband....I feel like my gender helps me a lot in criminal cases; you have these young people who come before you, you know, first time offenders, I look at them, I see my children, or their friends. I'm sure men have their skills and I think women look at things—we make just as good decisions, but many times we're not as objective as the men because we have that emotional quotient that comes in there just naturally. It gives us a different view. You know, I think we all come up with the same decision at the end, but we come to it from a different way. (Judge E)
>
> I do sometimes have a reflection…that I am being tough because I don't want to be perceived as being soft and I try to examine whether that is what I am doing and I usually decide that it is not. I enumerate the reasons for my sentence. I write down what the sentence is and the basis. But I'm just giving myself a margin of error and I'm suggesting that I don't think we know ourselves absolutely and that there is a possibility that sometimes that concern about how others perceive us is more weighty than I think it is. But I believe and I hope that generally my sentences are fair and are based on objective reasons and not on any fear that I have on how people will perceive me. (Judge B)

During the in-depth interviews, judges responded to a variety of questions pertaining directly to issues of law that affect women. Time after time, the judges responded that although gender should *not* play a role, nonetheless it might. They expressed the belief that women judges may also be able to empathize more, particularly with female victims. Actions by male judges, on the other hand, particularly the ones who continue to operate within a historical and stereotypical context of victim-blaming when facing violent crimes committed by men against women, might reflect their own (male) assumptions and experiences in a culture that often trivializes women's experiences and victimizations. For instance, the women were asked if they believed it makes a difference for male judges or women judges to preside over rape cases.

> I don't know. I would hope not. I would hope that any judge would be able to look at the evidence fairly and impartially and direct the jury in the same way. It's not as much of an issue if you realize that 99% of the time rape cases are going to be tried by a jury. And a

jury is made up, generally, of both men and women and we assume that all members of that jury will decide the case fairly and impartially according to the evidence presented. If we can assume that in laypeople, why should we not assume that of judges who are not only trained in the law, but through their experience as judges, expected to behave in a fair and impartial manner? (Judge D)

Whether it does or not, I don't know. I suppose that the reality is I suppose on some level, it's probably even on a subconscious level more frightening for a female because you can imagine it happening to yourself. (Judge C)

Yes I do. Now there again, there are of course I think our new breed of males may be a little different, but so many men I've heard them say "oh, she asked for it", or "what's the big deal" and things like that. I don't know that the men have caught on yet that rape is such a violent act, it's not really a sexy act. It's an act of violence against the woman....I can only tell you of how I can translate these into domestic violence cases that we hear all the time and some of my own colleagues, some of the comments they make, make me realize how insensitive they are. You know, I've even heard them say [she pretends to sound like a man while saying this], "Well, you know, women like to be roughed up," and "you don't understand—a lot of women *like* that." Until they get away from that attitude, until they realize, then, we have a problem. (Judge E)

Domestic violence had earlier been identified as an area in which all of the judges expressed strong interests. The judges focused on the enforcement aspect, reflecting the trend to arrest batterers rather than relying on alternatives to law enforcement such as separation and mediation. The female judges' responses sharply contradicted empirical research that has shown in the past that the (male) judiciary has not treated domestic violence cases with any more seriousness than have other players in the criminal justice system (i.e., police and prosecutors) (cf. Dobash & Dobash 1992; Price & Sokoloff, 1995).

Well, it depends on the circumstances. I think that the arrest option must be available to the victim. In other words, we have fought for many years now to finally get a law on the books that requires an officer to make the arrest and that permits such cases to be brought into criminal court in a manner that's workable and effective. That's not to say that there aren't other alternatives, or that other alternatives aren't appropriate in many cases. But sometimes, nothing short of arrest is going to work. And I think that that has to absolutely be available. (Judge A)

If someone has committed an act of domestic violence or if the victim has legitimate reasons of being in imminent danger or fear of imminent danger, then absolutely—we can't find out later that we should have had a warrant....If I have a domestic violence case on my docket and I put someone on probation and an order as a condition he has to move or stay away from the victim, not threaten, intimidate, harass or annoy, etc.

If I get a call, I don't take a chance. We've learned, I think, we have to make sure. I think too too many times these cases are not taken seriously, and people are really injured. (Judge E)

I have for years felt that it was important that victims of those kinds of crime be treated like victims or other crimes. I don't think just because it's between people who know one another that the option shouldn't be available....But I think that the option of an arrest and a trial and conviction is one that ought to be accessible to victims of domestic violence. And it ought to be used. (Judge B)

Overall, our interview data reveal a marked difference in judges' philosophies about gender-crime issues that may be atypical of traditional (male) judicial attitudes [for in-depth discussions of feminist jurisprudence related to gender differences in philosophical orientations, see Fineman and Thomadsen (1991), Frug (1992), and Hoff (1991)]. For years, advocates of women's rights, lawyers, and others have opposed and challenged the manner in which the criminal justice and legal systems treat female victims of violent crimes committed by male offenders. The extant literature demonstrates that the enforcers (police), interpreters (lawyers and judges), and punishers (corrections) are primarily male and have been socialized and trained to believe assumptions and expectations about appropriate gender roles in society (Price & Sokoloff, 1982; Stanko, 1985). The judges in this sample seem to recognize the results of this institutionalized and systemic sexism: victim-blaming and differential treatment of women. Part of this heightened understanding is shaped by their own experiences.

In summary, the judges' responses indicate the salience of the role that gender plays not only in the dynamics of specific crimes, but also in the responses to these crimes by members of our social and legal institutions (Allen & Wald, 1987; "Different voices," 1990; Merlo & Pollock, 1995). These beliefs are consistent with findings revealed in research on fourteen state supreme court justices that revealed that female judges tend to vote against the male majority on three issues: women's issues, criminal rights, and economic liberties; in fact, even when the court majority wished to curtail women's rights in sexual discrimination cases, female justices were steadfast in their position (Allen & Wald, 1987). Future research could explore whether or not judges respond to consciousness-raising about general social problems identified by society at large, or whether judges highlight specific issues because of their personal backgrounds, experience, and world views (cf. Tobias, 1990, 1991).

DISCUSSION AND CONCLUSIONS

In this chapter we have explored women judges in light of the gender task force findings as well as offering insight into the way that women judges view themselves within social and judicial contexts. For the component relating to women judges, despite the small sample size, the depth and richness of the interview data provide more detailed information than what is typically collected by close-ended survey instruments. The judges describe *their* own experiences and perceptions, which serve as a starting point in refining questions that should also be asked of male judges in future comparative studies as well as providing a complementary data set to quantitative research exploring sentencing decisions and gender.[7]

Most prior research that has identified gender-related differences among judges has focused exclusively on the types of sentences they impose. This kind of research hides the importance of background factors and experiences that shape one's world views and also ignores differences in the social construction of gender roles and expectations in our society. Gender alone may not exert significant influences on sentencing decisions per se, but the different experiences and philosophies that men and women have create a contextualized construct that may exert distinctions in judicial decision making (Davis 1992–1993; Sherry, 1986; R. L. West, 1991). The differences that men and women may bring to the bench typically remain unacknowledged because they contradict the model of the "impartial" arbiter. The information gleaned from the judges' voices here lends support to hopes that women's "emphasis on connection and contextuality might similarly transform law" (Sherry, 1986, p. 165), as well as to hopes of interrupting gender bias operating against women in the courts.

The judicial gender task forces succeeded in prioritizing the issue of gender bias at the state and federal levels. The reports and follow-up studies generated by this movement emphasize women's experiences in the court system and legal profession and portray how these experiences differ by gender. Collectively, the task force findings have demanded that the "halls of justice" take judicial notice of the problems created by gender discrimination within its courtrooms, administrative organizations, and legal profession as well as validating the perceptions of women (Resnik, 1996, p. 963).

For the women judges interviewed here, several important findings emerge. First, the voices of the women judges indicate that although they experience multiple obligations, they have succeeded in reconciling these diverse role strain pressures. The judges have reconceptualized the "traditional" care-taking role of motherhood to be one that offers excellent preparation for the bench. This interpretation differs greatly from "male" attributes of detachment and autonomy because it explicitly recognizes the benefits of familial and intimate experiences (Anleu, 1995).[8] This kind of characterization permits women judges to use their conventional sex roles to claim legitimacy in their nontraditional career choice.

The women assert that they have been successful at negotiating and balancing their personal and professional obligations. In fact, by imbuing women's traditional female roles with honor and insisting that these attributes are the reason for their greater clarity of judicial vision, the women judges present themselves as innovative mavericks who are more sensitive to situations of personal, familial, and/or economic injustice.

A second important finding that emerged concerns the judges' explicit perceptions about how they believe being a woman contributes to their decision making. Although the judges are quick to emphasize that their decisions are fair, equal, strict, and just, they recognize that being female may bring a uniquely feminine understanding to the situation. The judges interviewed in this study stressed that they believe both male and female judges ultimately reach the same legal conclusion but that they follow different paths to get there—paths that are indeed related to gender.[9] The judges describe their judicial style as patient, empathic, and reasonable, with a willingness and openness to hear all sides, and they recognize that these characteristics may be misperceived or misunderstood by others as indicating that they are lenient or coddle criminals (i.e., are "soft" on crime). The judges, however, insisted that this was not the case. Their rulings were simply shaped by different understandings of the situations and were *enhanced* by these understandings, not harmed or weakened. It is likely that defendants and victims felt that they were treated with more respect because of the judges' demeanor and style, regardless of case outcome. In fact, other research suggests that offenders who are treated with greater respect perceive greater procedural justice and satisfaction (Paternoster, Brame, Bachman, & Sherman, 1997). Nowhere are these unique understandings more apparent then when we examine the judges' opinions concerning women's rights. Their willingness to resist assimilation pressures to adopt male professional norms when confronting women's issues is noteworthy. Unlike the younger "careerist" women lawyers studied by Rosenberg, Perlstadt, and Phillips (1990), who rejected feminist objectives and labels and viewed gender as "inconsequential to their careers," the women judges in this study self-labeled as feminists and endorsed the centrality of gender and its role in shaping legal discourse and judicial action.[10]

Similar to the task force findings, the judges in our sample believed that the sexist comments and actions they experienced did contribute to an inhospitable working environment throughout their legal and judicial careers. They also described feeling isolated and alienated from males in the field as well as from other lawyers and judges. These working conditions may reflect the consequences of being treated as tokens due to their scarcity in numbers and heightened visibility, so that their "non-achievement character-istics...eclipse performance" (MacCorquodale & Jensen, 1993, p. 583). As such, these findings echo those of Rosenberg, et al. (1993) in their research on sexist work experiences of women lawyers: Gender disparagement and sexual harassment are manifestations of "gendered systems that maintain and reinforce inequalities between men and women on the job" (Rosenberg et al., 1993, p. 415).

By bringing their personal and professional experiences into the courtroom, the women revealed that they were able to dispense justice with a gentleness as well as a firmness that belied their own imaginings and expectations of a more humane courtroom setting. In fact, these views are consistent with findings reported in other studies which demonstrate women judges opt for more participatory management styles, in contrast to men's preference for more hierarchical courtroom styles, and that women judges are more likely to acknowledge others' emotions and fears than are male judges ("Different voices," 1990). Although quantitative studies may demonstrate that female judges' sentencing outcomes could be comparable or dissimilar to male judges' outcomes, the gendered paths that these follow—paths that are strikingly apparent in qualitative research, yet masked in statistical analyses—are distinctly different. Furthermore, an analysis of the task force findings provides insight into the "gendered machinery" of the court system and comple-ments the interviews of the female judges. Hearing the voices of women and the nature of their thinking and experiences offers a much richer context in which to explore the judicial process.

ACKNOWLEDGMENTS

The authors thank Georgia Scott and Estralita Jones for their valuable comments and suggestions.

NOTES

1. Colorado, Connecticut, Florida, Kentucky, Maryland, Massachusetts, New York, Minnesota, Vermont, and the state of Washington have all published procedural guidelines on how to address various types of gender bias. Additionally, judicial education programs, designed to eliminate gender bias and sexual harassment in the courts, have been enacted in the last twenty-six states.
2. The state of this study will not be identified, to ensure the confidentiality of the judges.
3. The other judges declined to participate because they were either too busy or because they were too concerned about confidentiality. Being approached to reveal examples of gender bias may have been perceived as threatening to their professional positions.
4. In the state of this study, the judicial selection process follows two steps: First, a nominating committee screens candidates and develops a list that is sent to the governor for each judicial vacancy. The nominating committees are comprised of attorney and lay members. Next, the governor makes appointments from these lists within a year of the occurrence of the vacancy.
5. While the females indicated that the nominating committee discriminates against women in terms of initial selection and criteria, the males contended that women have been given preferential treatment in the appointment process. The data reflect, however, that despite

sufficient numbers of eligible women lawyers, who are of an appropriate age for appointment, women are consistently overlooked at judicial appointment time.

6. According to the state committee, many lawyers and judges believed that a quota system applied to women judges in that "once 'enough' women have been appointed, no more need apply" (Special Joint Committee, 1989). The women believed that higher standards (especially with respect to professional experience) applied to women, and that inappropriate questions concerning family responsibilities, financial need, and spouse's occupations were asked of female candidates but not of the male candidates, and that these criteria disadvantaged women. Male attorneys, however, believed that women were selected over males who were far better qualified, and that women were favored "out of a misplaced sense of imbalance on the bench" (Special Joint Committee, 1989). The committee found no substantiation for these claims, and in fact, discovered that the opposite was true. (Due to honoring the request of the judges for confidentiality, the state special joint committee is not identified or listed in the references.)

7. Obviously, our research does not attempt to *compare* women's experiences and perceptions with those of their male counterparts on the bench, although this avenue may be a potentially fruitful inquiry to pursue in future studies.

8. Feminist scholars no doubt recognize that just as essentialist positions about women are problematic, there are also potential problems when introducing essentialist characteristics of men.

9. This is a puzzling contradiction: At the same time that the women judges admit that they may have greater insight and empathy related to women's legal issues, they maintain that these strengths do *not* influence their final outcomes.

10. It may also be the case that as women attain higher-status positions, such as judgeships, they feel safe in being more outspoken than do aspiring careerist lawyers.

REFERENCES

ALLEN, D., & WALD, D. (1987). The behavior of women state supreme court justices: Are they tokens or outsiders. *Justice System Journal, 12*(1), 232–244.

ANLEU, S. L. R. (1995). Women in law: Theory, research, and practice. In B. R. Price & N. J. Sokoloff (Eds.), *The criminal justice system and women offenders, victims, and workers*. New York: McGraw-Hill.

BAUNACH, P. J., & RAFTER, N. H. (1982). Sex-role operations: Strategies for women working in the criminal justice system. In N. H. Rafter & E. A. Stanko (Eds.), *Judge, lawyer, victim, thief*. Boston: Northeastern University Press.

BELKNAP, J. (1991). Women in conflict: An analysis of women correctional officers. *Women and Criminal Justice, 2*, 89–115.

BELKNAP, J. (1996). *The invisible woman: Gender, crime, and justice*. Cincinnati, OH: Wadsworth Publishing.

BERKSON, L. (1982, January). Women on the bench: Brief history. *Judicature 65*, 286–293.

COOK, B. B. (1978). Women judges: The end of tokenism. In W. Hepperle & L. Crites (Eds.), *Women in the courts*. Williamsburg, VA: National Center for State Courts.

COONTZ, P. (1995). Gender bias in the legal profession: Women "see" it, men don't. *Women and Politics, 15*(2), 1–22.

DAVIS, S. (1992–1993). Do women judges speak "in a different voice?": Carol Gilligan, feminist legal theory, and the Ninth Circuit. *Wisconsin Women's Law Journal, 7–8*, 143–173.

Different voices, different choices? The impact of more women lawyers and judges on the judicial system. (1990). *Judicature, 74*(3), 138–146.

DOBASH, R. E., & DOBASH, R. P. (1992). *Women, violence and social change*. New York: Routledge.

EPSTEIN, C. F., SAUTE, R., OGLENSKY, B., & GEVER M. (1995). Glass ceilings and open doors: Women's advancement in the legal profession. *Fordham Law Review, 64*(2), 291–449.

FARR, K. A. (1988). Dominance bonding through the good old boys sociability groups. *Sex Roles, 18*, 259–277.

FEINMAN, C. (1986). *Women in the criminal justice system* (2nd ed.). New York: Praeger.

FINEMAN, M. A., & THOMADSEN, N. S. (1991). *At the boundaries of law: Feminism and legal theory.* New York: Routledge.

FLYNN, E. E. (1982). Women as criminal justice professionals: A challenge to tradition. In N. H. Rafter & E. A. Stanko (Eds.), *Judge, lawyer, victim, thief.* Boston: Northeastern University Press.

FRUG, M. J. (1992). *Postmodern legal feminism.* New York: Routledge.

GILLIGAN, C. (1982). *In a different voice.* Cambridge, MA: Harvard University Press.

GITHENS, M. (1995). Getting appointed to the state court: The gender dimension. *Women and Politics, 15*(4), 1–24.

HOFF, J. (1991). *Law, gender, and injustice.* New York: New York University Press.

KEARNEY, R., & SELLERS, H. (1996). Sex on the docket: reports of state task forces on gender bias. *Public Administration Review, 56*(6), 587–593.

KEARNEY, R., & SELLERS, H. (1997). Gender bias in court personnel administration. *Judicature, 81*(1), 8–14.

LAMBER, J. S., & STREIBE, V. L. (1974). Women executives, managers, and professionals in the Indiana criminal justice system. *Indiana Law Review, 8*, 353.

MACCORQUODALE, P., & JENSEN G. (1993). Women in the law: Partners or tokens? *Gender and Society, 7*, 583–593.

MARTIN, S. E. (1980). *Breaking and entering: Policewomen on patrol.* Berkeley, CA: University of California Press.

MARTIN, S. E., & JURIK, N. C. (1996). *Doing justice, doing gender: Women in law and criminal justice occupations.* Thousand Oaks, CA: Sage Publications.

MERLO, A. V., & POLLOCK, J. M. (1995). *Women, law, and social control.* Boston: Allyn & Bacon.

MESSERSCHMIDT, J. W. (1993). *Masculinities and crime: Critique and reconceptualization of theory.* Lanham, MD: Rowman & Littlefield.

MOYER, I. L. (1992). *The changing roles of women in the criminal justice system.* Prospect Heights, IL: Waveland Press.

PATERNOSTER, R., BRAME, R., BACHMAN, R., & SHERMAN, L. (1997). Do fair procedures matter? The effect of procedural justice on spouse assault. *Law and Society Review, 31*(1), 163–204.

PRICE, B. R., & SOKOLOFF, N. J. (1995). *The criminal justice system and women: Women offenders, victims, and workers.* New York: McGraw-Hill.

RESNIK, J. (1996). Asking about gender in courts. *Signs: Journal of Women in Culture and Society, 21*(4), 952–990.

RIGER, S., FOSTER-FISHMAN, P., NELSON-KUNA, J., & CURRAN, B. (1995). Gender bias in courtroom dynamics. *Law and Human Behavior, 19*(5), 465–480.

ROSENBERG, J., PERLSTADT, H., & PHILLIPS, W. R. F. (1990). Politics, feminism and women's professional orientations: A case study of women lawyers. *Women and Politics, 10*, 19–48.

ROSENBERG, J., PERLSTADT, H., & PHILLIPS, W. R. F. (1993). Now that we are here: Discrimination, disparagement, and harassment at work and the experience of women lawyers. *Gender and Society, 7*, 415–433.

SCHAFRAN, L. H. (1987). Practicing law in a sexist society. In L. L. Crites & W. L. Hepperle (Eds.), *Women, the courts, and equality.* Newbury Park, CA: Sage Publications.

SHERRY, S. (1986). The gender of judges. *Law and Inequality, 4*, 159.

STANKO, E. A. (1985). *Intimate intrusions: Women's experience of male violence.* London: Routledge & Kegan Paul.

TIEDNA, M., SMITH, S., & ORTIZ, V. (1987). Industrial restructing, gender segregation, and sex differences in earning. *American Sociological Review, 52*, 195–210.

TOBIAS, C. (1990). The gender gap on the federal bench. *Hofstra Law Review, 19*(1), 171–184.

TOBIAS, C. (1991). More women named federal judges. *Florida Law Review, 43*, 477–486.

WEST, R. L. (1991). The difference in women's hedonic lives: A phenomenological critique of feminist legal theory: In M. A. Fineman & N. S. Thomadsen (Eds.), *At the boundaries of law: Feminism and legal theory*. New York: Routledge.

WILSON, N. K. (1982). Women in the criminal justice professions: An analysis of status conflict. In N. H. Rafter & E. A. Stanko (Eds.), *Judge, lawyer, victim, thief*. Boston: Northeastern University Press.

ZIMMER, L. E. (1986). *Women guarding men*. Chicago: University of Chicago Press.

5

In Defense of Affirmative Action for Women in the Criminal Justice Professions

Alida V. Merlo, Kate Bagley, and Michele C. Bafuma

R ecent attacks on affirmative action have raised questions about the goals of affirmative action and its effects. In this chapter the law of affirmative action is summarized and the need for affirmative action for women in criminal justice occupations is examined. The conclusion is that affirmative action must continue if women are to be fairly represented in the criminal justice field.

THE EVOLUTION OF AFFIRMATIVE ACTION

Affirmative action emerged in the 1960s as part of a series of efforts by the federal government to combat discrimination. The phrase *affirmative action* as it is used today made an early appearance in 1965 when President Johnson issued Executive Order 11,246 to prohibit discrimination by federal contractors. Section 202(1) of that order included a clause directing federal contractors to "take *affirmative action* to ensure that applicants are employed and that employees are treated during employment, without regard to their race, color, religion, sex, or national origin" (Zimmer, Sullivan, & Richards, 1988, p. 944; emphasis added). Under the Executive Order, federal contractors were required to develop *affirmative action programs* designed to create equal employment opportunity. Programs were to include an analysis of any deficiencies in the contractor's employment of minorities and women. If deficiencies were discovered, contractors had to take good faith action to develop goals and timetables that, when achieved, would correct those deficiencies (see *Legal Aid Society v. Brennan*, 1979).

Johnson's Executive Order applied only to federal contractors, but the passage a year earlier of the Civil Rights Act of 1964 provided a potent weapon against discrimination by private employers. Title VII of the act as originally enacted prohibited private employers from discriminating against job applicants and employees on the bases of race, gender, ethnicity, national origin, and religion. Section 706(g) of Title VII authorizes courts to "order such affirmative action as may be appropriate." In 1972 the act was amended to extend its protections to public employees, opening the door to government workers to file complaints of discrimination under Title VII. Today, Title VII "is the most comprehensive and most litigated of the federal employment discrimination laws" (Kaplin, 1989, p. 121).

Affirmative action has also been used in educational admissions policies, particularly in higher education. Both Title VI of the Civil Rights Act of 1964 and Title IX of the Education Amendments of 1972 prohibit discrimination by public and private educational institutions receiving federal funds. Race (but not gender) discrimination is also prohibited in private schools even if they do not receive federal funds, under 42 U.S.C. § 1981. According to Kaplin (1989), both Title VI and Title IX either permit or require educational institutions to use affirmative action. It is required when an institution has discriminated in the past. It has been permitted, even when the institution has not engaged in discrimination, as a means of overcoming wider societal discrimination. As a result of some recent federal court decisions, discussed below, the voluntary use of affirmative action by public institutions to address "societal" discrimination may no longer be permissible.

These laws, their accompanying regulations, and their implementation by employers and higher education administrators have been tested in federal courts. Since the U.S. Supreme Court is the final authority in federal cases, cases decided by the Supreme Court apply to all jurisdictions. The Court has decided a number of cases dealing with affirmative action, not all of which deal with gender-based affirmative action programs. However, even when an affirmative action case does not speak directly to the use of gender-based affirmative action, there are likely to be legal consequences for those programs and policies. The Court's response to affirmative action has been mixed. As we shall see, in recent years the Court has become less willing to support affirmative action programs.

Affirmative Action and the Court

The first test of gender-based affirmative action in employment to reach the U.S. Supreme Court was *Johnson v. Transportation Agency of Santa Clara County* (1987). Johnson, a white man, claimed that he was the victim of reverse discrimination when a woman was hired for a position for which he had applied. The agency had voluntarily created an affirmative action plan to remedy the effects of past discrimination against women and to prevent future discrimination. The plan provided that "in making promotions to positions within a traditionally segregated job classification in which women have been significantly underrepresented, the Agency is authorized to consider as one factor the sex of a qualified applicant" (*Johnson*, at 621). No quotas (*quota* refers to "hiring and promotion ratios and goals based on race and sex" (Lindgren & Taub, 1993, p. 248) were created. The Supreme Court upheld the county's affirmative action plan, stating that it "represents a moderate, flexible case-by-case approach to effecting a gradual improvement in the representation of minorities and women in the Agency's work force. Such a plan is fully consistent with

Title VII, for it embodies the contribution that voluntary employer action can make in eliminating the vestiges of discrimination in the workplace" (*Johnson*, at 642).

Johnson, however, included a ringing dissent by Justice Scalia, who described the Santa Clara County plan as "state-enforced discrimination." He rejected out of hand the argument that gender-segregation in the job categories at issue (road maintenance crews and their dispatchers) resulted from gender discrimination. (Gender segregation in employment refers to the clustering of women and men in different jobs. For example, clerical jobs such as secretary and administrative assistant are held primarily by women, while construction jobs and top management positions are held primarily by men.) Instead, Scalia pointed to "longstanding [*sic*] social attitudes" that caused women not to see such jobs as desirable (*Johnson*, at 668). Thus Scalia saw no evidence of overt discrimination against women and blamed women themselves (or "longstanding social attitudes") for their underrepresentation in these traditionally male-dominated occupations.

Clearly, one important goal of affirmative action is "to eliminate the discriminatory effects of the past" (*Albemarle Paper Co. v. Moody*, 1975). This goal may be achieved by making good-faith efforts to attract and hire qualified members of protected groups (groups that have been subjected to illegal discrimination) until the employer's workforce is "balanced" compared to the number or percentage of persons from that group in the "community, state, section, or other area" [42 U.S.C. § 2000e-2(j)].

Many businesses and nonprofit organizations engage voluntarily in affirmative action because they see it as good practice However, when an employer or labor union has been found to have engaged in purposeful discrimination, they may be ordered by a court to establish hiring goals. [See *Local 28, Sheet Metal Workers' Int'l Ass'n v. E.E.O.C.* (1986), holding that Title VII "does not prohibit a court from ordering, in appropriate circumstances, affirmative race-conscious relief as a remedy for past discrimination....[S]uch relief may be appropriate where an employer or labor union has engaged in persistent or egregious discrimination, or where necessary to dissipate the lingering effects of pervasive discrimination."]

As noted above, affirmative action programs have also been used in higher education admissions. The first U.S. Supreme Court case to consider such a policy was *Regents of the University of California v. Bakke* (1978). Bakke, a white male, had been denied admission to the University of California–Davis medical school. He challenged the university's admissions policy, which provided for "special admissions" for "disadvantaged" students (typically, members of four minority groups: African-American, Asian, Native American, and Hispanic). The special admissions program purported to serve the purposes of "(i) reducing the historic deficit of traditionally disfavored minorities in medical schools and in the medical profession, (ii) countering the effects of societal discrimination; (iii) increasing the number of physicians who will practice in communities currently underserved; and (iv) obtaining the educational benefits that flow from an ethnically diverse student body" (*Bakke*, at 307).

Although six different opinions were written in *Bakke*, none commanding a majority of the Court, the special admissions policy at UC Davis was struck down as a violation of Title VI of the Civil Rights Act of 1964. The university had essentially established a quota of minority applicants who were accepted over white applicants, such as Bakke, with higher test scores. The Court concluded that Bakke had been excluded on racial grounds. Although the Court recognized that there might be circumstances in which race could be used in this way, the university would have had to show both that the four goals listed above represented "a compelling state interest" (something the Court assumed was true) *and* that the racial classification it used to reach those goals was "narrowly tailored" to achieve those compelling goals. The Court found that the university, as a state institution, had not met the second part of this test, and concluded that the university could have used other, less burdensome methods not involving racial quotas in its efforts to recruit disadvantaged students. But *Bakke* did not prohibit the consideration of race and ethnicity in admissions decisions in appropriate situations.

Thus we have seen that goals and timetables for hiring (or for college admissions and federal, state, and municipal contracts), whether developed voluntarily or imposed by court order, have been attacked as "reverse discrimination." Critics of affirmative action often define it as mandating "strict quotas" and allowing "unqualified" minorities and women to displace "qualified" white men. Although the U.S. Supreme Court has not taken this view of affirmative action, it has moved in recent years to narrow its interpretation of the law of affirmative action. We turn now to a consideration of these criticisms and attacks and the Court's response.

ATTACKS ON AFFIRMATIVE ACTION

Affirmative action has been under concerted attack since Ronald Reagan's run for the Presidency in 1980. Reagan was against affirmative action because he saw it as requiring the use of race, ethnicity, and gender, rather than "merit," in employment decisions and educational admissions policies. Once elected, he cut the budgets of enforcement and oversight agencies (Mills, 1994). He hoped that the U.S. Supreme Court would follow his lead by ending affirmative action and by narrowing the scope of antidiscrimination law. For example, as Lindgren and Taub (1993) point out, the Reagan administration argued that Title VII's protections applied only to the actual victims of past discrimination. Thus affirmative action programs designed to prevent future discrimination or to create a balanced workforce should not be permitted. The Court rejected this argument in 1986 in *Local 28, Sheet Metal Workers.*

By the time that George Bush became President, however, the Court had begun to adopt a less favorable view of affirmative action. In *City of Richmond v. J.A. Croson Co.* (1989), the Court ruled that Richmond's minority set-aside program (which required that a certain percentage of city contracts be awarded to minority-owned firms or to firms employing a sizable proportion of minorities for city contracts) was unconstitutional because the city failed to provide direct evidence of past race discrimination in the awarding of contracts. However, the Court did not go so far as to abolish affirmative action. Again, Justice Scalia, who concurred with the Court's judgment but would have liked the Court to go further, called for an end to the use of affirmative action by state and local governments. He wrote, "We have in some contexts approved the use of racial classifications by the Federal Government to remedy the effects of past discrimination. I do not believe that we must or should extend those holdings to the States." (*Croson,* at 522)

By the end of the 1980s, then, affirmative action remained viable, although its use by state and local governments had been curtailed (but not ended, despite Scalia's wishes) by *Croson.* As the law stood, affirmative action plans were permitted "where: (a) there is a firm basis to believe that the employer to which the plan applies has discriminated against the group favored by the plan in the past; (b) the plan is impartial, in the sense that it aims only to eliminate discriminatory practices; and (c) the plan is temporary" (Lindgren & Taub, 1993, p. 259).

Devins (1996) argues that affirmative action remained viable throughout the decade of the 1980s and during the Bush administration (1988–1992) because it continued to have the support of a number of powerful forces, including the Congress, civil rights organizations, large corporations, and state and local governments. In 1987, Congress, allied with civil rights groups, succeeded in blocking the appointment of Robert Bork to the Supreme Court—an appointment which, if successful, would almost certainly have added a strong antiaffirmative action voice to the Court. Big business and labor, for the most part, were also supporters of affirmative action. However, after the Clinton administration had been in office for two years, signs began to emerge that affirmative action was in trouble. An indication of trouble was the Supreme Court's opinion in *Adarand Constructors*.

In *Adarand Constructors, Inc. v. Pena* (1995) the Court struck down a federal program that set aside a percentage of federal construction contracts for minority-owned firms. The Court's decision is most important for the standard it used to examine the set-aside program. For the first time, the Court held that a "strict scrutiny" standard must be applied to voluntary *federal* affirmative action programs based on race (the Court had earlier applied strict scrutiny to state and local governments' affirmative action programs in *J.A. Croson*). Strict scrutiny requires that a racial classification be "narrowly drawn" to meet a "compelling governmental objective." (Although Justice Powell's opinion in *Bakke* applied the strict scrutiny standard to the University of California–Davis's special admissions program, that opinion did not garner the votes of a majority of the Court. Therefore, although influential, the *Bakke* decision could not be read as requiring the use of the strict scrutiny test for such programs.) In the case of federal voluntary affirmative action programs, the Court ruled that these programs must remedy the effects of specifically documented discrimination and could not be used to remedy "societal discrimination." Generally, any use of the strict scrutiny test for a governmental racial classification is fatal, resulting in a finding that it violates the U.S. Constitution, and that was the case in *Adarand*.

After the Republicans won control of the House of Representatives in 1994, giving them majorities in both houses of Congress, congressional support for affirmative action diminished substantially. One sign of weakened congressional support was the Civil Rights Bill of 1997, introduced by Senator McConnell (R-KY) and Representative Canady (R-FL). Although the bill died in committee, if it had passed it would have eliminated all federal affirmative action programs for women and minorities (see S. 950 and H.R. 1909) (Leadership Conference on Civil Rights Online Center, 1997). Depending on the results of the next congressional election, we can expect to see continued efforts by Congress to end or sharply curtail affirmative action programs.

In addition to congressional attacks on affirmative action, battles to eliminate such programs have been waged at the state level. Two states that deserve particular attention are California and Texas. In Texas, Cheryl Hopwood, a white woman, and three other whites challenged the affirmative action admissions policy at the University of Texas School of Law. She and the others claimed that the policy represented unlawful racial discrimination in violation of the Fourteenth Amendment to the U.S. Constitution. After losing at the U.S. District Court (*Hopwood v. Texas*, 1994), Hopwood's claim was upheld by the

Fifth Circuit Court of Appeals (*Hopwood v. Texas*, 1996). The U.S. Supreme Court refused to grant certiorari and let stand the Fifth Circuit's ruling (*Hopwood v. Texas*, 1996). The Fifth Circuit used strict scrutiny to examine the racial classifications in the admissions policy, asking whether the classification served a compelling governmental interest and whether it was narrowly tailored to reach that goal. The University of Texas had cited two goals of its admissions policy: to achieve a diverse student body and to remedy the effects of past discrimination at the University of Texas and in Texas public education. Citing as authority a number of U.S. Supreme Court cases dealing with affirmative action, including *Adarand* and *Croson*, the Fifth Circuit held that the goal of "achieving a diverse student body is not a compelling interest under the Fourteenth Amendment" (Id., at 944). With respect to the goal of remedying past discrimination, the court held that the state had failed to offer sufficient evidence of a need for this particular kind of remedial action.

In discussing the use of racial classifications in admission to state-supported schools, the Fifth Circuit did say that "state-supported schools may reasonably consider a host of factors, some of which may have some correlation with race in making admissions decisions" (Id., at 945). Factors that the court mentioned included special musical and athletic talents, relationship to alumni, home state, and the applicant's social and economic background (Id.). Although the Fifth Circuit cited *Bakke* in its opinion, it went further than *Bakke* in saying that strict scrutiny should be applied to any race-based affirmative action admissions policy used by a public university or college. It also went further than *Bakke* in ruling that a state's interest in achieving a racially and ethnically diverse student body is not a "compelling interest" and thus could not justify a racial classification under the strict scrutiny test.

The far-reaching nature of the court's language resulted in an end to all race- and ethnicity-based affirmative action admissions programs in Texas public higher education. In an effort to continue to provide some additional opportunities for minority students, the Texas legislature passed a law requiring that all students in the top 10 percent of their high school graduating class would be eligible for admission to Texas public colleges and universities (Healy, 1998). The legislation does not provide for grants or financial assistance typically earmarked for lower-income minority students, and it does not fund remedial assistance through summer programs designed to facilitate the academic transition from high school to college and to prepare academically disadvantaged students for their college careers (Healy, 1998, p. A31). This law, however, does not affect public graduate schools, such as the School of Law at the University of Texas. In any case, it does not appear to have increased in a meaningful way the number of minority students admitted to Texas public colleges and universities (Healy, 1998). Because the Fifth Circuit covers Louisiana and Mississippi as well as Texas, the Hopwood case may well affect admissions policies in those states' public colleges and universities.

In California, voters passed Proposition 209 in the fall of 1996, which amended the California constitution to prohibit the use of "race, sex, color, ethnicity, or national origin as a criterion for either discriminating against, or granting preferential treatment to, any individual or group in the operation of the state's system of public employment, public education, or public contracting" (Morris, 1996, p. 190, quoting California State Office of Research, 1995). The amendment effectively ended existing affirmative action programs by any state or local governmental entity in California, including, most notably, the public system of higher education.

The University of California (UC) system, one of the outstanding systems of public higher education in the country, had already experienced the end of affirmative action. In 1995, the Regents of the University of California system, under pressure from Governor Pete Wilson, ordered that all affirmative action policies at all branches of the UC system be ended. In arguing for the ban, Governor Wilson stated that "we are happily in a time when a number of the compensations that were earlier advanced to make up for earlier discrimination are no longer needed" (Morris, 1996, p. 187, quoting Decker, 1995). This position—that discrimination occurred in the past and that the present generation should not have to pay for it—is one of the three themes that Morris has detected in critical discussions of affirmative action (the other two are ignoring the preferential treatment that whites and men continue to enjoy, and unconscious racism).

As part of their charge to the president of the UC system, the regents ordered him to develop admissions policies that did not use affirmative action but did achieve diversity in the student body. Faced with this daunting task, the UC president issued "Guidelines for Implementation of University Policy on Undergraduate Admissions" in July 1996 (University of California, 1996). The guidelines listed those factors that would be used in admitting freshmen beginning in the fall of 1998. Nine academic factors, with an emphasis on grade-point average (GPA) and test scores, would be used to admit "academically qualified" freshmen (the other seven factors included such things as recent improvement in GPA, quality of senior year program in high school, and performance in honors and advanced placement courses). If, after admitting academically qualified students, seats for first-year students were still open, each branch of the UC system could then accept other, presumably "less qualified" students. This group of applicants would be evaluated on the nine academic factors as well as on four additional factors, which included special talents, awards, and achievements in art, athletics, community service, and the study of other cultures (including proficiency in more than one language); academic accomplishments in light of special circumstances, such as being the first family member to attend college, coming from a low-income family or disadvantaged social or economic background; and high school location. These additional factors were designed to promote diversity in the freshman class without specifically taking into account race, ethnicity, national origin, color, and gender.

What has been the impact of California's antiaffirmative action policies on the makeup of the student body entering the UC system? Ethnic and racial diversity has diminished markedly at the two flagship campuses of the UC system: UC Berkeley and UCLA. At Berkeley, 191 black freshmen were offered admission in the fall of 1998, down from 562 in the fall of 1997. Six hundred Hispanics were offered admission, down from 1200 in 1997. Eight hundred African-American, Hispanic, and American Indian applicants, all with 4.0 GPAs (a straight "A" average) were turned away at Berkeley—presumably these students were among the "less qualified" who would have been "unfairly" admitted under the old affirmative action guidelines. At the prestigious Boalt Hall, the law school at UC Berkeley, only one African-American first-year student entered in the fall of 1997 (others who were admitted chose to attend other schools, perhaps because they believed that the climate had become more hostile at the UC system) (*PBS Newshour*, April 1, 1998).

In another example of state-based attacks on affirmative action, Washington State passed Initiative 200 in November 1998, which prohibits "...preferences based on race or sex in state contracting, hiring and admission to public colleges and universities" (Holmes, 1998b, p. A1).

So pervasive is the concern for eliminating affirmative action programs that bills were introduced (but not enacted) in thirteen states during the legislative sessions in 1996–1997 (Holmes, 1998b, p. A15). Clearly, the future of affirmative action programs on the state and federal level appears tenuous. Given all these attacks on affirmative action, especially by those that claim that discrimination is in the past and that affirmative action represents reverse discrimination, what does the evidence show? Has affirmative action resulted in a "reversal of fortune" for white men? Have women and minorities moved in large numbers into positions formerly held primarily by white men? Have women and minorities gained economically to the point where white men's economic superiority has been overcome and their financial well-being threatened?

WHAT THE EVIDENCE SHOWS

The undeniable gains that women have made, and the lack of attention paid by the mass media to the barriers that women continue to face in education and employment, have contributed to the perception that women, especially white middle-class women, have "made it," that they can now "have it all." We are told that we have moved into a postfeminist period and that feminism is no longer (if it was ever) relevant [see Faludi (1991) , who discusses this phenomenon and explodes the myths that underlie it]. Unfortunately, the evidence shows that progress, while real, has been slow. White men still benefit from an educational system and a workplace that are tilted in their favor. Governor Wilson's comment that we have reached a time when special efforts to help minorities and women are no longer necessary is disingenuous, at best.

Women in Higher Education

A study of admissions to Harvard College in 1988 found that 200 children of alumni who were given preference in admissions would not have been admitted under the standard criteria. This number exceeded the total number of blacks, Mexican-Americans, Puerto Ricans, and Native Americans admitted to Harvard College in that year (Morris, 1996). Bergmann (1996) notes that preferences in college admissions have traditionally been given to the children of alumni, to applicants from different regions of the country, and to athletes, among others, and that these preferential practices have usually not been challenged as "unfair to innocent individuals," a charge often leveled against affirmative action by its critics.

Affirmative action and related policies probably have resulted in an improvement in the chances of securing higher education for women and minorities, particularly in opening up elite institutions and professional schools to these groups. Women of color have certainly benefited from affirmative action in college admissions. But we need to remember that women began moving into higher education in increasing numbers prior to the advent of affirmative action and the passage of the Civil Rights Act of 1964. In 1920, ironically, the percentage of bachelor's degrees awarded to women (40 percent) was higher than in 1950 (about 25 percent). Since 1950, the percentage of bachelor's degrees awarded to women has increased steadily, and today more than 50 percent of those degrees are awarded to women (Fox, 1995, p. 224).

Affirmative action may have had more effect on the hiring of women as professors, especially in fields traditionally dominated by men, than on prompting women to go to college and graduate school. As affirmative action and laws against discrimination began to influence hiring and promotion in the workplace, and as occupations that had been male-dominated were opened up to women (grudgingly, in many cases), these developments have probably affected the decisions that women make about their training and education, and encouraged them to enroll in majors and training programs once dominated by men.

Women and Minorities Employed by the Federal Government

In 1991 the U.S. Senate held hearings on a General Accounting Office survey on women and minorities in federal agencies. That survey, better known as "The Glass Ceiling Report," documented the progress that had been made in the federal workplace, but also recorded the problems that remained to be addressed (*The Glass Ceiling*, 1993). While the survey found that workers in federal agencies had become a more diverse group, it also found that the degree of diversity varied from one agency to another. At the higher civil service ranks of GS-13 and above, little diversity existed. This was the "glass ceiling" to which the survey pointed—"[s]ubtle discrimination in training, promotions, assignments and reward structures that keeps women and minorities out of the executive suites" (*The Glass Ceiling*, 1993, p. 2). In his testimony before the Senate hearings, Bernard L. Ungar, Director, Federal Human Resources Management Issues, General Accounting Office, con-cluded that "agency affirmative action programs have failed to correct the imbalances in the federal workforce, particularly at higher grade levels" (*The Glass Ceiling*, 1993, p. 87). He criticized the Equal Employment Opportunity Commission (EEOC) for approving agency affirmative action plans even when the plans did not comply with the EEOC's requirements, and he went on to enumerate the inadequacies of federal agencies' affirmative action planning and implementation.

Other witnesses also pointed out that women and minorities were overrepresented in clerical and lower administrative positions in federal employment and that this created the misleading impression of progress toward a balanced workforce. At the highest civil service levels, women made up only 10.3 percent of senior executive service positions in 1989 (*The Glass Ceiling*, 1993, p. 124).

In 1990, men received higher average salaries than women in executive branch agencies worldwide, and this was true even when race was factored in. White men in federal white-collar occupations received an average salary of $39,211, black men $26,690, Hispanic men $31,757, Asian men $37,217, and Native American men $29,348. For women in federal white-collar occupations, average salaries were $26,637 for white women, $23,638 for black women, $23,384 for Hispanic women, $27,480 for Asian women, and $21,949 for Native American women (*The Glass Ceiling*, 1993, p. 147). Note that only Asian women had an average salary higher than any group of men, black men in this case. Similar differences were found in the average salaries of men and women in federal blue-collar occupations except that no group of women had an average salary higher than any group of men. The witness who presented these statistics pointed to occupational gender segregation as the main reason for these discrepancies.

Occupational Gender Segregation and the Effects of Affirmative Action

Occupational gender segregation "refers to the degree to which men and women are concentrated in occupations in which workers of one sex predominate" (Renzetti & Curran, 1995, p. 259). In the U.S. workplace today, workers are much more likely to work with other workers of the same gender (and race) than to work in mixed groups. This segregation is reflected in the terms *women's work* and *men's work*. One survey of occupational segregation done in 1989 found that "[j]obs in which 100 percent of the incumbents were male or 100 percent were female together accounted for 70 percent of all jobs....Only 14 percent of the respondents held jobs in which males and females worked together in numbers approximating their share of the workforce" (Bergmann, 1996, pp. 42–43).

However, women are moving into traditionally all-male occupations, for which affirmative action must be credited. For example, in 1960 women were 0.8 percent of engineers; in 1990 women made up 9.1 percent of engineers. Women have gone from comprising 2.5 percent of lawyers and judges in 1960 to 20 percent of that group in 1991. Among police and detectives, women made up 2.7 percent in 1960; they were 8.1 percent of that group in 1990. For carpenters, women increased from 0.3 percent in 1960 to 1.7 percent in 1990 (Flanagan & Maguire 1992, p. 41; Thornborrow & Sheldon, 1995, p. 211; U.S. Bureau of the Census, 1997, p. 215). Clearly, women have made gains, but it is also clear that progress has come more easily and rapidly in some occupations than in others. Thornborrow and Sheldon report that gender segregation in the workplace has been more persistent than racial segregation.

In 1995, President Clinton commissioned a review of affirmative action and its effects. The report clearly demonstrated that affirmative action, coupled with other efforts to eliminate discrimination, has benefited women. For example, the report pointed to an increase in the percentage of female police officers in the San Francisco Police Department from 4 percent in 1979 to 14.5 percent in 1985 and credited a court-ordered affirmative action plan that resulted from a lawsuit brought by the Department of Justice against the city of San Francisco (*Affirmative Action Review*, 1995).

The report asked whether discrimination against women and minorities still existed and found good evidence to answer in the affirmative. For example, a study of the hiring practices at top restaurants in Philadelphia found that male applicants were twice as likely to be interviewed as equally qualified female applicants, and that males were five times more likely to be offered jobs (*Affirmative Action Review*, 1995, citing Neumark et al., 1995). Women with master's degrees, on average, earn the same as men with associate's degrees, on average (*Affirmative Action Review*, 1995, citing 1990 census data compiled by the Office of Federal Contract Compliance in 1995). A study of the 1972–1975 graduates of University of Michigan's law school who had been in practice for fifteen years found that men earned 13 percent more than women, even when grades in law school, hours of work, family responsibilities, experience, and area of practice were controlled (*Affirmative Action Review*, 1995, citing Wood, Corcoran, & Courant, 1993).

In addition to occupational gender segregation, and related to it, is the wage gap between men and women. We have included some statistics on the wage gap above. More generally, in 1995 white women's wages were 73 percent of white men's; black women's were 63 percent of white men's (Bergmann, 1996). Bergmann attributes the gap to a number of factors, including education, experience, residence in low-wage regions, and discrimination. She calculates the residual gap (the gap that remains after all factors but discrimination have been eliminated) as about $3000 per year for black men and $5000 per year for black and white women.

WOMEN'S PROGRESS IN CRIMINAL JUSTICE

Women as Attorneys

There is no doubt that women have made great strides in the legal profession over the last twenty-five years. They are currently well represented in law schools, and the number of women practicing law has increased dramatically. In 1970, women were only 3 percent of all attorneys admitted to the bar. By 1980, women's share had risen to 8 percent, and by 1991, women comprised 20 percent of all attorneys (U.S. Bureau of the Census, 1997, p. 215). President Clinton's appointment of Janet Reno as the Attorney General is one manifestation of how much progress women attorneys have made.

But as Kaufman (1995) points out, while there are more female attorneys than ever before, they are clustered in specialties with lower status and pay, such as tax and trusts and estates. Recently, women have made significant gains in criminal law. As criminal lawyers, women are more likely to work as prosecutors or public defenders where the pay is typically low. However, these jobs can be steppingstones to a more prestigious career (Merlo & Pollock, 1995).

Women as Judges

Because so few women have been attorneys until recently, it is not surprising that women are still underrepresented on the bench. President Carter was the first President to appoint a significant number of women to the federal bench. Where Nixon and Ford had appointed only a few women to federal district court seats (0.6 percent and 1.9 percent of all such appointments, respectively), 14.4 percent of President Carter's appointments were women. In 1977, when Carter was inaugurated, women held 10 of 583 federal judicial appointments. By 1980, when he left office, that number had increased to 44 out of 648. (Flynn, 1982, p. 318).

President Reagan entered the White House in 1981. During his two terms in office he appointed fewer minorities and women than had Carter. The percentage of women appointed to the federal bench dropped to 7.4 percent under Reagan. But under President Bush, who succeeded Reagan, the number of female appointees again increased—nearly 20 percent of Bush's appointments were women. And under President Clinton the upward trend continues. Women made up 30 percent of Clinton's appointments to the bench of federal district courts by 1996 (Maguire & Pastore, 1997, p. 62)

Members of racial and ethnic minority groups have not fared as well as women (some of whom are, of course, members of these groups). Under the Carter administration, African-Americans were appointed to 13.9 percent of federal district court judgeships, but during the Reagan years this number plummeted to 3.9 percent. Bush's appointments were 6.8 percent minority. Clinton has made a major effort to appoint minorities to the bench, and during 1993–1996, 19.5 percent of his appointments to district court seats were African-Americans (Maguire & Pastore, 1997, p. 62).

Presidential appointments to the U.S. Courts of Appeals show a similar pattern. Presidents Nixon and Ford did not appoint any women or minorities to the courts of appeals. On the other hand, of Carter's appointments, 19.6 percent were women and 16.1 percent were African-American. Reagan took the opposite tack: From 1981 through 1984 only 3.2 percent of his appointments went to women; the percentage increased from 1985 to 1988 to 6.4 percent, but during this period not one minority was appointed as a judge in the courts of appeals. Bush, however, raised these percentages to 18.9 percent for women and 10.8 percent for African-Americans and Hispanics. Clinton's rate of appointing minorities and women has been even higher; during 1993–1996, 31 percent of his appointments were women and 24.1 percent were African-American and Hispanic (Maguire & Pastore, 1997, p. 61).

Women in Policing

Women's Progress in Obtaining Employment in Police Departments.   In the area of law enforcement, women have made limited progress over the past twenty-six years. Much of this progress, however, may be attributed to court-ordered recruiting and hiring practices implemented to increase the diversity of police forces across the country. In 1972, women were 1.5 percent of all police officers. By 1979, approximately 3.4 percent of all police officers were women (Feinman, 1986, p. 92). This figure grew to 5.9 percent in 1983, with women representing 6.9 percent of the police in larger cities (with populations over 250,000) (U.S. Department of Justice, 1984, p. 252). In 1993, women were 8.8 percent of all full-time sworn personnel in local police departments and 10.1 percent in 1996 (Maguire & Pastore, 1997, p. 38; U.S. Department of Justice, 1997, p. 290).

A recent survey conducted by the National Center for Women and Policing found that Pittsburgh, Pennsylvania leads the nation in the number of female officers with women representing 25 percent of the police force. Other cities with the highest rates of female officers include Washington, DC (24.8 percent), as well as Detroit and Philadelphia (21.6 percent). The survey entitled *Equality Denied: The Status of Women in Policing* notes that eight out of the ten police departments with the largest numbers of women on the force are either currently under mandatory hiring policies regarding women or had followed such court orders in the past (Fuoco, 1998). As such quota policies fall out of political favor and are discontinued, the rate of female police recruits in these cities will probably drop significantly. The federal court order regarding the hiring of minorities by the Pittsburgh Police Department was lifted in 1991. Since that year, females have made up 8.2 percent of new officers hired, a figure below the national average (Fuoco, 1998).

Research on the employment of women police officers in other states has documented similar patterns. In their research on women in law enforcement in Florida in 1988, Poulos and Doerner found that when the police agency was under a court-imposed affirmative action plan, there was a greater presence of women. Additionally, when a police department has a firm minority presence, there are likely to be more women officers (Poulos & Doerner, 1996, p. 30).

Although the strides women have made in large metropolitan police departments are encouraging, their inclusion in a number of state police departments is minimal. For example, in 1997, women made up 2.9 percent of the state police force in New Jersey, 3.8 percent in Pennsylvania, 3.8 percent in Virginia, 1.4 percent in Oklahoma, and 0.8 percent in North Carolina (Fuoco, 1998, p. A10). In Pennsylvania, there are currently 158 women state police officers compared to 4051 men. Some growth has occurred since 1983, when women represented 2 percent of the Pennsylvania State Police; in 1998, they represented 3.9 percent of the force (McKinnnon, 1998, p. A10). Only one state, Wisconsin, reported that women comprised 10 percent of all state police in 1996 (U.S. Department of Justice, 1997, p. 291). These data suggest that women's entry and assimilation into the state police forces across the nation have been limited at best.

Recent data on women's representation among federal law enforcement agencies suggest that women have made some progress. As of June 1996, women comprised 14 percent of all federal officers who have arrest and firearms authority (Reaves, 1997, p. 5). The agency with the largest percentage of women on the federal level was the Internal Revenue Service, which reported that 23.4 percent of its employees were women (Reaves, 1997, p. 5). Three federal agencies with low percentages of women were the Fish and Wildlife Service (8.2 percent) and the Park Police and the Secret Service, which each reported that women comprised 8.8 percent of their employees (Reaves 1997, p. 5).

These modest gains were probably facilitated, in part, by affirmative action programs. If affirmative action ceases to exist, women's representation will probably diminish. Rather than setting quotas as is frequently characterized, affirmative action programs simply made these agencies more accessible to women and minorities.

Gender Discrimination and Sexual Harassment Litigation in Law Enforcement. In the first edition of this book, Hale and Menniti (1993) discussed gender discrimination and sexual harassment directed against women police officers. Their review of a number of legal cases brought by female police officers shows how widespread these discriminatory practices were and how the law could be used by victims of discrimination to change the policies of police departments and the behavior of individual police personnel.

Unfortunately, not all departments seem to have gotten the message. Three female officers and three male officers in New York City initiated a lawsuit in which they allege that eleven department officials and supervisors engaged in sexual harassment and violated Title VII by engaging in employment discrimination (Raab, 1998). The case is scheduled to go to trial next year. One of the plaintiffs alleges that she has been the victim of sexual harassment for twelve years, beginning when she was a rookie. In one of the incidents recounted in the lawsuit, Officer Stacey Maher contends that when she resisted the squad commander's "attempts to grope her, she was given a 'punishment post' of foot patrol by herself on the Brooklyn Bridge in the dead of winter" (Raab, 1998).

A recent Westlaw search performed by one of the authors of this chapter (Bagley) found that outrageous behavior continues to be directed against female employees, both police officers and civilians, in police departments. For example, in *Hurley v. Atlantic City Police Department* (1996), Sergeant Hurley, a woman, claimed that she had been subjected to gender discrimination and sexual harassment, beginning while she attended the police academy in the 1970s and continuing into the early 1990s after she had been promoted to sergeant. She was the first female sergeant in the department. During her tenure in the department she was subjected to obscene graffiti and excluded from supervisory meetings other sergeants attended. Her radio transmissions were interrupted or cut off, the captain who supervised her made demeaning comments about her in the presence of other personnel, and a sanitary napkin with sergeant's stripes was hung over her roll-call podium. When she complained, she was transferred to an undesirable assignment in the property room. The Atlantic City Police Department never investigated her charges, never punished anyone, and never took any real action except to paint over the obscene graffiti months after it appeared. At trial, the captain who supervised Hurley dismissed this behavior as "childish." The appeals court disagreed and upheld the verdict below for Hurley.

In a case involving a female civilian employee of a police department (*Wilson v. Susquehanna Township Police Department*, 1995), the court describes the "sexually charged atmosphere" in that police department:

> ...the circulation on a daily basis of sexually explicit drawings, and the posting of obscene notes, some referring to female employees by name. Sexual conversations with female employees accompanied by leering were common place [*sic*]. A professional X-rated movie was shown, as well as graphic home videos. The female employees were called to the break room by officers to join them in viewing these pornographic films. The Chief talked about the sex life of some of the officers as well as his own, even commenting adversely about his own anatomy. The Chief also made other sexual comments offensive to women, if not also to men. These comments were about the anatomy of female employees and their physiological and sexual differences. Ms. Wilson testified about an indecent assault on her by an officer. When she complained to Chief Bell he laughingly dismissed it. (at 126, 128)

These cases demonstrate that discrimination and harassment against women police officers and other women working in police departments have not disappeared and are not a relic of the past, despite what Governor Pete Wilson and others may wish to believe. Although women's increased presence in police departments around the country is undeniable and can certainly be credited to affirmative action as well as to other efforts to combat discrimination, they have not reached parity with men, either in numbers or in acceptance. We can assume, with the judge in *Hurley*, that "[a]s women increasingly enter workplaces historically reserved for men, particularly those which value traditionally 'male' virtues such as physical strength and courage, it is not surprising that some male employees will by word or deed display their displeasure at this female 'intrusion'" (at 401). These cases probably represent only the tip of the iceberg of harassment and discrimination directed against women in policing.

Women in Corrections

Women in Correctional Institutions: Correctional Officers and Wardens.
Women have had a long history of employment within correctional institutions, but until recently were employed only in those housing female offenders (Pollock-Byrne, 1990; Rafter and Stanko, 1982). The enactment of Title VII of the Civil Rights Act, and its application to the public employment sector, opened up opportunities for women to work within correctional facilities in all capacities. The percentage of female correctional officers in

state adult systems rose from 9.2 percent in 1973, to 12.7 percent of all corrections officers in 1979 (Chapman, Minor, & Ricker, cited in Zupan, 1992, p. 327; Feinman, 1986, p. 155). By 1985, women were 10 percent of corrections officers in state prisons and 10 percent in federal prisons (Jamieson & Flanagan, 1989, p. 42).

In the 1990s, women made greater strides in the correctional officer ranks. Maguire, Pastore, and Flanagan reported that by mid-1992, women were 17 percent of corrections officers in male and female prisons (1993, p. 98; Beichner & Merlo, 1998, p. 11). More recently, women have attained greater representation in the position of correctional officer. However, that progress varies considerably from the federal government to individual states. For example, in 1996, 12 percent of all employees (1 in 8) in the Federal Bureau of Prisons were women who had arrest and firearms authority (Reaves, 1997, p. 5). Camp and Camp (1997, p. 102) report that as of January 1, 1997, women comprised 20 percent of all correctional officers (line staff) in adult institutions on the federal and state level. The percentage of women who work as correctional officers (line staff) ranged from a low of 4.2 percent in Utah to a high of 46.6 percent in Mississippi (Camp & Camp, 1997, p. 103). Some of the states with the largest prison populations, such as Pennsylvania, report small percentages of women in correctional officer positions (8 percent) (Camp & Camp, 1997, p. 112).

At the present time, women are more represented than ever before in corrections, yet they face more than a challenging job dealing with a difficult population; they often face a variety of gender-related issues, such as tokenism and unacceptance by male co-workers (Zupan, 1992). Because they are easily identified, women correctional officers are often more closely observed and analyzed throughout their daily activities than male guards (Zupan, 1992). Women within corrections also must deal with resistance to their presence by their male counterparts (Pollock-Byrne, 1990).

Improving the education and training of offficers may help to dispel some myths about female correctional officers and reduce instances of sexism in the workplace. The best method to change attitudes is to increase the presence of female correctional officers in male facilities (Pollock-Byrne, 1990). Unfortunately, with the antagonism toward affirmative action programs, women may once again be faced with few opportunities to pursue a career in corrections.

It should also be noted that these increases in the number and the percent of female correctional officers do not necessarily mean that women correctional officers have achieved parity with their male counterparts, or that large numbers of women are working in male institutions. Beichner and Merlo found that the increases in women correctional officers were largely due to the increase in the number of women offenders. While the number of women incarcerated in prison increased twelvefold between 1973 and 1997, the number of women correctional officers increased eightfold (1998, p. 12). The research suggests that it is the demand for more women correctional officers to guard the burgeoning population of women offenders rather than affirmative action that is fueling the demand for women correctional officers (Beichner & Merlo, 1998).

Women whose work experience is only in female institutions do not have the same opportunity for promotion as their male counterparts. The range of experiences that women correctional officers have in a single women's institution which houses all levels of inmate custody cannot compare to those of a male correctional officer who can be re-assigned to a variety of male institutions or who can work in a very large male institution

(Beichner & Merlo, 1998, p. 12). Clearly, women are disadvantaged by their segregation in women's institutions.

Part of the problem has been the belief that women are incapable of handling the rigors of male institutions, the issue of inmates' rights to privacy, and the belief that women do not want to work with male inmates. There is no evidence which indicates that women are incapable of doing the same job as men in men's institutions. Yet this myth persists and is sometimes communicated within the ranks and reinforced by supervisors. Although both inmates and correctional officers have initiated litigation to prevent cross-gender correctional supervision in prison, this has not prevented male correctional officers from working in women's institutions, and this continues today. Women's reluctance to apply for positions in all-male institutions may be due to the fact that their reception and treatment there by their supervisors and colleagues are disheartening at best and harassing at worst (Beichner & Merlo,1998; Britton, 1997).

African-American women have made small gains in this field, but Hispanic women have lost ground. In 1996 white women made up 10 percent of corrections officers in state-run adult facilities (Maguire & Pastore, 1997, p. 88). African-American women were 5.9 percent of corrections officers in adult facilities in 1989 and 7 percent in 1996. The percentage of female corrections officers who are Hispanic declined during the same period, from 4.5 percent in 1989 to 1 percent in 1996 (Maguire & Flanagan, 1990, p. 94; Maguire & Pastore, 1994, p. 94; 1997, p. 88).

Women have marginally increased their presence as wardens and supervisors in corrections facilities for adults. White women were 11 percent of wardens and supervisors in 1996, an increase from 8.3 percent in 1989. Women of color held 3.4 percent of warden/supervisor positions in 1990 and 5 percent in 1996 (Maguire & Flanagan, 1990, p. 96; Maguire & Pastore, 1994, p. 96; 1997, p. 89).

On the other hand, the proportion of wardens and superintendents who are women decreased over the same period (1989–1996) in juvenile facilities. In 1989, white women were 16.3 percent of administrators in these facilities. By 1996, the proportion had dropped to 15 percent. Among African-American women in those positions, the proportion was 6.7 percent in 1989 and 4 percent in 1996. In contrast, the numbers for African-American men went from 10 percent in 1989 to 12 percent in 1996, while white men held 59 percent of these positions in 1990 and 64 percent in 1996 (Maguire & Pastore, 1990, p. 97; Maguire & Pastore, 1994, p. 97; 1997, p. 89).

Women in Probation and Parole.   Women hold a much larger proportion of probation and parole staff positions than they do corrections officer positions. According to Maguire and Pastore (1996), women probation officers outnumbered men probation officers in Hawaii and Indiana in 1994. In those states where probation and parole are combined in one office, women probation and parole officers outnumbered male probation and parole officers in Maryland, Vermont, and Wisconsin (Maguire & Pastore, 1996, p. 81). However, complete data on women in probation and parole officer positions were unavailable because eight states did not report the gender breakdown of their officers.

The number of probation and parole officers varies from state to state. For example, Florida reported employing 2434 parole and probation officers, and 48 percent of the total were women. By contrast, Alaska reported a total of 76 probation and parole officers, and

45 percent were women (Maguire & Pastore, 1996, p. 81). Not all the states that reported gender breakdowns have such a proportionate representation of men and women. Pennsylvania's record is especially troubling. There were 242 parole officers in Pennsylvania in 1994, and 96 percent were men (Maguire & Pastore, 1996, p. 81).

According to Camp and Camp (1996, p. 130), the percentage of all employees in probation, parole, and probation and parole agencies who were women on January 1, 1996 was 53 percent. Women were most likely to work in probation departments where they comprised 54 percent of the probation staff and slightly less likely to work in parole where they comprised approximately 52 percent of the parole staff (Camp & Camp, 1997, pp. 128–129).

Women's greater representation in probation departments and parole agencies probably reflects the view that probation is a kind of "social work" and therefore more suitable for women. In fact, probation was the only criminal justice profession to encourage the pursuit of a master's in social work for its staff in the 1950s. Clearly, the social work orientation made the profession very appealing to and receptive to women, especially when compared to police work, the legal profession, and correctional officer positions.

It should also be noted that women have traditionally occupied the majority of the clerical positions in these agencies and that these figures reflect the large number of women who work as secretaries and administrative assistants as well as probation and parole officers. Camp and Camp found that in 1996 support staff made up 14 percent to 19 percent of the total probation, parole, and probation and parole staffs; and that between 9 and 18 percent of the staff in these agencies were designated as "other staff" who worked as paraprofessionals (Camp & Camp, 1997, p. 132).

In terms of minority representation, parole departments reported the highest percentage of African-American parole staff (approximately 29 percent). African-Americans comprised a total of 21 percent of the combined probation, parole, and probation and parole staff positions (Camp & Camp, 1997, pp. 128–130). Once again, these data do not separate African-American probation, parole, and probation and parole officers from clerical, support, and other (paraprofessional) staff members.

CONCLUSIONS

The evidence shows that women have made gains over the past twenty-five years but that there is still much more to be accomplished. In the criminal justice professions of law enforcement, the judiciary, and corrections, their gains have been modest. Women still encounter blatant discrimination and harassment as they move into these historically male-dominated fields. There is no reason to believe that the attitudes and behaviors that have kept women from moving into these occupations have been entirely eliminated. Indeed, lawsuits brought by women who have been subjected to discrimination and harassment continue to demonstrate how entrenched gender discrimination is, not only in the criminal justice field but in society in general. And occupational gender segregation is still the norm.

Given the slow progress that women have made, we can reject the suggestion made by some critics to end affirmative action and replace it by a program that targets only the economically disadvantaged for special consideration in employment and education. Perhaps such a program should be implemented, but this is not a reason to discard affirmative action based on race, ethnicity, and gender. Bergmann (1996) argues that proposals to replace race- and gender-based affirmative action with affirmative action for the economically disadvantaged will not succeed in leveling the playing field. Because of existing racial and gender prejudice and discrimination, deciding who is "disadvantaged" and how slots should be allocated to them may simply perpetuate racial and gender inequalities. She points out that "[w]hites already win most of the well-paying jobs that go to low-skilled people of modest backgrounds" (Bergmann, 1996, p. 168).

According to Bergmann, simply enforcing the laws against discrimination will not be adequate either, unless a much greater commitment of resources is made to agencies such as the Equal Employment Opportunity Commission. We know, too, that the victims of discrimination are often hesitant to bring charges because they fear retaliation and because they may not have the resources needed to find and retain legal assistance. Victims must also be informed about the law so that they will know their rights. Complaints of sexual harassment rose steeply after the Hill–Thomas hearings were televised, which seems to prove that a good deal of discrimination goes unreported either because of lack of knowledge or fear of the consequences of reporting.

Within criminal justice, employment opportunities have risen due to the development and expansion of community policing, the dramatic increase in the number of inmates (especially women), the boom in prison expansion, the increase in the juvenile offender population, and the explosion in the courts. Policymakers and administrators must continue to take the steps necessary to assure that women are represented equally in all segments of the criminal justice professions.

Although the current political climate seems to hold out little hope for affirmative action, the picture may not be as dismal as some think (or hope). In April 1997, in the face of a barrage of attacks on affirmative action (see the discussion above), a number of major U.S. corporations placed full-page advertisements in the *Wall Street Journal* in support of affirmative action. The corporations included Lucent Technologies, Shell Oil, Sony, Boeing, IBM, and others ("Reaffirming Affirmative Action," 1997, p. A17).

Even more recently, the major broadcasting corporations, including CBS, NBC, ABC, Fox, Time-Warner (which owns CNN), and large owners of radio and television stations announced that they would continue voluntarily to practice affirmative action (Holmes, 1998a). This announcement followed a ruling by the U.S. Court of Appeals for the District of Columbia Circuit barring the Federal Communications Commission (FCC) from requiring broadcasters to follow the FCC's affirmative action guidelines (see *Lutheran Church–Missouri Synod v. F.C.C.*, 1998). The broadcasters' actions demonstrate a continuing strong commitment to, and support for, affirmative action, not only in the business community but in the larger society.

In the Gallup Poll "Social audit on black/white relations" in the United States, published in June 1997, 82 percent of blacks and 51 percent of whites agreed that we should "increase" affirmative action programs in this country or "keep the same." In the National Opinion Research Center's poll "Public opinion on race and affirmative action" published in December 1996, 79 percent of respondents supported affirmative action and 74 percent agreed that affirmative action means "making equal opportunities for everyone including women and minorities." Only a small proportion of respondents, 24 percent, saw affirmative action as giving women and minorities an unfair advantage (Leadership Conference on Civil Rights Online Center, 1997).

In their comprehensive study of affirmative action, Bok and Bowen (1998) studied 45,000 students who entered college at 28 of the most selective universities in the United States in 1976 and 1989. Their data strongly suggest that the continuation of affirmative action programs is critical. They contend that shifting to "a 'race neutral' admission policy would be disastrous for American society, reducing black percentages at top colleges to less than 2 percent from 7 percent" (Bronner, 1998).

One of the often undocumented results of affirmative action policies in college and university admissions is the role that they play in teaching students the importance of integration (Bronner, 1998). Both black and white student respondents in Bok and Bowen's study indicated significant social interaction while attending college, which they contend "...helped them relate to members of different racial groups later in life" (Bronner, 1998).

According to Lester Thurow, "[t]he rules of football are written down, they are not axiomatic. It is the same thing with the economy. How do you acquire skills? How do you get to use those skills? Can you create a monopoly or can you not create a monopoly? All those decisions have to be made. If somebody is winning all the time and it becomes too inegalitarian, like the Rockefellers in the 1890's, we change the rules to stop this kind of behavior..." (Rabin, Silverstein, & Schatzki, 1988, pp. 168–169, quoting Thurow, 1986).

Such is the case for affirmative action. It was the inegalitarian nature of education and employment that had to be addressed. The ability to relate to members of different racial groups is very important in all professions and particularly so in the criminal justice professions. To decide at this juncture that we no longer need to actively recruit women and minorities to work in criminal justice because we now have a level playing field and to suggest that they are adequately represented would be a grave injustice. If we are seriously committed to maintaining equal opportunities for women and minorities, we have to ensure that programs designed to assist in the recruitment of women and minorities and their retention in the profession continue.

Without affirmative action, it is unlikely that women and minority-group members will ever achieve greater representation in criminal justice professions. There is ample evidence that only limited gains have been made. Recent ballot initiatives and court decisions will erode these programs, and women and minority group members will continue to lose ground. It is shortsighted and too premature to consider ending affirmative action programs in education and employment.

REFERENCES

Affirmative Action Review. (1995). Report to the President. Available: www.whitehouse.gov/WH/EOP/OP/html/aa.

BEICHNER, D. M., & MERLO, A. (1998, March 12). *Women in corrections: Twenty-five years after Title VII*. Paper presented at the annual meeting of the Academy of Criminal Justice Sciences, Albuquerque, NM.

BERGMANN, B. R. (1996). *In defense of affirmative action*. New York: Basic Books.

BOWER, W. G., & BOK, D. (1998). *The shape of the river: Long-term consequences of considering race in college and university admissions*. Princeton, NJ: Princeton University Press.

BRITTON, D. M. (1997). Perceptions of the work environment among correctional officers: Do race and sex matter? *Criminology, 35*(1), 85–105.

BRONNER, E. (1998, September 9). Study strongly supports affirmative action in admissions to elite colleges. *New York Times*, p. A24.

CALIFORNIA STATE OFFICE OF RESEARCH. (1995). Taking a look at affirmative action. Sacramento, CA.

CAMP C. G., & CAMP G. M. (1997). *The corrections yearbook, 1997*. South Salem, NY: Criminal Justice Institute.

DECKER, C. (1995, February 19). Affirmative action: Why battle erupted." *Los Angeles Times*, p. A2.

DEVINS, N. (1996). *Adarand Constructors, Inc. v. Pena* and the continuing irrelevance of Supreme Court affirmative action decisions. *William and Mary Law Review, 37*, 673–721.

FALUDI, S. (1991). *Backlash: The undeclared war against American women*. New York: Doubleday.

FEINMAN, C. (1986). *Women in the criminal justice system* (2nd ed.). New York: Praeger.

FLANAGAN, T., & MAGUIRE, K. (EDS.). (1992). *Sourcebook of criminal justice statistics, 1991*. U.S. Department of Justice, Bureau of Justice Statistics. Washington, DC: U.S. Government Printing Office.

FLYNN, E. E. (1982). Women as criminal justice professionals: A challenge to change tradition. In N. H. Rafter & E. A. Stanko (Eds.), *Judge, lawyer, victim, thief* (pp. 305–340). Boston: Northeastern University Press.

FOX, M. F. (1995). Women and higher education: Gender differences in the status of students and scholars. In J. Freeman (Ed.), *Women: A feminist perspective* (5th ed., pp. 220–237). Mountain View, CA: Mayfield Publishing.

FUOCO, M. A. (1998, May 28). City force no.1 in women in blue. *Pittsburgh Post-Gazette*, pp. A1–A10.

HALE, D., & MENNITI, D. J. (1993). Discrimination and harassment: Litigation by women in policing. In R. Muraskin & T. Alleman (Eds.) *It's a crime: Women and justice* (pp. 177–189). Englewood Cliffs, NJ: Regents/Prentice Hall.

HEALY, P. (1998, April 3). Admissions law changes the equations for students and colleges in Texas. *Chronicle of Higher Education, 44*, pp. A29–A31.

HOLMES, S. A. (1998a, July 30). Broadcasters vow to keep affirmative action. *New York Times*, p. A12.

HOLMES, S. A. (1998b, May 4). Washington state is stage for fight over preferences. *New York Times*, pp. A1, A15.

JAMIESON, K. M., & FLANAGAN, T. (EDS.). (1989). *Sourcebook for criminal justice statistics, 1988*. Bureau of Justice Statistics, U.S. Department of Justice. Washington, DC: U.S. Government Printing Office.

JAMISON, T., & BALU, R. (1995, Fall). Is it the beginning of the end for affirmative action? *Human Rights, 22*, 14–19.

KAPLIN, W. A. (1989). The law of higher education (2nd ed.). San Francisco: Jossey-Bass.

KAUFMAN, D. R. (1995). Professional women: How real are the gains? In J. Freeman (Ed.), *Women: A feminist perspective* (5th ed., pp. 287–305). Mountain View, CA: Mayfield Publishing.

Leadership Conference on Civil Rights Online Center. (1997). *A majority of Americans support affirmative action programs for women and people of color*. Available: www.civilrights.org/lccr.html

LINDGREN, J. R., & TAUB, N. (1993). *The law of sex discrimination* (2nd ed.). Minneapolis, MN: West Publishing.

MAGUIRE, K., & FLANAGAN, T. (EDS.). (1990). *Sourcebook of criminal justice statistics, 1990*. Bureau of Justice Statistics, U.S. Department of Justice. Washington, DC: U.S. Government Printing Office.

MAGUIRE, K., & PASTORE, A. (EDS.). (1994). *Sourcebook of criminal justice statistics, 1994*. Bureau of Justice Statistics, U.S. Department of Justice. Washington, DC: U.S. Government Printing Office.

MAGUIRE, K., & PASTORE, A. (EDS.). (1996). *Sourcebook of criminal justice statistics, 1995*. Bureau of Justice Statistics, U.S. Department of Justice. Washington, DC: U.S. Government Printing Office.

MAGUIRE, K., & PASTORE, A. (EDS.). (1997). *Sourcebook of criminal justice statistics, 1996.* Bureau of Justice Statistics, U.S. Department of Justice. Washington, DC: U.S. Government Printing Office.

MCKINNON, J. (1998, May 28). PA ranks 9th lowest for women troopers. *Pittsburgh Post-Gazette,* p. A10.

MERLO, A. V., & POLLOCK, J. M. (EDS.). (1995). *Women, law and social control.* Boston: Allyn & Bacon.

MILLS, N. (1994). Introduction: To look like America. In N. Mills (Ed.), *Debating affirmative action: Race, gender, ethnicity and the politics of inclusion,* pp. 1–34. New York: Delta.

MORRIS, K. (1996). Through the looking glass: Recent developments in affirmative action. *Berkeley Women's Law Journal, 11,* pp. 182–193.

NEUMARK, D., BANK, R. J., & VAN NORT, K. (1995, February). *Sex discrimination in restaurant hiring: An audit study.* Working Paper 5024. XX: National Bureau of Economic Research. Available: http://nberws.nber.org/papers/w5024

PBS Newshour (1998, April 1).

POLLOCK-BYRNE, J. (1990). *Women, prison and crime.* Pacific Grove, CA: Brooks/Cole.

POULOS, T. M., & DOERNER, W. G. (1996). Women in law enforcement: The distribution of females in Florida police agencies. *Women and Criminal Justice, 8*(2), 19–33.

RAAB, S. (1998, September 14). Lawsuits depict police harassment and cover-ups. *New York Times,* p. A29.

RABIN, R. J., SILVERSTEIN, E., & SCHATZKI, G. (1988). *Labor and employment law.* Minneapolis, MN: West Publishing.

RAFTER, N. H., & STANKO, E. A. (1982). *Judge, lawyer, victim, thief.* Boston: Northeastern University Press.

Reaffirming affirmative action. (1997, April 16). *Wall Street Journal,* p. A17.

REAVES, B. A. (1997, December). Federal law enforcement officers, 1996. *Bureau of Justice Statistics Bulletin,* pp. 1–11.

RENZETTI, C. M., & CURRAN, D. J. (1995). *Women, men, and society.* (3rd ed.). Boston: Allyn & Bacon.

Reverse discrimination complaints rare, a labor study reports. (1995, March 31). *New York Times,* p. A10.

The glass ceiling in federal agencies: A GAO survey on women and minorities in federal agencies. (1993). Hearings before the Committee on Governmental Affairs, U.S. Senate, 102nd Congress, May 16 and October 23, 1991. Washington, DC: U.S. Government Printing Office.

THORNBORROW, N. M., & SHELDON, M. B. (1995). Women in the labor force. In J. Freeman (Ed.), *Women: A feminist perspective* (5th ed., pp. 197–219). Mountain View, CA: Mayfield Publishing.

THUROW, L. (1986). Policy recommendations concerning the second draft of the pastoral letter. *St. Louis University Public Law Forum, 5,* 281–296.

UNIVERSITY OF CALIFORNIA, OFFICE OF THE PRESIDENT. (1996). *About affirmative action at the University of California.* Available: www.ucop.edu/sas/aa

U.S. BUREAU OF THE CENSUS. (1995). *Statistical abstract of the United States, 1995* (115th ed.). Washington, DC: U.S. Government Printing Office.

U.S. BUREAU OF THE CENSUS. (1997). *Statistical abstract of the United States, 1997.* (117th ed.). Washington, DC: U.S. Government Printing Office.

U.S. DEPARTMENT OF JUSTICE. (1984). *Uniform crime report for the United States, 1983.* Federal Bureau of Investigation. Washington, DC: U.S. Government Printing Office.

U.S. DEPARTMENT OF JUSTICE. (1995). *Uniform crime report for the United States, 1994.* Federal Bureau of Investigation. Washington, DC: U.S. Government Printing Office.

U.S. DEPARTMENT OF JUSTICE. (1997). *Uniform crime report for the United States, 1996.* Federal Bureau of Investigation. Washington, DC: U.S. Government Printing Office.

WOOD, R., CORCORAN, M., & COURANT, P. (1993, July). Pay differentials among the highly paid: The male–female earnings gap in lawyers' salaries. *Journal of Labor Economics, 11,* 417–441.

ZIMMER, M. J., SULLIVAN, C. A., & RICHARDS, R. F. (1988). *Cases and materials on employment discrimination* (2nd ed.). Boston: Little, Brown.

ZUPAN, L. (1992). The progress of women correctional officers in all-male prisons. In I. Moyer (Ed.), *The changing roles of women in the criminal justice system* (2nd ed., pp. 323–343). Prospect Heights, IL: Waveland Press.

CASES

Adarand Constructors, Inc. v. Pena, 115 S. Ct. 2097 (1995).

Albemarle Paper Co. v. Moody, 422 U.S. 405 (1975).

City of Richmond v. J.A. Croson Co., 488 U.S. 469 (1989).

Hopwood v. Texas, 861 F. Supp. 551 (W.D. Tex. 1994)

Hopwood v. State of Texas, 78 F.3d 932 (5th Cir. 1996), cert. denied, 578 U.S. 1033, 116 S. Ct. 2580, 135 L. Ed. 2d 1094 (1996).

Hurley v. Atlantic City Police Department, 933 F. Supp. 396 (D.N.J. 1996).

Johnson v. Transportation Agency of Santa Clara County, 480 U.S. 616 (1987).

Legal Aid Society v. Brennan, 608 F.2d 1319 (9th Cir. 1979).

Local 28, Sheet Metal Workers' Int'l Ass'n v. E.E.O.C., 106 S. Ct. 3019 (1986).

Lutheran Church–Missouri Synod v. F.C.C 154 F.3d 494 (D.C. Cir. 1998).

Regents of the University of California v. Bakke, 438 U.S. 265 (1978).

Wilson v. Susquehanna Township Police Department, 55 F.3d 126 (3rd Cir. 1995).

6

Postpartum Syndromes

Disparate Treatment in the Legal System

Cheryl L. Meyer, Tara C. Proano, and James R. Franz

Postpartum syndromes are rarely acknowledged by the psychological and medical communities, resulting in a lack of definitive criteria for recognition or diagnosis. This lack of "general acceptance" by scientific communities has made it difficult for postpartum syndromes to meet *Frye* or *Daubert* standards of admissibility in criminal courts. Although postpartum syndromes are considered mitigating factors in criminal responsibility in other countries such as England, they are generally precluded from consideration in U.S. criminal courts. However, since rules of evidence are typically less strict in civil courts, postpartum syndromes are admitted into evidence during these proceedings. This has created a disparate situation wherein postpartum syndromes can be used to harm women, such as through loss of custody, but cannot assist women in mitigating their loss of liberty. This chapter outlines the medical and psychological ambiguities regarding postpartum syndromes, and the legal inconsistencies created by these ambiguities. In addition, the politics of gender are addressed. Finally, the impact that recognition of these symptoms by the legal system could have on pathologizing normal processes in women is explored.

Despite the heightened attention recently given to postpartum syndromes, they are not a new phenomenon. Hippocrates recorded the first known reports of postpartum syndromes 2000 years ago (Cox, 1986). In describing postpartum psychosis, he wrote that it was "a kind of 'madness,' caused by excessive blood flow to the brain" (Lynch-Fraser, 1983). Since that time, physicians have struggled with the etiology of the syndromes. For example, an interesting explanation for postpartum syndromes was provided by an eleventh-century gynecologist, Trotula of Salerno, who suggested that postpartum blues resulted from the womb being too moist, causing the brain to fill with water, which was then involuntarily shed as tears (Steiner, 1990). However, it was not until the nineteenth century that physicians described the symptoms of postpartum syndromes in detail and began to theorize there was a connection between physiological events and the mind (Hamilton, 1989). Marcé termed this connection *morbid sympathy* and provided the first clear description of the syndromes (Hamilton, 1989). However, physicians were unable to agree upon a classification system or even a pattern of symptoms.

Once psychologists began to study postpartum syndromes, they too struggled with developing a classification system. Similar to physicians, psychologists found that the postpartum syndromes defied easy definition and were too elusive, diverse, and inconsistent to classify (Hamilton, 1989). Therefore, in the early twentieth century, when it was suggested that there was not a connection between psychiatric disorders and childbirth, the argument persuaded the medical and psychological communities. When physicians began the task of creating a comprehensive list of all medical disorders, now known as the *International Classification of Diseases* (ICD), they excluded the postpartum syndromes. Similarly, when professionals in the mental health field created their own comprehensive list, called the *Diagnostic and Statistical Manual of Mental Disorders* (DSM), they too excluded the postpartum syndromes. These exclusions were particularly damaging since these manuals are the means by which professionals within the two fields communicate, produce research, and develop treatments.

Subsequent revisions of both the *ICD* and *DSM* ultimately began to mention postpartum syndromes. The *ICD-10*, the latest version of the *ICD*, lists three specific levels of mental and behavioral disorders associated with the puerperium, or childbirth, ranging from mild to severe. These terms are *postnatal depression, postpartum depression*, and *puerperal psychosis*. However, postpartum syndromes should only be diagnosed when the symptoms do not meet criteria for other disorders, such as depression (World Health Organization, 1992).

Although the *DSM-IV*, the latest version of the *DSM*, has increased the recognition of postpartum syndromes by indicating that a birth can trigger a major depressive episode, the syndromes are still subsumed under depression or are listed as an example of a catchall category such as Psychotic Disorder Not Otherwise Specified (American Psychiatric Association, 1994, p. 315). In this way, the postpartum syndromes are not adequately defined, despite research which suggests that postpartum syndromes are discrete entities.

To compensate for the inadequacies of the *DSM*, individual psychologists have proposed separate categories of postpartum syndromes, but they have difficulty agreeing on levels and/or a pattern of symptoms. Theorists have suggested from two to five levels of the syndromes, and the terms used to refer to these levels vary (Pfost, Stevens, & Matejcak, 1990; Steiner, 1990).

Not surprisingly, this lack of consistency between classification systems has resulted in conflicting research findings (Thurtle, 1995). Additionally, the tendency of the *DSM* series to understate the importance and distinction of postpartum syndromes also results in minimal research because resources and funding are not available for unrecognized syndromes. Since research provides a foundation for recognition, without research, the syndromes continue to be unrecognized. This cycle is especially problematic because treatment and prognosis for postpartum syndromes are radically different from those given for other mood disorders.

Despite these problems with classification, three separate syndromes seem to have some consensus in the professional communities. From the mild to the moderate to the severe end of the continuum, the syndromes are termed postpartum "blues," postpartum depression, and postpartum psychosis, respectively (Hamilton, 1989).

Postpartum blues is a mild affective syndrome that generally occurs in the first week after delivery. It is transitory and typically requires no intervention. The symptoms can include mild depression, anxiety, and restlessness and appear between the third and seventh day postpartum (Gitlin & Pasnau, 1989). The symptoms last approximately forty-eight hours and abate by the tenth day postpartum. Postpartum blues are considered a normal part of childbirth since they occur in 50 to 80 percent of new mothers (Harding, 1989).

Postpartum depression is often used as a catchall term for all three syndromes. In actuality, postpartum depression is a more severe form of postpartum blues, resembling the *DSM-IV* diagnosis criteria for a major depressive episode. Symptoms may include depression, insomnia, crying, irritability, subtle changes of personality, diminished initiative, and difficulty coping, especially with the baby (Baran, 1989; Hamilton, 1989). The anxiety regarding how to cope with the baby differentiates postpartum depression from other forms of depression (Baran, 1989). Postpartum depression develops slowly throughout the weeks following delivery (Hamilton 1989), with the highest frequency of new cases occurring between the third and ninth months postpartum (Steiner, 1990). Most investigators estimate that the syndrome affects one in ten new mothers (Hamilton, 1989; Harding, 1989).

The most serious of all the syndromes is *postpartum psychosis*. In one such case, Angela Thompson went from being an honor society member, her school's first female senior class president, and an athletic and sociable person to later being a mother who drowned her second child, a nine-month-old son, in a bathtub after hearing voices telling her that her child was the devil (Japenga, 1987). After Thompson gave birth to her first child, she also suffered hallucinations, panic, and obsessions. She even attempted suicide by jumping out of a moving vehicle and then jumping from a bridge thirty feet high, which led to psychiatric hospitalization. Unfortunately, when she became pregnant with her second child, her doctors told her to forget about her previous psychosis, saying that it would not happen again (Brusca, 1990). In another often cited case, Sharon Comitz suffered a similar psychosis following the birth of her first child, but no one took notice of the repeated symptomatology with her second child until it was too late. Comitz had reported her fears of reoccurrence and of being left alone with the baby, but she was ignored.

Postpartum psychosis symptoms usually appear within two weeks after delivery (Harding, 1989). Symptoms of postpartum psychosis include hallucinations, delusions, confusion, irritability, emotional liability, mania, obsessional thinking, feelings of hopelessness, insomnia, headache, agitation, violence, and early signs of depressive illness.

Hamilton calls postpartum psychosis mercurial for the rapidity with which moods and symptoms change (Hamilton, 1989). However, "the principal hazard of puerperal psychosis is violent, impulsive self-destruction. Infanticide is also a hazard, when the syndrome is unrecognized or disregarded, and the [mother] is left alone with her child" (Hamilton, 1989, p. 94). In addition, the bonding between mother and child may be interrupted, precipitating later behavioral disorders in the child (Steiner, 1990). Accordingly, mothers at high risk should be very closely monitored, especially the initial two to four weeks postpartum (Gitlin & Pasnau, 1989). With proper treatment, instances of suicide, infanticide, and child abuse are very rare (Steiner, 1990).

The cause of postpartum syndromes is unknown. There are, however, risk factors that increase a woman's chance of developing a disorder. One cluster of risk factors focuses on the hormonal shifts that occur during and around the birthing process and on a predisposition toward mental illness. Certain hormonal levels, such as those of estrogen and progesterone, may drop by a factor well over 100 (Gitlin & Pasnau, 1989). Although women normally experience these severe changes in body chemistry, women who have previously experienced a mental illness or have a history of mental illness in their family are at greater risk for developing postpartum psychosis. Harding (1989) indicates that "[t]he risk of developing a psychotic mental illness in the first 3 months after delivery is approximately 15 times as great as in nonpuerperal women, with nearly two of every 1000 women delivered requiring hospitalization for such a postpartum psychosis" (p. 110). This incidence has been consistent over time and across class and culture, suggesting a genetic etiology (Hamilton, 1989).

The second cluster of risk factors that increase the likelihood of developing postpartum syndromes are sociological factors (Thurtle, 1995). Sociological factors may include single motherhood, lack of support by a spouse, and other stressful life events (Harding, 1989; Thurtle, 1995). This viewpoint is given greater examination in a later section. Regardless of the proposed etiologies of the syndromes, the phenomenal aspect of postpartum syndrome cases often leads to interaction with the legal system.

THE LEGAL SYSTEM AND POSTPARTUM SYNDROMES

Postpartum syndromes have been admitted into evidence in both criminal and civil courts. Clearly, the use of postpartum syndromes in criminal cases has become more infamous. This could be due to the nature of the crime, usually infanticide (killing a child during the first year of life), or to the media frenzy that surrounds criminal cases involving the mental health of the defendant. The fact patterns of these cases are chillingly similar (see, e.g., Gardner, 1990). Generally, the defendant had no prior history of criminal activity and often went to great lengths, including using reproductive technologies, to become pregnant. In other words, these were planned pregnancies and wanted children. In many cases, the woman had become psychotic, often perceiving the child as a source of evil, such as the devil. The murders are particularly gruesome, including running over the child with the car, throwing the child in an icy river, and strangulation. Afterward, the mother purportedly has no recollection of the event and reports the child missing or kidnapped to the police.

It is difficult to estimate the frequency of infanticide in the United States. However, "...in the United States and throughout the world, the population under one year of age is at great risk of death from homicide. Their killers are more likely to be their own mothers than anyone else" (Oberman, 1996, p. 159). Still, relatively speaking, very few infanticide cases are tried since many defendants plea bargain to a lesser offense of manslaughter. Of those tried, few raise postpartum syndromes as a defense.

In colonial times, women who killed their infants were often executed (Gardner, 1990). In the eighteenth century, juries became reluctant to impose such a harsh penalty, especially if women had committed infanticide due to social and economic hardship. This resulted in an increasing number of acquittals. It was not until this century that postpartum syndromes became formally linked to infanticide under British law. The Infanticide Act of 1922 provided for a reduction in charge from murder to manslaughter for mothers who killed their newborns while suffering from the effects of childbirth. This act was amended in 1938 to include children up to 12 months of age and the effect of lactation. The English Infanticide Act served as a model for a similar Canadian Criminal Code provision that was enacted in 1948. There is no similar statute in the United States.

In the United States, postpartum syndromes can enter into the criminal proceedings at a variety of phases, including competency, pleading, and sentencing. At the outset, the competency of the woman to stand trial could be at issue. However, this does not fit the typical fact pattern for postpartum syndromes since most women are not continuing to experience postpartum effects at the trial. Moreover, this would probably be an ineffective defense strategy. Since the statute on murder never runs out, the defendant would simply remain in a treatment facility until competency could be achieved in order for a trial to take place. A treatment facility would be an inappropriate place for most defendants who previously had a postpartum syndrome, as postpartum syndromes are often transitory conditions.

More commonly, postpartum syndromes are used to exculpate a defendant. At issue is whether the defendant could have formed the requisite mental intent (mens rea) to commit murder. One way to negate the mental state requirement would be through use of an insanity defense. Since most of these cases are not federal cases, the jurisdictional test for legal insanity would be used. However, mental statutes are incredibly inconsistent regarding insanity. In fact, three states do not have insanity statutes. The remaining states have adopted tests (criteria) to determine insanity. There are numerous tests used in the United States, but at least half of the states use a variation of the M'Naghten test (Melton, Petrila, Poythress, & Slobogin, 1997).

The M'Naghten test is a cognitive test which primarily addresses the question of whether the defendant knew that her actions were wrong at the time she committed the crime. This is a relatively strict test of insanity, as even very debilitated individuals generally know that their actions are wrong. Under the M'Naghten test, it is difficult to prove insanity for mothers suffering postpartum syndromes. For example, in *People v. Massip* (1990), the defendant threw her colicky baby into the path of an oncoming car after voices told her to do so. When the car swerved and missed the infant, the defendant put the infant under the front tire of her own car and ran over him, disposing of his body in the trash. Under M'Naghten, the jury found her guilty of second-degree murder.[1]

Other states have an additional component to their insanity test. This component can take various forms (Melton et al., 1997) but generally focuses on whether a defendant could appreciate the wrongfulness of her conduct or could control her conduct. Such tests have a tendency to be more liberal than M'Naghten. For example, Angela Thompson, a nurse, claimed that voices told her to drown her 9-month-old son, and she did. The defendant was found not guilty of voluntary manslaughter and felony child abuse by reason of insanity but would probably have been deemed guilty by the M'Naghten test. An NGRI verdict means that the defendant is not guilty of the crime but may be sentenced to a treatment facility until she is deemed safe to be released. Thompson was committed to an inpatient facility for 90 days and required to receive outpatient follow-up with a psychiatrist for six years (Japenga, 1987).

As an alternative to the insanity defense, postpartum syndromes have also been used to assert diminished capacity, diminished responsibility, or automatism. These are mitigating factors pled to reduce a charge to a lesser offense. Evidence is admitted regarding whether the defendant had the capacity to form the required mental state necessary to be found guilty of the charge. However, only about half the states recognize diminished capacity defenses.

If the defendant is found guilty, sentencing following the use of postpartum symptoms as a defense is also disparate. Brusca (1990) reports that about half the women that raise postpartum psychosis as a defense are found not guilty by reason of insanity, one-fourth receive light sentences, and one-fourth receive long sentences. Alternatively, the defendant may be found guilty but mentally ill (GBMI). In general, a GBMI verdict holds the defendant responsible for the murder but the mitigating role of illness is recognized in sentencing. The defendant may serve the same sentence length as if she were found guilty but may stay in a treatment facility until she has recovered enough to be transferred to a prison.

In *Commonwealth v. Comitz* (1987), Sharon Comitz, who was discussed previously, pled GBMI to dropping her 1-month-old infant into the icy waters of a stream and then reporting the child's disappearance to police as a kidnapping. Only under hypnosis did she recall the killing. Under M'Naghten she would have been found guilty of murder, especially given the fabricated kidnapping. Comitz pled GBMI to third-degree murder and received an eight- to twenty-year sentence. About one-third of states have GBMI provisions, but support is dwindling for the alternative sentencing structure. In any case, this may not be a very functional strategy for women suffering from postpartum syndromes, as they are generally recovered by the time of the trial. As these verdicts indicate, the cases involving postpartum syndromes as a defense are very similar, but the outcomes are quite disparate.

THE USE OF POSTPARTUM SYNDROMES IN CIVIL CASES

The rules of evidence are very different in criminal and civil cases, as demonstrated in the well-publicized criminal and civil trials of O. J. Simpson. In criminal cases, postpartum syndromes have generally been subjected to the conditions of the Frye test (*Frye v. United States*, 1923). The Frye test requires general acceptance of the disorder by the medical and/or psychological community before a syndrome can be admitted into evidence. Recently, federal and numerous state courts have shifted to the *Daubert* standard of admissibility, which requires a pretrial hearing regarding the degree of professional acceptance and recognition of a disorder (*Daubert v. Merrell Dow Pharmaceuticals*, 1993). It is unlikely that postpartum syndromes will meet *Daubert* criteria.

In civil cases, information may be admitted into evidence without meeting *Frye/Daubert* criteria. In fact, in custody matters the trial court has broad discretion, particularly regarding the mental health of parents. Mental health can be considered and weighed in relation to other factors in custody decisions. Postpartum syndromes have been raised as a health consideration in many custody cases. It is difficult to estimate how frequently the issue is raised because undoubtedly many mothers abandon their pursuit of custody after the father indicates that he intends to make mental health an issue. In addition, it is impossible to determine how heavily postpartum syndromes weigh in the decision because trial court transcripts are often inaccessible and opinions are generally not formally written. If custody awards are appealed, the court's opinion becomes more accessible. However, custody awards are appealed infrequently.

In custody disputes involving postpartum syndromes, the father generally asserts that the mother is an unfit parent, due to her history of postpartum mental illness, even though the mother is not currently mentally ill and may have no other history of mental illness or unfit parenting. For example, in one of the first recorded cases (*Pfeifer v. Pfeifer*, 1955), the father appealed an order that gave care, custody, and control of the child to the mother, based solely on her potential threat to the child due to her history of postpartum psychosis. When the couple separated, Kent, their child, went to live with Mr. Pfeifer and the paternal grandparents. Ms. Pfeifer was recently recovered from postpartum psychosis, was trying to rebuild her life, and had no home to offer Kent. The paternal grandmother became Kent's primary caretaker. Mr. Pfeifer remarried and relocated, but Kent continued to live with his paternal grandparents. Ms. Pfeifer, who had also remarried, sued and eventually won custody of Kent. Mr. Pfeifer appealed the custody award, citing the mental instability of Ms. Pfeifer. At the time of the custody hearing the mother had been asymptomatic for five years and had no intention of having more children.

On appeal, the father claimed there had been no change in circumstances warranting modification of the original custody award. The court held "...the mother has remained in good mental health for more than two years without relapse; she has remarried, can offer the child a good home, and is willing to give up her profession to take care of him and her household. This change in the circumstance of the mother could in itself justify the change of custody ordered. Moreover, the father has also remarried and has moved out of the home of his parents to another neighborhood. The grandparents, with whom the child remained, have reached an age, which, notwithstanding their love and devotion, must make them less fit to educate a child of the age of Kent and compared to them, the mother has, if she is not unfit to have custody, certainly a prior claim to the child" (*Pfeifer v. Pfeifer*, 1955, at 56). Mr. Pfeifer's appeal was denied. However, several aspects of this opinion bear noting.

This case was appealed solely on the issue of postpartum psychosis. There was no other reason for Ms. Pfeifer not to be awarded custody. First, it was not Mr. Pfeifer who would have retained custody but the paternal grandparents. Had Mr. Pfeifer chosen to fight for custody, it is quite possible the court would have reached a different opinion. Second, Mr. Pfeifer had led Kent to believe that his stepmother was his biological mother. The court felt this posed a danger that Kent would never learn the identify of his real mother. This may have swayed the court's opinion. Third, Ms. Pfeifer's marriage was important to the court. It is questionable whether the court would have reached the same decision if Ms. Pfeifer had not been remarried or living "under supervision." Fourth, the paternal grandparents were becoming too elderly to care for the child. Fifth, Ms. Pfeifer had no intention of bearing another child. Sixth, Ms. Pfeifer had been asymptomatic for five years. It would have been difficult to deny Ms. Pfeifer custody under these circumstances. In contrast, consider the following case.

Susan and Gary Grimm were married for thirteen years and parented three children (*In Re the Marriage of Grimm*, 1989). Gary's occupation is unclear, but Susan was a licensed practical nurse. After the birth of each child, Susan suffered from postpartum depression and was hospitalized for treatment. During these hospitalizations, Susan phoned home daily to speak with her children and had personal visits with them. Following the last hospitalization in 1985, the Grimms separated. During the separation, the children resided with their father, while the mother lived nearby and visited daily. Susan organized, washed dishes, laundered and mended clothes, cooked for the children, and stayed with the children at night whenever Gary was working.

The Grimms petitioned for dissolution and each sought sole custody of the children. The custody evaluation submitted to the court indicated that both Grimms were evaluated as excellent parents. However, the court placed custody with Gary. Susan appealed and her treating psychiatrist testified that the depression was resolved and it had been two years since Susan's last postpartum hospitalization. The court affirmed the custody award.

It is clear that Susan Grimm's postpartum depression was an important factor in this custody award. Her treating psychiatrist was called to testify regarding her stability. No other testimony regarding the fitness of either parent was addressed. Similar to *Pfeifer v. Pfeifer* (1955), Susan Grimm had not been hospitalized for a long period prior to the custody hearing. In addition, Susan had been and wanted to continue to be actively involved with the children's lives.

It is unclear why *Pfeifer* and *Grimm* were decided differently, especially in light of the fact that the courts have refused to allow testimony regarding postpartum depression to be persuasive in other civil matters. For example, in a 1997 adoption appeal, a biological mother who had given her child up for adoption asserted that postpartum depression rendered her incompetent to consent to the adoption. The Tennessee Appellate Court stated: "We do not dispute that [the mother] was probably depressed or emotionally distraught following this rather traumatic experience, but it is not unusual for there to be depression and distress following the birth of a child, even under the best of circumstances. If emotional distress meant that a parent was always incompetent to consent to an adoption, we would rarely have adoptions in this state" (*Croslin v. Croslin*, 1997, at 10).

Similarly, the court did not find that postpartum depression nullified a woman's competency to consent to a postnuptial agreement. Kim and Anthony Latina had a 1-year-old son when Kim gave birth to a daughter, Jill, who was premature and had to be returned to the hospital daily for a short time after her birth. Kim was caring for both children and preparing to return to work while suffering from postpartum depression. Approximately three weeks after Jill was born, Kim had to be rushed to the hospital for severe hemorrhaging. Although she was not admitted to the hospital, the court acknowledged, "it was obviously a very frightening and traumatic experience" (*Latina v. Latina*, 1995, at 19). A few days after Kim was rushed to the hospital, less than one month postpartum, Anthony presented her with a postnuptial agreement. Regarding the effect of postpartum depression on Kim's capacity to consent, the Delaware Family Court indicated:

> "The break-up of a marriage never comes at a good time, and, as noted in many earlier opinions, usually separation agreements are signed in a highly charged atmosphere, thereby necessitating the precautions taken by the Delaware courts to ensure the agreements' fairness. However, if the courts could set aside agreements based upon their being signed during the emotional turmoil of a marriage splitting up, no separation agreement would ever be permitted to stand. Although the court recognizes Wife was extremely distraught and probably feeling somewhat vulnerable when she signed the agreement, the Court finds that Wife signed more because she did not understand the implications of the agreement than because she was coerced. It should be noted that the second agreement was signed by Wife approximately six weeks after the first agreement, by which time Wife's postpartum depression and concern for Jill's health should have lessened. (*Latina v. Latina*, 1995, at 19)

All of these cases are patronizing, paternalistic, and lack a clear understanding of postpartum syndromes. It is difficult to find other cases in which the court admitted in its opinion that a party was exposed to a trauma and yet proceeded to validate capacity to consent. Moreover, their inconsistencies simply reflect disparate treatment. How can a disorder be a key factor in one civil case but be easily dismissed in another? This is particularly confusing since court cases in which postpartum syndromes were given extensive consideration involved women who had been asymptomatic for several years. Conversely, the cases in which postpartum syndromes were easily dismissed involved women who made decisions in the midst of experiencing postpartum syndromes. Even more disconcerting is the fact that these cases were all heard in the civil system.

THE LEGAL DILEMMA

When evidence regarding postpartum syndromes is entered into civil cases, it is almost always in opposition to a woman's interests. When the admission of evidence could assist women's interests, such as in criminal cases, it is often barred from admission. The medical and psychological communities are partially responsible for this discrepancy by their lack of recognition of postpartum syndromes. However, this is compounded by legal ambiguities in the insanity laws and discrepancies in insanity criteria that foster subjectivity in insanity decisions. This can even be seen in cases that involve disorders which are recognized by the psychological/medical community, such as dissociative identity disorder (formerly multiple personality disorder) or posttraumatic stress disorder

(PTSD). When asserted in court, the validity of these recognized disorders and their exculpatory capability often become the subject of dispute between experts. This dispute may be problematic for experts whose credibility and authority in the court room are already under scrutiny (see, e.g., Wilson, 1997). Experts are in an even more difficult situation when disorders are ambiguous, as in the case of postpartum syndromes.

One argument against routine recognition of postpartum syndromes in criminal courts is the even greater vagaries that could be created in the already ambiguous area of mental health defenses. Courts strive for *bright lines* or clear criteria on which to base decisions. Bright lines are rare but are desirable because they reduce disparate treatment that results from subjectivity. Recognizing postpartum syndromes in the legal system could create relatively fine lines and slippery slopes. For example, would a woman accused of child abuse now be able to assert postpartum syndromes as an exculpatory defense? Would the defense be available for other crimes, such as assault or shoplifting?

Although at first glance it appears that recognition of postpartum syndromes could lead to such unwieldy outcomes, it is unlikely. First, this has not been the case in England, where the defense is rarely used. Second, and more important, perpetrators with postpartum psychosis have very specific crimes and victims. Additionally, the trigger does not have multiple origins as with PTSD, but is clearly due to one cause, pregnancy, and this cause is not likely to reoccur with any frequency in a defendant's lifetime. Third, the dangerousness is temporary. If anything, postpartum syndromes seem to have more specificity than already recognized defenses (such as PTSD and dissociate identity disorder) and represent much less threat to the integrity of the legal system.

Overall, recognition of postpartum syndromes in criminal cases would constitute a gender defense (Denno, 1994) and the court has not been responsive to recognizing or ameliorating gender biases against women in defenses. Criminal defenses, particularly with regard to murder, have always been more applicable to crimes committed by men ("irresistible impulse") than those committed by women. More men than women murder, but the fact that women represent a minority of murder defendants should not preclude their equal treatment under the law.

Courts could facilitate preventive action by the medical community if they acknowledged the importance of postpartum syndromes in their opinions. The courts have been able to address this issue directly in cases involving insurance and disability claims for postpartum syndromes. As far back as 1964, the court was asked to determine whether postpartum syndromes represented a sickness or mental illness (*Price v. State Capital Insurance Company*, 1964). If postpartum syndromes represent a sickness, the level of coverage under insurance and disability is generally expanded. Conversely, if they represent a mental illness, the coverage is generally restricted. The courts have routinely held that the cause of postpartum syndromes has not been proven to be physical and the treatment is generally psychological; therefore, postpartum syndromes are excluded from coverage (*Blake v. Unionmutual Stock Life Insurance Company*, 1990). The courts have also found that postpartum syndromes were outside the scope of pregnancy disability claims (*Barrash v. Bowen*, 1988). Therefore, the courts' decisions reinforce the lack of recognition of postpartum syndromes. The courts could address the issue of classification of postpartum syndromes in their opinions, perhaps facilitating a review of the status of these conditions by the medical and psychological communities, as well as clarifying insurance provisions. Instead, the court provides passive approval by not commenting on the ambiguities with the diagnosis.

THE MEDICAL AND PSYCHOLOGICAL DILEMMA

The lack of clear definitions for postpartum syndromes and inconsistencies in the medical and psychological literature probably become self-perpetuating by leading to the inaccurate education of health professionals. Small, Epid, Johnston, and Orr (1997) found that fourth- and sixth-year medical students had inaccurate or incomplete knowledge of postpartum syndromes. Medical students had a narrower view of the factors that contribute to postpartum depression than did women who had experienced postpartum depression. For example, students selected hormonal or biological factors and a "tendency to depression" as the most influential in the development of postpartum depression. The women, however, identified social and experiential factors, such as lack of support, as contributing the most significantly to postpartum depression. The biological focus endorsed by the students suggests a likelihood to overlook the wide range of social, physical health, and life-event factors in diagnosis and treatment (Small, et al., 1997). If health professionals are not aware that a lack of social support is common for women with postpartum depression, they will not realize that women who lack social support are at greater risk for postpartum syndromes and may not create an intervention for women with postpartum syndromes aimed at increasing their social support. As a result, women are disadvantaged on multiple levels: health professionals only recognize biological contributors to postpartum syndromes, reducing treatment effectiveness, while the court excludes biological components, preventing women from receiving disability or insurance coverage for postpartum syndromes.

The inadequate preparation of health professionals may be compounded by the fact that many women are reluctant to report symptoms of postpartum syndromes. Motherhood can be a stressful time for women because it entails the adoption of new roles and perhaps the loss of others. Gender roles in this society dictate that women understand and love everything about motherhood (Cox, 1988; Mauthner, 1993). This value can be overwhelming for new mothers, who may be feeling unsure of their caregiving abilities. Women may feel inept and inadequate if they do not instinctively know how to care for their child (Thurtle, 1995). Additionally, despite the happiness that motherhood often brings, many new mothers experience grief due to their loss of freedom (Hopkins, Marcus, & Campbell, 1984). Activities of interest and important projects may need to be put on hold or may have less time allotted to them.

Motherhood can also be a difficult time as women may feel societal pressure to make motherhood their primary role (Miles, 1988). This places women who work outside the home in a no-win situation: Working outside the home may be their only opportunity to be recognized by society since motherhood is generally unappreciated, yet mothers who work outside the home are often labeled as selfish and uncaring.

Mothers who decide to stop working outside the home may experience a loss of self-esteem related to loss of roles and lack of importance given to them. Additionally, these women may experience a further decrease in self-esteem, as studies have shown that women who do not work outside the home are more isolated, and are expected to complete work that is repetitive and frustrating (Gove, 1972). Mothers who continue to work outside the home may experience stress related to juggling multiple roles and finding adequate child care. Additionally, social pressure to make child care their sole responsibility may lead to guilt (Thurtle, 1995).

Women experiencing symptoms of postpartum syndromes, whether from biological, psychological, or societal factors, may be hesitant to disclose these symptoms because of societal expectations that they relish every aspect of motherhood. Women's reluctance to seek help for postpartum syndromes makes early detection difficult and may result in the increased severity of their symptoms, especially since lack of social support has been shown to contribute to depression (Inwood, 1985).

THE IMPACT OF INCREASED RECOGNITION OF POSTPARTUM SYNDROMES

Recognition of a condition that solely or primarily affects women creates the risk of pathologizing women with that condition. This phenomenon is seen with conditions such as premenstrual syndrome (PMS). Although the aim of increased recognition of premenstrual syndrome has been to provide more effective prevention and treatment for women, some argue that increased recognition has pathologized a normal life event so that it is seen as a defect in a woman's character (Rome, 1986). This viewpoint may then be used to justify patronizing women in situations involving education or career since women are seen as incapable of handling challenging situations. Additionally, some argue that increasing the role of the medical, psychological, and legal communities with regard to PMS has taken power away from women as diagnosis and treatment of this condition has come under the control of these professions.

Increasing the recognition of postpartum syndromes could have the same consequences as increased recognition of PMS. The medical, psychological, and legal systems in this country are controlled by males. Males have the power to invent and deny disorders, and they do so based on societal standards of male health. For instance, research has shown that the concept of a healthy male differs from the concept of a healthy female. Mental health professionals were asked to select traits characteristic of either a healthy male, healthy female, or healthy adult person. Results showed that the participants' concepts of a healthy, mature adult were similar to the concepts of a healthy male, but different from concepts of a healthy female (Broverman, Broverman, Clarkson, Rosenkrantz, & Vogel, 1981).

Using these same standards, health professionals indoctrinated in patriarchal practice then choose conditions to which they want to devote resources. Thus certain medical or psychological states receive more funding than others for research, education, or treatment. Because postpartum syndromes are conditions affecting women, there are no male norms with which to compare them. As a result, these syndromes are of little interest in the male-dominated health fields and are therefore provided with less financial support for research and education than other conditions.

Given the cons of increased recognition of postpartum syndromes, it appears that women are facing a dilemma: It seems as though the only way for women to receive treatment for postpartum syndromes is to pathologize women and take control away from them. However, this dilemma becomes less difficult when we recognize that women are already pathologized and have little control over treatment of their bodies.

The concern that the recognition of postpartum syndromes will provide an excuse for the sexist practices happening in this society seems unfounded since individuals supporting sexism will always be able to find an excuse to support their behavior. Sexism in this society is much more far-reaching than the issue of postpartum syndromes: Sexism permeates every aspect of society and has many supporters. Those in power are reluctant to equalize power between men and women because it would mean giving up some of their power. Thus, pathologizing and paternalizing will occur in the health professions, regardless of the recognition given to postpartum syndromes, just as sexism occurs in the society at large.

It seems unlikely that recognizing postpartum syndromes could worsen the situation for women. In fact, a recognition of these conditions could actually benefit women. Some pathologizing might actually be necessary in order for women to receive treatment and recognition for medical and psychological conditions. Without pathologizing, health providers minimize women's syndromes, causing women to feel "crazy" for believing that something is wrong with them and leading to further problems as women's conditions go untreated. Therefore, pathologizing may be seen as a means to an end: Inequity is being used to eventually gain equity between men and women. Additionally, pathologizing some types of postpartum syndromes and not others may decrease the overall level of pathology assigned to these conditions. Pathologizing postpartum psychosis, which is a rare and serious disorder, may increase the distinction between this condition and less severe types of postpartum syndromes, which are then able to be normalized.

Some may argue that even pathologizing one type of postpartum syndrome does an injustice to women. In response to this argument, it is important to remember that women with postpartum syndromes are already being pathologized. Additionally, without a clear distinction between postpartum psychosis and less severe types of postpartum syndromes, postpartum blues and postpartum depression are likely to be pathologized as well. Although increasing the distinction between postpartum psychosis and less severe postpartum conditions creates a small possibility that the few women with postpartum psychosis will risk greater stigmatization, it also creates a large possibility that the many women with postpartum blues and postpartum depression will have their conditions recognized for what they are: typical reactions to biological, psychological, and societal stressors.

It is also important to realize that by increasing the recognition of postpartum syndromes, we are able to increase awareness of the context in which these conditions develop. Thurtle (1995) suggests that both biological and psychological explanations focus on the individual woman, placing the blame solely on her, and neglect the overall position of mothers in society. In contrast, a sociological explanation views postpartum depression as the response to societal pressure placed on women at the time of childbirth and to the societal pressure constantly affecting women (Thurtle, 1995). By increasing recognition of postpartum syndromes and acknowledging the social variables that contribute to these conditions, we would be able to provide women with the help they need, without viewing their conditions as inherently pathological.

Regardless of whether one believes that increased recognition of postpartum syndromes will benefit women, it is important to recognize that it is time for women to take control of their bodies and the medical and psychological conditions affecting them. Women are currently relying on the paternalistic health care systems to equalize the power differential between men and women, neglecting to remember that these systems had a large role in creating inequality in the first place. If equality between men and women is to be gained, women must take an active role in defining and explaining conditions with which they are affected.

Encouraging women to become active with decisions affecting their bodies and their lives does not negate the influence and responsibility that men as well as medical, psychological, and legal professionals have with regard to postpartum syndromes. Women do not exist in a vacuum; therefore, a condition that affects women affects their families, friends, work, and eventually the larger society. These people and institutions influence the fate of women with postpartum syndromes; thus each is instrumental in helping to ameliorate the disparate treatment experienced by these women.

NOTE

1. However, the judge rendered a judgment notwithstanding the verdict and found her not guilty by reason of insanity. The prosecution then appealed this judgment to the state appellate and supreme courts. Eventually, the appeal was dismissed.

REFERENCES

AMERICAN PSYCHIATRIC ASSOCIATION. (1994). *Diagnostic and statistical manual of mental disorders* (4th ed.). Washington, DC: APA.

BARAN, M. (1989). Postpartum illness: A psychiatric illness, a legal defense to murder, or both? *Hamlin Journal of Public Law and Policy, 10,* 121–139.

BROVERMAN, I. K., BROVERMAN, D. M., CLARKSON, F. E., ROSENKRANTZ, P. S., & VOGEL, S. R. (1981). Sex-role stereotypes and clinical judgments of mental health. In E. Howell & M. Bayes (Eds.), *Women and mental health* (pp. 86–97). New York: Basic Books.

BRUSCA, A. (1990). Postpartum psychosis: A way out for murderous moms? *Hofstra Law Review, 18,* 1133–1170.

CANADIAN CRIMINAL CODE. (1970). 2 R.S.C. 216.

COX, J. (1988). The life event of childbirth: Sociocultural aspects of postnatal depression. In R. Kumar & I. F. Brockington (Eds.), *Motherhood and mental illness: Vol. 2. Causes and consequences* (pp. 64–77). London: Butterworth.

COX, J. L. (1986). *Postnatal depression: A guide for health professionals.* Edinburgh: Churchill Livingstone.

DENNO, D.W. (1994). Gender issues and criminal law: Gender crime and the criminal law defenses. *Journal of Criminal Law and Criminology, 85,* 80–173.

GARDNER, C. A. (1990). Postpartum depression defense: Are mothers getting away with murder? *New England Law Review, 24,* 953–989.

GITLIN, M. J., & PASNAU, R. O. (1989). Psychiatric syndromes linked to reproductive function in women: A review of current knowledge. *American Journal of Psychiatry, 146,* 1413–1422.

GOVE, W. R. (1972). The relationship between sex roles, marital status, and mental illness. *Social Forces, 51*, 34–44.

HAMILTON, J. A. (1989). Postpartum psychiatric syndromes. *Psychiatric Clinics of North America, 12*, 89–103.

HARDING, J. J. (1989). Postpartum psychiatric disorders: A review. *Comprehensive Psychiatry, 30*, 109–112.

HOPKINS, J., MARCUS, M., & CAMPBELL, S. (1984). Postpartum depression: A critical review. *Psychological Bulletin, 95*, 498–515.

INFANTICIDE ACT OF 1938. (1938). 1 & 2 Geo. 6, Ch. 26 sec. 1.

INWOOD, D. G. (1985). The spectrum of postpartum psychiatric disorders. In D. G. Inwood (Ed.), *Recent advances in postpartum psychiatric disorders*. Washington, DC: American Psychiatric Press.

JAPENGA, A. (1987, February 1). Ordeal of postpartum psychosis: Illness can have tragic consequences for new mothers. *Los Angeles Times*, p. 1.

LYNCH-FRASER, D. (1983). *The complete postpartum guide: Everything you need to know about taking care of yourself after you've had a baby*. New York: Harper & Row.

MAUTHNER, N. (1993). Towards a feminist understanding of "postnatal depression." *Feminism and Psychology, 3*, 350–355.

MELTON G. B., PETRILA, J., POYTHRESS, N. G., & SLOBOGIN, C. (1997). *Psychological evaluations for the courts: A handbook for mental health professionals and lawyers*. New York: Guilford Press.

MILES, A. (1988). *The neurotic woman*. New York: New York University Press.

OBERMAN, M. (1996). Mothers who kill: coming to terms with modern American infanticide. *American Criminal Law Review, 34*, 1–110.

PFOST, K. S., STEVENS, M. J., MATEJCAK, A. J., JR. (1990). Counselor's primer on postpartum depression. *Journal of Counseling and Development, 69*, 148–151.

ROME, E. (1986). Premenstrual syndrome (PMS) examined through a feminist lens. In V. L. Olesen & N. F. Woods (Eds.), *Culture, society, and menstruation* (pp. 145–151). Washington, DC: Hemisphere Publishing.

SMALL, R., EPID, G. D., JOHNSTON, V., & ORR, A. (1997). Depression after childbirth: The views of medical students and women compared. *Birth, 24*, 109–115.

STEINER, M. (1990). Postpartum psychiatric disorders. *Canadian Journal of Psychiatry, 35*, 89–95.

THURTLE, V. (1995). Post-natal depression: The relevance of sociological approaches. *Journal of Advanced Nursing, 22*, 416–424.

WILSON, J. Q. (1997). *Sliding down the slippery slope away from personal responsibility: The abuse excuse*. New York: Harper Collins.

WORLD HEALTH ORGANIZATION. (1992). *The ICD-10 classification of mental and behavioral disorders: Clinical descriptions and diagnostic guidelines*. Geneva: WHO.

CASES

Barrash v. Bowen, 846 F.2d 927 (4th Cir. 1988).

Blake v. Unionmutual Stock Life Insurance Company, 906 F.2d 1525 (1990).

Commonwealth v. Comitz, 530 A.2d 473 (Pa. Super. 1987).

Croslin v. Croslin, 1997 Tenn. App. Lexis 84.

Daubert v. Merrell Dow Pharmaceuticals, 509 U.S. 579 (1993).

Frye v. United States, 392 F. 1013 (D.C. Cir. 1923).

In Re the Marriage of Grimm, 1989 Minn. App. Lexis 143.

Latina v. Latina, 1995 Del. Fam. Ct. Lexis 48.
People v. Massip, 271 Cal. Rptr. 868 (Cal. App. 1990).
Pfeifer v. Pfeifer, 280 P.2d 54 (Cal. App. 1955).
Price v. State Capital Insurance Company, 134 S.E. 2d 171 (Sup. Ct. 1964).

7

The Legal System and Sexual Harassment[1]

Roslyn Muraskin

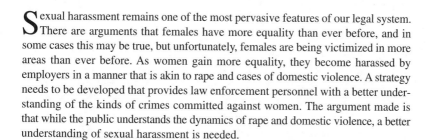

S exual harassment remains one of the most pervasive features of our legal system. There are arguments that females have more equality than ever before, and in some cases this may be true, but unfortunately, females are being victimized in more areas than ever before. As women gain more equality, they become harassed by employers in a manner that is akin to rape and cases of domestic violence. A strategy needs to be developed that provides law enforcement personnel with a better understanding of the kinds of crimes committed against women. The argument made is that while the public understands the dynamics of rape and domestic violence, a better understanding of sexual harassment is needed.

Historically, women have been discriminated against by the law, often by policies designed to protect them. During recent decades, women have found themselves in courts of law arguing for equality. The history of women's struggles has taught us that litigation becomes merely a catalyst for change. It does not guarantee results.

Rebecca West in 1913 stated: "I myself have never been able to find out precisely what feminism is. I only know that people call me a feminist whenever I express sentiments that differentiate me from a doormat." Women's basic rights are inextricably linked to our treatment by and with their participation in today's political world. Due to the fact that the lives of women are reflections of what they do, what they say, and how they treat each other, women as participating members of the human race are ultimately responsible for human affairs.

Throughout this work, we note that there is no way to allow both sexes automatically to enjoy the equal protection of the laws unless we are committed to the elimination of all gender discrimination. The criminal justice system has slowly come to grips with the needed understanding of women and justice. Today, courts need time for discovery of evidence and the opportunity to hear expert testimony in all cases of sexual violence.

Crimes such as rape, domestic violence, and sexual harassment are all part of the continuum of violence against women. Rape is not a crime of sex; it is a crime of power. It is "an act of violence, an assault like any other, not an expression of socially organized sexuality" (MacKinnon, 1979, p. 218). The fact that rape is acted out in sex does not mean that it is an act of male sexuality. Rape is an act of violence. The act of sexual harassment has drawn parallels to the crime of rape. If sex or sexual advances are unwanted, if they are imposed on a woman who is in no position to refuse, why is this act any different from the act of rape? It may be a lesser crime in the minds of many, including the courts, but it is nevertheless an act of violence against women. Sexual harassment is gender discrimination, and laws are needed to remedy such disparities. We see a current of public discussion about the cases of women accused and sometimes convicted of assaulting and killing partners who have battered them. The actual volume of cases is small, but the attention given these cases illuminates the larger problem for which they have come to stand: the common disparity of power between men and women in familial relationships.

According to MacKinnon (1979), "a crime of sex is a crime of power" (p. 220). Taken together, rape, domestic violence, and sexual harassment eroticize women's subordination. This continues the powerlessness in the criminal law of women as a gender. "If sexuality is set apart from gender, it will be a law unto itself" (p. 221).

From a historical point of view, there existed under the English common law the "rule of thumb," which allowed a husband to beat his wife with a whip or stick no bigger than his thumb. The husband's prerogative was incorporated into the laws of the United States. The sad fact is that several states had laws on the book that essentially allowed a man to beat his wife with no interference from the courts. Blackstone referred to this action as the *power of correction*. For too many decades women have been victims of sexual assaults. Each act of "sexual assault is recognized as one of the most traumatic and debilitating crimes for adults..." (Roberts, 1993, p. 362). The victimization of women has been more prevalent and problematic for the criminal justice system.

As point out by Susan Faludi (1991):

> Women's advances and retreats are generally described in military terms: battles won, battles lost, points and territory gained and surrendered. In times when feminism is at a low ebb, women assume the reactive role—privately and most often covertly struggling to assert themselves against the dominant cultural tide. But when feminism becomes the tide, the opposition doesn't simply go along with the reversal, it digs in its heels, brandishes its fists, builds walls and dams.

In past decades we have seen sexual assault reform legislation resulting "in several long-overdue improvements in the criminal justice processing of sexual assault cases, for example, passage of rape shield laws, confidentiality laws to protect communications between the victims and their counselors, and laws designed to preserve medical evidence" (Roberts, 1993, p. 370). In addition, we have seen the establishment of victim assistance programs.

SEXUAL HARASSMENT

The female represents half of the U.S. population. She is deserving of the same rights and opportunities as are afforded males. There exists the rhetoric of gender equality, but it has yet to match the reality of women's experiences. The case of Anita Hill and Judge Clarence Thomas brought to light the phrase *sexual harassment*, words that have gained new meaning.

Litigation is occurring. Though we do not have a federal equal rights amendment, there are states that recognize its potential value. As an example, the use of male terms to indicate both sexes is slowly being examined. There are those who choose to use gender-neutral terms. But gender discrimination is masked when such gender-neutral terms are used. Words are meant to have definitive meaning. "Words are workhorses of law" (Thomas, 1911, p. 116). Sexual harassment is a major barrier to women's professional lives and personal development, and a traumatic force that disrupts and damages their personal lives. For ethnic-minority women who have been sexually harassed, economic vulnerability is paramount. Women feel powerless, not in control, afraid, and not flattered by sexual harassment.

In 1980 the Equal Employment Opportunity Commission defined sexual harassment as occurring when unwelcome sexual advances, requests for sexual favors, and other verbal or physical conduct of a sexual nature are made a condition of employment, are used in employment decisions, affect an employee's work performance, or create an intimidating, hostile, or offensive working environment. The U.S. Supreme Court upheld these guidelines in 1986 in the case of *Meritor Savings Bank, FSB v. Vinson*, where it ruled that gender harassment is sexual discrimination and illegal under Title VII of the Civil Rights Act of 1964.

Throughout this country, committees have been established to combat the charges of sexual harassment. It was almost as if the Thomas–Hill hearings brought people "out of the closet." Cases that have come to light include *Wagenseller v. Scottsdale Memorial Hospital* (1990) in Arizona, where the Arizona Supreme Court overruled earlier law and recognized a public policy exception to discharge at will in the case of an emergency room nurse who allegedly was terminated because she refused to "moon" on a rafting trip.

A worker who continually harasses female co-workers and is discharged does not have a right to reinstatement for failure of the employer to follow the notice provisions of the contract (see *Newsday, Inc. v. Long Island Typographical Union*, 1991). In the case of *Ellison v. Brady* (1991) the trial court had dismissed as trivial "love" letters that the plaintiff had received from a co-worker along with persistent requests for dates. The Ninth Circuit Court disagreed, however, stating that the perspectives of men and women differ. Women, as indicated by the courts, have a strong reason to be concerned about sexual behavior, as they are potential victims of rape and sexual assault.

A court in Florida ruled in the case of *Robinson v. Jacksonville Shipyards, Inc.* (1991) that a display of nude women can lead to the creation of a hostile environment and is therefore deemed an act of discrimination. In the case of *Continental Can Co., Inc. v. Minnesota* (1980), the Minnesota Supreme Court upheld an action to stop harassment by fellow employees. In still another case, *E.E.O.C. v. Sage Realty Corp.* (1981), the court held that an employer may impose reasonable dress codes for its employees, but the employer cannot require its employees to wear "revealing and sexually provocative uniforms" that would subject the employee to a form of sexual harassment. This constitutes gender discrimination.

What has increased is the notice that sexual harassment is more than mere physical touching. It exists if any employer, supervisor, or co-worker subjects a person (usually a woman) to the following:

- Obscene pictures in the workplace or at a work-sponsored activity
- Leering at a person's body
- Sexually explicit or derogatory remarks
- Unnecessary touching, patting, or pinching
- Subtle pressure for sexual activities
- Demanding sexual favors for a good work assignment, performance rating, and/or promotion

In the case of *Bundy v. Jackson* (1981), the plaintiff had been subjected to sexual propositions by five of her supervisors during a period of two and one-half years. Because the plaintiff was unable to demonstrate that her rejection of the supervisors' advances had resulted in loss of job benefits or promotions, she lost in the lower courts; but reversing the decision of the lower courts, the judge held that an employer violates Title VII merely by subjecting female employees to sexual harassment in the absence of the deprivation of tangible job benefits.

In the cases of *Burlington Industries v. Ellerth* (1998) and *Faragher v. Boca Raton* (1998), the court decided a chaotic body of law in the area of sexual harassment, making it easier for women whose bosses harass them to sue under Title VII of the 1964 Civil Rights Act. Patricia Ireland, president of the National Organization for Women (NOW), stated that "the boss who paws, propositions and warns of retaliation takes away a woman's dignity...even if he doesn't take away her job" (1998).

In the *Burlington* case the claim was that the female endured a steady stream of sexual harassment from her supervisor's boss, "including pats on the buttocks, offensive sexual remarks and the threat that he could make her work life 'very hard or very easy.'" Although the employer's argument that she suffered no tangible job loss, the U.S. Supreme Court decided that her case could go forward because it was the employer's burden to prove that reasonable steps had been taken by the company and that the complainant had failed to follow proper reporting procedures.

While in *Faragher*, the complainant, Beth Faragher, claimed that while working at a remote lifeguard station she was harassed by male supervisors, "who repeatedly touched her, called her and other women 'bitches and sluts,' made comments about her breasts and threatened 'date me or clean toilets for a year.'" It was the city's claim that she was not entitled to damages, as she failed to go over her supervisors' heads and report the harassment. The U.S. Supreme Court reinstated her damages award, deciding that the city had not taken reasonable steps to prevent and correct the harassment. In the words of Patricia Ireland, "women's rights need to be written into the Constitution....[W]ithout it...women do not have a constitutional right to bodily integrity."

Originally thought to be limited to those relatively rare situations where women are compelled to trade sexual favors for professional survival, sexual harassment is now recognized more broadly as the "inappropriate sexualization of an otherwise nonsexual relationship, an assertion by men of the primacy of a woman's sexuality over her role as worker or student" (Muraskin, 1999, p. 373).

Legal scholars such as Catherine MacKinnon, a law professor at the University of Michigan, and activists such as Susan Brownmiller are credited with initiating a view of sexual harassment that has radically changed the way that sexual harassment complaints are treated under the legal system. Shifting the focus of sexual harassment from the belief that males' sexual pursuit of a woman in the workplace or the classroom is essentially biological and that sexual harassment is therefore a "normal" consequence of attraction between the sexes, MacKinnon, Brownmiller, and others advocate a "dominance" approach. *Sexual harassment* is *gender discrimination*. It occurs in the workplace wherever women are situated in an attempt to keep them in place.

> One way women have been stigmatized as inferior is through the identification of a sometimes erroneous, usually exaggerated, always exclusive set of feminine needs. Women's sexuality has been a prime example. It has been hard to avoid branding woman as inferior long enough to balance a grasp of her dignity with an analysis of her enforced inferiority, in order to address the specificity of her situation. (MacKinnon, 1979, p. 144)
>
> Women learn early to be afraid that men will not be attracted to them, for they will then have no future; they also learn early to be afraid that men will be attracted to them, for they may then also have no future. (p. 217)

MacKinnon continues to point out that the failings of the argument that sexual harassment is based solely on gender is because men are not placed in comparable positions to women (p. 216).

LITIGATION

The law sees and treats women the way that men see and treat women. The first litigation of sexual harassment claims did not occur until the mid-1970s. Title VII of the Civil Rights Act prohibiting sex discrimination in the workplace was followed eight years later by Title IX of the 1972 Higher Education Amendments, prohibiting gender discrimination in educational institutions receiving federal assistance. But in much of the early adjudication of gender discrimination, the phenomenon of sexual harassment was typically seen "as isolated and idiosyncratic, or as natural and universal, and in either case, as inappropriate for legal intervention." In was not until 1980 that the Equal Employment Opportunity Commission, in its *Guidelines on Discrimination*, explicitly defined sexual harassment under Title VII as a form of unlawful, gender-based discrimination.

Victims' rights to collect damages continue to be limited under federal law. Unlike the potential for damages available to victims of racial discrimination, damages for gender discrimination are capped at $50,000 for small companies and $300,000 for larger ones. As the law has been interpreted, prohibition against sexual harassment in the workplace technically covers any remark or behavior that is sufficiently severe and pervasive that not only the victim's but also a "reasonable person's" psychological well-being would be affected. A 1991 landmark ruling by the Court of Appeals for the Ninth Circuit in California held that the "appropriate perspective for judging a hostile environment claim is that of the 'reasonable woman' and recognized that a woman's perspective may differ substantially from a man's." There may be a difference between intent and impact. Many men may not intend it, but some things they do may be experienced by women as sexual harassment. A touch or comment can be viewed very differently.

While the 1991 Ninth Circuit Court ruling acknowledges that men and women may interpret the same behavior differently, in application this legal understanding is often overshadowed by a grave misunderstanding of the nature of sexual harassment as experienced by its victims. The people doing the judging are in no position to understand the position of those being judged. The powerful make judgments against the powerless.

The dilemma in applying the reasonable person standard to sexual harassment is that a reasonable woman and a reasonable man are likely to differ in their judgment of what is offensive. Men's judgments about what behavior constitutes harassment and who is to blame are likely to prevail. In terms of the court, what constitutes harassment and what determines the amount of awards for damages under state law and in the future under federal law ultimately depends on the perceptions of the judge rather than the victim, and the vestiges of the long-standing prejudices do not seem entirely absent from judicial as well as workplace forums.

RAPE, SEXUAL HARASSMENT, AND THE CRIMINAL JUSTICE SYSTEM

Like the crime of rape, sexual harassment is not an issue of lust; it is an issue of power. Sexual harassment does not fall within the range of personal or private relationships. It happens when a person with power abuses that power to intimidate, coerce, or humiliate someone because of gender. It is a breach of trust. In voluntary sexual relationships, everyone exercises freedom of choice in deciding whether to establish a close, intimate relationship. This freedom of choice is absent in sexual harassment (Paludi, 1992). Sexual harassment must be viewed as the art of a continuum of sexual victimization that ranges from staring and leering to assault and rape. Similar to rape, incest, and battering, sexual harassment may be understood as an extreme acting out of qualities that are regarded as supermasculine: aggression, power dominance, and force. Men who harass are not pathological but rather people who exhibit behaviors characteristic of the masculine gender role in U.S. culture. Most sexual harassment starts at the subtle end of the continuum and escalates over time. Each year, 1 percent of women in the U.S. labor force are sexually assaulted on the job. Yet cultural mythologies consistently blame the victim for sexual abuse and act to keep women in their place. Scholars have identified several similarities in attitudes toward rape and sexual harassment, especially revealing cultural myths that blame the victim:

1. Women ask for it.
    Rape: Victims seduce their rapists.
    Sexual harassment: Women precipitate harassment by the way they dress and talk.
2. Women say no but mean yes.
    Rape: Women secretly need and want to be forced into sex. They don't know what they want.
    Sexual harassment: Women like the attention.

3. Women lie.

    Rape: In most charges of rape, the woman is lying.

    Sexual harassment: Women lie about sexual harassment to get men they dislike into trouble.

Women who speak about being victims of sexual harassment use words such as *humil-iating, intimidating, frightening, financially damaging, embarrassing, nervewracking, awful,* and *frustrating.* These are not words that are used to describe a situation that one enjoys.

Historically, the rape of a woman was considered to be an infringement of the property rights of men. Sexual harassment should be viewed in the same light. The message is that changes are needed. We can no longer blame the messenger. We need to understand the message. There is no question that what is referred to as "women's hidden occupational hazard," sexual harassment, is gender victimization. The fact that sexual harassment exists demonstrates that it must be understood as part of the continuum of violence against women. In a typical sexual harassment case, the female accuser becomes the accused and the victim is twice victimized. This holds true in cases of rape and domestic violence, as well as in cases of harassment. Underlying the dynamics of the situation is the profound distrust of a woman's word and a serious power differential between the accused and the accuser. As indicated, sexual harassment is the most recent form of victimization of the woman to be redefined as a social rather than a personal problem, following rape and wife abuse.

Sexual harassment is a major barrier to women's professional and personal devel-opment and a traumatic force that disrupts and damages their personal lives. For ethnic-minority women who have been sexually harassed, economic vulnerability is paramount. Women feel powerless, not in control, afraid. There is nothing flattering about sexual harassment. Their emotional and physical well-being resembles that of victims of other sexual abuses (i.e., rape, incest, and battering). It must be stopped.

Women's issues infuse every aspect of social and political thought. It was Gloria Steinem who noted that cultural myths die hard, especially if they are used to empower one part of the population. The struggle of women continues under the law. There is no way to allow both sexes automatically to enjoy the equal protection of the laws unless we are committed to the elimination of all gender discrimination. Sexual harassment is gender discrimination. The criminal justice system over the years has slowly come to grips with the need to understand women in the context of justice and fairness.

Women continue to represent half the population. They are owed the same rights and opportunities as are afforded to men. For justice to be gained, the fight for freedom and equality must continue. Prevention is the best tool that the criminal justice system has to offer as long as it takes the action mandated by legislators. Dominance takes several forms. As stated so succinctly by Catherine MacKinnon (1979), "Sexual harassment (and rape) has everything to do with sexuality. Gender *is* a power division and sexuality is one sphere of its expression" (pp. 220–221). There is no logic to inequality.

NOTE

1. Much of the material for this chapter comes from "Women and the law: An agenda for change in the twenty-first century," In R. Muraskin and A. Roberts (Eds.), *Visions for change: Crime and justice in the twenty-first century.* Upper Saddle River, NJ: Prentice Hall, 1999).

REFERENCES

CORBIN, B., & BENNETT-HAIGNE, G. (1998, August 12). *Sexual harassment: Open season on working women.* Available: http://www.now.org/nnt/03-97/sexual.html

FALUDI, S. (1991). *Backlash: The undeclared war against American women.* New York: Crown Publishers.

IRELAND, P. (1998). *Sexual harassment: Open season on working women.*

MACKINNON, C. (1979). *Sexual harassment of working women.* New Haven, CT: Yale University Press.

MURASKIN, R., & ROBERTS, A. (1999). *Visions for change: Crime and justice in the twenty-first century.* Upper Saddle River, NJ: Prentice Hall.

PALUDI, M. A. (1992). Working nine to five: Women, men, sex and power. In R. Muraskin (Ed.), *Women's agenda: Meeting the challenge to change.* New York: Long Island Women's Institute, College of Management, C.W. Post Campus of Long Island University.

ROBERTS, A. (1993). Women: Victims of sexual assault and violence. In R. Muraskin and T. R. Alleman (Eds.), *It's a crime: Women and justice.* Upper Saddle River, NJ: Prentice Hall.

THOMAS, C. S. (1991). *Sex discrimination.* St. Paul, MN: West Publishing.

CASES

Bundy v. Jackson, 641 F.2d 934 (D.C. Cir. 1981).

Burlington Industries v. Ellerth, 123 F.3d 490 (1998).

Continental Can Co., Inc. v. Minnesota, 297 N.W. 2d 241 (Minn. 1980), 242.

E.E.O.C. v. Sage Realty Corp., 507 F. Supp. 599 (D.C. N.Y. 1981), 243.

Ellison v. Brady, 924 F.2d 872 (9th Cir. 1991), 119.

Faragher v. Boca Raton, 111 F.3d 1530 (1998).

Meritor Savings Banks, FSB v. Vinson, 477 U.S. 57, 106 S. Ct. 2399, 91 L. Ed. 2d 49 (1986), 239.

Newsday, Inc. v. Long Island Typographical Union No. 915, U.S. 111 S. Ct. 1314, 113 L. Ed. 2d 247 (1991), 195, 241.

Robinson v. Jacksonville Shipyards, Inc., 760 F. Supp. 1486 (M.D. Fla. 1991), 241.

Wagenseller v. Scottsdale Memorial Hospital, 147 Ariz. 370, 710 P.2d 1025 (Ariz. 1985), 194.

SECTION III

Women, Drugs, and AIDS

The rights of women as persons and the obligations of women as mothers emerge in this section as irreconcilable differences that serve to generate issues and debates that are central to women and the treatment accorded them by the criminal justice system. If close attention is paid to the arguments presented in this section, you will find the underlying issues to be emotion-provoking, the problems to be quite complex, and the solutions to be less than clear. The criminal justice system continues to rely principally on a simpleminded, punitive approach to the solution of very complex social problems. Many of the chapters in this section cover problems generated by the debate over the rights and obligations of women in contemporary society. At stake are the rights of women to bodily integrity. It is the combined images of being black, being on welfare, and using drugs that drive the punitive reaction toward pregnant women of all classes and races.

Drew Humphries examines certain ABC, CBS, and NBC evening news programs during the period 1983–1994 in her chapter, "Crack Mothers at 6: Prime-Time News, Crack/Cocaine, and Women." The data demonstrate that over time, news-framed maternal crack/cocaine use was demonstrated in three ways: (1) middle-class white women were presented as psychologically addicted, guilt-ridden for having exposed their babies to the drug cocaine, but motivated to gain treatment for their problems; (2) poor black women were represented as mindlessly addicted and unwilling to enter treatment; and (3) poor black women subsequently regretted prior drug use and were subsequently enthusiastic drug treatment clients in order to regain custody of their children. For the poor and minority women, the biological fact of pregnancy combined with drug addiction was used to override the reproductive rights of these women.

Women as offenders and women as victims are expected to play a significant role in the shaping of criminal justice policies used to deter the spread of AIDS. Joan Luxenburg and Thomas E. Guild in their chapter "Women, AIDS, and the Criminal Justice System" study prostitutes and their association with the AIDS epidemic. They contend that in the misguided belief that female prostitutes transmit the virus to their male clients, there are states that have enacted AIDS-specific statutes that target prostitutes. Prostitutes are incarcerated with no evidence that they are a vector of the virus. If we expand the laws to women who are victims of rape, we face an intrusion into the rights of defendants that will be challenged on constitutional grounds.

Inger Sagatun-Edwards, in "The Legal Response to Substance Abuse during Pregnancy," points out that criminal prosecution of fetal abuse does not protect the well-being of the fetus enough to violate important constitutional rights of the mother. Any interventions on behalf of the drug-exposed infant must be predicated on other indications of future harm, not past prenatal use. We may look at such indicators as a mother's failure to care for siblings, an unwillingness to participate in drug treatment programs and parenting classes, as well as a much needed support system.

In "HIV Disease and Women Offenders," Arthur J. Lurigio, James A. Swartz, and Ciuinal Jones describe first the HIV/AIDS epidemic with an emphasis on the disproportionate number of women of color who are infected with the disease. The authors indicate that the characteristics of women under correctional supervision and those of women with HIV and AIDS mirror each other. They indicate that women of color throughout the world have been devastated by the spread of the HIV virus. They conclude that women of color are not only one of the fastest-growing segments of the population with this disease, but that women of color with the AIDS virus are disproportionately represented in the correctional population. They present various strategies needed to be adopted to prevent the continuous onslaught of this disease.

8

Crack Mothers at 6

Prime-Time News, Crack/Cocaine, and Women[1]

Drew Humphries

This study examines ABC, CBS, and NBC evening news programs from 1983 to 1994 to understand the images associated with crack mothers (i.e., women who used crack or cocaine during pregnancy). Qualitative analysis shows that over time, the news framed maternal crack/cocaine use in at least three ways. First, middle-class white women were presented as psychologically addicted, as guilt-ridden for having exposed their babies to cocaine, and as motivated to succeed in treatment. Second, poor black women were represented as mindlessly addicted, as knowingly having exposed their fetuses to the adversity of crack, and as unwilling to enter treatment. Third, poor black women were subsequently represented as physically and spiritually depleted, as having regretted prior drug use, and as enthusiastic drug treatment clients, if only to regain custody of their children. Findings are discussed in terms of drug scares, racial disparity, and the reproductive rights of women.

Crack mothers, a media-coined phrase associated with the war on drugs, refers to women who continued to use cocaine or crack during pregnancy. Socially constructed as black and urban, the media demonized crack mothers as the threatening symbols for everything that was wrong in the United States. Its cities, its poverty, and its welfare dependency were laid at the door of crack mothers, who by their drug use undermined the family and drove up the rates of infant mortality and morbidity. Yet crack or cocaine mothers cannot be considered innocent. Drug use during pregnancy adds avoidable risk and violates the moral duties of motherhood (i.e., pregnant women are expected to prevent risk and encourage healthy development of the fetus). The issue is not risk or violation but rather how both were constructed. The news featured significant risk and egregious violations. To prevent these, warriors in the war on drugs invoked the law, using criminal sanctions to protect fetuses and babies from the effects of maternal drug use. More than 160 "crack mothers" were prosecuted in criminal court between 1988 and 1994. Rarely, if ever, have women triggered a drug scare of this magnitude.

Past drug scares have focused on males who used cocaine, marijuana, and heroin, but the construction of the problem across different antidrug crusades shows remarkable similarities. Social historians, for instance, suggest that during drug scares, drug use is identified with an unpopular minority, people are held responsible for their addiction, and addiction is cast as a broader threat (Levine, 1978; Musto, 1987). Reinarman and Levine (1995) have shown that the crack scare fits this model. Crack was constructed as the cause, not the symptom, of underlying problems. Legal liability—and mandatory prison sentences—fell to the crack addict, who epitomized a threatening underclass. As part of the larger scare, the crusade against crack mothers appealed to similar status resentments (Humphries, 1993; Humphries, Dawson, Cronin, Wisniewski, & Eichfeld, 1991). Reeves and Campbell (1994) have discussed the crack mother image as a racially defined composite, a "she-devil" image that borrows both from the welfare mother and from the sexually aggressive stereotype of black women, known as "Jezebels." Reeves and Campbell contrasted the she-devil image to the portraits of white mothers who used alcohol, showing racial disparities in coverage. It would have been better to compare race within the same category of drug user (e.g., black and white cocaine users), but this would have required a different approach to the problem. The longer time frame of this study permits racial comparisons among women who used cocaine or crack.

THE RESEARCH

The study surveys news segments shown on prime-time television during the war on drugs (1983–1994). ABC, CBS, and NBC were the networks sampled. A review of *Television News Index and Abstracts* yielded 84 news segments that referred to women and cocaine or crack. The media center at Vanderbilt University prepared the compilation tapes that included all 84 news segments. The tapes provide the data for this study. The tapes run 5 1/2 hours, this being the amount of time the major networks devoted to the story over nine years. Taken individually, the segments have a mean running time of 2 minutes, although segment duration ranges from 20 seconds to 6 minutes.

Because news connects people to a world beyond their experience, news images have considerable power in shaping perceptions. For this reason, media images are studied, but composite images are especially important. The power of a stereotype, such as mugger, to effectuate moral panic in England depended on converging images of race, poverty, the city, violence, and social menace (see Hall, Critcher, Jefferson, Clarke & Roberts, 1978). A similar convergence has been noted for the stereotype of crack mothers: Race, addiction, and poverty linked to sexuality and motherhood justify efforts to regulate pregnancy (Maher, 1991; Maher & Curtis, 1992).

This study focuses on news images, looking in particular for the special combination of race, class, gender (including motherhood), and addiction that created a pervasive sense of menace. To do this, the study looks at individuals shown on the videotaped segments as crack or cocaine addicts. To estimate the importance of maternal themes, the study also looks at the babies represented as drug exposed. A research assistant counted the babies and the people who used crack or cocaine.[2] For women, the assistant also determined race, ethnicity, and context. *Context* refers to the setting in which the addict or former addict is filmed. It includes civil society (ex-addict plays legitimate role in free society), drug life (addict is actively involved in drug use), treatment (addict participates in drug rehabilitation program), criminal court (addict awaits trial, is on trial, or is receiving posttrial punishment), and social services (addict is receiving help in the home from social workers or support groups). Other is a residual category.

The news narrative is also addressed in this article. Statements made by news anchors, news correspondents, experts, and interviewees form the narrative, the ongoing discussion about maternal drug use. That discussion consists of assertions about the drugs (crack or cocaine), the meaning of addiction (psychological and physical), and drug users, including motive, social class, and attitudes toward treatment or punishment.

News segments were coded for image and narrative. Coded entries have been located in a four-stage chronology of new coverage. The descriptive analysis identifies key aspects of image and narrative by stage.

FINDINGS

Drug scares and moral panics exhibit a typical pattern of news coverage: Volume increases, reaches a peak, and then trails off as other topics eclipse the story. As Figure 1 shows, the news about material drug use reveals a similar pattern. The four-stage model of news coverage shown in Table 1 is based on the frequency distribution of news segments and is used for comparative purposes.[3] Breaks between stages reflect data shifts, including a key event, a natural break, and a context change. Because the networks' discovery of crack changed the image of an addict, this key December 1985 event divides stage 1 and stage 2. News segments

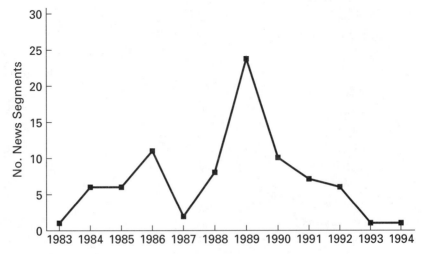

FIGURE 1   Distribution of news segments, 1983–1994.

dropped off in 1987, the natural break that separates stages 2 and 3. After 1991, the networks reduced coverage and introduced a new context, social services. Both are used to introduce stage 4.

Focusing on female crack or cocaine use, Table 1 shows a net increase in the proportion of female addicts from stages 1 to 4. That men were the majority in stage 2, however, reflects the discovery of crack and its identification as a male drug. The point at which the developing news story is clearly about maternal drug use occurs in stage 3: 63 percent of addicts shown on camera were women, and the maternal theme reached a peak with 93 babies shown on camera. Whereas white women defined the image of maternal drug use in the first two stages, black women defined it in the last two stages: 55 percent and 84 percent of the women were black in stages 3 and 4, respectively.[4] The last point concerns context. Table 1 shows that the treatment context provided a remarkable degree of continuity throughout the four-stage chronology, but as new contexts emerged, they are noted. Civil society provided a unique context for 37 percent of women who used cocaine in stage 1. As crack entered the picture in stage 2, 28 percent of the women were shown

TABLE 1   Summary of Descriptive Findings by Stage

	Stage							
	1		2		3		4	
Measure and Variables	n	%	n	%	n	%	n	%
Number of news segments	10	12	16	19	43	51	15	18
Number of crack/cocaine addicts								
Women	16	42	18	34	89	63	19	78
Men	22	58	35	66	53	37	6	24
Total	38	100	53	100	142	100	25	100
Maternal theme								
Babies	3		11		93		31	
Race/ethnicity—women								
White	12	75	13	72	28	31	3	
Black	3		2		49	55	16	84
Hispanic	1		3		2		0	
Unknown	0		0		10	11	0	
Context—women								
Civil society	6	37	1		7	8	3	
Drug life	2		5	28	23	26	4	21
Treatment	5	31	8	44	35	29	5	26
Criminal court	1		0		15	17	3	
Social services	0		0		0		4	21
Other	2		4		9	10	0	
Total women	16	100	18	100	89	100	19	100

using drugs against a background of drug supermarkets. At its stage 3 peak, the news used the criminal court to frame 17 percent of the women who used crack or cocaine. Finally, social services provided a new context for 21 percent of the women in stage 4.

Stage 1: Women, Cocaine, and the White Middle Class

Cindy, a middle-class white housewife, was the first cocaine mother to appear on network news (Brinkwater, 1984). She was, however, the third woman to be interviewed on an NBC Special Segment entitled "The Cocaine Epidemic." Like the two other middle-class white women, Cindy had not sought out the drug; rather, she, like the others, had been introduced to cocaine by the man in her life. Women used it to cope, explained Dr. Josette Mondonaro, a drug expert interviewed at a California treatment center. Women used cocaine to "pump up [their] low self-esteem," to feel better, to gain a competitive edge. But women did not fully appreciate cocaine's addictive potential. When Cindy discovered she was pregnant, she also discovered that she could not stop using cocaine. She sought drug treatment and succeeded in recovery. Interviewed in her home after the baby was born, Cindy was shown as a model mother, bathing a normal, healthy infant. An NBC correspondent, however, put the maternal scene in a darker context: When a woman used cocaine during pregnancy, the fetus could suffer from oxygen deprivation. Normal-looking babies such as Cindy's could still suffer the longer-term effects of cocaine.

Motherhood made Cindy atypical, but overall she resembled the other 15 women who admitted using cocaine, although stage 1 cocaine addicts, as shown in Table 1, were still as likely to be male (58 percent) as female (42 percent). The women tended to be white (75 percent). They appeared on camera as ex-addicts, but aside from this, they were represented as fulfilling legitimate roles as wives or professionals engaged in a variety of occupations. Maternal themes were not significant; only three babies were shown on camera in stage 1. Instead, female cocaine use served to illustrate the dangers associated with recreational drug use. The narrative suggested that an epidemic of middle-class cocaine addiction had resulted from misinformation and errors in judgment. In May 1984, CBS aired an interview with Dr. Mark Gold, cocaine expert and director of the Cocaine Hotline in New Jersey. Gold said that cocaine produces psychological dependence, although anywhere from 25 percent to 50 percent of cocaine users would become addicted. The more significant risk was death (Rather, 1984). CBS showed a film footage that outlined the results of animal research: A single monkey, free to move about its cage, repeatedly pushed a button to release cocaine intravenously into its bloodstream. The monkey injected so much cocaine that it fell into a state of seizure and died. Euphoria masked the deadly effects of cocaine, explained Dr. Gold. Humans were no different. The same CBS report introduced Kathryn, an ex-addict who recalled repetitive efforts to achieve the ultimate high. She used so much cocaine that she lost the desire to survive. She nearly died before she realized the problem.

Stage 2: The Discovery of Crack

Network news discovered crack in 1985; thereafter, the news tended to use terms—*crack, cocaine,* and *crack/cocaine*—interchangeably in referring to maternal drug use. Crack as a news story, however, pushed white women who used cocaine to the background. Even though Table 1 shows that most crack or cocaine addicts were men (66 percent), women addicted still tended to be white (72 percent). Maternal themes increased: Three middle-class mothers, all of whom resembled Cindy, were featured in stage 2, but the 11 babies shown on camera were still insignificant when compared with the 93 babies shown in stage 3. Less than half of the women appeared in the context of treatment, but the five women placed in the context of drug supermarkets were shown using crack.

The big news story was crack. Relying on street users and experts, the networks framed crack as the most dangerous drug in the United States. Crack produced the most powerful high. It was so good, according to one user, that he felt he could do anything (Palmer, 1985). Michael, a crack cook and dealer, said he got hooked the first or second time he tried the drug. He lost weight, became suicidal, and almost died (Jennings, 1986a). A recovering crack addict worried about relapse, explaining that his body would take over, compelling him to use it (Jennings, 1986b). Experts offered explanations (Palmer, 1985). Mitchell Rosenthal, president of the Phoenix House Foundation, reported that crack produced a short but powerful high, followed by a depression. To alleviate the depression, the user smoked more crack. Rosenthal predicted an increased rate of addiction.

The networks initially portrayed crack as everyone's drug. Crack smokers included people from all backgrounds, said Dennis Murphy, an NBC reporter (Brokaw, 1986). In the segment, a South Florida businessman claimed to have had an $1000-a-day crack habit and reported to have binged up to thirty hours at a time. The businessman appeared with two other white males before the camera cut to a litter-filled crack house in which police arrested black crack users. Film footage of a long black man smoking cocaine ended the segment. Other segments reported that the white middle class purchased crack. The New York Police Department impounded cars of out-of-state crack buyers, according to an NBC report (Chung, 1986). Film footage showed late-model cars and white drivers. Within a year, NBC had, however, redefined crack as an inner-city, minority, male drug (Brokaw, 1987). Crack spread from the largest seven to the largest forty cities in the country. But there was some good news, said Robert Stutman, spokesperson for the Drug Enforcement Administration. Crack use had leveled off in the suburbs. Stutman also said that he "did not believe it had leveled off in the inner city." Videotaped footage shown on camera included scenes of street trafficking, collection of crack vials, and black drug users. Black and Hispanic patients filled treatment centers.

Stage 3: Pregnancy, Crack, and Poor Women of Color

In October 1988, the television viewing public met its first crack mother (Brokaw, 1988). NBC introduced Tracy Watson, a pregnant black woman, who sat on a narrow bed in a bare New York City apartment and smoked crack. Tracy spent $100 a day on the drug and smoked up to twenty vials. Tracy spoke. She knew crack affected her pregnancy. She knew that the baby could be born prematurely. She knew that the baby might undergo with-drawal. All the while she smoked crack. Baring her protruding belly, Tracy said, "It kicks when I smoke. It tightens up on one side. It's kicking now."

Tracy Watson typified crack mothers, and as Table 1 indicates, her profile reflects the convergence of gender, maternal themes, and race. Women accounted for 63 percent of cocaine or crack addicts. Maternal themes reached a peak. Nine times more babies were shown during stage 3 (93) than were shown during stage 2 (11). And 55 percent of the women were black. News segments placed crack mothers in three different contexts. Active crack users such as Tracy Watson were shown smoking crack or placed in the context of drug supermarkets (26 percent). Crack addicts were more frequently placed in the context of treatment (39 percent) than in the context of criminal court (17 percent), but keep in mind that the criminal court required most defendants to enroll in a drug treatment program.

Network news hardened the concept of addiction. ABC reported that crack produced a "physical addiction," a permanent change in the brain (Jennings, 1988). Dr. Anna Rose Childress and Dr. Charles O'Brian, both of the Philadelphia Veterans Medical Center, noted that the rapid onset of euphoria, the rush, was the mechanism of change. To help the audience visualize the mechanism, the studio had supplied an outline of the human brain. The rush was represented by a moving wave of color swept across the brain. The brain permanently encoded the rush as memory, said Childress. This fact helped Dr. Jerome Jaffee, the director of the Addiction Research Center, explain the sudden relapses of people who had long since completed treatment.

Crack mothers were subjected to criminal prosecutions that the networks followed closely. In May 1989, CBS reported the case of Melanie Green (Rather, 1989). Winnebago County (Illinois) attorney Paul Logli had filed manslaughter charges against Melanie Green, following the death of her 2-day-old newborn. At birth, the infant had tested positive for cocaine, so Logli, operating on the theory that the cocaine was the cause of death, charged Green. According to Logli, there was no difference between an adult giving a child cocaine and a pregnant woman ingesting the drug to the detriment of the unborn child.

In July 1989, ABC reported that the trial of Jennifer Johnson was nearing a verdict (Sawyer, 1989). The anchor who inquired what should be done about crack mothers provided this answer: "You should know that some law enforcement authorities think it's time to prosecute, to consider those mothers as criminals." Jeffrey Deen, Florida State attorney, had filed felony criminal charges against Jennifer Johnson after her newborn tested positive for cocaine. The baby was Johnson's second cocaine-exposed child, an act that led Deen to take control. Lynn Paltrow, Jennifer Johnson's defense lawyer and a staff attorney for the Reproductive Freedom Project, took issue with prosecution's claims. "If the issue is harming the fetus, then you can arrest women for drinking alcohol, smoking cigarettes, working in places where chemicals are put into their bodies that harm fetuses, or even living with a husband who is a heavy smoker."

The last word, however, went to the babies. An ABC correspondent noted that another's right to privacy outweighed the right of a fetus to health but concluded that "a growing number of voices are crying out for change." This was said in voice-over as the camera panned rows of incubated newborns in a neonatal intensive care unit reported to care for crack babies.

Stage 4: Women, Crack, and Community-Based Programs

Betty Collins, a 24-year-old black woman and crack mother, was interviewed in prison for an NBC segment (Chung, 1994). "Nobody," she said, "should have to go through this just to get off drugs. It doesn't take jail." Collins's 3-week-old daughter had been taken from her by the state of South Carolina after cocaine was found in the child's stool. Despite Collins's efforts to get off drugs, she was still charged with child endangerment. An angry Collins complained: "They did not consider my efforts to improve myself. They just threw me in jail. I think that is very unfair. "Collins's attorney, Rauch Wise, told the CBS correspondent that his client had "abused her body in taking cocaine" and that she had "not abused her child." In prosecuting mothers whose babies tested positive for cocaine, Wise noted that the state of South Carolina was "playing a political and racist game." This and other statements by defense attorneys began to suggest that the prosecutions themselves might be part of the problem.

Betty Collins typified the news profile of crack mothers. As Table 1 indicates, crack mothers tended to be black (84 percent), and maternal themes continued to be important despite a precipitous reduction in the number of babies: from 93 in stage 3 to 31 in stage 4. Treatment and drug life provided a context for female addicts in stages 2, 3, and 4. What emerged as new for stage 4 were social service programs designed to manage the maternal crack or cocaine problem in the community or at a lower cost. ABC ran an *American Agenda* report in 1993 about an outreach program in Nashville, Tennessee (Jennings, 1993). In it, the community workers went door-to-door in a housing project to encourage drug-addicted black women to enter treatment programs. Even treatment had a community focus. A two-part NBC *American Close-Up* featured the Christian Community Youth against Drugs (Stone, 1992a, 1992b). This New Orleans program had been helped by a federal grant, but it ran on private donations and the profits from a car wash that employed program clients. Without additional state or federal spending, the program provided free drug treatment and long-term residential care for the poor. The Reverend Thomas Taylor, a charismatic Baptist minister, redefined addiction, taking it out of the realm of medical science and placing it in the realm of common sense and religion. Addiction represented physical problems. Drug use was hard on the body, but medical care, good food, and physical work could restore it. Addiction was also constructed as a spiritual problem. The drug lifestyle tested the spirit, so prayer, human contact, and charismatic leadership were part of the program. Group therapy and recovery classes dealt with residents' drug problems. High school equivalency classes promised them a brighter future. Independent evaluators judged the program a success. Such programs suggested that the black community had effectively solved its problems.

To summarize, this article surveyed television news images of maternal cocaine and crack use from 1983 to 1994. It showed three different images of maternal drug use as they emerged over the four-stage chronology of news. First, middle-class white women used cocaine during pregnancy without obvious consequences to their babies. Maternal themes, however, were relatively unimportant as the news segments addressed the cocaine epidemic among the middle class. The women, like other members of this class, were psychologically addicted and had responded to drug education by entering drug treatment. Second, poor black women used crack during pregnancy with severely damaging consequences to their babies. Active drug users appeared in the context of drug supermarkets; recovering crack addicts appeared in treatment settings. Maternal themes applied to active and recovering crack addicts. Like other members of the underclass, the women were physically addicted, indifferent to the effects of cocaine on themselves, their pregnancies, and others. They appeared as appropriate targets for punishment. Third, recovering crack mothers were also poor women of color. Maternal themes continued to be important, but by completing prison sentences or by entering treatments, mothers hoped to regain custody of their children. They suffered from a different kind of addiction, a spiritual as well as a physical problem. News coverage focused on community-based initiatives at getting women into treatment, although court-mandated treatment remained an issue.

DISCUSSION

Drug scares comprise a complex process that may take several years to unfold, but in the case of crack, events went quickly. The drug was immediately demonized. Addiction was promptly individualized (i.e., blamed on the addict). Within a year, crack use was associated with the urban underclass. Within four years, black women were put on trial for having used crack or cocaine during pregnancy. The war on drugs hastened the arrival of punitive measures but persuasive reactions were seemingly missing. The missing persuasive phase, however, reappears when crack and cocaine are treated as the same drug. Note that network news went to great lengths to differentiate the two drugs: Cocaine produced psychological addiction; crack, physical addiction. Normally, one speaks of addiction[5] or, using an alternative approach, one refers to psychoactive substances that produce a dependence of a psychological or physical type.[6] Using the terms interchangeably turns a manageable "dependence" into an intractable "addiction." Thus the war on drugs focused on cocaine, and news correspondents represented this drug as "addictive," a threatening enough term. If crack replaced cocaine as the most dangerous drug in America, then news teams had to invent a new set of superlatives; hence, physical addiction. Admittedly, the search was on in drug research circles for evidence that crack/cocaine caused the body to adapt permanently to the drug. And addiction research was a standard feature of news coverage. A news segment aired during stage 3 appeared to make the scientific case: With color-coded graphics, crack permanently encoded its euphoric rush on the brain. The segment had implications for how maternal crack/cocaine use was perceived. Black women who used crack during pregnancy presented a far more dangerous problem than did their white counterparts who had only used cocaine.

But to return to the missing persuasive phase in the crack mother scare, we can see that medical warnings and other persuasive strategies targeted middle-class white cocaine mothers. We can also see that punitive measures targeted poor women of color. Thus, the shift from persuasive to punitive approaches reflects suspect distinctions between crack and cocaine and differential reactions to white and black user populations. Crack mother images incorporated the hyperbole associated with crack, addiction, race, and its ties to the underclass, inner-city poverty, and welfare. But the study found no evidence for the presence of a Jezebel stereotype (Reeves & Campbell, 1994). Prime-time news did not cover the sex-for-crack exchanges, nor did it allude to women's alleged hypersexuality. News images of crack mothers reviewed for this study had more to do with errant motherhood than with sexuality. Pregnant women such as Tracy Watson smoked even though they knew that crack/cocaine would adversely affect their unborn babies. They violated basic rules of motherhood, but high-profile cases selected for criminal prosecution made extreme cases appear to be the norm. Melanie Green's drug use allegedly led to the death of her baby. Jennifer Johnson gave birth to not one but two cocaine babies. The network news broadcast images based on these cases into the homes of news viewers.

In retrospect, it is possible to compare media images of crack mothers to reality. Although the rate of drug use during pregnancy for black women was higher than it was for white women, the number of white women who used illicit drugs while pregnant greatly exceeded the number of minority women who used illicit drugs (National Institute of Drug Abuse, 1996). By sheer numbers, the newscasts should have focused on drug use by pregnant white women. Because the war on drugs targeted crack, news reports amplified racial disparities already entrenched in the hospital-based system for reporting maternal drug use. The key study on this point found that at their first prenatal examination, pregnant women of both races had comparable rates of drug use, but when admitted to the hospital for delivery, black women as opposed to white women were more likely to be tested for illicit drugs (Chasnoff, Landress, & Barrett, 1990). Because poor women go to public hospitals and because public hospitals are mandated to report drug use, poor women of color tend to be tested more frequently for drugs. When drug testing is discretionary, protocols have to be interpreted. Because hospital workers determine what constitutes incomplete prenatal care, biases about who uses drugs affect who gets tested. Public awareness of the drug problem—including awareness of maternal drug use—also affects the incidence of testing and the population tested.

We have yet to address crack mothers as freshly minted, recovering addicts. In the context of drug cases, this means asking how problems that once triggered panic are subsequently reframed as inoffensive, harmless, or resolved. In the last stage of coverage, the networks overhauled the image of the crack mother. Recovering addicts replaced women in the active phase of addiction. Recovery centers replaced street corners and hospital wards. Character traits changed as well. Hopefully, well-groomed women replaced sullen, disheveled ones. Crack mothers in recovery wanted to regain custody of their children. In that, they became a poor version of their middle-class counterparts. Both groups entered treatment: Poor black women went into publicly financed treatment programs (self-financed, community-based treatment featured in the news was atypical); affluent women entered private treatment centers financed through medical insurance. Both groups expressed regret for past conduct, seeing prior drug use as harmful. They warned others to avoid drugs. Warning, persuasive measures signaled the end of the problem, not because the problem had gone away but because menacing crack mothers had been remolded to fit middle-class stereotypes about recovering addicts.

CONCLUSIONS

As a window on the world, maternal drug use reveals how pregnancy and childbirth—biological potentials—can be used against women. Paternalism justified lenient treatment in cases of prenatal misconduct by middle-class women who had been misled about the recreational use of cocaine. For the poor and minority women, the biological fact of pregnancy combined with drug addiction served as a pretext to override fundamental reproductive rights. By denying public finding for abortion, the federal government eliminates the right to choose for poor women (Roberts, 1991). An affirmative step toward public financing in this area would guarantee the right to privacy and equalize access to women's health services, even though long-standing high infant mortality rates demonstrate that basic health care as well as reproductive services are sorely lacking in poor communities. On the other hand, federal and state governments have a history of terminating the paternal rights of the poor, citing a number of conditions, including maternal drug use, as grounds for removing children. For Kasinsky (1994), parallels between modern crusaders who hoped to save crack babies and nineteenth-century Progressives who tried to save immigrant children boil down to this: Middle-class standards of parenthood are used to dismiss the rights of poor and working-class parents. For women labeled crack mothers, pregnancy and childbirth triggered both kinds of infringement: the denial of reproductive and health services on one hand and the termination of parental rights on the other.

ACKNOWLEDGMENT

I thank Susan Caringella-MacDonald for her comments on earlier drafts of this article.

NOTES

1. This chapter is adapted from the author's article in *Violence Against Women, 4*(1), pp. 45–61 (February 1998). (c) 1998 Sage Publications, Inc.
2. Multiple counts, a clear set of protocols, the inclusion of an "unknown race or ethnic" category, and conferences to resolve problems overcame any limitations arising from using only one assistant to conduct the count.
3. Unequal time intervals underpin the four-stage model of news coverage. This study is descriptive and quite properly adopts a temporal framework that captures the shifts in the data. Equal time intervals are a requirement of hypothesis testing and do not necessarily apply to case studies.
4. The finding that 11 percent of the women could not be identified racially raises some questions about this finding. However, if one assumes that 11 percent of the women who could not be identified racially were white, the data would still show a pattern of racial disparity.
5. Addiction is marked by tolerance and withdrawal. Tolerance occurs when increased doses of a drug (e.g., heroin or alcohol) are required to achieve the original euphoric effects. Withdrawal refers to physical symptoms that appear following cessation of a drug. Withdrawal from alcohol is life-threatening; depression and irritation that follow the cessation of cocaine are not.
6. Cocaine produces rapid euphoria, followed by depression. Typically, it is said to produce a "psychological" pattern of dependence, meaning that it fosters a feeling of satisfaction that leads to continuous drug use. In contrast, physical dependence is associated with tolerance and withdrawal.

REFERENCES

BRINKWATER, T. (ANCHOR). (1984, August 10). The cocaine epidemic: Part II. *NBC Evening News.* On *Media services videotape, 1983–1994* [Compilation tape]. Nashville, TN: Vanderbilt University (1994).

BROKAW, T. (ANCHOR). (1986, May 23). Cocaine/crack. *NBC Evening News.* On *Media services videotape, 1983–1994* [Compilation tape]. Nashville, TN: Vanderbilt University (1994).

BROKAW, T. (ANCHOR). (1987, February 27). Drugs/crack. *NBC Evening News.* On *Media services videotape, 1983–1994* [Compilation tape]. Nashville, TN: Vanderbilt University (1994).

BROKAW, T. (ANCHOR). (1983, October 24). Cocaine kids: Part I. *NBC Evening News.* On *Media services videotape, 1983–1994* [Compilation tape]. Nashville, TN: Vanderbilt University (1994).

CHASNOFF, I., LANDRESS, H. J., & BARRETT, M. E. (1990). The prevalence of illicit drug or alcohol use during pregnancy and discrepancies in mandatory reporting in Pinellas County, Florida. *New England Journal of Medicine, 322,* 1202-1206.

CHUNG, C. (ANCHOR). (1986, August 4). Cocaine/crack. *NBC Evening News.* On *Media services videotape, 1983–1994* [Compilation tape]. Nashville, TN: Vanderbilt University (1994).

CHUNG, C. (ANCHOR). (1994, March 10). Eye on America (Medicine: Crack babies). *CBS Evening News.* On *Media services videotape, 1983–1994* [Compilation videotape]. Nashville, TN: Vanderbilt University (1994).

HALL, S., CRITCHER, C., JEFFERSON, T., CLARKE, J., & ROBERTS, J. (1978). *Policing the crisis: Mugging, the state, and law.* London: Macmillan.

HUMPHRIES, D. (1993). Crack mothers, drug wars, and the politics of resentment. In K. D. Tunnel (Ed.), *Political crime in contemporary America: A critical approach* (pp. 39–41). New York: Garland Publishing.

HUMPHRIES, D., DAWSON, J., CRONIN, V., WISNIEWSKI, C., & EICHFELD, J. (1991). Mothers and children, drugs and crack: Reactions to maternal drug dependency. *Women and Criminal Justice, 3,* 81–99.

JENNINGS, P. (ANCHOR). (1986a, July 15). Cocaine, *ABC Evening News.* On *Media services videotape, 1983–1994* [Contemporary tape]. Nashville, TN: Vanderbilt University (1994).

JENNINGS, P. (ANCHOR). (1986b, September 17). Cocaine. *ABC Evening News.* On *Media services videotape, 1983–1994* [Compilation tape]. Nashville, TN: Vanderbilt University (1994).

JENNINGS, P. (ANCHOR). (1988, July 13). Drugs/Starr death/"crack" cocaine rush. *ABC Evening News.* On *Media services videotape, 1983–1994* [Compilation tape]. Nashville, TN: Vanderbilt University (1994).

JENNINGS, P. (ANCHOR). (1993, June 10). American agenda (Drugs: Sisters program). *ABC Evening News.* On *Media services videotape, 1983–1994* [Compilation tape]. Nashville, TN: Vanderbilt University (1994).

KASINSKY, R. G. (1994). Child neglect and "unfit" mothers: Child savers in the Progressive era and today. *Women and Criminal Justice, 6,* 97–129.

LEVINE, H. G. (1978). The discovery of addiction: Changing conceptions of habitual drunkenness in America. *Journal of Studies on Alcohol, 39,* 143–174.

MAHER, L. (1991). Punishment and welfare: Crack cocaine and the regulation of mothering. *Women and Criminal Justice, 3,* 35–70.

MAHER, L., & CURTIS, R. (1992). Women on the edge of crime: Crack cocaine and the changing contexts of street-level sex work in New York City. *Crime, Law, and Social Change, 18,* 221–258.

MUSTO, D. F. (1987). *The American disease: Origins of narcotic control.* New York: Oxford University Press.

NATIONAL INSTITUTE OF DRUG ABUSE. (1996). *National pregnancy and health survey: Drug use among women delivering live births, 1992* (NIH Publ. 96-3819). Rockville, MD: National Institute of Health, U.S. Department of Health and Human Services.

PALMER, J. (ANCHOR). (1985, December 1). Cocaine/crack. *NBC Evening News.* On *Media services videotape, 1983-1994* [Compilation tape]. Nashville, TN: Vanderbilt University (1994).

PHILLIPS, S. (ANCHOR). (1992a, December 29). American close-up: Crack/cocaine: Part I. *NBC Evening News.* On *Media services videotape, 1983–1994* [Compilation tape]. Nashville, TN: Vanderbilt University (1994).

PHILLIPS, S. (ANCHOR). (1992b, December 30). American close-up: Crack/cocaine: Part II. *NBC Evening News.* On *Media services videotape, 1983–1994* [Compilation tape]. Nashville, TN: Vanderbilt University (1994).

RATHER, D. (ANCHOR). (1984, May 31). Cocaine: Part II. *CBS Evening News.* On *Media services videotape, 1983-1994* [Compilation tape]. Nashville, TN: Vanderbilt University (1994).

RATHER, D. (ANCHOR). (1989, May 26). Illinois/Greene cocaine case. *CBS Evening News.* On *Media services videotape, 1983–1994* [Compilation tape]. Nashville, TN: Vanderbilt University (1994).

REEVES, J. L., & CAMPBELL, R. (1994). *Cracked coverage: Television news, the anti-cocaine crusade, and the Reagan legacy.* Durham, NC: Duke University Press.

REINARMAN, C., & LEVINE, H. G. (1995). The crack attack: America's latest drug scare, 1986-1993. In J. Best (Ed.), *Images and issues* (pp. 147–190). New York: Aldine.

ROBERTS, D. E. (1991). Punishing drug addicts who have babies: Women of color, equality, and the right to privacy. *Harvard Law Review, 104,* 1419–1482.

SAWYER, D. (ANCHOR). (1989, July 12). American agenda (Medicine, crime: Pregnant women and drugs). *ABC Evening News.* On *Media services videotape, 1983–1994* [Compilation tape]. Nashville, TN: Vanderbilt University (1994).

9

Women, AIDS, and the Criminal Justice System

Joan Luxenburg and Thomas E. Guild

❖

Women as offenders and women as victims can be expected to play a significant role in the shaping of criminal justice policy to deter the spread of AIDS. For the woman as offender, we look at prostitutes and their association with the AIDS epidemic. For the woman as victim, we look at the offense of sexual assault and the controversy surrounding mandatory HIV testing (and disclosure).

Cumulatively speaking, the leading cause of HIV infection among women in the United States is intravenous drug use, followed by sexual contact with an infective intravenous (IV) drug user. This fact has tremendous policy implications for drug treatment programs as alternatives to incarceration, especially in cities where waiting lists for such treatment are prohibitive.

The association between non-IV drug use and AIDS cannot be ignored. Street prostitutes who are crack-addicted are likely candidates to exchange unprotected sex for crack. However, this group represents a very small percentage of prostitutes. In the misguided belief that female prostitutes transmit the virus to their male clients, several states have enacted AIDS-specific statutes that target prostitutes. With no scientific evidence indicating that prostitutes are a vector for transmission of the virus, they are needlessly incarcerated.

The criminal justice system has targeted sexual assault defendants for mandatory HIV antibody testing and disclosure to victims. With further expansion of these laws, women as the victims of rape will be granted medical information regarding the rapists. This seemingly necessary intrusion into the rights of defendants will no doubt be challenged on constitutional grounds.

The epidemic of acquired immune deficiency syndrome (AIDS) has had an impact on every facet of the criminal justice system (Blumberg, 1990b). We address two legal issues surrounding AIDS that are very specific to women. One topic (prostitution) involves women as criminal offenders. The other topic (sexual assault) involves women as the victims of crime. Although men are also arrested for prostitution, the offense is clearly a female-dominated activity. In fact, prostitution is the only crime for which the arrest rate for females is higher than the arrest rate for males (Yablonsky, 1990, p. 84). Similarly, we recognize that men are the victims of rape. However, only an estimated 10 percent of rapes occur to men (*Face-to-Face*, 1990). This percentage may be larger, since overall, three to ten rapes go unreported for every rape that is reported (President's Commission on the Human Immunodeficiency Virus, 1988).

Our focus on prostitution and AIDS deals with whether prostitutes are at greater risk than other sexually active women for contracting the AIDS virus (also known as human immunodeficiency virus, or HIV), and whether prostitutes are vectors for transmitting the virus to their customers. We examine legislation that targets prostitutes for mandatory HIV antibody testing or that targets HIV antibody-positive prostitutes for enhanced criminal penalties. For the issue of sexual assault, we look at the debate over requiring HIV antibody testing of accused and/or convicted rapists and disclosure of such test results to the alleged and/or proven victims.

WOMEN AND AIDS

Women's concerns in the AIDS epidemic had gone virtually ignored until 1990. During the 1980s (the first decade of the AIDS epidemic), the public minimized the role of women and their relationship to this public health crisis. Women were merely viewed as the principal caregivers for persons with AIDS (PWAs), for example, as nurses in hospitals or as mothers welcoming their homosexual sons home to spend their remaining days with family. This picture changed when in 1990, AIDS was recognized as the leading cause of death among black women in New York and New Jersey, and it was predicted to become the fifth-leading cause of death among U.S. women of childbearing age by 1991 ("AIDS deaths soaring," 1990; "More women getting AIDS," 1990). During the summer of 1990, the World Health Organization (WHO) estimated that 3 million women and children would die of AIDS during the 1990s, a figure representing more than six times their numbers of AIDS deaths in the 1980s ("More women, children," 1990). The rising death rate for women with AIDS is now apparent. Whereas only eighteen women in the United States (between the ages of 18 and 44) died of AIDS during the year 1980, for the year 1988 the number was 1430 ("AIDS deaths soaring," 1990). In the United States prior to 1983, only ninety women (13 years old and older) had been diagnosed with AIDS (Miller, Turner, & Moses 1990, pp. 50–51). However, by November 1990, the cumulative figure for all U.S. women (regardless of age) was 16,394 (Oklahoma State Department of Health, 1991).

In recognition of the increase in the number of women with HIV infection, World AIDS Day (December 1, 1990) proclaimed its focus to be on "Women and AIDS." Earlier that year, the sixth International AIDS Conference (held in San Francisco in June) became a forum for the Women's Caucus of the AIDS Coalition to Unleash Power (ACT-UP) to voice their grievances about women's issues related to HIV infection. By November 1990, the American Civil Liberties Union (ACLU) added to its staff a lawyer assigned to work exclusively with issues involving HIV infection among women and children (Herland Sister Resources, 1990). Many of the ACLU's concerns deal with civil liberties debates not easily reconcilable.

PROSTITUTION AS A TRANSMISSION CATEGORY

The AIDS literature on prostitution has concentrated almost exclusively on female heterosexual prostitutes rather than on male (homosexual) prostitutes. Because the clientele of male prostitutes are principally males, the AIDS literature treats male prostitutes for discussion under the heading of homosexuals (Centers for Disease Control, 1987b; Turner, Miller, & Moses, 1989, p. 14). Stereotypically, male and female prostitutes have been cast as intravenous drug users (IVDUs) or the sexual partners of IVDUs when, in fact, only a small percentage may fall into the category of IVDUs. In actuality, street prostitution accounts for an estimated 20 percent of all prostitution, and an estimated 5 to 10 percent of prostitutes are addicted (Cohen, Alexander, & Wofsy, 1990, p. 92; Leigh, 1987, p. 180). It is likely that those who are addicted (to IV drugs or to "crack") disregard safer sex practices in order to support their habit. For HIV-infected women in general, 75 percent acquired the virus through IV drug use or through sexual relations with IVDUs ("AIDS deaths soaring,"1990). The majority of U.S. women with AIDS live in New York, New Jersey, Florida, and California (Shaw, 1988).

Self-reported findings suggest that prostitutes may be more likely to use a condom with their customers rather than with their regular sex partners (Miller et al., 1990; Rowe & Ryan, 1987, pp. 2–20; Cohen et al., 1990). However, when Project AWARE (Association of Women's AIDS Research and Education) conducted its San Francisco General Hospital comparison of prostitutes and other sexually active women, it found a slightly lower seropositive rate for prostitutes (Leigh, 1987). The association between HIV-antibody-positive status and IV drug use (rather than with prostitution) was clearly found in the Centers for Disease Control (CDC)–coordinated seroprevalence studies of prostitutes in ten U.S. cities, including New York, San Francisco, Jersey City, Miami, and Los Angeles (Centers for Disease Control, 1987a).

Although our discussion focuses on street prostitution, it is worthwhile to note seroprevalence findings from other types of prostitution. In a study of New York City call girls, one in eight was HIV-antibody-positive and that person was an IVDU (*Geraldo*, 1990). When the state of Nevada conducted testing of all prostitutes employed in legal brothels, not a single case of HIV-antibody-positive results occurred in over 4500 tests of approximately 500 prostitutes (Hollibaugh, Karp, & Taylor, 1987, p. 135). Licensed houses of prostitution in Nevada (in addition to screening prospective employees for IV drug use) are required by law (since March 1986) to conduct preemployment HIV-antibody screening and monthly testing after employment; and employment is denied to HIV-antibody-positive applicants (Centers for Disease Control, 1987a; "Infection not reported," 1987).

The CDC has not reported any documented cases of HIV transmission from a female prostitute to a male customer through sexual contact (Cohen et al., 1990). Probably the most common means of an infected prostitute transmitting the virus to another person is through sharing infected IV drug paraphernalia (AIDS and Civil

Liberties Project, 1990). In the United States, female-to-male transmission of the AIDS virus through sexual contact is less efficient than is male-to-female transmission (Eckholm, 1990a). For the period 1981 to October 1985, the CDC concluded that only one-tenth of 1 percent of all U.S. cases of AIDS were the result of female-to-male sexual transmission (Schultz, Milberg, Kristal, & Stonebruner, 1986, p. 1703). As of January 1988, only six of the 11,000 cases of AIDS in New York City males traced back to female-to-male sexual contact, although it is impossible to ascertain from the published data whether prostitutes were involved (AIDS and Civil Liberties Project, 1990). Randy Shilts (1987, pp. 512–513) reported on a case of a San Francisco IV drug-using prostitute who continued working while carrying the AIDS virus for ten or eleven years, until her death in 1987, yet during that same period, only two male heterosexual contact cases of AIDS had occurred in San Francisco.

In a CDC study of spouses of transfusion-acquired PWAs, 16 percent of wives were infected, whereas only 5 percent of husbands were infected; and although 10 percent of those studied had more than 200 sexual contacts with an infected partner, the uninfected spouse remained seronegative (Stengel, 1987). It must be remembered that the chances of becoming infected are greater in repeated sexual contact (for example, with a spouse) as opposed to a one-time encounter (e.g., with a street prostitute). The ACLU estimates that 200,000 female prostitutes participate in some 300 million sexual transactions per year in the United States, yet the incidence of men contracting the AIDS virus from prostitutes in the United States is virtually nil (AIDS and Civil Liberties Project, 1990, p. 102). Early reports among U.S. servicemen are probably most responsible for having implicated pros-titutes in the spread of the virus (Redfield, et al., 1985). Critics of these reports were quick to reply that military men would be reluctant to report IV drug use or homosexual behav-ior (Potterat, Phillips, & Muth, 1987).

AIDS LAW AND PROSTITUTES

The ACLU's position on coercive measures against prostitutes is that such measures are futile and serve to drive the disease further underground (AIDS and Civil Liberties Project, 1990). History reveals that government crackdowns on prostitutes to stop the spread of other sexually transmitted diseases (STDs) have been ineffective (Brandt, 1985;1988, p. 370). Nevertheless, prostitutes have been the target in some states for mandatory HIV-anti-body testing and for enhanced criminal penalties for HIV-antibody-positive prostitutes who continue to practice their trade while knowing their seropositive status.

By 1990, approximately twenty-two states had criminalized the act of knowingly exposing another person to the AIDS virus ("More states," 1990). From the authors' own observations in Oklahoma, the utility of an AIDS-specific law seems questionable. The Oklahoma law [*Okla. Stat. Ann.* Tit., 21, § 1192.1 (West 1989)], which took effect July 1, 1988, states:

A. It shall be unlawful for any person to engage in any activity with the intent to infect or cause to be infected any other person with the human immunodeficiency virus.

B. Any person convicted of violating the provisions of this section shall be guilty of a felony, punishable by imprisonment in the custody of the Department of Corrections for not more than five (5) years.

In January 1990, the first person to be charged under this new law was a 34-year-old Tulsa prostitute, Lynnette Osborne (a.k.a. Lynette Love). Osborne had apparently been reported to police by other prostitutes who work in the same general location (Tulsa's red-light district). Four undercover Tulsa police officers had interactions with Osborne, resulting in four counts of soliciting between October 1989 and January 1990. Upon Osborne's arrest (under the new law), a search warrant was issued allowing authorities to test her blood for the HIV antibodies (Brus, 1990; "Charge filed," 1990). Unfortunately, the Osborne case does not lend itself to us for analysis of the first trial of its kind in Oklahoma, because the defendant pled guilty in February 1990 to all four felony counts in exchange for four three-year prison terms, to run concurrently ("Prostitute goes to jail,"1990).

Several states have enacted AIDS legislation that specifically targets prostitutes. In Florida, as of October 1986, convicted prostitutes are mandatorily tested for HIV antibodies (and other STDs). In that state, engaging in prostitution after having been informed of one's seropositivity results in a misdemeanor, separate from the charge of prostitution [Bowleg & Bridgham, 1989; Centers for Disease Control, 1987a; Fla. Stat. Ann., 14A, § 381.609, 3(i)(1)(a) (West 1990)]. Georgia law provides that a person who is aware of his or her seropositivity and subsequently offers to engage in sexual intercourse or sodomy for money, without disclosing (prior to the offer) the presence of the HIV infection, is guilty of a felony punishable upon conviction by not more than ten years. Georgia law also permits HIV-antibody testing by court order for anyone convicted of or pleading no contest to any HIV-transmitting crime, including prostitution (Bowleg & Bridgham, 1989). Idaho law mandates HIV-antibody testing for defendants being held in any county or city jail who are charged with certain offenses, including prostitution (Bowleg & Bridgham, 1989).

Illinois law requires HIV-antibody testing for those convicted of a sex-related offense, including prostitution, solicitation, patronizing a prostitute, and operating a house of prostitution (Thomas, 1988). One may question the relevance of testing the operator of a house if he or she is not exchanging his or her own bodily fluids with the customers. Similarly, the state of Washington's law requires anyone convicted of prostitution or "offenses relating to prostitution under chapter 9A.88 RCW" to submit to HIV-antibody testing. Included (in 9A.88 RCW) are the offenses of "promoting prostitution" and "permitting prostitution" [Wash. Rev. Code, § 70.24.340, 70.24.340(1)(b) (Supp. 1988)]. Under such a law, even persons who engage in no actual sexual act but who advance prostitution are required to take the HIV-antibody test. The Washington law has yet to be subjected to a "reasonableness test," where probable cause (e.g., that the defendant had actually engaged in an HIV-transmitting act with his or her own bodily fluid) would need to be established (Weissman & Childers, 1988–1989).

Michigan's law provides that those convicted of crimes capable of transmitting the AIDS virus (including prostitution) will be examined for HIV antibodies upon court order unless the court determines such testing to be inappropriate (Bowleg & Bridgham, 1989). Nevada law requires that anyone arrested for prostitution to be tested for HIV antibodies. If the arrest results in a conviction, the defendant pays $100 for the cost of the testing. After receiving notification of a positive test, if the person is subsequently arrested and found guilty of another charge of prostitution, the new conviction is for a felony punishable by one to twenty years in prison and/or a $10,000 fine [Nev. Rev. Stat. Ann., § 201.356, 201.358 (Michie 1987)]. Rhode Island and West Virginia each have laws requiring any individual convicted of prostitution to be tested for HIV antibodies (Bowleg & Bridgham, 1989).

California's law requires convicted prostitutes (and certain other sex offenders) to be tested for the HIV antibodies. If a prostitute receives positive test results and later receives a subsequent conviction for prostitution, the subsequent conviction is a felony [(Calif. Penal Code, § 647 f (West Supp. 1989)]. Despite California's law, some counties in that state have opted not to conduct such testing. For instance, the Alameda County Health Department has declined to test convicted prostitutes, partly because that county's budget does not permit it. Recently, Alameda County's policy came into the public limelight surrounding the highly publicized case of Oakland prostitute Linda Kean. Kean had posed for a picture in a *Newsweek* article in which she claimed to be an HIV-antibody-positive heroin-using prostitute who continues to service customers (Cowley, Hager, & Marshall, 1990). A zealous Oakland vice-squad sergeant, Mike Martin, read the *Newsweek* article and promptly arrested Kean for attempted murder after he witnessed her getting into a car with a suspected customer. Dr. Robert Benjamin, Director of the Communicable Disease Division of the Alameda County Health Department, referred to Kean's arrest as "scape-goating" and a "witch hunt." According to Benjamin, it is the customer's personal responsibility to use a condom. Benjamin further pointed out that testing prostitutes for HIV antibodies would send a "false message," suggesting to the public that those prosti-tutes who are still on the street have a clean bill of health.

Critics of the AIDS-specific laws targeting prostitutes suggest that enhancing penalties for subsequent convictions of HIV-antibody-positive prostitutes is an unpro-ductive, punitive strategy aimed at a politically powerless group that shows no epi-demiological evidence that they are contributing significantly to the sexual transmission of the AIDS virus. The laws clearly stem from a false perception that prostitutes pose a major risk to their customers.

ALTERNATIVES TO COERCION

The government's paternalistic concern can be helpful in assisting grass-roots efforts to educate disenfranchised segments of the population to reduce risk behaviors. Among IVDUs, the Community Health Outreach Worker (CHOW) has been most successful in educating this population; CHOWs are usually recovering addicts indigenous to the community and ethnically matched to the population they try to reach. CHOWs provide referrals for drug treatment programs, condoms, instructions for cleaning drug parapher-nalia, and so on. Several organizations, such as Cal PEP (California Prostitutes Education Project), have utilized prostitutes and ex-prostitutes in a similar manner (*Geraldo*, 1990). Clearly, funding and expansion of such programs appear to be worthy areas in which the government can invest its resources wisely. Education with dignity appears to have worked in Pumwani, a crowded slum in Kenya, where some 400 prostitutes can be found working on any given day (Eckholm, 1990b). More than 80 percent of Pumwani prostitutes have tested positive for the HIV antibodies. Knowing that the HIV reinfection or other STDs can worsen their health, these women have cooperated with health officials and are using condoms, reportedly 80 percent of the time (Eckholm, 1990b). Since African prostitutes are transmitters of the AIDS virus, thousands of new HIV infections are being avoided by these efforts. Only about 30 percent of the male truckers at a nearby weighing station (outside Nairobi) report that they "sometimes" use the free condoms handed to them; and one in four of those drivers (who consent to testing) show HIV antibodies (Eckholm, 1990b). Stubborn male customers are not confined to Pumwani. In the United States, there is a need to educate the clients of prostitutes as well as to monitor these men to learn the incidence and prevalence of HIV infection among them (Miller et al., 1990). While noncoercive government intervention shows promise for persuading prostitutes to reduce high-risk behaviors, the strategy may work only because we are dealing with consensual (though commercialized) sexual relations. For nonconsensual sexual relations, coercive measures may be appropriate.

AIDS LAW AND SEXUAL ASSAULT

Several states have enacted legislation that requires either accused or convicted sexual offenders to submit to HIV-antibody testing; and in some cases, the victim or alleged victim is entitled to the defendant's test results. Without AIDS-specific laws to address this topic, courts found themselves inconsistently deciding whether or not to permit testing of defendants accused of sexual assaults. In 1987, a Texas Court of Appeals ruled that a district court did not have the statutory (or constitutional) power to order an HIV-antibody test for a defendant charged with aggravated sexual assault, nor did the district court have the authority to release the results to alleged victims on a "need to know basis" (*Shelvin v. Lykos*, 1987). Subsequent to this appellate decision, Texas passed legislation (during a second, special session in 1987) granting statutory power to trial courts to order such tests and to disclose the results to alleged victims [Tex. Crim. Proc. Code Ann., Art. 21.31 (Vernon 1988)]; Thomas, 1988). According to Texas law, a person indicted for sexual assault and aggravated sexual assault can be directed by a court to be examined and/or tested for STD, AIDS, or HIV antibodies. The court can direct such examination and/or testing on its own motion or at the request of the alleged victim. The results may not be used in any criminal proceeding regarding the alleged assault. The court may not release the results to any parties other than the accused and the alleged victim.

In the state of New York, before similar legislation was introduced and defeated, that state's courts appeared to favor the victim's need to know over the defendant's right to privacy. In 1988, a New York Supreme Court ruled that it is not violative of a defendant's right to privacy for the state to divulge a rape defendant's HIV-antibody test results to the victim when such testing is done during routine processing of the person into the prison population (*People of New York v. Toure*, 1987). Further, the court, in its "balancing test," decided that the fears and health concerns of the victim outweighed the minimal intrusion to the defendant. Similarly, a county court decided in New York in 1988 that a defendant who had pled guilty to attempted rape could be ordered to submit to HIV-antibody testing and that the victim had a right to know the results (*People of New York v. Thomas*, 1988). In that case, the court concluded that the testing was not unreasonable search and seizure under the Fourth Amendment and that the intrusion to the defendant was minimal.

Two New York City cases gained national attention in 1990 on the issue of the victim's need to know the accused sexual offender's HIV-antibody status. In one case, a 17-year-old Columbia University coed was raped at knife point in her dormitory room by a former Columbia University security guard, 28-year old Reginald Darby (Glaberson, 1990; Salholz, Springen, DeLaPena, & Witherspoon, 1990). In this case, a Manhattan assistant district attorney plea-bargained a first-degree rape case for a reduced sentence, contingent upon the defendant's submitting to an HIV-antibody test and making the results available to the district attorney's office and to "other appropriate parties." The reduced sentence was for no more than five to fifteen years rather than the maximum sentence of eight and one-third to twenty-five years. One legal expert on women's rights criticized such agreements as creating a "windfall" for defendants and their attorneys (Glaberson, 1990). Rape defendants and their attorneys will have additional leverage for striking plea agreements and can even imply an AIDS risk where there is none. Clearly, AIDS-specific legislation would be preferable to this type of plea bargain. However, bills requiring HIV-antibody testing of rape defendants (and disclosure to victims) were defeated in New York's legislature in 1990 (Glaberson, 1990); and a principal opponent to the proposed laws was the Lambda Legal Defense Fund, a gay rights organization (*Face-to-Face*, 1990). Lambda's position was that no one should be "forced" to take an HIV-antibody test. However, more recently Lambda is reportedly willing to support such testing when the rape victim is pregnant (*Face-to-Face*, 1990). The other New York City case to gain attention in 1990 involved a victim of a March 31, 1988 burglary and rape whose assailant was apprehended at the scene by police after he fell asleep in the victim's bed. The defendant (32-year old Barry Chapman), an IVDU and career offender on parole for rape and burglary, was eventually convicted. The victim, who had witnessed a hypodermic needle fall out of Chapman's jacket when police searched it, wanted him tested. Chapman refused two requests, by the Manhattan District Attorney's office, to be tested. Even after Chapman died of AIDS in Sing Sing Prison in 1990, the victim remained unaware of the cause of death until CBS News obtained the autopsy report and informed the victim. More than two years after her attack, the victim continued to test negative for HIV antibodies.

In 1988, when Connecticut failed to pass a bill that would have forced rape defendants to be tested, those opposing the measure pointed out the unclear message that would result from a negative test (Hevesi, 1988). Because of the long "window period," the time between becoming infected and actually showing antibodies to the virus, a negative test does not rule out the presence of the virus in the rapist. For this reason, the victim is probably the most logical one to be tested (and retested every six months). With regard to repeated testing of the rapist, legislation can be worded to include this. For instance, Kansas law provides that if the test results are negative for persons convicted of offenses capable of transmitting the AIDS virus, the court will order the person to submit to another HIV-antibody test six months after the first test (Bowleg & Bridgham, 1989). This second test may actually be of dubious usefulness to the victim, because a positive test for the offender at this juncture may be the result of sexual activity after incarceration.

As of late 1990, very few states provided for HIV-antibody testing of accused sexual assaulters (prior to conviction). Colorado law provides that those who, after a preliminary hearing, are bound over for trial for sexual offenses (involving penetration) will be ordered by court to be tested for HIV antibodies. The court reports the test results to victims upon the victim's request. If the accused voluntarily submits to an HIV-antibody test, such cooperation is admissible as mitigation of sentence if the offense results in conviction [Colo. Rev. Stat. 8B, § 18-3-415 (1990)]. Florida law provides that any defendant in a prosecution for any type of sexual battery, where a blood sample is taken from the defendant, will have an HIV-antibody test. The results of the test cannot be disclosed to anyone other than the victim and the defendant [Fla. Stat. Ann, 14A, § 381.609 3(i)(6)

(West 1990)]; "Rape suspect," 1990). Idaho law requires the public health authorities to administer an HIV-antibody test to all persons confined in any county or city jail who are charged with "sex offenses" (Bowleg & Bridgham, 1989).

The length of time between testing the accused and/or convicted offender and notifying the victim (where allowed) does not appear to be addressed adequately by most states' laws. A case profiled on national television (*Face-to-Face*, 1990) illustrated the problem of timing. The case involved a victim of a rape and attempted murder in a suburban Seattle Park who was three months pregnant at the time of the knife-point attack. The conviction took place two days before the victim gave birth to a baby girl (six months after the attack). However, it took another six months until the victim was notified of the negative test results. The victim wanted to know the defendant's HIV-antibody status prior to his conviction, to decide whether to terminate the pregnancy. However, Washington is not one of the states where an accused rapist must be tested prior to conviction.

The President's Commission on the Human Immunodeficiency Virus Epidemic, in its June 1988 report, made several recommendations concerning HIV-antibody testing (and disclosure) in cases of sexual assault. Among its recommendations, the commission favored mandatory testing "at the earliest possible juncture in the criminal justice process" (Blumberg, 1990b, p. 76) and that there be disclosure to those victims (or their guardians) who wish to know. It is likely that more states will include such provisions in their laws.

As of January 1991, the CDC had no documented case of a rape victim becoming infected with the AIDS virus as a consequence of a sexual assault (Blumberg, 1990a; *Sally Jessy Raphael*, 1991). According to Mark Blumberg, who has written extensively on AIDS and the criminal justice system, the risk of HIV infection to female survivors of rape is remote. Most rape victims have been subjected to vaginal rather than anal intrusion—and (citing a 1988 *JAMA* article) Blumberg asserts that the chances are 1 in 500 for a female to contract the AIDS virus from a single male-to-female episode of vaginal intercourse (Blumberg, 1990a, p.81). Nevertheless, rape has taken on an added threat to life in the AIDS epidemic and, consequently, places its survivors in a tormented frame of mind.

SUMMARY AND CONCLUSIONS

Since no scientific evidence implicates U.S. female prostitutes significantly in the transmission of the AIDS virus through sexual contact with their male customers, it may be futile, politically and legally, to use punitive legislative measures to "control" such activity. Coercive and punitive measures are unlikely to alter the behavior of women engaged in consensual sexual relations with their customers, especially where such activity constitutes their livelihood. Where they exist, it is unlikely that punitive strategies will stop the spread of the AIDS virus, since there has yet to be a documented case of a female U.S. prostitute sexually transmitting the virus to a male customer.

Certainly, noncoercive measures such as education would contribute at least as much to public health as coercive measures against such prostitutes. Since data indicate that transmission via IV drug use is a greater risk than sexual transmission as far as female prostitutes are concerned, education in this area as well as distribution of clean needles might do more to assure public health than all the coercive and punitive measures presently on the books. Of course, proponents of the present trend of punitive legislation might point out that even if the risk of sexual transmission is small, all possible measures must be taken to check the AIDS virus. They might also argue that just because no cases have yet been documented, this does not mean sexual transmission has not occurred. Since many female prostitutes live a somewhat nomadic urban lifestyle, statistics and documentation may be extremely difficult to gather.

As far as state legislation requiring either accused or convicted sexual offenders (mostly male) to submit to HIV-antibody testing, several problems are raised. First, if we are testing accused offenders on an involuntary basis, we are eviscerating the presumption of innocence for the criminally accused. To conduct such testing, the government ought to have a compelling governmental interest before infringing on a criminal defendant's fundamental constitutional right to be presumed innocent. The right of a victim to obtain such information seems to fall short of such a compelling state interest. As for defendants who are convicted of sexual assault, convicts have traditionally lost many civil libertarian protections after conviction and it seems more within the U.S. constitutional tradition to then use coercive HIV-antibody testing. The contribution to public health and the victim's peace of mind seem to be sufficient justification for such postconviction testing and limited disclosure.

Clearly, the AIDS health crisis is a serious and growing epidemic. Rational and effective policies should be followed with the purpose of safeguarding both individual constitutional rights and public health of the United States.

REFERENCES

AIDS AND CIVIL LIBERTIES PROJECT, AMERICAN CIVIL LIBERTIES UNION. (1990). Mandatory HIV testing of prostitutes: Policy statement of the American Civil Liberties Union. In M. Blumberg (Ed.), *AIDS: The impact on the criminal justice system* (pp. 101–107). Columbus, OH: Merrill Publishing.

AIDS DEATHS SOARING AMONG WOMEN. (1990, July 11). *Daily Oklahoman*, p.5.

BLUMBERG, M. (1990a). AIDS: Analyzing a new dimension in rape victimization. In M. Blumberg (Ed.), *AIDS: The impact on the criminal justice system* (pp. 78–87). Columbus, OH: Merrill Publishing.

BLUMBERG, M. (ED.). (1990b). *AIDS: The impact on the criminal justice system.* Columbus, OH: Merrill Publishing.

BOWLEG, I. A., & BRIDGHAM, B. J. (1989). *A summary of AIDS laws from the 1988 legislative sessions.* Washington, DC: George Washington University, Intergovernmental Health Policy Project, AIDS Policy Center.

BRANDT, A. M. (1985). *No magic bullet: A social history of venereal disease in the United States since 1880.* New York: Oxford University Press.

BRANDT, A. M. (1988, April). AIDS in historical perspective: Four lessons from the history of sexually transmitted diseases. *American Journal of Public Health, 78*(4), 367–371.

BRUS, B. (1990, January 22). Tulsa official hopes arrest to slow AIDS. *Daily Oklahoman*, p.1.

CENTERS FOR DISEASE CONTROL. (1987a, March 27). Antibody to human immunodeficiency virus in female prostitutes. *Morbidity and Mortality Weekly Report, 36*(11), 159.

CENTERS FOR DISEASE CONTROL. (1987b, December 18). Human immunodeficiency virus infection in the United States: A review of current knowledge. *Morbidity and Mortality Weekly Report, 36*(5–6), 8.

CHARGE FILED UNDER ANTI-AIDS LAW. (1990, January 21). *Sunday Oklahoman*, p. A18.

COHEN, J. B., ALEXANDER, P., & WOFSY, C. (1990). Prostitutes and AIDS: Public policy issues. In M. Blumberg (Ed.), *AIDS: The impact on the criminal justice system* (pp. 91–100). Columbus, OH: Merrill Publishing

COWLEY, G., HAGER, M., & MARSHALL, R. (1990, June 25). AIDS: The next ten years. *Newsweek*, pp. 20–27.

ECKHOLM, E. (1990a, September 16). AIDS in Africa: What makes the two sexes so vulnerable to epidemic. *New York Times*, p. 11.

ECKHOLM, E. (1990b, September 18). Cooperation by prostitutes in Kenya prevents thousands of AIDS cases. *New York Times*, p. A6.

Face-to-face. (1990, December 10). Columbia Broadcasting System.

Geraldo. (1990, May 11). Have prostitutes become the new Typhoid Marys? *Tribune Entertainment.*

GLABERSON, W. (1990, July 9). Rape and the fear of AIDS: How one case was affected. *New York Times*, p. A13.

HERLAND SISTER RESOURCES. (1990). ACLU AIDS project to focus on women and children with AIDS. *Herland Voice, 7*(10), 4.

HEVESI, D. (1988, October 16). AIDS test for suspect splits experts. *New York Times*, p. 30.

HOLLIBAUGH, A., KARP, M., & TAYLOR, K. (1987). The second epidemic. In D. Crimp (Ed.), *AIDS: Cultural analysis/cultural criticism* (pp. 127–142). Cambridge, MA: MIT Press.

INFECTION NOT REPORTED AMONG LEGAL PROSTITUTES. (1987, November 18). *AIDS Policy and Law*, pp. 2–3.

LEIGH, C. (1987). Further violations of our rights. In D. Crimp (Ed.), *AIDS: Cultural analysis/cultural criticism* (pp. 177–181). Cambridge, MA: MIT Press.

MILLER, H. G., TURNER, C. F., & MOSES, L. E. (1990). *AIDS: The second decade.* Washington, DC: National Academy Press.

More states establishing laws allowing AIDS assault cases. (1990, October 22). *Daily Oklahoman*, p.20.

More women, children expected to die from AIDS. (1990, July 29). *Edmond Sun*, p. A9.

More women getting AIDS, study says. (1990, November 30). *Daily Oklahoman*, p.6.

OKLAHOMA STATE DEPARTMENT OF HEALTH. (1991, January). *Oklahoma AIDS Update, 91*(1), 6.

POTTERAT, J. J., PHILLIPS, L., & MUTH, J. B. (1987, April 3). Lying to military physicians about risk factors for HIV infections. [To the Editor]. *JAMA, 257*(13), 1727.

PRESIDENT'S COMMISSION ON THE HUMAN IMMUNODEFICIENCY VIRUS. (1988). Sexual assault and HIV transmission: Section V of Chapter 9: Legal and ethical issues. *Report of the President's Commission on the Human Immunodeficiency Virus.* Submitted to the President of the United States, June 24, 1988. Reprinted in M. Blumberg (Ed.), *AIDS: The impact on the criminal justice system* (pp. 73–77). Columbus, OH: Merrill Publishing, 1990.

Prostitute goes to jail in AIDS case. (1990, February 14). *Daily Oklahoman*, p.31.

Rape suspect due AIDS test. (1990, July 23). *Daily Oklahoman*, p.7.

REDFIELD, R. R., MARKHAM, P. D., SALAHUDDIN, S. Z., WRIGHT, D. C., SARNGADHARAN, M. G., & GALLO, R.C. (1985, October 18). Heterosexually acquired HTLV-III/LAV disease (AIDS-related complex and AIDS): Epidemiologic evidence for female-to-male transmission. *Journal of the American Medical Association, 254*(15), 2094–2096.

ROWE, M., & RYAN, C. (1987). *AIDS: A public health challenge: State issues policies and programs, Vol. I: Assessing the problem.* Washington, DC: George Washington University, Intergovernmental Health Policy Project, AIDS Policy Center.

SALHOLZ, E., SPRINGEN, K., DELAPENA, N., & WITHERSPOON, D. (1990, July 23). A frightening aftermath: Concern about AIDS adds to the trauma of rape. *Newsweek*, p. 53.

Sally Jessy Raphael (1991, January 21). Multimedia Entertainment.

SCHULTZ, S., MILBERG, J. A., KRISTAL, A. R., & STONEBRUNER, R. L. (1986, April 4). Female-to-male transmission of HTLV-III [To the Editor]. *Journal of the American Medical Association, 255*(13), 1703–1704.

SHAW, N. S. (1988, October–December). Preventing AIDS among women: The role of community organizing. *Socialist Review, 18*(4), 76–92.

SHILTS, R. (1987). *And the band played on: Politics, people and the AIDS epidemic.* New York: St. Martin's Press.

STENGEL, R. (1987, June 8). Testing dilemma: Washington prepares a controversial new policy to fight AIDS. *Time,* pp. 20–22.

THOMAS, C. (1988). *A synopsis of state AIDS laws enacted during the 1983–1987 legislative sessions.* Washington, DC: George Washington University, Intergovernmental Health Policy Project, AIDS Policy Center.

TURNER, C. F., MILLER, H. G., & MOSES, L. E. (1989). *AIDS: Sexual behavior and intravenous drug use.* Washington, DC: National Academy Press.

WEISSMAN, J. L., & CHILDERS, M. (1988–1989). Constitutional questions: mandatory testing for AIDS under Washington's AIDS legislation. *Gonzaga Law Review, 24,* 433–473.

YABLONSKY, L. (1990). *Criminology: Crime and criminality* (4th ed.). New York: Harper & Row.

CASES

People of New York v. Thomas, 529 N.Y.S. 2d 439 (Co. Ct. 1988).

People of New York v. Toure, 523 N.Y.S. 2d 622 (Sup. 1987).

Shelvin v. Lykos, 741 S.W. 2d 178 (Tex. App.-Houston 1987).

10

The Legal Response to Substance Abuse during Pregnancy

Inger Sagatun-Edwards

❖

The concept of *fetal abuse* raises complex legal and ethical questions. Society has responded to these dilemmas in three different ways: (1) holding that fetal abuse is a form of child abuse with criminal prosecution of the mother, (2) juvenile court dependency court intervention for the purposes of protecting the child, and (3) social services and medical treatment approaches with no court intervention. Often two or more of these approaches may be combined. Focusing on the problem of maternal substance abuse during pregnancy, various approaches to criminalizing maternal substance abuse during pregnancy and the basis for juvenile court or civil court intervention are discussed. The rationales and legal bases for each of these approaches and relevant legislation and recent cases are also discussed. It is concluded that criminal prosecution of fetal abuse does not protect the well-being of the fetus enough to violate important constitutional rights for the mother. Fetal abuse should not automatically come under mandatory child-abuse reporting laws, and juvenile court intervention should be used only in the most serious cases to protect the child. A comprehensive public health approach is the best way to deal with this problem.

In this chapter we focus on substance abuse during pregnancy, which, in turn, may affect the fetus. Numerous public policy issues are raised by the births of drug-exposed or drug-addicted infants. Should the state intervene on behalf of the baby? Should the criminal justice system take action to protect the child and punish the mother for her conduct? Should the child welfare system take action to protect the baby? Or should the mother be left to the medical and public health systems, which should deal with the problem?

The concept of fetal abuse raises complex legal and ethical questions. Meeting obligations to the unborn child may require placing limitations on the mother's conduct that would not be there if she were not pregnant (Robertson, 1989). The mother's right to privacy and her autonomy must be balanced against her baby's welfare. Should the right of the fetus be recognized at the risk of sacrificing the right of the mother? Is the mother's right of privacy worth the possible lifelong suffering of the child and perhaps staggering costs to society?

Society has responded to these dilemmas in three different ways: (1) criminalization of the mother's conduct for the purpose of punishing the mother and deterring future substance abuse during pregnancy, (2) juvenile court dependency intervention for the purpose of protecting the child, and (3) drug treatment according to a medical or public health model. In some cases, combinations of these approaches may be used. Before discussing the legal response to the problem of substance abuse during pregnancy, in this chapter we first briefly examine the extent and seriousness of maternal substance abuse and the issue of "fetal rights."

MATERNAL SUBSTANCE ABUSE DURING PREGNANCY

Early medical studies concluded that crack/cocaine had very negative effects on the fetus (Chasnoff, Burns, Schnoll, & Burns, 1986). The wisdom that sprang up in the late 1980s and early 1990s was that crack/cocaine addiction among pregnant mothers causes serious, often irreparable medical problems in their babies, and that this condition was extremely widespread and extremely costly to society. According to several studies, prenatal substance abuse could cause a wide range of serious medical complications for the infant, such as withdrawal, physical and neurological deficits, low birth weight, growth retardation, cardiovascular abnormalities, spontaneous abortion, and premature delivery, as well as long-term developmental abnormalities (Howard, Kropenske, & Tyler, 1986; Petitti & Coleman, 1990; Weston, Ivens, Zuckerman, Jones, & Lopez, 1989). Early hospital studies by the National Association on Perinatal Addiction Research and Education estimated that about 375,000 drug-exposed infants are born each year, at least one of every ten births in the United States (Chasnoff, Burns, Schnoll, & Burns, 1985; Dixon, 1989). A federal study in 1991 found that the number of young foster children who had had prenatal exposure to drugs grew from 17 percent in 1986 to 55 percent in 1991 (U.S. General Accounting Office, 1994). Most states also reported dramatic increases in the numbers of children victimized by parental drug involvement (Daro & McCurdy, 1992).

However, both early estimates of the widespread nature of maternal drug use during pregnancy and the conclusion that poor fetal outcomes are caused solely by illegal drugs have come under attack. One critic points out that the early hospital estimates were based on a survey of 36 hospitals, accounting for only 5 percent of all U.S. births in 1989 (Farr, 1995). Another notes that the women surveyed had used a number of different drugs and that the incidence of fetal exposure in different hospitals varied substantially (Gustafson, 1991). The extent to which the children's medical problems are actually due to illegal drugs is also difficult to determine. Many drug users are polydrug abusers, mixing illegal drugs with legal drugs such as cigarettes and alcohol, all known contributors to poor fetal outcomes. Often, such factors are compounded by family poverty, poor nutritional status and general health, sexually transmitted diseases, and little or no prenatal care (Lutiger, Graham, Einarson & Koren, 1991). When the lifestyles, social background, and other covariates of cocaine use are taken into consideration, it becomes clear that cocaine use per se may not affect infant outcomes (Richardson & Day, 1991). Although the initial paper by Chasnoff et al. (1985) had pointed out the many medical problems of drug-exposed infants, a later paper by the same author found that babies exposed to cocaine only in the first semester of pregnancy weighed the same as babies from a control population (Chasnoff, Landress, & Barrett, 1990).

A problem with early studies on the babies of mothers who used powdered cocaine and crack was that there were no control groups. The effects of cocaine are particularly difficult to identify because of the high probability of a total lack of prenatal care (Inciardi, Lockwood, & Pottieger, 1993). It is clear that the impact of prenatal drug use on fetal health is mediated by diet, prenatal care, and other factors associated with social class (Bingol, et al., 1987; Mathias, 1992). A more recent study gives support to this view. Hurt, Brodsky, Braitman, and Giannetta (1995) studied 105 cocaine users and their infants of thirty-four weeks' gestation or more at an urban hospital in Philadelphia. Although cocaine-exposed infants had an increased incidence of congenital syphilis, increased admission to the neonatal ICU, and lower birth weights and head circumference, the data showed that these children did not differ from the controls in the incidence of severe growth retardation. The researchers concluded that the data did not support the theory that cocaine alone increases the risk of growth retardation. Nicotine, a legal drug, was found to be an independent predictor of small head circumference. In a study of chronic cocaine use among pregnant subjects, Tuboku-Metzger et al. (1996) found no direct effects on the health or development of newborns. Woods et al. (1993) found no differences in neurobehavioral performance of cocaine-exposed infants compared to nonexposed infants. According to Hutchins (1997), knowledge concerning the biological effects of drug exposure on the newborn is inconclusive at present. Similarly, in a computerized assessment of the scientific literature, Lester et al. (1997) concluded that knowledge about the existence or extent of effects of prenatal cocaine exposure on child outcome is limited, scattered, and compromised by methodological shortcomings. Thus the effects often attributed to fetal exposure to illegal drugs may as likely be due to a host of other factors or be nonexistent.

TRADITIONAL FETAL RIGHTS

The fetal rights movement, which seeks to define the fetus as a person, grew out of the attempt to hold women liable for prenatal conduct that may cause harm to a fetus (Beckett, 1995). Within this movement, drug babies are seen as separate entities from their mothers and in need of protection from their substance-abusing parent. However, whether a fetus has any legal rights is a controversial issue. Most current laws seek to protect children from harm after their birth, and the applicability of current child abuse and neglect laws to prenatal conduct is uncertain. In most jurisdictions, fetuses have few, if any, legal rights since as fetuses they are not considered to be children. The fetus therefore has traditionally had a very precarious legal position: A much debated issue is whether prenatal conduct that affects the fetus should come under the same legislation intended for children after birth, or if new laws should be created that are specifically directed at the protection of the fetus.

The nonrecognition of the fetus as a legal entity is embodied in the "born alive" rule, which states that the fetus has to be born alive as a precondition to legal personhood. Underlying this rule is the assumption that the mother and fetus constitute a unit whose legal interests are coextensive (McNulty, 1987–1988). Historically, the law declined to extend any legal rights to the fetus except in narrowly defined situations and except when rights were contingent on live births (*Roe v. Wade*, 1973). Since the law viewed the fetus as part of the mother, it was only after birth that the child acquired any legal rights independent of those of the mother (Rickhoff and Cukjati, 1989).

To be actionable child abuse under traditional criminal law, the conduct that causes the injury or creates the dangerous situation must occur after the birth of a live child (*Reyes v. Superior Court*, 1977). In this case the court found that child-endangerment statutes did not apply to prenatal conduct, since this was not expressly stated in the relevant statute (*California Penal Code*, 1977).

Increasingly, however, the born alive rule in child abuse and child neglect laws has come under attack. In *Commonwealth v. Cass* (1984), the court held that a viable fetus was a person within the protection of the state's vehicular homicide statute. Several states, including California, Illinois, Iowa, Michigan, Mississippi, New Hampshire, Oklahoma, Utah, Washington, and Wisconsin, now have "feticide" statutes.[1] More important, in a recent case from South Carolina (*Whitner v. South Carolina*, 1996; Condon, McIntosh, Zelenka, Avant, & DeLoach, 1997) fetal abuse was included under general criminal child abuse laws. This landmark case is discussed in more detail later in the chapter.

In civil law, fetal rights have already been well established. A majority of states consider fetuses that have died in utero to be "persons" under wrongful death statutes, and therefore parents may sue people who harmed the fetus in utero, causing the death (McNulty, 1987–1988). Courts have also long recognized "wrongful life" actions. However, most of these cases involve harm caused by a third person, not the mother, and are therefore not directly applicable to the issue of maternal substance abuse during pregnancy. In general, parents are protected from civil suits for fetal harm by the doctrine of parental immunity (e.g., *Chambess v. Fairtrace*, 1987). Some courts have refused to recognize this immunity. In *Grodin v. Grodin* (1981), a child brought suit against his mother for prenatal injuries because of the mother's negligence in failing to secure prenatal care. The court held that the injured child's mother should bear the same liability as a third person for negligent conduct that interfered with the child's right to begin life with a sound mind and body (Balisy, 1987).

THE LEGAL RESPONSE TO SUBSTANCE ABUSE DURING PREGNANCY

Criminalization of Maternal Substance Abuse during Pregnancy

Proponents of criminalization argue that there are three compelling interests that justify prosecuting women for their conduct during pregnancy: (1) the state's interest in protecting the fetus's right to potential life, (2) the state's interest in protecting the newborn's right to be born healthy, and (3) the state's interest in protecting maternal health (Sagatun-Edwards, 1997). There is also a fourth compelling state interest in the criminalization of fetal injury by pregnant drug users: (4) the state's interest in protecting society from the burden of providing for injured newborns (Wright, 1990). Proponents believe that even under strict scrutiny standards the state's interests in protecting the health and the life of the unborn child take precedence over maternal privacy rights.

In a series of consecutive decisions the U.S. Supreme Court has firmly established a strict scrutiny in privacy decisions affecting the spheres of family, marriage, and procreation, and the right to control one's own body (*Eisenstadt v. Baird*, 1972; *Griswold v. Connecticut*, 1965; *Roe v. Wade*, 1973). These and subsequent abortion decisions make clear that any decision or statute that infringes upon a constitutionally protected privacy right must undergo strict scrutiny review and it will be upheld only if it is narrowly tailored to achieve a compelling state interest (Harvard Law Review Association, 1998).

As of 1995, at least 167 women in twenty-four states have been prosecuted for taking illicit drugs while pregnant (Beckett, 1995). These prosecutions have typically involved creative applications of existing statutes, such as (1) delivery of a controlled substance to a minor, or (2) some form of child endangerment or abuse. Most prosecutions under both types of existing law have ultimately been unsuccessful, with the notable important exception of *Whitner v. South Carolina* (1996). The courts have concluded that these laws were not meant to apply to the situation of drug use during pregnancy, and prior to *Whitner* all cases prosecuted successfully at the trial level have been thrown out by either the appellate or superior court of the relevant state. Many of these attempts to prosecute women criminally for illicit drug use during pregnancy have foundered on the question of nonrecognition of fetal rights as discussed above, the perception that existing laws were not intended to include fetal abuse, or that the constitutionally protected maternal rights to privacy were more important than the state's interest in protecting the unborn.

Prosecution under Controlled Substance Statutes

As stated above, many criminal prosecutions have been based on existing criminal laws, which were not designed or intended to govern prenatal conduct. These include statutes that prohibit drug use, sale, possession, or delivery of drugs to minors, which apply to all adults, males and females. *Johnson v. Florida* (1992) was the first case of this kind that was prosecuted successfully at the trial level using a "delivery of drugs to a minor" statute to apply to drugs being transferred through the umbilical cord at birth. The mother appealed and the appellate court affirmed her conviction. The Florida Supreme Court, however, reversed the conviction on a variety of grounds, including legislative intent. The court held that the legislature did not intend the word *deliver* to include the passage of blood through the umbilical cord. The Florida Supreme Court adopted the language of the justice who dissented in the lower appellate court decision when she wrote that

> [t]he Legislature never intended for the general drug delivery statute to authorize prosecution of those mothers who take illegal drugs close enough in time to childbirth that a doctor could testify that a tiny amount passed from mother to child in the few seconds before the umbilical cord was cut. Criminal prosecution of mothers like Johnson will undermine Florida's express policy of "keeping families intact" and could destroy the family by incarcerating the child's mother when alternate measures could protect the child and stabilize the family. (*Johnson v. Florida*, 1992), at 1294).

The Florida Supreme Court decision noted that drug abuse is a serious national problem and that there is a particular concern about the rising numbers of babies born with cocaine in their systems as a result of maternal substance abuse. But the court pointed out the negative aspects of prosecuting pregnant substance abusers. Women who are substance abusers may simply avoid prenatal care for fear of being detected when the newborns of these women are, as a group, the most fragile and sick and most in need of hospital neonatal care.

Decisions from higher courts since the Florida Supreme Court reversal in *Johnson* have followed the same path (i.e., the courts have consistently refused to apply drug delivery statutes to pregnant women).

Prosecution under Child Abuse and Neglect (Child Endangerment Statutes)

Until very recently, prosecutions based on criminal child abuse statutes had also had infrequent success. Courts repeatedly held that a fetus is not a "child" within the means of statutes prohibiting acts endangering the welfare of children. An example of such a decision is a case from the Supreme Court of Kentucky, *Commonwealth of Kentucky v. Connie Welch* (1993), where the high court reversed the trial court that had found Ms. Welch guilty of a criminal child abuse count. The Court of Appeals affirmed her convictions for possession of a controlled substance but vacated her conviction on the criminal abuse charge. The Kentucky Supreme Court affirmed the decision of the Courts of Appeals by noting that

> [t]he mother was a drug addict. But, for that matter, she could have been a pregnant alcoholic, causing fetal alcohol syndrome; or she could have been addicted to self-abuse by smoking, or by abusing prescription painkillers, or over the counter medicine; or for that matter she could have been addicted to downhill skiing or some sport creating serious risk of prenatal injury, risk which the mother wantonly disregarded as a matter of self-indulgence. What if a pregnant woman drives over the speed limit, or as a matter of vanity doesn't wear prescription lenses she knows she needs to see the dangers of the road? The defense asks where do we draw the line on self abuse by a pregnant woman that wantonly exposes risk to her unborn baby?...
>
> [I]t is inflicting intentional or wanton injury upon the child that makes the conduct criminal under the child abuse statutes, not the criminality of the conduct, per se....In short, the District Attorney's interpretation of the statutes, if validated, might lead to a "slippery slope" whereby the law could be construed as covering the full range of a pregnant woman's behavior—a plainly unconstitutional result that would, among other things, render the statutes void for vagueness. (*Commonwealth of Kentucky v. Connie Welch*, 1993, at 282)

The Supreme Court of Kentucky concluded that their state drug delivery statutes and child endangerment statutes did not intend to punish as criminal conduct self-abuse by an expectant mother potentially injurious to the baby she carries. In a similar decision, the Supreme Court of Nevada (*Sheriff v. Encoe*, 1994) explicitly held that the constraints of federal due process notice requirements prohibited reinterpreting the child neglect statutes to include fetal abuse.

In a departure from the state supreme court decisions noted above, a recent landmark case from a Supreme Court of South Carolina, *Whitner v. South Carolina* (1996) upheld the prosecution of a woman who ingested crack cocaine during the third trimester of her pregnancy under child abuse and endangerment statutes by concluding that a fetus does have legal rights on its own.

The procedural history of the case is as follows: On February 6, 1992, Cornelia Whitner, a 28-year-old African-American woman, was arrested for a violation of S.C. Code Ann 20-7-50 for "unlawful neglect of a child." Whitner had given birth to a son on February 2, 1992. The hospital test showed the presence of cocaine in his bloodstream. The Pickens Court Grand Jury indicted Whitner on April 7, 1992 for the same offense, and she pled guilty to "unlawful neglect of a child" on April 20, 1992. She was then sentenced to eight years imprisonment. No objections were made to the charge or jurisdiction of the court, and Whitner did not appeal her conviction or sentence.

On May 10, 1993, Whitner filed a state postconviction application with the South Carolina Court of Common Pleas. Another judge held a hearing on November 1, 1993, and issued an order vacating the convictions on November 22, 1993. The state appealed the judge's order. Following briefing and oral argument, the South Carolina Supreme Court reversed the granting of postconviction relief on July 15, 1996, based solely on state law issues. The court later granted Whitner's petition for a rehearing and issued an amended opinion on October 27, 1997, which addressed both state and federal claims in reversing the Court of Common Pleas conviction. The State Supreme Court denied a rehearing from that opinion on November 19, 1997.

In its 3–2 opinion the South Carolina Supreme Court noted that South Carolina law has long recognized that viable fetuses are persons holding certain rights and privileges for purposes of homicide laws and wrongful death statutes and that it would be absurd not to recognize a viable fetus as a person for the purposes of statutes proscribing child abuse. The court argued that "the consequences of abuse or neglect which take place after birth often pale in comparison to those resulting from abuse suffered by the viable fetus before birth" (1996 WL 393164, at 2). In reaching this conclusion the court relied on the harms reported by early articles in the *New England Journal of Medicine* (e.g., Chasnoff et al., 1985; Volpe, 1992). The perception that the defendant endangered the "life, health and comfort of her child" through ingesting crack cocaine led the court to uphold the prosecution under the criminal child neglect statute. In contrast, the dissent argued that a fetus is not a person, and that the distinction of a "viable fetus" is absurd in that it would then be legal for a woman to ingest cocaine early on in the pregnancy when presumably the fetus is most at risk for harmful substances.

The implications of the South Carolina decision were far-reaching. First, a viable fetus (24 weeks) is now a child for the purposes of the South Carolina Code (*Whitner*, 328 S.C. 1, at 22). Second, this decision could render women criminally liable for a myriad of acts that the legislature had not passed into law, such as failure to obtain prenatal care or failure to quit smoking and/or drinking. As noted in the dissenting opinion, this case also highlighted the irony of incarcerating a woman up to ten years for ingesting drugs while pregnant, yet the maximum for an illegal abortion (killing a viable fetus) is only a two-year maximum (*Whitner*, at 23).

In November 1991, another woman in South Carolina, Melissa Ann Crawley, was arrested under similar circumstances and pled guilty to the same charge. She was sentenced to five years imprisonment and did not appeal her conviction or sentence. In September 1994, Crawley filed a state petition for writ of habeas corpus. At the conclusion of her hearing, the judge vacated her conviction and sentence. The state of South

Carolina appealed the judge's order. On December 1, 1997, in an unpublished opinion, relying on the decision in *Whitner*, the State Supreme Court reversed the granting of state habeas relief and reinstated Crawley's conviction and sentence (*Crawley v. Evatt*, 1997). The State Supreme Court denied her petition for rehearing on January 8, 1998.

Both Whitner and Crawley subsequently petitioned the U.S. Supreme Court to review the decisions of the South Carolina Supreme Court (*Whitner v. South Carolina,* and *Crawley v. Evatt; Condon et al.,* 1997), on the grounds that they had pled guilty to a crime that does not exist in South Carolina. They argued that they had been indicted for child abuse for giving birth to a child who had cocaine in his system, when the child abuse statute did not apply to a fetus.

Several prominent national and state medical, health, social welfare, legal services, substance abuse treatment organizations, and social policy organizations wrote briefs to the U.S. Supreme Court in support of Whitner's and Crawley's petition for a writ of certiorari urging the Court not to let the decision in South Carolina stand.[2] They argued that if left to stand, the ruling in *Whitner* would require for the first time in the nation that physicians, health care providers, and social service workers, under threat of criminal penalties, divulge to state authorities, for possible prosecution, the identities and medical information of pregnant women who engage in conduct or activities that may adversely affect the welfare of their fetuses. They warned that the *Whitner* decision would deter pregnant women from obtaining adequate prenatal care, including substance abuse treatment, and that it would seriously compromise the doctor–patient relationship. The result would be damaged health, increased suffering, escalating health care costs, and decreased life expectancy. The *Whitner* decision, they argued, also created an intolerable dilemma for physicians and health care providers; either risk jail by upholding the confidentiality of medical care, or disclose clients' identities in compliance with state reporting requirements (Tracy, Frietsche, Abrahamson, Boyd, & Risher, 1997).

Similarly, the Center for Constitutional Rights and the American Civil Liberties Union also wrote a brief in support of the petition for a writ of certiorari on more legal and constitutional grounds (Olshansky, Davis, Paltrow, Paul-Emile, & Wise, 1997). They argued that *Whitner* had created an intolerable conflict among state high courts in that previous courts (e.g., Kentucky and Nevada, as described above) have refused to include fetal abuse under existing child abuse statutes without directives from state legislatures. They argued that the *Whitner* court misconstrued the federal guarantee of due process notice in that both petitioners had been unaware that fetal abuse was included in the state statutes on child abuse and neglect. Finally, they argued that Whitner misconstrued the prohibition against vague criminal statutes.

In a brief opposing the petition for writ of certiorari, the Attorney General of South Carolina argued that there was no conflict among the states concerning the application of child abuse laws to viable fetuses because the cases from other jurisdictions turn upon an interpretation of legislative intent (Condon et al., 1997). Since South Carolina already had included fetal rights under civil statutes, the state argued that the legislature would also have included such rights under child abuse and neglect laws. The *Whitner* case concerned a question of state law rather than federal law, and the decision had turned on interpretations of state law rather than federal constitutional grounds. Second, the petitioners' convictions satisfied due process requirements because the previous decisions of the State Supreme Court gave them adequate notice that a viable fetus was protected by the unlawful neglect statute. Finally, the state's brief in opposition to the petition for certiorari argued that Crawley had failed to raise her federal constitutional claims in a timely manner and that she had therefore defaulted these issues for certiorari review.

The U.S. Supreme Court declined to grant certiorari, and the decision of the South Carolina Supreme Court therefore stands. According to a brief from the group of medical and social welfare organizations, at least two alcohol and drug treatment programs in South Carolina have experienced precipitous drops in the number of pregnant women seeking admissions. It remains to be seen what the far-reaching consequences of this decision will be, but it is generally expected that other state courts may follow suit and that legislation will be enacted to specifically include fetal abuse in child abuse and child neglect statutes.

New Legislation to Criminalize Use of Drugs during Pregnancy

Although many observers who favor prosecutions of fetal abuse applaud the *Whitner* decision, many also feel that legislation specifically aimed at maternal substance abuse during pregnancy should be enacted rather than relying on courts' interpretations of existing law. Courts can only interpret the law after the fact, and "court-written" law is inherently unstable. Many states have therefore considered such new legislation, and several states have proposed statutes designed to criminalize maternal drug use during pregnancy. Proposed bills in some states would make it a felony to give birth to a drug-addicted child (e.g., Georgia, Louisiana, Ohio, Colorado), and several members of Congress have also supported such legislation. However, as of this date no state has yet passed a statute that explicitly criminalizes fetal abuse (although this could soon change in light of the *Whitner* decision). For example, in California, a bill to define drug use in late pregnancy as criminal child abuse failed in committee in April 1998 (Pasternak, 1998). Such failures may be because there are serious social policy concerns and constitutional difficulties with such bills, and because many medical and legal scholars have strongly criticized the use of any criminal sanction to address the problem of prenatal drug use. Indeed, several important medical, legal, and civil rights groups have voiced their opposition to policies aimed at the criminalization of pregnant drug users.[3] Class and racial biases in the testing and reporting of such cases have also been demonstrated (Chasnoff et al., 1990) and in prosecutions (Paltrow, 1992; Roberts, 1991).

Almost a decade ago Paltrow (1990) argued that no criminal statute on fetal abuse could be tailored narrowly enough to protect a woman's right to privacy or her due process rights. A recent article by the Harvard Law Review Association (1998) also concludes that in balancing the maternal privacy interests against the state's interest in protecting the life and health of the fetus, courts should only uphold narrowly drawn statutes targeted at specific, egregious conduct, and that in general, prosecutions for fetal abuse will not enhance fetal health and thus serve state interests. Through analyzing the legal status of maternal privacy rights versus fetal rights, this article assesses the constitutionality of criminal statutes that punish women for negligent or reckless conduct that harms or may harm their fetuses. The constitutional body of privacy law in general, and abortion law in particular, strongly suggests the existence of a maternal privacy interest that would be infringed by such statutes, thus requiring strict scrutiny by the courts (p. 994). Fetal abuse statutes would implicate two different aspects of the right to privacy: both the right to make decisions that affect the spheres of family, marriage, and procreation, and the right to control one's own body.

The article uses the viability decision in *Roe v. Wade* (1973) and subsequent abortion cases to provide a framework for analyzing the conflicts between maternal privacy rights and the state interest in protecting fetuses, and weighing the two to determine when the latter becomes compelling. *Roe's* holding that the state's interest in the birth of a fetus does not become compelling during the first two trimesters of pregnancy does not necessarily rule out the existence of a compelling state interest in ensuring that fetuses that will be carried to term are born unharmed. States may have a greater interest in preventing future suffering of those who will be born than in ensuring that any particular fetus will be born. Conversely, *Roe's* holding that states are allowed to protect fetuses from abortion in the third trimester does not necessarily imply that states have an equally compelling interest in protecting fetuses from all other harms during that period. Furthermore, fetuses are most vulnerable in the earliest stages of pregnancy and should require more protection then. Thus prosecutions of substance abuse by pregnant women in the third trimester after viability (as in *Whitner*) makes less sense than prosecutions at an earlier stage.

Ironically, *Roe v. Wade* has been used to argue in favor of the fetal rights movement. In this decision, the U.S. Supreme Court held that after the first trimester of pregnancy, the interests of potential life become important, and that after viability, the state has a legitimate and important interest in the unborn. After viability, the state may protect fetal life by prohibiting all abortions that are not necessary to protect the life and health of the mother. Thus, both proponents and opponents of the criminalization of fetal abuse can draw on different parts of *Roe v. Wade* to support their cause. *Webster* (1980) subsequently rejected the rigid trimester scheme for establishing viability, thus giving ammunition to those who argue that states may constitutionally criminalize pregnant women who abuse substances known to harm fetuses (Wright, 1990).

Criminalization of maternal conduct during pregnancy also violates a woman's rights to equal protection under the law. Because evidence of a newborn's positive toxicology screen is used only in cases against women, women would be punished because of their drug use and their ability to get pregnant. A statutory requirement that women resolve all health care decisions in favor of the fetus would hold women to a much higher standard (Sagatun-Edwards, 1997).

Farr (1995) argues that prosecuting women under laws that were not intended for the prosecution of substance abuse during pregnancy violates the due process clause of the Fourteenth Amendment. This clause guarantees a person the right to fair notice that his or her conduct is criminal. Thus, prosecuting women under existing laws, such as those dealing with delivery of drugs to a minor which do not specify the delivery of drugs to a fetus, violates the due process clause (see briefs cited in the *Whitner* case as well). Additionally, criminal laws require that punishment be imposed when there is both a criminal act and a culpable mental intent. Assuming that the state has a right to maintain a reasonable standard of fetal health, it seems logical that the state could only punish those women who willfully, intentionally, or knowingly create a substantial risk of harm to their fetus. Both the facts that the harmful effects of drug use alone have been called into question, and that many women may not even know that they are pregnant when they ingest the drug, therefore argue against such prosecutions.

Finally, the Harvard Law Review Association (1998) also analyzed the policy considerations that legislatures and courts should take into account when deciding whether to enact criminal fetal abuse statutes or to read fetal protection into existing legislation. The long-established constitutional rights of the individual to control procreative and familial decisions should also apply to the maternal decisions potentially infringed upon by fetal abuse legislation. Broad fetal abuse statutes that are patterned on child abuse statutes, those that make neglecting or abusing a crime without specifying what constitutes neglect or abuse, would be unconstitutional. They would be void for vagueness, and they require an infringement on maternal rights not justified by the fetal protection they offer; thus they would not be narrowly tailored enough to survive strict scrutiny. For example, a child abuse statute that included fetuses could be interpreted to punish the taking of drugs that are essential to the mother's health but harmful to the fetus (p. 1005). One possible avenue is to add additional penalties to conduct that is already criminal: for example, on pregnant women who take heroin. As long as the state could establish that the harm to the fetus is significant and that no lesser ban would protect fetuses adequately, such a statute would be constitutional. However, limiting the imposition of criminal liability to conduct already criminalized makes little sense as a practical matter because the deterrent effect of such an extra penalty is at best unclear and would penalize pregnancy more than any other factor (p. 1007). To pass the strict scrutiny test the state must show that any statute prohibiting fetal abuse in fact serves that interest. Because a fetal abuse statute may provide a powerful incentive to women to stay away from doctors in order to avoid detection and prosecution, statutes that criminalize pregnant women's conduct actually may thwart rather than serve the state's interest in protecting the fetus (p. 1008). The authors conclude, as did the authors of the briefs supporting Whitner and Crawley, that educating women and funding prenatal care are better approaches to the problem. Unlike criminal liability, these solutions foster positive social attitudes toward the role of women and family relationships.

Juvenile Court (Civil Court) Involvement

Although criminal prosecutions of pregnant drug users have been largely unsuccessful, thousands of women have had their children removed from their custody as a result of prenatal use of drugs (Paltrow, 1992). While the stated purpose of the criminal court is to punish the offender, the stated purpose of the juvenile court is protection of the child. Until recently, juvenile law and the jurisdiction of juvenile court did not extend to unborn children. In *In Re Stevens S.* (1981), the Court of Appeals in California overturned a juvenile court decision, finding that an unborn fetus was not a person within the meaning of the child abuse or child neglect statutes. However, in Michigan (*In Re Baby X*, 1980) an appellate court reasoned that since prior treatment of one child can support neglect allegations regarding another child, prenatal treatment can be considered probative of child neglect. In *Re Troy D.* (1989), the California Supreme Court let stand an earlier appellate decision that the use of drugs during pregnancy is alone sufficient basis to trigger a child abuse report and to support juvenile court dependency jurisdiction. This decision was later negated by passage of the Perinatal Substance Abuse Services Act in California (1991), which does not endorse the view that prenatal substance abuse is by itself indicative of future child abuse and neglect (see the description later in the chapter). However, several other states have passed civil child abuse and child neglect statutes that declare drug and/or alcohol use during pregnancy to be predictive of child abuse (Paltrow, 1992). Issues of concern for juvenile court or family court jurisdiction are the criteria for testing, whether positive tests should be included under mandatory reporting laws for child abuse and neglect, and the criteria used to remove a child from the mother.

Entry to Juvenile Court.   The first point of entry of drug-exposed infants and their families into the juvenile court system is often right after birth. Some states specifically require physicians to test and report pregnant women to child protective services for illicit substance abuse when toxicology tests on newborns are positive. Many hospitals now perform neonatal toxicology screens when maternal drug use is suspected. Typically, hospital protocols dictate that such screens are performed when the newborn shows signs of drug withdrawal, when the mother admits to drug use during pregnancy, or when the mother has had no prenatal care (Robin-Vergeer, 1990). Based on a positive toxicology test, the hospital may report the case to the child protective services, which in turn may ask the court to prevent the child's release to the parents while an investigation takes place. If further investigation reveals a risk to the child, the court may assume temporary custody of the child, and in the most serious cases, parental rights may be terminated (Sagatun-Edwards, Saylor, & Shifflett, 1995).

There are several problems with testing of mothers and children for the presence of illegal drugs. First, there is the invasion of privacy problem. Second, such testing is notoriously unreliable, and the results may depend on what type of drug was ingested and how soon after the ingestion the drug test was administered (Gomby & Shiono, 1991). Third, there may be both racial and social class biases in both the testing procedures and the reports of the testing. A study by Chasnoff et al. (1990) found that African-American women were almost ten times as likely to be reported to county health authorities for alcohol and drug use during pregnancy as Caucasian women. This occurred despite the fact that urine samples of the pregnant women collected at their first prenatal visit revealed no significant differences between black and white patients, or between low-income and upper-income women.

As of this date, no states require mandatory testing for drugs of all pregnant women. Minnesota is one state that has chosen universal screening of neonates while limiting maternal testing to women with pregnancy complications that suggest drug use (Sagatun-Edwards et al., 1995). Most states condition testing on a physician's suspicion of prenatal drug use, based on obstetric complications or assessment of mother and baby. Such discretionary testing is, however, most often done in public hospitals on poor and minority mothers. If routine testing is to be done at all, it should be universal testing of all newborns, thus negating the criticism of bias against minorities and the poor. However, compelling arguments against universal screening include cost, lack of informed consent, lack of reliability, and overemphasizing illegal drugs over equally dangerous drugs, such as alcohol. Most important, the threat of screening may influence a woman's decision to seek prenatal care (Sagatun-Edwards, 1997).

Mandatory Reporting under Child Abuse and Neglect Reporting Laws

In the wake of *Whitner v. South Carolina* and the state's Child Protection Reform of 1996, South Carolina now requires mandatory reporting of cases suspected of abuse or neglect involving unborn, yet viable, fetuses, defined as 24 weeks gestation with an illegal drug in their system (Condon, 1998). The policy distinguishes between a prebirth protocol and a postbirth protocol. The prebirth protocol is (1) reporting the incident, (2) investigation by the Department of Social Services, (3) treatment/intervention/documentation, and (4) continued services by the Department of Social Services after the birth of the child as stated in the postbirth protocol. The postbirth protocol is (1) reporting/investigation, and (2) an amnesty-type program (the mother is asked to seek treatment and counseling voluntarily). The protocol gives mother a chance to sober up; failure to rehabilitate will cause the mother to be prosecuted for violation of criminal child abuse and child neglect.

In Minnesota the definition of child abuse has been amended to include prenatal exposure to drugs [Minn. Stat. Ann., § 626.556 (1990)]. If the results on a toxicology screen of either mother or child are positive, the physicians are required to report the results to the Department of Health, and local welfare agencies are then mandated to investigate and make any appropriate referrals (§ 626.5561). If a woman is still pregnant and refuses to cooperate, civil commitment is authorized under Minnesota statute 253B.05. However, a recent study of the actual implementation of the Minnesota law concluded that Minnesota in effect has eschewed the punitive provisions embodied in the law (Pearson & Thoennis, 1996).

Other states, such as Florida, Massachusetts, Oklahoma, Utah, and Illinois have also included fetal abuse under their mandatory child abuse reporting laws.[4] Florida responded to the crack/cocaine hysteria of the late 1980s by amending its child abuse laws to underscore the specific risks associated with maternal drug use. Simultaneously, the Department of Health and Rehabilitative Services issued a policy requiring reports of newborn drug dependency and created a specialized unit to investigate drug-affected infants. Although these laws and policies established Florida's reputation as being tough on maternal substance abuse, many child protection service (CPS) workers and legal personnel in a study by Pearson and Thoennis (1996) characterized Florida as being a lenient climate due to gaps in the law, treatment voids, and court backlogs. CPS workers reported that most drug-affected infants were released to their mothers with a voluntary treatment contract and with no penalty for failure to comply. Lack of resources for case supervision, court oversight, and treatment also contributed to limited interventions. However, CPS workers also reported that due to the discretionary testing law in Florida, testing occurs only in publicly funded health care facilities among poor and nonwhite populations, thus mirroring the earlier race and social class bias reported by Chasnoff et al. (1990).

Illinois amended its child abuse reporting laws in 1989 so that any child born with any illegal drug in its system would be defined as a "neglected child." This eliminated the need to prove any harmful effects of maternal cocaine use and created the legal basis for filing a neglect petition. However, the Pearson and Thoennis study (1996) reports that these statutory changes did not revolutionize case handling. Administrators said that while reports of positive toxicology were routinely indicated by the CPS agency, such reports were often perceived to be racist and not acted upon unless there was other evidence of parental insufficiency. Most cases reported to CPS were not opened for services, and mothers were urged to explore drug treatment sources on their own. When placement was made, it tended to be with relatives. Finally, there was a perceived lack of treatment resources and an underuse of existing ones. Similar relative placements were made in the large majority of cases in a large urban county in California, often with the mother residing in the same house (Sagatun-Edwards, 1996).

In California, the Perinatal Substance Abuse Services Act of 1990 emphasizes the desirability of medical services and drug treatment, and it does *not* endorse mandatory reporting of positive toxicology screens. This law modified the existing child abuse reporting laws in California to specify that a positive toxicology screen at the time of delivery of an infant is not in and of itself a sufficient basis for reporting child abuse or neglect. Instead, any indication of maternal substance abuse will lead to an assessment of the needs of the mother and her infant. Any indication of risk to the child as determined by the assessment will then be reported to county welfare departments (Perinatal Substance Abuse Services Act of 1990, effective July 1, 1991; California Senate Bill 2669).[5]

The state of Washington treats perinatal substance abuse as a public health issue. The state has eschewed legislation requiring routine testing of babies, relying instead on hospitals to flag, test, and report cases to CPS when the risk of child abuse is high. As a result of the Omnibus Drug Act of 1989, Washington made pregnant women a priority for treatment of chemical dependency (Pearson and Thoennis, 1996). Drug-exposed infants are referred primarily when other children and the family have already been referred to CPS for other reasons.

Legal Criteria for Removing a Child from the Parents

In determining what to do with a child, social services and juvenile courts in all states must now follow the new directives of Public Law 105-89, or the Adoption and Safe Families Act of 1997. This is an amendment of the earlier Adoption Assistance and Child Welfare Act of 1980, which required states to exercise reasonable efforts to avoid out of home placement.[6] Under the new law, children's safety is now the paramount concern that must guide all child welfare services. State welfare agencies are mandated to make reasonable efforts to prevent a child's placement in foster care, and if foster care is necessary, the state must make efforts to reunite the family during specified time periods. If such reunification is not possible, the law further requires permanency planning for the child, which may include termination of parental rights to make adoption possible. The juvenile courts are required to determine whether or not the agency has made these efforts (McCullough, 1991). However, reasonable efforts toward reunification are not required if the child has been subjected to aggravated circumstances, if a parent has murdered or been responsible for the unlawful death of another, if a parent has committed a felony assault that resulted in serious bodily injury to the child, or if a parent has had his or her parental rights involuntarily terminated before. Where reasonable efforts to reunite have been made, permanency hearings must be held within twelve months, down from the earlier eighteen months. Substance abuse during pregnancy is not addressed specifically in the act, except that it calls for expansion of child welfare demonstration projects, including projects that are designed to "identify and address parental substance abuse problems that endanger children and result in the placement of children in foster care, including placement of children in residential facilities" (Adoption and Safe Families Act of 1997, § 301). Whereas the earlier act emphasized the importance of placing children with their biological parents, this act now emphasizes the safety of children. While an earlier longitudinal study in California found that in cases where the child is now 5 to 6 years old, it was not uncommon for such reunification to be attempted more than once (Sagatun-Edwards, 1996), the timeline for drug-exposed infants in California has now been shortened to six months in order to provide for permanent placement at an earlier date.

Despite the mandated reunification policy, drug-exposed cases tend to show a higher risk of removal (Leslie, 1993), court involvement (Sagatun-Edwards et al., 1995), and foster care placement (Feig, 1990). Taylor (1995) found that it was much more common for a drug-abusing parent to lose the right to visitation and custody than for nonabusing parents to do so. The assumption that drug use during pregnancy causes "imminent" danger to the fetus reinforces the perception of pregnant women's drug use as child abuse and neglect (Pollitt, 1990). According to Beckett (1995), the majority of the lower and appellate civil court rulings have supported the state's removal of infants from their mother's custody based on a positive drug toxicology.

SUBSTANCE ABUSE TREATMENT AND PRE- AND POSTNATAL CARE

Very few adequate drug rehabilitation services are available for pregnant substance abusers or for mothers with young children, and the ones that are available may not serve their particular needs. Opponents and proponents of criminalization and/or juvenile court involvement alike agree that the most effective solution to the problem of prenatal drug abuse is drug treatment and rehabilitation. The major problem here is that appropriate drug treatment programs are often unavailable or unaffordable, and when they are available, there are long waiting lists to get in.

Existing treatment programs often discriminate against pregnant women. In a survey of seventy-eight drug treatment programs in New York City, Chavkin (1991) found that 54 percent refused to treat pregnant women; of those that treated pregnant women, 67 percent refused to treat pregnant women on Medicaid, and 87 percent had no services available for Medicaid patients who were both pregnant and addicted to crack. Although this survey is now several years old and more treatment facilities have become available to pregnant women, the situation is still much the same. The financial cost involved alone is one reason that court-ordered drug rehabilitation services through the juvenile court currently may be the only way that a mother can afford to undergo drug rehabilitation programs (Larson, 1991).

Some states have moved toward detaining women during their pregnancy. The Wisconsin legislature recently passed a law that will allow authorities to protect fetuses by detaining pregnant women who abuse drugs or alcohol. The courts can order the expectant mother confined to a treatment program, a physician's office, a hospital, or a relative's home (Pasternak, 1998). In South Dakota it is now legal to commit substance abusers involuntarily for almost the entire period of their pregnancy, and such a law has been in existence in Minnesota since 1988 (Pasternak, 1998). As described earlier, the current protocol in South Carolina is to prosecute women for violation of criminal child abuse and child neglect statutes if they fail to rehabilitate. However, such laws, which punish women if they do not seek treatment, may easily backfire. Women may be afraid to consider such treatment if they know that they will be detained. Ideally, what is needed are free prenatal care and drug counseling in a nonpunitive setting, available to all, and geared to different ethnic and cultural subgroups. One of the most effective weapons against infant mortality is early, high-quality, comprehensive prenatal care.

CONCLUSIONS

A wide variety of legal responses to maternal substance abuse have been discussed: from criminal prosecution under existing drug-delivery laws and criminal child abuse and child neglect statutes, the constitutional issues involved in creating new fetal abuse legislation, to juvenile court jurisdiction and mandatory testing and reporting, to child protective services. Any legal response should depend on the gains to the fetuses and children relative to the harms to maternal rights that might arise from such a policy. Although the health of a fetus is important, criminalizing fetal abuse in most cases will not serve the intended purpose. It would probably jeopardize, rather than secure, the fetal health. Women at risk would not seek medical advice, for fear of being punished and of losing their children. More important, the mother's constitutional guarantees of right to liberty and privacy would be violated. The constitutionally protected rights to liberty, privacy, and equality prohibit any legal recognition of the fetus that would diminish women's decision-making autonomy of their right to bear children. Criminalization of conduct during pregnancy is simply a wrong policy; it is unconstitutional, sexist, and serves no social policy purpose.

Protection of children after birth is important. The states should have the right to interfere under juvenile court jurisdiction once family maintenance programs and other treatment forms of intervention have been explored. Infants who have severe symptoms of drug addiction and whose parents are unable to care for them should be reported to the child protective services. However, this should only be a last resort, and mothers should not be detained simply for failing treatment. Any intervention on behalf of the drug-exposed infant must be predicated on other indications of future harm, not past prenatal use. Such indicators might include the mother's failure to care for the siblings, unwillingness to participate in a drug treatment program and parenting classes, and the unavailability of a support system. The goal should always be to provide pregnant women with effective drug treatment and comprehensive pre- and postnatal care so that they may maintain custody of their own children. Intervention should be limited to protect children who are at great risk, so that loss of constitutional rights and societal costs may be prevented.

In general, the best policy to be followed is the one in the state of Washington which treats perinatal substance abuse as a public health problem. Free and nonpunitive pre- and postnatal care should ideally be available to all. Government expansion of educational and medical services aimed at all pregnant and especially substance-abusing women will avoid the infringement on maternal privacy rights and in the long run prove less costly and intrusive than criminal liability and/or long-term juvenile court intervention.

NOTES

1. State codes containing feticide statutes include: Cal. Penal Code, § 187 (1986); Ill. Ann. Stat. Ch. 38, § 9-1.1 (1985); Iowa Code Ann., § 707.7. (1979); Mich. Comp. Laws Ann., § 705.322 (1968); Miss. Code. Ann. § 97-3-37 (1973); N.H. Rev. Stat. Ann, § 585: 13 (1974); Okla. Stat. Ann. Tit. 21, § 713 (1983); Utah Code Ann. § 76-5-201 (1983); Wash. Rev. Code Ann. § 9A. 32.060 (1977); Wis. Stat. Ann. § 940.04 (1987).

2. Organizations supporting the petition for writ of certiorari as *amici curiae* in *Whitner v. South Carolina* were the National Association of Alcoholism and Drug Abuse Counselors, South Carolina Association of Alcoholism and Drug Abuse Counselors, American College of Obstetricians and Gynecologists, National Association of Social Workers, Inc., American Nurses Association, South Carolina Nurses Association, American Medical Women's Association, National Association for Families and Addiction Research and Education, Association for Medical Education and Research in Substance Abuse, American Academy on Physician and Patient, Society of General Internal Medicine, National Council on Alcoholism and Drug Dependency, Inc., National Center for Youth Law, Legal Services for Prisoners with Children, Coalition on Addiction, Pregnancy, and Parenting, NOW Legal Defense and Education Fund, Legal Action Center, Women's Law Project, Drug Policy Foundation, and Alliance for South Carolina's Children (Tracy et al., 1997). Organizations joining in a reply brief in support of petition for a writ of certiorari for both Whitner and Crawley were the Center for Constitutional Rights and the American Civil Liberties Union of South Carolina Foundation, Inc. (Olshansky et al., 1997).

3. These organizations include the Children's Defense Fund, the American Public Health Association, the American Medical Association, the American Nurses Association, the Center for the Future of Children, the National Association on Alcoholism and Drug Abuse, the National Black Women's Health Project, and the National Association for Perinatal Addiction Research.

4. Fla. Stat. Ann., § 415.503 (Supp. 1988); Mass. Laws Ann. Ch.119, § 51A (West Supp. 1988); Omnibus Crime Bill, Ch. No. 290, H.F. No. 59, Minn. Stat. 1988 at 626.5561 and 5562; Okla. Stat. Ann. Tit. 21, § 846 (A) (West Supp. 1988); Utah Code Ann. § 78-36-3.5 (1989 Cum. Supp); Ill. H.B. 2590, P.A. 86-659 § 3 (1989).

5. Perinatal Substance Abuse Services Act of 1990, effective July 1, 1991; California Senate Bill, 2669.

6. Adoption and Safe Families Act of 1997, Public Law 105-89, 42 U.S.C. (ASFA).

REFERENCES

BALISY, S. (1987). Maternal substance abuse: The need to provide legal protection for the fetus. *Southern California Law Review, 60*, 1209–1238.

BECKETT, K. (1995). Fetal rights and "crack moms": Pregnant women in the war on drugs. *Contemporary Drug Problems, 22*, 587–612.

BINGOL, N., SCHUSTER, C., FUCHS, M., ISOSUB, S., TURNER, G., STONE, R., & GROMISCH, D. (1987). The influence of socioeconomic factors on the occurrence of fetal alcohol syndrome. *Advances in Alcohol and Substance Abuse, 6*(4), 105–118.

CALIFORNIA PENAL CODE. (1977). St. Paul, MN: West Publishing.

CHASNOFF, I. J., BURNS, W. J., SCHNOLL, S. H., & BURNS, K. A. (1985). Cocaine use in pregnancy. *New England Journal of Medicine, 393*(11), 666–669.

CHASNOFF, I. J., GRIFFITH, D. R., MACGREGOR, S., DIRKES, K., & BURNS, K. A. (March, 1986). Temporal patterns of cocaine use in pregnancy: Perinatal outcome. *Journal of the American Medical Association, 261*(12), 1741–1744.

CHASNOFF, I. J., LANDRESS, H. J., & BARRETT, M. E. (1990). The prevalence of illicit drug or alcohol during pregnancy and discrepancies in mandatory reporting in Pinellas County, Florida. *New England Journal of Medicine, 322*(17), 1202–1206.

CHAVKIN, W. (1991). Testimony presented to House Select Committees on Children, Youth and Families. U.S. House of Representatives. New York: Columbia University School of Public Health.

CONDON, C. (1998, April). *Use of illegal drugs detected pre-birth.* Columbia, SC: The State of South Carolina, Office of the Attorney General.

CONDON, C., MCINTOSH, J., ZELENKA, D., AVANT, D., & DELOACH, C. R. (1997). Brief in opposition to petition for writ of certiorari. *Whitner v. State of South Carolina, and Crawley v. Moore,* No. 97-1562, U.S. Supreme Court, October Term, 1997.

DARO, D., & MCCURDY, K. (1992, August). *Current trends in child abuse reporting and fatalities: NCPCA's 1991 annual fifty state survey.* Chicago: National Committee for Prevention of Child Abuse.

DIXON, S. (1989). Effects of transplantal exposure to cocaine and methamphetamine on the neonate. *Western Journal of Medicine, 150,* 436–442.

FARR, K. A. (1995). Fetal abuse and the criminalization of behavior during pregnancy. *Crime and Delinquency, 41*(2), 235–245.

FEIG, L. (1990). *Drug exposed infants and children: Service needs and policy questions.* Working paper. Office of Social Services Policy, Division of Children, Youth and Family Policy, Office of the Assistant Secretary for Planning and Evaluation. Washington, DC: U.S. Department of Health and Human Services.

GOMBY, D., & SHIONO, P. (1991). Estimating the number of substance-exposed infants. *The Future of Children, 1*(1), 17–26.

GUSTAFSON, N. (1991). Pregnant chemically dependent women: The new criminals. *Affilia, 6,* 61–73.

HARVARD LAW REVIEW ASSOCIATION. (1998, March). Note: Material rights and fetal wrongs: The case against the criminalization of "fetal abuse." *Harvard Law Review, 101,* 994–1015.

HOWARD, J., KROPENSKE, V., & TYLER, R. (1986). The long term effects on neurodevelopment in infants exposed prenatally to PCP. *National Institute of Drug Abuse Monograph Series, 64,* 237–251.

HURT, H., BRODSKY, N. L., BRAITMAN, L. E., & GIANNETTA, G. (1995, July–August). Natal status of infants of cocaine users and control subjects: A prospective comparison. *Journal of Perinatology, 15*(14), 297–305.

HUTCHINS, E. (1997). Drug use during pregnancy. *Drug Issues, 27,* 463–465.

INCIARDI, J., LOCKWOOD, D., & POTTIEGER, A. (1993). *Women and crack cocaine.* New York: Macmillan.

LARSON, C. (1991). Overview of state legislative and judicial responses. *The Future of Children, 1*(1), 73–83.

LESLIE, B. (1993). *Parental crack use: Demographic, familial and child welfare perspectives: A Toronto study.* North York, Ontario, Canada: Children's Aid Society of Metropolitan Toronto.

LESTER, B. M., ET AL. (1997). Data base of studies of prenatal cocaine exposure and child outcome. *Drug Issues, 27,* 487–585.

LUTIGER, B., GRAHAM, K., EINARSON, T., & KOREN, G. (1991). The relationship between gestational cocaine use and pregnancy outcome: A meta-analysis. *Teratology, 44,* 405–414.

MATHIAS, R. (1992). Developmental effects of prenatal drug exposure may be overcome by postnatal environment. *NIDA Notes, 7*(1), 14–17.

MCCULLOUGH, C. (1991). The child welfare response. *The Future of Children, 1*(1), 61–72.

MCNULTY, N. (1987–1988). Pregnancy police: The health policy and legal implications of punishing pregnant women for harm to their fetuses. *Review of Law and Social Change, 16*(2), 277–319.

OLSHANSKY, B., DAVIS, L., PALTROW, L., PAUL-EMILE, K., & WISE, C. R. (1997). Reply brief in support of petition for a writ of certiorari. *Whitner v. South Carolina, and Crawley v. Moore*, no. 97-1562, U.S. Supreme Court, October Term, 1997.

PALTROW, L. (1990). When becoming pregnant is a crime. *Criminal Justice Ethics, 9*(1), 41–47.

PALTROW, L. (1992). *Criminal prosecutions of women for their behavior during pregnancy.* New York: Center for Reproductive Law and Policy.

PASTERNAK, J. (1998, May 2). Wisconsin o.k's civil detention for fetal abuse. *Los Angeles Times,* pp. A1, A13.

PEARSON, J., & THOENNIS, N. (1996). What happens to pregnant substance abusers and their babies? *Juvenile and Family Court Journal, 1,* 15–28.

PETITTI, D., & COLEMAN, M. (1990). Cocaine and the risk of low birth weight. *American Journal of Public Health, 80*(1), 25–28.

POLLITT, K. (1990). Fetal rights: A new assault on feminism. *The National, 247*(12), 455–460.

RICHARDSON, G. & DAY, N. (1991, July–August). Maternal and neonatal effects of moderate use of cocaine during pregnancy. *Neurotoxicology and Teratology, 13,* 455–460.

RICKHOFF, T., & CUKJATI, E. (1989). Protecting the fetus from maternal drug and alcohol abuse: A proposal for Texas. *St. Mary's Law Journal, 21*(2), 259–300.

ROBERTSON, J. (1989, August). *American Bar Association Journal,* p. 38.

ROBERTS, D. (1991). Punishing drug addicts who have babies: Women of color, equality and the rights of privacy. *Harvard Law Review, 104*(7), 1419–1482.

ROBIN-VERGEER, B. I. (1990). The problem of the drug exposed newborn: A return to principled intervention. *Stanford Law Review, 42*(3), 745–809.

SAGATUN-EDWARDS, I. (1996). *Family reunification for drug-exposed infants: Interim report.* Grant 95-9239. Los Altos, CA: Packard Foundation.

SAGATUN-EDWARDS, I. (1997). Crack babies, moral panic, and the criminalization of behavior during pregnancy. In E. Jensen and J. Gerber (Eds.), *The construction and impact of the war on drugs.* Cincinnati, OH: Anderson Publishing.

SAGATUN-EDWARDS, I., SAYLOR, C., & SHIFFLETT, B. (1995). Drug exposed infants in the social welfare system and the juvenile court. *Child Abuse and Neglect: The International Journal, 19*(1), 83–91.

TAYLOR, M. (1995). Parent's use of drugs as a factor in award of custody of children, visitation rights, or termination of parental rights. *American Law Reports, 5,* 535—668.

TRACY, C., FRIETSCHE, S., ABRAHAMSON, D., BOYD. G., & RISHER, M. (1997). On petition of writ of certiorari. *Whitner v. State of South Carolina,* no. 97-1562, U.S. Supreme Court, October Term, 1997.

TUBOKU-METZGER, A. J., ET AL. (1996). Cardiovascular effects of cocaine in neonates exposed prenatally. *American Journal of Perinatology, 13,* 1–20.

U.S. GENERAL ACCOUNTING OFFICE. (1994, April). *Foster care: Parental drug use has alarming impact on young children.* Washington, DC: Report to the Chairman, Subcommittee on Ways and Means, House of Representatives.

VOLPE, J. J. (1992, August). Effects of cocaine use on the fetus. *New England Journal of Medicine, 327,* 399–407.

WESTON, D. R., IVENS, B., ZUCKERMAN, B., JONES, C., & LOPEZ, R. (1989). Drug exposed babies: Research and clinical issues. *National Center for Clinical Infant Programs Bulletin, 9*(5), 7.

WOODS, N. S., ET AL. (1993). Cocaine use during pregnancy: Maternal depressing symptoms and infant neurobehavior over the first month. *Infant Behavior and Development, 16,* 83–92.

WRIGHT, L. (1990). Fetus vs. mother: Criminal liability for maternal substance abuse during pregnancy. *Wayne Law Review, 36,* 1285–1317.

CASES

Chambess v. Fairtrace, 158 Ill. App. 3d 325, 511 N.E. 2d 839 (1987).

Commonwealth of Kentucky v. Connie Welch, 864 S.W. 2d 280 (1993).

Crawley v. Evatt, Mem. Op. No. 97-MO-117 (S.C. December 1, 1997).

Eisenstadt v. Baird, 405 U.S. 438 (1972).

Griswold v. Connecticut, 381 U.S. 479 (1965).

Grodin v. Grodin, 102 Mich. App. 369, 301 N.W. 2d 869 (1981).

In re Baby X, 97 Mich. App. 111, 293 N.W. 2d 736 (1980).

In re Stevens, 178 Cal. Rptr. 525, Cal. Ct. App. (1981).

In re Troy D., 215 Cal. App. 3d 889, 263 Cal. Rptr. 868 (1989).

Johnson v. Florida, 602 So. 2d 1288, Fla. (1992).

Reyes v. Superior Court, 75 Cal App. 3d 214, 141 Cal. Rptr. 912 (1977).

Roe v. Wade, 410 U.S. 113 (1973).

Sheriff v. Encoe, 110 Nev. 1317, 885 p.2d 596 (1994).

Webster, 109 S. Ct. 3040 (1980).

Whitner v. South Carolina, 328 S.C. 1, 492 S.E. 2d 777 (S.C. 1997; 1996 WL 393164).

11

HIV Disease and Women Offenders

Arthur J. Lurigio, James A. Swartz, and Ciuinal Jones

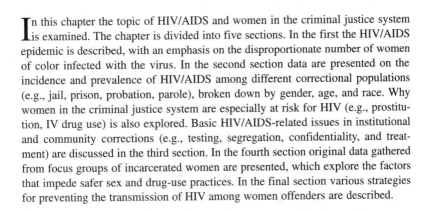

In this chapter the topic of HIV/AIDS and women in the criminal justice system is examined. The chapter is divided into five sections. In the first the HIV/AIDS epidemic is described, with an emphasis on the disproportionate number of women of color infected with the virus. In the second section data are presented on the incidence and prevalence of HIV/AIDS among different correctional populations (e.g., jail, prison, probation, parole), broken down by gender, age, and race. Why women in the criminal justice system are especially at risk for HIV (e.g., prostitution, IV drug use) is also explored. Basic HIV/AIDS-related issues in institutional and community corrections (e.g., testing, segregation, confidentiality, and treatment) are discussed in the third section. In the fourth section original data gathered from focus groups of incarcerated women are presented, which explore the factors that impede safer sex and drug-use practices. In the final section various strategies for preventing the transmission of HIV among women offenders are described.

The current chapter is about HIV disease among women in the criminal justice system. The characteristics of women under correctional supervision and those of women with HIV and AIDS mirror each other in important ways. Both groups consist of disproportionate numbers of poor women of color. Women in both groups are also more likely to use intravenous drugs and to have sex with intravenous drug users (American Correctional Association, 1990). The overlap between these two groups has influenced the content and organization of this chapter. Hence, in several places, our discussions regarding HIV transmission and prevention transcend women offenders and pertain to all women, especially women of color, particularly African-American women, one of the fastest-growing segments of both the HIV/AIDS and the criminal justice populations in the United States (Chesney-Lind, 1995). In addition, our suggestions for HIV program implementation, although discussed in the context of a HIV program for women inmates, are also germane to HIV programs for incarcerated men.

The chapter is divided into four major sections. In the first section we describe the causes of HIV and the prevalence of HIV disease in general and among women and women of color. In the second section we examine HIV and drug use, present data on HIV and women in prison, and discuss the value of drug treatment in stemming the spread of HIV. The third section focuses on HIV education and findings from a study of an HIV education program for women probationers. In the fourth section we enumerate practical guidelines for developing and implementing HIV programming for women in jail and prison settings.

SPREAD OF HIV DISEASE

Infection with the human immunodeficiency virus (HIV), the cause of acquired immunodeficiency syndrome (AIDS), is perhaps the most profound public health crisis that the nation and the world will ever face (Institute of Medicine, 1988). In 1996, AIDS was the eighth-leading cause of death overall in this country, the second-leading cause of death among Americans aged 25 to 44, and the leading cause of death among African-Americans between the ages of 25 and 44 (Centers for Disease Control, 1996a, 1998b). Since the first AIDS cases were reported to the Centers for Disease Control in 1981, scientists have learned a great deal about the etiology, clinical manifestations, and progression of HIV disease (Cohen, 1998).

HIV is a retrovirus that destroys the body's T-1 helper cells, which are the mainstays of the immune system. Untreated HIV disease results in significant immunosuppression that is irreversible and inexorable, rendering infected persons highly susceptible to a variety of opportunistic microbes and cancers that typically are harmless to persons with healthy immune systems (Fauci, 1988). HIV is spread through unprotected sexual contact, transfusions of infected blood or blood products, and perinatal passage from infected mother to fetus. AIDS is the late or end stage of the clinical spectrum of HIV disease, which includes asymptomatic HIV infection and acute HIV-related illnesses without life-threatening sequela. Estimates suggest that 78 to 100 percent of HIV-infected persons will progress to AIDS within fifteen years following their initial exposure to the virus (Douglas & Pinsky, 1992).

As of December 1997, 641,086 AIDS cases had been reported and 390,692 persons had died from AIDS in the United States (Centers for Disease Control, 1998a). An estimated 250,000 Americans are living with AIDS and between 650,000 and 900,000 are HIV positive. Because of successful prevention efforts that target persons at higher risk for HIV infection and the introduction of efficacious combination drug therapies to slow the progression of HIV disease, the incidence of AIDS is increasing at a yearly rate of 5 percent, compared with yearly rates of 65 to 95 percent during the early years of the HIV epidemic (Centers for Disease Control, 1998a).

HIV Disease and Women

Women have accounted for an increasing number of newly reported AIDS cases in the United States (Centers for Disease Control, 1997). The spread of HIV through sexual intercourse occurs more readily from men to women than from women to men. Women's risk of infection through heterosexual contact increases when they engage in anal sex or when they have a vaginal infection at the time of vaginal intercourse. Women with HIV are more likely than uninfected women to contract more often—and more severe—cases of vaginal infections, genital ulcers, genital warts, pelvic inflammatory disease, and cervical cancer.

A number of HIV-related diseases are different in women than they are in men. Men with AIDS, for example, are eight times more likely than women with AIDS to develop Kaposi's sarcoma, one of the AIDS-defining illnesses. Women with AIDS, however, are significantly more likely than men with AIDS to develop thrush as well as genital cancers, warts, and herpes (New Mexico AIDS InfoNet Fact Sheet, 1997).

HIV can be transmitted from women to children perinatally during pregnancy, labor, or delivery or postpartum through breast feeding. Exactly when transmission occurs from mother to child is unknown (Rogers, Mofenson, & Moseley, 1994). Women who contract HIV have approximately a 20 to 30 percent chance of having an HIV-infected child (Arras, 1990), and perinatal transmission of HIV is higher in minority women (Selik, Castro, & Pappaioanou, 1988).

AIDS is the seventh-leading cause of death among children aged 1 to 4 in the United States. By 1995, nearly 7000 cumulative pediatric AIDS cases had been reported in the United States; 82 percent of the cases involved children of color. The overwhelming majority (90 percent) of pediatric AIDS cases were the result of maternal transmission of HIV. Among women who transmitted HIV perinatally, 60 percent had contracted HIV through injection drug use or sex with an injection drug user (Centers for Disease Control, 1995b).

Rates of HIV infection and AIDS among male and female inmates in jails and prisons are significantly higher than the rates found in the general population. The rate of confirmed AIDS cases in the U.S. population is 0.08 percent, whereas the rate among state and federal prison inmates is 0.51 percent. Jail and prison inmates with the highest rates of HIV infection were arrested for drug offenses (and hence more likely to be using drugs at the time of admission) and were more likely to report that they had used drugs in the month before their current offenses (Bureau of Justice Statistics, 1997). The rate of HIV infection is higher among women state prison inmates than it is among men state prison inmates, 4.0 percent versus 2.6 percent. Moreover, between 1991 and 1995, the number of HIV-infected female prisoners increased at a rate of 88 percent; over the same time period, the number of HIV-infected male prisoners increased 28 percent.

Incarcerated females with HIV are concentrated in five northeastern states, each with infection rates among women inmates of 10 percent or higher: New York (23 percent), Rhode Island (15 percent), Connecticut (13 percent), New Hampshire (11 percent), and Massachusetts (10 percent). New York was the only state in which the infection rate among men state prison inmates exceeded 10 percent (Bureau of Justice Statistics, 1997).

Rates of HIV infection and AIDS among arrestees also have been found to be higher than the rates in the general population. A study of 831 adult male and 162 adult female arrestees in six Illinois counties, for example, found that the HIV infection rates in the sample were higher than the general population rates from the same Illinois counties. The rates for male and female arrestees were comparable: approximately 2 percent of the urine samples collected from the men and women tested positive for HIV.

HIV Disease and Women of Color

The HIV epidemic has had a devastating impact on women of color throughout the world (Maldonado, 1997). Women from developing countries constitute more than 90 percent of the cumulative AIDS cases among women worldwide (UNAIDS, 1996). Paralleling epidemiologic trends in the developing world, women of color in the United States are disproportionately affected by HIV disease. Although women of color represent approximately one-fourth of the female population in this country, they accounted for 77 percent of the new AIDS cases and 76 percent of the cumulative AIDS cases reported among women in 1995 (U.S. Department of Health and Human Services, 1995). The most rapidly expanding transmission category among women is heterosexual contact with HIV-infected men (Conrad, 1997).

The HIV epidemic has struck particularly hard at women in the African-American community. By year end 1995, for example, African-American women constituted 12 percent of the country's female population but accounted for approximately 55 percent of both the new and the cumulative AIDS cases found among women (Centers for Disease Control, 1995b). In 1995, the case rate among African-American women was 59 per 100,000, 16 times higher than the rate for white women and more than twofold higher than the rate for Hispanic/Latino women (Centers for Disease Control, 1995b). Estimates suggest that by the year 2000, African-American women will be 20 times more likely than non-African-American women to have AIDS (Walker, 1997). Valleroy (1998) recently reported that HIV prevalence among young African-American women is seven times higher than it is among young white women and eight times higher than it is among young Hispanic women.

The higher rates of HIV infection among women of color might be attributable to several factors, including their greater risk of contact with intravenous drug users, which we discuss in the next section, their negative perceptions of condom use (e.g., belief that condoms are symbols of sexual promiscuity), and their difficulty in maintaining stable sexual partnerships because of the significant gender imbalance in the African-American community, especially in the lowest-income areas (Mays & Cochran, 1988). Kline, Kline, and Oken (1992) reported that women of color weighed their chances of contracting HIV against expectations that condom use would be physically uncomfortable for them and would reduce their sexual pleasure. Among minority women who deal every day with a host of social problems such as poverty, violence, crime, and drug use, the risk of contracting HIV can seem relatively remote or trivial (Nyamathi & Lewis, 1991). In addition, Quinn (1993) found that a high percentage of poor women lacked knowledge about HIV protective behaviors but only half indicated they were "worried about getting AIDS."

Women's use of condoms to prevent HIV is quite low in general. Osmond et al. (1993), for example, estimated that the majority of women use condoms in fewer than half of the occasions in which they have sexual intercourse. To decrease their own HIV risk through condom use, women must influence the sexual practices of men, an often serious and frustrating challenge (Cochran, 1989; Ellerbrock, Bush, Chamberland, & Oxtoby, 1991). Many men, especially men of color, are reluctant to use condoms because of stereotypic cultural notions about masculinity that militate against such use (Osmond, et al., 1993; Peterson, Catania, Dolcini, & Faigeles, 1993). The lack of gender equality and socially encouraged passivity in heterosexual relationships might also preclude women from asking their male partners to use condoms (Amaro, 1995; Stein, 1990). Furthermore, women might perceive that such demands imply a lack of trust in their partners' sexual fidelity, causing conflicts in relationships that can have severe financial and emotional consequences for women (Kane, 1990; Shayne & Kaplan, 1991). And studies have shown that women's demands for condom use can result in physical and sexual assaults (O'Leary & Jemmott, 1995; Wermuch, Ham, & Robbins, 1992).

Osmond et al. (1993) reported that positive attitudes toward condom use were unrelated to reductions in women's risky sexual behaviors. Instead, the researchers found that a combination of HIV knowledge, motivation to reduce HIV risk, high self-esteem, and assertiveness in their sexual relationships influenced women's HIV-related sexual practices.

HIV AND DRUG USE

Unlike the developing world, in which three-fourths of HIV infections stem from unprotected heterosexual contact, intravenous drug use plays a central role in the spread of HIV in the United States, especially among women (Maldonado, 1997). Nearly three-fourths of new HIV infections overall are directly or indirectly attributable to illicit drug use (Kolata, 1995). Illicit drug users transmit HIV to each other through sharing HIV-contaminated needles or injection paraphernalia; through heterosexual contact with their uninfected, and often unsuspecting sexual partners; and through the exchange of sex for drugs, a behavior commonly seen among women who use crack/cocaine (McCoy, Miles, & Inciardi, 1995).

Women, Drugs, and HIV

In 1995, equal percentages of new AIDS cases among women were associated with injection drug use and heterosexual contact with an HIV-infected partner: 38 percent within each mode of transmission. More than one-fourth (27 percent) of all the women infected through heterosexual contact contracted HIV from having sex with injection drug users. Nearly half (47 percent) of the cumulative AIDS cases among women by 1995 were attributable to women's injection drug use; 78 percent of the cumulative AIDS cases stemming from injection drug use were among women of color (U.S. Department of Health and Human Services, 1995). Throughout the past decade, AIDS incidence among African-American women infected through injection drug use increased at a rate of 10 to 20 percent each year (Centers for Disease Control, 1998c). As data strongly suggest, therefore, the epicenter of the AIDS epidemic in the United States has shifted from the gay male population to drug addicts and their sex partners.

Offenders and HIV

The prevalence of drug use among offenders is significantly higher than it is among members of the general population (Leukefeld, 1985), which places offenders at greater risk for HIV infection. According to the Drug Use Forecasting Study, which has tested arrestees for drug use in more than twenty cities, the proportions of women testing positive for drugs often has equaled or exceeded those of men even for intravenous drug use (e.g., Decker & Rosenfeld, 1992).

HIV infection has been thoroughly documented among intravenous drug users, but researchers have reported increased risks of HIV disease among nonintravenous crack users as well. Booth, Watters, and Chitwood (1993), for example, reported that women who smoked crack/cocaine had more sexual partners and were more likely to engage in prostitution to obtain money for drugs than were women who did not smoke crack. Cocaine use also has been associated with the risk of contracting other sexually transmitted diseases (Rolfs, Goldberg, & Sharrar, 1990), the presence of which increases a person's susceptibility to HIV (Centers for Disease Control, 1997). Stall (1988) reported that heavy users of alcohol and noninjection drugs placed themselves at greater risk for HIV because of the disinhibitory effects that these substances exert on sexual behaviors. Whereas drug users accurately perceive their elevated HIV risk as a result of intravenous drug use, they tend to underestimate their risk of contracting HIV from unprotected sex (Kline & Strickler, 1993).

Over approximately the same time period that addicts and their sex partners have become the primary at-risk populations for HIV disease, staggering numbers of drug-abusing and drug-dependent persons have been processed through the criminal justice system (Belenko, 1990). Partly as a result of the most recent war on drugs and widely adopted mandatory minimum sentencing practices for drug crimes, state and federal prisons in the United States now house nearly 2 million offenders. Another 4 million offenders are on probation or parole supervision (Proband, 1998).

Incarcerated women are much more likely than men to be serving time for drug offenses (Bureau of Justice Statistics, 1994), an offense category that is related to higher rates of drug use. In particular, women offenders have very high rates of cocaine abuse and dependence. According to the 1997 Arrestee Drug Abuse Monitoring Program's annual report (National Institute of Justice, 1998), which is based on urinalysis results, adult female arrestees had higher rates of cocaine use in eighteen of the twenty-one reporting sites. They also had higher rates of heroin use compared with male arrestees in fifteen of the twenty-one reporting sites; however, these differences between men and women were not as large as they were for cocaine use.

A 1994 study of Illinois prison inmates was conducted by Treatment Alternatives for Safe Communities (TASC), which is a community-based, not-for-profit organization serving high-risk populations (including addicted offenders), and the Survey Research Laboratory of the University of Illinois. Men and women who entered the Illinois Department of Corrections at each of the state's four reception and classifications centers were randomly selected for in-depth interviews that explored their current and past drug use and their knowledge and attitudes regarding their risk for HIV infection.

Figure 1 shows the results for inmates' lifetime drug dependence. Women had a higher rate of lifetime dependence (i.e., ever dependent on the drug) on any drug (61 percent) compared with men (55 percent). Male admissions had higher rates of dependence on alcohol and marijuana. Drug-use findings for female admissions to Illinois prisons were consistent with the national ADAM result, that is, women had a much higher rate of lifetime dependence on cocaine (45 percent) than that of with men (27 percent). Moreover, according to the number of DSM-III R (American Psychiatric Association, 1987) symptoms reported, women had more severe drug dependencies than men.

The pattern and magnitude of the lifetime drug dependence found in the sample of Illinois prison admissions were very similar to the patterns of drug dependence found in

1995 for male and female arrestees from six Illinois counties (Illinois Criminal Justice Information Authority, 1996). Female arrestees had higher rates of lifetime dependence when all drugs were considered and were especially likely to be dependent on cocaine. And as would be expected, urinalysis results showed that women used cocaine at a much higher rate than men. In summarizing across the Illinois prisoner and arrestee studies, researchers noted that "…on average, approximately two-fifths of all adult Illinois males and three-fifths of all adult Illinois females who become involved with the criminal justice system are dependent on alcohol or other drugs at or near the time of their arrests" (Illinois Criminal Justice Information Authority, 1996, p. ix).

Drug-using female offenders are different from drug-using male offenders in other respects that compound their risk for HIV infection. Data that compared Chicago men (*n* = 7673) and women (*n* = 1929) who were referred for a TASC assessment over the past two years showed that women were more likely than men to report crack cocaine (48 percent compared with 29 percent) and injection drug use (8 percent compared with 5 percent). Other studies have found that criminally involved and addicted men and women also differ on how they are initiated into drug use, the length of time between initial use and drug dependency, and the likelihood of being involved with sex partners who also use drugs (e.g., Bowis, Griffiths, Gossop, & Strang, 1996; Hser, Anglin, & McGlothlin, 1987).

Women tend to be initiated into drug use by their boyfriends or husbands, whereas men are more likely to be initiated into drug use by their friends. After drug use has been initiated, women become addicted more quickly than men and are also more likely to be involved with sex partners who use drugs. Furthermore, women who inject drugs are also more likely than their male counterparts to report that they share needles with their partners.

These results indicate that female offenders are among the groups at greatest risk for HIV primarily because of their heavy use of drugs, especially cocaine, the exchange of sex

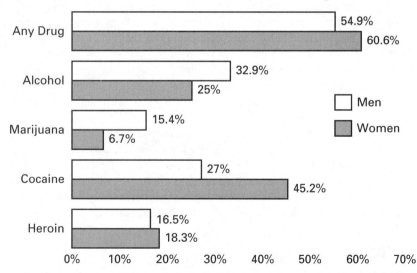

FIGURE 1   Comparison of the prevalence of lifetime drug dependence between men and women admitted to the Illinois Department of Corrections, by drug. (From Treatment Alternatives for Safe Communities, 1994.)

for drugs that often accompanies cocaine use (McCoy, Miles, & Inciardi, 1995), and their involvement with addicted men with whom they have sex and share injection equipment (Choi & Wermuch, 1991). Many women involved with addicted partners perceive themselves as being at low risk for HIV as long as they remain monogamous with their primary sex partners. Ethnographic studies (e.g., Ramos, Shain, & Johnson, 1995), however, suggest that addicted men often deceptively live nonmonogamous lives, placing themselves and their uninformed female partners at risk for HIV infection.

Drug Treatment and HIV

As we have just discussed, elevated HIV-risk among women offenders is directly or indirectly tied to drug use. Drug treatment, therefore, is an important means for controlling the spread of HIV in this highly vulnerable population (Batki & London, 1991; Brown & Needle, 1994; Guydish, Golden, & Hembry, 1991). The criminal justice system has great potential for encouraging women offenders to enroll in drug treatment programs and to obtain HIV-related services (e.g., HIV testing and counseling), which they would be less likely to do voluntarily. Moreover, addicts are often poorly motivated for treatment, and community-based drug treatment resources typically are scarce (Brown, 1990–1991). Hence, one of the best opportunities for engaging women addicts in drug treatment occurs while they are under the control of the criminal justice system.

Drug treatment programs for addicted women offenders have, historically, been designed "by men, for men" because of the preponderance of men in the criminal justice system and in need of drug interventions. Male-oriented drug treatment programs are generally inappropriate for and ineffective with women and have been characterized as hierarchical, punitive, and psychologically destructive for addicted women, who tend to have more serious self-esteem issues than those of addicted men (e.g., Ramlow, White, Watson, & Leukefeld, 1997). Consequently, drug treatment programs that are more suitable for women offenders are less confrontational and provide more nurturing experiences for participants.

In single-parent homes, women are more likely than men to bear the primary responsibility for raising children. To participate in drug-treatment programs, many women require child-care services. Because addicted women frequently live with and are strongly influenced by their addicted partners, women's drug treatment programs also must deal with the issue of how to manage this relationship (or terminate it) so that these women can achieve lasting recovery.

Treatment programs that are more sensitive to women's needs have become more available; however, they can be expensive if they include outpatient child-care arrangements or residential services that allow children to live with their mothers during treatment. Because of this expense and because men are still the preponderate population in the criminal justice system, it appears that drug-addicted and criminally involved women, and hence women at high risk for HIV infection, remain underserved.

Attitudes toward HIV

The 1994 Illinois Department of Corrections survey findings suggest that gender-sensitive HIV programs also need to respond to women's perceptions about HIV risk. Men and women inmates were significantly different in their attitudes toward HIV risk. Women were more likely to report that they would not have sex with a *new* partner unless he wore a condom but that they would have unprotected sex with their current partners. And, in general, higher proportions of women than men indicated that they were practicing safer sex and were more concerned about infecting someone else with HIV. At the same time, the women were almost three times more likely than the men to report that no matter what they did, they were ultimately going to be infected with HIV. Thus although more of the women than men inmates reported that they practiced safer sex, the women still felt that they were at high risk for contracting HIV, and many perceived that they were powerless to prevent themselves from contracting HIV.

According to a widely used model for understanding risk behavior, individuals are less likely to change their risk behaviors if they feel that doing so will have no positive consequences (Catania, Kegeles, & Coates, 1990). Hence HIV programs for women should focus on the fatalistic sense that they have regarding HIV infection, whereas programs for men need to address their unrealistic perceptions of invulnerability to HIV.

HIV EDUCATION

In the absence of a cure for or vaccine against HIV disease, prevention is crucial in combatting the HIV epidemic (Jemmott, Jemmott, & Fong, 1992; Fauci, 1988), a goal that is best achieved through education (Fineberg, 1988). The Institute of Medicine (1988) underscored the importance of educating various target populations at high risk for HIV because of injection drug use and unprotected sex, such as criminal offenders (Lanier & McCarthy, 1989). As Hammett and Moini (1990) have noted: "Education and training programs still represent the cornerstone of efforts to prevent transmission of HIV infection in prisons and jails, as well as in the population at large. In fact, the actual and potential role of education affects decisions on virtually all of the other AIDS issues and policy options in correctional facilities."

Because of the higher HIV risk of persons who come in contact with the criminal justice system, owing mostly to injection drug use and sex work, Hammett, Hunt, Gross, Rhodes, and Moini (1991) contended that "the CJS [criminal justice system] may assemble and identify a higher concentration of persons at risk for exposure to and transmission of HIV than will any other private or public agency" (p. 106). In a similar statement, the AIDS Research Institute (1995) declared that "prisons and jails would seem to be an ideal venue for drug treatment and education. There are more injection drug users in correctional facilities in the U.S. than in drug treatment centers, hospitals, or social services" (p. 1). Nonetheless, Hammett et al. (1991) found that the majority of corrections agencies did not provide comprehensive HIV education programs for offenders. Moreover, the percentage of state and federal prisons offering HIV education declined significantly from 1990 to 1994, and a large number of the programs relied on written materials rather on than live instruction, which is a more effective means of HIV prevention (Centers for Disease Control, 1996b).

Other researchers have stressed the importance of the criminal justice system in providing HIV education and referral services (e.g., Polonsky, Kerr, Harris, Gaiter, Fichtner, & Kennedy, 1994; Joint Subcommittee on AIDS in the Criminal Justice System, 1989; Lurigio, 1989). The relationship between high-risk behaviors and knowledge of HIV has been studied in both juvenile and adult offender populations (e.g., Morrison,

Baker, & Gillmore, 1994). And HIV education programs have been implemented success-fully in jail (Baxter, 1991) and in community corrections settings (Griffin, Lurigio, & Johnson, 1991).

HIV education for offenders can be quite effective. Lurigio, Petraitis, and Johnson (1992), for example, successfully educated probationers in Cook County (Chicago) about HIV. Offenders who participated in an HIV education session, compared with a control group of non-HIV-educated offenders, had more knowledge of HIV prevention and trans-mission and were more willing to undergo HIV testing, to use condoms, and to refrain from sharing needles. Other prevention programs aimed at increasing knowledge of HIV among offenders have had limited success, however. Among boot camp participants, for example, HIV education did not significantly affect offenders' perceived risk of HIV or attitudes toward high-risk sex activities (Burton, Marquart, Cuvelier, Alarid, & Hunter, 1993), which according to researchers, might be more difficult to change through HIV-intervention programs than are risky drug-use practices (e.g., Turner, Heather, & Moses, 1989).

HIV Education for Women Probationers

Jones and Lurigio (1996) evaluated an HIV education program for African-American women on probation. Brief education sessions, conducted as part of offenders' monthly reporting requirements, were designed to increase their knowledge about HIV and to reduce their risky behaviors. The researchers hypothesized that the participants would score significantly higher on an HIV knowledge test than a comparison group of women probationers and would retain that knowledge on follow-up assessment. Jones and Lurigio (1996) also explored why women fail to engage in risk-reduction behaviors despite their knowledge of HIV prevention strategies. To examine this question, they conducted extensive interviews with the study's participants, eliciting their attitudes toward safer sex practices and drug use and their decision-making styles in sexual relationships.

Jones and Lurigio (1996) found that the vast majority of women in the study were already knowledgeable about basic HIV facts. At pretest, more than 80 percent already knew that HIV can be transmitted by sharing needles and having unprotected sex and that it cannot be transmitted through casual contact (e.g., shaking hands). Significantly lower percentages of women at pretest gave correct responses about the chances of contracting HIV by donating blood or engaging in mutual masturbation. More important, more than two-thirds of the probationers at pretest believed than animal skin condoms were more effective than latex condoms in preventing HIV, and more than half of the women were incorrect about proper placement of a condom on a man's penis.

As predicted, the educated group's knowledge increased significantly at posttest, whereas the control group's did not. The attitudes and behaviors of the HIV-educated probationers also were more likely to change. At one-month follow-up, the educated group was more likely than the control group to report that they had bought condoms, had sex with condoms, and had asked their partners to use condoms since the education session. Moreover, the educated group was more likely to report that they were worried about contracting HIV and that they had been tested for HIV since the education session.

Interviews with women probationers identified a number of obstacles to safer sex practices. Contrary to conventional wisdom, several of the women believed that condom use would detract from *their* sexual pleasure but not necessarily from their partners' enjoyment.

As found in previous research, the women stated that they were afraid to ask their partners to use condoms because of the implications and consequences of such a request. In the words of one woman, "if I ask him [boyfriend] to use a condom, you know, he will think that I don't trust him anymore. It would be insulting to him…we might start fighting over it." Another probationer reported that "[asking her partner] to put on a condom would piss him off. He then starts to accuse me of sleeping around and starts hittin' on me, and [might] leave me for a few days."

With regard to effective HIV education programs for women offenders, probationers made two important observations. The first was that facts about HIV risk behaviors will be largely ignored by women who are actively using or addicted to illicit drugs. The overwhelming need to use drugs precludes women from "hearing" or applying any HIV-prevention measures. The women also reported that when they were "high" and "on the streets," obtaining drugs and surviving from one day to the next were immediate concerns, whereas HIV risk seemed a distant or obscure threat.

The second was that peer educators, especially those with seropositive status, are regarded as the most credible instructors. According to probationers, the educators' background and experiences are more important than the content of the sessions with regard to influencing their HIV-related behaviors. Offenders noted that messages about protection are particularly forceful when delivered by African-American women who had contracted HIV by engaging in unprotected sex or using intravenous drugs, the same behaviors that place them at risk for infection.

As Jones and Lurigio (1996) and other studies suggest, increasing HIV knowledge alone might be insufficient in decreasing women's risk of HIV contraction. Instead, interventions focused on women offenders must also increase their self-efficacy in making decisions with their male partners about condom use. In addition, factors that immediately affect women's well-being, such as lack of financial resources, shelter, and food, might cause them to view their risk of HIV as unimportant and far removed relative to other pressing concerns. Therefore, HIV-intervention programs in the criminal justice system must address these aspects of women's lives as well. Finally, educational efforts must focus on the power differential between men and women in sexual relationships, which has been posited as a factor in influencing women's high-risk sexual behaviors and another reason why their knowledge of HIV-prevention strategies might not affect their actual HIV-related behaviors (Stein, 1990).

HIV RISK-REDUCTION PROGRAM FOR WOMEN INMATES

TASC was awarded a three-year noncompetitive grant from the Centers for Disease Control to provide HIV education and outreach services to substance-abusing women offenders in the Cook County (Chicago) Sheriff's Female Furlough Program (SFFP). TASC's program, which is called Project Roots, was implemented in December 1997.

In partnership with the Cook County Department of Corrections, TASC serves a daily average of 70 women in Project Roots. Participants are required to report to Roots five days per week as a part of the SFFP pretrial diversion program and to remain drug-free. The program provides women from the SFFP with group HIV interventions that focus on the causes of high-risk behaviors and on participants' intimate and family relationships.

The program also provides direct and referral services to participants' family members and significant others. Through a comprehensive network of community-based providers, TASC links participants to a variety of medical and habilitative services.

To assist program participants in their recovery from substance abuse, Roots holds, on site, weekly Narcotics Anonymous and Alcoholics Anonymous meetings. A stress management series also has been added to Roots. The program benefits greatly from a strong client advocacy board (peer council) and a community agency advisory committee. As Project Roots has demonstrated, HIV risk-reduction programs can be developed successfully in correctional settings by focusing on program content, staff performance, service goals, and open communication with jail administrators and personnel.

Based on our experiences in Project Roots, we discuss ways to develop and provide HIV-prevention services for female offenders and to address the challenges that such programming is likely to encounter in correctional institutions. These activities are important in the planning and implementation of a HIV risk-reduction program for women: Locate the program's funding source, select the program's target population, develop a program work plan, establish a program implementation committee, address impediments to program development and implementation, determine the role of the correctional facility in program planning and implementation, develop an educational curriculum that is age, gender, culture, and language appropriate, convene a peer council to guide and support the program, identify HIV interventions or other services that are already offered in the correctional institution, draw lessons from successful HIV programs for similar populations, and conduct evaluations of program operations and outcomes. Following these guidelines, which we describe in more detail below, can help outside agencies in planning effective HIV education and service programs for women in jails or prisons (Centers for Disease Control, 1995a).

Locate a Funding Source

Program developers must determine whether the initiative will be funded internally by the correctional institution, externally through grant funding, or by a combination of funds from both sources. If the funding source is the correctional institution, program staff can be highly confident that the institution is receptive to and supportive of the program. If an external source of funding is being sought, information about the prospective program as well as the granting agency's expectations regarding program operations, services, and matching funds should be discussed with correctional staff before any plans are made for designing or implementing the program. The most successful programs involve correctional staff from the onset in searching for funding sources and in writing grant applications.

Define the Target Population

Staff must specify the criteria that will be used to select women for the program (e.g., race, risk behaviors, sexual orientation, offense). When targeting female offenders for HIV programs, it is advantageous initially to select women who are currently participating in other self-improvement programs within the correctional institution. Long-standing drug treatment, furlough, or parenting programs afford a solid foundation on which to build an HIV program, which can benefit significantly from a strong structural base of existing programming that emphasizes participant self-control, program compliance, and skills building.

Staff should select a small group of women to pilot the HIV program. Potential participants should complete an initial HIV risk assessment to determine seroprevalance rates and participants' risks for future HIV infection. Collaboration with an institution's medical services unit will allow the program to offer confidential HIV testing with pre- and posttest counseling. HIV testing and counseling will become even more important as participants increase their knowledge of HIV and their willingness to be tested. If no HIV testing capacity exists in the institution, program administrators should contact local county or city health departments for assistance. Although correctional facilities are designed primarily for discipline and safety, AIDS advocates have always underscored the need for HIV-related health care and counseling services as well.

Determine the Role of the Correctional Facility

Most jail or prison administrators will probably choose to be highly involved in HIV program planning, implementation, and participant selection. Some administrators, however, might prefer to be minimally involved in these activities or to be consulted only on program safety or security issues. To provide good-quality HIV programming, correctional staff should strike a balance, being supportive but not overly demanding in their involvement with program planners and practitioners.

Program policies should be consistent with the larger policies of the correctional setting. The first step in ensuring compliance with facility regulations is to discuss them fully with jail or prison administrators. HIV program staff should know who to contact regarding programming issues that might affect the institution. For example, a participant of the HIV program communicates that she is HIV positive. In this case, program providers should be aware of the jail's or prison's protocol regarding HIV-positive disclosures and should use institutionally approved procedures for HIV testing and follow-up. In short, HIV program staff should be aware of all the institution's policies that affect the program directly.

Develop a Work Plan

A program work plan should be developed, providing a blueprint that identifies what will be accomplished as the program progresses. The work plan describes the roles, duties, and responsibilities of staff involved in program operations and the methods that will be employed to achieve program goals and objectives. The work plan also specifies when staff meetings occur and who should be present at those meetings, when reports and curricula should be submitted to funders, when participant recruitment should begin and end, and when and to what departments HIV referrals should be made. The work plan serves as a barometer, keeping the program staff and institutional support persons informed about program progress and needs.

Establish an Implementation Committee

An implementation committee should be formed with representatives from all areas of the jail or prison that are affected by or involved in the implementation of the HIV initiative. During the development phases of the program, representatives from all areas of the facility should be present for monthly meetings. Widespread involvement in program development fosters strong internal linkages between institutional and program staff.

The most important function of the implementation committee is to write program policies and procedures. The charge of the implementation committee is also to oversee execution of the program; however, when the program is under way successfully, the committee will probably focus its attention on larger policy issues, such as the handling of confidential HIV test results, HIV-related referrals to outside service agencies, and the housing and treatment of HIV-infected inmates.

Address Program Barriers

Barriers to HIV prevention in correctional settings are similar to those present in the community: misinformation, lack of information, and stigmatization of HIV-infected persons. To overcome these barriers, facility personnel should be educated about HIV before inmate programming begins. Furthermore, facility administrators must be cognizant of all the logistical issues surrounding program implementation in order to provide the support and assistance that is needed to make the program work effectively. A program to educate inmates about HIV risk behaviors, for example, might encounter the following questions:

- Will the length of the initial presentations to inmates interfere with any jail-related orientations?
- Can a physical space be secured that is conducive to discussing the topics of HIV and AIDS?
- Will correctional officers be present during the educational sessions?
- Are written program materials appropriate, and have they been approved by jail or prison administrators? (Prior approval might be necessary in some facilities.)
- Are latex barriers considered contraband even if they are not being distributed?

If possible, the implementation committee should address these questions during the planning phase.

Develop Curriculum and Follow-up Activities

Specific, measurable, and attainable goals and objectives for learning should be written throughout the curriculum. The curriculum should also identify clearly the types of inmates being reached and the different modes of interventions that will be used in the program (e.g., education, case management, and medical assessment). In addition, the curriculum should include a variety of teaching methodologies that are responsive to the specific needs of particular types of learners. In correctional settings it is important to offer non-literacy based HIV education sessions for persons with reading deficiencies or learning disabilities (Kantor, 1990).

Program content should emphasize the dangers of HIV transmission posed by needle sharing and oral, anal, and vaginal sex. The curriculum should repeat basic HIV facts using consistent, simple, and easily remembered messages. Programmers should be creative in developing participant-focused and interactive curricula. For example, educators can conduct hands-on exercises in which participants practice applying a condom to a penis model, which is an effective way to demonstrate and reinforce correct condom use. Again, program staff should know in advance if this type of activity is allowed in the facility because condoms are contraband in many correctional settings.

Educators should encourage inmates to participate in group and self-exploration exercises. The program should also employ videos and lectures. Videos, however, should be used sparingly and should be no longer than 20 minutes in length. Longer films often fail to hold participants' attention and can lead to disruptive participant behaviors and lost teaching opportunities.

A follow-up program or intervention in the community must be developed to provide a continuum of care for program participants. Released inmates should be linked to supportive services in the community where they can continue to receive HIV information. Community follow-up is critical to the long-term success of any corrections-based HIV education program.

Convene a Peer Council

A peer council can facilitate greatly the success of an HIV program for incarcerated women. They can help to develop the curriculum, to encourage inmates to participate in sessions, to support HIV-infected inmates, and to identify problems or obstacles to program implementation. Peer council members should have previous experiences with one or more of the following: alcohol and substance abuse; incarceration; HIV experiences on an individual, family, or community level; relationship difficulties; and decision-making skills relating to safer drug use and sex practices. Peer counselors are effective at relating directly to the participants, providing a level of support that is unmatched, even by the staff. It may be necessary initially to select women from outside the facility to join the peer council (e.g., former inmates who have made a successful adjustment in the community). After the program has been established and has worked with a group of successful inmates, the peer council can be fully constituted from within the institution.

The most important contribution that peer counselors can make is as HIV educators. Peer education has proved effective in correctional settings (e.g., Centers for Disease Control, 1996b). Peer educators can also stress to inmates the importance of HIV testing and can be instrumental in disclosing HIV-positive results to those infected. Hence the selection and training of a small group of inmates motivated to work with program staff can be a critical addition to the program. Peer educators are often the key to program success, especially if the program is lacking a racially and linguistically diverse staff that is able to relate effectively to the inmate population.

Peer groups from other jail or prison programs might be available to cover topics such as drug use or parenting problems, which are common issues among incarcerated women. Peers from other program areas must be educated fully about HIV as the necessary first step in developing a strong HIV peer council in a correctional setting. Peer council members should take their responsibilities seriously: inducting them through a special ceremony can be helpful in solidifying their commitment to the program. Peer council members also should have clearly defined job descriptions and roles.

Identify Other HIV Interventions

Many correctional settings are large, making communication difficult from one division or complex to another. The program implementation committee should determine whether similar programs are operating in the facility and should be aware of any previous barriers or obstacles that these programs faced during planning or implementation. Staff from other HIV programs can provide committee members with helpful advice and direction.

Instead of "reinventing the wheel," program developers should ascertain if other institutions have created similar HIV programs and are willing to provide technical support or consultation. Existing HIV programs can offer refreshing programmatic ideas as well as valuable community networks and resources. It might benefit program staff to join other committees or initiatives that are aimed at helping women inmates.

Evaluate the Program

An evaluation plan should be a central component of HIV programming. The plan should involve a process evaluation that studies program operations and interventions and an outcome evaluation that examines whether the program has achieved its objectives and goals. The process evaluation provides staff with useful, ongoing information for improving the content and delivery of services. The outcome evaluation provides practitioners and funders with data regarding program success, which holds the program accountable and can help to guide future programming. When coupled effectively with a process evaluation, an outcome study informs staff about the most and least effective aspects of their program and recommends strategies for better interventions.

Evaluators determine whether a program was implemented as planned and whether participants have completed the program successfully. Measures of longer-term success in changing behaviors can be particularly difficult to obtain in jails because of the highly transient nature of the population. Therefore, evaluators must formulate strategies for measuring whether women on furlough, house arrest, or released status have internalized HIV risk-reduction messages.

SUMMARY

The spread of HIV disease is a major public health problem in the United States. Women of color are one of the fastest-growing segments of the population with HIV and AIDS and also are represented disproportionately in the criminal justice system. Research demonstrates that women arrestees and inmates in jails and prisons have significantly higher rates of HIV infection compared with members of the general population mostly because of intravenous drug use and sex with intravenous drug users.

The criminal justice system can play a major role in stemming the spread of HIV among high-risk women by implementing HIV prevention and drug treatment programs. To be most effective, prevention programs must increase women's knowledge about safer sex and drug-use practices as well as change their attitudes and perceptions about condom use and their notions about personal susceptibility to HIV. Because the use of intravenous and other types of drugs contribute greatly to HIV risk, drug treatment is an essential component of HIV prevention efforts for women. HIV programming for women offenders must be gender-specific and culturally sensitive, owing to the large number of minority women under correctional control. In addition, programming should be designed to accommodate the special needs of women with self-esteem and literacy problems.

HIV programming can be implemented successfully in jails, prisons, and probation departments—settings in which high-risk women can be provided with prevention and treatment services. Programs for incarcerated women should be carefully planned and designed with the input and support of facility administrators and staff. Furthermore, HIV program staff should be aware of all facility policies and protocols that can affect program operations. HIV program curricula should contain measurable goals. Basic educational messages should be simple and factual and they should be repeated several times and in different ways. Finally, peer educators can be quite effective in educating women about HIV prevention and in communicating the results of HIV testing and therefore should be brought into HIV programming whenever possible.

REFERENCES

AIDS RESEARCH INSTITUTE. (1995). *HIV prevention needs*. San Francisco: University of California Press.

AMARO, H. (1995). Love, sex, and power: Considering women's realities in HIV prevention. *American Psychologist, 6*, 437–447.

AMERICAN CORRECTIONAL ASSOCIATION. (1990). *The female offender: What does the future hold?* Washington, DC: St. Mary's Press.

AMERICAN PSYCHIATRIC ASSOCIATION. (1987). *Diagnostic and statistical manual of mental disorders* (3rd ed. rev.). Washington, DC: APA.

ARRAS, J. (1990). AIDS and reproductive decisions: Having children in fear and trembling. *Milbank Quarterly, 68*, 353–382.

BATKI, S. L., & LONDON, J. (1991). Drug abuse treatment for HIV-infected patients. In J. L. Sorensen, L. A. Wermuth, D. R. Gibson, K. Choi, J. R. Guydish, & S. L. Batki (Eds.), *Preventing AIDS in drug users and their sexual partners* (pp. 77–98). New York: Guilford Press.

BAXTER, S. (1991). AIDS education in the jail setting. *Crime and Delinquency, 37*, 48–63.

BELENKO, S. (1990). The impact of drug offenders on the criminal justice system. In R. Weisheit (Ed.), *Drugs, crime and the criminal justice system* (pp. 27–78). Cincinnati, OH: Anderson Publishing.

BOOTH, R. E., WATTERS, J. K., & CHITWOOD, D. D. (1993). HIV risk-related sex behaviors among injection drug users, crack smokers, and injection drug users who smoke crack. *American Journal of Public Health, 83*, 1144–1148.

BOWIS, B., GRIFFITHS, P., GOSSOP, M., & STRANG, A. (1996). The differences between male and female drug users: Community samples of heroin and cocaine users compared. *Substance Use and Misuse, 31*, 529–543.

BROWN, B. S. (1990–1991). AIDS and the provision of drug user treatment. *International Journal of the Addictions, 25*, 1503–1514.

BROWN, B. S., & NEEDLE, R. H. (1994). Modifying the process of treatment to meet the threat of AIDS. *International Journal of the Addictions, 25*, 1739–1752.

BUREAU OF JUSTICE STATISTICS. (1994, March). *Women in prison* (U.S. DOJ Publ. No. NCJ 145321). Washington, DC: U.S. Government Printing Office.

BUREAU OF JUSTICE STATISTICS. (1997, August). *HIV in prisons and jails*, 1995 (U.S. DOJ Publ. No. NCJ 164260). Washington, DC: U.S. Government Printing Office.

BURTON, V. S., MARQUART, J. W., CUVELIER, S. J., ALARID, L. F., & HUNTER, R. J. (1993). A study of attitudinal change among boot camp participants. *Federal Probation, 57*, 46–52.

CATANIA, J. A., KEGELES, S. M., & COATES, T. J. (1990). Towards an understanding of risk behavior: An AIDS risk reduction model (ARRM). *Health Education Quarterly, 17*, 53–72.

CENTERS FOR DISEASE CONTROL. (1995a). *Guidelines for health education and risk reduction activities.* Atlanta, GA: CDC.

CENTERS FOR DISEASE CONTROL. (1995b). *U.S. HIV and AIDS cases reported through December 1995.* Atlanta, GA: CDC.

CENTERS FOR DISEASE CONTROL. (1996a). *HIV/AIDS surveillance report, February.* Atlanta, GA: CDC.

CENTERS FOR DISEASE CONTROL. (1996b). HIV/AIDS education and prevention programs for adults in prisons and jails and juveniles in confinement facilities: United States, 1994. *Morbidity and Mortality Weekly Report, 45*, 27–41.

CENTERS FOR DISEASE CONTROL. (1997). *Report on the global HIV/AIDS epidemic.* Atlanta, GA: CDC.

CENTERS FOR DISEASE CONTROL. (1998a). *HIV/AIDS surveillance report: Cases reported through December 1997.* Atlanta, GA: CDC.

CENTERS FOR DISEASE CONTROL. (1998b). *CDC update: HIV/AIDS in the African American community.* Atlanta, GA: CDC.

CENTERS FOR DISEASE CONTROL. (1998c). *Geneva '98, combatting complacency: A closer look at HIV trends by gender and race.* Atlanta, GA: CDC.

CHESNEY-LIND, M. (1995). Rethinking women's imprisonment: A critical examination of trends in female incarceration. In B. R. Price and N. J. Sokoloff (Eds.), *The criminal justice system and women: Offenders, victims, and workers* (pp. 71–88). New York: McGraw-Hill.

COCHRAN, S. (1989). Women and HIV infection. In V. Mays, G. Albee, & S. Schneider (Eds.), *Primary prevention of AIDS* (pp. 27–42). Newbury Park, CA: Sage Publications.

COHEN, P. T. (1998). *Understanding HIV disease: Hallmarks, clinical spectrum, what we need to know.* Available: HIV InSite: AIDS Knowledge Base

CONRAD, R. (1997). *African Americans suffer disproportionately from AIDS.* Washington, DC: National Center for Public Policy Research.

DECKER, S., & ROSENFELD, R. (1992). Intravenous drug use and the AIDS epidemic: Findings from a 20-city sample of arrestees. *Crime and Delinquency, 38*, 492–509.

DOUGLAS, P. H., & PINSKY, L. (1992). *The essential AIDS fact book.* New York: Simon & Schuster.

ELLERBROCK, T. V., BUSH, T. J., CHAMBERLAND, M. E., & OXTOBY, M. J. (1991). Epidemiology of women with AIDS in the United States, 1981 through 1990. *Journal of the American Medical Association, 265*, 2971–2975.

FAUCI, A. (1988). The human immunodeficiency virus: Infectivity and mechanisms of pathogenesis. *Science, 239*, 617–622.

FINEBERG, H. V. (1988). Education to prevent AIDS: Prospects and obstacles. *Science, 239*, 592–596.

GRIFFIN, E., LURIGIO, A. J., & JOHNSON, B. R. (1991). HIV policy for probation officers: An implementation and evaluation program. *Crime and Delinquency, 37*, 36–47.

GUYDISH, J. R., GOLDEN, E., & HEMBRY, K. (1991). Needle sharing, needle cleaning, and risk behavior change among injection drug users. In J. L. Sorensen, L. A. Wermuth, D. R. Gibson, K. Choi, J. R. Guydish, & S. L. Batki (Eds.), *Preventing AIDS in drug users and their sexual partners* (pp. 28–42). New York: Guilford Press.

HAMMETT, T. W., & MOINI, S. (1990). *Update on AIDS on prisons and jails.* Washington, DC: National Institute of Justice.

HAMMETT, T., HUNT, D., GROSS, M., RHODES, W., & MOINI, S. (1991). Stemming the spread of HIV among IV drug users, their sexual partners, and children: Issues and opportunities for criminal justice agencies. *Crime and Delinquency, 37*, 101–124.

HSER, Y., ANGLIN, M. D., & MCGLOTHLIN, W. (1987). Sex differences in addict careers: 1. Initiation of use. *American Journal of Drug and Alcohol Abuse, 13*, 33–57.

ILLINOIS CRIMINAL JUSTICE INFORMATION AUTHORITY. (1996, July). *Results of the 1995 Illinois drug use forecasting study.* Chicago: ICJIA.

INSTITUTE OF MEDICINE. (1988). *Confronting AIDS: Update 1988*. Washington, DC: National Academy Press.

JEMMOTT, J. B., JEMMOTT, L. S., & FONG, G. T. (1992). Reductions in HIV risk-associated sexual behaviors among black male adolescents: Effects of an AIDS prevention intervention. *American Journal of Public Health, 82*, 372–377.

JOINT SUBCOMMITTEE ON AIDS IN THE CRIMINAL JUSTICE SYSTEM. (1989). *AIDS and the criminal justice system: A final report and recommendations*. New York: The committee.

JONES, M. E., & LURIGIO, A. J. (1996). *Combatting HIV in the suburbs: An intervention for African American women probationers*. Paper presented at a grantee meeting of the Cook County Department of Health, South Holland, IL.

KANE, S. (1990). AIDS, addictions and condom use: Sources of sexual risk for heterosexual women. *Journal of Sex Research, 27*, 427–444.

KANTOR, E. (1990). AIDS and HIV infection in prisoners: Epidemiology. In P. T. Cohen, M. A. Sande, & P. A. Volberding (Eds.), *The AIDS knowledge base* (pp. 86–99). San Francisco: Medical Publishing Group.

KLINE, A., KLINE, E., & OKEN, E. (1992). Minority women and sexual choice in the age of AIDS. *Social Science and Medicine, 34*, 447–456.

KLINE, A., & STRICKLER, J. (1993). Perceptions of risk for AIDS among women in drug treatment. *Health Psychology, 12*, 313–323.

KOLATA, G. (1995, February 28). New picture of who will get AIDS is crammed with addicts. *New York Times*, pp. A17–A18.

LANIER, M. M., & MCCARTHY, B. R. (1989). AIDS awareness and the impact of AIDS education in juvenile corrections. *Criminal Justice and Behavior, 16*, 395–411.

LEUKEFELD, C. G. (1985). The clinical connection: Drugs and crime. *International Journal of Addictions, 20*, 1049–1064.

LURIGIO, A. J. (1989). Practitioners' views on AIDS in probation and detention. *Federal Probation, 53*, 16–24.

LURIGIO, A. J., PETRAITIS, J. M., & JOHNSON, B. R. (1992). HIV education for probationers. *AIDS Education and Prevention, 4*, 205–218.

MALDONADO, M. (1997). Trends in HIV/AIDS among women of color. *Update special edition: Women of color and HIV/AIDS policy*. Washington, DC: National Minority AIDS Council.

MAYS, V., & COCHRAN, S. (1988). Issues in the perception of AIDS risk and risk reduction activities by black and Hispanic/Latina women. *American Psychologist, 41*, 949–957.

MCCOY, H. V., MILES, C., & INCIARDI, J. (1995). *Survival sex: Inner-city women and crack-cocaine*. New York: Roxbury Publishing.

MORRISON, D. M., BAKER, S. A., & GILLMORE, M. R. (1994). Sexual risk behavior, knowledge and condom use among adolescents in juvenile detention. *Journal of Youth and Adolescence, 23*, 271–288.

NATIONAL INSTITUTE OF JUSTICE. (1998). *ADAM 1997 annual report on adult and juvenile arrestees*. Washington, DC: NIJ.

NEW MEXICO AIDS INFONET FACT SHEET. (1997). *Women and HIV*. Available: http://hivsite.UCSF.edu/medical/factsheets

NYAMATHI, A., & LEWIS, C. (1991). Coping of African American women at risk for AIDS. *Women's Health Issues, 1*, 53–62.

O'LEARY, A., & JEMMOTT, L. S. (1995). General issues in the prevention of AIDS in women. In A. O'Leary & L. S. Jemmott (Eds.), *Women at risk: Issues in the primary prevention of AIDS* (pp. 114–129). New York: Plenum Press.

OSMOND, M. W., WAMBACH, K. G., HARRISON, D. F., BYERS, J., LEVINE, P., IMERSHEIN, A., & QUADAGNO, D. M. (1993). The multiple jeopardy of race, class, and gender for AIDS risk among women. *Gender and Society, 7*, 99–120.

PETERSON, J. L., CATANIA, J. A., DOLCINI, M. M., & FAIGELES, B. (1993). Multiple sexual partners and condom use among African Americans in high-risk cities of the United States: The National AIDS Behavioral Surveys. *Family Planning Perspectives, 25*, 263–267.

POLONSKY, S., KERR, S., HARRIS, B., GAITER, J., FICHTNER, R. R., & KENNEDY, M. G. (1994). HIV prevention in prisons and jails: Obstacles and opportunities. *Public Health Reports, 109*, 615–625.

PROBAND, S. C. (1998). Corrections populations near 6 million. *Overcrowded Times, 9*, 4–5.

QUINN, S. C. (1993). AIDS and the African American women: The triple burden of race, class, and gender. *Health Education Quarterly, 20*, 305–320.

RAMLOW, B. E., WHITE, A. L., WATSON, D. D., & LEUKEFELD, C. G. (1997). The needs of women with substance use problems: An expanded vision for treatment. *Substance Use and Misuse, 32*, 1395–1403.

RAMOS, R., SHAIN, R. N., & JOHNSON, L. (1995). "Men I mess with don't have anything to do with AIDS": Using ethno-theory to understand sexual risk perception. *Sociological Quarterly, 36*, 483–504.

ROLFS, R., GOLDBERG, M., & SHARRAR, R. (1990). Risk factors for syphilis: Cocaine use and prostitution. *American Journal of Public Health, 80*, 853–857.

SELIK, R., CASTRO, K. G., & PAPPAIOANOU, M. (1988). Racial/ethnic differences in the risk of AIDS in the United States. *American Journal of Public Health, 78*, 1539–1545.

SHAYNE, V. T., & KAPLAN, B. J. (1991). Double victims: Poor women and AIDS. *Women and Health, 17*, 21–37.

STALL, R. (1988). The prevention of HIV infection associated with drug and alcohol use during sexual activity. *Advances in Alcohol and Substance Abuse, 7*, 73–88.

STEIN, Z. (1990). HIV prevention: The need for methods women can use. *American Journal of Public Health, 80*, 460–462.

TREATMENT ALTERNATIVES FOR SAFE COMMUNITIES. (1994). *A survey of the level of need for substance abuse treatment among Illinois State Prison inmates*. Unpublished raw data.

TREATMENT ALTERNATIVES FOR SAFE COMMUNITIES. (1996). *Final results of the 1995 Illinois drug use forecasting study*. Report published by the Illinois Criminal Justice Information Authority.

TURNER, C., HEATHER, G., & MOSES, L. (1989). *AIDS: Sexual behavior and intravenous drug use*. Washington, DC: National Academy Press.

UNAIDS. (1996). *The HIV/AIDS situation in mid 1996: Global and regional highlights*. Joint United Nations Program on HIV/AIDS fact sheet. Geneva: UNAIDS.

VALLEROY, L. A. (1998). Young African American women at high risk for infection. *Journal of Acquired Immune Deficiency and Human Retrovirology, 18*, 25–48.

WALKER, J. (1997). *The AIDS crisis among African Americans*. New York: Balm in Gilead.

WERMUTH, L. A., HAM, J., & ROBBINS, R. L. (1992). Women don't wear condoms: AIDS risk among sexual partners of IV drug users. In J. Huber & B. E. Schneider (Eds.), *The social context of AIDS* (pp. 78–91). Newbury Park, CA: Sage Publications.

SECTION IV

Women in Prison

Since the 1980s, the number of women imprisoned in the United States has doubled. Increases in the number of women incarcerated have surpassed the male rates of increase for the past decades, and an unprecedented number of expensive prison spaces have been built for women

In the past, women prisoners were often ignored because of the paucity of their numbers. Now, with increasing numbers of female prisoners and overcrowded facilities, the number of women's prisons continues to grow. Since the extraordinary increases in women's imprisonment have been a product of criminal justice policy shifts, rather than significant changes in women's criminal behavior, dramatic reductions of incarcerated women ought to be within reach. But significant prison population reductions through the use of alternatives to incarceration are not yet to be realized.

Women present a special challenge as prisoners because their needs and interests are different from those of men. Socially, women come from situations where they are already "imprisoned" as a result of lower wages, inadequate housing, and unequal opportunities for education and employment. Prisons provide an atmosphere that doubly and often triply imprisons women, particularly when they are separated from their children. The social consequences of imprisoning large numbers of women is magnified when the effects on families and dependent children are taken into consideration.

The treatment of women in prison is in many ways an extension of the way women are treated generally in society. The images, roles, and stereotypes of women carry over into our correctional facilities, where women are either ignored and treated as unimportant or given that special attention that casts them as dependent beings who must be "rehabilitated" to their traditional familial roles as wives and mothers. The ways in which women are treated as prisoners, particularly by correctional officers, reflect in a rather direct way the inequality and subservience of women in general. Prison and its policies continue to represent a fertile area of research of women and their roles in society.

In their chapter "Women in Prison: Vengeful Equity," Barbara Bloom and Meda Chesney-Lind describe the conditions that women experience in prison as being the "worst of both worlds" correctionally. Litigation is used to justify the kind of treatment that women receive in prison (i.e., parity with men prisoners, thus putting women in both boot camps and chain gangs). They conclude that relying on correctional facilities is not the answer. We need to seek alternatives for women who commit crimes.

Zina T. McGee, in her chapter "The Pains of Imprisonment: Long-Term Incarceration Effects on Women," hypothesizes that the effects of incarceration are greater for long-term than for short-term inmates, and that black females report fewer emotional difficulties than do white females. McGee posits some questions: Are there significant differences in the emotional well-being of short- and long-term female offenders? Does the frequency of contact with family members differ from among black and white long-term offenders? She concludes that future research should address the questions of emotional difficulties faced by long-term female offenders.

Mona J. E. Danner, in "Three Strikes and It's *Women* Who Are Out: The Hidden Consequences for Women of Criminal Justice Policy Reforms," describes how it is women who pay the lion's share of any criminal justice reform. Women appear to remain invisible during debates surrounding criminal justice reforms, but they become the ones harmed by such reforms. It is pointed out that some states continue to build beds in women's prisons at a higher rate than they do for beds in shelters for women and children. Danner concludes that it is women who receive the least from the wars on crime and drugs, with women bearing most of the burdens.

In her chapter "Disparate Treatment in Correctional Facilities," Roslyn Muraskin demonstrates how litigation has won the right for women to be treated on a par with men inmates. The providing of services and programs is deemed to be part of good detention practices, ensuring that those inmates who do return to society can be reintegrated into society. However, even with more women being incarcerated than a decade ago, there are still conflicts between the administrators of these facilities for women and their population. Disparate treatment still exists, and the alternatives of no incarceration for many of these women remains a very good recommendation.

What is the male inmate preference? In "The Dislike of Female Offenders among Correctional Officers: A Need for Specialized Training," Christine E. Rashe describes how both male and female correctional officers look to avoid working with female offenders. Little or no training is offered to the correctional officers on how to handle female inmates. Tactics that are used and taught are primarily for the male inmate and do not necessarily work with the female offender. Special training is needed for correctional officers who are to work in facilities housing female inmates.

All the contributors in this section talk about the rise in the female inmate population. Zelma W. Henriques and Evelyn Gilbert, in their chapter "Sexual Abuse/Assault of Women in Prison," discuss the rise in the female inmate population due to mandatory drug laws. Inevitably, many of these women will be housed in facilities with male correctional officers, and sexual assault is one of the many victimizing experiences that women inmates incur. They point out that while confined, women have fewer resources than are available to victims of sexual assault outside the correctional facility. They conclude that women in prison have a right not to be victims of "sexploitation."

Capital punishment is a subject of interest to researchers and students alike. It is the severest punishment meted out by our system. What then of "Women on Death Row"? Etta F. Morgan explores the importance of gender in the criminal justice system and the experiences of women on death row. She points out that women as second-class citizens have carried this very status into the penal system. Limited research is available on women sentenced to death. Although women continue to be in the minority with regard to the commission of crimes, women nevertheless are arrested and sentenced to death. Women who suffer discrimination while serving time in the correctional facilities continue to suffer continued discrimination while on death row. We have been lulled into believing that though many of the women have their death sentences commuted, we should not "really" be concerned with such inmates, but with more women facing the death penalty in the future, we need to concentrate our efforts on their treatment.

12

Women in Prison

Vengeful Equity

Barbara Bloom and Meda Chesney-Lind

The number of women in U.S. prisons has increased dramatically in recent decades, rising nearly sixfold since 1980. In addition, the increase in women's imprisonment has outstripped the male increase every year since the mid-1980s. As a result, women's share of the correctional population has also increased significantly. In the face of such increases, the authors question whether changes in the character of women's crime, measured either by arrest or commitment data, signal a change in the seriousness of women's offenses. A review of these data suggests a significant increase in the proportion of women with drug offenses serving time in state and federal prisons. Additionally, large numbers of women are imprisoned for property offenses.

A review of the conditions that women experience in prison suggests that they are experiencing the "worst of both worlds" correctionally. On the one hand, recent "parity"-based litigation has been deployed to justify treating women inmates the same as men—resulting in women on chain gangs and in boot camps. On the other hand, details of women's experience of prison underscore the persistence of gender as a theme in their situations both inside the prison and in their relationships with their families. Finally, the need to seek actively to reduce our nation's reliance on imprisonment as the primary response to women's crime is discussed.

In recent years, movie audiences have been entertained by Hollywood's newest construction of women, "the rampaging female" (Birch, 1994, p. 1). Films such as *Thelma and Louise, Fatal Attraction, Basic Instinct, Set It Off*, and *Bound*, among others, have introduced images of women—African-American and white, heterosexual and lesbian, working and middle class—seeking and apparently getting revenge, money, excitement, control, and "liberation" through criminal activity. While notions of womanhood that appear in popular culture, particularly movies, have always been problematic (Douglas, 1994; Haskell, 1973), the last two decades has seen a particular and determined focus on the lethally violent woman, who has become the "new cliché of Hollywood cinema, stabbing and shooting her way to notoriety" (Birch, 1994; p. 1; Holmlund, 1995). There is no denying the fact that women's violence fascinates the general public at the same time that it perplexes feminist scholars (White & Kowalski, 1994), but its chief attribute is its relative rarity. As an example, women killers have accounted for about 10 to 15 percent of all homicides for centuries (Holmlund, 1994, p. 131), and there is even some evidence that the number of adult women killing men actually decreased rather sharply in the last few years. One estimate of this decline is 25 percent (Holmlund, 1994, p. 131). Hollywood's female crime wave has occurred in the absence of a dramatic change in the level of women's violence or serious crime for that matter (see also Chesney-Lind, 1997). It has, however, accompanied a different change, one that may explain the need to construct women as more culpable, blameworthy, and aggressive: a dramatic increase in the number of imprisoned women.

THE NATIONAL CONTEXT: GETTING TOUGHER ON WOMEN'S CRIME

Historically, women under criminal justice supervision were correctional afterthoughts, often ignored because their numbers were extremely small in comparison to those of men under supervision (Rafter, 1990). Indeed, in the mid-1970s, only about half the states and territories had separate prisons for women, and many jurisdictions housed women inmates in male facilities or in women's facilities in other states.

This pattern shifted dramatically during the 1980s, and since then, the nation has seen the number of women in U.S. prisons increase sixfold. In 1980 there were just over 12,000 women in U.S. state and federal prisons. By 1996 there were almost 75,000 (Bureau of Justice Statistics, 1997a). Since 1985 the annual rate of growth of female prisoners averaged 11.2 percent higher than the 7.9 percent average increase in male prisoners.

Women's share of imprisonment has also increased. At the turn of the century, women were 4 percent of those imprisoned; by 1970 this had dropped to 3 percent, and women accounted for only 3.9 percent of those in prison in 1980; but by 1996, women accounted for 6.3 percent of those in prison (Bureau of Justice Statistics, 1997a, p. 6; Callahan, 1986).

California led the nation with 10,248 women in prison, followed by Texas, with 9933, New York with 3728, and Florida with 3302 incarcerated women (Bureau of Justice Statistics, 1997a, p. 6). As of October 12, 1997, the number of women incarcerated in California state prisons reached over 11,000 (California Department of Corrections, 1997).

The rate of women's imprisonment is also at an historic high, increasing from a low of 6 sentenced female inmates per 100,000 women in the United States in 1925 to 51 per 100,000 in 1996 (Bureau of Justice Statistics, 1997a, p. 5; Callahan, 1986). As we shall see, the soaring increase in the imprisonment of women is not explained by changes in the character and seriousness of women's offending. In fact, despite media images of violent women offenders, the proportion of women serving sentences in state prisons for violent offenses declined from 48.9 percent in 1979 to 32.2 percent in 1991. In states such as California, which operates the two largest women's prisons in the nation, the decline is even sharper. In 1992, only 16 percent of the women admitted to the California prison system were incarcerated for violent crimes, compared to 37.2 percent in 1982 (Bloom, Chesney-Lind, & Owen, 1994).

What does explain the increase? The so-called war on drugs has become a largely unannounced war on women, particularly women of color, and this has clearly contributed to the explosion in the women's prison population (Bloom et al., 1994). A decade and a half ago (1979), one in ten women in U.S. prisons was serving time for drugs. Now it is one out of three (32.8 percent), and while the intent of "get tough" policies was to rid society of drug dealers and "kingpins," over a third (35.9 percent) of the women serving sentences for drug offenses in the nation's prisons are serving time solely for "possession" (Bureau of Justice Statistics, 1988, p. 3).

Under current punishment philosophies and practices, women are also increasingly subject to criminalization of noncriminal actions and behaviors. For example, large numbers of poor and homeless women are subject to criminalization as cities across the nation pass ordinances prohibiting begging and sleeping in public places. Many of these women are mothers. Additionally, pregnant drug-addicted women are increasingly being sentenced to prison. Possibly the most dramatic targets of the war on drugs are pregnant women using illegal drugs, who are characterized as "evil women" willing to endanger the health of their unborn children in pursuit of drug-induced highs.

PROFILE OF WOMEN PRISONERS

The characteristics of U.S. women prisoners reflect a population that is triply marginalized by race, class, and gender. Imprisoned women are low income, disproportionately African-American and Latina, undereducated and unskilled with sporadic employment histories. Moreover, they are mostly young, single heads of households, with at least two children (Owen & Bloom, 1995). Women prisoners have a host of medical, psychological, and financial problems and needs. Substance abuse, compounded by poverty, unemployment, physical and mental illness, physical and sexual abuse and homelessness, often propels women through the revolving door of the criminal justice system.

Table 1 describes the characteristics of state female inmates as follows: African-American women comprise 46 percent of women prisoners, white women 36.2 percent of women in prison, and Hispanic women 14.2 percent of women in prison. The median age of women in prison is approximately 31 years.

The majority of imprisoned women were unemployed prior to arrest (53.3 percent) and 22.7 percent had completed high school. The majority of incarcerated women were also unmarried (45 percent never married). More than three-fourths have children, two-thirds of whom are under age 18 (Bureau of Justice Statistics, 1994). The majority of the children of imprisoned mothers live with relatives, primarily grandparents. Approximately 10 percent of the children are in foster care, a group home or other agency. About 8 to 10 percent of women are pregnant when they are incarcerated (Bloom & Steinhart, 1993).

Women under criminal justice supervision frequently have histories of childhood or adult abuse. Forty-three percent of women inmates reported being physically or sexually abused at some time in their lives prior to incarceration. More than four in every ten women reported that they had been abused at least once before their current admission to prison (Snell & Morton, 1994, p. 5). Compared to men, imprisoned women were at least three times more likely to have been physically abused and at least six times more likely

TABLE 1   Characteristics of Female State Prison Inmates, 1991[a]

Characteristic	Percent
Race/origin	
White non-hispanic	36.2
Black non-hispanic	46.0
Hispanic	14.2
Other	3.6
Age	
17 or younger	0.1
18–24	16.3
25–34	50.4
35–44	25.5
45–54	6.1
55 and older	1.7
Median age	31.0
Marital status	
Married	17.3
Widowed	5.9
Divorced	19.1
Separated	12.5
Never married	45.1
Education	
Eighth grade or less	16.0
Some high school	45.8
High school graduate	22.7
Some college or more	15.5
Prearrest employment	
Employed	46.7
Full-time	35.7
Part-time	11.0
Unemployed	53.3

Source: Snell and Morton (1994).

[a]Number of inmates, 38,796.

to have been sexually abused since age 18. For most women under correctional supervision, their problems begin as girls; another national study of women in U.S. prisons and jails indicated that nearly half (46.7 percent) had run away as girls—and two-thirds of these women ran away more than once (American Correctional Association, 1990). Table 2 illustrates the family lives of women inmates prior to prison.

Incarcerated women use more drugs and use them more frequently than do men. About 54 percent of the women used drugs in the month before their current offense, compared to 50 percent of the men. Women prisoners are also more likely than their male counterparts to use drugs regularly (65 percent versus 62 percent), to have used drugs daily in the month preceding their offense (41 percent versus 36 percent), and to have been under the influence at the time of the offense (36 percent versus 31 percent). Nearly one in four female inmates reported committing their offense to get money to buy drugs, compared to one in six males (Bureau of Justice Statistics, 1994, p. 7).

The rate of HIV infection is higher for women prisoners than for men prisoners. At the end of 1995, 4.0 percent of female state prisoners were infected with HIV compared to 2.3 percent of male prisoners. From 1991 to 1995, the number of male state inmates infected with HIV increased 28 percent, while the number of female inmates infected with HIV increased at the much faster rate of 88 percent (Bureau of Justice Statistics, 1997b, p. 6).

MOTHERS BEHIND BARS

It is estimated that between 75 percent and 80 percent of women prisoners are mothers (Bloom & Steinhart, 1993) and that two-thirds of those who are mothers have at least one child under age 18 (Snell & Morton, 1994). A similar percentage of male prisoners, approximately 65 percent, are fathers (Bureau of Justice Statistics, 1994). When a father is incarcerated, responsibility of his children is typically assumed by their mother.

The problems facing incarcerated mothers and their children have been the focus of studies spanning more than three decades. The research has consistently shown that mothers who are prisoners face multiple obstacles in maintaining their relationships with their children. In addition to correctional systems, mothers in prison must also deal with child welfare agencies.

A mother's incarceration is more disruptive to children since mothers are frequently the primary caretakers of their children prior to incarceration. The majority of these mothers are single parents who had custody of their children (73 percent) prior to incarceration. Many of these women never see their children during the period that they are incarcerated.

TABLE 2   Childhood Households of Female Inmates and Abuse Experienced before Prison, 1991

	Percent of Female Inmates
Grew up in a household with both parents present	58
Ever lived in a foster home or institution	17
Parents or guardians abused alcohol or drugs	34
Immediate family member ever incarcerated	47
Ever physically or sexually abused	43

Source: Snell and Morton (1994).

According to a national study (see Bloom & Steinhart, 1993), over 54 percent of the children of incarcerated mothers never visited their mothers during incarceration. For mothers who were separated from their children prior to arrest, the no-visit rate was 72 percent.

Bloom and Steinhart (1993) found that 17 percent of children whose mothers were incarcerated lived with their fathers, nearly half (47 percent) lived with their grandparents, 22 percent were with relatives or friends, and about 7 percent had been placed in foster care. Incarcerated mothers whose children are in foster care must overcome numerous obstacles to maintain their parental rights (Barry, 1995). Children are often in multiple-foster-care placements and siblings are separated, making it difficult for mothers to determine the whereabouts of their children. This situation is exacerbated when the social services caseworker does not maintain timely communication with the mother. Distance from the prison, lack of transportation, and limited economic resources on the part of the caregiver can pose barriers to regular visitation by children. This, coupled with inadequate family reunification services during incarceration and inability to meet contact requirements and statutory schedules for reunification, put many incarcerated mothers at considerable risk of losing custody of their children (Gabel & Johnston, 1995).

A mother who is incarcerated may not have access to resources such as parent education, drug treatment, counseling, and vocational training to meet the other reunification requirements commonly imposed by dependency courts. Additionally, while continuing contact between mother and child may be the most significant predictor of family reunification following incarceration, as mentioned previously, mothers in prison often have little or no contact with their children while incarcerated.

Although no studies have systematically examined the extent of this issue, the Center for Children of Incarcerated Parents has found that involuntary termination of parental rights occurs disproportionately among women. About 25 percent of women offenders whose children participate in the center's therapeutic programs lost their parental rights (Johnston, 1992).

The Personal Responsibility and Work Opportunity Reconciliation Act of 1996 (PRA) is likely to cause further disruption to incarcerated women and their families. For example, PRA specifically denies federal assistance to two categories of women offenders, drug felons and probation and parole violators. First, PRA imposes a lifetime ban on receiving food stamps or assistance from the federal grant for anyone convicted of a drug felony. Pregnant women can receive benefits while pregnant but not after the child is born. PRA also prohibits benefits to persons violating the conditions of probation and parole. In 1996 there were 515,600 women on probation and 79,300 on parole (Bureau of Justice Statistics, 1997a), and many of them are at high risk of technical violations due to failure to report or drug relapse. The ban does not distinguish between minor technical violations and serious violations such as committing a new crime. These provisions pose significant consequences for women in prison and their families since women incarcerated for drug offenses are the fastest-growing population in women's prisons (Katz, 1997).

CURRENT OFFENSES

Studies have consistently shown that women generally commit fewer crimes than men and that their offenses tend to be less serious. Gilfus (1992); Bloom, Chesney-Lind, and Owen (1995); and Pollock (1994) argue that women's patterns of criminal activity differ from those of men in both the type and amount of crime committed by women. Nearly half of all women in prison are currently serving a sentence for a nonviolent offense and have been convicted in the past only of nonviolent offenses (Snell & Morton, 1994, p. 1). The offenses for which women are arrested and incarcerated are primarily property and drug offenses. When women do commit acts of violence, it is most likely against a spouse or partner and in the context of self-defense (Browne, 1987; Bureau of Justice Statistics, 1994).

As noted earlier, contrary to media-spawned images of the "new violent female criminal," the proportion of women imprisoned for violent offenses continues to decline. Meanwhile, the proportion of women in prison for drug-related offenses has increased substantially. When women do commit violent offenses, they often do so in self-defense and as a response to domestic violence. Additionally, women prisoners are far more likely to kill intimates or relatives (49 percent) than strangers (21 percent), whereas men are more likely to kill strangers (50.5 percent) than intimates or relatives (35.1 percent) (Bureau of Justice Statistics, 1994). The nature of women's violence is often intertwined with their own histories and experiences of abuse, and consequently, their acts of violence take on a different significance than men's violence (Stark & Flitcraft, 1996; Websdale & Chesney-Lind, 1997).

The war on drugs, coupled with the development of new technologies for determining drug use (e.g., urinalysis), plays another less obvious role in increasing women's imprisonment. Many women parolees are being returned to prison for technical parole violations because they fail to pass random drug tests. Of the 6000 women incarcerated in California in 1993, approximately one-third (32 percent) were imprisoned due to parole violations. In Hawaii, 55 percent of the new admissions to the Women's Community Correctional Center during a two-month period in 1991 were being returned to prison for parole violations, due largely to drug violations. Finally, in Oregon, during a one-year period (October 1992–September 1993), only 16 percent of female admissions to Oregon institutions were incarcerated for new convictions; the remainder were probation and parole violators. This pattern was not nearly so clear in male imprisonment; 48 percent of the admissions to male prisons were for new offenses (Anderson, 1994).

Nowhere has the drug war taken a larger toll than on women sentenced in federal courts. In the federal system, the passage of harsh mandatory minimums for federal crimes, coupled with new sentencing guidelines intended to "reduce race, class and other unwarranted disparities in sentencing males" (Raeder, 1993), have operated in ways that distinctly disadvantage women. They have also dramatically increased the number of women sentenced to federal institutions. In 1989, 44.5 percent of the women incarcerated in federal institutions were being held for drug offenses. Only two years later, this increased to 68 percent. Twenty years ago, nearly two-thirds of the women convicted of federal felonies were granted probation, but in 1991 only 28 percent of women were given straight probation (Raeder, 1993, p. 927). The mean time to be served by women drug offenders increased from 27 months in July 1984 to a startling 67 months in June 1990 (Raeder, 1993, p. 929). Taken together, these data explain why the number of women in federal institutions has skyrocketed since the late 1980s. In 1988, before full implementation of sentencing guidelines, women comprised 6.5 percent of those in federal institutions; by 1992 this figure had jumped to 8 percent. The number of women in federal institutions increased by 97.4 percent over a three-year period (Bureau of Justice Statistics, 1989, p. 4; 1993b, p. 4).

Snell and Morton (1994) found many women are serving time in state prisons for larceny–theft. Indeed, of the women serving time for property offenses (28.7 percent of all women in prison), well over a third (36.7 percent) are serving time for larceny–theft. This compares to only 18 percent of men who are serving time for property crimes. Fraud is another significant commitment offense for women, accounting for 35 percent of women's but only 9.7 percent of men's most serious property offenses. Men serving time for property offenses are more likely to be serving time for burglary (52.4 percent).

California again gives us a closer look; over a third (34.1 percent) of women in California state prisons in 1993 were incarcerated for property offenses for which "petty theft with a prior" is the most common offense. This generally includes shoplifting and other minor theft. One women in ten in California prisons is doing time for petty theft. In total, one women in four is incarcerated in California for either drug possession or petty theft with a prior (Bloom et al., 1994, p. 3).

ARREST PATTERNS

The pattern of women's arrests provides little evidence that women's crimes are increasing in seriousness and frequency, which would, in turn, explain the dramatic increase in women's imprisonment. As an example, arrests of adult women increased by 36.5 percent between 1986 and 1995 (Federal Bureau of Investigation, 1996, p. 213). During that same period, the number of women held in state and federal prisons increased by 179 percent (Bureau of Justice Statistics, 1997a).

Most of the increase in women's arrests is accounted for by more arrests of women for nonviolent property offenses such as fraud, forgery, and theft, as well as for drug offenses. The arrest data also support the notion that the war on drugs has translated into a war on women. Between 1986 and 1995, arrests of adult women for drug abuse violations increased by 91.1 percent compared to 53.8 percent for men (Federal Bureau of Investigation, 1996, p. 213). In the last decade, arrests of women for drug offenses and other assaults have replaced fraud and disorderly conduct as the most common offenses for which women are arrested (see Table 3). Women's share of arrests for serious violent offenses went from 10.8 percent to 12.3 percent between 1983 and 1992 (Federal Bureau of Investigation, 1992).

These figures, however, should not be used to support notions of dramatic increases in women's crime. As an example, while the number of adult women arrested between 1994 and 1995 did increase, it was only by 4 percent (Federal Bureau of Investigation, 1996, p. 216). Turning specifically to trends in the arrests of women for Part One or "index" offenses (murder, rape, aggravated assault, robbery, burglary, larceny–theft, motor vehicle theft, and arson), these did increase by 16.2 percent (compared to an increase in male arrests of 4.5 percent) between 1986 and 1995 (Federal Bureau of Investigation, 1993, p. 222). While these figures may appear to be dramatic, recall that this category includes larceny–theft, which some contend often involves such minor offenses that it should not be confused with serious crime (see Steffensmeier & Allan, 1995).

Moreover, looking at these offenses differently reveals, if anything, a picture of stability rather than change over the past decade. Women's share of these arrests as a proportion of all those arrested for these offenses rose from 21.8 percent to 23.4 percent between 1986 and 1995. Women's share of arrests for serious violent offenses moved from 11 percent to 15 percent during this same period (Federal Bureau of Investigation, 1996, p. 213).

Overall, the increase in women's arrests is largely accounted for by more arrests of women for nonviolent property offenses such as shoplifting (larceny–theft), which was up 8.1 percent; check forgery (forgery or counterfeiting), which was up 41.9 percent; welfare fraud, which was up 13.5 percent; and most important, drug offenses, which were up 100.1 percent (Federal Bureau of Investigation, 1996, p. 213). Here the increases in arrests are real, since the base numbers are large, and as a result, these offenses comprise a large portion of women's official crime. Whether they are the product of actual changes in women's behavior over the last decade or changes in law enforcement practices is an important question to which we now turn.

THE NATURE AND CAUSES OF WOMEN'S CRIME

As represented in official arrest statistics, women's crime is remarkably similar to the pattern seen in girls' arrests. Essentially, adult women have been, and continue to be, arrested for minor crimes and what might be called "deportment" offenses (prostitution, disorderly conduct, and "driving under the influence"). Their younger counterparts are arrested for essentially the same crimes, as well as status offenses (running away from home, incorrigibility, truancy, and other noncriminal offenses for which only minors can be taken into custody). Like arrests of girls, arrests of adult women have shown an increase in both aggravated and other assaults. Finally, and most important, adult women's arrests for drug offenses have surged.

Where there have been increases in women's arrests for offenses that appear to be nontraditional, as in the case of assault or drug offenses, careful examination of these trends reveals the connections between these offenses and women's place.

English (1993) approached the issue of women's crime by analyzing detailed self-report surveys that she administered to a sample of 128 females and 872 male inmates in Colorado. She examined both the participation rates and crime frequency figures for a wide array of offenses. She found few differences in the participation rates of men and women, with the exception of three property crimes. Men were more likely than women to report participation in burglary, while women were more likely than men to have participated in theft and forgery. Exploring these differences further, she found that women "lack the specific knowledge needed to carry out a burglary" (English, 1993, p. 366).

Women were far more likely than men to be involved in forgery. Follow-up research on a subsample of high-crime rate female respondents revealed that many had worked in

TABLE 3   U.S. Rank Order of Adult Male and Female Arrests, 1986 and 1995

Male				Female			
1986 Arrests	Percent of Total	1995 Arrests	Percent of Total	1986 Arrests	Percent of Total	1995 Arrests	Percent of Total
(1) Other offenses	24.3	(1) Other offenses	28.7	(1) Other offenses	21.0	(1) Other offenses	26.2
(2) DUI	17.1	(2) DUI	11.3	(2) Larceny–theft	18.0	(2) Larceny–theft	14.5
(3) Drunkenness	9.4	(3) Drug abuse	11.0	(3) DUI	11.3	(3) Drug abuse	9.7
(4) Drug abuse	7.9	(4) Other assaults	8.8	(4) Fraud	8.4	(4) Other assault	8.1
(5) Larceny–theft	7.4	(5) Larceny–theft	6.8	(5) Drug abuse	6.8	(5) DUI	8.0

Source: Compiled from the Federal Bureau of Investigation (1996, p. 213).

retail establishments and therefore "knew how much time they had between stealing the checks or credit cards and having them reported (English, 1993, p. 370). The women said that they would target strip malls, where credit cards and bank checks could be stolen easily and used in nearby retail establishments. The women reported that their high-frequency theft was motivated by a "big haul," which meant a purse with several hundred dollars in it as well as cards and checks. English concludes that women's overrepresentation in low-paying, low-status jobs increases their involvement in these property crimes (English, 1993, p. 171).

English's findings with reference to two other offenses where gender differences did not appear in participation rates are worth exploring. She found no difference in the participation rates of women and men in drug sales and assault. However, when examining these frequency data, English found that women in prison reported significantly more drug sales than men reported, but this was not because they were engaged in big-time drug selling. Instead, the high number of drug sales was a product of the fact that women's drug sales were "concentrated in the small trades (i.e., transactions of less than $10)" (English, 1993, p. 372). Because they made so little money, English found that 20 percent of the active women dealers reported twenty or more drug deals per day (English, 1993, p. 372).

A reverse of the same pattern was found when she examined women's participation in assault. Here, slightly more (27.8 percent) of women than men (23.4 percent) reported an assault in the last year. However, most of these women reported only one assault during the study period (65.4 percent) compared to only about a third of the men (37.5 percent).

In sum, English found that both women's and men's crime reflected the role played by economic disadvantage in their criminal careers. Beyond this, though, gender played an important role in shaping women's and men's response to poverty. Specifically, women's criminal careers reflect "gender difference in legitimate and illegitimate opportunity structures, in personal networks, and in family obligations" (English, 1993, p. 374).

WOMEN AND THE DRUG CONNECTION

The majority of female arrests are for drug offenses and crimes committed to support a drug habit, particularly theft and prostitution. According to Drug Use Forecasting (DUF) data, more than half of women arrestees test positive for drugs. Drug-related arrests contribute to increases in the female prison population (Bureau of Justice Statistics, 1991). Federal Bureau of Investigation (FBI) data suggest that women accounted for 20 percent of the increase in drug arrests between 1980 and 1989. From 1982 to 1991, the number of women arrested for drug offenses increased by 89 percent, compared with an increase of 51 percent for men during the same period (Mauer & Huling, 1995).

Studies show that women are more likely to use drugs, use more serious drugs more frequently, and are more likely than men to be under the influence of drugs at the time of their offenses (Bureau of Justice Statistics, 1991, 1992). Although it is commonly assumed that women addicts will probably engage in prostitution to support their drug habits, their involvement in property crimes is even more common. In their sample of 197 female crack/cocaine users in Miami, Inciardi, Lockwood, and Pottieger (1993) found that in the women's last 90 days on the street, 76 percent engaged in drug-related offenses, 77 percent committed minor property crimes, and 51 percent engaged in prostitution (p. 120). The reliance on prostitution to support drug habits was also not confirmed in Anglin and Hser's sample (1987). According to the FBI, arrests for prostitution decreased between

1983 and 1992 (Federal Bureau of Investigation, 1993). Anglin and Hser (1987) found that the women in their sample supported their habits with a variety of crimes, in addition to property crimes, to raise money. Although theft is the crime of choice for women drug users, the researchers found that drug dealing was one of the criminal activities in which their respondents engaged (p. 393).

Data from state and federal court convictions also suggest that women are being arrested, convicted, and sentenced to prison for drug and property crimes but that both crime categories appear to be related to drug use. Felony conviction data for most serious offenses from state courts in 1990 illustrate that the highest percentage of women were convicted of fraud, which includes forgery and embezzlement (38 percent), followed by drug possession (17 percent) and trafficking (15 percent) (Maguire, Pastore, & Flanagan, 1993, p. 528). In terms of the numbers of offenders sentenced in the federal courts in 1992 under the U.S. Sentencing Commission Guidelines, the largest numerical category for females was drug offenses.

SENTENCE LENGTH AND TIME SERVED

Because female prisoners tend to receive shorter sentences than men overall, it has been assumed that women benefit from chivalrous treatment by sentencing judges. Recent research and available data suggest that shorter sentences for women are in fact a result in gender differences in the offenses for which women are incarcerated, criminal histories, and crime roles. On average, women incarcerated in state prisons in 1991 had fewer previous convictions than men, and their record of past convictions was less violent. Women were more likely than men to be in prison for drug and property offenses, and less likely than men to be incarcerated for violent offenses (Mauer & Huling, 1995).

The Bureau of Justice Statistics (1991, 1994) provides some information on time served and sentence length. Overall, average time served for those released in 1986 was sixteen months. Violent offenders served an average of twenty-seven months, with property offenders serving about thirteen months on average and drug offenders serving around fourteen months. In the 1991 sample, women received somewhat shorter maximum sentences than men, with half of the female prisoners serving a sentence of sixty months or less versus half of the men serving a sentence of 120 months or less. Twenty-four percent of the female prison population received sentences of less than thirty-six months. For women's drug offenses, the median sentence received was fifty-four months (with a mean of seventy-nine months); property offenders received a median sentence of forty-four months (with a mean of seventy-four months); and violent offenders received a median sentence of 180 months (mean 178 months). For all female prisoners, the median sentence received was sixty months, with a mean of 105 months (Bureau of Justice Statistics, 1994).

RACE, CLASS, AND GENDER DISPARITIES

Contemporary feminist theorists argue for the integration of race, class, and gender in any analytic framework used to study the experiences of women in the criminal justice system. Without such a framework it is impossible to draw a truly accurate picture of their experiences.

Only a few research efforts, however, have focused on the combined effects of race, class, and gender disparities among women in the criminal justice system. The stark realities of race, class, and gender discrimination touch the lives of all women and appear throughout the criminal justice process. Racial bias is a factor in arrests, pretrial treatment, and differential sentencing of women offenders. Women of color are disproportionately incarcerated in the United States. African-American women are incarcerated at a rate seven times that of white women (143 versus 20 per 10,000), and women of color represent more than 60 percent of the adult women in state and federal prisons nationwide (American Correctional Association, 1990). Women of color are also disproportionately represented on the death rows of this country relative to their proportion in the general population.

Mann (1995) documents disproportionality in prison sentences by comparing arrest rates with sentencing rates of women offenders in three states, California, Florida, and New York. She found that in all three states, women of color, particularly African-Americans, were disproportionately arrested. Mann asserts that women of color face double discrimination because of their gender and race/ethnicity. When class level is included, these women often face triple jeopardy.

A recent review of the literature addressing differential sentencing of African-American women and men notes the dearth of research on the possible interactive effects of gender and ethnicity and the inconclusiveness of the available information on the influence of race and ethnicity on criminal justice dispositions (Odubekun, 1992). The few studies that do report race-specific gender differences indicate more punitive treatment of women of color.

Foley and Rasche (1979) found that African-American women received longer sentences (55.1 months) than white women (52.5 months) in their study of one Missouri institution over a sixteen-year period. When the same offense was committed, Foley and Rasche found differences based on race. For example, white women imprisoned for murder served one-third less time than African-American women incarcerated for the same offense.

According to Mann (1989), in 1979, 32 percent of the women arrested and sentenced to prison in California were African-American, 14.9 percent were Hispanic, 0.8 percent were Native American, and 52.4 percent were white. By 1990, felony prosecutions of women of color in California had increased to 34.4 percent for African-Americans, 19 percent for Hispanics, and 2.5 percent for other women of color; prosecutions of white female felons had decreased to 43.8 percent. California female convictions in 1990 were fairly consistent across racial and ethnic subgroups.

In a study of sentencing outcomes for 1034 female defendants processed in a northern California county between 1972 and 1976, Kruttschnitt (1980–1981, p. 256) reports that in three of the five offense categories studied, a defendant's race or income affected her sentence. "Specifically, African-American women convicted of either disturbing the peace or drug law violations are sentenced more severely than their white counterparts."

In a study of gender differences in felony court processing in California in 1988, Farnsworth and Teske (1995) found that white women defendants were more likely to have charges of assault changed to nonassault than were women of color. Also, class and race often come together, as defendants are often African-American or Latina, and poor. Similar to arrest figures, sentencing statistics may also reflect the race and gender bias that occurred in the earlier decision-making stages of the criminal justice process.

THE WAR ON DRUGS: A WAR ON WOMEN OF COLOR

The declared intention to get rid of drugs and drug-related crime has resulted in federal and state funding being allocated for more police officers on the streets, more federal law enforcement officers, and the building of more jails and prisons rather than funds for prevention, education, and treatment. Poor women of color have become the main victims of these efforts in two ways. As mothers, sisters, daughters, and partners, they are trying to hold their families and communities together while so many men of color are incarcerated, and in addition, they are increasingly imprisoned themselves.

The incarceration of women of color, especially African-Americans, is a key factor in the increase in the number of women in prison. Women serving sentences for possession and possession for sale constitute the majority of women in prison for drug offenses.

According to a recent study by the Sentencing Project, from 1989 to 1994, young African-American women experienced the greatest increase in criminal justice control of all demographic groups studied. The 78 percent increase in criminal justice control rates for black women was more than double the increase for black men and for white women, and more than nine times the increase for white men (Mauer & Huling, 1995). Nationally, between 1980 and 1992 the number of black females in state or federal prisons grew 278 percent while the number of black males grew 186 percent; overall, the inmate population increased by 168 percent (Mauer & Huling, 1995).

Mauer and Huling (1995) present compelling evidence to support their contention that much of this increase can be laid at the door of the war on drugs, which many now assert has become a war on women, particularly women of color. Their analysis of Justice Department data shows that between 1986 and 1991, the number of black non-Hispanic women in state prisons for drug offenses nationwide increased more than eightfold, from 667 to 6193 (see Table 4). This 828 percent increase was nearly double the increase for black non-Hispanic males and more than triple the increase for white females (see Table 4).

TABLE 4   State Prisoners Incarcerated for Drug Offenses by Race or Ethnic Origin and Gender, 1986 and 1991

	1986		1991		Percent Increase	
	Male	Female	Male	Female	Male	Female
White (non-Hispanic)	12,868	969	26,452	3,300	106	241
Black (non-Hispanic)	13,974	667	73,932	6,193	429	828
Hispanic	8,484	664	35,965	2,843	324	328
Other	604	70	1,323	297	119	324
	35,930	2,370	137,672	12,633	283	433

Source: Mauer and Huling (1995).

"EQUALITY WITH A VENGEANCE": IS EQUAL TREATMENT FAIR TREATMENT?

Pollock (1994) asks if women are receiving more equal treatment in the criminal justice system today. If equal treatment relates to equal incarceration, the answer appears to be a resounding *yes*. It is certainly true that many more women offenders are likely to be incarcerated than at any other time in U.S. history. The criminal justice system appears to be more willing to incarcerate women.

There is a continuing debate among feminist legal scholars about whether equality under the law is necessarily good for women. To recap this debate (see Chesney-Lind and Pollock-Byrne, 1995, for a full discussion), some feminist legal scholars argue that the only way to eliminate the discriminatory treatment and oppression that women have experienced in the past is to push for continued equalization under the law, that is, to champion equal rights amendments and to oppose any legislation that treats men and women differently. It is argued that while equal treatment may hurt women in the short run, in the long run it is the only way to guarantee that women will ever be treated as equal partners in economic and social realms. For example, MacKinnon (1987, pp. 38–39) states: "For women to affirm difference, when difference means dominance, as it does with gender, means to affirm the qualities and characteristics of powerlessness." Even those who do not view the experience of women as one of oppression conclude that women will be victimized by laws created from "concern and affection" that are designed to protect them (Kirp, Ydof, & Franks, 1986).

The opposing argument maintains that women are not the same as men and that because it is a male standard that equality is measured against, women will always lose. Therefore, the position calls for recognizing the differential or "special" needs of women. This would mean that women and men might receive differential treatment as long as it did not put women in a more negative position than the absence of such a standard.

Yet another position points out that both the equal treatment and special needs approaches accept the domination of male definitions. For example, equality is defined as rights equal to those of males, and differential needs are defined as needs different from those of males. In these cases, women are the "other" under the law; the "bottom line" is a male one (Smart, 1989). Eisenstein (1988) writes: "Difference in this instance is set up as a duality: woman is different from man and this difference is seen as a deficiency because she is not man" (p. 8).

While these scholars are identifying the limitations of an equal-treatment model in law or in research in legal practices, that model and the evidence on which it is based are the centerpiece for sentencing reforms throughout the United States. These gender-neutral sentencing reforms aim to reduce sentencing disparity by punishing like crimes in the same way. By emphasizing parity, and then utilizing a male standard, more women are losing their freedom (Daly, 1994).

PRISONS AND PARITY

Initially, the differential needs approach was the dominant correctional policy. From the outset, the correctional response to women offenders was to embrace the Victorian notion of "separate spheres" and to construct and manage women's facilities based on what were seen as immutable differences between men and women (Rafter, 1990). Women were housed in separate facilities, and programs for women prisoners represented their perceived role in society. Thus they were taught to be good mothers and housekeepers; vocational education to prepare for employment was slighted in favor of domestic training. Women were hired to supervise female prisoners in the belief that only they could provide for the special needs of women prisoners and serve as role models to them. To some degree, this legacy still permeates women's prisons.

Sentencing practices also treated women and men differently. Women typically were much less likely to be imprisoned unless the woman offender did not fit the stereotypical female role; for example, she was a bad mother or did not have a family to care for (Chesney-Lind, 1987; Eaton, 1986).

The differential treatment of women in sentencing and prison programming was challenged by an emerging "parity" perspective during the 1970s. As a result of prisoner rights' litigation based on the parity model (see Pollock-Byrne, 1990), women offenders are being swept up in a system that seems bent on treating women "equally." This equity orientation translated into treatment of women prisoners *as if they were men*. Since this orientation did not change the role of gender in prison life or corrections, women prisoners receive the worst of both worlds.

For example, boot camps have become very popular as an alternative to prison for juvenile and adult offenders. New York operates a boot camp for women that is modeled on boot camps for men. This includes uniforms, short hair, humiliation for disrespect of staff, and other militaristic approaches.

Chain gangs for women have also become fashionable. In Alabama, male chain gangs were reinstated and corrections officials in that state were threatened with a lawsuit brought by male prisoners suggesting that the practice of excluding women from chain gangs was unconstitutional. The response from the Alabama Corrections Commissioner was to include women in chain gangs (Franklin, 1996). The corrections commissioner was ultimately forced to resign, but the debate about the value of male chain gangs continues in the state.

A serious and persistent allegation that has been associated with women's imprisonment is sexual abuse of women inmates at the hands of male correctional officers. The sexual victimization of women in U.S. prisons is the subject of increasing news coverage and, more recently, international scrutiny. Scandals have erupted in Georgia, Hawaii, California, Ohio, Louisiana, Michigan, Tennessee, New York and New Mexico (Craig, 1996; Curriden, 1993; Lopez, 1993; Meyer, 1992; Sewenely, 1993; Stein, 1996; Watson, 1992). This issue is of such concern that it has attracted the attention of organizations such as Human Rights Watch (1993).

Institutional subcultures in women's prisons, which encourage correctional officers to "cover" for each other, coupled with inadequate protection accorded women who file complaints, make it unlikely that many women prisoners will formally complain about abuse. Additionally, the public stereotype of women in prison as "bad girls" also makes it difficult for a woman inmate to support her case against a correctional officer in court. Finally, what little progress has been made is now threatened by recent legislation that has curtailed the ability of prisoners and advocates to sue about prison conditions (Stein, 1996, p. 24; see also Human Rights Watch, 1996).

Reviewing the situation of women incarcerated in five states (California, Georgia, Michigan, Illinois, and New York) and the District of Columbia, Human Rights Watch (1996) concluded:

> Our findings indicate that being a woman prisoner in U.S. state prisons can be a terrifying experience. If you are sexually abused, you cannot escape from your abuser. Grievance or investigatory procedures, where they exist, are often ineffectual, and correctional employees continue to engage in abuse because they believe that they will rarely be held accountable, administratively or criminally. Few people outside the prison walls know what is going on or care if they do know. Fewer still do anything to address the problem. (p. 1)

Human Rights Watch (1996) also noted that investigators were "concerned that states' adherence to U.S. anti-discrimination laws, in the absence of strong safeguards against custodial sexual misconduct, has often come at the fundamental rights of prisoners" (p. 2).

Ironically, despite the superficial emphasis on equity in contemporary corrections, it appears that women today are also recipients of some of the worst of old separate spheres abuses, particularly in the area of social control. As an example, McClellan (1994) examined disciplinary practices at prisons housing Texas male and female inmates. McClellan (1989) constructed two samples of inmates (271 males and 245 females) from Texas Department of Corrections records and followed them for a one-year period. She found gender-related differences in treatment between the sexes. For example, she documented that while most men in her sample (63.5 percent) had no citations or only one citation for a rule violation, only 17.1 percent of the women in her sample had such records. McClellan (1994) noted that women prisoners were more likely to receive numerous citations and for different sorts of infractions than men. Most frequently, women were cited for "violating posted rules," while males were cited most often for "refusing to work" (p. 77). Women were more likely than men to receive the most severe sanctions.

McClellan (1994) notes that the wardens of the women's prisons in her study state quite frankly that they demand total compliance with every rule on the books and punish violations through official mechanisms. She concluded that there exist "two distinct institutional forms of surveillance and control operating at the male and female facilities" (p. 87).

DOING TIME: ADAPTATION AND COPING IN CONTEMPORARY WOMEN'S PRISONS

Very little research has been conducted on women prisoner subcultures in over two decades since the classic research of Ward and Kassebaum (1965), Giallombardo (1966), and Heffernan (1972). Owen (1998) describes the world of women's prisons today. As Owen explains, the day-to-day world of female prisons now requires a new description and analysis. She attempts to answer several critical questions: How do women in prison do time? How has prison culture for women changed from the findings of earlier research? How have the contemporary problems of overcrowding, the war on drugs, gangs, and racial division among prisoners affected the way women do time? Owen observed that women prisoners organize their time and create a social world that is quite different from contemporary men's prisons. She suggests that imprisonment and its subsequent response are gendered.

As cited in Owen (1998), the early work of Ward and Kassebaum (1965) and Giallombardo (1966) focused on a social structure based on the family, traditional sex roles, and same-sex relationships. Later studies (Larsen & Nelson, 1984; Leger, 1987; Propper, 1982) described the female prisoner culture in terms of pseudofamily structure and homosexual relations, following themes developed by Ward and Kassebaum and Giallombardo. These studies suggest that women create lives in prison that reflect elements of traditional family roles and the street life. This social structure revolves around their sexual identify and attendant social roles, mirroring their relations with males on the outside.

Owen explains that Heffernan (1972) found that the existing descriptive and theoretical models of prison culture were based on a male version of the prison and therefore were inadequate for describing life in a women's prison. Employing Syke's (1958) hypotheses, Heffernan looked for key roles and norms that enable the prisoner social system to act cohesively and to reject those who don't adopt the roles and norms. Although she found no support for Syke's role adaptations among the women prisoners in her study, Heffernan described adaptation to the inmate world in terms of three orientations: "the square," a woman who was tied to conventional norms and values; "the cool," a person doing time in a way that involved control and manipulation; and "the life," someone who embraced a more deviant criminal identity based on the culture of the streets.

Similar to Irwin (1970), Heffernan argues that a woman's initial orientation to prison was often based on preprison identities. She found that women who created a family life in prison were most apt to adapt to prison life and that the family was a critical element to the social order of the prison.

The imprisonment of women is tied directly to their status under patriarchy (Kurshan, 1992). Kurshan states that while prisons are used as social control for both men and women, the imprisonment of women "as well as all other aspects of our lives, takes place against a backdrop of patriarchal relationships" (p. 230). Following this theme, Owen (1998) suggests that "the study of women in prison must be viewed through the lens of patriarchy and its implications for the everyday lives of women."

According to Owen (1998), little has changed in women's prison culture. Personal relationships with other prisoners, both emotionally and physically, connections to family and loved ones, and commitments to preprison identities continue to shape the core of prison culture among women. "The world of the women's prison is shaped by pre-prison experiences, the role of women in contemporary society, and the ways women rely on personalized relationships to survive their prison terms" (p. 7). Economic marginalization, histories of abuse, and self-destructive behavior form the pathway to women's imprisonment. The degree to which these behaviors continue to shape their lives, in turn, is dependent on the nature of one's experience in the prison and attachment to competing systems and identities (p. 8).

Contemporary women's prisons also differ from men's prisons in terms of gang activity. Owen (1998) found a lack of organized gangs at her study site, the Central California Women's Facility. She attributed this to the prison family structure and the activities surrounding this structure, which may meet the survival needs of women prisoners that are often met by street gangs.

CONCLUSIONS: PROGRAM AND POLICY IMPLICATIONS

The expansion of the women's prison population has been fueled primarily by increased rates of incarceration for drug law violations and other less serious offenses. The majority of imprisoned women in the United States are sentenced for nonviolent crimes, which often reflect their marginalized status. Women prisoners share many of the problems of their male counterparts, but they also endure unique issues as a result of their race, class, and gender. This threefold jeopardy is manifested in several ways: (1) women offenders are more likely to be victims of physical, sexual, and emotional abuse; (2) they are at greater risk of incarceration due to substance abusing behavior; and (3) they are most likely to be the sole caretakers of dependent children and they are economically marginalized.

Women prisoners have a host of medical, psychological, and financial problems and needs. Substance abuse, compounded by poverty, unemployment, physical and mental illness, physical and sexual abuse, and homelessness often propels women through the revolving door of the criminal justice system. Rather than affording an ameliorative approach to these complex issues, the law enforcement response often exacerbates these problems, causing further psychological and social stress.

Changes in criminal justice policies and practices over the last decade have clearly contributed to dramatic growth in the female prison population. Mandatory prison terms and sentencing guidelines are gender-blind, and in their crusade to get tough on crime, policymakers have gotten tough on women, drawing them into jails and prisons in unprecedented numbers.

The data summarized in this chapter, as well as other research, suggest that women may be better served in the community due to the decreased seriousness of their crimes and their amenability to treatment. By focusing on strategies that directly address the problems of women in conflict with the law, the overuse and overcrowding of women's prisons can be avoided.

Women prisoners have experienced a history of neglect in the development and implementation of correctional programming targeted to their situations. Historically, programs for women offenders were based on male program models without consideration as to their appropriateness for women. Thus we have very little empirical evidence indicating what works for female offenders.

Research supported by the National Institute of Corrections by Austin, Bloom and Donahue (1992) identified a series of effective strategies for working with women offenders in community settings. This study reviewed limited program evaluation data and found that "promising approaches" are multidimensional and deal with the gender-specific needs of women. Austin et al. found that promising community programs combined supervision and services to address the specialized needs of female offenders in safe, structured environments. These programs and strategies use an "empowerment" model of skill building to develop competencies to enable women to achieve independence.

A recent study (Koons, Burrow, Morash, & Bynum, 1997) provides characteristics of promising programs serving women offenders. "A sizable number of promising models approached the treatment of women offenders using a comprehensive and holistic strategy for meeting their needs" (p. 521). Program components included elements such as the use of continuum of care, individualized and structured programming, and an emphasis on skill building.

A review of the backgrounds of women in prison suggests more effective ways to address their problems and needs. Whether it be more funding for drug treatment programs, more shelters for the victims of domestic violence, more family-focused interventions, or more job training programs, the solutions are available. However, changes in public policy are needed so that the response to women's offending is one that emphasizes human needs rather than focusing solely on punitive sanctions. The tax dollars saved by reducing women's imprisonment could be reinvested in programs designed to meet their needs, which would enrich not only their lives but the lives of their children and future generations.

REFERENCES

AMERICAN CORRECTIONAL ASSOCIATION. (1990). *The female offender: What does the future hold?* Washington, DC: St. Mary's Press.

ANDERSON, S. (1994). *Comparison of male and female admissions one year prior to the implementation of structured sanctions.* Salem, OR: Oregon State Department of Corrections.

ANGLIN, M., & HSER, Y. (1987). Addicted women and crime. *Criminology, 25,* 359–394.

AUSTIN, J., BLOOM, B., & DONAHUE, T. (1992). *Female offenders in the community: An analysis of innovative strategies and programs.* Washington, DC: National Institute of Corrections.

BARRY, E. (1995). Legal issues for prisoners with children. In K. Gabel & D. Johnston (Eds.), *Children of incarcerated parents* (pp. 147–156). New York: Lexington Books.

BIRCH, H. (Ed.). (1994). *Moving targets: Women, murder and representation.* Berkeley, CA. University of California Press.

BLOOM, B., CHESNEY-LIND, M., & OWEN, B. (1994). *Women in California prisons: Hidden victims of the war on drugs.* San Francisco: Center on Juvenile and Criminal Justice.

BLOOM, B., & STEINHART, D. (1993). *Why punish the children? A reappraisal of the children of incarcerated mothers in America.* San Francisco: National Council on Crime and Delinquency.

BROWNE, A. (1987). *When battered women kill.* New York: Free Press.

BUREAU OF JUSTICE STATISTICS. (1988). *Profile of state prison inmates, 1986.* Washington, DC: U.S. Department of Justice.

BUREAU OF JUSTICE STATISTICS. (1989). *Prisoners in 1988.* Washington, DC: U.S. Department of Justice.

BUREAU OF JUSTICE STATISTICS. (1991). *Women in prison in 1986.* Washington, DC: U.S. Department of Justice.

BUREAU OF JUSTICE STATISTICS. (1992). *Women in jail in 1989.* Washington, DC: U.S. Department of Justice.

BUREAU OF JUSTICE STATISTICS. (1993). *Prisoners in 1992.* Washington, DC: U.S. Department of Justice.

BUREAU OF JUSTICE STATISTICS. (1994). *Women in prison.* Washington, DC: U.S. Department of Justice.

BUREAU OF JUSTICE STATISTICS (1997a). *Prisoners in 1996.* Washington, DC: U.S. Department of Justice.

BUREAU OF JUSTICE STATISTICS. (1997b). *HIV in prisons and jails, 1995.* Washington, DC: U.S. Department of Justice.

CALIFORNIA DEPARTMENT OF CORRECTIONS. (1997, October 15). *Weekly report of population.* Data Analysis Unit, Offender Information Services Branch. Sacramento, CA: The department.

CALLAHAN, M. (1986). *Historical corrections statistics in the United States, 1850–1984.* Washington, DC: Bureau of Justice Statistics.

CHESNEY-LIND, M. (1987). Female offenders: Paternalism reexamined. In L. Crites & W. Hepperele (Eds.), *Women, the courts and equality* (pp. 114–140). Newbury Park, CA: Sage Publications.

CHESNEY-LIND, M. (1997). *The female offender: Girls, women and crime.* Thousand Oaks, CA: Sage Publications.

CHESNEY-LIND, M., & POLLOCK-BYRNE, J. (1995). Women's prisons: Equality with a vengeance. In J. Pollock-Byrne & A. Merlo (Eds.). *Women, law and social control* (pp. 155–175). Boston: Allyn & Bacon.

CRAIG, G. (1996, March 23). Advocates say nude filming shows need for new laws. *Rochester Democrat and Chronicle*, pp. A1, A6.

CURRIDEN, M. (1993, September 20). Prison scandal in Georgia: Guards traded favors for sex. *National Law Journal*, p. 8.

DALY, K. (1991, April). *Gender and race in the penal process: Statistical research, interpretive gaps, and the multiple meanings of justice.* Mimeo.

DALY, K. (1994). *Gender, crime and punishment.* New Haven, CT: Yale University Press.

DOUGLAS, S. (1994). *Where the girls are: Growing up female with the mass media.* New York: Random House.

EATON, M. (1986). *Justice for women?* Milton Keynes, England: Open University Press.

EISENSTEIN, Z. (1988). *The female body and the law.* Berkeley, CA: University of California Press.

ENGLISH, K. (1993). Self-reported crime rates on women prisoners. *Journal of Quantitative Criminology, 9,* 357–382.

FARNSWORTH, M., & TESKE, R. (1995). Gender differences in felony court processing: Three hypotheses of disparity. *Women and Criminal Justice 6*(2), 23–44.

FEDERAL BUREAU OF INVESTIGATION. (1992). *Crime in the United States, 1991.* Washington, DC: U.S. Department of Justice.

FEDERAL BUREAU OF INVESTIGATION. (1993). *Crime in the United States, 1992.* Washington, DC: U.S. Department of Justice.

FEDERAL BUREAU OF INVESTIGATION. (1996). *Crime in the United States,1995.* Washington, DC: U.S. Department of Justice.

FOLEY, L., & RASCHE, C. (1979). The effect of race on sentence, actual time served and final disposition on female offenders. In J. Conley (Ed.), *Theory and research in criminal justice.* Cincinnati, OH: Anderson Publishing.

FRANKLIN, R. (1996, April 26). Alabama to expand chain gangs—adding women. *USA Today*, p. 3A.

GABEL, K., & JOHNSTON, D. (EDS.). (1995). *Children of incarcerated parents.* New York: Lexington Books.

GIALLOMBARDO, R. (1966). *Society of women: A study of a women's prison.* New York: Wiley.

GILFUS, M. (1992). From victims to survivors: Women's routes of entry and immersion into street crime. *Women and Criminal Justice, 4*(1), 62–89.

HASKELL, M. (1973). *From reverence to rape: The treatment of women in the movies.* New York: Holt, Rinehart and Winston.

HEFFERNAN, E. (1972). *Making it in prison: The square, the cool, and the life.* New York: Wiley.

HOLMLUND, C. (1995). A decade of deadly dolls: Hollywood and the woman killer. In H. Birch (Ed.), *Moving targets: Women, murder and representation.* Berkeley, CA: University of California Press.

HUMAN RIGHTS WATCH. (1996). *All too familiar: sexual abuse of women in U.S. state prisons.* New York: HRW.

INCIARDI, J., LOCKWOOD, D., & POTTIEGER, A. (1993). *Women and crack cocaine.* New York: Macmillan.

IRWIN, J. (1970). *The felon.* Englewood Cliffs, NJ: Prentice Hall.

JOHNSTON, D. (1992). *The children of offenders study.* Pasadena, CA.: Pacific Oaks Center for Children of Incarcerated Parents.

KATZ, P. (1997). The effect of welfare reform on incarcerated mothers and their families. In *Family and Corrections Network Report 14,* 3, 6.

KIRP, D., YUDOF, M. & FRANKS, M. (1986). *Gender justice*. Chicago: University of Chicago Press.

KOONS, B., BURROWS, J., MORASH, M., & BYNUM, T. (1997). Expert and offender perceptions of program elements linked to successful outcomes for incarcerated women. *Crime and Delinquency 43*(4), 512–532.

KRUTTSCHNITT, C. (1980–1981). Social status and sentences of female offenders. *Law and Society Review, 15*(2), 247–265.

KURSHAN, N. (1992). Women and imprisonment in the U.S. In W. Churchill & J. Vander Wall (Eds.), *Cages of steel* (pp. 331–358). Washington, DC: Maisonneuve Press.

LARSEN, J. & NELSON, J. (1984). Women, friendship, and adaptation to prison. *Journal of Criminal Justice, 12*(5), 601–615.

LEGER, R. (1987). Lesbianism among women prisoners: Participants and nonparticipants. *Criminal Justice and Behavior, 14*, 463–479.

LOPEZ, S. (1993, July 8). Fifth guard arrested on sex charge. *Albuquerque Journal*, pp. A1, A2.

MACKINNON, C. (1987). *Feminism unmodified: Discourse on life and law*. London: Harvard University Press.

MAGUIRE, K., PASTORE, A., & FLANAGAN, T. (1993). *Sourcebook of criminal justice statistics, 1992*. U.S. Department of Justice, Bureau of Justice Statistics. Washington, DC: U.S. Government Printing Office.

MANN, C. (1989). Minority and female: A criminal justice double bind. *Social Justice, 16*(3), 95–114.

MANN, C. (1995). Women of color and the criminal justice system. In B. Price & N. Sokoloff (Eds.). *The criminal justice system and women* (pp. 118–135). New York: McGraw-Hill.

MAUER, M., & HULING, T. (1995). *Young black Americans and the criminal justice system: Five years later*. Washington, DC: The Sentencing Project.

MCCLELLAN, D. (1994). Disparity in the discipline of male and female inmates in Texas prisons. *Women and Criminal Justice, 5*(2), 71–97.

MEYER, M. (1992, November 9). Coercing sex behind bars: Hawaii's prison scandal. *Newsweek*, pp. 23–25.

ODUBEKUN, L. (1992). A structural approach to differential gender sentencing. *Criminal Justice Abstracts, 24*(2), 343–360.

OWEN, B. (1998). *In the mix: Struggle and survival in a women's prison*. Albany, NY: State University of New York Press.

OWEN, B., & BLOOM, B. (1995). Profiling women prisoners: Findings from national surveys and a California sample. *Prison Journal, 75*(2), 165–185.

POLLOCK, J. (1994, April). *The increasing incarceration rate of women offenders: Equality or justice?* Paper presented at Prisons 2000 conference, Leicester, England.

POLLOCK-BYRNE, J. (1990). *Women, prison, and crime*. Pacific Grove, CA: Brooks/Cole.

PROPPER, A. (1982). Make-believe families and homosexuality among imprisoned girls. *Criminology, 20*(1), 127–139.

RAEDER, M. (1993). Gender and sentencing: Single moms, battered women and other sex-based anomalies in the gender free world of federal sentencing guidelines. *Pepperdine Law Review, 20*(3), 905–990.

RAFTER, N. (1990). *Partial justice: Women, prisons, and social control*. New Brunswick, NJ: Transaction Books.

SEWENELY, A. (1993, January 6). Sex abuse charges rock women's prison. *Detroit News*, pp. B1, B7.

SINGER, L. (1973). Women and the correctional process. *American Criminal Law Review, 11*, 295–308.

SMART, C. (1989). *Feminism and the power of law*. London: Routledge & Kegan Paul.

SNELL, T., & MORTON, D. (1994). *Women in prison*. Special report. Washington, DC: Bureau of Justice Statistics.

STARK, E., & FLITCRAFT, A. (1996). *Women at risk: Domestic violence and women's health*. London: Sage Publications.

STEFFENSMEIER, D., & ALLAN, E. (1995). Gender, age and crime. In J. Sheley (Ed.), *Handbook of contemporary criminology* (pp. 88–116). New York: Wadsworth.

STEIN, B. (1996, July). Life in prison: Sexual abuse. *The Progressive*, pp. 23–24.

SYKES, G. (1958). *Society of captives*. Princeton, NJ: Princeton University Press.

WARD, D., & KASSEBAUM, G. (1965). *Women's prison: Sex and social structure*. Chicago: Aldine-Atherton.

WATSON, T. (1992, November 16). Georgia indictments charge abuse of female inmates. *USA Today*, p. A3.

WEBSDALE, N., & CHESNEY-LIND, M. (1997). Doing violence to women: Research synthesis on the victimization of women. In L. Bowker (Ed.), *Masculinities and violence*. Thousand Oaks, CA: Sage Publications.

WHITE, J., & KOWALSKI, R. (1994). Deconstructing the myth of the nonaggressive woman: A feminist analysis. *Psychology of Women Quarterly, 18*, 487–508.

13

The Pains of Imprisonment

Long-Term Incarceration Effects on Women in Prison[1]

Zina T. McGee

This study examines differences in reported emotional problems among short- and long-term female inmates. Results suggest (1) that long-term female inmates are more likely to experience emotional problems than are short-term female inmates, and (2) that white females serving a long-term sentence are more likely to report emotional problems than are black females serving a long-term sentence. Additional support is found for the extended-kin network that is characteristic of black females compared to whites, in that subjects reported greater personal contact with families and a higher level of satisfaction with their child's living arrangement. It is suggested that the kinship network also serves as a coping mechanism for black female inmates, which may account for the decrease in emotional problems reported among this group. In addition, in light of these findings it is suggested that future studies continue to examine the effects of long-term incarceration of female inmates.

Recent studies have shown that in the United States, rates of female arrests and subsequent incarceration are increasing (see, e.g., Allen & Simonsen, 1998; Gilliard & Beck, 1998; Henriques, 1995; Watterson, 1996). In 1994 the FBI reported a 24 percent increase in the arrest rate of females betwee 1986 and 1991, in addition to a 75 percent increase in the rate of female incarceration during the same period (Snell, 1994). Figures released by the Bureau of Justice Statistics (BJS) indicate that in 1997 the number of women under the jurisdiction of state and federal prison authorities grew from 74,970 to 79,624 (Gilliard & Beck, 1998). With regard to the rate of growth among female inmates in proportion to the male counterparts, additional statistics released by the BJS suggest that during 1997, the number of male inmates increased 5.2 percent, while the number of female inmates increased 6.2 percent (Gilliard & Beck, 1998). These figures, which indicate that a substantial number of women are jailed each year, suggest that if a woman is arrested, she will probably be incarcerated for her crime (Allen & Simonsen, 1998).

Although studies have suggested that compared to men, *addicted* women are increasingly committing crimes of violence, researchers continue to argue that the overall increase in female detainees is not the result of greater involvement in more serious crime. Instead, changes in sentencing laws and practices such as mandatory minimum sentencing have contributed greatly to rising imprisonment rates among women (Allen & Simonsen, 1998; McClellan, Farahee, & Crouch, 1997; Rosenblatt, 1996; Snell, 1994). In fact, with the exception of larceny–theft, rates of arrest and detainment among females have increased faster for drug offenses than for any other category within the crime index (see Allen & Simonsen, 1998; Chesney-Lind, 1997). In a historical analysis of women's confinement, Rosenblatt (1996) argues that the increase in felony drug charges among females can be viewed primarily as a response to deteriorating economic conditions. Thus impoverished women are often forced to engage in drug crimes to survive since they are the primary caretakers of their children.

Despite recent increases in the female offender population and attention to the impact of imprisonment on mothers and children, little is known about the multiple occurrence of factors that can affect a woman's adjustment to prison life. Further, few studies have examined programs designed to create successful outcomes such as economic independence, family reunification, and reduced criminal involvement. It is the intention of the author to examine the psychological effects of imprisonment on women and their children. Emphasis is placed on the conditions of confinement as well as on the strategies used by female offenders to cope with incarceration. Finally, we provide an analysis of racial differences among female detainees forced to cope with the pains of imprisonment.

REVIEW OF THE LITERATURE

Although female offenders became the subjects of extensive research in the 1960s, studies examining their adjustment to imprisonment today have received minimal attention. Research continues to focus primarily on the effects of incarceration on male prisoners, suggesting that the female inmate remains a "forgotten offender" (Iglehart & Stein, 1985; MacKenzie, Robinson, & Campbell, 1989, 1995). Those studies that have focused on the female inmate, however, have shown that the impact of imprisonment is more severe on women than on men, especially if they have family responsibilities (Durham, 1994; Edwards, 1984). Nearly two-thirds of women in prison have at least one child under 18, many of whom were the sole caretakers of their children prior to incarceration (Chesney-Lind, 1997; Koons, Burrow, Moresh, & Bynum, 1997). Watterson (1996) suggests that the greatest source of tension in prison for women is the concern they have about their children, particularly among those incarcerated for long periods of time who face the risk of losing their children. In an analysis of imprisoned women and their children, Henriques (1995) also suggests that separation from children is a major concern for imprisoned mothers. Inmate mothers are thought to lose their sense of identity when the parental role is threatened by incarceration, and in many instances the mother–child relationship is permanently damaged (Henriques, 1995). In a study of the difficulties faced by women in prison, Sobel (1982) reported a high incidence of nervous disorders resulting from the strain experienced by female inmates, most of which was due to a separation from children. In a similar study of the female offender, Flowers (1987) also found enforced separation to be the greatest problem faced by mothers in prison. His results further suggested that the behavior exhibited by incarcerated mothers resembled those of a person suffering a loss due to death, divorce, or other mother–child separations, characterized by such symptoms as anger and guilt (Flowers, 1987). Morris (1981) also found the prison experience to be more severe for women than for men, particularly because of their concern with the care and upbringing of their children. Her findings indicated that female prisons had a tendency to destroy a woman's emotional and physical well-being in addition to her relationships with family members and friends (Morris, 1981). Finally, Kurshan (1996) suggests that incarceration has severe ramifications for women, particularly in terms of the intense pain of forced separation from children, many of whom are placed in foster care. Since most data suggest a significantly higher rate of female inmates with children than of men, the effects of imprisonment on them remains an important issue.

While research on women and their adjustment to prison life remains limited, studies of the female inmate serving a long-term sentence seem nonexistent (MacKenzie et al., 1989, 1995). Recent figures compiled by the Bureau of Justice Statistics suggest that the average maximum length of felony sentences imposed by state courts for females is thirty-five months, while the average maximum length of felony sentence imposed by state courts for males is fifty-four months (Maguire & Pastore, 1996). Although these figures may suggest that the female offender is more likely to serve a short-term sentence for her crime, recent studies have shown that the number of long-term offenders in the United States is increasing at a faster rate than for those serving short-term sentences (Chesney-Lind, 1997; MacKenzie & Goodstein, 1985; Negy et al., 1997; MacKenzie et al., 1989, 1995). Since research has indicated that the pains of imprisonment are harsher for incarcerated mothers, one would expect the effects of a long-term sentence to be even more severe for this group.

Despite the growing number of long-term offenders in the United States, studies continue to focus primarily on the male long-term offender, with little emphasis being placed on females. Since few studies have examined issues of coping among women within the prison setting, very little is known about the special concerns of female inmates, including those relating to the need to maintain a parental role within the family (see, e.g., Sheridan, 1996). Those studies that have focused on long-term female offenders, however, have had inconsistent results with regard to the effects of long-term sentencing. In a study of female offenders, Carlen (1985) found that long-term inmates were more likely than short-term inmates to engage in one of four responses to the pains of imprisonment, including death, institutionalization, self-mutilation, and madness. Her results indicated further that the primary means of survival for long-term female offenders involved the formation of relationships with other prisoners (Carlen, 1985). In contrast, MacKenzie et al. (1989, 1995) found no difference in the level of anxiety experienced by women serving both short- and long-term sentences, regardless of their time served in prison. In addition, they found the establishment of relationships with other inmates, or "play families," to be a coping mechanism only for newly entered inmates as opposed to those having served their sentences for a longer period of time. These studies suggest that coping behavior and prison adjustment may in some cases differ among short- and long-term female inmates, although a specific response to long-term incarceration cannot be generalized to the entire female prison population.

The present study examines the effects of long-term incarceration on the emotional well-being of black and white female inmates. Studies have suggested that compared to white women in prisons and jails, black women face greater problems in that they are more likely to be single, living on welfare, and responsible for young children (Feinman, 1986; Flowers, 1987; Morris, 1987; Rosenblatt, 1996). In a study of detainees at Rikers Island Correctional Facility, Richie (1996) suggests that the intersection of gender, race, and violence creates an effective system that leaves many black women vulnerable to public and private subordination. With regard to the coping strategies of female prisoners, however, additional studies have shown that black women have stronger ties to their families and children than do white women, as indicated by increased visits, phone calls, and letters (Baunach, 1985; Feinman, 1986). In addition, studies have shown that black and white mothers in prison tend to show important differences in their psychological responses to enforced separation. Baunach (1985), for example, found that black children were more likely to live with their mother's parents, whereas white children more often lived with their fathers and nonrelatives. Moreover, black mothers appeared to be more satisfied with their child's living arrangements than were white mothers (Baunach, 1985). These findings suggest the importance of the extended-kin network as a coping mechanism for black female inmates, and it is anticipated that the negative effects of enforced separation from children may be lessened when these factors are taken into account.

In summary, it is suggested that studies of the long-term offender lack sufficient research on incarcerated mothers, who, as previous studies have shown, suffer more from the pains of imprisonment than any other group. In an effort to reintroduce the "forgotten offender" as an integral part of the research on long-term incarceration, the present study addressed the following questions:

1. Are there significant differences in the emotional well-being of short- and long-term female offenders?
2. If so, are there significant differences in reported emotional problems among black and white long-term female offenders?
3. Does the frequency of contact with family members differ among black and white long-term female offenders?
4. Do differences exist in children's living arrangements among black and white mothers serving a long-term sentence?

It is hypothesized that the effects of incarceration will be greater for long-term than for short-term inmates, and that black females will report fewer emotional difficulties than will white females in the presence of the extended-kin network. In addition, it is expected that coping strategies among female inmates will be linked to closer ties to families as well as to satisfaction with a child's placement within the family.

DATA AND METHOD

Data for this study were collected from the *Survey of Inmates of Local Jails, 1989* [United States]. Information was collected by the Bureau of Justice Statistics (1990) on 5785 inmates (3992 male and 1793 female) located in 407 institutions throughout the United States. Variables include current offenses, prior criminal record, detention status, drug and alcohol use, demographic and socioeconomic characteristics, military service, jail activities, and health care provided by the jails. For the present study, emphasis is placed specifically on female inmates serving both short- and long-term sentences. Differences in demographic characteristics among the two groups of women are examined, in addition to an analysis of the variation in reported emotional difficulty. With regard to race, emphasis is placed on (1) differences in the degree of reported emotional difficulty among long-term inmates, and (2) differences in the degree of familial contact and the location of a child as two coping strategies used by long-term inmates.

Variables

Detention Status.   Female offenders were divided into categories of short- and long-term sentencing. Those serving a sentence of two years or less ($n = 161$) were classified as short-term offenders, while those serving a sentence of eight years or more ($n = 176$) were classified as long-term offenders (see MacKenzie et al., 1989, 1995).

Mental Health Status.   Respondents were asked to report a series of health problems that required a doctor's care on a regular basis. Emphasis is placed specifically on those respondents who reported having emotional problems as a measure of mental health status.

Coping Strategies.   Respondents were asked the extent to which they received phone calls, letters, and visits from family members and friends as a means of coping with long term imprisonment. Responses range from more than three times a month to never, and emphasis is placed solely on those respondents reporting the greatest frequency on familial contact. Satisfaction with a child's placement serves as a second means of coping with long-term imprisonment, in which respondents were asked to report whether their child (or children) lived with a father, grandparents, other relatives, friends, or elsewhere. To remain consistent with studies focusing on the kinship network and to compare racial differences, emphasis is placed on mothers reporting their children as living with fathers or grandparents.

ANALYSIS AND FINDINGS

Table 1 presents a comparison of demographic characteristics and mental health status among short- and long-term offenders. With regard to the demographic variables, the findings remain consistent with previous studies that have found no significant differences in the age, race, and number of children found in each category (see MacKenzie &

TABLE 1   Demographic Characteristics and Mental Health Status among Short- and Long-Term Female Inmates

Demographics	Short-Term Sentence (*n* = 161)	Long-Term Sentence (*n* = 176)
Mean age	28.9	29.5
Race (%)		
White	48.4	53.4
Black	47.8	46.6
Other	3.7	0.0
Mean number of children	2.2	3.0
Mental health status		
Emotional difficulty (%)	8.1	20.0*

*Significantly different from short-term sentence at *p* <0.05.

Goodstein, 1985; MacKenzie et al., 1989, 1995). In contrast, results show a significant difference in the mental health status of short-term and long-term inmates, in that those serving long-term sentences are more likely to report emotional difficulties (20.0 percent) than are those serving a short-term sentence (8.1 percent).

Table 2 provides a comparison of reported emotional problems among black and white long-term offenders. Results suggest that black females serving a long-term sentence are less likely to report emotional difficulties (14.3 percent) than are white females (25.0 percent) also serving a long-term sentence.

Table 3 examines differences in the degree of familial contact and location of a child as coping mechanisms among long-term female inmates of both races. Results suggest that among long-term offenders, white females are more likely to receive phone calls or letters from their families (25.0 percent and 37.5 percent respectively), while black females are more likely to receive personal visits (14.3 percent). In addition, the findings indicate that among long-term offenders, the children of white mothers are more likely to be placed with their fathers (37.5 percent), while the children of black mothers are more likely to be

TABLE 2   Mental Health Status of Long-Term Female Inmates by Race

	Race	
	Whites (*n* = 94)	Blacks (*n* = 82)
Emotional difficulty (%)		
Yes	25	14.3*
No	75	84.7

*Significantly different from white female inmates at *p* <0.05.

TABLE 3   Variation in the Degree of Familial Contact and Location of
Child(ren) among Black and White Long-Term Female Inmates

	Race	
	Whites ($n = 94$)	Blacks ($n = 82$)
Familial contact (more than three times per month, %)		
Phone calls	25.0	14.3*
Letters	37.5	12.4
Visits	07.9	14.3
Location of child		
Father	37.5	20.2*
Grandparents	25.0	42.9

*Significantly different from white female inmates at $p < 0.05$.

placed with their grandparents. Consistent with previous research, these findings suggest that significant differences in children's placement exist for white and black female inmates. Further, the results indicate the importance of familial contact as a source of coping among females incarcerated for extended periods of time.

DISCUSSION AND CONCLUSIONS

The results of this study support the contention that long-term incarceration has a greater effect on the emotional well-being of female inmates than does short-term incarceration. Although this finding is inconsistent with some studies of long-term incarceration, it does suggest that future research should examine the effects of long-term sentencing on mental health status. In a review of prisoners' rights, McLaren (1997) suggests that a humane system of corrections should make efforts to minimize the damage to the bond between mother and child. Similarly, Allen and Simonsen (1998) argue that contact with family members is central to the well-being of female inmates, many of whom are at the lowest point of their lives. Therefore, further research on long-term sentencing is necessary to understand the psychological ramifications of imprisonment among mothers.

Results of this study also indicate that white female inmates serving long-term sentences are more likely to exhibit emotional difficulties than are black female inmates serving long-term sentences. This finding is inconsistent with Feinman's (1986) assertion that minority women face more serious problems than do white women in prison, particularly where mental health status is concerned. In addition, results indicate that black female inmates are more likely to receive personal visits from family members, which is consistent with Baunach's (1985) finding that closer ties exist among black female prisoners and their families. This finding may in part suggest that decreased emotional difficulties experienced by black female inmates may be the result of greater personal contact with family members as a means of coping with long-term incarceration.

Results further show support for the extended-kin networks found among black women. Those serving long-term sentences tend to have children living with their grandparents as opposed to their fathers. This finding is also consistent with Richie's (1996) gender identity development model, which suggests that close family ties have a significant effect on black women's identity and their ability to cope with imprisonment. Further, while research suggests that black female prisoners are more likely to be single mothers than are white female prisoners, studies continue to demonstrate that black females are more likely to be satisfied with their child's living arrangement. Thus it is suggested that dissatisfaction with a child's living arrangement may enhance the likelihood of emotional difficulty, particularly among long-term inmates. Since studies continuously show that the effects of imprisonment are more severe for females, it seems plausible that future research should address these questions when examining the impact of long-term confinement among female offenders.

Thirty years of "get tough on crime" policies that increase the likelihood and length of incarceration, such as mandatory minimum sentences and Three Strikes laws, appear to be either gender blind or beneficial to women. In fact, these reforms contain significant consequences for women. A portion of the costs of prison construction and maintenance are paid for by cutting social services from which women benefit. In addition, since women are more likely to be employed in social services and men are more likely to be employed in criminal justice, the increase of the criminal justice system at the expense of the social service system places women's employment opportunities in jeopardy. Finally, the incarceration of parents leaves behind children who may be traumatized and whose emotional and economic care is left to women.

NOTE

1. The data used in this chapter were made available by the Inter-university Consortium for Political and Social Research. The data for the *Survey of Inmates of Local Jails, 1989* [United States] were originally collected by the Bureau of Justice Statistics (1990). Neither the collector of the original data nor the Consortium bear any responsibility for the analyses or interpretations presented here.

REFERENCES

ALLEN, H. E., & SIMONSEN, C. E. (1998). *Corrections in America: An introduction.* Upper Saddle River, NJ: Prentice Hall.

BAUNACH, P. J. (1985). *Mothers in prison.* Piscataway, NJ: Transaction Books.

BUREAU OF JUSTICE STATISTICS. (1990). *Survey of inmates of local jails, 1989.* Washington, DC: U.S. Government Printing Office.

CARLEN, P. (1985). *Criminal women: Autobiographical accounts.* New York: Blackwell.

CHESNEY-LIND, M. (1997). *The female offender: Girls, women, and crime.* Thousand Oaks, CA: Sage Publications.

DURHAM, A. M. (1994). *Crisis and reform: Current issues in American punishment.* Boston: Little, Brown.

EDWARDS, S. S. M. (1984). *Women on trial: A study of the female suspect, defendant, and offender in criminal law and the criminal justice system.* Dover, England: Manchester University Press.

FEINMAN, C. (1986). *Women in the criminal justice system.* New York: Praeger.

FLOWERS, R. B. (1987). *Women and criminality: The woman as victim, offender, and practitioner.* New York: Greenwood Publishing.

GILLIARD, D. K., & BECK, A. J. (1998). *Prisoners in 1997.* U.S. Department of Justice, Bureau of Justice Statistics. Washington, DC: U.S. Government Printing Office.

HENRIQUES, Z. W. (1995). Imprisoned mothers and their children: Separation–reunion syndrome dual impact. *Women and Criminal Justice, 8,* 77–95.

IGLEHART, A. P., & STEIN, M. P. (1985). The female offender: A forgotten client? *Social Casework: The Journal of Contemporary Social Work, 66,* 152–159.

KOONS, B. A., BURROW, J. D., MORASH, M., & BYNUM, T. (1997). Expert and offender perceptions of program elements linked to successful outcomes for incarcerated women. *Crime and Delinquency, 43,* 512–532.

KURSHAN, N. (1996). Behind the walls: The history and current reality of women's imprisonment. In E. Rosenblatt (Ed.), *Criminal injustice: Confronting the prison crisis.* Boston: South End Press.

MACKENZIE, D. L., & GOODSTEIN, L. (1985). Long-term incarceration impacts and characteristics of long-term offenders: An empirical analysis. *Criminal Justice and Behavior, 12,* 395–414.

MACKENZIE, D. L., ROBINSON, J. W., & CAMPBELL, C. S. (1989). Long-term incarceration of female offenders: Prison adjustment and coping. *Criminal Justice and Behavior, 16,* 223–238.

MACKENZIE, D. L., ROBINSON, J. W., & CAMPBELL, C. S. (1995). Long-term incarceration of female offenders: Prison adjustment and coping. In T. J. Flanagan (Ed.), *Long-term imprisonment: Policy, science, and correctional practice.* Boston: Northeastern University Press.

MAGUIRE, K., & PASTORE, A. L. (1996). *Sourcebook of criminal justice statistics, 1995.* U.S. Department of Justice, Bureau of Justice Statistics. Washington, DC: U.S. Government Printing Office.

MCCLELLAN, D. S., FARAHEE, D., & CROUCH, B. M. (1997). Early victimization, drug use, and criminality: A comparison of male and female prisoners. *Criminal Justice and Behavior, 24,* 455–476.

MCLAREN, J. (1997). Prisoners' rights: The pendulum swings. In J. M. Pollack (Ed.), *Prisons: Today and tomorrow.* Gaithersburg, MD: Aspen Publishers.

MORRIS, A. (1981). *Women and crime: Papers presented at the Cropwood Round-Table Conference, December 1980.* Cambridge: University of Cambridge Press.

MORRIS, A. (1987). Women, crime, and criminal justice. Malden, MA: Basil Blackwell.

NEGY, C., WOODS, D. J., & CARLSON, R. (1997). The relationship between female inmates' coping and adjustment in a minimum-security prison. *Criminal Justice and Behavior, 24,* 224–233.

RICHIE, B. (1996). *Compelled to crime: The gender entrapment of battered black women.* New York: Routledge.

ROSENBLATT, J. (1996). *Criminal justice.* Boston: South End Press.

SHERIDAN, M. J. (1996). Comparison of the life experiences and personal functioning of men and women in prison. *Families in Society: The Journal of Contemporary Human Services, 6,* 423–434.

SNELL, T. (1994). *Women in prison.* U.S. Department of Justice, Bureau of Justice Statistics. Washington, DC: U.S. Government Printing Office.

SOBEL, S. B. (1982). Difficulties experienced by women in prison. *Psychology of Women Quarterly, 7,* 107–118.

WATTERSON, K. (1996). *Women in prison: Inside the concrete womb.* Boston: Northeastern University Press.

14

Three Strikes and It's *Women* Who Are Out[1]

The Hidden Consequences for Women of Criminal Justice Policy Reforms

Mona J. E. Danner

Thirty years of "get tough on crime" policies that increase the likelihood and length of incarceration, such as mandatory minimum sentences and three strikes laws, appear to be either gender blind or beneficial to women. In fact, these reforms contain significant consequences for women. A portion of the costs of prison construction and maintenance are paid for by cutting social services from which women benefit. In addition, since women are more likely to be employed in social services and men are more likely to be employed in criminal justice, the increase in the criminal justice system at the expense of the social service system places women's employment opportunities in jeopardy. Finally, the incarceration of parents leaves behind children who may be traumatized and whose emotional and economic care is left to women.

The 1994 Federal Crime Control Act marks the twenty-sixth year of the "get tough on crime" movement initiated with the passage of the 1968 Crime Control and Safe Streets Act (Donziger 1996, p. 14). The 1984 crime bill increased penalties for drug offenses, thereby engaging the war on drugs and initiating the centerpiece of law-and-order legislative efforts to control crime: mandatory minimum and increased sentence lengths. "Three strikes and you're out" laws, in particular, captured the imagination of the public, the press, and the politicians. State legislators in thirty-seven jurisdictions proposed three strikes laws in 1993 and 1994, often as part of their own state crime bills. By February 1995, fifteen jurisdictions had enacted these laws, and California voters had made three strikes part of their constitution (Turner, Sundt, Applegate, & Cullen 1995). The new sentencing laws contained in the federal and state crime bills increased the dramatic expansion of the criminal justice system already under way, especially in corrections.

In 1995, the United States recorded over 5.3 million adults in the correctional population (U.S. Department of Justice, 1996). Our nation now incarcerates over 1.5 million of its citizens in federal and state prisons, more than a fourfold increase in just twenty years; another one-half million people are in local jails. Over 120,000 of those imprisoned are women (Gilliard & Beck, 1996). In the 1980s, the rate of women's imprisonment increased nearly twice as much as that of men's, and thirty-four new women's prison units were opened (Immarigeon & Chesney-Lind, 1992). African-Americans, who account for 13 percent of the population, are 48 percent of those incarcerated (Maguire & Pastore, 1995, p. 546); twenty years ago they were 35 percent of those locked up (Maguire, Pastore, & Flanagan 1993, p. 618). Black men and women are seven times more likely to be imprisoned than are white men and women (U.S. Department of Justice, 1995); the expansion of mandatory and increased sentences for drug law violations accounts for much of the increase (Mauer, 1990). Young African-American men are particularly hard hit by the rhetoric and ensuing policies associated with the war on drugs and three strikes laws (Tonry, 1995). Nearly all of those behind bars are poor.

The result of "lock 'em up" policies is that U.S. prisons currently operate at 114 percent to 126 percent capacity (Gilliard & Beck, 1996). Across the country, federal and state governments are engaged in an enormous and costly prison construction program. In fact, prisons represent "the only expanding public housing" in our country ("The prison boom," 1995, p. 223). One truism of prison and jail construction remains: "If you build it, they will come." So the costs associated with maintaining these facilities and incarcerating citizens—especially geriatrics, as lifers age—will quickly dwarf the costs of construction.

The rationale behind the crime bills and the resulting expansion of the criminal justice system cannot be found in the crime rate. Despite political rhetoric at the national and state levels and the carnage shown daily and repeatedly in all forms of news and entertainment media, the violent crime rate remained relatively stable over the last twenty years as measured by the National Crime Survey (Bureau of Justice Statistics, 1994a).

Throughout it all, however, the consequences for women of the expansion of the criminal justice system remain largely unconsidered and invisible in public policy discussions. This chapter makes women visible in the identification of the hidden costs to women of the expansion of the criminal justice system. In brief, I argue that one way or another, it is *women* who will pay the lion's share of criminal justice reform.

LOOKING FOR WOMEN

The feminist revolution in society and the academy is about making women visible, interrogating and deconstructing the manner in which women do appear, and calling for progressive action to benefit women. In criminal justice, feminist analysis has largely focused on women as offenders, victims, and workers (Price & Sokoloff, 1995), with the issues and debates centered around building theory, containing men's violence against women, and the equality/difference concern (Daly & Chesney-Lind, 1988). This chapter advances feminist perspectives in criminal justice in analysis of the ways in which supposedly gender-blind crime control writ large affects *all* women.

Women are not readily visible in current criminal justice policy debates. The use of a baseball analogy—"three strikes and you're out"—to refer to the policy of mandatory life sentences for those persons convicted of three felonies illustrates the exclusion of women from the crime debates. Although it's called the "national pastime," women don't identify much with baseball, have no significant presence in the sport, and reap few of its economic benefits (facts true of all professional sports). Yet it is in this sense that baseball represents an excellent analogy to the crime bills since women remain largely invisible from the debates surrounding criminal justice reforms. When women do appear, it is often as diversionary props which only barely resemble the realities of the lives of women and girls. Recent public debates in some states regarding increasing the availability of concealed weapons provide one illustration of this phenomenon.

During the 1995 legislative year, Virginia enacted a "right to carry" law requiring that judges grant permits for concealed weapons to nearly anyone who applies (Snider, 1995). Lobbyists for the National Rifle Association (NRA), along with sympathetic legislators, repeatedly invoked the image of the lone woman walking to her car at night who might need a gun to protect herself from the lurking stranger ready to pounce on her at any moment. This image of a woman served as a diversionary prop to obscure the protests of police and judges who objected to the law because of safety concerns and the restriction on judicial discretion. The image also diverted attention away from the vested interests of the NRA and state politicians who benefit from NRA contributions. This is simply one example of the way in which women are used in debates surrounding criminal justice policies. Women's lives and the realities of potential dangers are distorted, and in the process, women are left out of the debate and policies are enacted that will not only *not* benefit women, but will, in fact, harm women.

Nearly all of the political rhetoric about crime focuses on making our streets and neighborhoods safe again and protecting our homes from vicious, dangerous intruders. The focus on stranger crimes ignores the fact that it is the ones whom they know and love who represent the greatest danger to women's lives. Although women are much less likely than men to become victims of violent crimes in general, when women are assaulted, robbed, or raped, the best guess is to look to loved ones (Bachman, 1994). Of these violent crimes that women experience, the perpetrator is a husband, boyfriend, ex-husband, or ex-boyfriend 28 percent of the time; the comparable figure for men is 2 percent. Adding in other relatives increases the figure for women to 34 percent; for men, it is 5 percent. Expanding the definition to include other persons known reveals that 72 percent of the times that women are the victims of violent crimes the assailant is known to the victim as either an acquaintance, a relative, or an intimate partner; for men this figure is 54 percent. The offender is a stranger in just one-fourth of the occasions when women are victims of violent crime. In violent crimes occurring between spouses, lovers, ex-spouses, and ex-lovers, 90 percent of the time, the victim is a woman. And a woman is the victim in 70 percent of murders between intimate partners (Bureau of Justice Statistics 1994b, p. 2).

Women need far less protection from strangers than from supposed protectors, especially intimate partners, relatives, and acquaintances. But the debates surrounding the crime bills and recent research demonstrate that women are also at risk from the law-makers and even some law enforcers (Kraska & Kappeler, 1995), most of whom are men, nearly all of them white, and with respect to politicians, legislators, and judges, members of the elite social classes. Lawmakers do not pay attention to the data but, like the public, fall victim to popular myths about crime, especially the myth that it is strangers who are most responsible for violent victimizations, particularly those committed against women.

The result is that this myth and others like it are used to shape public debate and craft public policies that ignore women's lives and force women to bear the brunt of the financial and emotional costs for such policies.

The *New York Times* called women the "quiet winners" in the U.S. Crime Bill because of inclusion of the Violence Against Women Act (Manegold, 1994). This portion of the national crime bill budgets $1.6 billion for a national hot line for domestic violence victims and education programs aimed at police, prosecutors, and judges. It includes provisions that encourage mandatory arrests in domestic violence complaints, sex offender registration programs, and the release to victims of the results of rapists' HIV tests, and it allows women to file civil suits in cases of gender-bias crimes.

The Violence Against Women Act makes women's victimization visible and crafts public policies to assist women. The act represents an important step in public recognition of, and response to, male violence against women. But examination of the crime bills and their accompanying public debate reveals no sign of women other than as victims of domestic violence. Feminist interrogation about how criminal justice policies affect women's lives calls us to make visible more of the ways in which criminal justice policies affect women. Considering the unintended consequences and hidden costs of the crime bills and current public policies suggests that women are less likely to be quiet winners in criminal justice reforms as a whole, than to be quiet and big-time losers.

And so we return to the baseball analogy. "Three strikes and you're out" doesn't just refer to the policy of mandatory life sentences following a third felony conviction. It also refers to three ways in which women will be hurt by, and forced to pay for, criminal justice reform.

STRIKE 1: OFF THE ROLLS

The first strike against women comes in the decisions regarding which government services will be sacrificed to pay for the expansion of the criminal justice system. The emphasis on budget balancing and deficit reduction at the national and state levels means that money targeted for tough-on-crime proposals comes at the expense of other government programs. RAND researchers concluded that implementation of California's three strikes law would require cuts in other government services totaling more than 40 percent over eight years, a move that would leave the state of California "spending more money keeping people in prison than putting people through college" (Greenwood et al., 1994, p. 34). The hardest-hit programs, however, are those in social services, especially those targeted to the poor, most of whom are women and children.[2]

Discussion about entitlements to the poor is to some extent a separate debate about the causes of poverty and the state's responsibility, or lack thereof, to help alleviate misfortune and suffering. But it is also a debate that remains close to the debates about crime and criminal justice. Like criminal offenders and prisoners, women on welfare and their families are demonized as lazy, unwilling to work for their keep, immoral, and criminal. Both groups—composed disproportionately of poor and minority persons—are scapegoated as the source of numerous social ills while public attention draws away from inequitable economic and political conditions (Sidel, 1996). Blaming the victims of structural conditions justifies cutting welfare for the poor and funneling savings elsewhere.

Social services that benefit women are sacrificed to accommodate the expenditures associated with expansion of the criminal justice system. Chesney-Lind (1995) notes that New York continued to build beds in women's prisons at the same time that it had an insufficient number of beds for women and children in shelters. Adequate social services can reduce those life stressors associated with criminality; legal changes and battered women's shelters helped reduce the rates of women's homicide of male partners (Browne, 1990, as cited in Chesney-Lind, 1995).

The rhetoric surrounding cuts in social programs reveals class as well as race/ethnic and gender bias. The Welfare Reform Bill of 1996 imposes a limitation on the length of time that poor women may receive AFDC (Aid to Families with Dependent Children). After two years most women will be kicked off the rolls under the assumption that they will find work. Overall, few provisions are made for ensuring that either jobs or day care are available. We see social class operating here. Politicians, pundits, and religious leaders commonly argue that children should be cared for at home by the mother. Apparently, this is true, however, only for middle-class mothers and their children; poor mothers are admonished and will be legally required to leave their children so that they may return to work in order to save the tax coffers.

In 1994, at the same time that Virginia first instituted welfare reform, the state also passed its crime bill and accompanying criminal justice reforms. Plans called for the building of twenty-seven new prisons at a cost of $1 billion over ten years (later estimates placed these costs at $2 to 4 billion) as well as three strikes and other provisions for increasing the length of sentences for violent offenses and repeat offenses. The bill also called for the abolition of parole as of January 1, 1995, but the governor's new parole board had already, in effect, abolished parole as it drastically reduced the number of paroles granted—at a cost of $77 million in just six months (LaFay, 1994). Virginia prisons were so overcrowded that they could not accept new inmates housed in local jails awaiting transfer to the state system. This, in turn, led to such pressures in the jails that sheriffs sued the state to force it to assume its responsibility and take custody of its charges (Jackson, 1995). One way in which Virginia, like all states, deals with the problem of overcrowding is to ship inmates to other states and pay them the costs associated with incarceration (LaFay, 1995).

The expenditures associated with the expansion of the criminal justice system are being paid for in part by the savings to come from reforms that cut the social safety net of welfare. Further, an "iron triangle" of interests—politicians, job-starved communities, and businesses that build and service prisons—benefits from tough-on-crime rhetoric and policies (Thomas 1994). Neither military, corporate, nor middle-class subsidy programs are targeted for payment in support of the prison industrial complex; rather, social service programs—with their disproportionately poor, minority, and female recipients—remain those responsible for picking up the check.

Women are the majority of direct beneficiaries of various social service programs, but we know that they steer nearly all of those benefits to their dependents, especially their children, but also the elderly and disabled adults in their lives. Simply put, women and those who depend on them will lose their social security, in part so that politicians can appear to be tough on crime and imprison more men and women. It is poor women—who are also disproportionately minority, especially African-American women—and their families who in this way will pay a disproportionate share of the hidden costs associated with the war on crime and drugs. Strike 1.

STRIKE 2: JOBS FOR WHOM?

Women are not only more likely than men to be the recipients of social services, women are also more likely to be employed in social service agencies as social workers, case-workers, counselors, and support staff. The implications of this fact represent the second strike against women. Sixty-nine percent of social workers are women, and women comprise an even larger portion of front-line caseworkers and clerical personnel (U.S. Bureau of the Census, 1994, p. 407). Thus, as social services are cut back, women work-ers will be affected disproportionately.

Critics will respond that the expansion of the criminal justice system means increased employment opportunities for women. After all, 24 percent of law enforcement employees in the United States are women (Maguire & Pastore, 1995, p. 55). Even greater opportunities appear to exist in corrections, where 30 percent of employees in adult corrections are women (Maguire & Pastore, 1995, p. 92). However, most women employed in law enforcement and corrections agencies work in traditional pink-collar ghettos as low-wage clerical or support staff. Practically speaking, the only way to advance to upper levels of administration in either policing or corrections is through line employment as a police or correctional officer. And although 72 percent of law enforce-ment employees are police officers, only 9 percent of police officers are women (Maguire & Pastore, 1995, p. 55), and women make up just 18 percent of correctional guards (p. 92).

There remains a long-standing bias against women in policing and corrections. Even after women's more than twenty years of proven effectiveness as officers on the streets and in the prisons, male co-workers and supervisors persist in their bias against women. They use harassment and masculine work cultures that marginalize women to resist efforts to increase the representation of women on these forces (Martin & Jurik, 1996; Morash & Haarr, 1995).

The attacks on affirmative action in the current political climate further endanger women's employment possibilities in the criminal justice system (Martin, 1995). In addition, the definition and nature of work in criminal justice are being restructured to emphasize punitiveness and dangerousness. In Virginia, probation and parole counselors were renamed officers and may now carry weapons (Va. Code, § 53.1-145). Virginia's Director of Corrections since 1994 insists that probation and parole clients as well as inmates be called "convicts" or "felons." These moves emphasize punishment and the untrustworthiness of offenders; they stand in sharp contrast to the need to develop positive relationships in order to encourage social adjustment. Such practices also emphasize masculinity as a requirement for the job, thereby creating a climate that further discourages women in the work.

Three strikes and no-parole policies have at least three implications for police and correctional officers. For the police, three strikes may influence people likely to be caught in the web of these laws to take more desperate measures than ever to evade arrest. For correctional guards, abolishing parole first means overcrowding in the prisons; it also means the loss of incentives and rewards for good behavior and the loss of faith in the future. In turn, these conditions produce an increase in the likelihood of prison violence and uprisings.

Thus real increases in fear and the loss of hope among offenders become coupled with politically inspired attitudes about the dangerousness of offenders and the punitive goals of the work. Combined with attacks on affirmative action, bias against women in traditionally male occupations and the resulting stress on women employees, these factors may be surprisingly effective in bringing about actual *decreases* in women's employment in precisely those positions in policing and corrections that lead to advancement and higher pay.

The crime bills represent a government jobs program—criminal justice is, in fact, "the only growing public-sector employment" ("The prison boom," 1994, p. 223)—but the new jobs created come at the cost of other public-sector jobs, such as those in social services, which are more likely to be held by women. And the new jobs created by the expansion of the criminal justice system are overwhelmingly jobs for men. Strike 2.

STRIKE 3: FAMILY VALUES?

Men and women who commit crimes for which they are convicted and sentenced to prison have not lived their lives solely in criminal gangs; they do not structure their entire days around illegal activity; they are not *only* criminals. They are also sons and daughters, fathers and mothers. In short, they are responsible for caring for others who depend on them, and most of them do their best to meet these responsibilities because they do, in fact, love their families.

Sixty-seven percent of women and 56 percent of men in state prisons in 1991 had children under the age of 18; most of these women (72 percent) and men (53 percent) lived with their children before entering prison (Maguire & Pastore, 1994, p. 616). Imprisoned adults cannot contribute to their families' financial or psychological well-being. In a very few cases, children are committed to foster homes or institutions (Maguire & Pastore, 1994, p. 616). But most of the time another family member takes over care of those children and any elderly or disabled adults left behind—and that family member is usually a woman. This fact represents the third strike against women.

Because most of those imprisoned are men, it is the women in their lives—wives, girlfriends, and mothers—who are left with the responsibility of providing for the economic and emotional needs of the children and any dependent adults, a task these women must accomplish on their own. And when women are imprisoned, it is generally their mothers who take over the care of the children.

As we imprison increasing numbers of men and women, we saddle more women with sole responsibility for care of the next generation. The problem is exacerbated when the state, due to overcrowding, moves prisoners out of its system and to other states, thereby leaving the women and children bereft of even emotional support from incarcerated parents.

Today in the United States, "there are at least 1.5 million children of prisoners and at least 3.5 million children of offenders on probation or parole" (Johnston, 1995a, p. 311). The women who care for these children, as well as the children themselves, must be recognized as paying some of the hidden costs of punitive criminal justice policies. Parental arrest and incarceration endures as a traumatic event for all involved. It can lead to inadequate child care due to persistent and deepening poverty. In addition, children may suffer from problems with which the women who care for them must cope: developmental delay, behavioral and emotional difficulties, feelings of shame and experiences of stigmatization, distrust and hatred of police and the criminal justice system, and subsequent juvenile delinquency (Carlson & Cervera, 1992; Fishman, 1990; Johnston, 1995b). In effect, children suffer from post traumatic stress disorder when their parents are imprisoned (Kampfner, 1995). Effective programs to address the needs of children of incarcerated parents and their caregivers remain few in number and endangered.

As politicians get tough on crime, it is women and children who do the time, alone. Remembering the first two strikes against women discussed earlier, it emerges as strikingly clear that women will not be able to look to the federal or state government for either public assistance or public employment. Strike 3. It's *women* who are out.

FINAL THOUGHTS: AN EVERY WOMAN'S ISSUE

It remains far too easy to be lulled into complacency when it comes to women and criminal justice. After all, women represent a very small number of offenders. And despite male violence against women, most victims of crime are men. Yet the social construction of crime and criminals and the political nature of their control are neither gender blind nor gender neutral. We are finally and fully confronted by the harsh reality that criminal justice *is* about women, *all* women. Although it occasionally operates as an important resource for women, the criminal justice system most frequently represents a form of oppression in women's lives. It attacks most harshly those women with the least power to resist it. As Jean Landis and I wrote several years ago:

> [I]t is time to recognize that in real life...offenders do not exist as exclusive objects. They are connected in relationships with other people, a major portion of whom are women—mothers, wives, lovers, sisters and daughters. Any woman who fights to keep her wits, and her roof, about her as she helplessly experiences a loved one being swept away by the currents of criminal justice "knows" the true brutality of the system and the extensiveness of its destruction. If she is a racial/ethnic minority person, which she is likely to be, and/or if she is poor, which she surely is, she intuitively knows the nature of the interaction between criminal justice practices and the racist and/or classist [as well as sexist] structure of her society, as well as its impact on her life, her family, and her community (Danner and Landis, 1990, pp. 111–112)

She also knows that precious little assistance exists for her, and those who depend on her, in the form of either welfare or employment from the larger community as represented by the state. In addition, it is every woman, no matter who she is, who will pay for the dramatic expansion of the criminal justice system. Clearly, criminal justice *is* a women's issue.

The get tough, lock 'em up, and three strikes policies will not reduce crime or women's pain associated with crime. They will only impoverish communities as they enrich politicians and corporations associated with the new prison industrial complex. Although women have largely been left out of the debate, it is women who are the quiet losers—the big-time losers—in the crime bills. Criminal justice reforms such as these are politically motivated, unnecessary, ineffective, and far, far too costly. Finally and most important, it is women who receive the least from the wars on crime and drugs, and it is women who bear most of their hidden burdens.

ACKNOWLEDGEMENTS

This paper was originally prepared as the 1995 Women's Studies Junior Faculty Lecture, Old Dominion University; I thank Anita Clair Fellman, Director of Women's Studies, for that invitation. Thanks to Marie L. VanNostrand (Virginia Department of Criminal Justice Services) and Lucien X. Lombardo (Old Dominion University), who were most gracious in providing materials. The members of Our Writing Group and COOL provided much encouragement and entertainment. An earlier version was presented at the 1995 American Society of Criminology meetings, Boston, Massachusetts.

NOTES

1. This chapter is adapted from the author's chapter in Susan L. Miller (Ed.), *Crime Control and Women: Feminist Implication of Criminal Justice Policy*, Susan L. Miller (Newbury Park, CA: Sage Publications, 1998).

2. Entitlements to the poor include Aid to Families with Dependent Children (AFDC); the Women, Infants and Children (WIC) nutritional program; food stamps; school breakfast and lunch programs; Medicaid; public housing and emergency grants; and social security for disabled and dependent persons, as well as other programs. Each of these programs is under attack and will almost certainly be cut back, just as has welfare.

REFERENCES

BACHMAN, R. (1994). *Violence against women: A national crime victimization survey report.* Washington, DC: U.S. Department of Justice.

BROWNE, A. (1990, December 11). Assaults between intimate partners in the United States. Testimony before the United States Senate, Committee on the Judiciary, Washington, DC.

BUREAU OF JUSTICE STATISTICS. (1994a). *Criminal victimization in the United States: 1973–1992 Trends.* Washington, DC: U.S. Department of Justice.

BUREAU OF JUSTICE STATISTICS. (1994b). *Violence between intimates.* Washington, DC: U.S. Department of Justice.

CARLSON, B. E., & CERVERA, N. (1992). *Inmates and their wives: Incarceration and family life.* Westport, CT: Greenwood Press.

CHESNEY-LIND, M. (1995). Rethinking women's imprisonment: A critical examination of trends in female incarceration. In B. R. Price & N. J. Sokoloff (Eds.), *The criminal justice system and women: Offenders, victims, and workers* (2nd Ed., pp. 105—117). New York: McGraw-Hill.

DALY, K., & CHESNEY-LIND, M. (1988). Feminism and criminology. *Justice Quarterly, 5*, 497–538.

DANNER, M., & LANDIS, J. (1990). Carpe diem (Seize the day!): An opportunity for feminist connections. In B. D. MacLean & D. Milovanovic (Eds.), *Racism, empiricism and criminal justice* pp. 109–112. Vancouver, British Columbia, Canada: Collective Press.

DONZIGER, S. A. (ED.). (1996). *The real war on crime: The report of the National Criminal Justice Commission.* New York: HarperPerennial.

FISHMAN, L. T. (1990). *Women at the wall: A study of prisoners' wives doing time on the outside.* New York: State University of New York Press.

GILLIARD, D. K., & BECK, A. J. (1996). *Prison and jail inmates, 1995.* U.S. Department of Justice, Bureau of Justice Statistics. Washington DC: U.S. Government Printing Office.

GREENWOOD, P. W., FYDELL, C. P., ABRAHAMSE, A. F., CAULKINS, J. P., CHIESA, J., MODEL, K. E., & KLEIN, S. P. (1994). *Three strikes and you're out: Estimated benefits and costs of California's new mandatory-sentencing law.* Santa Monica, CA: RAND Corporation.

IMMARIGEON, R., & CHESNEY-LIND, M. (1992). *Women's prisons: Overcrowded and overused.* San Francisco: National Council on Crime and Delinquency.

JACKSON, J. (1995, January 11). Sheriffs suing state to relieve overcrowding in city jails. *The Virginian-Pilot,* pp. A1, A6.

JOHNSTON, D. (1995a). Conclusion. In K. Gabel & D. Johnston (Eds.), *Children of incarcerated parents* (pp. 311–314). New York: Lexington Books.

JOHNSTON, D. (1995b). Effects of parental incarceration. In K. Gabel & D. Johnson (Eds.), *Children of incarcerated parents* (pp. 59–88). New York: Lexington Books.

KAMPFNER, C. J. (1995). Post-traumatic stress reactions in children of imprisoned mothers. In K. Gabel & D. Johnston (Eds.), *Children of incarcerated parents* (pp. 89–100). New York: Lexington Books.

KRASKA, P. B., & KAPPELER, V. E. (1995). To serve and pursue: Exploring police sexual violence against women. *Justice Quarterly 12,* 85–111.

LAFAY, L. (1994, December 9). New, low parole rate has cost Va. $77 million. *The Virginian-Pilot,* pp. A1, A24.

LAFAY, L. (1995, February 17). State sends 150 inmates to Texas. *The Virginian-Pilot,* pp. A1, A9.

MAGUIRE, K., & PASTORE, A. L. (EDS.). (1994). *Sourcebook of criminal justice statistics, 1993.* U.S. Department of Justice, Bureau of Justice Statistics. Washington, DC: U.S. Government Printing Office.

MAGUIRE, K., & PASTORE, A. L. (EDS.). (1995). *Sourcebook of criminal justice statistics, 1994.* U.S. Department of Justice, Bureau of Justice Statistics. Washington, DC: U.S. Government Printing Office.

MAGUIRE, K., PASTORE, A. L., & FLANAGAN, T. J., (EDS.). (1993). *Sourcebook of criminal justice statistics, 1992.* U.S. Department of Justice, Bureau of Justice Statistics. Washington, DC: U.S. Government Printing Office.

MANEGOLD, C. S. (1994, August 25). Quiet winners in house fight on crime: Women. *New York Times,* p. A19.

MARTIN, S. E. (1995). The effectiveness of affirmative action: The case of women in policing. *Justice Quarterly 8,* 489–504.

MARTIN, S. E., & JURIK, N. D. (1996). *Doing justice, doing gender: Women in law and criminal justice occupations.* Thousand Oaks, CA: Sage Publication.

MAUER, M. (1990). *Young black men and the criminal justice system: A growing national problem.* Washington, DC: The Sentencing Project.

MORASH, M., & HAARR, R. N. (1995). Gender, workplace problems, and stress in policing. *Justice Quarterly 12,* 113–140.

PRICE, B. R., & SOKOLOFF, N. J. (1995). *The criminal justice system and women: Offenders, victims, and workers* (2nd ed.). New York: McGraw-Hill.

SIDEL, R. (1996). *Keeping women and children last: America's war on the poor.* New York: Penguin Books.

SNIDER, J. R. (1995, December 13). Have gun, will travel.... *The Virginian-Pilot.*

The prison boom. (1995, February 20). *The Nation,* pp. 223–224.

THOMAS, P. (1994, May 12). Making crime pay. *Wall Street Journal,* pp. A1, A6.

TONRY, M. H. (1995). *Malign neglect: Race, crime, and punishment in America.* New York: Oxford University Press.

TURNER, M. G., SUNDT, J. L., APPLEGATE, B. K., & CULLEN, F. T. (1995). "Three strikes and you're out" legislation: A national assessment. *Federal Probation, 59,* 16–35.

U.S. BUREAU OF THE CENSUS. (1994). *Statistical abstract of the United States, 1994.* Washington, DC: U.S. Government Printing Office.

U.S. DEPARTMENT OF JUSTICE. (1995, December 3). State and federal prisons report record growth during last 12 months. Press release.

U.S. DEPARTMENT OF JUSTICE. (1996, June 30). Probation and parole population reaches almost 3.8 million. Press release.

15

Disparate Treatment in Correctional Facilities

Roslyn Muraskin

It is estimated that 500,000 women are locked up in local jails across our nation annually. Approximately 20,000 women are detained in jail to await trial or to serve sentences of less than one and one-half years. In prisons, women inmates constitute a small but growing percentage of the total inmate population. These women inmates housed in jails must live in correctional institutions established largely by and for men. Litigation has been the means used in an effort to eliminate what has been claimed to be discriminatory treatment against delivery of services for women. Even when legal action has been deemed successful, there has been no guarantee that compliance as well as implementation has occurred.

The providing of services and programs is all part of good detention practice; it ensures that those inmates returning to society can be reintegrated into society. Equality or parity of treatment between men and women still does not exist in correctional institutions. How women prisoners have sued and have taken their cases to court is outlined. It is demonstrated here that services legally mandated by the states has not been fully delivered.

In the United States, no constitutional obligation exists for all persons to be treated alike. The government frequently, and in fact, does treat disparate groups differently. However, this does not excuse invidious discrimination among potential recipients (Gobert & Cohen, 1981, pp. 294–295). What is required is that where unequal treatment exists, the inequalities must be rational and related to a legitimate interest of the state (Pollack & Smith, 1978, p. 206). Laws create categories in which some people may be treated unequally. These categories include women incarcerated in correctional facilities. The question that arises is "whether the inequalities by the law are justifiable—in legal terms whether the person upon whom the law's burden falls has been denied equal protection of the law" (Pollack & Smith, 1978, pp. 206–207).

Since the decision in *Holt v. Sarver* (1970), in which the court declared an entire prison to be in violation of the Eighth Amendment and imposed detailed remedial plans, the judiciary has taken an active role in the administration of correctional facilities. Some of the most recent cases challenge the inequity of treatment between male and female prisoners.

Ostensibly, the needs of male and female prisoners would appear to be the same. They are not. Although some inmate interests are similar, others are separate and distinct. In many institutions, criteria developed for men are applied automatically to women, with no consideration for gender differences. Research shows that female inmates experience more medical and health problems than do male inmates. Classification officials note that female offenders need help in parenting skills, child welfare, pregnancy and prenatal care, home stability, and understanding the circumstances of their crime. But typically, assignments to programs and treatment resources in correctional facilities have been based more on what is available than on what should be available.

A review of the literature of the cases and issues dealing with disparate treatment reveals that each takes note of the fact that women represent a small minority in both prisons and jails. Yet the effects of incarceration are in many but not all respects similar for men and women. Each suffers the trauma of being separated from family and friends. When either a man or a woman becomes imprisoned, he or she experiences a loss of identity as well as a devaluation of his or her status. Regardless of the inmate's sex, prison life coerces conformity to an environment alien to the individual and in which one's every movement is dictated each and every minute (Muraskin, 1989).

Most challenges to prison conditions have neglected the special needs of female prisoners, especially in jails. Historically, correctional facilities for women have not received funding comparable to that of correctional facilities for men. Education and vocational-training programs for women have been seriously underfunded. "Benign neglect [has]…created a situation of unequal treatment in many states" (Hunter, 1984, p. 133). Correctional administrators have insisted that "the small number of female offenders [has] made it too expensive to fund such programs." The courts, however, have ruled "that cost is not an acceptable defense for denying equal treatment" (Hunter, 1984, pp. 133–134). Females have been subjected to policies designed for the male offender. "Women have deferred to males in the economic, social, political spheres of life. In the legal realm, more specifically in the imprisonment of the female, women have been forced into the status of being less than equal" (Sargent, 1984, p. 83).

REVIEW OF THE CASES

When inmates similarly situated find themselves being treated differently, there may exist a violation of equal protection. A review of the cases discussed below demonstrates for us that "discretion in such matters as classification, work assignments, and transfers may not be exercised discriminatorily or in an arbitrary or capricious manner" (Gobert & Cohen, 1981, p. 293).

Constitutionally, no obligation exists for the government to provide any benefits beyond basic requirements. However, this principle is not an excuse for invidious discrimination among potential recipients (Gobert & Cohen, pp. 294–295). Case law indicates that benefits afforded some cannot be denied others based solely on race or sex.

In any equal-protection challenge, the central question raised is the "degree of state interest which can justify disparate treatment among offenders" (*Reed v. Reed*, 1971). As established, the "classification must be reasonable, not arbitrary and must bear a fair and substantial relation to the object of the legislation or practice" (*Reed v. Reed*, 1971). Courts, for example, have found sex classifications to be irrational because they appear to be enacted solely for the convenience of correctional administrators (see *Craig v. Boren*, 1976[1]; *Weinberger v. Wisenfeld*, 1975[2]; and *Eslinger v. Thomas*, (1973).[3] Existing differences in conditions, rules, and treatment among inmates have proven fertile ground for equal protection challenges. Administrative convenience is not an acceptable justification for disparity of treatment (*Cooper v. Morin*, 1979, 1980), nor is lack of funds an acceptable justification for disparate treatment (*State ex rel Olson v. Maxwell*, 1977).

Legal uprisings against intolerable conditions in correctional facilities and prisoners' rights litigation were initiated by male attorneys and male prisoners. In the early stages of this litigation, females inmates did not turn to the courts, nor did officials at female institutions fear lawsuits, condemnation by the public, or inmate riots. With so few women incarcerated, there was little the women felt they could do. This situation has changed. Female prisoners have sued and have demanded parity with male prisoners (Aron, 1981, p. 191). The Fourteenth Amendment of the Constitution, in particular the equal protection and due process clauses, is the legal basis for presenting issues of disparity in correctional facilities. The Fourth Amendment is the source for issues of violation of privacy, while the Eighth Amendment is used for cases involving cruel and unusual punishment.

Differential sentencing of similarly situated men and women convicted of identical offenses has been found to violate the equal protection clause. A review of cases dealing generally with sentencing in correctional institutions includes *United States ex rel Robinson v. York* (1968), which held that it was a violation of the equal protection clause for women who were sentenced to indeterminate terms under a Connecticut statute to serve longer maximum sentences than men serving indeterminate terms for the same offenses. In *Liberti v. York* (1968), the Court held that female plaintiff's indeterminate sentence of up to three years violated the equal protection clause because the maximum term for men convicted of the same crime was one year. In *Commonwealth v. Stauffer* (1969), a Pennsylvania court held that the practice of sentencing women to state prison on charges for which men were held in county jail to be a violation of a woman's right to equal protection. In a reverse of disparate treatment in *United States v. Maples* (1974), a male co-defendant's sentencing of fifteen years was held to violate his equal protection rights when his female co-defendant received only a ten-year term. The trial judge had expressly stated that gender was a factor in imposing the lighter sentence.

In *Williams v. Levi* (1976), dealing with disparate treatment in the issue of parole, male prisoners in the District of Columbia were placed under the authority of the D.C. Board of Parole, whereas women prisoners were placed under the authority of the U.S. Board of Parole's stricter parole standards for women. In *Dawson v. Carberry* (1973), it was held that there must be substantial equivalence in male and female prisoners' opportunities to participate in work-furlough programs.

In *Barefield v. Leach* (1974), women at the Women's Division of the Penitentiary of New Mexico claimed that conditions there violated their rights to an uncensored press, to have their persons free from unreasonable searches, to be free from cruel and unusual punishment, and to be allowed due process and equal protection of the law regarding disciplinary procedures and rehabilitative opportunities, respectively. The court held that "[w]hat the equal protection clause requires in a prison setting is parity of treatment as contrasted with identity of treatment, between male and female inmates with respect to the conditions of their confinement and access to rehabilitative opportunities." *Barefield* is especially important, as it was the first case to enunciate the standard against which disparity of treatment of men and women in prison was to be measured.

Still further, in *McMurray v. Phelps* (1982), there was a challenge to conditions for both men and women at the Ouachita County Jail, where the jail ordered an end to the disparate treatment of female detainees. And in *Mary Beth G. v. City of Chicago* (1983), a strip-search policy under which female arrestees underwent a full strip-search while men were not stripped without reason to believe that a weapon or contraband was present was ruled to be a violation of the equal protection clauses as well as the Fourth Amendment.

In *Bounds v. Smith* (1977), the court held that access to the courts by prisoners was a fundamental constitutional right. The court noted that there existed an affirmative obligation on the part of state officials to ensure court access by providing adequate law libraries or some alternative involving a legal-assistance program. It was further noted in the court's decision that females inmates had less access to library facilities than did male inmates. This situation was ordered remedied. In *Cody v. Hillard* (1986), the court held that inmates at the state women's correctional facility, which had neither a law library nor law-trained assistants, were denied their constitutional right of meaningful access to the courts.

In a case dealing with the transfer of female inmates out of state because of a lack of facilities (*State ex rel Olson v. Maxwell*, 1977), female inmates filed a petition for a supervisory writ challenging the North Dakota practice of routinely transferring them to other states to be incarcerated, alleging a denial of equal protection and due process. It was held that North Dakota must not imprison women prisoners outside the state unless and until a due process waiver hearing is held or waived and the state admits that it cannot provide women prisoners facilities equal to those of male prisoners. While in *Park v. Thompson* (1973), the court ruled that there must be substantial equivalence for male and female prisoners in the distance of the place of incarceration from the place of sentencing.

"From a policy perspective, discriminatory distribution of prison privileges...will appear counter-rehabilitative, fueling inmate-administration animosity and generating inmate-peer jealousies" (Gobert & Cohen, 1981, p. 295). Male prisoners may be assigned to maximum, medium, or minimum security units, whereas female prisoners, regardless of the severity of their crimes, will be sent to the same institution. Problems have arisen with the provision of proper treatment as well as the need for rehabilitative programs. The cases indicate a need for parity of treatment. This is evidenced again in *Molar v. Gates* (1979), a class action suit that challenged the county's practice of providing minimum-security jail facilities for men but not for women. It was held that the practice violated the equal protection clauses of the state and federal constitutions. Women prisoners were awarded the same rights of access to minimum-security facilities as men. Over the years, the courts have been very critical of differences in men's and women's correctional facilities (*Mitchell v. Utreiner*, 1976).

In *Canterino v. Wilson* (1982, 1983), it was indicated that "restrictions imposed solely because of gender with the objective of controlling the lives of women inmates in a way deemed unnecessary for male prisoners" would not be tolerated. In areas such as work programs, vocational education, and training and community programs, disparate treatment was found to exist between male and female prisoners. Inferior programs as they existed and discrimination in the area of privileges were to be remedied. The court concluded that "males and females must be treated equally unless there is a substantial reason which requires a distinction be made" (1982). Such a distinction was not found by the courts. Case law has established that discriminatory selection for work release when based on race, religion, gender, or even mental impairment is not an acceptable practice. Any arbitrary or capricious selection for participation in work programs has been prohibited by the courts.

Due to the small numbers of women in men's correctional facilities, services and treatment programs appeared to have been reduced. Such reduced services included medical services. Generally, there was always a wider range of medical services for male than for female inmates. Thus in both *Todaro v. Ward* (1977) and *Estelle v. Gamble* (1976), the issues were medical. In the former case, the medical system in the Bedford Hills Correctional Facility was found to be unconstitutionally defective, while in the latter, there was found to be deliberate indifference to the medical needs of the females. This was found to be a violation of the Eighth Amendment.

In *Bukhari v. Huto* (1980), it was held that no justification existed for disparate treatment based on the fact that women's prisons serviced a smaller population and the cost would be greater to provide programs equivalent to the men's institutions. Cost could not be claimed as an excuse for paucity of services.

The landmark case on women's prison issues was *Glover v. Johnson* (1979). This was a comprehensive case challenging a disparate system of educational, vocational, work, and minimum-security programs in the Michigan prison systems based on due process and equal protections. The Court ruled that female prisoners must be provided program opportunities on a parity with male prisoners. The case resulted in an order requiring the state to provide postsecondary education, counseling, vocational programs, and a legal-education program (in a companion case, *Cornish v. Johnson* 1979) as well as other relief. "[I]nstitutional size is frankly not a justification but an excuse for the kind of treatment afforded women prisoners" (*Glover*, 1979).

In a facility in Nassau County, New York, in the case of *Thompson et al. v. Varelas, Sheriff, Nassau County et al.* (1985), the plaintiffs asked for

> declaratory and injunctive relief regarding the discriminatory, oppressive, degrading and dangerous conditions of…their confinement within the Nassau County Correctional Center.…alleged in their action was the existence of inadequate health care, lack of private attorney visiting facilities, inadequate and unequal access to employment, recreation and training; unequal access to library facilities and newspapers, and excessive confinement; unsanitary food preparation and service; and, inadequate and unequal access to religious services.…

They claimed that lack of these facilities and services violated their rights as guaranteed by the First, Fifth, Sixth, Eighth, Ninth, and Fourteenth Amendments to the Constitution of the United States and various provisions of the state law. The *Thompson* case began in 1979, but it was not until September 1985 that a consent judgment was entered in the *Thompson* case. *Thompson* makes a further argument for the needs of a checklist of standards against which to assess what constitutes disparate treatment in the correctional facilities.

Prior to these cases the female prisoner was the "forgotten offender." Testimony by a teacher in the *Glover* case indicated that whereas men were allowed to take shop courses, women were taught at a junior high level because the motto of those in charge was "keep it simple, these are only women."

While litigation has provided the opportunity for inmates to have a role in altering their conditions of confinement, a judicial opinion does not necessarily bring about change. Viewed from a nonlegal perspective, litigation is simply a catalyst for change rather than an automatic mechanism for ending wrongs found. All the cases discussed have held that invidious discrimination cannot exist. A review of the nonlegal literature (below) in the field indicates that the reasoning of the courts is supported by social scientists.

REVIEW OF THE LITERATURE

There are indications that significant differences have existed at all levels of men's and women's services in relation to living conditions, medical and health services, vocational and educational programs, religious practices, psychological counseling, work-release programs, legal and recreational services, postrelease programs, drug and alcohol counseling, and the actual management of the correctional facilities.

Prior to any discussion of the literature, it is necessary to note the distinctions between jails, prisons, and reformatories. A *jail* is generally defined as a facility "which detains persons for more than forty-eight hours, [and is] used both as a detention center for persons facing criminal charges and as a correctional facility for persons convicted of misdemeanor and felony crimes" (American Correctional Association, 1985, p. xvii). Such facilities usually hold persons convicted of a crime for up to one year. It is generally intended for adults, although it sometimes contains juveniles. Jails hold both persons detained pending adjudication of their cases and those sentenced to one year or less of incarceration. A *prison* is defined as a facility housing those sentenced to one year or more. Prisons tend to have more programs than jails, due to the lengthier prison sentences. A *reformatory* is a type of prison and has been called "an historical fad that merely reflects the spirit of the times" (Williams, Formby, & Watkins, 1982, p. 387). These "prisons" were built during a time when penologists want to stress their commitment to their idea of rehabilitation (Williams et al., 1982). The reformatory era represents a treatment philosophy of corrections. The view was that offensive behavior represented manifestations of "various 'pathologies' and psychological 'maladies'," all of which could be corrected by therapeutic intervention (Inciardi, 1984, p. 582). The importance of these three distinctions is that the courts have accepted different standards for different types of institutions.

The first penal institution for women opened in Indiana in 1873. By the beginning of the twentieth century, women's correctional facilities had opened in Framingham, Massachusetts, in Bedford Hills, New York, and in Clinton, New Jersey. The Federal

Institution for Women in Alderson, West Virginia, opened in 1927, and the House of Detention for Women (the first separate jail for women) opened in New York City in 1931. These institutions all shared one thing in common, "traditional values, theories and practices concerning a woman's role and place in society....The staffs, architectural design and programs reflected the culturally valued norms for women's behavior" (Feinman, 1986, p. 38).

Historically, disparate treatment of male and female inmates started when state penitentiaries first opened. "Female prisoners...were confined together in a single attic room above the institution's kitchen. [They] were supervised by the head of the kitchen below. Food was sent up to them once a day, and once a day the slop was removed. No provision was made for privacy or exercise and although the women were assigned some sewing work, for the most part they were left to their own devices in the 'tainted and sickly atmosphere'" (Rafter, 1983, p. 135). Female convicts were morally degraded to a greater extent than were male convicts. The reformatories built for female prisoners "established and legitimated a tradition of deliberately providing for female prisoners treatment very different from that of males" (Rafter, 1983, p. 148).

Lown and Snow (1980) describe the disparate treatment of females in prison. "Traditional theories of women's crime and imprisonment tend to focus on biological, psychological and social factors to explain criminal activity. From Lombroso to the present, criminological thought has been wrought with the sexism inherent in assuming that there exists only two distinct classes of women—those on pedestals and those in the gutter" (p. 195). A double standard has persisted traditionally in both the law and treatment of inmates: "Overlooking, letting go, excusing, unwillingness to report and to hold, being easy on women are part of the differential handling of the adult female in the law enforcement process from original complaints to admission to prison. The differential law enforcement handling seems to be built into our basic attitudes toward women. The operation of such attention can be called euphemistically the chivalry factor" (Reckless, 1967).

This chivalry factor meant that women should be treated more leniently than men. The nature of treatment and programs for female inmates appears to indicate the assumption of such a theory. Theories abound concerning the causes of criminality by female offenders. Certainly, the chivalry factor does not appear to be held in favor today. Once the female enters the correctional facility, she does not necessarily benefit from the benevolence of the criminal justice system. The theories of female crime continue to emphasize the natural differences between men and women but fail to explain why women commit the crimes they do. Sarri concluded that "discrimination and sexism are serious and pervasive problems in statutes, law enforcement, courts, and correctional agencies. All society is being harmed by a series of overkill in the processing of females and by the inhuman conditions which continue to prevail in correctional agencies" (Sarri, 1979, p. 194). It is clear that female prisoners have historically been treated differently and sometimes worse than male prisoners. Often, as an alternative to differential treatment, the model followed is that of the men's prison, which frequently ignores the obvious physical differences of female inmates. An almost total lack of enforcement of standard exists for the confinement of women. What has occurred, then, at the local correctional facilities represents but a sample of those problems characterizing state prisons for women. The literature and cases both indicate that "the plight of the female behind bars is often a difficult one" (Allen & Simonsen, 1978, pp. 325–327).

In addition to the poor quality and minimal services that have been made available to female inmates, they still suffer the same miserable conditions of incarceration as do male inmates. Women suffer even more because in jails, regardless of classification, they are normally housed together in the same area (for lack of adequate space), while men, who are classified according to minimum, medium, and maximum security, find themselves housed in separate areas. Women have always lived in crowded facilities, often finding themselves under squalid conditions, lacking privacy, faced with insensitive visiting rules, callous treatment, and the threat of, or actual, sexual abuse. Two other stresses on the female inmate stem from her being separated from her family and children (although in some institutions children are allowed visits) and from having special health and medical needs (Wood, 1982, p. 11).

In 1971, suggestions were put forth by the National Advisory Commission for the Correctional Facilities to reexamine policies, procedures, and programs with the objective of making them relevant to the problems and needs of female inmates. At that time, it was strongly urged that:

> Facilities for women offenders should be considered an integral part of the overall correctional system....
>
> Each state should determine differences in the needs between male and female offenders and implement differential programming.
>
> Appropriate vocational training programs should be implemented.
>
> Classification systems should be investigated to determine their applicability to the female offender.
>
> Adequate diversionary methods for female offenders should be implemented.
>
> State correctional agencies with such small numbers of women inmates as to make adequate facilities and programming uneconomical should make every effort to find alternatives to imprisonment for them.
>
> Programs within the facility should be open to both sexes (where both sexes are being held). (Flynn, 1971, p. 113)

Much of the neglect in assessing disparate treatment is attributed by writers believing that the experiences in prison for both men and women are the same and are not areas calling for special investigation. As Rafter (1983) had pointed out in an article, "Prisons for Women, 1790–1980" it was not until the 1970s that literature dealing with women in prison began to take notice of their special problems (p. 130). Singer's (1979) bitter protest regarding the treatment afforded women inmates and her indictment of the criminal justice system's refusal even to recognize the existence of women is still quite evident. Arditi and associates (1973) complied a staggering catalog of sex discrimination in prisons throughout the country. Gibson (1973) took a "first step toward historical research on women's prisons...." Feinman (1982) indicated that for the most part, programs in correctional facilities for women continued to be based on the belief that "the only acceptable role for women is that of wife/mother" (p. 12). The female offender has been described as being poor, African-American, Hispanic, or other, undereducated, and lacking in both job skills and self-confidence. As we approach the twenty-first century, indications are that more women are involved in committing crimes than ever before. And yet when women are released back into the community, studies show that men still represent a disproportionate majority in community programs. The way these community programs are structured continues to provide evidence of the lack of sensitivity and the differential treatment afforded women (Lewis, 1982, p. 49).

Historically, the women's prison system is not to be a replica of men's but rather, should differ somewhat radically along "a number of key dimensions, including its historical development, administrative structures, some of its disciplinary techniques, and the experience of inmates" (Rafter, 1983, p. 132). In her work in the 1980s, Suzanne Sobel (1980) assessed the mental health needs of inmates and concluded that " women incarcerated in state or federal prisons are the victims of a sexist correctional system that delivers fewer services and offers fewer opportunities than those available to male prisoners" (p. 336).

Writing in 1971, Jessica Mitford stated that "the entire criminal justice system for all offenders in the United States could not be characterized as a just or humane system, but in the case of the female offender its ineffectiveness and inhumanity are even more apparent." Fabian (1980) pointed out that "the reform movement for women prisons was aimed at refining their standards of sexual mobility to a level acceptable to society, while that for men was aimed at reaching the young felon before he became a permanent danger to the community" (p. 173).

It is specifically this attitude that has persisted throughout the literature over these many years dealing with disparate treatment. Historically, women have been regarded as moral offenders, while men continue to assert their masculinity. "[I]nstitutional incarceration needs to become more reflective of the ongoing changing social climate" (Sargent, 1984, p. 42). Most states continue to have one (in some cases, two) facilities for women, which, of necessity, must be of maximum security; local jails house both men and women. Population size has become a justification for ignoring the plight of women prisoners. However, size is but "an excuse for the kind of treatment afforded women prisoners" (*Glover v. Johnson*, 1979, at p. 1078). The disparate treatment of female and male prisoners "is the result of habitual and stereotypic thinking rather than the following of a different set of goals for incarceration" (Lown and Snow, 1980, p. 210).

If administrators in corrections continue to assign women's corrections low priority in budget allocation, staff development, and program development, continued conflict can be expected between the needs of the correctional facilities and such treatment afforded or not afforded women, even as we head into the next century. It may well be that because of overcrowding in both types of facilities, men's and women's equality will become less of an issue, thereby producing equally undesirable conditions for both. Regardless, as demonstrated in the research, disparate programs continue to permeate the correctional institutions of today, and changes are needed. Indeed, the literature and cases both indicate that the plight of the female serving time behind bars is often a difficult one. Standards have been developed over the years to guide correctional institutions in providing proper care and treatment. Adequate care and continuity in the delivery of services to all inmates is most important. Standards must be applied equally. Such standards as developed over the years are meant to serve efficiency, provide greater cost-effectiveness, and establish better planning than we have at present. If the cases are the catalyst for change, change must occur. Words have little meaning if actions do not follow (Muraskin, 1989, p. 126).

NOTES

1   In *Craig v. Boren* (1976) it was held to "withstand [a] constitutional challenge under the equal
    protection clause of the Fourteenth Amendment, classification by gender must serve important
    governmental objectives and must be substantially related to achievement of those objectives."

2. *Weinberger v. Wisenfeld* (1975) was a case in which a widower was denied benefits for him-
    self on the ground that survivors' benefits were allowable only to women under 42USCS §
    4029g): "a provision, header 'Mother's insurance benefits,' authorizing the payment of bene-
    fits based upon the earnings of a deceased husband and father covered by the Social Security
    Act, to a widow who has a minor child in her care." The Court held that "(1) the sex-based
    distinction of 42USCS § 402(g), resulting in the efforts of women workers required to make
    social security contributions producing less protection for their families than was produced by
    the efforts of men, violated the right to equal protection under the due process clause of the
    Fifth Amendment, and (2) the distinction could not be justified on the basis of the 'noncon-
    tractual' character of social security benefits, or on the ground that the sex-based classifica-
    tion was one really designed to compensate women beneficiaries as a group for the economic
    difficulties confronting women who sought to support themselves and their families."

3. *Eslinger v. Thomas* (1973) was an action brought by a female law student who alleged that
    she was denied employment as a page because of her gender. Citing *Reed*, the Court indicated
    that "the Equal Protection Clause (denies) to States the power to legislate that different treat-
    ment be accorded to persons placed by a statute into different classes on the basis of criteria
    wholly unrelated to the objective of that statute."

    The Court quoted from an article by Johnson and Knapp that "on the one hand, the
    female is viewed as a pure delicate and vulnerable creature who must be protected from expo-
    sure to criminal influences; and on the other, as a brazen temptress, from whose seductive
    blandishments the innocent must be protected. Every women is either Eve or Little Eva—and
    either way, she loses" (Johnson & Knapp, 1971).

    The decision of the lower court was reversed, there being no "fair and substantial 'rela-
    tion between the object of the resolution,' which was to combat the appearance of impropri-
    ety, and the ground of difference, which was sex...."

REFERENCES

ALLEN, H. E., & SIMONSEN, C. E. (1978). *Corrections in America: An introduction.* Criminal
    Justice Series. Encino, CA: Glencoe.

AMERICAN CORRECTIONAL ASSOCIATION. (1985, April). Standards for adult local detention facilities
    (2nd ed.). In cooperation with the Commission on Accreditation for Corrections.

ARDITI, R. R., GOLDBERG, F., JR., PETERS, J., & PHELPS, W. R. (1973). The sexual segregation of
    American prisons. *Yale Law Journal, 6*(82), pp. 1229–1273.

ARON, N. (1981). Legal issues pertaining to female offenders. In N. Aron (Ed.), *Representing pris-
    oners.* New York: Practicing Law Institute.

FABIAN, S. L. (1980). Women prisoners challenge of the future. In N. Aron (Ed.), *Legal rights of
    prisoners.* Beverly Hills, CA: Sage Publications.

FEINMAN, C. (1986). *Women in the criminal justice system.* New York: Praeger.

FEINMAN, C. (1982). Sex role stereotypes and justice for women. In B. Raffel Price & N. J.
    Sokoloff (Eds.), *The criminal justice system and women* (pp. 131–139). New York: Clark
    Boardman Company, Ltd.

FLYNN, E. E. (1971). *The special problems of female offenders.* Paper presented at the National
    Conference on Corrections, Williamsburg, VA: Virginia Division of Justice and Crime Prevention.

GIBSON, H. (1973). Women's prisons: Laboratories for penal reform. *Wisconsin Law Review.*

GOBERT, J. J., & COHEN, N. P. (1981). *Rights of prisoners.* New York:McGraw-Hill.

HUNTER, S. (1984, Spring–Summer). Issues and challenges facing women's prisons in the 1980's. *Prison Journal, 64*(1).

INCIARDI, J. A. (1984). *Criminal justice.* Orlando, FL: Academic Press.

JOHNSON, J., & KNAPP, J. (1971). Sex discrimination by law: A study in judicial perspective. 46 N.Y.U. Law Rev. 675, 704–5.

LEWIS, D. K. (1982). Female ex-offenders and community programs. *Crime and Delinquency, 28.*

LOWN, R. D., & SNOW, C. (1980). Women, the forgotten prisoners: *Glover v. Johnson.* In *Legal Rights of Prisoners.* Beverly Hills, CA: Sage Publications.

MITFORD, J. (1971). *Kind and unusual punishment.* New York: Alfred A. Knopf.

MURASKIN, R. (1989). *Disparity of correctional treatment: Development of a measurement instrument.* Doctoral dissertation, City University of New York. Doctoral Dissertation Abstracts International.

POLLACK, H., & SMITH, A. B. (1978). *Civil liberties and civil rights in the United States.* St. Paul, MN: West Publishing.

RAFTER, N. (1983). Prisons for women, 1790–1980. In M. Tonry & N. Morris (Eds.), *Crime and justice: An annual review of research* (Vol. 5). Chicago: University of Chicago Press.

RECKLESS, W. (1967). *The crime problem.* New York: Appleton-Century-Crofts.

SARGENT, J. P. (1984, Spring–Summer). The evolution of a stereotype: Paternalism and the female inmate. *Prison Journal, 1.*

SARRI, R. C. (1979). Crime and the female offender. In E. S. Gomberg & V. Frank (Eds.), *Gender and disordered behavior: Sex differences in psychopathology.* New York: Brunner/Mazel.

SINGER, L. (1979). Women and the correctional process. In F. Adler & R. Simon (Eds.), *The criminality of deviant women.* Boston: Houghton Mifflin.

SOBEL, S. B. (1980). Women in prison: Sexism behind the bars. *Professional Psychological, 2.*

WILLIAMS, V. L., FORMBY, W. A., & WATKINS, J. C. (1982). *Introduction to criminal justice.* Albany, NY: Delmar Publishers.

WOOD, D. (1982). *Women in jail.* Milwaukee, WI: Benedict Center for Criminals.

CASES

Barefield v. Leach, Civ. Action No. 10282 (1974).

Bounds v. Smith, 430 U.S. 817 (1977).

Bukhari v. Huto, 487 F. Supp. 1162 (E.D. Va. 1980).

Canterino v. Wilson, 546 F. Supp. 174 (W.D. Ky 1982) and 562 F. Supp. 106 (W.D. Ky. 1983).

Cody v. Hillard, 799 F.2d 447 (1986).

Commonwealth v. Stauffer, 214 Pa. Supp. 113 (1969).

Cooper v. Morin, 49 N.Y. 2d 69 (1979), cert. denied, 446 U.S. 984 (1980).

Cornish v. Johnson, No. 77-72557 (E.D. Mich. 1979).

Craig v. Boren, 429 U.S. 190 (1976).

Dawson v. Carberry, No. C-71-1916 (N.D. Cal. 1973).

Eslinger v. Thomas, 476 F.2d (4th Cir. 1973).

Estelle v. Gamble, 429 U.S. 97 (1976).

Glover v. Johnson, 478 F. Supp. 1075, 1078 (1979).

Holt v. Sarver, 309 U.S. F. Supp. 362 (E.D. Ark. 1970).

Liberti v. York, 28 Conn. Supp. 9, 246 A.2d 106 (S. Ct. 1968).

Mary Beth G. v. City of Chicago, 723 F.2d 1263 (7th Cir. 1983).

McMurray v. Phelps, 535 F. Supp. 742 (W.D.L.A. 1982).

Mitchell v. Untreiner, 421 F. Supp. 887 (N.D. Fla. 1976).

Molar v. Gates, 159 Ca. Rptr. 239 (4th Dist. 1979).

Park v. Thompson, 356 F. Supp. 783 (D. Hawaii 1973).

Reed v. Reed, 404 U.S. 71 (1971).

State ex rel Olson v. Maxwell, 259 N.W. 2d 621 (Sup. Ct. N.D. 1977).

Thompson et al. v. Varelas, Sheriff, Nassau County et al., 81 Civ. 0184 (JM) (September 11, 1985).

Todaro v. Ward, 431 F. Supp. 1129 (S.D. N.Y. 1977).

United States ex rel Robinson v. York, 281 F. Supp. 8 (D. Conn. 1968).

United States v. Maples, 501 F. Ed. 985 (4th Cir. 1974).

Weinberger v. Wisenfeld, 420 U.S. 636, 43 L. Ed. 2d 514 (1975).

Williams v. Levi, Civ. Action No. Sp. 792-796 (Superior Court of D.C. 1976).

16

The Dislike of Female Offenders among Correctional Officers

Need for Specialized Training

Christine E. Rasche

Work with *women*offenders? Oh, they are the *worst*! I hate to admit it, but I would rather have a caseload of male rapists than a caseload of WOMEN petty offenders!

Female community corrections officer

A pervasive phenomenon in corrections, here termed the *male inmate preference*, is discussed in this chapter. It is evidenced by the almost unanimous desire on the part of correctional officers, male and female, to *avoid* working with female offenders or in women's prisons, despite the fact that female inmates are usually housed in smaller facilities and are less likely to physically attack correctional officers. It is argued that this male inmate preference is probably a product of the fact that most states provide no specialized training for correctional officers on how to work with female inmates, despite the fact that it is well established that male and female inmates are quite different in prison. Most training given to correctional officers is focused on rules and security management, and even the inmate supervisory techniques that are taught seem to emphasize intimidating tactics which may backfire when applied to female prisoners. It is argued that correctional officers who work in women's prisons need specialized training in order to do their jobs better, which would also probably help to offset the male inmate preference.

There is a widespread phenomenon in corrections that has not been well researched scientifically. Anecdotally, this phenomenon shows up in conversations with correctional line staff, both those who work in prisons and those who work in community corrections. Although correctional leaders seem mostly to regard it as a curiosity with little real relevance to correctional practice, I think this phenomenon *does* have an impact on both correctional officers and administrators. More important, it has a direct impact on inmates at prison facilities for women. This phenomenon is the pervasive tendency among correctional workers to dislike working with female offenders or to avoid working at women's prisons, and to view such duty as undesirable.

This dislike of female offenders appears to be very widespread in corrections and is well known by almost all those who work in the field. As Pollack (1984) has noted, "there is informal agreement among correctional personnel that female offenders are somehow 'harder to work with' than male offenders" (p. 84). One has only to ask correctional officers whether they prefer working with male or female offenders. Spontaneously, most correctional officers (both male and female) tend to state a clear preference for working with male offenders.

Logically, this preference might seem somewhat counterintuitive. After all, male inmates are much more likely than female inmates to be housed in very large facilities where supervision is somewhat more difficult, and male inmates are also more likely to physically attack and injure correctional staff. A layperson might well expect that correctional staff would prefer to work in smaller facilities with inmates who are unlikely to physically harm them. However, all the available evidence suggests that the opposite is true.

The layperson might also expect that a such preference for working with male inmates would be widespread only among male correctional officers, given the macho-oriented nature of our culture in general and criminal justice professions in particular. A layperson might easily assume that at least female correctional officers would prefer working with female inmates, either for ideological reasons or because of a desire for less physically risky work. Again, however, this does not seem to be true. With a few notable exceptions discussed below, most female correctional officers also seem to express a clear preference for working with male inmates instead of female inmates. For the purposes of this discussion, I call this widespread phenomenon the *male inmate preference*.

As far as can be determined, the male inmate preference is found among both male and female correctional officers, among both high- and low-ranking officers, among officers working at both male and female inmate facilities, and among officers in all regions of the country. It appears among both those correctional personnel working in prisons and those in community corrections. When this preference is expressed, it usually seems to be articulated immediately, seeming to require little or no thought on the part of respondents. Indeed, a question about their working preferences usually elicits from correctional staffers a prompt, strong, even passionate response, such as the quotation that opened this chapter. Laughter and boisterous exclamations about their working experiences often result, along with unsolicited explanations for their preferences in the form of horror stories.

In fact, often the only correctional staff who do not seem to express the male inmate preference, at least in my experience, are long-time female staff members working at female-only correctional facilities. Such staff are often women who began their careers before institutional staffs were gender-integrated, and many have spent their entire careers working at institutions for female offenders. In general, their preference for working with female inmates seems to arise from long and successful experience in working with female offenders. However, some also express a strong ideological commitment to working with women offenders. This ideological commitment among the older, long-time female staffers is sometimes feminist in nature, but it can also be religious. It should be noted that some *younger* correctional female staff members at female facilities (as well as a few *male* staffers) also express such an ideological commitment to working with female offenders. But outside of these comparatively few ideologically committed or long-time women's prison staff members, my experience is that most other correctional personnel clearly express the male inmate preference, even though they will often simultaneously agree that male inmates are more likely to represent a hazard to their own personal safety.

The fact that the male inmate preference has not been well researched scientifically does *not* mean that it represents a new phenomenon. Observations about the comparatively greater difficulty of working with female inmates appear in the literature dating back at least to the mid-nineteenth century. For example, Pollack (1986) cites one prison matron's description of female inmates in the 1860s:

> It is a harder task to manage female prisoners than male…They are more impulsive, more individual, more unreasonable and excitable than men; will not act in concert, and cannot be disciplined in masses. Each wants personal and peculiar treatment, so that the duties fall much more heavily on the matrons than on the warders; matrons having thus to deal with units, not aggregates, and having to adapt themselves to each individual case, instead of simply obeying certain fixed laws and making others obey them, as in the prison for males. (citing Prison matron, 1862).

Somewhat more recently, Charles Turnbo, who served as the warden of the female prison at Pleasanton, California, from the late 1970s to the early 1980s, recalled that when he was made the warden in 1978, he "received as many condolences as congratulations" (Turnbo, 1993, p. 13). He was also subjected to hearing the war stories of other colleagues who had pulled duty in women's facilities, since "many wardens want nothing to do with an all-female prison population" (p. 13). By way of explanation, Turnbo quoted Heffernan in observing that "women are seen as a persistent and continuing problem in corrections for two reasons: one, their small numbers, and two, their perceived nature" (Heffernan, 1978, cited in Turnbo, 1993, p. 13).

By far the most exhaustive scientific research on this phenomenon has been done by Pollack (1984, 1986). Her research on correctional officers' attitudes revealed that what I call the male inmate preference is a real component of what she calls the prevailing modern "CO culture." Two-thirds (68 percent) of her sample of forty-five experienced correctional officers who had worked in both male and female facilities stated preferences for working with male inmates, and two-thirds (67 percent) also agreed that female inmates were harder to supervise. Interestingly, female correctional officers generally expressed a *stronger* preference for working with male inmates than did male correctional officers (f = 72 percent, m = 66 percent) and were *more* likely than their male colleagues to agree that women inmates were more difficult to manage (f = 83 percent, m = 55 percent) (Pollack, 1986).

However, male and female correctional officers may not always have the same reasons for holding the same preference. As shown in Table 1, Pollack (1986) found that the reasons given by male officers for a male inmate preference included perceived difficulties in supervising the opposite sex and fear of being framed for rape. Male officers also perceived the need to modify their normal behavior when working with women inmates (e.g., curbing their speech, being careful about the use of force). By contrast, the reasons given by *female* officers for a male inmate preference included perceptions that male inmates were more likely to treat women officers with respect and that male inmates

---

TABLE 1   Reasons Given by Correctional Officers for the Male Inmate Preference

---

Reasons given by male officers for preferring to work with male inmates included:

1. Difficulties in supervising the opposite sex and fear of being framed for rape
2. The need to modify their behavior toward women inmates (e.g., curb their speech, be careful about the use of force)

Reasons given by female officers for preferring to work with male inmates included:

1. Male inmates were seen as more likely to treat women officers with respect
2. Male inmates were seen as appreciating them as women, which made the job more enjoyable

Reasons give by both male and female officers for the male inmate preference included:

1. Women inmates are more demanding
2. Women inmates complain more
3. Women inmates are more likely to refuse orders

Source: Pollack (1986).

---

seemed to appreciate them as women, which made the job more enjoyable. In short, male correctional officers were likely to perceive more potential penalties for working with female inmates, while female correctional officers saw more rewards in working with male inmates. Interestingly, however, reasons given by both male and female officers for disdaining work with female inmates included perceptions that women inmates are more demanding and tended to complain more than male inmates, and that women inmates are more likely to refuse orders.

Pollack (1986) also found that there were a few correctional officers in her sample who preferred to work with women inmates, even though they agreed that women inmates were more difficult to supervise. These officers indicated that they enjoyed the challenge of trying to deal with the demands and problems of female inmates. These atypical correctional officers also stated that they enjoyed the "variety, unpredictability, and constant turmoil that was likely to be present in settings for women" (p. 99). Normally, qualities such as "constant turmoil" are *not* listed as desirable job attributes!

As part of her research, Pollack (1984, 1986) explored correctional officers' views of male and female inmates by giving officers lists of adjectives which they applied to different types of inmates. As Table 2 shows, Pollack (1986) found that some adjectives were applied frequently to both male and female inmates. Thus both male and female prisoners were seen as being defensive, distrustful, and manipulative. However, female inmates specifically were characterized as emotional, temperamental, moody, manipulative, quarrelsome, demanding, changeable, complaining, argumentative, excitable, immature, and noisy. By comparison, choosing from this same list of adjectives, male inmates were characterized by correctional officers as active, defensive, boastful, aggressive, and manipulative. Pollack (1986) noted that "only three adjectives for males were agreed upon by more than 60 percent of the officers, whereas

60 percent or more officers agreed on twelve adjectives for females" (pp. 34–35). This greater consensus among the correctional officers about which adjective labels to apply to female inmates "raises the possibility that officers possess a stereotype of females. It is not unusual to obtain a high rate of agreement among those who possess a common stereotype of a group; likewise, one is less likely to get consensus on a description of any group for which a stereotype is not operating, since people interact and perceive each other differently" (p. 35).

Ultimately, Pollack found three "themes" emerging from the adjective descriptions of female inmates selected by correctional officers. As shown in Table 3, the first theme was *defiance*, which involved selecting descriptions of women inmates as being likely to oppose the officers in various ways. This included descriptions of women inmates as being argumentative, less likely to follow rules, demanding, and harder to handle. In the closed

---

TABLE 2   Adjectives Used by Correctional Officers to Describe Female and Male Inmates

---

Some adjectives were applied frequently to both male and female inmates:

　　Defensive (54.5%)

　　Distrustful (50%)

　　Manipulative (65%)

But female inmates also were characterized as:

　　Emotional (83%)

　　Tempermental (76%)

　　Moody (74%)

　　Manipulative (71%)

　　Quarrelsome (64%)

　　Demanding (69%)

　　Changeable (67%)

　　Complaining (81%)

　　Argumentative (69%)

　　Excitable (64%)

　　Immature (62%)

　　Noisy (64%)

By comparison, male inmates were characterized as:

　　Active (64%)

　　Defensive (60%)

　　Boastful (57%)

　　Aggressive (55%)

　　Manipulative (60%)

Source: Pollack (1986).

TABLE 3   Themes in the Description of Female Inmates by Correctional Officers

1. *Defiance:* descriptions of the women as opposing the officers, which included women inmates described as being argumentative, less likely to follow rules, demanding, harder to handle, questioning rules, more troublesome, more complaining, confronting verbally, more critical, less respectful, and harder to reason with.

2. *Open display of emotion:* descriptions of women inmates as expressing more feelings, being louder/noisier, screaming/hollering more, having a greater tendency to cry, having spur-of-the-moment outbreaks, fighting spontaneously and easily, being ready to explode, being crybabies, being explosive, losing their tempers easily.

3. *Gratification seeking:* described women as needing and wanting more from their environment, needing/wanting both material and personal commodities such as attention, friendship, or sympathy, wanting things with little or no patience, emotionally demanding, less independent, more childish, having critical demands and a greater need for friends.

Source: Pollack (1986).

world of the prison, defiant inmates are uniformly disliked by correctional officers, whose jobs often hinge on the degree to which they are able to manage inmates smoothly.

The second theme Pollack (1986) found emerging from the adjectives correctional officers chose to describe female offenders was *open display of emotion*. This involved characterizations of women inmates as expressing more feeling, being louder and noisier, having a greater tendency to cry, erupting in spur-of-the-moment outbreaks, fighting spontaneously and easily, and losing their tempers easily. Clearly, such boisterous displays are viewed by correctional officers as management problems, particularly when the emotional outburst of one inmate can result in emotional displays among others.

The third theme characterizing female offenders in the eyes of correctional officers, according to Pollack (1986), was that female inmates were seen as *gratification seeking*. This described women inmates as needing and wanting both material and personal commodities, such as attention, friendship, or sympathy, more than males, and wanting things immediately with little or no patience or willingness to wait. Such impatient and demanding inmates are, once again, viewed by correctional officers as "management problems," who tend to create a major fuss over minor problems and who therefore make supervision more difficult. Overall, Pollack (1986) found that there was strong agreement among her respondents that men and women inmates required different styles of supervision (91 percent), and that there could be situations where they as correctional officers needed to respond to men and women in different fashions (73 percent).

Interestingly, when asked to account for why these perceived differences between male and female inmates exist, Pollack (1984, 1986) found that correctional officers referred to general "sex differences (whether biological or socialization) rather than institutional factors" (1986, p. 116). In other words, women inmates and women in general were seen as being similar.

> The inmates' behavior, in other words, is taken for granted, and the officers see themselves as doing their best within the confines of that assumption. Attempts to change behavior by changing procedures, policies, or other situational components are unlikely to be viewed as effective since it is assumed that the behavior is not situationally induced. We could, therefore, expect the officers to view inmate-generated problems with exasperated resignation, which indeed, appears to be their attitude. (Pollack, 1986, p. 116)

In short, correctional officers did not think there was anything they could do about the greater difficulty posed by female inmates because it was a product of nature. Women inmates were just being women.

Pollack's (1984, 1986) reports on correctional officers' different attitudes toward male and female inmates are by far the most scientific analyses of a sentiment that both experienced correctional workers and outside observers readily assert runs throughout the field. This tendency to view female inmates as more difficult to manage leads to the perpetuation of what I have called the male inmate preference.

PERCEPTIONS VERSUS REAL DIFFERENCES

The question that follows is whether there are real differences between male and female inmates in terms of supervision and management requirements, or whether correctional officers are merely articulating unfounded prejudices and stereotypes. As it turns out, there is a considerable literature on the differences between men and women in captivity. There are at least three dimensions of this difference.

The first dimension of difference between male and female inmates is their *demographic profiles*. The demographic characteristics of women who are in prison are different in some important ways from those of males who are in prison. First, while African-Americans are clearly overrepresented in U.S. prisons in general, there is some evidence that there may be a larger percentage of African-Americans among women in prison than among men (Binkley-Jackson, Carter, & Rolison, 1993; Goetting & Howsen, 1983; Rafter, 1985; Sarri, 1987). Overall, women inmates as a group have tended to be slightly older than male inmates. Women inmates have also tended to be slightly better educated than their male counterparts, although this is not saying much, since both male and female inmates tend to be less academically skilled when tested than their respective completed years of formal education would suggest. Women inmates are highly likely to have minor children in the home prior to imprisonment and were usually the primary caregivers for their dependent children, which is much less true of male inmates with dependent children (Koban, 1983). Compared to male inmates, female inmates have tended to be imprisoned more often for economic and drug-related crimes than for assaultive crimes. Women inmates are less likely to have been legitimately employed compared to their male counterparts, despite the fact that they were often the sole support for their minor children.

In recent years, women prisoners also have been shown to have a higher likelihood of drug addiction/abuse than males, especially addiction to heroin, cocaine, and other intravenous drugs. In the light of this, it is perhaps not so surprising to find out that new women prisoners have had higher levels of HIV infection than new male prisoners. Also in recent years, women prisoners have been found to have had very high levels of sexual and/or physical abuse as either children or adults, or both; usually, these are much higher levels than even the high levels reported for males (American Correctional Association, 1990; Arnold, 1990; Carlen, 1983; Chesney-Lind & Rodriguez, 1983, Fletcher, Shaver, & Moon, 1993; Gilfus, 1992; Immarigeon 1987a, 1987b; Sargent, Marcus-Mendoza, & Yu, 1993).

In addition to such differences in their *demographic profiles*, a second dimension of difference between male and female inmates is that they have quite dissimilar *needs during incarceration*. Some differences between the sexes are obvious and expected. For example, women have needs for gynecologically related goods and services, such as menstrual supplies, annual gynecological checkups, prenatal care for those who are pregnant, and postnatal care and counseling for those who give birth in prison. Only recently have prison systems begun to acknowledge that pre- and postnatal care and counseling needs to be both of the normal variety, which might be given to any woman before and after giving birth, and somewhat specialized care, given to women with greater needs. Specialized care is needed partly because of the large proportion of prison pregnancies that are "high risk" in nature. That is, women who are pregnant in prison are more likely than those in the general population to have been in ill health previously, to have received little prior prenatal care, and to suffer from a variety of chronic conditions that increase risk during pregnancy or afterward (Resnick & Shaw, 1980; Ross & Fabiano, 1986). However, specialized care is also required because following a prison birth there is (in all but a few women's prisons) an inevitable "loss" of the newborn, who will immediately be taken away from the mother and placed outside the prison with foster caregivers. Although the child lives, its physical loss immediately following birth may be experienced as almost "deathlike" by the imprisoned mother. Special health care, both physical and mental, is required under such considerations. Male inmates, obviously, do not require such services.

Also among the obvious and expected differences between the sexes in needs during incarceration are that women inmates need different sorts of routine health and beauty aids and different types of clothing. Women prisoners also express a much higher need for privacy than do male inmates. Furthermore, women generally need a different kind of diet, with fewer calories and carbohydrates overall and more of certain vitamins and minerals than men require.

Less obviously, it is only recently that have we begun to realize that women inmates need specialized counseling for sexual and/or physical abuse that most received as children and/or adults. Indeed, women are more likely than men to be in prison precisely for killing an adult abuser, particularly a spouse, lover, or other family member. They are also somewhat more likely to be imprisoned for having killed their own children; many women who kill their own children explain their actions as a form of "mercy" killing in the face of what they saw as intolerably brutal conditions. Also, because they were often the primary caregivers to their minor children prior to their imprisonment, women inmates seem to need more help than do male inmates in dealing with the separation from their children, which many view as the harshest single aspect of being imprisoned. There is now considerable evidence that for all these reasons women inmates need more counseling and psychiatric services overall than do male inmates.

In part because of all these unique stressors, women inmates seem to need different kinds of supervision techniques from correctional officers. Because so many women inmates have an abusive history, correctional staff may unwittingly trigger "flashbacks" of painful past abuses if they utilize the common in-your-face approach favored for handling male inmates. Male correctional staff may be more likely to run into this problem, since women inmates are likely to have been abused primarily by the males in their lives, but it should be noted that even female staff can employ supervisory tactics that backfire when used with female offenders.

In discussing these first two dimensions of difference between male and female inmates, *demographic profile differences* and *different needs during incarceration*, it is noteworthy that we have not made any references to the third dimension, *differences in personality*. This is important because we have already seen that there are big differences in the ways staff perceive the personalities and behaviors of incarcerated men and women in general. As it turns out, there is evidence to suggest that some of these perceived differences are real. For example, some researchers (Joesting, Jones, & Joesting, 1975; McKerracher, Street, & Segal, 1966) have found that women prisoners are more likely than male prisoners to engage in what is usually called "acting-out" behaviors (e.g., extremely emotional outbursts). A higher level of emotionality is, indeed, a consistent theme among writers describing women prisoners, including higher levels of emotional attachment between female inmates than is usually found between male inmates (Giallombardo, 1966; Lekkerkerker, 1931; Ward, & Kassebaum, 1965). This higher level of emotionality is perceived by correctional officers as problematic because "emotions displayed by the inmates may translate into hostility toward the officer...." (Pollack, 1984).

It seems clear that there are many real differences between male and female offenders in prison, which could translate into differences in required management and supervisory approaches. If we add the third dimension, *differences in personality*, it would seem that not only must the overall management of an institution be revised in certain significant ways to accommodate female offenders, but the day-to-day business of direct inmate supervision might need to be altered significantly for things to go as smoothly as possible.

SHOULD INMATE DIFFERENCES LEAD TO SPECIALIZED STAFF TRAINING?

In 1996 there were at least sixty-eight state prison facilities in the United States that housed female offenders only, plus another ninety-seven state "co-correctional" facilities housing both male and female inmates. At least two additional female-only institutions are run by the Federal Bureau of Prisons, which also operates sixteen co-correctional institutions. In short, at least 183 penal institutions in the United States house a female inmate population (American Correctional Association, 1998). Most of these facilities house hundreds of inmates each, although in 1993 the numbers ranged from as few as one female inmate in Nome, Alaska and Hilo, Hawaii, to as many as 2393 in Chowcilla, California (Maquire & Pastore, 1994, pp.109–111).

Of course, men still vastly outnumber women behind bars in the United States (by about 20 to 1). But the *number* of women incarcerated by the states and the federal government has increased at a much faster rate than did the number of men during the 1980s, resulting in most states now having record-high numbers of women prisoners. Prior to 1980, most states had only one separate women's prison facility. and some states did not even have that, continuing instead to house women in small separate units within larger men's prisons, in coeducational facilities, or even sending them to women's prisons in adjoining states. Due to the huge population growth of prisoners in the 1980s, however, some states opened multiple women's institutions by the 1990s. Indeed, by 1996 at least seventeen states had two or more women's prisons, and two states had at least four female-only institutions (American Correctional Association, 1998). Most states added to their correctional workforce exponentially in the 1980s in the effort to keep pace with burgeoning prison populations, and thousands of correctional staff are now employed by these women's institutions and coeducational facilities. Add to this the correctional officers in the thousands of jails around the nation that house one or more women detainees, and the number of correctional officers affected by the management differences required for female versus male inmates is enormous.

Furthermore, the inmate population boom of the 1980s led to some remarkable and dramatic facilities changes. In some states, within the span of just a few years, facilities changed from housing male inmates only, to housing co-correctional inmate populations, to housing females only as inmate populations grew or shifted. This meant that correctional officers who were experienced in working with male inmates have sometimes found themselves suddenly supervising female offenders with little advanced preparation. Given all the differences between male and female inmates noted above, we might expect that correctional systems would be concerned about providing specialized preparation to those correctional staff members assigned to work with female offenders. However, there seems to be little evidence of specialized training for correctional staff assigned to female facilities.

The American Correctional Association recognized this in the mid-1980s when it noted that the "requirements and opportunities for staff development often overlook the needs of administration and staff for professional, on-going training in managing the female offender" (American Correctional Association, 1986, p. 29.). Modern researchers on women in prison have also noted the lack of specialized training for staff in women's prisons:

> Typically, state correctional systems have moved from an approach that isolates and differentiates the women's institution to an approach that alleges that all inmates and all prisons are the same in terms of rules, supplies, assignments and other factors. This latter approach is no more helpful than the benign neglect that previously characterized the central office's attention to facilities for women; women's prisons obviously have unique needs, different from men's institutions. (Pollack-Byrne, 1990, p. 115)

Of course, the counter-argument to the claim that specialized training is needed for staff working in women's prisons is that regular correctional training is sufficient. That is, if the routine training given to new correctional officers includes training for the different supervisory requirements of female and male inmates, no specialized training would be needed for those assigned to women's institutions.

THE CONTENT OF ROUTINE CORRECTIONAL TRAINING

The idea of requiring any training at all for correctional officers to prepare them for their duties is not a very old one. The first correctional training school was begun in New York in 1930 by the Federal Bureau of Prisons (Schade, 1986). Both prior to and after that, the states apparently hired correctional officers directly into their jobs, with little or no formal training of any kind except that received on the job. Official reviewers and reform-minded critics of corrections often complained about the quality of the correctional staff, but they usually recommended remedies in the form of taking more care about who was hired rather than expressing concern about what preparation was given after hiring. For example, shortly after the Civil War, prison reformers Wines and Dwight (1867) set forth guidelines for the hiring of prison officers, in which they asserted that

> [p]rison officers should be men of strict and uniform sobriety....They should be men of mild temper, quiet manners, and pure conversation....They should be men of decision and energy....They should be men of humane and benevolent feelings....They should be men having a sincere interest in those placed under their care....They should be men of high moral principle, and distinguished by habits of industry, order and cleanliness....They should be men possessing a knowledge of human nature in its various aspects and relations....They should be men of sterling and incorruptible honesty....They should be men of experience....They must be men of a just and steadfast purpose, free from prejudice and partiality....They should be men of untiring vigilance....They should have a liking for the occupation in which they are employed....Finally, prison officers should be men duly impressed with religious principles; men who fear God, and are in the habit, as the expression of that reverence, of attending the services of some religious body. (pp. 120–122)

It is only after this long recitation about what kind of *men* corrections should seek to hire that Wines and Dwight (1867) provide a brief paragraph on *female* officers, about whom they recommend:

> The qualifications of female officers are, in many respects, the same as those of males. It is especially important, however, that female officers should be distinguished for modesty of demeanor, and the exercise of domestic virtues, and that they should possess that intimate knowledge of household employment, which will enable them to teach the ignorant and neglected female prisoner how to economize her means, so as to guard her from the temptations caused by waste and extravagance. (pp. 123–24)

These are certainly descriptions of outstanding prospective employees. Such exemplary persons, both then and now, might possibly be attracted to high-paying high-prestige jobs. But what was the likelihood that corrections was able to attract large numbers of such inherently good and skilled workers in the nineteenth century—or could even do so now? Modern writers Hawkins and Alpert (1989) have provided a much more brutally frank description of a modern correctional officer's job:

> A candid job description for a correctional officer position would read something like this: Excellent employment opportunity for men and women who are willing to work eight-hour shifts at varying times (early morning, afternoon, and late nights) on a rotating basis. Applicants must enforce numerous rules with few guidelines. They must be willing to risk physical harm, psychological harassment, and endure the threat of inmate law suits, which could involve civil liability. They must be willing to spend eight hours each day among people who do not like them. They will not be allowed to fraternize with these people, but are expected to control as well as help them. Applicants must accept that they have little or no input into the rules they will be asked to enforce, nor will they be privy to the policy rationale for these rules. They should realize that management will probably not listen to their complaints. Work superiors, located in a military chain of command, are likely to have a great deal of time invested in organizational rules and therefore will resist employee innovations. The person at the top of the chain of command is likely to be a political appointment, but applicants are not allowed to

engage in political activity. Promotion is infrequent and opportunities for advancement in the organization are very limited. All applicants are considered untrustworthy: frequent questioning and searches of private possessions are designed to reduce corruption. Applicants must give up some civil rights for employment to continue. Women and minority groups are encouraged to apply, but will be discriminated against once on the job. (pp. 338–339)

This "job description" of a correctional officer is exaggerated, of course, but there is some evidence that persons who seek correctional employment are entering into an employment area that does *not* have much inherent attractiveness. For example, Smith (1974) found that the social position of the correctional officer had very little prestige compared with other occupations or careers (cited in Farmer, 1977, p. 239). This low prestige may be not so much a reflection of the low pay and minimal qualifications that corrections work has traditionally involved, as it is a reflection of the *object* of that work: prison inmates. Jacobs and Retsky (1975) observed that the job of prison guard is not entirely unlike other guard jobs, except that "bank guards and Secret Security Agents derive some measure of esteem from the objects they guard, while 'close contacts with convicted felons seems morally profaning for the (prison) guard.'" (p. 10, as cited in Farmer, 1977, p. 238). There is ample evidence that the commitment to the job at the lower levels of correctional work is not generally very great and that the field suffers from relatively high turnover rates (McShane, Williams, Schichor, & McCain, 1991). This may be because of the lower prestige of the field and its less desirable working conditions. But it also may be because there is some evidence that a significant proportion of persons who enter correctional work do so out of economic necessity (Shannon, 1987); in other words, most people do not enter correctional work out of a zeal to work with prisoners. Interestingly, the degree to which economic necessity plays a role in correctional recruitment may vary somewhat by gender. In at least one study, a much larger proportion of women indicated that they had sought correctional employment because they were interested in human service work (f = 55%, m = 14%), whereas males more frequently indicated that they took the job because there was no alternative work available to them (m = 14%, f = 3%) (Jurik & Halemba, 1984). Overall, however, it may be concluded that the dedication of correctional officers to their work varies greatly and that there is little internal incentive to seek more difficult or challenging posts, such as assignment to women's prisons.

As of the spring of 1993, preservice correctional training in the United States varied from a minimum of two weeks (in Louisiana, North Dakota, and Wyoming) to a maximum of sixteen weeks (only in Michigan), with the average being about five and a half weeks (for forty-eight states that reported plus the Federal Bureau of Prisons) (Maquire & Pastore, 1994, pp. 101–107). What is the content of that training? Wicks (1980) has noted that the emphasis in recent decades has been on standardizing correctional training in the United States, so that there can be some assurance that all correctional officers have received basic training in certain skills and knowledge areas that are consistent with state policies and procedures. Shaver (1993) observed that training in Oklahoma, for example, consisted of four weeks of intensive, centralized group training of new recruits, followed by another three to five days of in-house training and orientation once new correctional officers arrived at their actual work site. However, "[v]ery little of this training is directly related to their new positions. Rather, the training focuses on the policies, rules, regulations and values of the correctional agency" (p. 122). There is no reason to assume that Oklahoma is a training aberration in this regard.

Shannon (1987) found that only 85 percent of his Ohio correctional officer respondents reported that they had received forty hours of training prior to starting their position, although the American Correctional Association (ACA) has stipulated that forty hours of preservice training is the minimum. Only 60 percent of Shannon's respondents indicated that they had received 120 hours of training during their first year on the job as required by the ACA. Even fewer (42 percent) indicated that they had received the required forty hours of in-service training per year since starting their jobs.

When asked about the content of the training they had been given, Shannon's respondents indicated that the training they most frequently received had to do with firearms training, housing and body searches, contraband hunting, report writing, rules and regulations of the institution, self-defense training, key and tool control, riot control tactics, and CPR certification (Shannon, 1987, p. 174) (see Table 4). In general, Shannon notes that "[t]he officer's formal training consists primarily of instruction in the skills and mechanics of security procedures and the handling of inmates to maintain order and prevent trouble. The real learning (training) occurs on the job under inmate testing and manipulation attempts" (p. 173). Of course, it is after formal preservice training that the new correctional

TABLE 4   Specific Training Reportedly Received by Correctional Officers[a]

Subject	Percent
Firearms training	97
Housing and body searches	93
Contraband hunting	92
Training in report writing	88
Rules and regulations of the institution	85
Self-defense training	84
Key and tool control	78
Riot control tactics	67
Valid CPR certification	66
Legal authority training	64
Suicidal inmate recognition	62
Emergency prevention training	61
Techniques for protecting prison property	59
Inmates' rights training	57
Valid first-aid certification	56
How to behave if taken hostage	56
Radio communications	54
Identifying mental illness	52

[a]All other specific training was completed by less than half of respondents.

Source: Shannon (1987, p. 174).

officer learns about and enters into the "officer subculture," which may well train the recruit somewhat differently than did the academy. For example, while the academy trains rookies in approved ways to handle inmates, the officer subculture "encourages officers to use intimidating behavior to establish authority over inmates" (Shannon, 1987, p. 173). It also provides working definitions of the kinds of inmates the new correctional officer can expect to confront, and anecdotal evidence of what techniques work best with different kinds of inmates. There is increasing evidence that institutional socialization processes have a significant impact on correctional officer attitudes toward inmates (Jurik, 1985).

In short, while most academy training focuses on mechanical skills and operational procedures, the real "wisdom" about inmate handling comes from on-the-job inculcation into an officer subculture that may emphasize stereotypes and extreme examples. It is perhaps not at all surprising that such training leaves most correctional officers ill-prepared to deal with the unique needs and demands of working with female offenders in custody.

THE NEED FOR SPECIALIZED TRAINING FOR STAFF WORKING WITH FEMALE OFFENDERS

So far, we have seen that there is a variety of circumstances that combine to produce the widespread presence of the male inmate preference among correctional officers: the perceptions of and stereotypes about female inmates that are conveyed in the correctional officer subculture; the very real supervisory differences posed by the needs of female inmates compared to their male counterparts; and the limited and largely operations-oriented training given to officer recruits. All these conspire to virtually ensure that most correctional officers are somewhat biased against, and certainly unskilled in dealing with, female offenders in custody.

Little wonder, then, that so many correctional officers report unsatisfactory experiences in working with female offenders or, in the absence of actual experience in female prisons, much anticipatory prejudice against such assignments. Little wonder, additionally, that women inmates continue to be viewed as more difficult to manage, since little (if any) routine training is aimed at helping correctional officers understand their female inmate charges or what supervisory techniques might be more effective with this population. Finally, little wonder that charges of sexual harassment and inappropriate behavior from correctional officers toward inmates has emerged in the 1990s as one of the more problematic features of managing female institutions. Many state correctional systems have found themselves facing such charges—either in the media or in the courtroom—from individual inmates, interest groups representing inmates, or the federal government.

Suffice it to say that confronting the problem of male inmate preference and all that it means *should* become a high priority of all correctional systems housing female offenders. The costs of defending the system against lawsuits and media reports are high. But there is little evidence that absent media attacks or lawsuits, most correctional systems are taking preventive measures by providing appropriate specialized training to their correctional staff members in women's institutions. Although the costs of such specialized training would be comparatively modest, it appears that most correctional leaders still regard the male inmate preference as an anecdotal curiosity with little effect on daily operations. Since their systems are always populated predominantly by male inmates, the fact that correctional officers overwhelmingly prefer duty with male inmates does not seem to be a problem. Those comparatively few correctional officers assigned to women's institutions, and their discontent with such duty, seems like a small problem in an ocean of correctional difficulties facing the modern correctional administrator. The result, however, is that those correctional staff members who are assigned to women's prisons continue to work with inmates about whom they hold highly negative perceptions and for whose management they have never been properly trained. If nothing else, it is these correctional officers and the female inmates they supervise who are the losers.

REFERENCES

AMERICAN CORRECTIONAL ASSOCIATION. (1986). *Public policy for corrections: A handbook for decision makers*. College Park, MD: ACA.

AMERICAN CORRECTIONAL ASSOCIATION. (1990). *The female offender: What does the future hold?* Arlington, VA: Kirby Lithographic Company.

AMERICAN CORRECTIONAL ASSOCIATION. (1998). *Directory: Juvenile and adult correctional departments, institutions, agencies and paroling authorities, United States and Canada, 1997.* College Park, MD: ACA.

ARNOLD, R. (1990). Processes of victimization and criminalization of black women. *Social Justice, 17*, 153–166.

BINKLEY-JACKSON, D., CARTER, V. L., & ROLISON, G. L. (1993). African-American women in prison. In B. R. Fletcher, L. D. Shaver, & D. G. Moon (Eds.), *Women prisoners: A forgotten population* (pp. 65–74). Westport, CT: Praeger.

CARLEN, P. (1983). *Women's imprisonment: A study in social control*. London: Routledge & Kegan Paul.

CHESNEY-LIND, M., & RODRIGUEZ, N. (1983). Women under lock and key. *Prison Journal, 63*, 47–65.

FARMER, R. E. (1977). Cynicism: a factor in corrections work. *Journal of Criminal Justice, 5*, 237–246.

FLETCHER, B. R., SHAVER, L. D., & MOON, D. G. (1993). *Women prisoners: A forgotten population.* Westport, CT: Praeger.

GIALLOMBARDO, R. (1966). *Society of women: A study of a women's prison*. New York: Wiley.

GILFUS, M. E. (1992). From victims to survivors to offenders: Women's routes of entry and immersion into street crime. *Women and Criminal Justice, 4*, 63–90.

GOETTING, A., & HOWSEN, R. M. (1983) Women in prison: A profile. *Prison Journal, 63*, 27–46.

HAWKINS, R., & ALPERT, G. P. (1989). *American prison systems: Punishment and justice.* Englewood Cliffs, NJ: Prentice Hall.

HEFFERNAN, E. (1978). *Female corrections: History and analysis.* Paper presented at the Confinement of Female Offenders Conference, Lexington, KY.

IMMARIGEON, R. (1987a). Women in prison. *Journal of the National Prison Project, 11*, 1–5.

IMMARIGEON, R. (1987b). Few diversion programs are offered female offenders. *Journal of the National Prison Project, 12*, 9–11.

JACOBS, J., & RETSKY, H. (1975). Prison guard. *Urban Life, 4*, 5–29.

JOESTING, J, JONES, N., & JOESTING, R. (1975). Male and female prison inmates' differences on MMPI scales and revised beta I.Q. *Psychological Reports, 37*, 471–474.

JURIK, N. (1985). Individual and organization determinants of correctional officer attitudes toward inmates. *Criminology, 23*, 523–539.

JURIK, N., & HALEMBA, G. J. (1984, Autumn). Gender, working conditions and job satisfaction of women in non-traditional occupations: Female correctional officers in men's prisons. *Sociological Quarterly, 25*, 551–566.

KOBAN, L. (1983). Parent in prison: A comparative analysis of the effects of incarceration on the families of men and women. *Research in Law, Deviance and Social Control, 5*, 171–183.

LEKKERKERKER, E. (1931). *Reformatories for women in the United States*. Groningen, The Netherlands: J.B. Wolters.

MAQUIRE, K., & PASTORE, A. L. (EDS.). (1994). *Sourcebook of criminal justice statistics, 1993*, U.S. Department of Justice, Bureau of Justice Statistics. Washington, DC: U.S. Government Printing Office.

MCKERRACHER, D. W., STREET, D. R. K., & SEGAL, L. S. (1966). A comparison of the behavior problems presented by male and female subnormal offenders. *British Journal of Psychiatry, 112*, 891–899.

MCSHANE, M., WILLIAMS, F. P., SCHICHOR, D., & MCCLAIN, K. L. (1991, August). Early exits: Examining employee turnover. *Corrections Today, 53*, 222–225.

POLLACK, J. M. (1984). Women will be women: Correctional officers' perceptions of the emotionality of women inmates. *Prison Journal, 64*, 84–91.

POLLACK, J. M. (1986). *Sex and supervision: Guarding male and female inmates*. New York: Greenwood Press.

POLLACK-BYRNE, J. M. (1990). *Women, prison and crime*. Pacific Grove, CA: Brooks/Cole.

PRISON MATRON. (1862). *Female life in prison*. New York: Hurst & Blackett.

RAFTER, N. H. (1985). *Partial justice: Women in state prisons, 1800–1935*. Boston: Northeastern University Press.

RESNICK, J., & SHAW, N. (1980). Prisoners of their sex: Health problems of incarcerated women. In I. P. Robbins (Ed.), *Prisoners' rights sourcebook*. New York: Clark Boardman.

ROSS, R. R., & FABIANO, E. A. (1986). *Female offenders: Correctional afterthoughts*. Jefferson, NC: McFarland.

SARGENT, E., MARCUS-MENDOZA, S., & YU, C. H. (1993). Abuse and the women prisoner. In B. R. Fletcher, L. D. Shaver, & D. G. Moon (Eds.), *Women prisoners: A forgotten population* (pp. 55–64). Westport, CT: Praeger.

SARRI, R. (1987). Unequal protection under the law: Women and the criminal justice system. In J. Figueira-McDonough & R. Sarri (Eds.), *The trapped woman: Catch-22 in deviance and control* (pp. 55–64). Newbury Park, CA: Sage.

Schade, T. (1986). Prison officer training in the United States: The legacy of Jesse O. Stutsman. *Federal Probation, 50*(4), 40–46.

SHANNON, M. J. (1987, April). Officer training: Is enough being done? *Corrections Today, 49*, 172–175.

SHAVER, L. D. (1993). The relationship between language, culture and recidivism among women offenders. In B. R. Fletcher, L. D. Shaver, & D. G. Moon (Eds.), *Women prisoners: A forgotten population*. Westport, CT: Praeger.

SMITH, W. (1974). *Some selective factors in the retention of prison guards*. Unpublished masters thesis written in 1963 and reported in E. Johnson, *Crime, corrections and society*. Homewood, IL: Dorsey Press.

TURNBO, C. (1993). Differences that make a difference: Managing a women's correctional institution. In American Correctional Association, *Female offenders: Meeting the needs of an neglected population* (pp. 12–16). College Park, MD: ACA.

WARD, D. A., & KASSEBAUM, G. G. (1965). *Women's prison: Sex and social structure*. Chicago: Aldine.

WICKS, R. J. (1980). *Guard! Society's professional prisoner*. Houston, TX: Gulf Publishing.

WINES, E. C., & DWIGHT, T. W. (1867). *Report on the prisons and reformatories of the United States and Canada*. Albany, NY: Van Benthuysen and Sons Steam Printing House. Reprinted by AMS Press, New York, 1973.

17

Sexual Abuse and Sexual Assault of Women in Prison

Zelma Weston Henriques and Evelyn Gilbert

By the end of 1994, 794,100 women were in prison, jail, or on probation/parole. This number represents 1 of every 130 women in the total population. In 1995 the population of women in prison was 6.3 percent of the overall prison population (Bureau of Justice Statistics, 1995). As of June 30, 1996, there were 73,607 women in federal and state prisons and 63,500 women in local jails. Further, 51 percent of the female jail population were still awaiting trial (Bureau of Justice Statistics, 1997). Flowers (1987) observed that while the crimes of women in jail are mainly misdemeanors and victimless crimes, their fate behind bars is anything but victimless and is perhaps the greatest criminal justice system paradox.

The numbers are indisputable evidence that the paternalistic gloves of the criminal justice system have been removed. The public has accepted a punitive response to women who step outside the bounds of their socially prescribed role. But are women to be subjected to all the degradations of punishment that characterize male offenders? Some believe that incarcerated women have always experienced harsher punishment than men. The suggestion is that the harsh punishment of women is evidenced by the number of penal facilities; geographic placement; lack of variety in female institutions; absence of educational, treatment, and vocational programming in women's prisons; and the virtual absence of transitional or alternative programs. On the other hand, some believe that imprisonment and its accompanying deprivations are the "just deserts" of persons who violate the criminal law. Do all deprivations equal just deserts?

Since the first system of laws was developed, punishment has been officially sanctioned as a means of regulating behavior (Allen & Simonsen, 1995, p. 69). While most people agree that those who violate societal standards must be sanctioned, few understand that the significance of punishment flows from the perspective of the one being punished. If the punishment is perceived as undeserved, unjust, or too harsh, and other inmates reinforce this belief, offenders' deviant behavior is more likely to be reinforced by punishment. It is incumbent upon the state and its representatives (i.e., correctional officers) to be irreproachable paragons of community citizenship, to champion superior values, and to foster conformist behavior (Allen & Simonsen, 1995, pp. 71, 72), even in the punishment of criminals.

A century ago, women reformers advocated the creation of separate correctional institutions for women. The reformers were repulsed by the abuse of female inmates at the hands of male guards. They abhorred the widespread practice of abuses in the male-dominated prison system. Elizabeth Fry (1790–1845), a British Quaker, is attributed with early prison reform. She felt that female custodial officers in prison would prevent sexual assault of female inmates by male guards (Freedan, 1974, p. 79). According to Pollock (1997, p. 43), sexual abuse was disturbingly common in custodial prisons run by men. Women might be fondled at intake and raped in their cells by their male keepers. On other occasions, guards would make sport of their sexual encounters with their female captives ("An illustrated history," 1871).

Separate penal facilities for women are still dominated by male custodial officers, and there is no evidence that sexual assaults have diminished with the introduction of female correctional officers. According to Flowers (1987, p. 161), sexual and physical abuse and harassment of female prisoners is "a common practice" in many small jails, especially in the South. An example is the case of Joan Little, a black female inmate in a North Carolina county jail, who killed her white jailer after he tried to sexually assault her. For this woman, the penalty under law for murder was a less severe punishment than the sexual assault at the hands of the custodial officers. Patsy Sims, an investigative journalist, found Joan Little's experience not unique among incarcerated women. In interviews of more than fifty incarcerated women, Sims (1976) heard stories of oral sex through the jail bars, trespass of male trustees into women's cells, and offers of reduced sentences in exchange for sexual favors.

It would appear that sexual assault and harassment of women by male correctional officers is not an issue in correctional management. Sims (1976) describes the system response as less than apathetic. This type of response contributes to the harshness of punishment for imprisoned women. Additionally, women in custodial regimes are "...probably lonelier and certainly more vulnerable to sexual exploitation, easier to ignore because so few in number, and viewed with distaste by prison officials, women in custodial units were treated as the dregs of the state prisoner population" (Rafter, 1990, p. 21). The literature on imprisoned women recognizes their exploitation and the fact that they have little or no choice but to submit to the predations of their keepers (Pollock, 1997). Women are imprisoned for punishment. Their exploitation by male custodial officers is an additional degradation of imprisonment. Lack of recourse to prevent the sexual assault makes the imprisonment severe punishment. While imprisonment may be just deserts for the crime committed, forced sexual assault is undeserved, unjust, and harsh punishment. Sexual assault of female inmates by male correctional staff is inconsistent with the goals of retribution, deterrence, incapacitation, or rehabilitation.

DEFINITION OF THE PROBLEM

Sexual assault is the gender-neutral term now used to refer to the sexual violation of both women and men. It is meant to capture the traditional legal concept of rape as well as the traditional notion of homosexual rape. Rape may be defined as the forced carnal knowledge of a woman by a man. Homosexual rape referred to male-on-male sodomy. Despite the statutory differences, by state, in the term used to refer to traditional rape, a generic definition of the offense *criminal sexual assault* is "any genital, anal, or oral penetration, by a part of the accused's body or by an object, using force or without the victim's consent" (Tuite, 1992). *Sexual abuse* is sometimes used interchangeably with *sexual assault*. While both refer to sexual crimes, *assault* is a specific incident and *abuse* indicates a pattern of behavior. *Sexual harassment* is a pattern of sexual abuse.

Erez and Tontodonato (1992) cite the National Advisory Council on Women's Education Programs' categorization of sexual harassment into five levels. According to this categorization, the nearly total authority used by guards in their interaction with female inmates, as documented in the recent report by Human Rights Watch, equates with the third and fourth levels of sexual harassment. Level three includes a solicitation for sex with the promise of reward. Level four introduces the notion of punishment for failure to comply with a request for sexual favors. Negative consequences ensue for noncooperation. This type of situation is generally thought of as the quintessential sexual harassment (Erez & Tontodonato, 1992, p. 233).

MAGNITUDE OF THE PROBLEM

Scholars and practitioners agree that the precise number of sexual assaults committed yearly is unknown. The medical profession recognizes sexual assault as a violent crime that claims a victim every 45 seconds in this country. Based on this crime clock, more than 700,000 women are sexually assaulted yearly, resulting in two-thirds of these victims under the age of 18 (American Academy of Pediatrics Committee on Adolescence, 1994). In stark terms, one in five women has been the victim of a sexual assault by the time she reaches her twenty-first birthday (Ester & Kuznets, 1994). A former president of the American Medical Association observed that "the crime is shrouded in silence, caused by unfair social myths and biases that incriminate victims rather than offenders."

Official estimates of sexual assault closely parallel those of the medical profession. The evidence from the National Crime Victimization Survey (Bureau of Justice Statistics, 1995) is that at least 500,000 women were victims of attempted rape or rape, and the number not reported ranges from two to six times those reported. While women are ten times more likely than men to be sexual assault victims, the Survey recorded 49,000 men as victims.[1] All women are potential victims of sexual assault; however, sexual assault victims are characteristically young, low income, and single, separated, or divorced[2]; and African-American women are disproportionate sexual assault victims (Bureau of Justice Statistics, 1994).

Sexual assault is recognized as an increasing problem in the general population. By extension, it is reasonable to believe that the number of sexual assaults among the incarcerated is astronomical. Many women were sexually abused (rape, incest) prior to their incarceration (American Correctional Association, 1990, p. 6; Arnold, 1990; Carlen, 1983; Chesney-Lind & Rodriquez, 1983; Gilfus, 1992; Greenfeld & Minor-Harper, 1991, p. 6; Immarigeon, 1987; Sargent, Marcus-Mendoza, & Yu, 1993). Their continued abuse at the hands of their keepers is therefore an issue that warrants attention and redress. The ACA reports that the average female offender has probably been a victim of sexual abuse (36 percent) a minimum of three to eleven times or more (55 percent) between the ages of 5 and 14 (57 percent). She probably was sexually abused by a male member of the immediate family (49 percent) such as a father or stepfather (23 percent). Reporting the incident resulted in no change or made things worse (49 percent). Greenfeld and Harper-Minor reported that an estimated 22 percent of the women in prison in 1984 said that they had been sexually abused prior to the age of 18. Their study found that women serving time for a violent offense are the most likely of the prisoners to report having experienced prior physical or sexual abuse.

The exact number of male and female prisoners sexually assaulted is unknown. Surveys conservatively estimate more than 290,000 inmates are sexually assaulted behind bars each year (Donaldson, 1993). In 1995, there were 69,028 women in prison and an estimated 135,000 rapes of female inmates nationwide (Bureau of Justice Statistics, 1995). The problem is serious and chronic but has not been adequately studied. Although there are no statistics to document the magnitude of sexual abuse[3] of women in jails, there is reason to believe that the majority of assaults go unreported. Sims (1976) contends that the stories she heard from incarcerated women are substantiated by attorneys, correction officers, and law enforcement personnel. A Manhattan lawyer concedes: "Inmates are in a completely vulnerable position and are very susceptible to sexual advances by guards for a variety of reasons" (Golding, 1998). For example, between January 1990 and June 1995, seventy-six sexual misconduct complaints were filed by inmates at the Albion State Correctional Facility near Rochester, New York. Albion is New York State's largest prison for women, and male custodial officers outnumber female correctional officers by a 3-to-1 ratio. Of the seventy-six complaints, fifty-six were dropped (mainly because inmates refused to talk when questioned), but fourteen cases were substantiated. As a result, six officers were transferred from Albion and one officer received counseling. Six cases remain open (Williams, 1996).

Absent empirical data, anecdotal reports of custodial sexual assault of females are rich sources of the magnitude and nature of the problem. An example from New York is worthy of note. Twenty-two-year-old inmate Felita Dobbins, serving time at Bedford Hills, accused a correction officer of sexually abusing her. To substantiate her claim, she retained the officer's semen in a perfume bottle. According to the assaulted inmate, the officer threatened to kill members of her family, including her 2-year-old daughter, if she reported the incident. Upon arrest for forcible sodomy, the officer resigned from his job. He pled guilty to the lesser charge of sexual abuse and received five years probation. Of her experience, the inmate lamented: "In their eyes I was the criminal, so why not go with the officer?" (Williams, 1996). This is a common experience among female inmates, as the following case demonstrates. A Delaware inmate, Dorothy Carrigan, accused a prison guard of raping her. When the guard finished, he tossed the used condom on the inmate's bed and told her to flush it down the toilet. The inmate turned the used condom in to prison officials. Although the custodial officer was charged under a Delaware law that prohibits sex between prisoners and correctional workers, prison officials and prosecutors alleged that the female inmate consented to engage in sex with the officer (Holmes, 1996).

Apparently, in prison there is a fine line between consensual and nonconsensual sex. Whether or not female inmates can overcome the "willing participant" hurdle, they are still punished for making the accusation. Consider the Delaware inmate. After making the accusation of rape, Dorothy was immediately transferred from a minimum-security section of the women's prison to the maximum-security section. While in maximum-security, she was beaten and harassed by guards; as a result, she jumped from the second-floor tier of cells to the floor (Holmes, 1996). In addition to assaults, inmates are sexually abused, sometimes as a matter of policy. Although required, the strip search of newly admitted prisoners may be conducted in such a way as to dehumanize inmates. LeBlanc (1996) reports a typical search as described by an inmate:

> To be searched the inmate spreads her legs while the female officer slides a mirror on the end of a long instrument, like an oversize spatula, on the floor. The inmate squats over it and coughs. She also opens her mouth, runs her fingers along her gums and under her breasts and through her pubic hairs. She folds back her ears and wiggles her toes. Then she bends over, as if to touch her toes, and spreads her buttocks and coughs again. (p. 39)

The inmate who provided the description of the search stated that she appreciates it when the officer doesn't stare. At Albion State Facility in New York, strip searches were videotaped from January 1994 to July 1994 in response to inmate complaints of abuse. However, videotaping as a solution to the problem of sexual abuse led to additional issues related to sexual harassment. According to inmates, the tapings represented a systemwide pattern of sexual harassment of women inmates (including incidents of inmates being impregnated by guards) by correctional officers (Rutenberg & Stasi, 1995). A lawsuit filed on behalf of the inmates at Albion State Correctional facility resulted in a settlement from the state in the amount of $1000 per incident to the women involved in each of eighty-five documented videotaped strip searches (Rutenberg & Stasi, 1995).

Perhaps, women inmates are subjected to harsh punishment because their presence in prison proves that they are not members of the "gentler sex"; that is, they have violated gender-role expectations. After all, nice girls don't exhibit behaviors and engage in those activities that cause them to be incarcerated. For Sims (1976), "much of the abuse—sexual and otherwise—is due to an attitude that women prisoners, especially black ones, are little better than animals."[4]

Female inmates who become pregnant as a result of a sexual assault in prison are encouraged to have abortions, while the officers accused of the impregnation are usually allowed to resign (Holmes, 1996; Williams, 1996). If the inmate does continue the pregnancy, she will not be allowed to keep the baby. In either scenario, the woman's right to make decisions about her body and offspring is usurped by the correctional system. Even for women in the general population, being deprived of the ability to make a decision to get pregnant and keep the baby is harsh treatment. For female inmates this amounts to severe punishment and there is no corollary for incarcerated men; it is undeserved and unjust.

Experts acknowledge that it is difficult to measure the extent of the problem but admit that even one such case is too many. Many cases go unreported "partly because of fear, partly because the jailer is considered more believable" than a woman locked up for committing a crime. Dorothy Q. Thomas, director of the Human Rights Watch Women's

Rights Project, says that sexual abuse of women in prison by guards is a "hidden, largely accepted, standard operation procedure, and there are very little express administrative rules or laws to prohibit, punish and remedy it." Women who had been imprisoned in the Federal Correctional Institution in Dublin, California, sued the BOP and were awarded monetary damages for their sexual victimization. The women were serving time for nonviolent crimes (drug-related and credit card conspiracy) but were isolated in the men's solitary confinement unit as discipline for fighting. In a civil rights suit, three women alleged that prison officials (guards, lieutenants, a captain, the warden, and regional director of BOP) facilitated and encouraged a prostitution ring in which "guards took money from inmates in return for access to the women" (Opatmy, 1996). Although the regional director was transferred to Denver and the guards left the Dublin prison, available information suggests that none of those named in the suit have been criminally prosecuted or fired from the BOP.

Elaine Lord, the superintendent at New York's Bedford Hills Correctional Facility, states: "The system creates a need to get things and there are too many things to be bargained for." A recent report prepared by Human Rights Watch (1996) notes that guards use their nearly total authority to provide or deny goods and privileges to female prisoners to compel them to have sex, or in other cases, to reward them for having done so.

RESPONSE TO THE PROBLEM

Even when assaults are reported, the response is usually to give more credence to the accused than to the victim. Treating the sexual assault as though it is victim-precipitated is usually a response when a female inmate does make an allegation. However, the traditional response to charges of sexual assault brought against prison employees is to subject the female inmate to punishment (e.g., administrative, disciplinary, or protective confinement).

Since 1979, New Jersey has had a statute that criminalizes sex between inmates and prison employees. Connecticut has had such a law since 1972. Delaware also has such a law. In New York, such a law was enacted in 1996. This law classifies all sex between prison employees and inmates as rape ("Ending sexual abuse," 1996; Golding, 1997). Despite the laws, sexual assaults continue. Few male[5] prison staff who engage in sexual relations with female prisoners ever face legal action (Flowers, 1987, p. 161).

Some women inmates also use sex to demand privileges and favors from guards ("Ending sexual abuse," 1996; Sims, 1976). In her investigation, Sims found women who admitted that some of the sex is by force, while others admitted that the sex was consensual or bartered to obtain better treatment, or to get needed or wanted things such as a candy bar or a Coke. In the Beaufort county jail, there were stories regarding how a jailer named Alligood offered sandwiches or whiskey in exchange for touching a breast (Sims, 1976, p. 137).

Inmates

In confinement, women have fewer resources than are available to victims of sexual assault outside prisons or jails. The victim-response protocol is well known even though most women choose not to invoke the protocol by not reporting the assault. The medical community recommends that sexual assault victims seek help within the first seventy-two hours after an attack to facilitate treatment. Treatment is critical because the victimization causes "lasting emotional distress, self-destructive behavior, interpersonal problems and behavioral disorders" (American Medical Association, 1995).

Female inmates have taken legal action in recent years (Holmes, 1996). Prisons in California, Georgia, and the District of Columbia have reached out-of-court settlements in class-action suits brought on behalf of women alleging sexual harassment and sexual assault by guards while incarcerated. The landmark class-action suit against prison officials because prison inmates were victims of sexual assault was brought by men who had been incarcerated in a Florida prison.[6] In *LaMarca v. Turner* (1987), ten inmates of Glades Correctional Institution claimed that they suffered "unconstitutional conditions of confinement" because of the "deliberate indifference" of the superintendent. The alleged sexual assault or sexual abuse cases of each of the inmates were similar; LaMarca's allegations, outlined in the court's opinion, are indicative:

> On May 14, 1982, Anthony LaMarca, then an inmate at GCI, filed a handwritten *pro se* complaint in the district court stating that he had "been countlessly approached, threatened with physical violence and assaulted by other inmates at [GCI] because [he] refused to participate in homosexual activities, or pay protection to be left alone." He alleged that "a severe lack of protection" existed at GCI and that "the institution seem[ed] unable or unwilling to handle the situation."

The court agreed that conditions of confinement precipitated and sustained violence, thus were unconstitutional:

> *First*, every plaintiff was attacked or threatened with a weapon, typically a knife. The evidence establishes the prevalence of such weapons and Turner's failure to take reasonable measures designed to control such contraband. *Second*, the long duration of several of the attacks, the places in which they occurred, and possibly the fact that they occurred in the first place, are functions of Turner's failure to take even minimal steps to ensure that GCI was adequately patrolled (Aldred raped in shower for fifteen to twenty minutes; Durrance led away at knifepoint from place between bunks which was concealed by hanging blanket; Bronson raped with baseball bat on recreation field in broad daylight; Saunders raped in bathroom for twenty-five to thirty minutes; Harper raped in top bunk; Cobb stabbed in front of canteen in fight lasting ten to twelve minutes). *Third*, Turner's failure to implement adequate reporting procedures for rapes and assaults was a legal cause of plaintiff's psychological and possibly physical damage (Aldred reported rape to several officers with no results; Aldred not given protective confinement; Durrance and Bronson did not report out of fear of consequences; Saunders raped by two inmates who previously had attacked him; Saunders reported rape and received inadequate treatment and no investigation; inmates identified as assailants by LaMarca were not confined for investigation and continued to assault him; classification officer told Johnson to take protective confinement or to get a weapon and fight back). *Fourth*, Turner's callous indifference to the obvious and rampant indicia of homosexual activity was the proximate cause of rapes, attacks, or repeated harassment (Aldred, Durrance, Bronson, Saunders, and Harper raped; Bronson forced to commit nonconsensual sexual act in movie trailer; Johnson sexually harassed and later attacked four times; constant threats and sexual solicitation caused LaMarca to escape, take protective confinement, and receive disciplinary reports; Cobb injured in fight over homosexual). *Fifth*, Turner's failure to adequately supervise correctional officers up to the lieutenant level

resulted in corruption and incompetence among the officers and a lack of reasonable protection of inmates (Cobb's assailant worked as an "enforcer" with GCI staff and was protected by them; LaMarca complained to Barrett about threats and assaults and was given a knife by Barrett; Bronson afraid to report rape because he had witnessed inmates exchanging money and drugs with guards).

The court accepted inmates' evidence of sexual assault or sexual abuse and said that the superintendent was aware of the problems at the prison but did not take actions to protect inmates from violence. The court found that the inmates had been subjected to cruel and unusual punishment in violation of the Eighth Amendment protection from violence and ordered monetary awards to the inmates: "[D]ue to [their] very nature as acts of violence, the rapes that occurred are not isolated incidents of sexual conduct, but rather flow directly from the lawless prison conditions at GCI....[These conditions created] the background and climate which...preordained homosexual rapes and other inmate assault[s]."

Finally, the court established two committees to recommend additional actions. The penological committee was required to find out if there were other rape victims in the prison and to prevent further sexual assaults. A committee composed of psychiatrists and psychologists was charged with (1) prescribing treatment for the inmates who brought suit, and (2) developing a prison strategy to provide support for rape victims.

Organizations and advocacy groups have taken up the cause of female inmates sexually assaulted. Examples include the American Civil Liberties Union's Prison Project, National Women's Law Center (both in Washington, DC), California Prison Focus (based in San Francisco), National Lawyers' Guild, and Amnesty International Americas Regional Program. The inmates at Chowchilla Valley State Prison for Women sent a grievance to the California Prison Focus detailing "sexual assault, improper touching, leering at women in showers, intimidation and constant verbal harassment" (California Prison Focus, 1998) by male corrections officers. The sexual assault or sexual abuse took place in the solitary confinement unit at the prison. After an on-site investigation of the inmates' complaints, the California Prison Focus contacted the director of the prison and (1) demanded a response to the allegations, (2) asked for the removal of male custodial officers from the solitary confinement unit, and (3) requested a meeting to discuss their preliminary findings.

The inmate alone must cope with feelings of shame, anger, and guilt for being victimized. As with women who are not incarcerated, the victim of sexual assault is viewed as culpable in letting the assault happen. Similarly, the assaulted inmate experiences isolation, fear, and helplessness as she struggles with the question "Where can I go for help and protection?" The experience is most likely to be difficult to survive since the inmate may be isolated from and shunned by other female inmates.

Correctional Officers

The prison work environment requires that the corrections officer function as a social control agent who has primary responsibilities of custody, security, and control. Correctional staff are organized along rigid paramilitary lines consisting of a chain of command of structure composed of the ranks of officer trainee, officer, sergeant, lieutenant, captain, major, deputy for custody, and the superintendent or warden. Officers are the line staff responsible for the direct supervision of inmates and daily enforcement of all policy and procedures set forth by the managerial staff (Lombardo, 1981, p. 310). Lombardo used the term *people worker* to analyze the role of the correctional officer, noting that the officer must work with inmates on a personal level in an environment of physical closeness over long periods of time (p. 311).

Many correction officers are drawn to the job to help other human beings and to engage in activities that are intrinsically worthwhile. Johnson (1996) notes: "They hunger for opportunities to improve the quality of life in the prison community and grasp them when they can. Like most of us, they want to be people who matter." (p. 224)

The organizational goals of American prisons directly proscribe or indirectly influence the role of the correctional officer (Hepburn & Albonetti, 1980). Historically, prisons have emphasized the custody functions of control and security (Lombardo, 1981, p. 317). In recognition of the complexity of their duties, guards are now called correctional officers, and training academies routinely provide new hires with weeks of orientation and sophisticated training covering such skill areas as the use of physical force, report writing, and sensitivity to cultural diversity. In addition, there are some correctional managers who have instituted ongoing professional training for employees and membership in organizations such as the American Society of Criminology (Pollock, 1997, p. 294).

Most correctional facilities combine the dual roles of custody and treatment. This duality creates role conflict for the correctional officer. The goal of custody demands that the principal rule of interaction between officers and inmates is to maintain maximum social distance (Lombardo, 1981, p. 318). Beginning in the 1960s, rehabilitation became an important goal of prisons. The introduction of treatment as a goal required nonpunitive control of inmates, relaxed discipline, a willingness to form affective ties, informal relationships that resulted in minimized social distance with inmates, and the exercise of discretion based on individual characteristics and situations (p. 318). The central goal of the treatment role entails flexibility, the use of discretionary justice, and the ability to secure inmate compliance through informal exchange relationships that deviate from the written rules (p. 319). Administrators formally and informally create an expectation that correctional officers should define themselves as agents of change who will use discretion as they engage in the daily process of helping the treatment staff to rehabilitate inmates while maintaining security and enforcing the roles (Cressey, 1965; Poole & Regoli, 1981; President's Commission, 1967). Correctional officers are expected to exercise professional judgment and flexibility in performing their job and are subject to disciplinary action if they themselves violate the rules or permit inmates to violate the numerous official rules and procedures of the prison (Hepburn, 1985).

Yet Poole and Regoli (1981) note that introducing such rehabilitation-related practices as due process rights in disciplinary actions, limited use of solitary confinement, and formal inmate grievance mechanisms has undermined the ability of the correctional officer to use coercive power, with a corresponding loss of officer control, and provided inmates with a countervailing power. This places the officer in the stressful position of having to serve two masters. Many officers express the opinion that administrators and treatment staff have more respect and affinity for inmates than for officers, suggesting that the social distance between correctional officers and administrators may even be greater than that between officers and inmates (Lombardo, 1981, p. 321).

The relationship between the correctional officer and inmate is one of *structured conflict* (Jacobs & Kraft, 1978). Inmates do not want to be incarcerated and naturally resent the staff assigned to control them (p. 309). The corrections officer is both a manager and a worker: a low-status worker in relationship to superior officers, but a manager of inmates. As the lowest level in the correctional hierarchy, the officer is under surveillance by corrections management and the scrutiny of inmates. Officers often experience a sense of emotional isolation. They work alone or as a part of a small team, but always with the expectation that they are capable of performing the functions of the job independently (Jacobs & Kraft, 1978, p. 311). Officers possess power in relation to inmates. In discussing the bases of control, Poole and Regoli (1981) identify and define legitimate power and coercive power. These authors note that "legitimate power is rooted in the legal authority given the officer to exercise control over inmates because of their structural relationship within the prison." The position of the officer in this relationship confers the right to have orders obeyed and authority respected. The position of the inmate in the relationship conveys the duty to obey orders.

Coercive power, on the other hand, is based on the inmate perception that officers have the ability to punish rule violators, either formally (through the use of written reports of misconduct) or informally (by beating or other forms of physical and psychological abuse). Although this power is limited by the possibility of legal or administrative action against the officer, it nevertheless serves to remind the inmate that coercion is a basis of power within the prison. This is demonstrated by cell searches, assignment to disciplinary units, random strip searches, and lethal force to accomplish compliance (Poole & Regoli, 1981, p. 314). Upon arrival at the correctional facility, inmates are informed that they are expected to follow all the rules or suffer the consequences (Poole & Regoli, 1981, p. 315).

Criminal Justice System

Many states have laws criminalizing sexual assault or sexual abuse of prisoners. The effectiveness of these laws has yet to be determined, but it is interesting to note several of the laws. When New York State introduced the legislation, The New York State Department of Correctional Services took the position that because inmates are under the control of employees twenty-four hours a day, they cannot give free consent, and without consent it is a crime ("Ending sexual abuse," 1996). Prior to the enactment of the 1996 law, the union pledged support for the bill only if it included an amendment that would safeguard against false accusations made by inmates; make false accusations a felony rather than a misdemeanor. Republican Assemblyman Michael Balboni of Nassau County, New York, has expressed skepticism about accusations by inmates, acknowledging that people in prison are not particularly believable and that by their presence in prison they have demonstrated they're not going to play by the rules (Williams, 1996). Former New York City Commissioner of Corrections, State Senator Catherine Abate, one of the sponsors of the bill, resisted the amendment, arguing that further penalties on inmates may increase their reluctance to come forward since many women already submit to sex as a "condition of confinement" ("Ending sexual abuse," 1996).

In 1997, the Federal Bureau of Prisons amended its policy statement on sexual assault "to include instances of staff-on-inmate sexual abuse/assault" (Federal Bureau of Prisons, 1997) in recognition of the vulnerability of inmates to their keepers. The policy defines two types of sexual abuse or assault: inmate-on-inmate and staff-on-inmate. The BOP considers the latter type illegal and the first type a prohibited act. Annual reporting of the number of sexual assaults is required. While reporting, treatment, and investigation and prosecution protocols are established, the policy does not include specific statements about actions to be taken when the aggressor in the sexual abuse or assault is correctional staff.

The Justice Department filed lawsuits in the federal district courts in Phoenix and Detroit alleging that Arizona and Michigan failed to protect female inmates from rape and sexual assault by prison guards and staff members in violation of the federal Civil Rights of Institutionalized Persons Act of 1980. Both lawsuits seek court orders requiring that the states protect female inmates from rapes, sexual assaults, and other improper contact by the state ("Government sues," 1997).

RECOMMENDATIONS

In addressing the sexual assault or abuse of women in prison, several issues must be considered. New York State Senator Catherine Abate noted that male officers, by virtue of their position, have a great deal of power over female prisoners. Acknowledging that many of these women have been in abusive relationships, Abate identified the need for change. She noted a need for greater numbers of female officers so that men aren't frisking women (Rutenberg & Stasi, 1995). For example, at Central California Women's Facility, only 2 percent of the guards are women. At New York State Albion Correctional Facility, male officers outnumber female officers by a 3-to-1 ratio. There is also a need for greater integration of the correctional workforce.

The majority of women in prison are there for drug-related crimes (Bureau of Justice Statistics, 1997). Rather than incapacitation, isolation, and confinement, treatment programs are needed. Women are considered to be less dangerous and have historically been arrested and incarcerated for fewer and less serious offenses (Muraskin & Alleman, 1993; Pollock, 1990). It is therefore important that mandatory sentencing and other sentencing policies that have had a disproportionate impact on women, especially women of color, be examined. Alternatives to incarceration should be sought. In cases where it is necessary to imprison women, and especially in cases where women are to be searched, the policy should be to have two officers conduct the search, one of whom must be female. Although this is currently the policy in some institutions (e.g., Central California Women's Facility), this should become the policy throughout the criminal justice system. LeBlanc (1996) notes that many women in prison are accustomed to coercive relationships and that the problem worsens when they are placed in a highly sexualized, paramilitary setting in the custody of mostly men.

Ethics should be emphasized as a focus of training in the academy. All staff should be trained regarding their role in preventing rape and other forms of sexual abuse. Although the possibility exists for prostitutes and others to seduce correctional employees, these people should be guided by a standard of professionalism in their dealings with all inmates. In the same way that prostitution is the crime that might have landed women in jail, rape or other sexual violations by the correctional employee should result in the violator also being sanctioned. Sexual violations by correctional employees should therefore be viewed as criminal and punished accordingly. Services, including rape counseling, should be made available to women who are victims of sexual abuse while they are in custody and upon their release to the community.

CONCLUSIONS

According to Pollock-Byrne (1990, p. 41), there were additional reasons why Fry, along with other American reformers, supported the idea that prisons should be run by women superintendents, called warders. One reason is that women warders would set a proper moral example of true womanhood for women inmates who had fallen from grace. Another reason is that warders would provide a sympathetic ear for female inmates.

Walker (1989) acknowledges women's marginality in U.S. society and cites the vast amount of violence against women as evidence of this marginality. It therefore stands to reason that if women in general are marginalized, women in prison are marginalized to a greater degree.

How then can a woman in prison convincingly report and explain that she has been raped? Among the issues to be considered are (1) trust, (2) credibility, (3) shame, guilt, anger, and (4) isolation, fear, helplessness. Trust is the most crucial issue facing the assaulted inmate who must decide: "Is it safe to tell?" and "Who can be told?" Credibility is an issue shared by the inmate and authorities. For the inmate, the question becomes "Will I be believed?" For correctional authorities, the question is: "Why should she be believed?" The justice system is designed and operated based on a male model. Men, therefore, can easily tell their stories using the rules of the legal system (Walker, 1989, p. 257).

Battered women are failed by the court system because it is based on a male model of how to determine fact. Women often have trouble "separating discrete factual events from the general patterns of their lives" (Walker, 1989, p. 258). If, for women in general, physical and sexual abuse are events that have shaped their lives from early on, it should not be difficult to understand the power of such patterns over their lives and its influence even more so when they are in prison, stripped of their freedom, and in addition, have been sexually abused. Women in prison have a right[7] not to be victims of sexual exploitation.

N O T E S

1. Although there are no official counts of sexual assaults on homosexuals, the National Gay and Lesbian Task Force reports that lesbian and gays are more likely to be targeted for violent attacks today that they were ten years ago.

2. Marital sexual assault is a serious aspect of family violence and appears to be more common among couples living below the poverty line, particularly when men are unemployed (Crime Victims Research and Treatment Center, 1992).

3. Lesbian relationships are excluded because they have been recognized as a distinguishing feature of the female prison subculture. Lesbian relationships are voluntary and consensual and represent attempts to create family (including marital) units. The description of prison lesbian relationships by Stephen Donaldson (1990) is notable:

The "penitentiary turnout" is the inmate who resorts to lesbian relationships because the opposite sex is unavailable; in contrast, the "lesbian" prefers homosexual gratification even in the outside world, and this is equated with the queen in the men's prison. The lesbian is labeled as sick by some of the other inmates because the preference in a situation of choice is deemed perversion. The participant in lesbian relations who does so for lack of choice is not so stigmatized.

The "femme" or "mommy" is the inmate who takes the female role in a lesbian relationship, a role highly prized because most of the inmates still wish to play the feminine role in a significant way in prison....The complement is the "Stud broad" or "daddy" who assumes the male role, which in its turn is accorded much prestige.

When a stud and a femme have established their union, they are said to be "making it" or to "be tight," which is to say that other inmates recognize them socially as a "married" pair. Since the prisoners attach a positive value to sincerity, the "trick"—one who is simply exploited sexually or economically—is held in low esteem by the inmate subculture. Tricks are also regarded as "suckers" and "fools" because their lovers dangle unkept promises in front of them. The "commissary hustler" is the woman who establishes more than one relationship; besides an alliance with an inmate in the same housing unit, she also maintains relations with one or more inmates in other housing units for economic advantage. The other women, labeled tricks in the prison argot, supply her with coveted material items which she shares only with the "wife" in her own unit. The femme may even encourage and guide the stud in finding and exploiting tricks. The legitimacy of the primary pseudo-marriage is not contested, though the tricks may anticipate replacing the femme when a suitable opportunity arises.

4. Mauer and Huling (1995) attribute the current increase in the number of women in the criminal justice system to the war on drugs launched by the Republican administrations of Reagan and Bush. Although the United States has historically had a disproportionate number of African-Americans in prison (Brinkley-Jackson, Carter, & Rolison, 1993; Free, 1996; French, 1983; Mann, 1993), this disparity is exacerbated by the get-tough-on-crime policies of recent decades. The 78 percent increase in the number of African-American women under criminal justice supervision between 1989 and 1994 (Mauer, 1995) has less to do with increased criminality and more to do with the social and economic environments (poverty, limited economic opportunities, and abuse) shaping the lives of African-Americans. According to Arnold (1990, p. 139), black women are victims of gender and class oppression, as well as sexual violence at the hands of stepfathers and father-substitutes. The latter victimization conditions the women to rigid, patriarchal family relationships, relations that are replicated in prison with male custodial officers. This socialization contributes to the continued vulnerability to sexual assault while in confinement of African-American women.

5. Women custodial staff also sexually assault female inmates, as the following story posted on the Stop Prison Rape Web page demonstrates:

I hear this women's voice everyday. She has victimized other girls here as well + no one will lift a finger to stop her. She runs this + if one displeases her, they are victimized. I believe the officials are scared of her + the obvious power she holds. Knowing her the way I do, I sincerely believe she is blackmailing someone to get away with what she has + is still doing.

No one cares what happens to a prisoner. Everyone has the attitude that prisoners complain too much + have unreal expectations in wanting to live as a human being. That we somehow deserve all that happens to us. I know this attitude well; because I used to have this view before my incarceration.

I have done all I can possibly do to help myself...+ it is useless....No one here is interested in your organization. The major reason for that is homosexuality is blatant +

89% of the inmate population engages in free, casual sex + damn anyone who doesn't. Inmates-to-inmates + inmates-to-officials. It's sickening.—Clara, Florida.

6. Another interesting case is that of a transsexual. See *Farmer v. Brennan* (1970).

7. Dane County, Wisconsin (1998), has created the "Sexual assault victim's bill of rights," which is instructive as an exemplar for the criminal justice system. The Bill of Rights is available on the Web at http://danenet.wicip.org/dcccrsa/bill2.html

REFERENCES

ALLEN, H., & SIMONSEN, C. (1995). *Corrections in America* (7th ed.). Englewood Cliffs, NJ: Prentice Hall.

AMERICAN ACADEMY OF PEDIATRICS COMMITTEE ON ADOLESCENCE. (1994). Sexual assault and the adolescent. *Pediatrics, 94*, 761–765.

AMERICAN CORRECTIONAL ASSOCIATION. (1990). *The female offender: What does the future hold?* Washington, DC: St. Mary's Press.

AMERICAN MEDICAL ASSOCIATION. (1995, November 6). AMA reports "silent violent epidemic" of sexual assault throughout the U.S. Press release, Chicago.

An illustrated history and description of state prison life by one who has been there. Written by a convict in a convict's cell [Prison Life, 1865–1869]. New York: Globe.

ARNOLD, R. A. (1990). Process of victimization of black women. *Social Justice, 17*, 153–166.

BRINKLEY-JACKSON, D., CARTER, V. L., & ROLISON, G. L. (1993). African American women in prison. In B. R. Fletcher, L. D. Shaver, & D. B. Moon (Eds.), *Women prisoners: A forgotten population* (pp. 65–74). Westport, CT: Praeger.

BUREAU OF JUSTICE STATISTICS. (1994, January). *Violence against women: a national crime victimization survey report*. Washington, DC: U.S. Department of Justice.

BUREAU OF JUSTICE STATISTICS. (1995). *National crime victimization survey*. Washington, DC: U.S. Department of Justice.

BUREAU OF JUSTICE STATISTICS. (1997). *Prison and jail inmates at midyear, 1996*. Washington, DC: U.S. Department of Justice.

CALIFORNIA PRISON FOCUS. (1998, June 8). California prison focus exposes sexual abuse at Valley State Prison. Press release, San Francisco.

CARLEN, P. (1983). *Women's imprisonment: A study in social control*. London: Routledge & Kegan Paul.

CHESNEY-LIND, M. (1991. Spring–Summer). Patriarchy, prisons, and jails: A critical look at trends in women's incarceration. *Prison Journal*, Vol. 71, 63.

CHESNEY-LIND, M., & RODRIQUEZ, N. (1983). Women under lock and key. *Prison Journal, 63*(2), 47–65.

CRIME VICTIMS RESEARCH AND TREATMENT CENTER. (1992). *The national women's study*. Charleston, SC: Medical University of South Carolina.

CRESSEY, D. R. (1965). Prison organization. In J. March (Ed.), *Handbook of organizations* (pp. 1023–1070). Chicago: Rand McNally.

DANE COUNTY, WISCONSIN. (1998). *Dane County sexual assault victim's bill of rights*. Available: http://danenet.wicip.org/dcccrsa/bill2.html

DONALDSON, S. (1990). Prisons, jails, and reformatories. In W. Dynes (Ed.), *Encyclopedia of homosexuality*. New York: Garland Publishing.

DONALDSON, S. (1993, December 29). The rape crisis behind bars. *New York Times*.

Ending sexual abuse in prison. (1996, April 27). *New York Times*, 22:1.

EREZ, E., & TONTODONATO, P. (1992). Sexual harassment in the criminal justice system. In I. Moyer (Ed.), *The changing roles of women in the criminal justice system: Offenders, victims, and professionals* (2nd ed., pp. 227–252). Prospect Heights, IL: Waveland Press.

ESTER, A., & KUZNETS, N. (1994). *AMA guidelines for adolescent preventive services [GAPS]: Recommendations and rationale.* Baltimore: Williams & Wilkins.

FEDERAL BUREAU OF PRISONS. (1997). *PS 5324.04 sexual abuse/assault prevention and intervention programs.* Washington, DC: U.S. Department of Justice.

FLOWERS, R. B. (1987). *Women and criminality.* New York: Greenwood Press.

FREE, M. D. (1996). *African Americans and the criminal justice system.* New York: Garland Publishing.

FREEDAN, E. B. (1974). Their sisters' keepers: An historical perspective on female correctional institutions in the United States, 1870–1900. *Feminist Studies, 2,* 77–95.

FRENCH, L. (1983). A profile of the incarcerated black female offenders. *The Prison Journal, 63*(2), pp. 80–87.

GILFUS, M. E. (1992). From victims to survivors to offenders: Women's routes of entry and immersion into street crime. *Women and Criminal Justice, 4,* 63–90.

GOLDING, B. (1997, April 25). Correction officer is charged with misconduct. *Gannett Newspaper,* pp. 1B, 12A.

GOLDING, B. (1998, January 4). Group uges action to stop sex abuse in female prisons. *Gannett Newspaper,* pp. 1A, 14A.

Government sues 2 states over women's prisons. (1997, March 11). *New York Times,* p. A16(2).

GREENFELD, L., & MINOR-HARPER, S. (1991). *Women in prison.* Bureau of Justice Statistics Special Report. Washington, DC: U.S. Department of Justice.

HEPBURN, J. (1985). The exercise of power in coercive organizations: A study of prison guards. *Criminology, 23*(1), 146–164.

HEPBURN, J., & ALBONETTI, C. (1980). Role conflict in correctional institutions: An empirical examination of the treatment-custody dilemma among correctional staff. *Criminology, 17*(4), 445–459.

HOLMES, S. A. (1996, December 27). With more women in prison, sexual abuse by guards becomes greater concern. *New York Times,* p. 9.

HUMAN RIGHTS WATCH. (1996). *All too familiarly: Sex abuse of women in U.S. prisons.* New York: HRW.

IMMARIGEON, R. (1987). Women in prison. *Journal of the National Prison Project, 11,* 1–5.

JACOBS, J. B., & KRAFT, L. (1978). Integrating the keepers: A comparison of black and white prison guards in Illinois. *Social Problems, 25,* 304–318.

LEBLANC, A. N. (1996, June 2). A woman behind bars is not a dangerous man. *New York Times Magazine,* pp. 33–40.

LOMBARDO, L. (1981). *Guards imprisoned: Correctional workers at work.* New York: Elsevier.

MANN, C. (1993). *Unequal justice: A question of color.* Bloomington, IN: Indiana University Press.

MAUER, M. (1995, October 16). Disparate justice imperils a community. *Legal Times.*

MAUER, M., & HULING, T. (1995). *Young black Americans and the criminal justice system.* Washington, DC: The Sentencing Project.

MURASKIN, R., & ALLEMAN, T. (1993). *It's a crime: Women and justice.* Englewood Cliffs, NJ: Regents/Prentice Hall.

NATIONAL GAY AND LESBIAN TASK FORCE. (1992). *A study of 5 cities: New York, Chicago, San Francisco, Boston and Minneapolis.* NGLTF.

OPATMY, D. (1996, September 29). 3 women sue, allege sex slavery in prison. *San Francisco Examiner,* p. C1.

POLLOCK, J. (1990). *Prisons: Today and tomorrow.* Gaithersburg, MD: Aspen Publishers.

POLLOCK-BYRNE, J. (1990). *Women, prison and crime.* Belmont, CA: Brooks/Cole Publishers.

Poole, E., & Regoli, R. (1981). Alienation in prison: An examination of the work relations of prison guards. *Criminology, 19*(2), 251–270.

President's Commission on Law Enforcement and Administration of Justice. (1967). *Task force report: Corrections*. Washington, DC: U.S. Government Printing Office.

Rafter, N. H. (1990). *Partial justice: Women, prisons, and social control* (2nd ed.). Boston: Northeastern University Press.

Rutenberg, J., & Stasi, L. (1995, September 10). Prison strip. *Daily News*, pp. 4,5.

Sargent, E., Marcus-Mendoza, S., & Yu, C. (1993). Abuse and the woman prisoner. In B. Fletcher, L. Shaver, & D. Moon (Eds.), *Women prisoners: A forgotten population* (pp. 55–64). Westport, CT: Praeger.

Sims, P. (1976). Women in southern jails. In L. Crites (Ed.), *The female offender* (pp. 137–147). Lexington, MA: D.C. Heath.

Tuite, P. (1992). *Ignorance is no excuse*. Chicago: Nelson-Hall Publishing.

Walker, L. E. (1989). *Terrifying love: Why battered women kill and how society responds*. New York: Harper & Row.

Williams, M. (1996, April 23). Bill seeks to protect inmates from guards who seek sex. *New York Times*, pp. A1, B4.

CASES

Farmer v. Brennan, 114 S. Ct. (1970).

LaMarca v. Turner, 662 F. Supp. 647 (1987).

Larmarca v. Turner, 995 F. 2d. 1526 (1993).

18

Women on Death Row

Etta F. Morgan

Capital punishment is a controversial issue in society, yet it is the most severe punishment that our courts can administer. The purposes of this chapter are to (1) provide an historical overview of capital punishment, (2) explain capital punishment using Girard's theory of culture, (3) examine the influence of the Supreme Court regarding capital punishment, (4) discuss the importance of gender in the criminal justice process, and (5) review the literature on executed females as well as share some of the experiences and problems of female death row inmates.

Ironically, every aspect of our society is influenced by the social and cultural perspectives that dominate our being. These influences are also prevalent in the administration of our prisons. Women, as second-class citizens in society, carry this status into the penal system, which openly ignores their needs in more ways than one. One prime example would be that most states have only one prison for women, and some have none. Female criminality and experiences have often been described based on men's experiences. Previous research (Erez, 1989; Kruttschnitt, 1982; Mann, 1984; Pollock-Byrne, 1991; Visher, 1983; Zingraff & Thompson, 1984) suggests that as a group, women have been treated more leniently than men in the criminal justice system. If this is true, it may explain the disproportionate number of women sentenced to death in relation to the number of men sentenced to death. Female offenders have often been a forgotten population in research as well as in reality.

Limited research has focused on women sentenced to death. Victor Streib publishes a quarterly report, which details demographics about the offender, a brief statement about the offense, and the current status of the inmates (i.e., reversals, commutations). Other authors (Fletcher, Dixon, Shaver, & Moon, 1993; Mann, 1984) tend to devote only a few pages in textbooks to a discussion of women on death row. Perhaps this is due to the fact that women do not commit violent crimes at the same rate as men.

There appears to be an increase in female crime based on the current *Uniform Crime Reports* (*UCR*), but it is unclear whether this increase is due to actual offenses or changes in reporting practices by law enforcement agencies. Cautiously interpreting the *UCR* data, there seems to be an increase in violent crimes by females, but basically, female crime is still concentrated in the area of property crimes. Upon closer examination of violent crimes, it is found that women homicide offenders tend to kill persons of the same race, usually an intimate male associate. As a group, women murderers are not as common as their male counterparts, which could possibly influence the treatment they receive in the criminal justice system. In examining the imposition of death sentences in this country, it is obvious that women are not sentenced to death or executed at the same rate as men.

The death penalty has and continues to be a controversial issue in the United States. It is the ultimate sentence that can be imposed for a criminal offense. Proponents of the death penalty suggest that it is needed to deter would-be criminals, while opponents believe that it is an inhumane act on the part of society in administering justice. In the past, the death penalty was withdrawn because some states were unfairly targeting specific populations of offenders. Although it was reinstated by the Supreme Court in 1976, the controversy has not been settled as to whether or not the death penalty should be used as a form of punishment.

HISTORICAL OVERVIEW

Capital punishment is a controversial issue nationally as well as internationally. It is believed to have been in existence before societies became organized. After the organization of society, legal codes were established in an attempt to provide rules and regulations for social control. Capital punishment has been included in legal codes since the period of the Old Testament continuing on to the Code of Hammurabi, Assyrian laws, Athenian Codes, European laws, and the code established in the thirteen colonies (Koosed, 1996).

Capital punishment in the United States has been greatly influenced by English traditions, and research has shown it to be an Anglo-American custom (Paternoster, 1991). The practice of capital punishment in the colonies reflected the ideology of the American people in regard to the types of crime that were considered capital offenses. Because there was no uniform criminal code throughout the colonies, each state had different capital statutes (Kronenwetter, 1993; Paternoster, 1991). In some instances, states declared fewer offenses (five to eight) capital offenses if committed by whites while identifying seventy offenses as capital offenses if committed by blacks (Paternoster, 1991). After the American Revolution, states began to restrict the number of offenses that could be classified as capital offenses. States also narrowed the application of capital punishment by establishing degrees of murder and giving juries more discretion in sentencing, thereby permitting the jury to sentence people to death in only the most serious murders (Paternoster, 1991).

Along with the passage of discretionary statutes for capital crimes, this period of U.S. capital punishment has two distinct characteristics: (1) executions were public events, and (2) local authorities were responsible for performing all executions. Executions were performed as public events until the end of the nineteenth century, although some public executions were performed as late as 1936 and 1937 (Paternoster, 1991). At the turn of the century we find a shift from public executions controlled by local authorities to executions controlled and conducted by the state (Paternoster, 1991).

Capital punishment's historical significance is related not only to punishment but also to social control. Capital punishment was often administered upon those identified as members of problem populations. It was believed that these populations did not respect established authority. In many instances, these populations were viewed as threatening or dangerous to established authority. Capital punishment also had an extralegal form that was lynching. According to Paternoster (1991), "[l]ynching, primarily by vigilante groups, was frequently used by majority groups to keep minorities oppressed" (p. 8). Use of this extralegal form of capital punishment claimed more lives than legal executions (Paternoster, 1991). Although we experienced a decline in lynchings with the centralization of the death penalty, there were more executions between 1930 and 1940 than were noted for the following twenty years. During the 1960s and 1970s, there was a decline in executions followed by a moratorium on capital punishment (Paternoster, 1991).

Over time there have been regional differences in imposition of the death penalty. Historically, the South has performed more executions than any other region. In examining capital offenses and capital statutes during the pre-modern era, Paternoster (1991) states: [o]ne interesting feature about the imposition of capital punishment for different offenses is that the region of the country and the race of the offender has been, at least in the past, an important correlate" (p. 15). Statistics (Flanagan & Maguire, 1989) suggest that race may have been an overriding factor in the imposition of the death penalty for particular offenses in the South, resulting in racially biased applications of the death sentence. As in previous years, it has also been suggested that capital punishment continued to be used as a form of social control for specific groups.

Capital punishment, as the ultimate sentence, has also created problems for juries. Specifically, juries were at odds with the harshness of the laws and as a result found themselves mitigating that fact instead of the case. In later years, juries were given discretionary powers with the understanding that they were to consider any and all factors related to the case which could support a death sentence as well as factors supportive of a noncapital sentence (Paternoster, 1991). This unbridled reign led to irrational and discriminatory practices in the imposition of death sentences. The uncontrolled sentencing freedom enjoyed by juries and the misapplication of death sentences "led to the temporary suspension of the death penalty in the United States" (p. 17).

The modern era of capital punishment represents the return to the imposition of death sentences. During the moratorium on capital punishment, the Supreme Court ruled that the discretionary powers given to juries were unconstitutional, along with the procedures used for the imposition of death sentences. A thorough examination of the U.S. Supreme Court's position as it relates to capital punishment is examined in more detail later using Girard's theory of culture.

THEORETICAL ANALYSIS

The debate over capital punishment remains unresolved in U.S. society. Some believe that capital punishment deters would-be criminals, while others contend that persons should be punished based on the doctrine of retribution. Another possible explanation for the existence of capital punishment in our society may be the need for ritualized violence as a method of social control. Although controversial, Rene Girard's theory of culture (1977) based on religious thought, anthropology, psychology, literary criticism, and other social sciences appears to explain the importance of the death penalty in our society. According to Girard (1987):

> In the science of man and culture today there is a unilateral swerve away from anything that could be called mimicry, imitation, or mimesis. And yet, there is nothing, or next to nothing, in human behavior that is not learned, and all learning is based on imitation. If human beings suddenly ceased imitating, all forms of culture would vanish....The belief is that insisting on the role of imitation would unduly emphasize the gregarious aspects of humanity, all that transforms us into herds. There is a fear of minimizing the importance of everything that tends toward division, alienation, and conflict. If we give a leading role to imitation, perhaps we will make ourselves accomplices of the force of subjugation and uniformity. (p. 7)

The theory that human behavior is, to some extent, learned behavior resulting from imitating the behavior of others has also been advanced by theorists, such as Aristotle, Plato, Tarde, and Sutherland. Although Plato's description of imitation, as well as his followers, failed to identify specific behaviors involved in appropriation, Girard (1987) states that "if imitation does indeed play the fundamental role for man, as everything seems to indicate, there must certainly exist an acquisitive imitation, or, if one prefers, a possessive mimesis whose effects and consequences should be carefully studied and considered" (p. 9), not overlooked. It is indisputable that imitation brings about conflict, but in many instances, persons have learned to control and dispense imitated behavior in acceptable ways.

Society determines which behaviors are authorized, thereby identifying behaviors that may or may not be imitated. In other words, there are restricted imitations. These prohibitions exist because some behaviors are just plain absurd or threaten the safety of society (Girard, 1987). It has been suggested that primitive societies understood that there was a relationship between mimesis and violence unlike modern society (Girard, 1987). The theory of culture advanced by Girard (1987) claims that "there is a connection between conflict and acquisitive mimesis. Modern society tends to view competition and conflict differently from primitive society mainly because we tend to see differences emerge from the outcome of a conflict...[and] we tend to focus on the individual act" (pp. 11–12). By focusing on the individual act instead of the act and its context, we (modern society) are able to view violence as an isolated crime. In doing so, we fail to truly understand the context in which the act was committed and its relationship to the violence experienced. Instead, we depend on the power of our judicial institutions to mandate adherence to the rules of social order, which does little, if anything, to increase our understanding of imitative violence or the importance of external factors to violent behavior(s). The purpose of these judicial institutions seems to imply that all persons in a society will abide by the laws that have been established and agreed upon by the members of society, but this is not true, especially since laws tend to represent the wishes of those persons who have power and wealth in society (the elite) in an attempt to control the masses.

It has been suggested that without these institutions, "the imitative and repetitious character of violence becomes manifest once more; the imitative character of violence is in fact most manifest in explicit violence, where it acquires a formal perfection it had not previously possessed" (Girard, 1987, p. 12). For example, in previous societies, a murder expanded substantially in the form of blood feuds. Violent acts, such as blood feuds and other rivalries, had to be curtailed in order to reunite the community, and the solution had to be dramatic and violent. Basically, the idea was and remains that violence begets violence.

In *McGautha v. California* (1971) a violent solution was also suggested by one justice as the only means by which violence could be ended even though it was noted that violence is self-propagating. Fortunately or unfortunately, our society has established a judicial institution in the form of the death penalty as a means to end violence (sanctioned self-propagating violence). Society has proscribed the method, time, and deliverer of the punishment for the sanctioned ritualized killing of another person (Girard, 1987). As such, the death penalty is a dramatic and violent solution used to reunite the community, but fails unless the targeted community is the victim's family, not society as a whole. Beschle (1997) states: "[M]odern legal systems seek to break the cycle of imitative violence by directing the punitive urge of all members of society toward a common enemy" (p. 521). The common enemy becomes the "new victim" in the community-sanctioned ritualized violence.

In order to proceed through the various phases of the ritualized killing, there must first be some type of relationship established between the "new victim" and the community. As part of the ritualized killing, it is important that the person to be executed (the new victim) is viewed as the cause of the community's discord and that his or her death will somehow restore peace in the community. Girard (1987) also suggests that "at the moment when violence ceases and peace has been established, the community has the whole of its attention fixed on the victim it has just killed" (p. 81), which leads one to surmise that in some instances there is a fascination with some executed persons, such as Gary Gilmore and Ted Bundy.

In addition to the symbol of intense interest in the executed victim, there are many symbols associated with the death process. For example, the tradition of the *last meal* is viewed as a special privilege or a ritualized privilege granted by the community to one who for a brief period is perceived as special and worthy of this treatment. Additionally, the person who has received the death sentence most often is a typical member of the community but is also significantly different because of his or her criminal act. This being the case, most members of the community lack compassion for and do not identify themselves with the offender. Having used Girard's theory of culture to explain the symbolism in the death process, we will now use his theory to examine the shift in the rulings of the Supreme Court.

Girard's (1987) theory can be used as a plausible explanation for the shift in the courts from being concerned with guilt to focusing more on expediting executions. As justices are replaced on the U.S. Supreme Court, we find that the new member is expected to bring to the Court a particular view that is shared by the controlling political party. The justice then merely advances the opinions shared by those who are not in office that share the same beliefs. In many instances, justices have been accused of relying on personal feelings or previous policy decisions, which purportedly expressed the public's desires, in order to write opinions for various cases. This being the case, it is safe to assume that some of the opinions rendered by the Court have not only been influenced by public opinion but also mirror public opinion, thereby extending the theory of imitation to the Court. For this reason, we are able to link Girard's theory of culture to the shift in Supreme Court decisions based on the makeup of the Court and the political climate under which it has operated. Girard (1987) noted that society does not desire to be perceived as in a state of constant revenge, but is more interested in providing an effective judicial system, which allows permissible social constraints. The apparent shift in the Supreme Court suggests that some, if not all, of the justices believe that there must be little or no interference from the Supreme Court in lower-court decisions. This "hands-off" approach has evolved over time as the Supreme Court has decided various cases. In the following sections we discuss briefly this evolutionary process of the Supreme Court.

THE INFLUENCE OF THE SUPREME COURT

One phase that the Supreme Court entered into can be identified as the period of constitutionality. By this, we mean that the Court was concerned with the issue of whether or not the death penalty itself was against the Constitution of the United States. *Powell v. Alabama* (1932) (the right to appointed counsel in capital cases) is said to represent the beginning of the Court's reform efforts concerning the death penalty. It is during this period that the Court used broad interpretations of the Fourteenth Amendment to bring about changes in criminal justice systems throughout the states in relation to capital cases. However, the main issue of whether or not the death penalty was in violation of the Constitution was often *not discussed*. It was not until Justice Goldberg's dissenting opinion in *Rudolph v. Alabama* (1963) that there was even any hint of a constitutional issue.

The Court continued to avoid the issue of constitutionality until there was an active campaign against the death penalty initiated by the NAACP Legal Defense Fund, which resulted in a moratorium against executions. During this period, the Court, in *Witherspoon v. Illinois* (1968), ruled that juror exclusion could not be based solely on a potential juror's personal objections to the death penalty. It is also in *Witherspoon* that we find the first written opinion (by Justice Stewart) in a case decision that questions the propriety of the death penalty. Without ruling specifically on whether or not the death penalty was against the Constitution of the United States, the Court suggested that morally sound jurors would not impose the death penalty upon another human being, and therefore a decision concerning the matter was not warranted by the Court (Burt, 1987). The Court presumed that U.S. society was harmonious and stable and would work in such a manner as to maintain social order (Burt, 1987). The implication was that the maintenance of social order would deter and/or reduce crime and there would be no need for administering the death penalty. Therefore, the Court would not have to address the constitutionality issue concerning the death penalty.

However, four years later in *Furman* (1972), the majority of the justices declared that the death penalty as administered was in violation of the Eight Amendment protection against cruel and unusual punishment. The rationale for this conclusion varied among the justices, but the main concern was the application of the death penalty under the existing standards at that time. The Court failed, however, to declare the death penalty unconstitutional based on a different set of standards. By 1976, the Court in *Gregg, Proffitt*, and *Jurek* ruled that the sentence of death was not an unconstitutional punishment and for a brief period began scrutinizing imposed death sentences upon appellate review. According to Burt (1987), "this kind of closely detailed, sustained observation by the Supreme Court was itself 'aberrational'" (p. 1780).

Beginning in 1983, the Court turned resolutely away from this pursuit, instead appearing intent on affirming capital punishment in order to suppress "the seeds of anarchy— of self help, vigilante justice, and lynch law" (Burt, 1987, p. 1780). The Court not only seemed to support capital punishment, but it also began closing avenues previously open to inmates seeking federal constitutional relief. State appellate courts were encouraged to (1) spend less time reviewing cases, (2) overlook admitted errors in death penalty proceedings, and (3) disregard the proportionality review process (Burt, 1987). Then, in 1985, the Court made another shift in the capital punishment debate.

In *Wainwright v. Witt* (1985) the Court dismantled the opinion it rendered in *Witherspoon* concerning death-qualified jurors and, instead, concluded that there was a presumption of correctness on the part of state judges in excluding jurors. This action by the Court blocked federal constitutional review unless the defense attorney could show that the trial judge had erred. Given the resources available to defense attorneys in capital cases, the likelihood of a challenge to the presumption of correctness lies moot. The Court continued to tear down the tenets of the *Witherspoon* decision in its ruling of *Lockhart v. McCree* (1986). It ruled that even if a death-qualified jury is more conviction prone than other juries, that fact alone *does not* raise a constitutional issue for review by the Court. According to Burt (1987), the Court's ruling in *Lockhart* reveals that "the Court is now content on suppressing rather than exploring doubts about capital punishment" (pp. 1788–1789).

It is not surprising that the controversy surrounding capital punishment continues when the justices of the Supreme Court cannot deal effectively with the issue. If there are constitutional safeguards to ensure that inmates are afforded those rights, why should judges be instructed to overlook such safeguards? Does this mean that the justices of the Supreme Court view persons convicted and sentenced to death as less than human and therefore should not be afforded the rights guaranteed by the Constitution? It seems fair to say that the chaos that has plagued the Court concerning capital punishment is representative of the confusion and inconsistencies that prevail in society about capital punishment. Perhaps the chaos that plagues us (society) could be diffused by simply treating those persons sentenced to death as human beings until death if an execution is forthcoming. After all, what does society have to lose if death is what one seeks? Does acknowledging that these people are human stir up emotions that one tries hard to suppress? Is that why we prefer not to read or hear about the conditions of incarceration? Facing the reality that death row inmates are humans, just like the rest of us, makes it hard to accept the inadequacies of prison life.

THE ADMINISTRATION OF LAW

In any society, laws define behaviors that are deemed unacceptable based on the morals and values of the community at large. They also determine who will be punished (Price & Sokoloff, 1995). In societies that are not very complex, informal rather than formal methods are used as means of social control. Both society and individuals are presumably protected by the laws. These laws may prescribe punishments, direct or restrain certain actions, and access financial penalties (Reid, 1995). Price and Sokoloff (1995) state that "the law protects what those in power value most" (p. 14). Laws are created and passed by legislative bodies composed mainly of rich white men and persons who share their interests (Price & Sokoloff, 1995). Laws are the mechanism by which the dominate class ensures that its interests will be protected (Quinney, 1975). However, challenges to specific laws are not uncommon (Price & Sokoloff, 1995).

Historically, women have been considered the property of their fathers or husbands without full acknowledgment of them as individuals with rights granted by the Constitution (Price & Sokoloff, 1995). Several cases have come before the Supreme Court concerning the rights of women. In the landmark case of *Reed v. Reed* (1971), the Supreme Court ruled that women were indeed persons and should be treated as such under the U.S. Constitution. The Court stated that the Fourteenth Amendment clause "does not deny to States the power to treat different classes of persons in different ways....[it] does, however, deny to States power to legislate that different treatment be accorded to persons placed by a statute into different classes on the basis of criteria wholly unrelated to the objective of that statute. A classification "must be reasonable, not arbitrary, and must rest upon grounds of difference having a fair and substantial relation to the object of the legislation....(*Reed v. Reed*, 404 (1971). According to the justices, preference based on gender that is used merely to reduce the number of court hearings that could arise because two or more persons are equally entitled is directly in violation of the Fourteenth Amendment clause forbidding arbitrariness, nor can gender be used as a preventive measure against intrafamily controversies (*Reed v. Reed*, 1971). Based on this ruling, the Court recognized women as individuals with the right to individualized treatment, but it did not identify gender in relation to the suspect-classification argument under the Fourteenth Amendment.

It was not until *Frontiero v. Richardson* (1973) that the Court came close to ruling that gender was a suspect classification that "must be subjected to strict judicial scrutiny" (at 677). This case involved differential treatment of men and women in the military in regards to their respective spouses being classified as dependents. The ruling by the Court also stated that the current statute was in violation of the due process clause of the Fifth Amendment. Justice Powell suggested that the Court should not rule on gender as a suspect classification because the Equal Rights Amendment (ERA) had been approved by Congress and it would eliminate the need for such a classification (*Frontiero v. Richardson*, 1973). Unfortunately, the states did not ratify the ERA. It is difficult to imagine the extent to which gender discrimination would have evolved without the protection afforded women in *Frontiero*.

Women were still seeking equal rights during the Ford and Carter administrations. The Court ruled in *Craig* that "classification by gender must serve important governmental objectives and must be substantially related to achievement of those objectives" (*Craig v. Boren*, 1976). Yet this case did not a have true impact on constitutional law; instead, it most notably suggested that there were changes in alliances among the justices. These cases represent only small legal gains by women.

According to Hoff (1991), "some of the most disturbing gender-biased decisions the Supreme Court has reached in the last seventeen years have involved pregnancy cases....Other recent decisions are either discouraging or disquieting for the cause of complete female equality, especially where redistributive economic issues are at stake" (p. 251). Knowing that many households are now headed by women has not moved Congress or the Supreme Court to address the comparable worth issue properly. Instead, they avoid the comparable worth issue as though it were a plague. Women must decide "whether they prefer equal treatment as unequal individuals (when judged by male standards) or special treatment as a protected (and thus implicitly) inferior group" (Hoff, 1991, p. 274). The legal system has not always treated women and girls fairly, and this could be due in part to the perceptions that men (who are the majority in the legal system) have of females

(Price & Sokoloff, 1995). Roberts (1994) states that "the criminal law most directly mandates socially acceptable behavior. Criminal law also helps to shape the way we perceive women's proper role" (p. 1). Women who do not adhere to prescribed gender roles and commit criminal offenses are viewed differently by our criminal justice system. This issue is discussed more fully in the following section on female criminality.

FEMALE CRIMINALITY

Female crime is not as prevalent as that of males, and previously had not been considered a social problem (Belknap, 1996). Women are also more likely to commit fewer and less serious violent crimes than males (Belknap, 1996; Mann, 1984; Pollock-Byrne, 1990; Simon & Landis, 1991). Yet we have been led to believe that female crime has reached outlandish proportions and far exceeds male crime. The basis for this information has been the *Uniform Crime Reports* (*UCR*) complied by the FBI from data supplied by law enforcement agencies.

According to Steffensmeier (1995), these data (*UCR*) are problematic in assessing female crime patterns. Steffensmeier (1995) suggests the following: (1) the changes in arrest rates may be related more to "public attitudes and police practices..." than actual behaviors; (2) because of the broadness of categories they include "dissimilar events and...a range of seriousness"; and (3) the definition of serious crime as used by the *UCR* tends to lead one to believe that serious female crime has risen dramatically, when in fact, women have been arrested more for the crime of larceny, especially for shoplifting (p. 92), than for any other type I offense. Previous research (Mann, 1984; Naffine, 1987; Simon & Landis, 1991; Steffensmeier, 1980) has revealed that overall female crime rates have remained fairly stable in most areas. The notable changes are in the areas of "less serious property offenses and possibly drugs" (Belknap, 1996, p. 58).

To better assess the rate of female crime, Steffensmeier (1995) completed a thirty-year study of arrest statistics. Although the study examined trends in individual offenses, of particular importance here are the trends by type of crime based on male/female arrests. The type of crimes chosen to develop trends for male/female arrests were "violent, masculine, Index ('serious'), and minor property" (Steffensmeier, 1995, p. 94). He found that female participation in masculine crimes increased slightly, which led to more arrests, but this was not the case for violent crimes. Steffensmeier (1995) again attributes the increase in arrests for index crimes to an increase in the number of women committing larcenies. Women have also had an increase in arrest rates for minor property crimes (Belknap, 1996; Steffensmeier, 1995). Simpson (1991) suggests that violent behavior varies among females, and it is difficult to separate the individual influences of race, class, and gender because they are so intermingled. For the purposes of this chapter, we will examine only the influence of gender in the administration of law.

Having examined briefly female criminality, we now turn our attention to the processing of female criminal cases by the criminal justice system. It has been suggested (Chesney-Lind, 1982; Farnworth & Teske, 1995; Frazier, Bock, & Henretta, 1983; Harvey, Burnham, Kendall, & Pease, 1992; Spohn & Spears, 1997; Steffensmeier, 1980) that women receive differential treatment during the processing of criminal cases. The differential treatment may be negative or positive. For example, Steffensmeier (1980) suggested that the likelihood of future offending and the perceived danger to the community influenced the preferential treatment of women in the criminal justice process and as a result increased their chances of receiving probation instead of prison. Yet Chesney-Lind (1982) discovered that female juveniles have always received negative differential treatment. She noted that the females were processed into the juvenile justice system as a result of status offenses and received institutionalization more often than male juveniles.

Frazier et al. (1983) examined the effect of probation officers in determining gender differences in sentencing severity. In their study, they collected data from presentence investigation reports with various information concerning the offender as well as recommendations from the probation officers regarding sentences. According to Frazier et al. (1983), "there is a strong relationship between gender of offender and final criminal court disposition....Probation officers' recommendations have major effects and...being female greatly increases the likelihood of receiving a nonincarceration sentence recommendation " (pp. 315–316). In an international comparison of gender differences in criminal justice, Harvey et al. (1992) found that women were processed out of the criminal justice system more often than men. Their study also revealed that men who were processed through the criminal justice system were convicted and imprisoned at a higher rate than women worldwide. Harvey et al. (1992) note "that criminal justice worldwide operates differentially by gender (but not necessarily in a discriminatory way)" (p. 217).

In another study, Farnworth and Teske (1995) found some evidence of gender disparity in relation to charge reductions if there was no prior criminal history. The absence of prior offending was noted to increase the possibility of probation for females. Based on the selective chivalry thesis, Farnworth and Teske (1995) discovered "that white females were twice as likely as minority females to have assault charges changed to nonassault at sentencing" (p. 40). There was also supportive evidence which suggested that the use of discretionary powers influenced informal rather than formal decisions (Farnworth & Teske, 1995).

More recently, Spohn and Spears' (1997) study of the dispositions of violent felonies for both men and women revealed that more men (71.4 percent) than women (65.0 percent) were prosecuted, but their conviction rates were very similar and major differences appeared in sentencing. For example, males were incarcerated 77.4 percent of the time versus 48.2 percent for females. Overall females normally served "428 fewer days in prison" (p. 42) than males. This study also found that charge reduction or total dismissal of charges was more likely for females than males. Spohn and Spears (1997) state: "Females were more likely than males to have injured their victims....Female defendants were much less likely than male defendants to have a prior felony conviction. Females were charged with and convicted of less serious crimes and were less likely....to be charged with or convicted of more than one offense....less likely than males to have used a gun to commit the crime or to have victimized a stranger....Females were more likely to have private attorneys and to be released prior to trial" (p. 42). Based on their findings, Spohn and Spears (1997) suggest that violent female offenders are looked upon differently by judges for various reasons, such as that (1) females may be perceived as less dangerous to the community, (2) females may have acted as an accomplice instead of being the primary perpetrator, (3) the risk of recidivism is less for females, and (4) there is better chance of rehabilitating female offenders.

WOMEN AND CAPITAL PUNISHMENT

The imposition of the death penalty is not just racially biased but is also gender biased. Streib (1990) states that gender bias is associated with two main sources: "(1) the express provisions of the law, and (2) the implicit attitudes, either conscious or subconscious, of key actors involved in the criminal justice process" (p. 874). Although gender is not mentioned specifically in state statutes, there are certain considerations that may be applied differently based on gender (Streib, 1990). For example, most male criminals have prior criminal histories that include violent acts, whereas women do not have significant prior criminal histories and tend to be less violent than their male counterparts. When women are arrested for murder, it is usually their first offense. Because there tends to be an absence of criminal behavior on the part of women, Mann (1984) and Steffensmeier (1980) suggest that women are not viewed as a threat to society. Another factor considered in capital cases is the defendant's mental state. Allen (1987) suggests that a commonly held belief is that female murderers are emotionally unbalanced at the time of the crime. Additionally, women are usually not the primary perpetrator; therefore, they are able to request consideration for this mitigating factor. According to Streib (1990), "even when all of the specific aggravating and mitigating factors are the same for male and female defendants, females still tend to receive significantly lighter sentences in criminal cases generally" (p. 879).

In examining the treatment of female defendants in the criminal justice system, Gillespie and Lopez (1986) found that "in one area, however, women have constantly been treated with unquestionable deference because of their sex—that of the death penalty. Women have been traditionally been considered a separate class, deserving of a brand of 'justice' all their own. Rather than execute them, they have been lectured, even released to the supervision of their husbands, and often never brought to trial" (p. 2). It has been suggested that this deference is directly related to the paternalistic attitudes of male power brokers in the criminal justice system. However, this idea only explains why some women receive preferential treatment. It is not useful in explaining the absence of this same treatment toward other women. It is this difference in the treatment received by other female defendants that makes them susceptible to harsh treatment in the criminal justice system. Research (Mann, 1984; Streib, 1990) has shown that women who are uneducated, poor, members of a racial minority group, and of the lower socioeconomic group tend not to receive preferential treatment in the criminal justice system. It is the women who have any or all of the aforementioned factors that are more likely to be condemned to death and in some instances, executed in our society.

Historically, we find that there is and has been an acceptance of executing female offenders in this country. Although executions of female defendants are rare, there have been 533 confirmed executions of women since 1632. This represents 2.7 percent of all executions in this country. Yet when we examine executions of females from other centuries, we find that fewer executions take place today than in the past. For example, women comprised only 0.5 percent of the executions during the twentieth century (Streib, 1998). In the following section, we discuss briefly the characteristics of executed women.

We find that 68 percent of the women who have been executed were white and 32 percent were black. Although some defendants were over 50, the average age was 38.7

years old. In terms of previous criminal history, only one had a prior homicide conviction while the others had only minor criminal histories. The motivation for the crimes was profit and emotion, but they were not always domestic situations (Gillespie & Lopez, 1986). Several patterns emerged related to executed women and the crimes. First, there was usually nothing unique or particularly heinous about the crime. Second, collecting insurance was the primary motive for the murder in many cases and in most instances, there was a male accomplice. Next, there seemed to be no established relationship between the victim and the defendant. Finally, the South has executed more women than any other region, while New York leads the states in the execution of women (Gillespie & Lopez, 1986).

In examining death sentences from 1973 to 1997, we find that women received only 117 death sentences compared to over 6210 death sentences for men (Streib, 1998). During the 1970s women received only twenty-one death sentences, but there was a dramatic increase (twenty-nine) in the number of death sentences imposed on women in the 1980s, for an overall total of fifty death sentences in the two decades following the resurgence of the death penalty. During 1989, there were eleven death sentences given to women, representing the single highest total of death sentences given women in any year from 1973 to 1997 (Death Penalty Information Center, 1998). In the 1990s we find a total of forty-five death sentences imposed and predict that the number of death sentences imposed on women in the 1990s will exceed the combined total of the two preceding decades. It is interesting to note that seventy-two of the death sentences imposed during 1973–1997 were either commuted to life imprisonment or reversed, while three of the death sentences were actually fulfilled (Death Penalty Information Center, 1998; Streib, 1998).

Currently (as of July 1, 1998) there are 3426 males and forty-three females on death row. Of the forty-three females currently on death row, five have had their sentences overturned. Women constitute 1.5 percent of the total death row population (NAACP Legal Defense and Educational Fund, 1998; Streib, 1998). Since capital punishment was reinstated in 1976, there have been 467 executions. Of these executions, only three women (Velma Barfield, 1984; Karla Faye Tucker, 1998; and Judy Buenoano, 1998) have been executed, representing 0.64 percent of the total number of executions.

Upon closer examination, we find that the women on death row range in age from 21 to 78. Thirty-five percent of the women on death row were between the ages of 20 and 29 at the time of the criminal act. Twenty-eight percent of the women were between 30 and 39 years old at the time of the crime. The racial breakdown of defendants reveals that 60 percent of the inmates are white and 33 percent are black. Latinas represent only 7 percent of the female death row population (Death Penalty Information Center, 1998)

Briefly, we should note that the victims were 69 percent white, 16 percent black, 10 percent Latinas, and 5 percent Asian. Overwhelmingly, the victim was male (65 percent) with females representing 33 percent of the victims. Four percent of the victims were not identified by sex, thereby creating an "unknown" category (Death Penalty Information Center, 1998).

The women who are currently serving a death sentence are subjected to the same inadequate environmental conditions as other women in prison: namely, poor medical care, inhumane treatment, and isolation from family. In many instances, people who are in correctional facilities become socialized to believe that they are (1) not human, (2) worthless, and (3) cannot be rehabilitated; in other words, they will always be criminals. Some critics also suggest that we should not permit persons on death row access to rehabilitative programs because they are serving a death sentence. We disagree, especially since the reversal rate on appeal for women is 97 percent.

Although the reversal rate for women is high, until their sentences are reversed, these women must survive within the confines of the institution. A major concern for death row inmates is medical care. First, to secure a form requesting a doctor's visit, a death row inmate has to wait until an officer makes a security check. Then a nurse decides whether or not the request will be granted. In many instances, this decision is based solely on the nurse's opinion, not on a preliminary evaluation of the inmate's medical condition. Inmates state that they often do not seek medical assistance because the officers accuse them of trying to get attention. One inmate was so worried that the officers were going to accuse her of trying to get attention that she did not seek medical assistance at the onset of a heart attack. Her cellmate finally called an officer against the sick woman's wishes to take her to the infirmary. Unfortunately, the nurse in the infirmary said there was nothing wrong with her and had the inmate returned to her cell. The inmate died later that night of a massive heart attack. This is only one story of the lack of concern shown by some people who are employed to provide medical care to inmates. Yet the media suggest that inmates have the best medical care available.

Like other inmates, death row inmates are seldom treated like persons by correctional officers and staff. Instead, they are made to feel like a burden that everyone wishes would go away. Because death row is isolated from the general population, the correctional officers are the only people these inmates interact with during the day. If an inmate is housed in the same cell unit as another death row inmate, they may visit and talk to each other. Some correctional officers speak to inmates in a manner that creates problems. By this, we mean that inmates expect to be treated like humans beings, not as animals or objects. Although their daily activities are programmed by the institution, some correctional officers add to the humiliation of the inmates by their conduct and handling of the inmate. It is at times like these that inmates need to be able to turn to family to cope with the dehumanization characteristic of prison life.

In some instances, families cannot withstand the pressures associated with having a family member incarcerated. In far too many cases, family relationships are strained because there is little to no contact with the person incarcerated. Research (Mann, 1984; Pollock-Byrne, 1991) shows that women tend to lose contact with their families more often than men because women's facilities are in remote, rural areas of the state. As a result, visitation is more difficult and more restricted for death row inmates. Women also experience severe emotional separation from family and friends due to their socialization process. Family support adds to the inmate's sense of humanity. Without this support, inmates do not have a buffer from the institutional process of dehumanization.

CONCLUSIONS

The reversal rate on appeal for women sentenced to death is approximately 97 percent (Streib, 1988). Because of the high reversal rate associated with female offenders, we have been lulled into believing that women would not be executed. Given the current attitude toward executing women, as we enter the twenty-first century, we can expect an increase in the number of women executed. We believe that this increase is inevitable because of the "ever lingering get tough on crime" mentality presently dominant in our society, along with recent legislation in Congress limiting appeals for defendants.

REFERENCES

ALLEN, P. (1987). Rendering them harmless: The professional portrayal of women. In P. Carlen & A. Worrell (Eds.), *Gender, crime and justice*. Philadelphia: Milton-Keynes.

BELKNAP, J. (1996). *The invisible woman: Gender, crime and justice*. Belmont, CA: Wadsworth Publishing.

BESCHLE, D. (1997). What's guilt (or deterrence) got to do with it? The death penalty, ritual, and mimetic violence. *William and Mary Law Review, 38*(2), 487–538.

BURT, R. (1987). Disorder in the court: The death penalty and the Constitution. *Michigan Law Review, 85*, 1741–1819.

CHESNEY-LIND, M. (1982). Guilty by reason of sex: Young women and the juvenile justice system. In B. Price & N. Sokoloff (Eds.), *The criminal justice system and women* (pp. 77–105). NY: Clark Boardman.

DEATH PENALTY INFORMATION CENTER. (1998). *Facts about the death penalty*. Washington, DC: DPIC.

EREZ, E. (1989). Gender, rehabilitation, and probation decisions. *Criminology, 27*(2), 307–327.

FARNWORTH, M., & TESKE, R. JR. (1995). Gender differences in felony court processing: Three hypotheses of disparity. *Women and Criminal Justice, 6*(2), 23–44.

FLANAGAN, T., & MAGUIRE, K. (1989). *Sourcebook of criminal justice statistics*. U.S. Department of Justice, Bureau of Justice Statistics. Washington, DC: U.S. Government Printing Office.

FLETCHER, B., SHAVER, D., & MOON, D. (1993). *Women prisoners: A forgotten population*. Westport, CT: Praeger.

FRAZIER, C., BOCK, E., & HENRETTA, J. (1983). The role of probation officers in determining gender differences in sentencing severity. *Sociological Quarterly, 24*, 305–318

GILLESPIE, L. & LOPEZ, B. (1986). *What must a woman do to be executed: A comparison of executed and non-executed women*. Paper presented at the annual meeting of the American Society of Criminology.

GIRARD, R. (1977). *Violence and the sacred*. (P. Gregory, trans). Baltimore: Johns Hopkins University Press.

GIRARD, R. (1987). *Things hidden since the foundation of the world*. London: Athlone Press.

HARVEY, L., BURNHAM, R., KENDALL, K., & PEASE, K. (1992). Gender differences in criminal justice: An international comparison. *British Journal of Criminology, 32*(2), 208–217.

HOFF, J. (1991). *Law, gender and injustice: A legal history of U.S. women*. New York: New York University Press.

KOOSED, M. (1996). *Capital punishment: The philosophical, moral, and penological debate over capital punishment*. New York: Garland Publishing.

KRONENWETTER, M. (1993). *Capital punishment: A reference handbook*. Santa Barbara, CA: ABC-CLIO.

KRUTTSCHNITT, C. (1982). Respectable women and the law. *Sociological Quarterly, 23*(2), 221–234.

MANN, C. (1984). *Female crime and delinquency*. Tuscaloosa, AL: University of Alabama Press.

NAACP LEGAL AND EDUCATION FUND. (1998). *Death row, U.S.A.* New York : NAACP.

NAFFINE, N. (1987). *Female crime: The construction of women in criminology*. Sydney, Australia: Allen & Unwin.

PATERNOSTER, R. (1991). *Capital punishment in America*. New York: Lexington Books.

POLLOCK-BYRNE, J. (1991). *Women, prison, and crime*. Pacific Grove, CA: Brooks/Cole.

PRICE, B., & SOKOLOFF, N. (1995). The criminal law and women. In B. Price & N. Sokoloff (Eds.), *The criminal justice system and women: Offenders, victims, and workers* (pp. 11–29). New York: McGraw-Hill.

QUINNEY, R. (1975). *Class, state and crime: On the theory and practice of criminal justice.* New York: Longman.

REID, S. (1994). *Crime and criminology* (7th ed.). Madison: Brown & Benchmark.

ROBERTS, D. (1994). The meaning of gender equality in criminal law. *Journal of Criminal Law and Criminology, 85*(1), 1–14.

SIMON, R., & LANDIS, J. (1991). *The crimes women commit, and the punishments they receive.* Lexington, MA: Lexington Books.

SIMPSON, S. (1991). Caste, class, and violent crime: Exploring differences in female offending. *Criminology, 29*(1), 115–135.

SPOHN, C., & SPEARS, J. (1997). Gender and case processing decisions: A comparison of case outcomes for male and female defendants charged with violent felonies. *Women and Criminal Justice, 8*(3), 29–59.

STEFFENSMEIER, D. (1980). Assessing the impact of the women's movement on sex-based differences in the handling of adult criminal defendants. *Crime and Delinquency, 26,* 344–357.

STEFFENSMEIER, D. (1995). Trends in female crime: It's still a man's world. In B. Price & N. Sokoloff (Eds.), *The criminal justice system and women: Offenders, victims, and workers* (pp. 89–104). New York: Clark Boardman.

STREIB, V. (1988). *American executions of female offenders: A preliminary inventory of names, dates, and other information* (3rd ed.). Cleveland, OH: Author.

STREIB, V. (1990). Death penalty for female offenders. *University of Cincinnati Law Review, 58*(3), 845–880.

STREIB, V. (1998). *Capital punishment for female offenders, names, dates, and other information* (3rd ed.). Cleveland, OH: Author.

VISHER, C. (1983). Chivalry in arrest decisions. *Criminology, 21*(1), 5–28.

ZINGRAFF, M., & THOMSON, R. (1984). Differential sentencing of men and women in the U.S.A. *International Journal of the Sociology of Law, 12,* 401–413.

CASES

Craig v. Boren, 429 U.S. 190, 197 (1976)

Frontiero v. Richardson, 411 U.S. 677 (1973)

Furman v. Georgia, 408 U.S. 238 (1972)

Gregg v. Georgia, 428 U.S. 158 (1976)

Jurek, 428 U.S. 262 (1976)

Lockhart v. McCree, 106 S. Ct. 1758 (1986)

McGautha v. California, 402 U.S. 183 (1971)

Powell v. Alabama, 287 U.S. 45 (1932)

Proffitt, 428 U.S. 242 (1976)

Reed v. Reed, 404 U.S. 71, 92 S. Ct. 251, 30 L. Ed. 2d, 255 (1971)

Rudolph v. Alabama, 375 U.S. 889 (1963)

Wainwright v. Witt, 469 U.S. 412 (1985)

Witherspoon v. Illinois, 391 U.S. 510 (1968)

SECTION V

Women: Victims of Violence

The amount of violence aimed at women is staggering and horrific. All women are affected by this violence, and women's behavior is controlled and limited by it. Over one-third of all women who cohabit with men are battered by men in their own homes. In many instances, the most dangerous place for a woman is in her own home.

The traditional stance of the criminal justice system toward incidents of domestic violence was to look the other way. The battering of women was perceived by police officers to be the outgrowth of a domestic dispute that was really none of their business. Domestic violence had to be redefined as an assault before new tactics and procedures emerged for dealing with offenders.

The civil rights movement of the 1960s and the women's rights movement a decade later sought to challenge existing stereotypes that ignored the problems of women. For example, pro-arrest procedures were adopted by many police departments. And, in the beginning, further acts of family violence appeared to be quelled by arrest and jail actions. However, findings from replication studies and other policy evaluation research offer little support for these early deterrence claims and raise serious questions about the efficacy of pro-arrest policies. Additionally, it has been found that arrest policies may be more detrimental to battered women from minority groups and women with fewer resources and opportunities. There continue to be efforts to develop effective criminal justice policies that are clearly dependent upon studying domestic violence while using a variety of perspectives and methodologies.

An underlying theme of the chapters in this section is the pervasive violence and fear that remain a part of so many women's lives. How we measure abuse, beatings, and crimes of "forced sexual intercourse," including stalking, are more prevalent today than ever before.

Susan L. Miller's chapter, "Arrest Policies for Domestic Violence and Their Implications for Battered Women," describes for us how both minority and lower-class women have traditionally placed greater reliance on the police to intervene in order to resolve conflicts within their intimate relationships. She points out that social class may be inextricably linked to race in the study of intimate violence. This, we are told, is because nonwhites are overrepresented in the lower socioeconomic groups and socioeconomic status affecting the options that women have: Women with greater income have greater access to resources to assist them in keeping their abuse private, while those in the lower socioeconomic class are denied a certain amount of privacy. It is entirely possible that mandatory and pro-arrest policies may disproportionately affect minority women, who have few places to turn.

In "Likelihood of an Arrest Decision for Domestic and Nondomestic Assault Calls: Do Police Underenforce the Law When Responding to Domestic Violence?" Lynette

Feder presents a study that focuses on the police's likelihood to arrest in jurisdictions that specify mandatory or the presumption in favor of arrest statutes. Her studies point to a low rate of arrest, which, in turn, leads many to conclude that the police are continuing to practice a subtle and insidious policy of nonenforcement when responding to domestic violence offenders. What is called for is a comparison of police response to domestic and nondomestic assault which is lacking for purposes of verifying whether police are selectively underenforcing domestic violence laws.

Stalking is a crime that can happen to anyone at any time. This act is more complex than simply following an intended victim before committing an act of violence. In her chapter, "Female Victims and Antistalking Legislation," Janice Joseph describes how the act of stalking involves psychological, physical, and legal issues that converge to form a course of conduct. Her chapter focuses on the effectiveness of the antistalking laws prescribed to "protect" females from a legal perspective. Stalking is a serious phenomenon that has only recently been brought before the attention of the public. Although states have reacted fairly quickly with the passage of legislation, the laws as stated often allow the stalker to evade punishment. And still the violence against women continues.

What do we mean when we talk of "forced sexual intercourse"? In "Forced Sexual Intercourse: Contemporary Views," Robert T. Sigler, Ida M. Johnson, and Etta F. Morgan suggest that this term is used to label four types of behavior which are substantially different. They discuss stranger rape, courtship or date rape, predatory rape, and spousal rape. Regardless, rape is rape. Rape is and continues to be a topic of relevance for women. By definition, rape is a crime perpetrated by men against women. There is the element of force in all rape cases. The authors in this chapter suggest that a model that addresses the different kinds of rape cases is needed. The argument advanced is that there are types or sets of related forms of forced sexual intercourse which are sufficiently different as to require separate explanatory models if the phenomena are to be effectively understood and examined.

19

Arrest Policies for Domestic Violence and Their Implications for Battered Women

Susan L. Miller

Historically, the criminal justice system has failed to respond adequately to woman battering. In response to criticisms, the system has moved toward emphasizing pro-arrest policies. Much of this redirection resulted from an outcry from feminist groups and the findings from the Minneapolis Domestic Violence Experiment, which indicated that arrest deters offenders at higher rates than separation or mediation. Consequently, in the ensuing years, many police departments have restructured their policies and procedures; replication efforts have tested the deterrence hypothesis using different samples and geographic sites. Several particular concerns have been raised as a result of these shifts in policy: first, the replication studies have failed to demonstrate convincingly that arrest of batterers deters repeat offenses from occurring in sites other than Minneapolis; arrest may in fact make the situation worse. Second, under mandatory arrest statutes, often both the victim and the offender are arrested despite preemptive aggression from the offender. Finally, pro-arrest policies may introduce disproportionately negative ramifications for women of lower socioeconomic classes and minority women.

In this chapter the changes in how the criminal justice system responds to women batterers, beginning with a review of the policy changes since the 1980s are explored. Next, the research conducted to evaluate pro-arrest policies is addressed. The implications for victims are assessed in terms of these studies and the differential impact that these policies may have for lower-class and minority women. Finally, a brief review of alternatives and supplements to arrest is conducted, such as coordinated community and criminal justice system response efforts.

Historically, the crime of intimate violence has been shrouded in secrecy, viewed as a private matter and not as a social problem. Both legal and social institutions have reinforced the "hands-off approach" that has characterized responses to woman battering. However, since the 1970s, efforts initiated by the battered women's movement have successfully propelled the issue of intimate violence into the national spotlight (see Schechter, 1982; Dobash & Dobash, 1977).[1] Much of the research and political activism has focused on identifying the correlates of abuse, providing services for victims, creating or strengthening domestic violence legislation, and improving the criminal justice system's responses to woman battering. One of the most compelling criticisms concerning the handling of woman battering has been leveled against police officers' failure to arrest woman batterers and protect victims adequately. Consequently, in the 1980s, innovative laws were introduced and policy efforts were designed to improve the criminal justice system's treatment of domestic disputes. Included was the move toward pro-arrest policies. This chapter focuses on the problems that facilitated these policy innovations, the pro-arrest strategies themselves, and reviews the current status of pro-arrest strategies. Special attention is paid to the different impact that these policies may have for lower-class and minority battered women. It concludes with a brief review of alternative dispositions (other than arrest) and their value to battered women.[2]

CRIMINAL JUSTICE SYSTEM'S RESPONSES TO WOMAN BATTERING

The handling of domestic disputes evokes deep feelings of frustration both from police officers responding to these calls *and* from battered women responding to police officers' inaction.[3] Since mediation or separation were the common modes of police response, batterers were not punished for their actions, and victims of their violence were not adequately protected (Stanko, 1985). These official responses were justified by cultural norms and gender role expectations, despite the accumulated evidence showing that unchecked intimate violence escalates in frequency and intensity, with some episodes resulting in the death of the victim (Walker, Thyfault, & Browne, 1982).[4]

For years, battered women faced police officers who routinely supported the offender's position, challenged the credibility of the victim—often blaming her for her own victimization—and trivialized her fears (Gil, 1986; Karmen, 1982). Police officer training manuals reinforced officer behavior, stressing the use of family crisis intervention or separation tactics (International Association of Chiefs of Police, 1967; Parnas, 1967). This policy emphasis sanctioned the discretion of police officers; it thus also sanctioned their reluctance to initiate criminal justice proceedings when officers thought that a reconciliation might occur and make arrest actions futile (Field & Field, 1973; Lerman, 1986). Not only did the police fail to respond formally to battering by invoking arrest; other components in the system responded similarly (e.g., prosecutors and judges).[5] Taken together, the failure of the system to respond appropriately to women battering perpetuated the silence surrounding intimate violence.

Statistics indicate that when police do retain the discretion to arrest in domestic assault incidents, officers largely do not arrest.[6] For example, three different studies indicate that for domestic violence incidents, police arrest rates were 10, 7, and 3 percent (see Buel, 1988). In Milwaukee, although 82 percent of battered women desired arrest of their abusers, police arrested only 14 percent of these offenders (Bowker, 1982). Similarly, in Ohio, police arrested only 14 percent of the cases, even though in 38 percent of these incidents, victims were either injured or killed (Bell, 1984). Overall, police in jurisdictions with pro-arrest policies still fail to arrest batterers (Balos & Trotzky, 1988; Ferraro, 1995; Lawrenz, Lembo, & Schade, 1988).

As a result of police departments' inadequate responses to treat battering as a serious offense, class-action suits were introduced against police departments by victims (Martin, 1978; Paterson, 1979). In fact, battered women who felt unprotected by police have received some satisfaction from this kind of court action, arguing successfully that the equal protection clause of the Fourteenth Amendment is violated when police treat women who are assaulted by an intimate partner differently from people assaulted by strangers.[7] Class-action suits, political activism by feminists, and victims' advocacy groups proved instrumental in challenging the efficacy and unresponsiveness of police departments (Schechter, 1982). The stage was set for researchers to explore new and different responses by police to battering, including advocating for pro-arrest or mandatory arrest policies.

MANDATORY ARREST POLICIES

Movement away from discretionary arrest policies and toward mandatory or pro-arrest policies is attractive for a variety of reasons. First, the psychological benefit to battered women cannot be overstated: Arrest demonstrates a willingness to assert officially that battering will not be tolerated. Second, some police officers believe that mandatory arrest laws assist in clarifying police roles by providing more guidance and training (Loving, 1980). Third, evaluations of jurisdictions that enact mandatory arrest laws indicate that rather than making police officers more vulnerable, police injuries decrease (National Criminal Justice Association, 1985); this decrease may be due to the advance notice or warning about the consequences of abusive behavior once mandatory arrest policies are in effect. Fourth, the onus of responsibility is transferred to police and does not remain solely on the battered woman's shoulders. Thus many believe that officer-initiated arrest empowers the victim (Buel, 1988): "Arrest can kindle the battered woman's perception that society values her and penalizes violence against her. This perception counteracts her experience of abuse....When a battered woman calls the police and they arrest the man who beats her, her actions, along with the officer's actions, do something to stop her beating....Now her actions empower. The woman may begin to believe in herself enough to endeavor to protect herself" (Pastoor, 1984).[8]

A fifth advantage of mandatory arrest policies is the feeling that more equitable law enforcement will result than with a discretionary-based arrest system. Buel (1988, p. 224) argues that mandatory arrest that is conducted whenever specific, objective conditions are met will "ensure that race and class distinctions are not the basis for determining how police intervene in family violence situations."[9] Sixth, strong police action can contribute to purposeful follow-through by the other components of the criminal justice system.

Finally, some early research findings indicate that recidivism of batterers dramatically decreases after instituting mandatory arrest policies. For instance, homicides decreased from twelve or thirteen annually to one in the initial six months of 1986 in

Newport News, Virginia (Lang, 1986); in Hartford County, Connecticut, the number of calls for police service for domestic violence incidents decreased by 28 percent (Olivero, 1987). Perhaps the most conclusive research findings have been attributed to the Minneapolis Domestic Violence Experiment, conducted by Sherman and Berk (1984).

The Minneapolis field experiment manipulated types of police response to misdemeanant domestic assault.[10] The research findings revealed that arrest is twice as effective a deterrent for batterers than the more traditional police strategies of separation or mediation (Sherman & Berk, 1984).[11] A subsequent national survey of police departments indicate that jurisdictions supporting arrest for minor domestic assault are increasing in numbers (from 10 percent in 1984 to 31 percent in 1986); eleven states attribute these policy changes to the publicized results of the Minneapolis experiment's success (Cohn & Sherman, 1986).[12]

NEW CONCERNS ABOUT MANDATORY ARREST POLICIES

Ostensibly, mandatory arrest policies appear to solve the dilemmas faced by battered women. In fact, it is difficult not to embrace wholeheartedly such a transformation of police procedure in dealing with women battering. However, there are at least three considerations that limit unconditional acceptance of the interpretation that arrest deters battering, or that mandatory arrest eliminates disparity in arrest practices. First, there are methodological problems associated with the original (first-wave) research, the Minneapolis Domestic Violence Experiment (MDVE) (Binder & Meeker, 1996; Sherman & Berk, 1984), which was instrumental in generating additional evaluations of mandatory-arrest policies. Second, there are problems identified with the NIJ-funded replication studies and contrary results reported from other (second-wave) studies (Dutton et al., 1996). Third, there may be unintended negative consequences of mandatory arrest for battered women themselves, particularly for women of color or women from lower-socioeconomic groups (Rasche, 1995; Miller, 1989). These concerns raise hesitations about fully accepting the conclusion that arrest of woman batterers deters subsequent acts of intimate violence.

METHODOLOGICAL PROBLEMS

Since the Minneapolis Domestic Violence Experiment remains the seminal study to inform public policy on police response to domestic violence, it is important to review the experiment and its findings. Methodological problems associated with the MDVE are now legion (see, e.g., Binder & Meeker, 1988; Fagan, 1989; Lempert, 1984). The most salient problem concerns the sample. The deterrent effect attributed to mandatory arrest was based on a small number of follow-up interviews completed by the battered women: Sherman and Berk (1984, p. 265) report a 62 percent completion rate for the initial face-to-face interviews and a 49 percent completion rate for the biweekly follow-ups for six subsequent months (161 respondents from a sample of 330 victims). L. Sherman and Berk (1984) contend that the experimental design of the research had no effect on the victim's participation decisions during the follow-up phase. It may be likely that further violence occurred but is undisclosed in follow-up interviews or simply lost due to case attrition. If these problems escape detection, a research artifact may be created during the follow-up stage, or the observed deterrent effect may be only temporary, contingent on pending charges (Jaffe, Wolfe, Telford, & Austin, 1986).

Victims may display reluctance in requesting police service after experiencing the consequences of official intervention once a mandatory-arrest policy becomes effective (Sherman & Berk, 1984, p. 269). This dynamic would mask continued violence in follow-up interviews and in official records, demonstrating a deterrent effect in reporting practices, but not actual battering incidences (Berk & Newton, 1985). In fact, Buzawa (1982) contends that once a woman loses control over the outcome of a domestic dispute, she may be deterred from calling the police.[13] Battered women who call the police for help may only desire the cessation of the immediate abuse; in these cases, arrest may be acknowledged by the woman as a possible alternative, but one that is not desirable. An unintended consequence may be that battering escalates as a result of an arrest, with increased intimidation, threats, or retaliation from the abuser, causing the victim to be silent (Goolkasian, 1986, p. 35).[14]

Findings of a deterrent effect may really be a result of displacement in which the original violent relationship has terminated, but the batterer simply moves into a new violent relationship with a new partner (Fagan, 1989; Reiss, 1985). This displacement effect is related to selective attrition problems identified by Elliott (1989, p. 453). These may occur if arrest affects the termination of the relationship, thereby limiting the deterrent interpretation of lower recidivism rates after a pro-arrest policy goes into effect. Ford (1984) offers support for this hypothesis with evidence that arrest may be correlated with breaking up, which is one successful way of stopping further violence. A displacement effect could also exist under the guise of a deterrent effect if the violence shifts its focus to other family members. If a relationship remains intact but the couple moves away from the area, their absence in official records may be misleading if it is interpreted as a deterrent effect (Lempert, 1984).

Given the plausibility of alternative explanations, some researchers have suggested caution in adopting such dramatic policy shifts based on the "success" of the Minneapolis experiment, fearing that the changes are not well thought out, not well grounded in empirical support, and are generated from research that is methodologically problematic (Binder & Meeker, 1988; Elliott 1989; Gelles & Mederer, 1985; Lempert, 1984).[15]

FAILURES AND PROBLEMS WITH REPLICATION STUDIES AND OTHER PRO-ARREST EVALUATIONS

In this section we explore the policy impacts of mandatory or presumptive arrest in a number of jurisdictions.[16] Researchers examining the impact of a pro-arrest policy change in London, Ontario, found that the numbers of cases in which the police initiated criminal charges of woman abuse increased dramatically (2.7 percent in 1979 to 67.3 percent in 1983), the numbers of cases dismissed or withdrawn decreased substantially, and victim self-reports revealed a decrease in subsequent violence for the year following the policy change and police intervention (Jaffe et al., 1986). However, results from a police officer survey indicated that only 21 percent of the police surveyed believed that the new policy was effective in stopping intimate violence, and 32 percent thought women stopped calling the police after the policy was enacted (Jaffe et al., 1986). Elliott (1989) addresses this contradiction, maintaining that the study is plagued by serious methodological problems that question the success of the new arrest policy, such as the absence of control groups to use for comparisons, and the unrepresentativeness of the sample of victims used. In light of these problems, it is difficult to conclude with any confidence that pro-arrest policies in Ontario facilitated victim reporting, or that the deterrent effects indicated were really true ones.

Buzawa and Buzawa (1990) contend that police officers are generally distrustful of police policy directives designed by outside political leaders or nonpolice personnel. This distrust is manifested in officer circumvention of laws or policies, which "extends to ignoring or subverting recognized rules of criminal procedure or explicit organizational goals and directives" (Buzawa & Buzawa, 1990, p. 100). Research that evaluates the impact of a presumptive arrest policy adopted by the Phoenix, Arizona police supports the idea that police circumvent policy (Ferraro, 1989b); despite the change in law and department policies, arrests were made in only 18 percent of the domestic assault cases. Ferraro (1989b) suggests that most of the noncompliance by the police was related to legal, ideological, and political considerations, which led them to ignore the policy change. In this analysis, Ferraro was able to gather detailed qualitative data through interviews with victims. These provided explanations as to why some battered women, particularly those from lower-class positions, would be less inclined to call the police if it meant their partners would be arrested, creating financial hardship for the family, including possible job loss.

In 1987, the District of Columbia's police department enacted new legislation that directed officers to arrest batterers. However, an evaluation conducted two years after its imposition found that police had failed to enforce the guideline, continuing to resort to mediating domestic disputes and keeping arrests at a minimum (Baker, Cahn, & Sands, 1989). These findings are based on interviews with almost 300 victims who sought protection at either the Superior Court or the Citizens Complaint Center. Similar to other pro-arrest policy implementation evaluations, police circumvented the policy. In the DC study, only 5 percent of the cases resulted in arrest; this rate remained low even when the complainant was seriously injured (requiring medical treatment) or had been threatened with knives, guns, or other weapons.[17] The most commonly cited reasons offered by police to explain their failure to arrest were that they believed that nothing could be done (23.7 percent), the police thought the case was "domestic" or the couple lived together (22.6 percent) (and thus the police did not want to get involved), or the victim was instructed to go to the Citizens Complaint Center (20.1 percent) to explore civil remedies.

Based on the questions and concerns generated by Sherman and Berk's Minneapolis experiment, the National Institute of Justice[18] funded six different replication studies to explore the deterrent effects of police response to battering (U.S. Department of Justice, 1985). It was hoped that these new studies would address and correct some of the important issues and problems raised by the Minneapolis experiment.[19] The replication studies have achieved equivocal results and in fact suggest that arrest may have no effect or even might escalate violence (see Berk, Campbell, Klap, & Western, 1992a, 1992b; Dunford, 1990; Dunford, Huizinga, & Elliott, 1990; Garner, Fagan, & Maxwell, 1995; Hirschel,

Hutchinson, & Dean, 1992a, 1992b; Pate, Hamilton, & Annan, 1991; Sherman, Smith, Schmidt, & Rogan, 1991; Sherman et al., 1991, 1992).[20]

The NIJ-funded replication studies evaluated various interventions; the results demonstrated different outcomes. For instance, the Milwaukee project used three treatment responses: arrest with a mean jail detention of 11.1 hours, arrest that resulted in an average release time of 2.8 hours; and no arrest (only issued a warning). An analysis of 1200 cases revealed no significant differences in arrest effects after a six-month follow-up period (Hirschel et al., 1992b), although there was a slight deterrent effect after 30 days. The researchers concluded that arrest affects people differently, with persons who have a greater stake in conformity because of their employment being more deterred by arrest than are unemployed persons with little stake in conformity (Sherman, 1992).

In its replication, the Omaha Police Experiment followed the design of the MDVE by randomly assigning cases to one of three police interventions: separation, mediation, or arrest. They developed two types of outcome measures: official recidivism (measured by new arrests or complaints noted in police records) and victim reports of repeat acts of violence (fear of injury, pushing–hitting, and physical injury) (Dunford et al., 1990, p. 188). Victims were interviewed twice over a six-month period, with the overall completion rate being 73 percent ($n = 242$).[21]

Several comparisons between the two experiments concerning the victim interview data are important to highlight: The proportion of initial interviews completed in Minneapolis was 62 percent, and in Omaha, the proportion was 80 percent; the proportion completing the six-month follow-up interview for Minneapolis was 49 percent, while in Omaha, the proportion was 73 percent. Additionally, only the Omaha experiment used face-to-face interviews. The researchers concluded that there are virtually no differences in the prevalence and frequency of repeat offending regardless of the police intervention assigned to the case (Dunford et al., 1990). Thus the Omaha experiment was unable to replicate the Minneapolis findings. Omaha researchers also sought to determine if one of the interventions (separation, mediation, or arrest) could delay a repeat of violence for a longer period of time than the other interventions. After conducting time-to-failure analyses, Dunford et al. (1990, p. 202) present that "[a]fter six months at risk, no one treatment group could be described as requiring more time to fail than any other treatment group." The conclusion reached in the Omaha Police Experiment provides ample caution for mandatory or presumptory arrest policies to be adopted in other jurisdictions: "[A]rrest in Omaha, by itself, did not appear to deter subsequent domestic conflict any more than did separating or mediating those in conflict. Arrest, and the immediate period of custody associated with arrest, was not the deterrent to continued domestic conflict that was expected. If the Omaha findings should be replicated in the other five sites conducting experiments on this issue, policy based on the presumptory arrest recommendation coming out of the Minneapolis experiment may have to be reconsidered" (Dunford et al., 1990, p. 204).[22] The last line in their article offers an admonition to both researchers and practitioners interested in the reduction of woman battering to begin considering new or additional strategies to cope with this problem.

Similar to findings reported in Milwaukee and Omaha, the Charlotte study found that arrest increased domestic violence recidivism rather than deterring it. The Charlotte replication retested three treatments: immediate arrest, issuing a citation for court at a later date and no formal action (separate and advise). An analysis of 650 cases revealed an increase in the proportion of repeat arrests across each group. Hirschel et al. (1992a) offered five reasons why the Omaha, Milwaukee, and Charlotte experiments failed to find evidence supporting arrest as an effective deterrent. First, a majority of offenders in these studies had previous criminal records, so arrest failed to deter because it was not a new experience. Second, many of the offenders studies were chronic abusers or had criminal histories, so arrest was unlikely to have any impact. Third, arrest may not be associated with a change in behavior, especially when the time served is relatively short and offenders have been arrested before. Fourth, the data revealed that few offenders were found guilty and sentenced to jail. Finally, these studies focused on whether arrest was an effective deterrent for all offenders and ignored the possibility that arrest may be effective for only certain types of abusers.

Researchers in Colorado Springs and Metro-Dade found limited support for the MDVE findings, but only with victim interview data (Schmidt & Sherman, 1996), and the response rate was low. Sherman (1992) suggests that if the response rate in the Colorado experiment was higher among the more stable, employed group of criminals (30 percent of offenders were known to be employed), the difference could be due to the kinds of people tapped by victim interviews versus official records. Conversely, Hirschel, Hutchinson, & Dean (1992b) argue that extensive comparisons conducted on interviewed versus non-interviewed cases showed the two groups to be similar. Confounding the interpretation of results in the Colorado experiment was the fact that the majority of crimes in the sample (58 percent) were based on the offender's nonviolent, harassing, or menacing behavior toward the victim (Sherman, 1992). These measures may be different from the physical attack required to arrest for battery in other replication studies.

Overall, these studies reviewed indicate that for a variety of reasons, mandatory (or presumptive) arrest policies do not provide the anticipated panacea to the woman-battering problem. Additionally, Buzawa and Buzawa (1990, pp. 102–105) cite several reasons for not supporting mandatory arrest policies: First, they argue that the benefits do not outweigh the costs because convictions will not increase dramatically. A victim may refuse to comply with prosecutorial efforts voluntarily; or if forced to testify, her recall ability may be deliberately vague or too incomplete to warrant further prosecution efforts (Ferraro, 1989b). Second, police may engage in arrest-avoidance techniques that would limit assistance to victims: "The net result may therefore be to shift help from some victims who receive no police assistance to another group who obtain the degree and type of help that a paternalistic system believes is appropriate, whether desired or not" (Buzawa & Buzawa, 1990, p. 103). Third, in cases in which a victim is not desirous of an arrest, mandatory policies perpetuate the belief that police disregard victims' preferences.[23] Buzawa and Buzawa suggest that victim preferences must be elicited out of earshot from the offender, and that police should be trained in other victim-sensitive skills. Fourth, these policies entrust too much power to police departments; "dual arrests" (of both the victim and offender) or threats of such an outcome might result.[24] For example, both Connecticut and Rhode Island experienced a significant increase in dual arrests for the first several years following the change to mandatory arrests. Some jurisdictions, such as Washington, DC, include specific language in their statutes, such as "primary aggressor," in order to reduce the likelihood of a dual arrest; Massachusetts requires written justification for the arrest of both the offender and the victim. Qualitative interviews with police administrators from 24 police departments across Massachusetts revealed dual arrests were more likely to occur when it was difficult for the officers to assign blame or the officer was assaulted by the victim (Mignon & Holmes, 1995). These last two reservations involve the potential for police to misuse their arrest powers; critics point out that police may make more trivial arrests of victims if they are called repeatedly to the same house. Policies may as well encourage judges not to treat the cases seriously. To support this last claim, the researchers refer to Ferraro's (1989a) finding that policies "created great uncertainty both for the judiciary and the department and tended to trivialize cases clearly warranting arrest" (Buzawa & Buzawa, 1990, p. 105).

RACE AND CLASS IMPLICATIONS

Another potential problem with mandatory arrest policies is that they may produce unanticipated and negative consequences for some women. Due to limited opportunities, resources, and alternatives, men who abuse women from minority or low-socioeconomic groups may be disproportionately arrested in jurisdictions favoring pro-arrest policies, creating added problems for battered women.[25] However, a discussion acknowledging the differential concerns of battered women from minority and low-income groups is absent from the domestic violence literature.[26] The responses of women from different racial, ethnic, class, and religious groups may indicate that policies designed to assist them may prove to be inadequate or inappropriate based on their cultural or community needs. Lockhart (1985) contends that any mainstream research on battering suffers from major shortcomings in design: "[R]acial comparisons made by these researchers were based on an implicit assumption that all groups in this country are homogeneous, regardless of their political, socio-historical, and economic experiences. *Researchers who ignore the fundamentally different realities of racial groups commit serious methodological and theoretical errors*" [italics added] (p. 40).

Hagan and Albonetti (1982) report that blacks and lower-socioeconomic-status persons are more likely than whites and higher-socioeconomic-status persons to perceive injustice operating against them by police, juries, and court personnel. Minority groups indeed have a long history of uneasy relations with police (see Overby, 1971; Rossi, Berk, & Edison, 1974). If a legacy of distrust exists between the minority community and law enforcement agents, minority women may not embrace the new arrest polices. Some minority-group women may object "…to mandatory arrest laws because they are viewed as providing police with yet another means of harassing minority group men rather than as protection for battered women" (Goolkasian, 1986, p. 37). Many black women themselves may be ambivalent about seeking relief from the criminal justice system: "The effects of racism and sexism seem too great to tackle in the face of having been victimized by a loved one. The woman oftentimes feels powerless to change her situation, tending to feel she is being forced to tolerate the situation longer because the very system which has historically served to subjugate and oppress her is the only system which can save her from the immediate abusive system" (Hearing on Violence Prevention Act, Formal Testimony, 1978, p. 521).[27] This testimony echoes informal conclusions regarding black women's reluctance to involve police in their personal lives: "All (abusive) men, regardless of race, should be dealt with, but black men are going to be dealt with more severely. Naturally, this troubles [black] victims. Black women know they don't want him (the abuser) in jail—all they want is for the abuse to stop...There's a lot of guilt involved when you're talking about reporting a man. There's a fear that it's not supporting black and other minority men and that they shouldn't be punished" (Williams, 1981, p. 22).

McLeod (1984) discusses two competing hypotheses concerning disproportionate representation of minority citizens and calls to the police: First is the differential participation hypothesis, which states that statistics accurately reflect that minorities are more involved in domestic violence incidents; and second is the differential notification hypothesis, which suggests that these statistics are misleading in that they only reflect reporting rates, not participation rates.

Research conducted by Block (1974) found that black victims have higher reporting rates than whites with assault-and-battery incidents and so are overrepresented in official police statistics. Similarly, Hindelang (1976) claims the statistics are misleading; they reflect assaults known to police only. *National Crime Survey* (*NCS*) data also seem to support the differential notification hypothesis: The data show overrepresentation of minorities in abuse victimizations (11.3 percent of the population are black; 17 percent of male victims are black) (McLeod, 1984).

With any assessment or pro-arrest policies, it is necessary to discern whether or not there are class differences in victims' reporting of intimate violence to the police. Schwartz (1988) tackles the issue of differential representation of minority and lower-class citizens reflected in victimization surveys. Essentially, he argues that there is evidence suggesting that the NCS is more likely to be biased in favor of showing more middle- and upper-class women's victimizations, rather than overrepresenting lower classes, citing Sparks' (1981) research: "[He] argues that black and lower-class persons systematically underreport assaults in NCS interviews, and that any findings which show a greater incidence of victimization of lower-class persons are in fact stronger than would be indicated by these data" (Schwartz, 1988, p. 378).

Additionally, Schwartz challenges the pervasive argument that there are *not* class differences in intimate violence vulnerability. He argues that this issue is largely ignored by feminists conducting research on battered women because they do not want to advance the myth that battered women are located primarily in the lower end of the economic spectrum. Schwartz contends that since feminist ideology embraces framing the issue within a context which insists that all women are equally oppressed and vulnerable to victimization in a patriarchal society, they refuse to investigate class distinctions. Feminists (and other researchers) are able to effectively criticize the methodology of studies that do find greater incidence rates among lower-class women. Schwartz contends that this is very easy to do (e.g., reporting artifacts or data sources, oversampling poorer persons, who are more likely to use services such as the police, courts, shelters, or other social service agencies; see Okum, 1986, p. 48).[28]

Conspicuously absent in the District of Columbia's mandatory arrest policy evaluation is any mention of the racial breakdowns of victims and offenders.[29] However, the study does offer some relevant economic information: 55.5 percent of the battering victims earned $15,000 or less; 79 percent earned less than $20,000. The authors assert that "[c]ontributions from other household members do not significantly increase these victims' financial security: Even with other family member's income, 63 percent of the victims live in households whose income was $20,000 or less per year" (Baker et al., 1989, pp. 29–30). Even more important is the finding that the victim whose abusers were arrested was even poorer: "These results reflect the fact that victims who have lower incomes do not have resources, other than the police and the Citizens Complaint Center, to escape domestic violence. They do not have lawyers to commence legal action: they do not have the option of moving their families to separate homes; they do not have the income to enter family counseling designed to stem the violence. The police response to their plight is possibly their only protection" (Baker et al., 1989, p. 30).

Both minority and lower-class women have traditionally placed greater reliance on police intervention to resolve conflicts within their intimate relationships. Social class may be inextricably linked to race in the study of intimate violence; this is because nonwhites are overrepresented in the lower socioeconomic groups, and socioeconomic status affects options (Lockhart, 1985, 1987). Women with more income have greater access to resources to assist them in keeping their abuse private; they have the ability to afford private physicians and safe shelters, which results in their being able to escape detection from law enforcement, hospital emergency rooms, or social service agencies (Asbury, 1987; Prescott & Letko, 1977; Stark, Flitcraft, & Frazier, 1979; Washburn and Frieze, 1981).

Findings from the National Commission on the Causes and Prevention of Violence suggest that "...lower-class people are denied privacy for their quarrels: neighborhood bars, sidewalks, and crowded, thin-walled apartments afford little isolation" (Eisenberg & Micklow, 1977, p. 142). Therefore, it is entirely plausible that mandatory and pro-arrest policies may disproportionately affect minority women and women from lower-socioeconomic statuses who may have fewer opportunities and alternatives available for settling disputes privately (Stanko, 1985). The economic consequences of arrest may be more devastating for lower-socioeconomic households. If the batterer is jailed, income may be lost, thus increasing the probability that a woman may not call the police if arrest would be imminent. Thus it seems clear that limited alternatives exist for economically disadvantaged battered women, especially women from minority groups, who are faced with the dilemma of being dependent on the police for assistance whenever their partners engage in violence against them.

BRIEF REVIEW OF ALTERNATIVES AND SUPPLEMENTS TO ARREST

Early efforts of the battered women's movement were designed to assist the victims of domestic violence by establishing shelters and crisis lines. Not all of these programs received unanimous support; shelters have been viewed (mostly by pro-family groups) as instrumental to the destruction of the family. Empirical assessments refute these contentions (Stone, 1984).[30] By the early 1980s, domestic violence legislation was enacted in most states (Morash, 1986). Included was a variety of programs or remedies: civil protection orders were established to provide effective procedures to ensure victim safety;[31] legal advocacy and job-training programs designed to empower women became readily accessible in shelters. However, not all of these options have been successful. Grau, Fagan, & Wexler (1984) report that restraining orders designed to provide civil court alternatives to formal sanctions are largely ineffective. Based on 270 victim interviews in four states, they argue that civil protection orders do little to prevent or reduce future violence, and the potential helpfulness of these orders is limited by implementation problems (e.g., long waiting periods and little or no protection offered to cohabitators or unmarried persons), circumvention by police officers who fail to enforce the orders, and an overall lack of coordination and integration of civil and criminal remedies (Grau et al.,1984). Harrell and Smith (1996), A. Klein (1996), and others have reported that although civil restraining orders were ineffective in protecting victims from future violence, they served an important symbolic feature. These conclusions are particularly important given Harrell and Smith's (1996) finding that the majority of women who seek restraining orders were victims or more seriously abused by their partners. In addition, researchers found that the potential helpfulness of these orders was hampered by the cumbersome process of obtaining a permanent restraining order, low arrest rates, and the lack of vigorous prosecution and significant sanctioning of offenders (Klein, 1996).

More recently, attention has shifted toward the relationship dynamics of battering, concentrating on providing treatment for offenders.[32] Many of these intervention or treatment efforts apply a feminist, antisexist, psychotherapeutic approach that challenges male batterers to examine traditional gender-role socialization, responses, and practices (see, e.g., Adams, 1989). Evaluations of counseling programs indicate much variability in recidivism rates, often as low as 2 percent in programs in which batterers were eager to participate (Dutton, 1987) to as high as 39 percent (Gondolf, 1984). Some of this variability is attributed to small sample sizes and different measures of recidivism. Deterrence may be most effective when both social *and* legal penalties are utilized (Fagan, 1989). For instance, one study that followed batterers who were arrested and participated in court-mandated counseling demonstrated low recidivism rates (as measured by wives' reports) after thirty months (Dutton, 1986b). Gondolf (1998) examined batterer treatment programs of varying interventions and lengths, and concluded that shorter programs may be just as effective as longer, more intensive programs. His research used a fifteen-month follow-up period, and he argues for the use of much longer follow-ups to determine the impact of programs.

Police policy changes cannot exist in a vacuum. Arrest is only the initial step in the criminal justice system continuum and can easily be circumvented by unresponsiveness from other key players in the system (Dutton, Hart, Kennedy, & Williams, 1996; Elliott, 1989). There has been some demonstrated success in reducing battering through innovative programming that provides a combination of services, including policies that involve the prosecutor taking responsibility for initiating prosecution and not the victim [see Lerman (1981, 1982, 1986) for a comprehensive review of these types of programs]. Fostering links between the criminal justice system and social service agencies might be helpful, especially for women with limited opportunities to explore other alternatives (see Hirschel et al., 1992a, 1992b). Mandated counseling programs may provide this link; they would add another official component, besides the arrest itself, to the increasing societal and institutional recognition that woman battering is an act of criminal proportions. It has been suggested that a collaboration of legal sanctions and social services, such as court-mandated counseling, generally tends to complement each other and correct power imbalances between victims and offenders, rather than being coercive (Dutton, 1986a; Miller & Wellford, 1997).[33] Third-party mediation programs are also being used as a method to formally mediate interpersonal disputes with the assistance of a trained mediator who strives to develop a way to solve disputes nonviolently.[34] Prosecutors' offices have introduced pretrial mediation programs as an alternative to formal criminal processing. The idea behind mediation is to informally educate both the victim and the offender about more effective methods for resolving conflict and to inform both parties about their legal rights. Some preliminary evaluations of mediation programs indicate they offer similar reductions in recidivism as more formal case processing (Bethel & Singer, 1981–1982). However, mediation programs have been criticized for their failure to assign blame, and for allowing violence to be seen as part of a dysfunctional family rather than as violence directed against women (Lerman, 1984).

Many prosecutors' offices have adopted a "pro-prosecution" policy to augment pro-arrest, which entails aggressive prosecution of domestic violence cases, even without victim cooperation, and the enhanced use of civil protection orders (Rebovich, 1996). However, prosecutors feel that protection orders are not very effective and that violators receive minimal punishment (Rebovich, 1996). Prosecutors' offices are very supportive of domestic violence diversion programs, offender counseling programs, and victim advocacy programs (Rebovich, 1996). Research in Indianapolis, however, found that court-mandated counseling as a condition of either probation or diversion was no more effective in reducing recidivism than was prosecution with conviction using presumptive sentencing (Ford & Regoli, 1992).

Despite training, it is still very rare for police to refer battered women to outside agencies (Donlon, Hendricks, & Meagher, 1986; Loving, 1980). Consistent police training for handling domestic violence cases, proper control over training course content, and funding support for this training are virtually nonexistent (Buzawa & Buzawa, 1990). Other research indicates that policy changes exert little influence over officer beliefs and practices: Ferraro (1989a) found that most of the male officers disliked the presumptive arrest policy enacted in Phoenix, Arizona, with most of the female officers feeling similarly. For women who perceive the consequences of arrest to represent a greater hardship than the actual physical battering itself, some intermediate interventions will be necessary. Otherwise, the possibility exists of women being left without effective remedies after the failure of official ones. Cromack (1996) asserts that interagency cooperation is necessary to deal effectively with domestic violence; for instance, some police trainings use role-playing exercises while civilian volunteers act as peer advocates (FBI Law Enforcement Bulletin, 1997). Interagency effectiveness rests on the police officers' commitment to arrest batterers. For instance, recent research indicated that in Florida, under a pro-arrest policy, offenders' presence at the scene increased the likelihood of arrest (44 percent when offender was present; 8 percent when offender was absent) (Feder, 1996).

Another fruitful avenue to explore involves the procedure of arrest itself. Paternoster, Brame, Bachman, & Sherman (1997) found that when police acted fairly, the rate of rearrest for domestic violence was significantly lower, regardless of the outcome. McCord (1992) calls for examining the sequentialization of domestic violence when an offender leaves a current violent situation and begins with a new target. She also believes that researchers have overlooked important victim characteristics, such as education, occupation, and family or emotional resources, that may affect relationship durability following interventions or arrests (McCord, 1992, p. 233).

It seems clear that to devise ways to deter domestic violence, policies, experiments, and ideas need to include studies that encompass victim characteristics, displacement concerns, interagency and coordinated community responses, treatment programs, and issues of procedural justice.

CONCLUSIONS

Mandatory arrest policies or laws may exacerbate an already difficult problem, despite good intentions or conventional wisdom. Given the inconsistent research findings and the negligible deterrence effects found in the policy evaluation research, it appears that many battered women will not benefit from mandatory arrest policies and that these policies might be particularly detrimental for battered women of color and/or women from lower-socioeconomic groups. Given these findings, expansion of state authority to intrude into peoples' lives may be unwarranted in the area of domestic violence unless a victim specifically requests such action. Efforts to improve police responses must be embedded within the context of emerging knowledge of the range of intimate violence remedies and the entire criminal justice system. Otherwise, operational changes that dictate police response to battering incidents will remain largely fractured, rhetorical, and ineffective.

ACKNOWLEDGMENT

Special thanks to Cassandra Rousonelos for her research assistance and Michelle L. Meloy for her helpful comments regarding an earlier draft of this chapter.

NOTES

1. Although methodologies vary, incidence rates of woman battering range from 16 percent using nationally representative household surveys (Straus, Geller, & Steinmetz, 1980) to 50 percent based on victimization surveys and interviews (Freize, Knoble, Washburn, & Zomnir, 1980; Russell, 1982; Walker, 1979). According to national household survey data, these percentages suggest that 1.5 million women are battered each year (Straus & Gelles, 1986; Straus, Gelles, & Steinmetz, 1980) while victimization data from the *National Crime Survey* provide estimates that 2.1 million women are battered annually, with violence recurring in 32 percent of the cases within six months of reporting (Langan & Innes 1986).

2. Although this chapter is focused explicitly on heterosexual violence perpetrated by men against women, there are other studies that explore similar issues for different samples [see Lobel (1986) and Renzetti (1987) for research on battered lesbians; see McLeod (1984) and Island and Letellier (1991) for discussions about battered heterosexual men and battered gay men, respectively]. Samples of battered lesbians or battered men, although different, share some commonalities, such as reasons that would inhibit victims' disclosure of violence. Both battered men and battered lesbians may fear social stigmatization; this fear compounds disclosure issues and isolation. For battered lesbians and gay men, reporting may be particularly risky, especially if their relationships are not socially

desirable or institutionally sanctioned. Additionally, traditional sources of help that are available for victims, such as shelters and laws, have been designed primarily to benefit women engaged in heterosexual relationships.

3. More thorough reviews of police responses to women battering are available elsewhere (see Buzawa & Buzawa, 1992, 1996; Elliott, 1989; Hirschel et al., 1992).

4. For instance, a study in Kansas City (Missouri) revealed that in 85 percent of domestic assault or homicide incidents, police were called in at least once before, and police had been called in at least five times before in 50 percent of these cases (Police Foundation, 1977).

5. For instance, see Ellis (1984), Field and Field (1973), Klein (1981), Kuhl and Saltzman (1985), Laszlo and McKean (1978), Lerman (1981), Lerman and Livingston (1983), Parnas (1970), Paterson (1979), Stanko (1982), Truninger (1971), and Vera Institute of Justice (1977).

6. However, see Smith's (1987) analysis of interpersonal violence that found particular extra-legal factors, such as race, gender, victim's preference, economic status of neighborhood, and demeanor of combatants toward officer, influenced police arrest decisions.

7. For more details on litigation by battered women, see Moore (1985) and Eppler (1986).

8. However, an alternative interpretation challenging Pastoor's empowerment hypothesis has been raised by MacKinnon (1983). Essentially, she argues that police intervention increases dependency on the state by battered women. Additionally, MacKinnon argues that manipulating police responses fails to "address...the conditions that produce men who systematically express themselves violently toward women, women whose resistance is disabled, and the role of the state in this dynamic (MacKinnon, 1983, p. 643). See also Rifkin (1980) for a discussion of the limitations of what the law can accomplish since it remains embedded in patriarchal foundations that do not challenge sexual stratification in society.

9. Buel (1988, p. 224) contends that officers disproportionately arrest batterers who are men of color and/or from the lower-socioeconomic classes; mandatory arrest would restructure this traditional police response.

10. The Minneapolis Domestic Violence Experiment randomly assigned police officers to deliver one of three possible responses to misdemeanant domestic assaults: mediation, separation, or arrest. Using a six-month follow up period, both victim reports and police reports indicate that arrest deterred offenders significantly more than did the alternative interventions (Sherman & Berk, 1984).

11. At least one effort to replicate this finding in a nonexperimental setting has been successful (see Berk & Newton, 1985).

12. However, a reexamination of the mandatory arrest policy enacted in Minneapolis revealed that despite the policy, out of 24,948 domestic assault calls in 1986, less than 3635 resulted in arrest; instead of arrest, officers used mediation techniques to dispense with cases (Balos & Trotzky, 1988; see also Buzawa & Buzawa, 1996; L. W. Sherman 1993).

13. Buzawa's (1982) position stems from an examination of aggregate domestic-assault arrest data from Detroit after an aggressive arrest policy went into effect. Considerably fewer calls for police assistance were made by victims after the policy was in place. This effect of victim deterrence may be more magnified in jurisdictions that have mandatory arrest policies because victims would have even less power to state their preference (Buzawa, 1982).

14. One way of assessing this hypothesis is to keep track of calls to domestic violence hot lines or shelters to see if these more informal responses increase after mandatory arrest policies go into effect. This would seem to indicate that battered women still desire help, but not in terms of official intervention. This issue might be even more complicated for some battered women (e.g., women of color or from lower-socioeconomic groups). This is addressed later in the chapter.

15. However, it is not always feasible to stall policy decisions while awaiting for results of repli-
     cation studies, in light of public sentiment and political pressures (see Sherman & Cohn,
     1989).

16. As of 1990, thirteen states had enacted mandatory arrest policies for domestic violence
     offenders (the application of arrest varies, depending on if the offense is a felony or misde-
     meanor, whether or not the crime is a first offense, for violation of restraining order, if victim
     is in danger, and for primary aggressor only) (Buzawa & Buzawa, 1992).

17. In fact, the police filed a report in only 16.4 percent of the incidents, arrests were made if the
     victim had broken bones or was taken to the hospital for her injuries, and only 27.2 percent of
     the abusers were arrested when they had threatened or attacked their partner with weapons
     (e.g., knives or guns), even if the weapon was visible to the police. "When the incident
     included an attack on a child, arrests were made only 11 percent of the time. However, when
     the incident included damage to the victim's car, the police made arrests in 25 percent of the
     cases....The single factor most highly correlated with whether an arrest is made is *whether
     the abuser insulted the police officer*. The arrest rate for such incidents was 32 percent."
     (Baker et al., 1989, pp. 2–3; emphasis is original).

18. The National Institute of Justice was the original funding source for the Minneapolis
     Domestic Violence Experiment (Sherman & Berk, 1984)

19. The replication sites were Dade County, Florida; Atlanta, Georgia; Charlotte, North Carolina;
     Milwaukee, Wisconsin; and Colorado Springs, Colorado.

20. Mandatory arrest limits police officer discretion while dictating arrest action; presumptive
     arrest is designed to strongly guide police officer discretion in the direction of arrest.

21. Follow-up interviews were also conducted after twelve months, but these findings are not
     reported in their 1990 article.

22. Moreover, Dunford et al. (1990, p. 204) also report that victim-based measures of repeat vio-
     lence indicated that victims who called the police were not placed in great danger of being the
     recipient of subsequent violence: "What the police did in Omaha after responding to cases of
     misdemeanor domestic assault (arrest, separate, mediate) neither helped nor hurt victims in
     terms of subsequent conflict."

23. On this point, Buzawa and Buzawa (1990, p. 103) suggest that "a mandatory-arrest policy
     merely appears to make victims and assailants pawns to larger policy goals formulated by
     administrative and well-meaning 'victim advocates,' whose goals may not be shared.
     Despite her emotional involvement and trauma, the victim is usually in a better position
     than patrol officers to determine the likely impact of an offender's arrest." It is likely that
     this consideration is magnified for certain groups of battered women, discussed under the
     next heading.

24. Buzawa and Buzawa (1990) acknowledge that adding "primary aggressor" clarifications to
     the statutes may eliminate this problem, but in doing so, police discretion would increase.

25. Supplemental approaches to exploring the ramifications of new policies have been suggested,
     entailing renewal of the dialogue between practitioners, battered women, and academics, and
     expanding present research designs and methodologies [see Miller (1989) for a more com-
     plete discussion].

26. There are some exceptions in research on battered women where differences in culture and
     their relationship to battering have been addressed: see Asbury (1987), Coley and Beckett
     (1988), and Lockhart (1985, 1987) for research concerning black women, Scarf (1983) on
     battered Jewish women, and Carroll (1980) for a comparison of battered Mexican-
     American and Jewish families; Lobel (1986) and Renzetti (1987) on battered lesbians;
     Feinman (1987) on battered Latino women; and "Response to wife abuse" (1985) on bat-
     tered women in New Zealand.

27. In the same vein, Tong (1984) contends that black women especially may question arrest policies with regard to the treatment of black men, based on other experiences with the law; for example, black rapists historically have received harsher treatment than white rapists (A. Y. Davis, 1981; Wolfgang & Riedel, 1975).

28. There exists even more of a split in the discourse between feminist analysis and more mainstream analysis regarding the issue of class differences in intimate-violence victimizations. Several researchers refuse to even raise the issue, positing that the question is inherently sexist and a form of victim blaming because of its assumption that victimization can be avoided if only one changed the victim's personal characteristics (see Dobash & Dobash, 1979; Stark et al., 1979; Wardell, Gillespie, & Leffler, 1983; N. J. Davis, Hatch, Griffin, & Thompson, 1987). However, see Breines and Gordon (1983) for an opposing—and more courageous—position.

29. According to 1990 census population counts for the District of Columbia, the racial distribution is 26.6 percent white, 65.8 percent black, and 4.6 percent other (American Indian, Eskimo or Aleut, Asian or Pacific Islander, and combined other races) (U.S. Department of Commerce, Bureau of the Census, 1991).

30. Stone (1984) conducted interviews of shelter residents to determine if shelters can be blamed for dissolving marriages. This research is important, given the recent pro-family criticisms that shelters persuade battered women to leave their spouse and family. Stone (1984) found that women who had made the decision to file for a divorce had decided prior to going to the shelter. Overwhelmingly, the battered women interviewed indicated that the shelter provided an opportunity to feel safe and protected while recovering from physical and emotional trauma, and a place where they could think and make rational decisions about their futures.

31. Since 1976, thirty-one states have enacted some form of civil protection order for battered women (Grau, 1982).

32. See Saunders and Azar (1989) for a review of treatment programs for family violence in general.

33. Similar to the research concerns raised by pro-arrest policies, research would need to be conducted with mandated counseling programs to discern any inherent class or race biases (see, generally, Marsella & Pedersen, 1981). Self-help style books that employ a multicultural perspective and are written by women from similar backgrounds which are designed to assist minority battered women may also benefit practitioners and policymakers, who may not understand the role that racism and racist stereotypes may play or the value of support systems within different cultural communities [for good examples of this, see White (1985) and Zambrano (1985)].

34. See Ray (1982) for a thorough review of such mediation programs.

REFERENCES

ADAMS, D. (1989). Stages of anti-sexist awareness and change for men who batter. In L. J. Dickstein & C. C. Nadelson (Eds.), *Family violence: Emerging issues of a national crisis* (pp. 63–97). Washington, DC: American Psychiatric Press.

ASBURY, J. (1987). African-American women in violent relationships: An exploration of cultural difference. In R. L. Hampton (Ed.), *Violence in the black family*. Lexington, MA: Lexington Books.

BAKER, K., CAHN, N., & SANDS, S. J. (1989). *Report on District of Columbia police response to domestic violence*. Washington, DC: D.C. Coalition against Domestic Violence and the Women's Law and Public Policy, Georgetown University Law Center.

BALOS, B., & TROTZKY, I. (1988). Enforcement of the domestic abuse act in Minnesota: A preliminary study. *Law and Inequality, 6*, pp. 83–125.

BELL, D. J. (1984). The police response to domestic violence: An exploratory study. *Police Studies, 3*, 23–30.

BERK, R. A., CAMPBELL, A., KLAP, R., & WESTERN, B. (1992a). Bayesian analysis of the Colorado Springs spouse abuse experiment. *Journal of Criminal Law and Criminology, 83*, 170–200.

BERK, R. A., CAMPBELL, A., KLAP, R., & WESTERN, B. (1992b). The deterrent effect of arrest incidents of domestic violence: A Bayesian analysis of four field experiments, *American Sociological Review, 57*, 698–708.

BERK, R. A., & NEWTON, P. J. (1985). Does arrest really deter wife battery? An effort to replicate the findings of the Minneapolis spouse abuse experiment. *American Sociological Review, 50*, 253–262.

BETHEL, C. A., & SINGER, L. R. (1981–1982). Mediation: A new remedy for causes of domestic violence. *Vermont Law Review, 6*(2) and *7*(1).

BINDER, A., & MEEKER, J. W. (1988). Experiments as reforms. *Journal of Criminal Justice, 16*, 347–358.

BINDER, A. & MEEKER, J. W. (1996). Arrest as a method to control spouse abuse. In E. S. Buzawa & C. G. Buzawa (Eds.). *Domestic violence: The criminal justice response* (pp. 129–140). Thousand Oaks, CA: Sage Publicatons.

BLOCK, R. (1974). Why notify the police: The victim's decision to notify the police of an assault. *Criminology, 11*, 555–569.

BOWKER, L. H. (1982). Police service to battered women: Bad or not so bad?" *Criminal Justice and Behavior, 9*, 476–486.

BREINES, W., & GORDON, L. (1983). The new scholarship on family violence. *Signs: Journal of Women in Culture and Society, 8*,(3), 490–531.

BUEL, S. M. (1988). Recent developments: Mandatory arrest for domestic violence. *Harvard Women's Law Journal, 11*, 213–226.

BUZAWA, E. S. (1982). "Police officer response to domestic violence legislation in Michigan. *Journal of Police Science and Administration, 10*(4), 415–424.

BUZAWA, E. S., & BUZAWA, C. G. (EDS.). (1990). *Domestic violence: The criminal justice response*. Westport, CT: Greenwood Press.

BUZAWA, E. S., & BUZAWA, C. G. (EDS.). (1992). *Domestic violence: The changing criminal justice response*. Westport, CT: Greenwood Press.

BUZAWA, E. S. & BUZAWA, C. G. (EDS.). (1996). *Domestic violence: The criminal justice response* (2nd ed.) Thousand Oaks, CA: Sage Publications.

CARROLL, J. C. (1980). A cultural-consistency theory of family violence in Mexican American and Jewish-ethnic groups. In M. A. Straus & G. T. Hotaling (Eds.), *The social causes of husband–wife violence* (pp. 68–81). Minneapolis, MN: University of Minnesota Press.

COHN, E. G., & SHERMAN, L. W. (1986). Police policy on domestic violence, 1986: A national survey. *Crime Control Reports*, no. 5. Washington, DC: Crime Control Institute.

COLEY, S. M., & BECKETT, J. O. (1988). Black battered women: A review of empirical literature. *Journal of Counseling and Development, 66*, 266–270.

CROMACK, V. (1996). The policing of domestic violence: An empirical study. *Policy and society, 5*, 185–199.

DAVIS, A. Y. (1981). *Women, race and class*. New York: Random House.

DAVIS, N. J., HATCH, A. J., GRIFFIN, C., & THOMPSON, K. (1987). Violence against women in the home: A continued mandate of control. *Violence, Aggression and Terrorism, 1*(3), 241–276.

DEFINA, M. P., & WETHERBEE, L. (1997, October). Advocacy and law enforcement: Partners against domestic violence. *FBI Law Enforcement Bulletin, 66*(10), 22–24.

DOBASH, R. E., & DOBASH, R. P. (1977). Love, honor and obey: Institutional ideologies and the struggle for battered women. *Contemporary Crises, 1*, 403–415.

DOBASH, R. E., & DOBASH, R. P. (1979). *Violence against wives: A case against the patriarchy.* New York: Free Press.

DONLON, R., HENDRICKS, J., & MEAGHER, M. S. (1986). Police practices and attitudes toward domestic violence. *Journal of Police Science and Administration, 14*, 187–192.

DUNFORD, F. W. (1990). System-initiated warrants for suspects of misdemeanor domestic assault: A pilot study. *Justice Quarterly, 7*, 631–653.

DUNFORD, F. W., HUIZINGA, D., & ELLIOTT, D. S. (1990). The role of arrest in domestic assault: The Omaha police experiment. *Criminology, 28*(2), 183–206.

DUTTON, D. (1986a). The outcome of court-mandated treatment for wife assault: A quasi-experimental evaluation. *Violence and Victims, 1*, 163–176.

DUTTON, D. (1986b). Wife assaulters' explanations for assault: The neutralization of self-punishment. *Canadian Journal of Behavioral Science, 8*(4), 381–390.

DUTTON, D. (1987). *The prediction of recidivism in a population of wife assaulters.* Paper presented at the 3rd International Family Violence Conference, Durham, NH.

DUTTON, D., HART, S. D., KENNEDY, L. W., & WILLIAMS, K. R. (1996). Arrest and the reduction of repeat wife assault. In E. S. Buzawa & C. G. Buzawa (Eds.), *Domestic violence: The criminal justice response* (2nd ed., pp. 111–127). Thousand Oaks, CA: Sage Publications.

EISENBERG, S. E., & MICKLOW, P. L. (1977). The assaulted wife: "Catch 22" revisited. *Women's Rights Law Reporter, 3*, 142.

ELLIOTT, D. S. (1989). Criminal justice procedures in family violence crimes. In L. Ohlin & M. Tonry (Eds.), *Family violence* (pp. 427–480). Chicago: University of Chicago Press.

ELLIS, J. W. (1984). Prosecutorial discretion to charge in cases of spousal assault: A dialogue. *Journal of Criminal Law and Criminology, 75*(1), 56–102.

EPPLER, A. (1986). Battered women and the equal protection clause: Will the constitution help them when the police won't? *Yale Law Journal, 8*, 788–809.

FAGAN, J. (1989). Cessation of family violence: Deterrence and dissuasion. In L. Ohlin & M. Tonry (Eds.)., *Family violence* (pp. 377–425). Chicago: University of Chicago Press.

FEDER, L. (1996). Police handling of domestic calls: The impact of offender's presence in the arrest decision. *Journal of Criminal Justice, 24*(6), 481–490.

FEINMAN, C. (1987). Domestic violence in Australia. Paper presented at the annual meeting of the American Society of Criminology, Montreal.

FERRARO, K. (1989a). The legal response to women battering in the United States. In J. Hamner, J. Radford, & E. Stanko (Eds.), *Women, policing, and male violence* (pp. 155–184). London: Routledge & Kegan Paul.

FERRARO, K. (1989b). Policing women battering. *Social Problems, 36*(1), 61–74.

FERRARO, K. J. (1995). Cops, courts, and woman battering. In. B. R. Price & N. J. Skoloff (Eds.), *The criminal justice system and women: Offenders, victims, and workers* (pp. 262–271). New York: McGraw Hill.

FIELD, M. H., & FIELD, H. F. (1973). Marital violence and the criminal process: Neither justice nor peace. *Social Service Review, 47*, 221–240.

FORD, D. A. (1984, August). Prosecution as a victim power resource for managing conjugal violence. Paper presented at the annual meeting of the Society for the Study of Social Problems, San Antonio, TX.

FORD, D. A., & REGOLI, M. J. (1992). The preventive impacts of policies for prosecuting wife batterers. In E. S. Buzawa & C. G. Buzawa (Eds.), *Domestic violence: The changing criminal justice response* (pp. 180–207). Westport, CT: Greenwood Press.

FRIEZE, I. H., KNOBLE, J., WASHBURN, C., & ZOMNIR, G. (1980). Types of battered women. Paper presented at the annual research conference of the Association for Women in Psychology, Santa Monica, CA.

GARNER, J., FAGAN, J., & MAXWELL, C. (1995). Published findings from the spousal assault replication program. *Journal of Quantitative Criminology, 11*, 3–28.

GELLES, R., & MEDERER, H. (1985). Comparison or control: Intervention in the cases of wife abuse. Paper presented at the annual meeting of the National Council on Family Relations, Dallas, TX.

GIL, D. G. (1986). Sociocultural aspects of domestic violence. In M. Lystad (Ed.), *Violence in the home: Interdisciplinary perspectives* (pp. 124–149). New York: Brunner/Mazel.

GONDOLF, E. W. (1984). *Men who batter: An integrated approach stopping wife abuse.* Holmes Beach, FL: Learning Publications.

GONDOLF, E. W. (1998). Do batterer programs work? A 15 month follow-up of multi-site evaluations. *Domestic Violence Reporter, 3*(5), 65–80.

GOOLKASIAN, G. A. (1986). *Confronting domestic violence: A guide for criminal justice agencies.* Washington, DC: U.S. Government Printing Office.

GRAU, J. L. (1982). Restraining order legislation for battered women: A reassessment. *University of San Francisco Law Review, 16*, 703–741.

GRAU, J., FAGAN, J., & WEXLER, S. (1984). Restraining orders for battered women: Issues of access and efficacy. *Women and Politics, 4*(3), 13–28.

HAGAN, J., & ALBONETTI, C. (1982). Race, class, and the perception of criminal injustice in America. *American Journal of Sociology, 88*(2), 329–355.

HARRELL, A., & SMITH, B. E. (1996). Effects of restraining orders on domestic violence victims. In E. S. Buzawa & C. G. Buzawa (Eds.), *Do arrests and restraining orders work?* (pp. 214–242). Thousand Oaks, CA: Sage Publications.

HEARING ON VIOLENCE PREVENTION ACT. (1978, March 17). Formal Testimony, Harriet Tubman Woman's Shelter presented by Kenyari Bellfield in U.S. Congress, House Subcommittee on Select Education of the Committee on Education and Labor, *Domestic Violence: Hearing on H.R. 7297 and H.R. 8498*, 95th Congress, 2nd session.

HINDELANG, M. J. (1976). *Criminal victimization in eight American cities: A descriptive analysis of common theft and assault.* Cambridge, MA: Ballinger.

HIRSCHEL, J. D., HUTCHINSON, I. W., III, & DEAN, C. W. (1992a). The failure of arrest to deter spouse abuse. *Journal of Research in Crime & Delinquency, 29*, 7–33.

HIRSCHEL, J. D., HUTCHINSON, I. W., III, & DEAN, C. W. (1992b). Female spouse abuse and the police response: The Charlotte, North Carolina experiment. *Journal of Criminal Law and Criminology, 83*, 73–119.

INTERNATIONAL ASSOCIATION OF CHIEFS OF POLICE (1967). *Training key 16: Handling disturbance calls.* Gaithersberg, MD: IACD.

ISLAND, D., & LETELLIER, P. (1991). *Men who beat the men who love them: Battered gay men and domestic violence.* New York: Harrington Park Press.

JAFFE, P., WOLFE, D. A., TELFORD, A., & AUSTIN, G. (1986). The impact of police charges in incidents of wife abuse. *Journal of Family Violence, 1*, 37–49.

KARMEN, A. (1982). Women as crime victims: Problems and solutions. In B. R. Price & N. J. Sokoloff (Eds.), *The criminal justice system and women* (pp. 185–201). New York: Clark Boardman.

KLEIN, A. (1996). Re-abuse in a population of court-restrained male batterers: Why restraining orders don't work. In E. S. Buzawa & C. G. Buzawa (Eds.), *Do arrests and restraining orders work?* (pp. 192–213). Thousand Oaks, CA: Sage.

KLEIN, D. (1981). Violence against women: Some considerations regarding its causes and its elimination. *Crime and Delinquency, 27*(1), 64–80.

KUHL, A., & SALTZMAN, L. E. (1985). Battered women in the criminal justice system. In I. L. Moyer (Ed.), *The changing role of women in the criminal justice system* (pp. 180–196). Prospect Heights, IL: Waveland Press.

LANG, P. (1986, July 21). How to stop crime the brainy way. *U.S. News and World Report*, pp. 55–56.

LANGAN, P. A., & INNES, C. A. (1986). *Preventing domestic violence against women* [Special report]. Washington, DC: U.S. Department of Justice, Bureau of Justice Statistics.

LASZLO, A. T., & MCKEAN, T. (1978). Court decision: An alternative for spousal abuse cases. In *Battered women: Issues of public policy* (pp. 327–356). Washington, DC: U.S. Commission for Civil Rights.

LAWRENZ, F., LEMBO, J. F., & SCHADE, T. (1988). Times series analysis of the effect of a domestic violence directive on the numbers of arrests per day. *Journal of Criminal Justice, 16*, 493–498.

LEMPERT, R. (1984). From the editor. *Law and Society Review, 18*(4), 505–513.

LERMAN, L. (1981). Criminal prosecution of wife beaters. *Response, 4*(3), 1–19.

LERMAN, L. (1982, May–June). Court decisions on wife abuse laws: Recent developments. *Response.*

LERMAN, L. (1984). Mediation of wife abuse cases: The adverse impact of informal dispute resolution of women. *Harvard Women's Law Journal, 7*, 65–67.

LERMAN, L. (1986). Prosecution of wife beaters: Institutional obstacles and innovations. In M. Lystad (Ed.), *Violence in the home: Interdisciplinary perspectives* (pp. 250–295). New York: Brunner/Mazel.

LERMAN, L., & LIVINGSTON, F. (1983). State legislation on domestic violence. *Response, 6*, 1–28.

LOBEL, K. (1986). *Naming the violence: Speaking out against lesbian battering*. Seattle, WA: Seal Press.

LOCKHART, L. L. (1985). Methodological issues in comparative racial analyses: The case of wife abuse. *Social Work and Abstracts, 21*, 35–41.

LOCKHART, L. L. (1987). A reexamination of the effects of race and social class on the incidence of marital violence: A search for reliable differences. *Journal of Marriage and the Family, 49*(3), 603–610.

LOVING, N. (1980). *Responding to spouse abuse and wife beating: A guide for police*. Washington, DC: Police Executive Research Forum.

MACKINNON, C. (1983). Feminism, marxism, method, and the state: Toward a feminist jurisprudence. *Signs: Journal of Women in Culture and Society, 8*, 635.

MARSELLA, A., & PEDERSEN, P. (1981). *Cross cultural counseling and psychotherapy: Foundations, evolutions, and cultural considerations*. Elmsford, NY: Pergamon Press.

MARTIN, D. (1978). Overview: Scope of the problem. In *Battered Women: Issues of Public Policy*. Washington, DC: U.S. Commission for Civil Rights.

MCCORD, J. (1992). Deterrence of domestic violence: A critical review of research. *Journal of Research in Crime and Delinquency, 29*(2), 229–239.

MCLEOD, M. (1984). Women against men: An examination of domestic violence based on an analysis of official data and national victimization data. *Justice Quarterly, 2*, pp. 171–193.

MIGNON, S. I., & HOLMES, W. M. (1995). Police response to mandatory arrest laws. *Crime and Delinquency, 41*(4), 430–442.

MILLER, S. L. (1989). Unintended side effects of pro-arrest policies and their race and class implications for battered women: A cautionary note. *Criminal Justice Policy Review, 3*(3), 299–316.

MILLER, S. L., & WELLFORD, C. F. (1997). Patterns and correlates of interpersonal violence. In A. P. Cardavelli (Ed.), *Violence between intimates: Patterns, causes, and effects* (pp. 16–28). Boston: Allyn & Bacon.

MOORE, T. (1985). Landmark court decisions for battered women. *Response, 8*(5).

MORASH, M. (1986, June). Wife battering. *Criminal Justice Abstracts*, pp. 252–271.

NATIONAL CRIMINAL JUSTICE ASSOCIATION (1985). Domestic violence arrests deter batterers. Police Agencies Report. *Justice Bulletin, 5*(3).

OKUM, L. (1986). *Women abuse: Facts replace myths*. Albany, NY: State University of New York Press.

OLIVERO, A. (1987, November 16). Connecticut's new family violence law may be one of the toughest—But is it tough enough? *Hartford Advocate*, p. 6.

OVERBY, A. (1971). Discrimination against minority groups. In L. Radzinowicz & M. E. Wolfgang (Eds.), *The criminal in the arms of the law* (pp. 569–581). New York: Basic Books.

PARNAS, R. E. (1967). The police response to the domestic disturbance. *Wisconsin Law Review, 31*, 914–960.

PARNAS, R. E. (1970). The judicial response to intra-family violence. *Minnesota Law Review, 54*, 585–645.

PASTOOR, M. K. (1984). Police training and the effectiveness of Minnesota "Domestic Abuse" Laws, *Law and Inequality, 2*, 557–607.

PATE, A., HAMILTON, E. E., & ANNAN, S. (1991). *Metro-Dade spousal abuse replication project draft final report*. Washington, DC: Police Foundation.

PATERNOSTER, R., BRAME, R., BACHMAN, R., & SHERMAN, L. W. (1997). Do fair procedures matter: The effect of procedural justice on spouse assault. *Law and Society Review, 31*(1), 163–204.

PATERSON, E. J. (1997). How the legal system responds to battered women. In D. M. Moore (Ed.), *Battered women* (pp. 79–100). Beverly Hills, CA: Sage.

POLICE FOUNDATION. (1977). *Domestic violence and the police: Studies in Detroit and Kansas City*, p. 9. Washington, DC: The foundation.

PRESCOTT, S., & LETKO, C. (1977). Battered: A social psychological perspective. In M. M. Roy (Ed.), *Battered women: A psychosociological study of domestic violence* (pp. 72–96). New York: Van Nostrand Reinhold.

RASCHE, C. E. (1995). Minority women and domestic violence: The unique dilemmas of battered women of color. In B. R. Price & N. J. Sokoloff (Eds.), *The criminal justice system and women* (pp. 246–261). New York: McGraw-Hill.

RAY, L. (1982). *Alternative means of family dispute resolution*. Washington, DC: Author.

REBOVICH, D. J. (1996). Prosecutorial responses to domestic violence: Results of a survey of large jurisdictions. In E. S. Buzawa & C. G. Buzawa (Eds.), *Do arrests and restraining orders work?* (pp. 176–191). Thousand Oaks, CA: Sage Publications.

REISS, A. J., JR. (1985). Some failures in designing data collection that distort results. In L. Burstein, H. E. Freeman, & P. H. Rossi (Eds.), *Collecting evaluation data: Problems and solutions*. Beverly Hills, CA: Sage Publications.

RENZETTI, C. (1987). Building a second closet: Official responses to victims of lesbian battering. Paper presented at the annual meeting of the Academy of Criminal Justice Sciences, San Francisco.

Response to wife abuse in four western countries. (1985). *Response to Violence on the Family and Sexual Assault, 8*(2), 15–18.

RIFKIN, J. (1980). Toward a theory of law and patriarchy. *Harvard Women's Law Journal, 3*, 83.

ROSSI, P., BERK, R. A., & EDISON, B. (1974). *The roots of urban discontent*. New York: Wiley.

RUSSELL, D. E. H. (1982). *Rape in marriage*. New York: Macmillian.

SAUNDERS, D. G., & AZAR, S. T. (1989). Treatment programs for family violence. In L. Ohlin & M. Tonry (Eds.), *Family violence* (pp. 481–546). Chicago: University of Chicago Press.

SCARF, M. (1983). Marriages made in heaven? Battered Jewish wives. In S. Heschel (Ed.), *On being a Jewish feminist*. New York: Schocken Books.

SCHECHTER, S. (1982). *Women and male violence: The visions and struggles of the battered women's movement.* Boston: South End Press.

SCHWARTZ, M. D. (1988). Ain't got no class: Universal risk theories of battering. *Contemporary Crisis, 12,* 373–392.

SHERMAN, L. W. (1992). *Policing domestic violence: Experiments and dilemmas.* New York: Free Press.

SHERMAN, L. & BERK, R. (1984). The specific effects of arrest for domestic assault. *American Sociological Review, 49,* 261–272.

SHERMAN, L. & COHN, E. G. (1989). The impact of research on legal policy: The Minneapolis domestic violence experiment. *Law and Society Review, 23*(1), 117–144.

SHERMAN, L. W., SCHMIDT, J. D., ROGAN, D. P., GARTIN, P. R., COHN, E. G., COLLINS, D., & BACICH, A. R. (1991). From initial deterrence to long term escalation: Short custody arrest for poverty ghetto domestic violence. *Criminology, 29,* 821–850.

SHERMAN, L. W., SCHMIDT, J. D., ROGAN, D. P., SMITH, D. A., GARTIN, P. R., COHN, E. G., COLLINS, D. J., & BACICH, A. R. (1992). The variable effects of arrest on criminal careers: The Milwaukee domestic violence experiment. *Journal of Criminal Law and Criminology, 83.*

SHERMAN, L. W., SMITH, D. A., SCHMIDT, J. D., & ROGAN, D. P. (1991). *Ghetto poverty, crime and punishment: Legal and informal control of domestic violence.* Washington, DC: Crime Control Institute.

SMITH, D. A. (1987). Police responses to interpersonal violence: Defining the parameters of legal control. *Social Forces, 65*(3) 767–782.

STANKO, E. A. (1982). Would you believe this woman: Prosecutorial screening for "credible" witnesses and a problem of justice. In N. H. Rafter & E. A. Stanko (Eds.), *Judge, lawyer, victim, thief: Women, gender roles and criminal justice* (pp. 63–82). Boston: Northeastern University Press.

STANKO, E. A. (1985). *Intimate intrusions: Women's experience of male violence.* London: Routledge & Kegan Paul.

STARK, E., FLITCRAFT, A., & FRAZIER, W. (1979). Medicine and patriarchal violence: The social construction of a "private" event. *International Journal of Health Services, 9,* 461–493.

STONE, L. H. (1984). Shelters for battered women: A temporary escape from danger or the first step toward divorce? *Victimology, 9*(2), 284–289.

STRAUS, M. A., & GELLES, R. (1986). Societal change and change in family violence from 1975 to 1985 as revealed by two national surveys. *Journal of Marriage and the Family, 48,* 465–479.

STRAUS, M. A., GELLES, R., & STEINMETZ, S. K. (1980). *Behind closed doors: Violence in the American family.* New York: Anchor Press.

TONG, R. (1984). *Women, sex, and the law.* Totowa, NJ: Rowman & Allanheld.

TRUNINGER, E. (1971). Marital violence: The legal solution. *Hastings Law Journal, 23,* 259–173.

U.S. DEPARTMENT OF JUSTICE (1985). *Replicating an experiment in specific deterrence: Alternative police responses to spouse assault: A research solicitation.* Washington, DC: U.S. Department of Justice, National Institute of Justice.

VERA INSTITUTE OF JUSTICE. (1977). *Felony arrests: Their prosecution and disposition in New York City's court.* New York: Vera Institute of Justice.

WALKER, L. (1979). *The battered woman.* New York: Harper & Row.

WALKER, L., THYFAULT, G., & BROWNE, A.. (1982). Beyond the juror's ken: Battered women. *Vermont Law Review, 7.*

WARDELL, L., GILLESPIE, D., & LEFFLER, A. (1983). Science and violence against wives. In D. Finkelhor, R. Gelles, G. Hotaling, & M. Straus (Eds.), *The dark side of families: Current family violence research* (pp. 69–84). Beverly Hills, CA: Sage Publications.

WASHBURN, C., & FRIEZE, I. H. (1981, July). *Methodological issues in studying battered women.* Paper presented at the First National Conference for Family Violence Researchers, University of New Hampshire, Durham, NH.

WHITE, E. C. (1985). *Chain chain change: For black women dealing with physical and emotional abuse.* Seattle, WA: Seal Press.

WILLIAMS, L. (1981, January–February). Violence against women. *The Black Scholar,* pp. 18–24.

WOLFGANG, M. E., & RIEDEL, M. (1975). Rape, race and the death penalty in Georgia. *American Journal of Orthopsychiatry, 45,* 658–668.

ZAMBRANO, M. M. (1985). *Mejor sola que mal acompanada: For the Latino in an abusive relationship.* Seattle, WA: Seal Press.

20

Likelihood of an Arrest Decision for Domestic and Nondomestic Assault Calls[1]

Do Police Underenforce the Law When Responding to Domestic Violence?

Lynette Feder

Domestic violence has historically been selectively ignored by both those within as well as outside the criminal justice system. Prior to the 1980s, research contrasted these incidents to comparable nondomestic assaults and found that police typically treated domestic violence cases more leniently. More recent research, however, has focused on the police's likelihood to arrest in jurisdictions that specify mandatory or presumption in favor of arrest statutes. These studies consistently find a low rate of arrest, which, in turn, leads many to conclude that police are continuing to practice a subtle and insidious policy of nonenforcement when responding to domestic violence offenders. But an actual and current comparison of police response to domestic and nondomestic assault calls is lacking. Without a basis for comparison, one cannot assume that police are selectively underenforcing domestic violent laws.

LITERATURE REVIEW

Historical analysis indicates that wife assault has a long and honored tradition in Western civilization (Davidson, 1977; Hillberman, 1980). Under English common law, the doctrine of coverture stated that when a man and woman married, they became a single entity. Accordingly, that entity was the husband's, as the wife thereafter lost all legal standing (Dobash & Dobash; 1978; Eisenberg & Micklow, 1977). This led, quite logically, to the view that the husband had a right to control his wife. As Blackstone noted: "For, as he is to answer for her misbehaviors, the law thought it reasonable to entrust him with the power of restraining her by chastisement" (Davidson, 1977).

The husband's right to beat his wife had a more circuitous legal history in the United States. Probably because the colonists were originally dependent on women to help sustain the family, combined with the fact that they were not well versed in the ways of the English common law, Puritans deviated from this tradition (Taub, 1983). However, by the nineteenth century, Blackstone's *Commentaries of the Laws of England* gained wider influence in the United States (Davidson, 1977; Taub, 1983). The result was that some state courts explicitly recognized a husband's right to chastise his wife, while others prohibited it (Eisenberg & Micklow, 1977; Fields, 1977–1978; Stedman, 1917). Gradually, though, a judicial shift took place and by the late nineteenth century most states disallowed wife beating (Davidson, 1977; Taub, 1983). Still, even as courts rejected this right, they held that "…if no permanent injury has been inflicted, nor malice, cruelty or dangerous violence shown by the husband, it is better to draw the curtain, shut out the public gaze, and leave the parties to forget and forgive" (*State v. Oliver*, 1873). Thus, although wifebeating was illegal in most states by the late 1800s, few incidents resulted in arrest or prosecution of the offender.

Given this contradictory legal history in the United States, it can hardly be surprising that law enforcement's response showed similar ambivalence in treating cases of wife abuse seriously. Furthermore, those outside the criminal justice system showed equal disinterest on the subject of domestic violence. Yet the magnitude of the problem has long suggested that this was a subject warranting serious attention.

Government figures based on domestic violent incidents reported to the police indicate that among all female victims of murders, more than one-fourth are believed to have been slain by their husbands or boyfriends (Harlow, 1991). Furthermore, approximately 2.1 million women are beaten each year (Friedman & Shulman, 1990). However, we know that these numbers greatly undercount the true amount of spousal violence, since they rely only on incidents that come to the police's attention. One well-regarded study indicated that victim interview surveys provided higher numbers of domestic violence incidents than those reported by the police (Hirschel, Hutchinson, & Dean, 1992). But victim interviews have also been shown to undercount the true incidence of violence committed at the hands of intimates (San Jose Methods Test, 1972).

Although the numbers indicated a large problem, research was surfacing which demonstrated that police were not responding as seriously to domestic assault cases as to comparable nondomestic assault calls. Black's critical study observed police–citizen encounters in three cities in 1966 and found that the victim–offender relationship was more important than the severity of the crime in accounting for variation in police likelihood to arrest (Black, 1978). He concluded that "[w]hen an offender victimizes a social intimate the police are most apt to let the event remain a private matter…" (p. 54).

Data from another large police observational study conducted in several cities in 1977 concluded that although police were as likely to arrest domestic as nondomestic offenders, legal variables (such as severity of offense and victim's cooperation) would argue for a higher rate of arrest in domestic assault cases. Therefore, the police were practicing a policy of underenforcement when responding to these calls (Oppenlander, 1982). Another researcher analyzed this same data set and found that a variety of extralegal factors entered into the police's decision to arrest, including the gender of the victim. Specifically, where the victim was female, police were less likely to invoke the law (Smith, 1987).

In summary, most of these earlier studies observed police handling of calls and found that police were less likely to arrest in cases of domestic versus nondomestic calls, even after legal variables had been taken into account. Probably these studies provided fuel for women's groups and other concerned citizens to lobby for changes in the laws. Simultaneously, a plethora of other factors were coalescing around this issue. For instance, results from an important study, the Minneapolis experiment, indicated that arrest led to lower rates of recidivism among domestic violent offenders (Sherman & Berk, 1984).

At the same time, litigation was also leading police to respond more proactively when dealing with domestic violence. Specifically, several important lawsuits were brought against large police departments alleging denial of equal protection under the law when the police failed to respond vigorously to assaults perpetrated upon women by their husbands and boyfriends (*Bruno v. Codd*, 1976; *Scott v. Hurt*, 1976; *Thomas v. Los Angeles*, 1979). Although police responded to these lawsuits by agreeing to treat domestic assault as a crime in the future, many observers still did not see any significant changes in police's handling of these cases. A few years later, though, the courts went even further. In *Thurman v. City of Torrington* (1984), the police were held liable (for the sum of $2.3 million) for the injuries that a battered wife sustained when the police failed to respond vigorously to her requests for help.

Previously, statutes had largely neglected the problem of spousal abuse. But in response to these and many other factors, beginning in the 1980s, state legislatures began to directly address the problem of domestic violence (Lerman, Livingston & Jackson, 1983). These new statutes varied greatly, although most dealt with ways in which the government could respond to the problem more effectively. As legislators wrote laws that mandated or presumed arrest when responding to domestic assault calls, researchers followed up with investigations on the impact of these laws on police behavior. Implicitly, there was an assumption that these agencies were not treating domestic violence cases as seriously as they were comparable nondomestic assault cases. Perhaps this implicit assumption explains why these newer studies did not explicitly compare police reactions to domestic versus nondomestic assault calls.

A variety of research approaches were used to assess police response to domestic violence in these jurisdictions. Researchers directly observed the police's handling of domestic calls (Ferraro, 1989; Smith, 1987; Worden & Pollitz, 1984), surveyed police on their self-reported likelihood to arrest (Breci & Simons, 1987; Dolon, Hendricks, & Meagher, 1986; Homant & Kennedy, 1985; Saunders & Size, 1986; Waaland & Keeley, 1985; Walter, 1981), analyzed police records (Bell, 1987; Berk & Loseke, 1980–1981; Erez, 1986; Lawrenz, Lembo, & Schade, 1988), or interviewed victims of domestic violence (Balos & Trotzky, 1988; Berk, Fenstermaker & Newton, 1988; Bowker, 1984; Brown, 1984; Gondolf & McFerron, 1989; Kennedy & Homant, 1983) to determine the law's success in getting police to respond legally to domestic assault calls.

The results from these studies consistently indicated a low rate of arrest, typically between 11 and 15 percent (Bell, 1985; Blount, Yegidis, & Maheux, 1992; Buzawa, 1982; Erez, 1986). This led those working in the field to conclude that the police were engaged, either implicitly or explicity, in a process of selective nonenforcement when responding to domestic assault calls (Davis, 1983; Ferraro, 1989; Oppenlander, 1982). For instance, Lerman (1982) noted that [t]hough written law gives the appearance that protection is available through the criminal justice system [for battered wives], many court and law enforcement officials whose duty it is to enforce the laws still believe that domestic violence is a private matter—that most abuse is too trivial to warrant intervention" (p. 3). And Taub (1983) stated: "As the preceding overview indicates, domestic violence has not merely been ignored by the legal system. Rather, it has been the subject of sex-based exemptions from laws of general applicability" (p. 165).

As already noted, these studies failed to make comparisons to police's likelihood to arrest when confronting similar nondomestic assault calls. However, it is widely known in criminological circles that arrest is a highly uncommon response in most police–citizen encounters (Sherman, 1992). Evidence of illegal behavior does not result automatically and inevitably in an arrest for a wide range of offenses (Black, 1978). As Sherman et al. (1992) aptly note: "The problem with the use of these facts as evidence of discrimination against women victims of domestic violence is that they are silent about disparity. One must look at whether there is a difference of probability of arrest for domestic violence and other offenses" (p. 141)

This study seeks to address this serious omission in the research literature. Police handling of domestic assault calls will be compared to nondomestic calls with controls introduced for legal and extralegal variables. The study seeks to determine (1) the likelihood of an arrest response for domestic and nondomestic assault calls in one police jurisdiction, and (2) whether different factors account for an arrest response when police deal with these two types of calls.

RESEARCH METHODOLOGY

As if to combat police's resistance to arrest when responding to domestic assault calls in Florida, a new law was implemented as of January 1, 1992. Florida State Statute 741.29 mandated several changes, including requiring a report to be made in all cases involving domestic violence calls, whether or not an arrest was effected. Additionally, the new law directed the officer to document and justify why an arrest was not made in cases where probable cause existed. Therefore, while Florida continues to have a nonmandatory arrest policy, it is clear that the intent of the statute is to combat the resistance that laws on police handling of domestic violence were meeting in various jurisdictions within the state.

The jurisdiction out of which the study was based represents one of the largest police agencies in South Florida. The department has achieved recognition for its professionalism and has gone on record, from the very top of the hierarchy, in support of a pro-arrest law enforcement stand in the handling of domestic assault. In fact, this agency had a written pro-arrest departmental policy long before the new legislation was implemented.

This research is part of a larger study whereby police in this jurisdiction were surveyed after implementation of the new law about their likelihood to arrest when responding to domestic violence calls (Feder, 1997). Later, in an attempt to compare different research approaches used to assess police response to domestic violence, the researcher returned to this jurisdiction and requested police records for the same seventeen-day time period (Feder, 1998a, 1998b). The data from this survey come exclusively from the police records.

Research indicates that domestic calls may be handled differently from the time the call is received by the police (Oppenlander, 1982). Additionally, it is possible that police records may be little more than after-the-fact reconstructions justifying previous police responses

(Dutton, 1988). This speaks to the problem of research relying exclusively on written police records. To circumvent this potential danger, the starting point for the sampling procedure was all calls for service received by this police department.

Whenever a citizen calls for help in this jurisdiction, the call is taken through their computer-assisted dispatch system (CADS). Regardless of whether or not an officer is dispatched to the site or makes a subsequent written police report, the CADS unit makes a written record of the call, which includes cursory information about the incident. Therefore, all calls for service coming into the department, and the records some of them generated subsequently, were collected. In this way, a comparison can be made between those calls where an officer was dispatched and a written police record made, and all other calls. This then allows for the possibility that domestic calls may be subtly winnowed out at an early point in the process, which would then go unrecognized if the research began at a later point in the system.

In ongoing conversations with the dispatchers it became clear that domestic assaults might originally be classified under many different headings. Therefore, it was decided to include all incoming calls for service labeled as *disturbance, domestic, fight,* or *assault.* For purposes of this research, *domestic* is defined according to Florida law. As such, it includes incidents where the victim and offender are or have been married, cohabiting, or romantically involved. therefore, cases involving parent–child or sibling relationships would not be included under this operationalization.

Several comparisons were conducted using this research methodology. First, a comparison was made between those calls for service that received the police's attention, along with a subsequent police record (referred to as the CADS and police records group), and those calls that did not receive further investigation (referred to as CADS with no police records group). Once again, this was necessary to ensure that domestic assault calls were not being devalued by the police at an early point in the process. We hypothesize that there are no significant differences in these two groups in terms of the type of call, their priority ratings, the victim–offender relationship, estimated level of violence, and similar factors.

Next we look at the profile of domestic assault calls and compare it to nondomestic assault calls (this includes all calls for service labeled *disturbance, fight,* and *assault*). We do this when the call is first received and the only available information comes from the CADS. This process is then repeated for information that becomes available through the police's follow-up visit and subsequent report. Once again, our null hypothesis is that there are no significant differences between the two groups in terms of legal and extralegal variables as reported in the CADS or police reports.

Finally, we conduct a logistic regression equation to assess those variables that are significant in accounting for variation in police's likelihood to arrest. Since the dependent variable is dichotomous (police's decision to arrest versus not arrest), logistic regression analysis was thought to be more suitable than multiple regression (Alba, 1987; Aldrich & Nelson, 1984; Knoke & Burke, 1980). This procedure is similar to multiple regression in that it allows an examination of the individual effects of several, simultaneously considered, independent variables on the dependent variable—the probability of being arrested. Conceptually, logit analysis fits a logistic function to the data in which the dependent variable is the natural logarithm of the odds of being arrested versus all other outcomes (e.g., mediated, separated, referred, etc.). We hypothesize that the victim–offender relationship will not be significant in accounting for variation in the police's decision to arrest.

RESEARCH RESULTS

During that seventeen-day period, the police received 627 calls for service that were classified as *disturbance, assault, fight,* or *domestic assault.* Of these calls, 57 percent ($n = 356$) involved incidents where the police were dispatched and wrote subsequent reports. The information that comes from CADS is cursory and sometimes proves to be incorrect once the police arrived. Still, that was the information that the CADS unit was working with when they made their decisions to dispatch officers. Therefore, that is the information that we follow in determining whether calls that received a police visit were different from those where no officer was dispatched.

Comparison of Calls Receiving and Not Receiving Police Dispatch

As can be seen from Table 1, significant differences maintained between those calls for service that received police dispatch ($n = 356$) and those where police did not attend to the call ($n = 271$). Those that received a police visit were more likely to be calls for service that CADS had classified as an assault or domestic assault [χ^2 (3, $n = 627$) = 89.12, $p <$ 0.001]. Additionally, those where police were dispatched were more likely to be in progress when the call came into the station [χ^2 (1, $n = 627$) = 3.91, $p < 0.05$]. Although those with higher-priority ratings were more likely to incur a police visit, calls with the lowest-priority ratings also received this follow-up response [χ^2 (3, $n = 627$) = 46.32, p <0.001]. However, contrary to previous research findings (Berk & Loseke, 1980–1981; Berk et al., 1988), this jurisdiction is more likely to dispatch police when the victim placed the call for service versus when anyone other than the victim called (63 percent versus 54 percent respectively) [χ^2 (3, $n = 464$) = 26.62, p <0.001]. Additionally, those calls where police are dispatched are more likely to involve female victims [χ^3 (3, $n = 627$) = 21.71, p <0.001]. According to these data, police are also more likely to be sent to an incident where the victim–offender relationship has been classified by the dispatcher as a domestic assault [χ^2 (1, $n = 340$) = 6.05, p <0.05]. But the data also indicate that legal variables are significant in accounting for the variation in police treatment. Specifically, dispatchers are more likely to send police to calls that are determined to be more violent [χ^2 (8, $n = 539$) = 65.23, p <0.001].

Comparison of Domestic and Nondomestic Assault Calls on CADS Variables

Next we turn our attention to whether significant differences appear in the CADS variables between those determined by the dispatchers to be domestic related and those classified as other than domestic. The dispatchers classified fully 57 percent ($n = 195$) of the incoming calls for service as domestic related. And once again, there were significant differences between these two groups.

As can be seen from a cursory review of Table 2, calls classified as domestic assaults were significantly more likely to be in progress when called in [χ^2 (1, $n = 340$) = 4.76, p <0.05] and were given a higher priority rating than nondomestic assault calls [χ^2 (3, $n = 340$) = 24.85, p <0.001]. Additionally, there was a tendency for the victim to have placed the call for service in a domestic assault. In terms of victim and offender

TABLE 1   Comparison of Calls for Service with and without Police Reports[a]

	CADS with No Report (n = 271) [% (no. cases)]		CADS and Police Report (n = 356) [% (no. cases)]	
Type of call*				
Disturbance	74	(98)	26	(35)
Assault	21	(25)	79	(96)
Fight	67	(24)	33	(12)
Domestic assault	37	(124)	63	(213)
Call in progress*				
Not in progress	46	(215)	55	(258)
In progress	36	(56)	64	(98)
Priority rating*				
Highest priority	42	(79)	58	(109)
Second highest	33	(8)	67	(16)
Second lowest	72	(76)	28	(29)
Lowest priority	35	(108)	65	(202)
Who called*				
Victim	37	(109)	63	(188)
Family/friend	22	(13)	78	(47)
Neighbor	68	(38)	33	(19)
Other	52	(26)	48	(24)
Victim gender*				
Male	43	(62)	57	(83)
Female	34	(88)	66	(173)
Unknown	55	(121)	45	(100)
Offender gender*				
Male	37	(114)	63	(195)
Female	31	(22)	69	(50)
Unknown	55	(135)	45	(111)
Victim offender relationship*				
Not domestic	42	(61)	58	(84)
Domestic	29	(57)	71	(138)
Highest level of violence*				
None	65	(58)	35	(31)
Shouting	59	(66)	41	(46)
Threatened, no weapon	48	(13)	52	(14)
Property damage	37	(7)	63	(12)
Minor/moderate physical	30	(61)	71	(146)
Threatened, with weapon	13	(2)	87	(13)
Used weapon	29	(2)	71	(5)
Severe physical harm	0	(0)	100	(18)
Weapon present				
No weapon present	40	(29)	60	(44)
Weapon present	16	(5)	84	(26)

[a]No correction factors were employed in the statistical tests where the numbers in the cell sizes were small.

*Significance at the 0.05 probability level.

TABLE 2   Comparison of Domestic and Nondomestic Assault Calls on CADS Variables ($n = 340$)[a]

	Domestic Assault Calls ($n = 195$) [% (no. cases)]		Nondomestic Assault Calls ($n = 145$) [% (no. cases)]	
Call in progress*				
Not in progress	69	(134)	79	(115)
In progress	31	(61)	21	(30)
Priority rating*				
Highest	33	(64)	23	(33)
Second highest	7	(13)	4	(6)
Second lowest	6	(12)	24	(35)
Lowest	54	(106)	49	(71)
Who called*				
Victim	79	(149)	69	(87)
Family/friend	13	(24)	18	(23)
Neighbor	5	(9)	5	(6)
Other	3	(6)	9	(11)
Victim gender*				
Male	20	(38)	37	(54)
Female	73	(143)	39	(56)
Unknown	7	(14)	24	(35)
Offender gender*				
Male	73	(143)	59	(86)
Female	19	(37)	16	(23)
Unknown	8	(15)	25	(36)
Highest violence level*				
No violence	14	(17)	24	(38)
Shouting	28	(34)	15	(24)
Threatened, no weapon	8	(10)	6	(9)
Property damage	8	(9)	4	(6)
Minor/moderate physical harm	34	(41)	44	(71)
Threatened, with weapon	3	(3)	6	(9)
Used weapon	3	(3)	1	(1)
Severe physical harm	3	(3)	1	(2)
Weapon present				
No weapon present	73	(35)	68	(21)
Weapon present	27	(13)	32	(10)

[a]In the remaining cases, missing data precluded their use in subsequent analyses.

*Significance at the 0.05 probability level.

characteristics, domestic assaults were more likely to involve female victims [χ^2 (3, $n =$ 340) = 63.47, p <0.001] and male offenders [χ^2 (3, $n = 340$) = 4.12, p <0.001]. Once again, there is a significant difference in terms of violence level: In all but a few cases, domestic assaults are classified as being less violent than nondomestic assaults [χ^2 (7, $n = 280$) = 17.27, p <0.05].

Comparison of Domestic and Nondomestic Assault Calls on Police Report Variables

Victim Characteristics.   Of the 356 calls for service where an officer was dispatched and a report was made, fully 94 percent ($n = 334$) provided information in the police's report on the victim–offender relationship. Table 3 provides an overview of those classified as domestic and those recorded as nondomestic in terms of victim characteristics. Domestic assault calls are significantly more likely than nondomestic calls to involve female victims [χ^2 (1, $n = 228$) = 43.32, $p < 0.001$]. No other significant differences emerge in terms of victim's age, race, belligerence to police, or use of drugs or alcohol for domestic and nondomestic calls.

Offender Characteristics.   Table 4 indicates that there are few significant differences in terms of offender characteristics for domestic and nondomestic calls. The only differences that achieve significance is that offenders in the nondomestic groups are more likely to become physical in front of the police (although the numbers involved are very small) [χ^2 (1, $n = 226$)

TABLE 3   Comparison of Domestic and Nondomestic Assault Calls on Police Report Variables: Victim Characteristics

	Domestic Assault Calls ($n = 189$) [% (no. cases)]		Nondomestic Assault Calls ($n = 145$) [% (no. cases)]	
Victim gender*				
Male	17	(21)	58	(59)
Female	84	(106)	42	(42)
Victim age	31.4 years		31.9 years	
Victim race				
White	83	(99)	81	(69)
Black	17	(20)	19	(16)
Victim belligerent	2	(2)	0	(0)
Victim use of drugs/alcohol	3	(4)	5	(5)

*Significance at the 0.05 probability level.

= 4.01, $p < 0.05$], while those in the domestic group are more likely to be known to their victims [χ^2 (1, $n = 226$) = 19.43, $p < 0.001$]. However, there are no meaningful differences between the two groups in terms of the offender's gender, age, race, presence at the scene when police arrive, noted use of drugs or alcohol, or belligerence to the police.

Incident Characteristics.   A comparison of domestic and nondomestic calls was also investigated in terms of characteristics related to the incident. As Table 5 indicates, there are very few variables that significantly differentiate between these two groups on incident-related variables. Specifically, domestic assaults are less likely to involve a physical fight [χ^2 (1, $n = 314$) = 5.26, $p < 0.05$], and therefore not surprisingly, amount to less severe injury[2] to the victim [χ^2 (2, $n = 228$) = 8.93, $p < 0.05$]. However, the analysis did not find differences in the level of violence involved or in the time required for police arrival between the two types of incidents. Additionally, no differences appeared in terms of victim preference for arrest, police effort to contact the offender, whether the offender was contacted, and the time police required to complete the call.

TABLE 4   Comparison of Domestic and Nondomestic Assault Calls on Police Report Variables: Offender Characteristics

	Domestic Assault Calls ($n = 189$) [% (no. cases)]		Nondomestic Assault Calls ($n = 145$) [% (no. cases)]	
Offender gender				
Male	84	(107)	81	(75)
Female	16	(21)	19	(18)
Offender age	32.8 years		31.3 years	
Offender race				
White	85	(98)	78	(55)
Black	15	(17)	23	(16)
Offender present				
Offender present	52	(66)	47	(46)
Offender not present	48	(62)	53	(52)
Offender use of drugs/alcohol	9	(12)	9	(9)
Offender belligerent	6	(8)	8	(8)
Offender physical in front of police*	1	(1)	5	(5)
Offender known*				
Offender known	98	(126)	82	(80)
Offender not known	2	(2)	18	(18)

*Significance at the 0.05 probability level.

TABLE 5   Comparison of Domestic and Nondomestic Assault Calls on Police
           Report Variables: Incident Characteristics

	Domestic Assault Calls (*n* = 189) [% (no. cases)]		Nondomestic Assault Calls (*n* = 145) [% (no. cases)]	
Arrival time	10.58 minutes		11.04 minutes	
Highest level of violence				
No violence	14	(25)	8	(11)
Harassing	5	(9)	7	(9)
Shouting	22	(39)	17	(23)
Threatened, no weapon	5	(9)	5	(7)
Property damage	6	(10)	4	(5)
Physical fighting	36	(63)	42	(59)
Threatened, with weapon	6	(10)	7	(9)
Used weapon	2	(4)	2	(3)
Severe physical harm	3	(6)	9	(13)
Involves physical fight*				
No physical fight	53	(92)	40	(55)
Physical fight	47	(83)	60	(84)
Victim injuries*				
No injuries	50	(63)	46	(46)
Some injuries	47	(60)	41	(41)
Severe injuries	3	(4)	14	(14)
Victim preference				
Does not want arrest	49	(53)	41	(40)
Prefers arrest	51	(55)	59	(57)
Police effort to contact offender				
No effort	55	(39)	61	(37)
Some effort	9	(6)	13	(8)
Great effort	37	(26)	26	(16)
Offender contacted				
Not contacted	41	(53)	47	(46)
Contacted by phone	1	(1)	2	(2)
Contacted in person	58	(74)	51	(49)
Completion time	44.07 minutes		44.5 minutes	

*Significance at the 0.05 probability level.

Police Handling of Domestic and Nondomestic Assault Calls

Looking at the call's outcome indicates that domestic and nondomestic calls could not be differentiated in terms of the police disposition (e.g., did nothing, separate or mediate, refer, or arrest). However, Table 6 does show an interesting twist. Where police outcome is dichotomized into those resulting in an arrest and those with all other possible outcomes (e.g., did nothing, separate or mediate, or refer), a significant difference is seen [χ^2 (1, $n = 334$) = 5.86, $p < 0.05$). Specifically, domestic calls are almost twice as likely to result in an arrest of the offender than are nondomestic calls, although the rates of arrest are still fairly low (23 percent versus 13 percent, respectively).

Table 7 lists the independent legal and extralegal variables used in this logistic regression analysis. Examining the main effects of the independent variables reveals that offenders who were present when the police arrived at the scene, offenders whose victims preferred an arrest response from the police, offenders who had physically injured their victims, and those who were belligerent to police were significantly more likely to face an arrest response. Odds ratios are provided to simplify interpreting the logit coefficients in this analysis. The odds ratio is the ratio of the probability that offenders with one charac-teristic will be arrested to the probability that others without this characteristic will be arrested, while controlling for all other factors.

As Table 7 indicates, offender's presence at the scene when police arrive had the largest impact on police response. Persons who were present were more than nineteen times more likely to be arrested than those who were not present when police arrived at the scene, even once all other variables in the equation were controlled. Continuing to review Table 7 indicates that where the victim preferred the police to arrest, the offender

TABLE 6   Comparison of Domestic and Nondomestic Assault Calls on Police Disposition

	Domestic Assault Calls ($n = 189$) [% (no. cases)]		Nondomestic Assault Calls ($n = 145$) [% (no. cases)]	
Police disposition				
Did nothing	61	(102)	64	(72)
Separate or mediate	11	(18)	15	(17)
Refer to another agency	5	(9)	7	(8)
Arrest	23	(38)	13	(15)
Arrest outcome*				
Did not arrest	77	(151)	86	(130)
Offender arrested	23	(38)	13	(15)

*Significance at the 0.05 probability level.

TABLE 7   Logit Model Statistics Describing Main Effects of Independent
Variables on Decision to Arrest

	Logit Coefficient	S.E.	Odds Ratio
Individual Variables			
Offender belligerent*	1.829	0.943	6.23
Offender use drugs/alcohol	0.099	0.873	1.10
Offender known to victim	5.990	21.507	399.42
Victim gender	0.533	0.717	1.70
Incident-related variables			
Offender present when police arrive*	2.961	0.642	19.31
Level of violence	0.146	0.930	1.16
Victim injured*	1.853	0.815	6.38
Domestic vs. nondomestic[a]	1.066	0.641	2.90
Victim preference for arrest*	2.523	0.635	12.46

$n = 155$

chi squared = 76.691

*Significance at the 0.05 probability level.

[a]A tendency, though not significant.

was more than twelve times more likely to be arrested. In a similar fashion, those offenders who injured their victims, and those who were belligerent to the police, were each six times more likely to face an arrest.

Surprisingly, the analysis also indicates that although not significant, where the victim–offender relationship can be characterized as "domestic" (e.g., current or past marital or romantic relationship), there is a tendency for police to be more likely to arrest the offender. Specifically, offenders in domestic assaults are almost three times more likely to face an arrest response than those in equivalent nondomestic assaults.

Just as important in this analysis is what failed to achieve significance in explaining an arrest decision by the police. The logistic regression indicates that offender's use of drugs or abuse of alcohol, offender being known to the victim, and victim's gender did not significantly affect the police's decision to arrest. Finally, the level of violence did not significantly distinguish between those cases where the police resounded with an arrest and those where they disposed of the case using other than an arrest response. Although this seems surprising at first, it must be remembered that the extent of victim injuries significantly distinguished an arrest from a nonarrest response. Therefore, police seem to be gauging the outcome of the violence rather than the level of the violence displayed.

Overall, this model correctly predicts 87 percent of the arrest decision. In fact, of the inmates who were not arrested, 94 percent were predicted correctly (of those arrested, 65 percent were predicted correctly) by this model. The formula

$$R^2 = \frac{\chi^2}{n + \chi^2}$$

provides an R^2 statistic for logistic regression which is analogous to the familiar R^2 statistic of OLS regression analysis. Although extreme caution should be exercised in using this statistic (Aldrich & Nelson, 1984), calculations indicate that entering these variables simultaneously into this model accounts for fully 33 percent of the variance in the police's decision to arrest when responding to these calls.

As a check of the logistical regression, a multiple regression analysis was conducted using police response (arrest versus nonarrest) as the dependent variable and entering all the other legal and extralegal independent variables into the equation. This procedure yields a less conservative estimate than the logit model and is being used only for comparative purposes. The results indicate that the equation explains 38 percent of the variation in police's decision to arrest. Additionally, the offender's presence when the police arrive, victim preference for a police arrest, extent of victim injuries, and the offender's demeanor to the police were all associated significantly and positively with an arrest decision.

SUMMARY AND DISCUSSION OF RESULTS

We originally hypothesized that there would be no significant differences between calls where police are dispatched and those where a police officer is not sent for follow-up investigation. The results of the analysis squarely indicate that there are significant differences leading to the conclusion that these are two very different types of incidents. Specifically, calls in which police are dispatched are more likely to be determined by CADS to be domestic related, they are more likely to be in progress at the time of the call, with a higher-priority rating and with the victim having placed the call for service. There are additional factors distinguishing the two types of calls. Those that receive police follow-up are more likely to involve female victims and to be judged by the dispatchers to involve a higher level of violence.

We also found that contrary to the null hypothesis, domestic and nondomestic calls could be differentiated significantly in terms of the CADS variables. Specifically, domestic assault calls were more likely to be in progress. Perhaps this is why they received a higher-priority rating from the dispatchers despite the fact that nondomestic calls involved a higher level of violence. Finally, victims were more likely to place the call to the police in domestic calls than in nondomestic calls.

Contrary to previous research indicating that dispatchers underreport the severity of domestic assaults (Oppenlander, 1982), this study finds no proof of this occurrence. Although a skeptic could point to the fact that the rating for the level of violence was significantly lower for domestics and argue that it was due to underreporting by the dispatchers, there seems to be no substance to such a charge in light of the fact that police were dispatched to 71 percent ($n = 138$) of the domestic calls and to only 58 percent ($n = 84$) of the nondomestic calls.

Finally, we hypothesized that there would not be significant differences in terms of victim, offender, or incident characteristics between domestic and nondomestic calls that police responded to upon assignment by the dispatchers. The null hypothesis stands in terms of victim and offender characteristics, with minor exceptions. Specifically, victims of domestic assaults are more likely to be female. This finding is consistent with previous research indicating that women are much more likely to be the victims of domestic violence than are men (Dutton, 1988; Gelles, 1979; Kurz, 1991).

There was little which significantly differentiated between the two offender groups. They showed no differences in terms of the gender, age, race, drug or alcohol use, belligerence to the officer, or their presence at the scene when police arrived. However, and not surprisingly, domestic offenders were more likely to be known by their victims than were nondomestic offenders.

Additionally, many incident-related variables also failed to achieve significance. Contrary to previous research findings (Oppenlander, 1982), police demonstrated similar arrival and completion times in handling domestic and nondomestic calls. There were no significant differences in terms of the highest level of violence, as indicated on the police report or in the victim's preference for an arrest. The fact that no significant differences were shown between domestic and nondomestic assault calls in terms of victim preference for arrest is noteworthy. It is commonly held that police failure to arrest domestic violent offenders reflects, to some extent, this particular victim's ambivalence (Dutton & Levens, 1977; Sherman, 1988). However, this study indicates that victims of domestic assault were not significantly less likely to desire an arrest outcome than were nondomestic assault victims.

Police also demonstrated about the same amount of effort, and met with similar amounts of success, in contacting domestic and nondomestic assault offenders. This finding does raise a question, however. Since the offender in a domestic call was known by his victim, we might expect significantly more effort and greater success on the police's part to contact a known rather than an unknown offender. Additionally, since fear of retaliation would seem to be more of an issue for victims of domestic assault, one would hope that the police would make an even greater effort to find the offender who has fled the scene. However, although we cannot know what this finding truly means, it is possible that it represents a shortage of personnel on the police's part (and therefore an inability to follow up) rather than a policy of treating domestic offenders leniently. Obviously, further research is necessary. Finally, only two variables significantly distinguished domestic from nondomestic calls: (1) nondomestic calls were more likely to involve a physical fight, and (2) therefore more likely to involve severe injuries to the victim.

The data indicate that police are almost twice as likely to arrest when responding to a domestic call than to a nondomestic call (23 percent versus 13 percent, respectively). Two things must be noted about this rate of arrest. First, the arrest rate for domestic assault calls in this study (23 percent) is significantly higher than found in previous studies (usually between 11 percent and 15 percent). What this increase represents cannot be ascertained by these data. Second, even though higher than indicated in past research, the rates of arrest remain relatively low. However, whereas previous research indicated that an arrest outcome was atypical when police responded to domestic assault calls, this research finds that police only infrequently utilize an arrest in all cases of assault, both domestic and nondomestic.

The logistic regression indicates that four variables, all incident related, were significant in accounting for this variation in police's likelihood to arrest: offender's presence at the scene when police arrive, victim's preference for an arrest outcome, extent of victim injuries, and offender's demeanor toward police. These findings are fairly consistent with previous findings. For instance, victim's preference for an arrest outcome has been found to be a leading correlate in the police's decision to arrest (Berk & Loseke, 1980–1981; Black, 1978; Smith & Visher, 1981). Additionally, the findings that extent of victim's injuries (Gondolf & McFerron, 1989; Waaland & Keeley, 1985) and offender's demeanor toward police (Smith, 1987; Smith & Klein, 1984; Worden & Pollitz, 1984) affect an arrest likelihood had been demonstrated in other research studies.

Less usual is the impact of the variable offender's presence at the scene on the police's decision to arrest. Although this variable made an arrest nineteen times more likely even once all other variables had been controlled, with few exceptions (see, e.g., Feder, 1996; Ferraro & Pope, 1993) it has received very little attention in recent years. This contrasts with earlier studies of this variable's impact on arrest outcome (Berk & Loseke, 1980–1981; Worden & Pollitz, 1984). Although the importance of studying offender's presence in the arrest decision may at first seem self-evident, its impact is critical to bear in mind. It must be remembered that in domestic cases the offenders were always known by their victims and therefore to police. Yet this study indicates that an offender could easily escape the consequences of his illegal behavior merely by ensuring that he was not there when police arrived.

Finally, although not significant, there was a tendency for the victim–offender relationship to affect the likelihood of an arrest response. Specifically, those victim–offender relationships that involved past or current marital or romantic relationships (i.e., domestics) were associated with a higher likelihood of arrest than were nondomestic calls, even after all other variables were controlled.

Perhaps these results should not come as such a big surprise. Despite claims that the family is treated as a sacred entity (Lerman, 1981), and assertions that police and prosecutors do not want to get involved in domestic cases (Buzawa, 1982; Buzawa & Buzawa, 1985; Davis, 1983), previous research comparing police response to domestic and nondomestic calls found no statistically significant differences in the police's likelihood to arrest (Smith & Klein, 1984). Dutton, after conducting an extensive review of the research literature, concluded "…that the winnowing effect of the criminal justice system for wife assault cases does not appear to be appreciably different than for other crimes" (Dutton, 1988, p. 199). Finally, a comparison of domestic and nondomestic cases and prosecutorial likelihood to prefer charges also failed to show significant differences in the handling of these cases (Schmidt & Hochstedler-Steury, 1987).

None of this is meant to argue that the police's rate of arrest when responding to domestic violence is sufficient. Instead, this research merely indicates that it is comparable to, and even a bit higher than, the rate for nondomestic calls. This finding probably should not come as a surprise. The legislation enacted made a nonarrest response difficult when responding to domestic rather than nondomestic calls, and this police department had gone on record in support of this legislative mandate. Therefore, perhaps we should not be surprised to find a higher rate of arrest when police responded to domestic violence calls in this particular department.

Two important points must be noted about this study and its results. First, the research methodology limits the generalizability of the study's findings. Specifically, we deal here with data from one specific police agency in South Florida—a state without a presumptive arrest statute—during a seventeen-day period. The department represents a highly professional law enforcement agency that had gone on record before the legislation was passed in support of an arrest policy when responding to domestic assault calls. There is no reason to believe that this particular jurisdiction is representative of police agencies nationwide. Instead, the study is intended to be exploratory, with the hope of encouraging additional research in other jurisdictions.

Furthermore, although this research indicates that police are more likely to arrest in domestic assault cases in comparison to nondomestic assault calls, all other things being equal, it still cannot answer whether police are arresting domestic violent offenders in sufficient numbers relative to the new legislation's intent. Only the public, through their legislators, can make that decision.

NOTE

1. A shortened version was presented in an earlier article published in *Crime and Delinquency* (1998), "Police Handling of Domestic and Non-Domestic Calls: Is There a Case for Discrimination?"
2. Severe injury was operationalized in this study as an injury requiring hospitalization for any length of time.

REFERENCES

ALBA, R. (1987). Interpreting the parameters of log-linear models. *Sociological Methods and Research, 16*, 45–77.

ALDRICH, J., & NELSON, F. (1984). *Linear probability, logit, and probit models.* Beverly Hills, CA: Sage Publications.

BALOS, B., & TROTZKY, K. (1988). Enforcement of the domestic abuse act in Minnesota: A preliminary study. *Law and Inequality, 6*, 83–125.

BELL, D. (1985). Domestic violence: Victimization, police intervention, and disposition. *Journal of Criminal Justice, 13*, 525–534.

BELL, D. (1987). The victim–offender relationship: A determinant factor in police domestic dispute dispositions. *Marriage and Family Review, 12*(1), 87–102.

BERK, R., FENSTERMAKER, S., & NEWTON, P. (1988). An empirical analysis of police responses to incidents of wife battering. In G. Hotaling, D. Finkelhor, J. Kirkpatrick, & M. Straus (Eds.), *Coping with family violence: Research and policy perspectives* (pp. 158–168). Newbury Park, CA: Sage Publications.

BERK, S. F., & LOSEKE, D. (1980–1981). "Handling" family violence: Situational determinants of police arrest in domestic disturbances. *Law and Society Review, 15*(2), 317–346.

BLACK, D. (1978). Production of crime rates. In L. Savitz & N. Johnston (Eds.), *Crime in society* (pp. 45–60). New York: Wiley.

BLOUNT, W., YEGIDIS, B., & MAHEUX, R. (1992). Police attitudes toward preferred arrest: Influences of rank and productivity. *American Journal of Police, 9*(3), 35–52.

BOWKER, L. (1984). Battered wives and the police: A national study of usage and effectiveness. *Police Studies, 7*, 84–93.

BRECI, M., & SIMONS, R. (1987). An examination of organizational and individual factors that influence police response to domestic disturbances. *Journal of Police Science and Administration, 15*(2), 93–104.

BROWN, S. (1984). Police responses to wife beating: Neglect of a crime of violence. *Journal of Criminal Justice, 12*(3), 277–288.

BUZAWA, E. (1982). Police officer response to domestic violence legislation in Michigan. *Journal of Police Science and Administration, 10*(4), 415–424.

BUZAWA, E., & BUZAWA, C. (1985). Legislative trends in the criminal justice response to domestic violence. In A. Lincoln & M. Straus (Eds.), *Crime in the family* (pp. 134–147). Springfield, IL: Charles C. Thomas.

DAVIDSON, T. (1977). Wifebeating: A recurring phenomenon throughout history. In M. Roy (Ed.), *Battered women: A psychosociological study of domestic violence* (pp. 2–23). New York: Van Nostrand Reinhold.

DAVIS, P. (1983). Restoring the semblance of order: Police strategies in the domestic disturbance. *Symbolic Interaction, 6*(2), 261–278.

DOBASH, R. E., & DOBASH, R. (1978). Wives: The "appropriate" victims of marital violence. *Victimology: An International Journal, 2*(3–4), 426–442.

DOLON, R., HENDRICKS, J., & MEAGHER, S. (1986). Police practices and attitudes toward domestic violence. *Journal of Police Science and Administration, 14*(3), 187–192.

DUTTON, D. (1988). Research advances in the study of wife assault: Etiology and prevention. *Law and Mental Health, 4*, 161–220.

DUTTON, D., & LEVENS, B. (1977). Domestic crisis intervention attitude survey of trained and untrained police officers. *Canadian Police College Journal, 1*(2), 75–92.

EISENBERG, S. & MICKLOW, P. (1977). The assaulted wife: "Catch 22" revisited. *Women's Rights Law Reporter, 3*, 138–164.

EREZ, E. (1986). Intimacy, violence, and the police. *Human Relations, 39*(3), 265–281.

FEDER, L. (1996). The importance of offender's presence in the arrest decision when police respond to domestic violence calls. *Journal of Criminal Justice, 24*(6), 1–10.

FEDER, L. (1997). Domestic violence and police response in a pro-arrest jurisdiction. *Women and Criminal Justice, 8*(4), 79–98.

FEDER, L. (1998a). Police handling of domestic and non-domestic violence calls: Is there a case for discrimination? *Crime and Delinquency, 44*(2), 139–153.

FEDER, L. (1998b). Police handling of domestic violence calls: An overview and further investigation. *Women and Criminal Justice, 10*(2).

FERRARO, K. (1989). Policing woman battering. *Social Problems, 36*(1), 61–74.

FERRARO, K., & POPE, L. (1993). Irreconcilable differences: Battered women, police and the law. In N. Z. Hilton (Ed.), *Legal responses to wife assault: Current trends and evaluation* (pp. 96–123). Newbury Park, CA: Sage Publications.

FIELDS, M. (1977–78). Wife beating: Facts and figures. *Victimology, 2*(3-4), 643–647.

FRIEDMAN, L., & SCHULMAN, M. (1990). Domestic violence: The criminal justice response. In A. Lurigio, W. Skogan, & R. Davis (Eds.), *Victims of crime: Problems, policies, and programs* (pp. 87–103). Newbury Park, CA: Sage Publications.

GELLES, R. (1979, October). The myth of battered husbands and new facts about family violence. *Ms., 66*, 71–75.

GONDOLF, E., & McFERRON, J. R. (1988). Handling battering men: Police action in wife abuse cases. *Criminal Justice and Behavior, 16*(4), 429–439.

HARLOW, C. W. (1991). *Female victims of violent crime.* Washington, DC: U.S. Department of Justice, Bureau of Justice Statistics.

HILBERMAN, E. (1980). Overview: The "wife-beater's wife" reconsidered. *American Journal of Psychiatry, 137*(11), 1336–1347.

HIRSCHEL, J. D., HUTCHINSON, I., & DEAN, C. (1992). The failure of arrest to deter spouse abuse. *Journal of Research in Crime and Delinquency, 29*(1), 7–33.

HOMANT, R., & KENNEDY, D. (1985). Police perceptions of spouse abuse: A comparison of male and female officers. *Journal of Criminal Justice, 13*, 29–47.

KENNEDY, D., & HOMANT, R. (1983). Attitudes of abused women toward male and female police officers. *Criminal Justice and Behavior, 10*(4), 391–405.

KNOKE, D., & BURKE, P. (1980). *Log linear models.* Beverly Hills, CA: Sage Publications.

KURZ, D. (1991). Corporal punishment and adult use of violence: A critique of "Discipline and Deviance." *Social Problems, 38*(2), 155–161.

LAWRENZ, F., LEMBO, J., & SCHADE, T. (1988). Time series analysis of the effect of a domestic violence directive on the number of arrests per day. *Journal of Criminal Justice, 16*, 493–498.

LERMAN, L. (1981). Criminal prosecution of wife beaters. *Response to Violence in the Family and Sexual Assault, 4*(3), 1–19.

LERMAN, L. (1982). Court decisions on wife abuse laws: Recent developments. *Response to Family Violence and Sexual Assault, 5*, 3–4, 21–22.

LERMAN, L., LIVINGSTON, F., & JACKSON, V. (1983). State legislation on domestic violence. *Response to Violence in the Family and Sexual Assault, 6*(5), 1–27.

OPPENLANDER, N. (1982). Coping or copping out. *Criminology, 20*(3-4), 449–465.

SAN JOSE METHODS TEST OF KNOWN CRIME VICTIMS. (1972). *Statistics Technical Report No. 1.* Washington, D.C.: National Institute of Law Enforcement and Criminal Justice Statistics Division, Law Enforcement Assistance Administration.

SAUNDERS, D., & SIZE, P. (1986). Attitudes about woman abuse among police officers, victims and victim advocates. *Journal of Interpersonal Violence, 1*(1), 25–42.

SCHMIDT, J., & HOCHSTEDLER-STEURY, E. (1987). Prosecutorial discretion in filing charges in domestic violence cases. *Criminology, 25*(1), 487–510.

SHERMAN, L. (1988). *Domestic violence.* Washington, DC: U.S. Department of Justice, National Institute of Justice.

SHERMAN, L. (1992). The influence of criminology on criminal law: Evaluating arrests for misdemeanor domestic violence. *Journal of Criminal Law and Criminology, 83*(1), 1–45.

SHERMAN, L., & BERK, R. (1984). The specific deterrent effects of arrest for domestic assault. *American Sociological Review, 49*, 261–272.

SHERMAN, L., SCHMIDT, J., ROGAN, D., SMITH, D., GARTIN, P., COHN, E., COLLINS, D., & BACICH, A. (1992). The variable effects of arrest on criminal on criminal careers: The Milwaukee domestic violence experiment. *Journal of Criminal Law and Criminology, 83*(1), 137–169.

SMITH, D. (1987). Police response to interpersonal violence: Defining the parameters of legal control. *Social Forces, 65*(3), 767–782.

SMITH, D., & KLEIN, J. (1984). Police control of interpersonal disputes. *Social Problems, 31*(4), 468–481.

SMITH, D., & VISHER, C. (1981). Street-level justice: Situational determinants of police arrest decisions. *Social Problems, 29*(2), 167–177.

STEDMAN, B. (1917). RIGHT OF HUSBAND TO CHASTISE WIFE. *VIRGINIA LAW REPORTER, 3*(4), 241–248.

TAUB, N. (1983). Adult domestic violence: The law's response. *Victimology: An International Journal, 8*(1–2), 152–171.

WAALAND, P., & KEELEY, S. (1985). Police decision making in wife abuse: The impact of legal and extralegal factors. *Law and Human Behavior, 9*(4), 355–366.

WALTER, J. (1981). Police in the middle: A study of small city police intervention in domestic disputes. *Journal of Police Science and Administration, 9*, 243–260.

WORDEN, R., & POLLITZ, A. (1984). Police arrests in domestic disturbances: A further look. *Law and Society Review, 18*(1), 105–119.

CASES

Bruno v. Codd, 90 Misc. 2d 1047, 396 N.Y.S.2d (Sup Ct 1997).
Scott v. Hurt, No. C-76-2395 (N.D. Cal., filed October 28, 1976).
State v. Oliver, 70 N.C. 60, 61-62 (1873).

21

Female Victims and Antistalking Legislation

Janice Joseph

S talking is a complex crime that involves the threat of violence. It is an act of
terrorism that includes telephone calls, letters, or following the victim. Stalking
does not have to end in death or injury, but it can cause a reasonable person to feel
threatened or fearful. Anyone can be a victim of stalking, but the majority of victims are females.

Stalking may occur in a domestic situation or it may involve a stranger.
Stalkers can be classified into various groups according to certain characteristics
and their relationship to the victim. Several states have enacted antistalking legislation to protect people from stalkers. However, these statutes appear to be ineffective
in protecting females from stalkers.

In this chapter the effectiveness of states' antistalking laws to protect
females is assessed critically by discussing the legal elements of stalking, criminal and civil remedies for the crime of stalking, constitutional issues raised by
these laws, and federal antistalking legislation and measures. The implications
are also discussed.

Stalking is a crime that can happen to anyone at any time. The act of stalking is more
complex than simply following an intended victim before committing an act of violence.
It involves psychological, physical, and legal issues that all converge to form a course
of conduct.

It was in the late 1980s and early 1990s, when numerous high-profile cases involving celebrities came to the attention of the media and politicians, that this behavior became

known as stalking. With the advent of blockbuster films such as *Fatal Attraction, Cape Fear*, and *Sleeping with the Enemy* and coverage by the news media, *stalking* has become a household word. This chapter evaluates the effectiveness of the antistalking laws to protect female victims by focusing on the legal elements of the crime as reflected in state statutes, constitutional issues of antistalking laws, and the federal antistalking legislation and measures.

SOCIAL DIMENSIONS OF STALKING

The history of stalking behavior is as old as the history of human relationships. What is new about stalking is that until recently, it was never labeled as a separate and distinct class of deviant behavior. Prior to its common usage and subsequent designation as a crime, stalking was referred to as harassment, annoyance or, in some cases, simply as domestic violence.

The legal definition of stalking is defined primarily by state statutes. Although statutes vary, most define stalking as a course of conduct that places a person in fear for his or her safety. However, the term *stalking* is more commonly used to describe specific kinds of behavior, such as harassing or threatening another person, directed at a particular person. Virtually any unwanted contact between a stalker and his or her victim that directly or indirectly communicates a threat or places the victim in fear can generally be referred to as stalking.

Extent of Stalking

Unlike most violent crimes, the Federal Bureau of Investigation and many state law enforcement officials do not categorize the incidences of stalking as separate offenses. Consequently, no one knows just how common stalking cases are in the United States. However, best estimates indicate that as many as 200,000 Americans are currently being stalked and 1 in 20 women will become targets of stalking behavior at least once during their lifetimes (Guy, 1993). Fifty-one percent of stalking victims are ordinary citizens, and 75 to 80 percent of stalking is domestic-related. Ninety percent suffer from at least one kind of mental disorder, 9.5 percent suffer from erotomania and 43 percent have love obsession with their victims (U.S. Congress Senate Committee on the Judiciary, 1992). With the passage of the 1994 Crime Bill by the U.S. Congress, which mandated the tracking and compilation of stalking crime statistics, experts will eventually be able to determine the prevalence of this crime.

The first national survey on stalking was recently conducted by the Justice Department. The study interviewed 8000 women and 8000 men regarding their experiences with stalking. The study found that stalking was more prevalent than previously thought; 8 percent of women and 2 percent of the men have been stalked at some time in their lives. Eighty percent of the stalking victims are women and most are between 18 and 29 years old. About 87 percent of the stalkers are men. The study also reported that an estimated 1 million women and 400,000 men are stalked every year and that women were likely to be stalked by their male "intimate partners," whereas men were likely to be stalked by a stranger or an acquaintance. In most cases the episodes lasted a year or less. Less than half of the victims were directly threatened, although the victim experienced a high level of fear. The study also indicated that there was strong relationship between stalking and other forms of violence in intimate relationships (Tjaden & Thoennes, 1998).

Nature of Stalking

Stalking behavior has many dimensions. It can include written and verbal communication, unsolicited and unrecognized claims of romantic involvement, surveillance, harassment, loitering, following, or appearing within the sight of another. It can also take the form of contacting the victim by telephone, sending mail or electronic mail, and appearing at the workplace or the residence of the victim.

Stalking is a gender-neutral crime, with both males and females as perpetrators and victims. However, most stalkers are men and most of the victims are females. There is no single psychological or behavioral profile of a stalker, and most experts believe that stalkers are different, making it difficult to categorize their behavior and to devise effective strategies to cope with such behavior. Stalkers, as a group, manifest a variety of psychological disorders, including erotomania (Zona, Sharma, & Lane, 1993) and schizophrenia (Dietz et al., 1991).

Stalking occurs in a variety of contexts, from situations in which the stalker and victim are intimately related, to those where there is a personal relationship, to those between complete strangers. Consequently, the victims can be grouped into four categories: (1) victims who were former lovers or spouses; (2) victims who are acquaintances of the stalkers, such as co-workers; (3) victims who are celebrities or well known but not known personally to the stalkers; and (4) victims who are strangers with no celebrity status (National Victim Center, 1997).

Stalkers can be dangerous to victims, and stalking sometimes escalates into violence. Stalking victims frequently live in fear and terror. Often, they are forced to alter their lives significantly in attempts to find safety and freedom from the harassing behavior of former lovers or spouses, acquaintances, and strangers.

Based on the discussion above, stalking can be defined as criminal behavior (terrorism, threatening, harassment, trespassing, pursuing) committed against a variety of victims and occurring in several contexts. The stalker can be from any social background and can manifest some level of mental illness or can be complete mentally sound. The victim of stalking could be a stranger, an acquaintance, or someone with whom the stalker had an intimate relationship.

ANTISTALKING LEGISLATION

Prior to the passage of antistalking legislation, police and prosecutors had few legal avenues available by which they could apprehend stalkers. At times, police could charge stalkers only with trespassing, harassment, disorderly conduct, terrorist threats, or intimidation. Protection orders were the only means of protection for stalking victims. These traditional measures were rarely effective because they penalized the perpetrator only after the harm had occurred. For these reasons, legislators across the nation have implemented antistalking legislation that is intended to protect people from stalkers.

In 1990, California became the first state to pass a law that specifically made stalking a crime. The law was passed in response to the 1989 stalking murder of actress Rebecca Schaeffer and other reports of stalking of high-profile celebrities. In each case the victim had notified the police of their stalker's threatening behavior. Yet in each case, the police said that unless the stalker acted on those threats, there was nothing they could do legally. The California antistalking law was intended to give law enforcement officers the legal tool they needed to intervene in stalking cases before offenders acted on their threats (National Institute of Justice, 1993).

Since the passage of that first stalking law in 1990, all fifty states have enacted stalking laws. While each state stalking statute differs in both definition and approach, virtually all proscribe behavior that constitutes a pattern of conduct seeking to harass and/or threaten the safety of another. These new laws were intended to give law enforcement agencies more powerful tools to arrest and prosecute stalkers and to offer victims of stalking much greater protection than was previously available for them.

Elements of State Legislation

State statutes differ in their definition and elements of stalking. Antistalking legislation makes it a crime to engage in a pattern of behavior that harasses and/or threatens other people. Its purpose is twofold: to eliminate perpetrator behavior that disrupts normal life for the victim; and to prevent such behaviors from escalating into violence.

Most antistalking laws define stalking as "the willful, malicious and repeated following or harassing of another person." Some states require the existence of both a *credible threat* (defined as a verbal or written threat of violence made against a person by the perpetrator) and the appearance that the perpetrator intends and has the ability to carry out that threat. Some state laws specify a *course of conduct* in which the perpetrator (or stalker) "knowingly, purposefully, and repeatedly" engages in a series of actions (such as maintaining visual or physical closeness or repeatedly conveying verbal or written threats) directed toward a specific person and which serves no legitimate purpose and "alarms, annoys, and causes a reasonable person to suffer fear and emotional distress" (National Institute of Justice, 1993). The elements of state antistalking legislation are described below.

Course of Conduct.   States' antistalking laws almost always require that the alleged perpetrator engages in a course of conduct, which consists of a series of acts over a period of time (National Institute of Justice, 1993). A few states specify how many acts must occur and over what period of time the conduct must occur to constitute stalking. Illinois refers to "acts done on at least two occasions" [Ill. Rev. Stat., §§ 5/12-7.3, 12-7.4, 110-6.3, 3-14.5 (1992)]. Kentucky states that course of conduct means a pattern of conduct composed of two or more acts [K. Rev. Stat. Ann., § 508.150 (1992)], while Connecticut law uses the term *repeatedly* [Conn. Gen. Stat., § 53a-181(c) and (d) (1992)].

Many states specify the prohibited behaviors. These include surveillance, following, "lying in wait," harassing, approaching, pursuing, and intimidating of a victim, trespassing, showing a weapon, vandalizing, disregarding warning by a victim, and confining or restraining another person (National Institute of Justice, 1993).

Purposeful Behavior. The acts must be done in a conscious manner. The course of conduct must be "intentional" [Tenn. Code Ann. 36-3-606 (1995)], "willful" [(Mich. Penal Code MCLA, § 650.411h (1993)], or done "maliciously" [Calif. Penal Code, § 649.9 (1993)]. Florida uses the words *willfully* and *maliciously* [Fl. Stat. Ann., § 784.048 (1992)]. Missouri and New Jersey only require that the defendant intend to cause alarm or annoyance [Mo. Rev. Stat. 565.225 (1993); N.J. Rev. Stat., § 209, 2C: 12-10 (1993)]. What all this means is that if a person is aware of what he or she is doing and has a conscious desire or objective to engage in the conduct, this element is met.

Threatening Behavior. Fourteen states require that the perpetrator make a threat against the victim. Thirty-three states and the District of Columbia include in their definition of stalking, behaviors that threaten another person, even if there are no verbal threats by the perpetrator. Hawaii, Texas, and Utah include threats to persons and property (National Institute of Justice, 1993).

Missouri and Nevada require a threat in order to prove aggravated stalking, but not to prove stalking. In some states the threat need not be written or verbal to instill fear (National Institute of Justice, 1993). Thirteen states require that the defendant have the intent and/or the ability to carry out the threat (National Institute of Justice, 1993). A few states incorporate a much lower standard than the defendant intended, merely to cause alarm or annoyance (Sohn, 1994).

Intent to Cause Fear of Injury or Death. The conduct must be more than simply an annoying series of acts. The victim must fear that he or she will be injured by the perpetrator's actions (National Institute of Justice, 1993). Thirteen states do not require that the defendant have the intent to cause fear, provided that he intends to do the act that results in fear. In these states, if the victim is reasonably frightened by the alleged perpetrator's conduct, an element of the crime is met (National Institute of Justice, 1993).

Some states extend the fear to the victim's family members. The actions may be directed at the victim or his or her family. Immediate family is normally considered to be spouses, children, or parents. For example, Idaho and Oklahoma statutes include behavior that threatens the victim or a member of the immediate family of the victim [Idaho Code, § 18-7905 (1992); Okla. Stat. Ann., Tit. 21, § 1173 (1993)].

Reasonable Person/Fear. Thirty-three states and the District of Columbia stipulate that the acts of stalking should cause a *reasonable* person to feel threatened or fearful (National Institute of Justice, 1993). States use such terms as "causes such other person reasonable fear for her (his) physical safety" [Conn. Gen. Stat., § 53a-181(c) and (d) (1992)]; "course of conduct must be such as would cause a reasonable person to suffer substantial emotional distress, and must actually cause substantial distress to the person" [N.J. Rev. Stat., § 209, 2C: 12-10 (1993)], and "with the intent of placing that person in reasonable fear of death or injury" [Fla. Stat. Ann., § 784.048 (1992)].

CIVIL AND CRIMINAL REMEDIES

Beyond this basic definition of the crime, statutes include a wide variety of additional stalking-related provisions. For example, state stalking statutes provide for automatic and emergency protective orders and allow victims to file civil litigation against stalkers. States allow police to make warrantless arrests in stalking cases where probable cause exists, make stalking a nonbailable offense under certain circumstances; establish sentencing enhancements in cases where the victim is a minor or when there is a protective order in place against the perpetrator, and create heightened crime classifications for stalkers who commit second stalking offenses. In general, state statutes provide for civil and criminal remedies for the crime of stalking.

Civil Remedies

Protective Orders.   *Protective orders* include "stay away" orders, "no contact" orders, restraining orders, and (in some states) antistalking orders. Basically, no-contact and stay-away orders are generated by judges as either conditions of a bond (before conviction) or conditions of probation (after conviction) or conditions of parole (after conviction and after a period of imprisonment). *Restraining orders* (or injunctions) are orders generated by the victim against a perpetrator and filed for in civil court. *Antistalking orders* are similar to *restraining orders* but are used specifically against alleged stalkers. They prohibit the offender from having any contact with the victim.

Protective orders allow a woman partial protection in that she can go to court to get the order before anything actually happens as long as there is the likelihood that it will happen. In such a case, the perpetrator becomes aware that the potential victim is taking precautions and that he can be charged with a crime the first time anything does happen to her (Morin, 1993; Thomas, 1993). They can serve as the first formal means of intervention in a stalking situation.

Protective orders have several inherent limitations. Until recently, a woman who moves to another state to get away from her stalker sometimes found that the second state could not enforce the restraining order issued in another state. The order could be enforced only in the jurisdiction in which it was issued, and to receive protection the victim had to obtain another protection order in the new state (National Institute of Justice, 1996).

Another limitation is that it may be difficult for a victim to obtain a protective order. All states have mechanisms for issuing emergency restraining orders, and many states have filing fees. In nonemergency situations, however, it may take several weeks for a victim to obtain a protective order, and the process sometimes involves prohibitively high legal fees and court costs, especially in nondomestic cases (National Institute of Justice, 1996).

Depending on the state law, protective orders may not be available to every victim of stalking. Although some states, such as Oregon, have amended their domestic abuse and/or protective order statutes to provide full issuance of protective orders in cases of stalking, in other states protective orders are available only to protect victims of spousal abuse or abuse from someone with whom the victim cohabited. Although most stalking occurs in a domestic setting, female victims of other types of stalking are left unprotected by these remedies (Ross, 1992).

Protective orders may be easy to avoid on technicalities because such orders, by their nature, are very specific. A determined stalker can simply alter his or her behavior to avoid the language of the order: for example, from following, to sending flowers. Although almost every state statute requires a threat of death or serious injury to the victim (as stated earlier), only a few states include a threat made on a family member of the victim. Therefore, in most states a stalker can avoid prosecution for stalking by harassing a family member of the victim (Sohn, 1994).

Protective orders are difficult to enforce. Even if the victim gets a protective order, she may still be faced with the threat of harassment or physical harm before the police can arrest the stalker. Protection orders sometimes fail to provide the anticipated protection for victims. Very often, women are killed despite the existence of a protective order. Their deterrent effect is weak against a perpetrator intent on committing a crime. In addition, violators often receive minimal jail time, if at all, and criminal contempt is seldom filed against them. Consequently, protection orders are sometimes viewed as "merely pieces of paper" or as "paper shields" (Kegan, 1993).

Realizing that waving a piece of paper in front of an obsessed stalker is probably of little value, many victims may be reluctant to risk his wrath. Furthermore, many victims may believe that orders can aggravate their stalkers and do little to protect them. Out of fear, they may not even seek court orders. In general, the obtaining of protective orders can be a complex and expensive task that may discourage victims from pursuing the protection they need (Topliffe, 1992).

Civil Litigation. Another civil alternative is civil litigation in which the victim sues the stalker for monetary damages, punitive as well as compensatory. The victim can file civil action against a stalker for physical, emotional, and psychological damage incurred as a result of the stalking, as well as for attorney fees and costs of the action. The victim can also file suit seeking these remedies regardless of whether the stalker has been charged or convicted for the crime of stalking (National Institute of Justice, 1993).

The major advantage of a civil suit is that the victim will be compensated financially for emotional distress, damage to property, and medical and legal costs. In addition, the burden of proof in a civil court is lower than in a criminal court. However, the major problem with civil litigation is the legal cost. Although people are allowed to represent themselves during a civil litigation proceeding, they are often advised not to do so but instead are encouraged to retain the services of an attorney. This is a costly undertaking and may be prohibitive to most victims of stalking, and many may be reluctant to file civil action against the stalker because of the cost involved in such an action. In addition, cases in civil court often take an extremely long time to come to trial. Furthermore, civil actions do not deter violent behavior. In general, civil actions seem to be inappropriate in stalking cases.

Criminal Remedies

Warrantless Arrests.   Warrantless arrests of stalking suspects are permitted in several states, provided that there is probable cause. Some also allow a warrantless arrest if there is a violation of a protective order. It is implicit in the statutes that the officer need not see the violation in order to arrest the person. Florida and Pennsylvania laws make such a provision (National Institute of Justice, 1993).

Bail and Pretrial Release Provisions.   Eleven states include bail provisions for stalking defendants in their stalking laws. Ohio lists specific factors that a court must consider in determining the amount and the conditions of bail. In Montana, the defendant cannot be released without appearing, and the victim must be notified of the pretrial release. Vermont considers stalking a violent crime, and the granting of bail to the defendant is determined according to state guidelines for violent crimes. Illinois allows the denial of bail if the defendant "poses a real and present threat to the physical safety of the alleged victim of the offense" [Ill. Rev. Stat., §§ 5/12-7.3, 12-7.4, 110-6.3, 3-4.5 (1992)]. In Georgia, as a condition of bail, the court may prohibit the defendant from appearing at the victim's school, work, or other location where the victim may be present. In addition, the state can deny bail to the defendant if he previously violated conditions of pretrial release, probation, or parole arising out of a stalking offense (National Institute of Justice, 1993).

Criminal Sanctions.   Generally, penalties for stalking can be a misdemeanor, a felony, or a misdemeanor for the first offense and a felony for any subsequent offense. Many states have both misdemeanor and felony classifications of stalking. Until recently, most stalking statutes were classified as misdemeanors. The rationale for this is based on the fact that no physical injury is required for the crime to be completed, and felonies should be reserved for the more serious property or personal crimes. Misdemeanors generally carry a jail sentence of up to one year. Felonies are punishable by imprisonment in state prison. Felony penalties from three to five years are typical, but some states allow ten- and twenty-year sentences. Enhanced penalties are available in most states if a stalker violates a protective order, brandishes a weapon, directs his conduct toward a victim who is under 16 years of age, or has committed a prior stalking offense. In fourteen states, the prior offense must have been against the same victim or directed against a child. Nine states permit enhanced penalties for stalking if the defendant has previously been convicted of another felony (Sohn, 1994; Wallace, 1996).

Iowa's law considers stalking convictions in other states as "previous violations" and allows for enhanced penalties in subsequent offenses, even if the first offense did not occur in Iowa. It also has no requirement that the second or subsequent offense be committed against the same person as the previous offense, a clause that punishes stalking *because of the act*, not because a specific victim is targeted. Iowa is also unusual because upon a third offense of stalking (with two previous *convictions*), there exists a "presumption of ineligibility for bail." The burden to prove that the offender will not "jeopardize the personal safety of other persons" then shifts to the defense and not to the state (National

Victim Center, 1997). The constitutionality of criminal remedies is discussed in the next section of the chapter.

EVALUATION OF STATE ANTISTALKING STATUTES

The effectiveness of a law is its ability to provide protection to potential victims. It appears that in response to public fear, states have enacted antistalking statutes that are poorly designed, constitutionally unsound, and practically unenforceable.

Problems with Legal Elements of Stalking

Course of Conduct.   Statutes that narrowly define the course of conduct and the circumstances under which they are made may only provide limited protection for female victims. In North Carolina, for example, the defendant must have received and ignored a reasonable warning to desist by, or on behalf of, the victim [N.C. Gen. Stat., § 14-277.3(a) (1992)]. Three states—Colorado, Illinois, and New Mexico—require that the perpetrator make a threat and then engage in additional act(s) in furtherance of the threat. If the circumstances above are not met (in the various states), there is no crime of stalking. Nebraska has enacted a statute that requires that the perpetrator violate an injunction, restraining order, or no-contact order before criminal liability arises [Neb. Rev. Stat., §§ 42-903,924 and 28-101 (1992)]. The Texas antistalking statute requires annoying or harassing conduct, or a threat, and that the conduct must occur after the victim reported the perpetrator to the police [Texas Crim. Code Proc. Ann., §§ 17.4b, 42.12, 42.8 (1993)]. One of the most narrowly written statutes is West Virginia's, which states that the victim must have resided with, cohabited with, or engaged in sexual or intimate contact with the perpetrator [W.Va. Code, § 61-2-9a (1992)]. If a woman, for example, has to wait to file charges of stalking until two acts of harassment have occurred after she has been threatened by a perpetrator, it may be too late. If the woman did not report it previously to the police, as in the case of Texas, or did not reside with him previously, she cannot file stalking charges against her perpetrator. These required circumstances do not provide protection for all females against stalkers.

Purposeful/Intentional Behavior.   In all states, the perpetrator's behavior must be intentional for it to be classified as stalking. The requirement of criminal intent creates a loophole for one group of offenders who are mentally disturbed. For example, an erotomanic, psychotic personality stalker, or a psychopathic personality stalker (all suffering from mental disturbances) may well believe that he is merely showing the victim how much he loves her, despite the fact that his intentions may be creating fear in the victim. He may not believe or realize that his behavior is causing fear. A prosecutor may have difficulty establishing such a stalker's guilt through criminal intent (Schaum & Parrish, 1995).

Explicit/Implicit Threats.   Some laws require that threats be made verbally or in written form. Such statutes ignore a range of nonverbal threatening behaviors. A stalker can convey a threat to the victim by sending her black roses, forming his hand into the shape of a gun and pointing it at her, or delivering a dead animal on the victim's doorstep. Sometimes these cues are subtle but powerful enough to cause fear, especially in domestic stalking cases. The context in which certain gestures are made can make them suggestive and frightening (Schaum & Parrish, 1995).

Fearful of Bodily Harm or Death.   Most statutes stipulate that the victim be fearful of bodily harm or death. This means that the victim has to believe that the stalker will injure, disfigure, or even kill her before the behavior can be considered stalking. This restrictive requirement ignores behaviors that may not be perceived as causing such extreme violence but nevertheless are frightening. Why should a threat of such extreme violence be required before a victim and her family members can be protected from stalkers?

Reasonable Person/Fear Standard.   Thirty-three states and the District of Columbia use the reasonable person/fear standard. This means that the victim will be judged by what a "reasonable" person would feel rather than on the victim's personal feeling and experiences. In addition, the term *reasonable* is not defined in the statutes. This is a critical element for many victims, especially victims of domestic stalking. An ex-wife who has had a prior violent relationship with the perpetrator may react fearfully to minor harassing incidents, whereas a co-worker of a stalker may ignore the same types of incidents. "Does this mean that the ex-wife or her fear is unreasonable? Not necessarily, but she could be viewed as being overly sensitive; thus a judge could considered her fear unreasonable. A batterer may whisper to his former wife: "Remember the gift I gave you last year for your birthday?" To a casual listener this may seem nonthreatening, but only the victim would be able to understand the real meaning of this statement. The former husband could be saying to his former wife: "Remember the beating that I gave you last year on your birthday?" The determination as to who is a "reasonable person" or what is "reasonable fear" is usually left to the discretion of the judge. However, the victim's perception of fear should be taken into consideration rather than how a "reasonable" person would respond to threats by a stalker. Lawmakers are now beginning to realize that the victim's perception of possible violence is the most accurate indicator of whether such violence will occur (Schaum & Parrish, 1995).

Constitutional Issues

State antistalking laws have raised concerns over their constitutionality. These issues include violation of the First, Fourth, and Eighth Amendments.

First Amendment.   The U.S. Supreme Court has ruled that to ensure that individuals' freedom of expression is guaranteed, a statute cannot be vague. Antistalking laws may be subjected to constitutional challenges for vagueness (Guy, 1993). The vagueness doctrine under the due process clauses for the Fifth and Fourteenth Amendments of the U.S. Constitution requires that all persons be given fair notice of conduct that is against the law and may subject them to criminal liability. The statute should define the behavior with such explicitness and in a manner that ordinary people can understand what conduct is prohibited and its enforcement does not encourage arbitrary and discriminatory practices. Statutes that do not meet these criteria can be voided on the grounds that they are too vague.

Several of the terms used to identify the course of conduct in many of the laws are vague. For example, such words as *follows, repeatedly, annoys*, and *alarms* are not clearly defined in some statutes. Similarly, such phrases as *explicit or implicit threat, intentionally and closely follows, lies in wait*, and *seriously alarms, annoys* or *harasses* have been used in many states without sufficient definition or clarity (Lingg, 1993). The Oregon statute was struck down for vagueness in 1993, but was amended in 1995 to remove the offending language. The Massachusetts stalking law was found to be unconstitutionally vague; the Kansas law suffered a similar fate in 1996 (National Institute of Justice, 1996).

Statutes can be voided because of their overbreadth. A statute is overly broad if in addition to proscribing activities that are not constitutionally protected, it includes protected freedoms of speech, conduct, movement, and association granted to persons under the First Amendment. There are two reasons for invalidating a statute that is overly broad: (1) citizens may be intimidated and therefore reluctant to exercise their First Amendment rights, and (2) it may give law enforcement officials the power to select certain citizens and punish them.

Antistalking legislation may be subjected to constitutional scrutiny because of overbreath. By their very nature, antistalking laws regulate the expression of ideas and thoughts. The stalker may engage in behavior that is intended to express his or her feelings of love or hate toward the victim. This conduct may involve following the victim, sending letters and flowers to the victim, phoning the victim proclaiming their undying love for that person, and other conduct that appears to be clearly protected by the First Amendment. However, only fifteen states make exceptions for "constitutionally protected activities" and nine exclude "conduct which occurs during labor picketing" (National Institute of Justice, 1993). The omission of such exceptions raises the issue of the overbreath of some stalking laws.

The Colorado statute, for example, is vulnerable to attack on grounds of overbreadth. The sectional issue states that stalking includes making a credible threat to another person and "in connection with such threat, repeatedly [making] any form of communication with that, person, whether or not a conversation ensues" [Colo. Rev. Stat. Ann., § 18-9-11(4)(a)(III) (1992)]. According to the literal language of the statute, if the stalker made an apology or attempted an explanation for his behavior; the perpetrator could be guilty of stalking. Ironically, if the defendant made a credible threat and did not attempt to apologize, he would not be guilty of stalking. The broad language of this provision of this law makes it vulnerable to constitutional attack in that it tends to inhibit unreasonably the exercise of the constitutionally protected right of freedom of speech (Sohn, 1994). As a general rule, courts have applied the overbreath doctrine reluctantly and sparingly. Although there have been several overbreath challenges, no court to date has struck down an antistalking law on that ground (National Institute of Justice, 1996).

In the case of *Commonwealth v. Camper* (1993), the Virginia antistalking statute has already been struck down on vagueness and overbreadth grounds. Virginia defines stalking as engaging in "conduct with the intent to cause emotional distress to another person by placing that person in reasonable fear of death or bodily injury" [Vir. Code Ann., § 18.2-60-3 (1992)]. Although it follows the trend of dealing exclusively with repeated behavior, the statute is significantly broader than most other statutes and does not include the detailed definitions. A district court judge found that the statute violated both vagueness and overbreadth principles. The judge's decision was based on the statute's failure to include definitions for the terms *engage in conduct, intent to cause emotional distress*, and *reasonable fear of death or bodily injury*. The Virginia judge found that much of the behavior prohibited by the Virginia statute was simply left to the imagination or is protected by the First Amendment. The court was particularly concerned that under the facts of this case, the defendant could effectively be arrested for attending the church of his choice (*Commonwealth v. Camper*, 1993). Most of the constitutional challenges so far revolved around vagueness and overbreath. Florida has had the highest number of constitutional challenges regarding vagueness and overbreath, but the statute was able to withstand constitutional scrutiny (National Institute of Justice, 1996).

Fourth Amendment Right.   The Fourth Amendment protects persons from unreasonable searches and seizures by law enforcement officers. Although states have the power to develop effective investigate crimes, they are prohibited from authorizing police conduct that violates the Fourth Amendment rights of citizens.

A number of states allow police to arrest an alleged stalker without an arrest warrant. Warrantless arrests give police the power to arrest someone purely on the basis of the alleged victim's word. This can lead to arbitrary and discriminatory enforcement. Under these laws an officer may choose to arrest a perpetrator based on his perception of credibility of the victim. Circumstances do exist where a suspect may legitimately be arrested without a warrant. Under common law, either a misdemeanor committed in the presence of an officer, or a felony committed in or outside the presence of an officer, justifies a warrantless arrest (*U.S. v. Watson*, 1976). In general, an arrest warrant is not required when an officer arrests a suspect in a public place and there is probable cause and the crime is a felony. Warrantless arrests are prohibited in public places when the crime is a misdemeanor unless it was committed in the officer's presence (Sohn, 1994).

Florida's statute, which provides for warrantless arrests of suspected stalkers if a law enforcement officer has probable cause to believe the accused is guilty of stalking [Fla. Stat. 784.048 (1996)], appears to violate the Fourth Amendment right. Stalking in Florida is both a misdemeanor and a felony under certain circumstances. Florida's statute appears to allow police officers much broader authority to execute an arrest than is permitted constitutionally because it grants police officers the power to arrest a stalking suspect without an arrest warrant, even if it is a misdemeanor that does occur in the presence of the officer.

Eighth Amendment.   In determining whether a statute violates the Eighth Amendment's prohibition against cruel and unusual punishment, a reviewing court must consider the "barbaric" nature of criminal sanctions and the proportionality of these sanctions to the crime committed. While bail, fines, and imprisonment are not barbaric punishments, these punishments may violate the Eighth Amendment if they are imposed disproportionately to the crime committed.

A few states deny bail to stalkers to protect the victim from further threats. While the Eighth Amendment does state that excessive bail should not be required, it is silent on whether bail should be granted to a defendant and under what conditions it should be granted. The denial of bail to protect the victim may be constitutionally unsound, especially if the state's definition of stalking is vague. Denial of bail is usually practiced in cases of capital crimes, to ensure the defendant's appearance in court and to prevent the defendant from fleeing the jurisdiction. It is seldom used to protect the community or the victim. In fact, Illinois' no-bail provision was considered unconstitutional under the Illinois Constitution (Bailey, 1993). Other state statutes with similar bail provisions are likely to be challenged. As a matter of fact, the National Institute of Justice recommends amendments to these statutes or constitutions to allow for pretrial bail in stalking cases (National Institute of Justice, 1993).

In determining whether criminal sanctions violate the Eighth Amendment, courts use three conditions: (1) the gravity of the offense and the harshness of the penalty, (2) the sentences imposed on other criminals in the same jurisdiction for similar offenses, and (3) the sentences imposed on criminals in other jurisdictions for the same crime. The Illinois statute has also been criticized on the grounds that it amounts to cruel and unusual punishment. Under the statute, a first offense is considered a class 4 felony, punishable by up to three years in jail and a $10,000 fine. Alabama and Massachusetts, which threaten even stricter penalties, are certainly subject to the same scrutiny (Sohn, 1994). The challenge to Wyoming's enhancement provision in its stalking law was upheld in 1993 (National Institute of Justice, 1996). It is still quite possible that there will be more constitutional challenges to the enhanced sentences for stalking stipulated in some states, especially since stalking in most cases involves threat of violence rather than infliction of the actual violence on another person. This will be true particularly if the stalking statute is vague.

Practical Issues

Some states' statutes cannot adequately protect a victim from further stalking. Twenty-nine states place no restrictions on the availability of registered drivers' home addresses. The twenty-one remaining states and the District of Columbia impose various restrictions on public access. Only the two remaining states—California and Virginia—completely prohibit individual access to drivers' records [Calif. Vehicle Code, § 1808 (1989); Va. Code Ann., § 462-212 (1993)]. In addition, most states and the District of Columbia allow the public to have access to voter registration lists with individuals' addresses. The information is available through the county recorder's office and through the state agency responsible for maintaining voter registries (U.S. Department of Justice, 1993). What this means is that in many states, stalkers can have public access to the address of a potential victim. If a victim changes his or her home address, the stalker can have access to the new one.

In a few states the alleged stalker will not be charged with an offense unless the victim first requests the perpetrator to cease his or her behavior and if the person fails to do so. This provision creates a major problem for victims in two ways: (1) many victims might justifiably be reluctant to confront their stalker with such a request, which could potentially place the victim in a dangerous situation, and (2) many victims may not have the opportunity to do so. For example, if a victim knows that she is being stalked by a stranger who never gets physically close to her, is she required to hold up a sign saying, "Please stop stalking me?" While the rationale behind requiring such a request seems relatively straightforward, its practical application is highly unlikely (Sohn, 1994).

Despite the above, there are a few statutes that provide some protection for victims. Some states have focused more on the stalker and his or her state of mind. Eight states broaden or eliminate entirely the *mens reas* requirement with such terms as *no intent necessary* [Colo. Rev. Stat. Ann., § 18-9-4(a)(II) (1992)], *in reckless disregard of risk of harassing* [Hawaii Rev. Stat., § 711-1106.5(3) (1992)], and *knows or reasonably should know that the victim is afraid* [Wash. Rev. Code, §§ 9a46.020 to 9a46.100 (1992)]. One of the harshest stalking laws exists in Michigan, where the victim need only establish a reasonable fear of harm to meet the statute's requirement. Michigan chooses to focus on the potential harm to the victim rather than the state of mind of the defendant. This eliminates the need for victims to convince authorities that the stalker intends to harm them [Mich. Penal Code, MCLA, § 650.411h (1993)]. These statutes allow the convictions of stalkers who, because of mental incapacity, lack the specific intent by many statutes.

Apart from family members being covered in some antistalking legislation, several states have provisions that protect certain types of victims. The Connecticut statute contains an enhancement that automatically raises the offense of stalking from a misdemeanor to a felony when the victim is under 16 years of age [Conn. Gen. Stat., § 53a-181(c) & (d) (1992)]. South Dakota has created a separate offense of stalking a child 12 years of age and over [S. Dak. Codified Laws, §§ 22-19A-2 to 22-19A-6 (1993)].

Federal Legislative Response

Because of the problems inherent in state antistalking statutes, the National Criminal Justice Association was asked by Congress to develop a model stalking act. The National Institute of Justice (1993) recommended a model stalking code for consideration by states when they amend their existing statutes. This model stalking code incorporated the rights of the alleged stalker as well as the rights of the victim. In short, the model viewed stalking as a "a course of conduct directed at a specific person that would cause a reasonable person to fear bodily injury to himself, herself or a member of his or her immediate family or to fear death to himself or herself or a member of his or her immediate family" (National Institute of Justice, 1993, p. 43). The model code extended the term *immediate family* to include "anyone who within the prior six months regularly resided in the household" (p. 43). Unlike state statutes, the model code does not include a list of the behaviors prohibited. It encourages the use of a continuum of charges that could be used by law enforcement officials to intervene at various stages—because a stalker's behavior is often characterized by a series of increasingly serious acts—and the creation of a felony classification for stalking (National Institute of Justice, 1993).

The model code was designed to assist the states in crafting and adopting stalking laws that are not so broad as to be unconstitutional nor so narrow as to be virtually meaningless. It encourages state legislators "to make stalking a felony offense; to establish penalties for stalking that reflect and are commensurate with the seriousness of the crime; and to provide criminal justice officials with the authority and legal tools to arrest, prosecute, and sentence stalkers" (National Institute of Justice, 1993, p. 43).

In the fall of 1994, Congress passed the Violent Crime Control and Law Enforcement Act. A part of this crime bill, the Violence against Women Act, encompassed a provision that makes it a federal crime for spouses to cross a state line (or to enter or leave Indian country) to harass or continue to abuse their spouses or intimate partners with the intent to injure the person and the person's immediate family. The provision also made it a crime for a person to cause his or her spouse or intimate partner to cross a state line (or to enter or leave Indian country) by "force, coercion, duress, or fraud," which then results in bodily injury to that person. This provision also makes it a federal crime to cross a state line (or to enter or leave Indian country) with the intent to do anything that violates the "portion of a protection order that involves protection against credible threats of violence, repeated harassment, or bodily injury" and then engages in such conduct [Public Law 103-322, Title IV, Subtitle B, Chap. 110A, §§ 2261 to 2266 (1994)]. This legislation also tripled existing federal funds for battered women's shelters, and it allowed victims of crimes to sue for civil damages in federal court if they can prove that they were targeted specifically due to their gender (Schaum & Parrish, 1995). This federal provision dealt with domestic stalking but did not address cases in which the victim is not related to the stalker.

In 1996, Congress expanded its 1994 legislation by enacting a measure (HR2980) prohibiting interstate stalking and stalking on federal property and other places within federal jurisdiction. This law also includes all victims, not just the spouses and intimate partners of offenders. It also would make restraining orders, against stalking, issued in any state valid in all other states [Public Law 104-201, § 1069, Title 18 U.S.C. 2261, 2261A, 2262 (1996)].

POLICY IMPLICATIONS

In general the present state antistalking statutes do not provide adequate protection for females against stalking. State antistalking statutes are seriously flawed and limited in their usefulness. One of the most important factors to be considered when developing antistalking legislation is the protection of the rights of the defendant while meeting the needs of the victim. In addition, such legislation should take into consideration the various behaviors that stalking encompasses.

Because of this, some states have already amended, or are currently in the process of amending, antistalking and harassment statutes to include broader protections to stalking victims. For example, West Virginia's original antistalking statute provided that a person could only be guilty of stalking provided that the perpetrator and the victims formerly resided or cohabited or with whom that person formerly engaged in a sexual or intimate relationship. A recently amended version of the statute removes this limitation [W.Va. Code, § 7 62-2-9a (h) (1993)]. South Dakota has increased the punishment level for stalking offenses and has eliminated the requirement that a threat causes the victim to have a reasonable fear for her safety [S.Dak. Codified Laws, §§ 22-19A-2 to 22-19A-6 1993)]. Once lawmakers realize the shortcomings of their initial attempts to criminalize stalking, more amendments and revisions should be forthcoming.

States that have the "credible threat" requirement in their definition of stalking need to remove such a requirement. It is too vague a term and is open to subjective interpretation: what constitutes a credible threat? In addition, the national survey found that stalkers do not often threaten their victims verbally or in writing but instead engage in a conduct of behavior that causes a reasonable person to feel fearful. The survey also found that although many of victims felt fear, the stalkers did not threatened directly by their stalkers (Tjaden & Thoennes, 1998). Given these findings, it appears that antistalking statutes that require an actual verbal or written threat makes the prosecution of stalkers difficult and should therefore be removed from all state statutes.

State should use language in their statutes to avoid constitutional challenges. The term *stalking* should be clearly defined in the statute. Words such as *following, repeatedly, reasonable, annoys,* and *intent* should be excluded. Constitutionally protected actions should be removed from all state antistalking legislation. Constitutionally unsound laws do not protect victims but rather, defendants. When states enact constitutionally valid antistalking legislation, they are protecting victims of stalking.

In revising their statutes, states should consider all types of potential victims. Some states' antistalking laws include family members as victims, whereas others do not. All state laws should include family members. In addition, states need to consider other victims, such as acquaintances and co-workers. Similarly, states need to include other categories of stalkers, such as juveniles.

States need to change their practices regarding restraining orders. States should eliminate much of the bureaucratic processes necessary to get a protection order against an alleged stalker. Although these orders are not foolproof, they can provide some measure of protection for victims. In addition, to deter alleged stalkers from engaging in further violent acts, law enforcement officers should arrest violators of protection orders.

State legislation needs to protect victims of stalking by providing them with confidentiality. As stated earlier, most states release the names and addresses of their citizens to the public. This enables stalkers to pursue their victims even if they move to a new location to escape the stalker. States can either include in their antistalking legislation a section on the protection of the confidentiality of personal information of victims, or they should prohibit the release of personal information of all citizens to the general public.

SUMMARY

Stalking is a serious phenomenon that has only recently become a national focus. In an attempt to tackle the problem, states have enacted antistalking legislation. Although the responsiveness of the states to victims of stalking are to be applauded for their efforts, the utility and validity to these laws have been the subject of much debate. The speed with which these laws were passed has sometimes resulted in the use of language that allows the stalker to evade punishment, or they raise constitutional issues (Thomas, 1993). Many of these laws are too vague, too narrow or too broad, and violate various constitutional rights. Because of their flaws, state antistalking laws are ineffective in protecting females against stalking. At the present time, however, some states are in the process of revising their antistalking laws to make them more effective.

State and federal legislative remedies are one solution to crime that can be potentially life threatening. Given the fact that laws will not necessarily be the panacea for crimes, victims and potential victims need to protect themselves. They need to be aware of the devices, skills, and services that can be used for protection. It is important that everyone works together to prevent the crime of stalking.

REFERENCES

BAILEY, D. (1993, February 5). Circuit judge finds no-bail provision of stalking law to be unconstitutional. *Chicago Daily Bulletin*, p. 1.

DIETZ, P. E., MATHEWS, D. B., VAN DUYNE, C., MARTELL, D. A., PERRY, C. D. H., STEWART, T., WARREN, J., & CROWDER, J. D. (1991). Threatening and otherwise inappropriate letters to Hollywood celebrities. *Journal of Forensic Sciences, 36*, 185–209.

GUY, R. A. (1993). Nature and constitutionality of stalking laws. *Vanderbilt Law School, 46*, 991–1029.

KEGAN, K. (1993, January 11). New focus on deadly stalkers. *San Francisco Chronicle*, p. A1.

LINGG, R. A. (1993). Stopping stalkers: A critical examination of antistalking legislation. *Saint John's Law Review, 67*(2), 347–381.

MORIN, K. S. (1993). The phenomenon of stalking: Do existing state statutes provide adequate protection? *San Diego Justice Journal, 1*, 123.

NATIONAL INSTITUTE OF JUSTICE. (1993). *Project to develop a model of antistalking code for states. Final Summary Report*. Washington, DC: U.S. Department of Justice.

NATIONAL INSTITUTE OF JUSTICE. (1996). Domestic violence, stalking, and antistalking legislation. Washington, DC: U.S. Department of Justice.

NATIONAL VICTIM CENTER. (1997). Stalking and the law. Infolink, Arlington, VA: NVC.

ROSS, E. (1992, June). Problem of men stalking women spurs new laws. *Christian Science Monitor*, p. 6.

SCHAUM, M., & PARRISH, K. (1995). *Stalked: Breaking the silence on the crime of stalking in America*. New York: Simon & Schuster.

SOHN, E. (1994). Antistalking statute: Do they actually protect victims. *Criminal Justice Bulletin, 30*(3), pp. 203–224.

THOMAS, K. R. (1993). How to stop the stalker: State antistalking laws. *Criminal Law Bulletin, 21*, 124–136.

TJADEN, P., & THOENNES, N. (1998). *Stalking in America: Findings from the national violence against women survey*. Washington, DC: National Institute of Justice, Centers for Disease Control and Prevention.

TOPLIFFE, E. (1992). Why civil protection orders are effective remedies for domestic violence but mutual protective orders are not. *Indiana Law Journal, 67*, 1039, 1047.

U.S. CONGRESS SENATE COMMITTEE ON THE JUDICIARY. (1992). *Antistalking legislation hearing before the Senate Judiciary Committee*. Washington, DC: U.S. Government Printing Office.

WALLACE, H. (1995). Stalkers, the Constitution, and victims' remedies. *Criminal Justice, 10*, 16.

ZONA, M. A., SHARMA, K. K., & LANE, J. (1993). A comparative study of erotomanic and obsessional subjects in a forensic sample. *Journal of Forensic Sciences, 38*(4), 894–903.

CASES

Commonwealth v. Camper, Case No. 93-2876, Gen. Dist. Ct. City of Richmond (April 4, 1994).

U.S. v. Watson, 423 U.S. 411, 418 (1976).

22

Forced Sexual Intercourse

Contemporary Views

Robert T. Sigler, Ida M. Johnson, and Etta F. Morgan

In this chapter some degree of clarity is introduced in an area noted for its lack of clarity. Forced sexual intercourse is generally treated as a single phenomenon. The authors suggest that this term is used to label four types of behavior which are substantially different. Stranger rape occurs when someone who is not known or who is casually known to the victim uses force to gain sexual access. Courtship or date rape occurs when someone who is developing a legitimate relationship with the victim uses force to gain sexual access. Predatory rape occurs when someone uses force to gain sexual access while pretending to engage in a legitimate courtship or dating activity (the pretense is used to maneuver the victim into a vulnerable position). Spousal rape occurs when someone uses force to gain sexual access with a spouse or with someone with whom he has a relatively permanent relationship. The authors will argue that these are different sets of phenomena which require different explanatory models and interventions. Each type is defined with reference to the relevant literature when appropriate. Recommendations are made for research foci for each type. A model that addresses courtship and dating forced sexual intercourse is presented.

Forced sexual intercourse has been growing steadily in importance as an area of concern for scholars. The definition of women's roles and the social values that define the relationships between men and women have been changing. Social service and criminal justice agencies have responded to these changes by moving to adopt policies and practices that are more sympathetic to female victims of domestic violence, courtship violence, and forced sexual intercourse. In the process, rape, the intentional or planned use of physical force to obtain sexual access against the wishes of a woman who was not intimately involved with her assailant, has been redefined to the extent that rape is no longer an accurate characterization of the behaviors that can be addressed by the justice system on the complaint of a victim.

Although the focus of this chapter is on the definition of types of forced sexual intercourse, it should be noted that the definition of rape that was common in the first half of this century has slowly evolved to include types of forced sexual intercourse which in the past were held to be of no interest to the justice system and to include offensive sexual behaviors less than intercourse. Sexual assault, the emerging concept, is broad, has been widely accepted, and specifies degrees of offensiveness. There is some recognition that offensive sexual behavior and forced sexual intercourse can be placed on a continuum based on degree of unacceptability of the offensive behavior. Although this evolution may have positive effects on the ability of the justice system to protect women from male offenders, it increases the confusion in definition that has characterized forced sexual intercourse by including a wide range of behaviors under one label. At the same time, the perspective that will be presented here suggests that the continuum of those behaviors identified as forced sexual intercourse is broader than generally accepted and may include offensive sexual behaviors which are tolerated by some of the victims. Specifically, some offensive sexual behavior occurs in the context of courtship and dating and is accepted, to some degree, by some of the victims.

Historically, theories that sought to explain rape focused on those cases in which a stranger sexually assaulted a relatively unknown victim. Sexual assaults were explained in terms of mental illness and generally asserted that rape was more a matter of serious mental defect or a matter of dominance and control of women than a matter of gaining sexual access.

Three major works, published in the 1980s, sought to explain the broader range of behaviors which had become defined as behaviors, that were sufficiently unacceptable that they should be subjected to the control of the justice system. Sunday and Tobach (1985) addressed the sociobiological approach to violence against women, including rape. Ellis (1989) shifted the emphasis from predatory stranger rape to acquaintance rape and recognized the influence of the feminist perspective as originally advanced by Brownmiller (1975). He grouped explanations for forced sexual intercourse into three general theoretical perspectives: feminist theory, learning theory, and evolutionary theory. Baron and Straus (1989) also sought to present theories that reflected the broader definition of rape that had emerged by the 1980s. They grouped explanations for sexual assault into four general theoretical perspectives: gender inequality, pornography, social disorganization, and legitimate violence. Readers who seek more comprehensive coverage of these perspectives should review these three earlier works as well as Brownmiller's 1975 book, *Against Our Will: Men, Women, and Rape*.

THEORETICAL PERSPECTIVES

The Feminist Perspective

The feminist movement produced, or at least influenced, much of the reform in the manner in which society relates to women. Feminists argue that sexual assault is defined as a legitimate or normal product of male-dominated societies. From this perspective, offensive behaviors that control women are defined as acceptable to the males who control the society. Feminist theorists argue that patriarchal societies define men as dominant over women. Women are assigned inferior social status, with relatively little power, while men are socially superior and dominate and control women (Dobash & Dobash, 1979; Friedan, 1963). Men's power over women historically was defined as not subject to control by society in even the most severe instances, thus came to be perceived as a right or at least as a privilege exercised by men. In this context, forced sexual intercourse becomes more a matter of dominance and control than a matter of sex (Brownmiller, 1975; Goth, 1979; Holdstrom & Burgess, 1980; Riger & Gordon, 1981; Scarpitti & Scarpitti, 1977). Men (male-dominated society) use the fear of rape to allow men to assert their dominance over women and rape to control nonconforming women as a means of maintaining the patriarchal system of male dominance (Adamec & Adamec, 1981; Barry, 1979; Brownmiller, 1975; Goth, 1979; Persell, 1984; Riger & Gordon, 1981; Russell, 1975; Thompson & Buttell, 1984; Weis & Borges, 1977). Studies supporting the feminist perspective have tended to measure the incidence of rape in relation to incidents of violence in general (Baron & Straus, 1984; Benderly, 1982; Kutchinski, 1988; Sanday, 1981; Schwendinger & Schwendinger, 1985; Sigelman, Berry, & Wiles, 1984). Self-report studies that ask rapists to report their motivation tend to contradict the feminist model. They find that rapists report motivation by desire for excitement, risk taking, and sex (Scully & Marolla, 1984) and report high levels of deviant sexual fantasies (Walker & Meyer, 1981) with high levels of sexual arousal reported by date rapists (Yegidis, 1986).

In the feminist model, behaviors such as forced sexual intercourse are defined as acceptable or justified. It is possible, however, to argue within the feminist perspective that the behaviors themselves are not defined as acceptable, but rather, they are defined as personal or private and not of interest to those outside the family. That is, men who force their wives or female friends to engage in sex are not defined as good or tolerated for the purposes of controlling women, but the offensive behavior that they exhibit is defined as private and personal and not suitable for control by society.

The feminist perspective can be seen as an application of social learning theory. Some authors suggest that traditional gender roles and expectations define forced sexual intercourse as a normal aspect of male female interaction, thus encouraging rape (Burt, 1980; Check & Malamuth, 1983a; Cherry, 1983, Curtis, 1975, Russell, 1975; Weis & Borges, 1977). Norms that define masculinity in terms of dominance and control and femininity in terms of passivity and submission define the use of force by men to control women as gender role expectations that support or encourage forced sexual intercourse (Gagnon & Simon, 1973).

The Social Learning Theory

From a learning theory perspective, forced sexual intercourse and the attitudes that support it are learned in the same ways that other behaviors are learned. Men who force women to have sex do so because they (and in some perspectives their victims) have learned that this is appropriate behavior. For the feminists, this learning is related to or associated with the set of values that supports the socioeconomic and political exploitation of women by men; nonfeminist social learning theorists see forced sexual intercourse as related to or associated with cultural traditions linked with interpersonal aggression, masculine roles, and sexuality.

Learning theory is a general term encompassing theories developed in a number of traditions, including symbolic interaction and cognitive attitude theory; however, much of the work that addresses rape is derived from Bandura's (1973) drive-based, psychoanalytic modeling theory, which addresses aggression. Ellis (1989, pp. 12–13) states that social learning theories of rape which assert that rape is a form of aggression state that these behaviors are learned in four ways: by imitating or modeling aggressive sexual behaviors that the learner has observed in real life or in media presentations (Huesman & Malamuth, 1986; Nelson, 1982); by observing sex and violence in the same context or presentation (Check & Malamuth, 1983b; Malamuth, 1981, 1984, 1986, 1988; Malamuth, Briere, & Check, 1986); by repeating or portraying rape myths that make rape acceptable (Burt, 1980); and by the desensitization of the learner to the victim's perspective through repetition of exposure to incidents of sex and violence or of violent sex (Donnerstein, Linz, & Penrod, 1987).

The Sociobiological Perspective

The sociobiological perspective asserts that humanity is a product of evolution in which both physical and social traits conducive to survival are selected and survive through a process of natural selection. Propagation is the key to survival of a trait, as a genetic predisposition can be passed on only through offspring. The linkage of sexual selection and rape with trait survival was first made by Deutsch (1944). Social traits that have been selected include female emphasis on child care and male emphasis on mating with as many partners as possible (Bateman, 1948; Chamove, Harlow, & Mitchell, 1967; Daly & Wilson, 1978; Hagen, 1979; Leshner, 1978; Smith, 1978; Symons, 1979; Trivers, 1972; G. C. Williams, 1975). From a sociobiological perspective, men have a lower commitment to gestation than women (Quinsey, 1984) but have a disadvantage in that they cannot definitely identify their children (Daly & Wilson, 1978; Dawkins, 1976; Durden-Smith & deSimone, 1983); thus an inclination to impregnate as many females as possible has gene survival value. In this model, forced sexual intercourse increases the survival of a male's genes, thus selecting a tendency to rape (Gibson, Linden, & Johnson, 1980; Hagen, 1979; Quinsey, 1984; Symons, 1979). On the other hand, females who resist males who impregnate them and move on to other females are more likely to pass on their genes. The use of force to gain sexual access reduces the ability of a female to choose a mate who will stay with her after insemination. The absence of a male partner decreases the likelihood of survival of her children (Mellen, 1981; Richard & Schulman, 1982; Symons, 1979; Thornhill, 1980; Wilder, 1982). From this, rape would be a particularly effective strategy in modern times for men who have limited resources with which to attract a mate (Shields & Shields, 1983; Thornhill & Thornhill, 1983).

Social Disorganization and Legitimate Violence

Baron and Straus (1989) advance two additional theoretical perspectives for explaining rape: social disorganization and legitimate violence. Social disorganization occurs when social institutions and norms that regulate social conduct become ineffective (Blumer, 1937; Martindale, 1957; Mower, 1941; Thomas & Zaniecki, 1927; Wirth, 1940). When society's social control is weakened, deviant behavior and crime, including rape, are more likely to occur. Baron & Straus (1989) constructed a social disorganization index and discovered that when their measure of social disorganization is high, rates of rape are high.

Legitimate violence begins with the recognition that some theoretical perspectives define rape as normatively permitted rather than as beyond the control of society. Baron and Straus (1989) note that the feminists argue the presence of such norms (Brownmiller, 1975; Scully & Marolla, 1985).

Baron and Straus (1989) also note that a number of perspectives suggest that the legitimacy of rape might be supported indirectly. They cite violent subculture theories (Gastil, 1971; Hackney, 1969; Messner, 1983; Wolfgang & Ferracuti, 1967) and cross-cultural theories that demonstrate a link between types of violence (Archer & Gartner, 1984; Huggins & Straus, 1980; Lambert, Triandis, & Wolf, 1959) and between violence and sexual violence (Sanday, 1981) as well as between violence and sexual violence in the United States (Amir, 1971). These findings are taken by Baron and Straus to support a cultural spillover theory of criminal violence. As the extent to which society approves the legitimate use of violence increases in some areas, the use of violence in rape and in collateral areas, such as personal assault, increases.

STATE OF THE ART

The theories that have been developed to explain forced sexual intercourse tend to treat forced sexual intercourse as a single type of behavior. Because forced sexual intercourse is seen as a single phenomenon, scholars have sought to develop a single theory. The theories that have been developed tend to be most effective in explaining incidents of forced sexual intercourse in which a man intends to force a woman to have sex when she does not want to have sex, when physical force or the threat of physical force is used, and when the woman defines her victimization as rape. If the nature of the interaction between the victim and offender is such that forced sexual intercourse produces different sets of phenomena, a single model theory will not be sufficient to describe accurately the phenomena under study.

The criminal status of forced sexual intercourse in marriage is still evolving. Historically, forced sexual intercourse in marriage was specifically excluded in definitions of rape to the extent that the "marital exemption" was an accepted legal principle (LaFave & Scott, 1972).

The rationales for the adoption of the marital rape exemption include the following:

1. The marriage contract in which some people would argue dissolves the woman's rights and enhances the rights of the husband as the head of the house. A woman's consent to marriage has been extended to imply consent to submit to the wishes of the husband and can only be revoked by divorce.

2. The legal definition of rape—historically, rape has been defined as a property crime and women were considered the property of their husbands or fathers. In

People v. Liberta (1984), the court stated that "the purpose behind the pro-scriptions [against rape] was to protect the chastity of women and thus their property value to their husbands and fathers" (p. 567).

3. Marital unity—the belief that husbands and wives become one after marriage. If this is true, a man cannot rape himself (Brown, 1995; Sitton, 1993). These rationales are no longer applicable to married women because the roles of women in society have changed dramatically.

Contemporary proponents of marital rape suggest that marital rape is not as serious as other types of rape (Sitton, 1993). It is argued that the closer the relationship between the victim and the perpetrator, the more a victim feels violated both physically and mentally. In fact, the victim may be more traumatized because of the relationship. Additionally, some proponents fear that having a marital rape classification would cause false rape claims to be made by angry wives who seek to damage or destroy their husband's reputation. Another issue raised in opposition to the inclusion of a marital rape classification was the possible impact on marital stability (Sitton, 1993). It is hard to imagine a marriage that is stable if the husband is raping his wife.

Regardless of which argument one examines concerning marital rape, the result is the same: Women are not equal beings in our society. According to Sitton (1993), "throughout our legal and cultural tradition, the woman is either a virgin or a whore, alter-natively someone to be placed on a pedestal or in the bedroom" (p. 268). Again, previous views and role expectations associated with women are no longer applicable. Fortunately, in *Trammell v. United States* (1980), the court ruled that women are not chattel and are no less than other human beings. Other reform measures toward gender equality have assisted in solidifying the legal status of women. Challenges to the marital rape exemption have been based on the constitutional right to privacy, a broad and private-sphere interpretation of the Thirteenth Amendment and the Fourteenth Amendment. For a more thorough examination of the arguments regarding marital rape based on the Constitution and its amendments, see Dailey (1986), McConnell (1992), *Merton v. State* (1986), *People v. Liberta* (1984), *Reed v. Reed* (1971), and West (1990).

The lines are clearly drawn from a social activist perspective: Forced sexual intercourse in marriage is either rape or a husband's privilege, depending on the per-spective of the speaker. It is more likely that this is an issue of public versus private interest rather than a matter of male rights. That is, few will actually believe that men who force their wives to engage in sex are behaving in an acceptable manner. The behavior is perceived as wrong but not a matter that should be resolved by the police and the criminal courts. Confusion is added by the prospect that there is an expectation of sexual access in marriage and a corresponding obligation of the wife to submit to her husband which is endorsed by both many men and many women (endorsement of "tra-ditional values") (Bullough, 1974; J. E. Williams, 1979). Setting the legal arguments aside, the question of behavioral similarity remains. Is forced sexual intercourse in marriage the same or more similar to the behavior exhibited when a stranger forces an unwilling victim, or the same as or more similar to forced sexual intercourse in a courtship setting? It is possible that forced sexual intercourse in marriage is not a matter of sexual access but a matter of power and domination. It is also possible that there are two types of forced sexual intercourse in marriage, the first reflecting power and dominance, the second reflecting forcing sexual access from an unwilling spouse.

TYPES OF FORCED SEXUAL INTERCOURSE

Some scholars have focused on the development of theoretical models that address forced sexual intercourse in dating or courtship settings. Most studies with a theoretical base attempt to identify factors that make types of assault more or less likely to occur. One effort (Shotland, 1992) develops a basic typology of date rape. Five different types of date rape are characterized, based on time, courtship violence, and degree of development of a relationship. Felson (1992) has developed a model that seeks to explain sexual assaults in terms of motives and goals. He identifies five paths, using factors such as social identity, bodily pleasure, personal justice, domination, sexual relations, and harm to target.

The present theories that focus on rape are not effective in describing all events presently included under the terms *date rape, acquaintance rape*, and *marital rape*. In some incidents that are identified as date rape, a man intentionally forces a woman to have sex when she doesn't want to using substantial force, and the woman defines her victimization as rape. In other instances that are identified as date rape, the man may not intend to force the woman to have sex, the degree of force may be less substantial, and the woman may not define her victimization as rape. In the first instance, a rape has occurred that can be explained with one or more of the existing models; the incident just happened to occur in a dating context. In the second instance, the behavior is offensive and unacceptable by standards that are emerging today, but the behavior cannot be explained accurately with existing theories. The inability to describe the nature of the phenomena accurately reduces the ability to effectively address what is clearly a contemporary social problem.

The data available from studies of forced sexual intercourse consistently have identified sets of incidents in which the forced sexual intercourse reported by victims is not identified as rape beginning with Russell's (1984) early study. About one-half of the women who indicated that they had experienced incidents which met the legal definition of rape in use at that time did not respond affirmatively when asked if they had been raped. Similar results were reported by a leading study in the area of date rape. Koss, Dinero, Seibel, and Cox (1988) reported 23.1 percent of the women victimized by men they knew labeled their victimization as rape, and 62 percent of these victims indicated that they did not view their victimization as any type of crime. Similar results have been reported by Johnson, Palileo, and Gray (1992), Doyle and Burfeind (1994), Johnson and Sigler (1998), and other studies that report findings for women's characterizations of their victimization.

A BEGINNING MODEL

We argue that all instances of forced sexual intercourse are not the same—that there are substantial differences among various sets of sexually offensive behaviors. While existing theories provide an effective basis for dealing with those cases in which a man intends to rape a woman who realizes that she is being raped, they are less effective in explaining many of the victimizations which are presently included under the labels of date or acquaintance rape.

At this point we suggest that alternative models should be developed to explain different types of forced sexual intercourse. Based on the knowledge available today, four types of forced sexual intercourse can be identified, which are substantially different from each other. These models are biased in that they assume that the victim is always a woman and the offender is always a man. Although the same models might apply to homosexual relationships or to cases in which a woman victimizes a man, the limited information available in these areas makes it difficult to attempt model development. We identify four types of forced sexual intercourse: rape, spousal rape, forced sexual intercourse, and predatory rape in a dating or courtship context.

Rape occurs when a man who is unknown or known casually to the victim uses physical force or threat of physical force to secure sexual access against the wishes of the victim. Both the offender and the victim tend to identify the behavior as rape. This form of forced sexual intercourse has been studied more extensively than other forms of forced sexual intercourse, and several models are available to explain the behavior, many of which suggest that the behavior is not sexual in nature.

Spousal rape occurs when a man uses physical force or the threat of physical force against a woman to secure sexual access against her will from a partner with whom he has established a relatively permanent relationship. Definition of the behavior as rape will vary from offender to offender and from victim to victim. A *relatively permanent relationship* is defined as a relationship which includes sexual intimacy as a part of the relationship and is not limited to couples who share the same living area (cohabitation). Very little information is available about this form of behavior. Most of the literature that addresses this issue focuses on the legal and ethical dimensions of the issue rather than on understanding the nature of the interaction between the actors. Placing this behavior in the context of marital disputes and spouse abuse may be more effective than addressing the issue in the context of forced sexual intercourse as a sexual act even when sexual access is the primary goal of the offender.

Forced sexual intercourse in a dating or courtship context occurs when a man uses physical force to secure sexual access without her consent from a woman with whom he is developing a relationship while the couple is engaged in a consensual intimate social context. Definition of the behavior as rape will vary from offender to offender and from victim to victim. This type of forced sexual intercourse applies only to events that occur as the relationship is developing. It is probable that sexual access is the primary motivator in these types of exchanges. In most cases the man does not enter the exchange with the intent of using force. These events tend to be characterized as involving loss of control and may be better understood in the context of courtship than as independent acts of sexual assault.

Predatory rape occurs when a man pretends to engage in legitimate dating or courtship behavior with the intent of using force to gain sexual access against the will of the woman if he cannot gain consent. The offender will tend to identify his behavior as rape, but the victim may or may not define the behavior as rape. In these cases, the offender is not seeking a personal or intimate relationship; rather, he is seeking sexual relief and has no concern for the feelings, rights, or needs of his victim. He intends to maneuver the victim into a comprising position so that she will not protest after the act has been completed and he will use almost any means necessary to achieve his goal. Very little is known about this behavior; thus the development of an accurate model is difficult. These men are identifiable in data that have been collected by the authors (Johnson & Sigler, 1998).

FORCED SEXUAL INTERCOURSE IN A COURTSHIP OR DATING CONTEXT

Sufficient data are now available to permit the development and testing of a model designed to explain the nature of forced sexual intercourse in a dating context. Although all factors that might operate in instances of forced sexual intercourse in these situations have not been clearly identified by contemporary efforts to examine forced sexual intercourse, sufficient information has been gleaned to permit the development of a tentative model that can be used to guide further research. The model only addresses behavior that has generally been characterized as date or acquaintance rape and does not address stranger rape, spousal rape, or predatory rape.

The model advanced here suggests that some forms of forced sexual intercourse should be examined in the context of courtship or dating. *Courtship* is defined as a set of activities that are undertaken with the intent of establishing a fairly permanent relationship. Although some undetermined portion of dating is primarily temporary and recreational in nature, much of dating has a courtship function. In many instances, participants in recreational dating are evaluating their partners in terms of potential suitability as long-term partners. Dating is an activity that leads to courtship when a potential partner is identified. Although this shift in emphasis is usually not formally noted, most of those who actively date are aware of the potential in their activity.

A couple progresses from casual dating to a committed, long-term, relatively permanent relationship in a process that can be characterized by degrees of increasing intimacy. Both partners tend to assume that at some point, sexual intimacy will become a part of the relationship as the relationship matures. For most couples, this assumption is not overtly recognized, the stages through which a relationship moves to maturity are not specified, and the circumstances under which sexual intimacy will occur are not addressed overtly. The process, in terms of increasing commitment, is one of advancing and retreating as the relationship moves toward the development of a relatively permanent relationship. Forced sexual intercourse can occur when the process of relationship formation gets out of control.

In Western society, women are expected to control the degree of sexual intimacy at each stage in the development of the relationship. Men are expected to seek increasing degrees of sexual intimacy as a relationship develops, and women are expected to resist male pressure until the relationship matures to the point at which the woman feels comfortable committing to sexual intimacy. Women have personal standards that must be met before they are willing to engage in increased sexual intimacy, particularly sexual intercourse. Couples generally do not discuss the conditions that must be met before complete sexual intimacy becomes a part of the relationship. Although these standards are individual, they can include such things as a determination with a high degree of certainty by the woman that this man is the person with whom she wishes to establish a permanent relationship; he will not abuse her at some later date, he is as committed to her as she is to him, and he (as well as her friends, his friends, and other significant others) will not label her negatively if she agrees to complete sexual intimacy. Men who are aware that such standards exist usually are not aware of the standards held by the person with whom they are seeking to establish a relatively permanent relationship.

"Real" men are expected to be aggressive. Men who express an unwillingness to be physically aggressive are generally labeled negatively. Aggression by men in the courtship process produces a situation in which men attempt assertively to move the courtship process to increasing levels of sexual intimacy, while women resist these efforts in favor of a more deliberate and cautious development of the relationship. Men place pressure on women to move forward with commitment to the relationship, while women want to move forward but not as fast as the men are requesting. Moving toward sexual intimacy is an interactive process frequently involving a trial-and-error process or advancing and retreating from complete sexual intimacy as the couple works to develop a long-term, stable, relatively permanent relationship. An out-of-control situation can develop that can produce forced sexual intercourse when unclear expectations produce unacceptable behavior, biological arousal reduces rational behavior for one or for both parties, or the level of male aggression is greater than the woman anticipated.

Some women consent to sexual intimacy when they do not really want to be intimate. There are a number of circumstances under which unwilling consent is given. This behavior may be more common in established sexually intimate relationships. Once a relationship has moved to a level including sexual intimacy, the man may desire sexual intimacy at times when the woman does not or more frequently than the woman prefers. Women sometimes will agree to sexual intimacy when they would rather not in order to meet the man's needs. In cases in which a relationship is developing, at times a woman may hesitate to commit to complete sexual intimacy although she has decided that she will become sexually intimate at some point in the relationship with the man she is dating. As the relationship develops, she may respond to the man's pressure to agree to sexual intimacy before she is certain that she is ready for the relationship to move to that particular level of intimacy. Men generally believe that if they are persistent, some women will consent when they are certain about their decision. Some men are not sufficiently sensitive to realize that they are forcing the women with whom they have a relationship to be sexually intimate.

The factors that have been advanced as important to a model which seeks to explain incidents of nonpredatory forced sexual intercourse include (1) the relationship formation process in which couples become increasingly intimate, (2) role expectations for aggressive behavior in courtship (more rapid development of the relationship), (3) role expectations for women to resist male aggression in courtship (less rapid development of the relationship), (4) women control (decide) when the relationship will move to more intense levels of sexual intimacy, (5) women have standards (conditions) that must be satisfied before they agree to sexual intimacy, (7) some women will consent to sexual intimacy when they don't really want to be sexually intimate, and (8) men are aware that women will consent at times when they don't want to be sexually intimate but men are usually not aware of or sensitive to the existence or of the nature of the standards or conditions that women hold for their own commitment to sexual intimacy. When these factors are applied to instances of forced sexual intercourse in courtship and dating, a number of patterns emerge (Johnson & Sigler, 1998).

In some situations, both the man and the woman anticipate and are moving toward eventual intense sexual intimacy. They engage in preliminary sexually intimate behavior, and at a point in the relationship, the situation gets out of control. The man forces the woman to have sex while they are engaging in consensual sexual activity. In these cases it is probable that neither the man nor the woman will label the behavior as rape, psychological damage will be minimal, and both the man and the woman may choose to continue to develop a long-term relationship and have positive images of each other (Johnson & Sigler, 1998).

In some instances, the woman considers intense sexual intimacy a possibility at some point, but she has not committed to the development of a permanent relationship at that point in the relationship. She engages in some exploratory sexual activity even though she may not anticipate a permanent relationship. During a period of intimacy, the man forces the woman to have intercourse. In these cases, both the woman and the man might or might not define the incident as rape. If the woman defines the incident as rape, she will terminate the relationship and have mixed or negative opinions of the man. Psychological damage will be moderate to high. If the woman does not define the incident as rape, she may continue the relationship and have mixed opinions of the man. Psychological damage will be low to moderate (Johnson & Sigler, 1998).

In some situations the women will hold a value that prohibits sexual intercourse before a firm permanent relationship is established, but she engages in some intimate sexual behavior in the process of seeking a relationship. During a period of consensual sexual activity the man forces the woman to have sexual intercourse. In these cases the woman will define the incident as rape, and the man may or may not define the incident as rape. The woman will terminate the relationship and have mixed but predominantly negative opinions of the man, in that there are characteristics that she found attractive which were not related to his sexual aggression. She will not continue the relationship, and in most cases, psychological damage will be high (Johnson & Sigler, 1998).

This model suggests that the development of an agreement to engage in consensual sexual intercourse in a dating or courtship setting is a negotiated process in which the woman grants sexual access to the man when specific personal conditions (personal standards) are met. It is acceptable for men to actively pursue sexual intercourse, and this pursuit is not channeled by the woman's conditions for agreeing to sexual intimacy because these conditions (woman's expectations) frequently are not clear.

The development of a relatively stable intimate relationship involves exploratory sexual behavior in which the couple approaches but does not necessarily engage in sexual intercourse. If this process gets out of control, forced sexual intercourse might occur because the man is larger and stronger and/or because the woman cannot manage to withdraw without permanently damaging a relationship she may want to preserve. When forced sexual intercourse occurs in this context, the woman may accept responsibility for the outcome, and the man might see this as an acceptable or anticipated outcome.

This model only addresses forced sexual intercourse that occurs during a legitimate pursuit of a relatively long-term relationship and does not address forced sexual intercourse labeled as predatory, blitz, or confidence rape. In the latter, a male predator engages in dating or courtship behavior to gain a position from which he can relatively safely force a women to submit to sexual intercourse. He does not intend to develop a long-term relationship but pretends to pursue a relationship in order to gain sexual access by trick or fraud. If his efforts to gain consensual sexual access are not successful, he might use whatever degree of force is necessary to gain sexual access. The characterization of this behavior as courtship behavior provides some protection from sanctioning for the offender. It should be noted that research to date has not indicated that women are able to distinguish between the predatory rapist and the legitimate suitor until after she has been successfully victimized, and it is possible that she may not be certain after her victimization. This behavior can be explained more successfully by traditional theories of rape than by a courtship model of forced sexual intercourse.

The model does not effectively address marital rape or rape that occurs in relatively stable relationships in which sexual intercourse has been accepted as a normal part of the relationship. Although sufficient empirical attention has not been devoted to an examination of this phenomenon to permit preliminary model development, it is probable that models which stress dominance and control rather than sexual access are more appropriate than other models. Power and dominance or sexual needs may drive the offender, but the behavior occurs in the context of a relatively permanent relationship and may be better understood in the context of the dynamics, particularly the dynamics of conflict resolution, than in the context of rape or the context of courtship and dating.

The courtship model advanced here will not effectively address situations in which sexual intercourse is a potential form of recreation rather than an activity that occurs in a relatively permanent relationship. In situations in which both the man and the woman define sexual intercourse as a recreational option in casual dating, the behavioral patterns might be similar but accelerated with different interpretations of expectations and processes held by the actors. If a man forces a woman to have sex in this setting, new models might need to be developed, or traditional theories of rape may be more effective in understanding and investigating the behavior. Little empirical attention has been directed toward this phenomenon, so any assessment is pure speculation at this point.

The model advanced here is a simplification of a very complex system of interactions that comprise dating and courtship. There is a need for extensive further research directed toward increasing our understanding of all forms of forced sexual intercourse. An effort must be made to determine if different types of phenomena are addressed under the labels of date rape and under the more general category of rape. If there are differences, are they such that if they were fully understood, effective strategies to protect women could be developed? The questions that must be addressed are extensive. What are the factors in the individual settings that are more likely to precipitate the use of physical force? What are the interactional characteristics of these situations? What are the factors that cause some people to be more likely than others to use physical force in intimate situations? When the relevant variables are identified, patterns can be defined and resources can be allocated effectively and efficiently. The model presented here can provide a focus for this research once it is more fully articulated and tested.

SUMMARY

Forced sexual intercourse has been perceived as a single phenomenon throughout history. There has been a great deal of evolution in the reaction of the justice system with many acts of forced sexual intercourse that were considered private matters becoming criminalized. All forms of forced sexual intercourse have been defined as parts of a social problem that has emerged because changing social values regarding the roles of women and men in society and in intimate relationships have created a change in the degree of public interest in women's victimization.

Before effective responses to all forms of forced sexual intercourse can be developed, this phenomenon must be understood. A first step in increasing understanding of the phenomenon is to recognize that the same behaviors may be different phenomena in different social contexts: that some forms of forced sexual intercourse occur between relatively intimate partners, and that one form of forced sexual intercourse might be substantially different from other forms of forced sexual intercourse. That is, types of forced sexual intercourse must be examined in the social context in which they occur.

Rape has been evaluated consistently in terms of aggression, dominance, control, and violence rather than in terms of sexual access. Historically, rape has been a crime that has been condemned, if not effectively prosecuted. Reforms in the past decade have introduced changes in the law that create different levels of sexual assault and that make cases of sexual assault easier to prosecute successfully. Social concern that accompanied reform efforts on intimate violence as well as on forced sexual intercourse has focused attention on the prevalence and nature of forced sexual intercourse.

Most theories that attempt to explain rape treat rape as a single phenomenon. All forms of forced sexual intercourse are seen as the same thing. The feminist perspective argues that rape is a characteristic of male-dominated patriarchal societies. Threat of rape functions to control and dominate women, forcing them into passive submissive roles.

From a number of perspectives, learning theories specify that the use of force in sexual encounters is learned in the same way that other behaviors and/or values are learned. The most prominent of these are drive-based psychoanalytic theories that are related to the work of Bandura. Most other learning theorists, sociologists, and criminologists have not applied their perspectives directly to the explanation of forced sexual intercourse.

Sociobiologists argue that males who use force in sexual intercourse will be more likely to pass their genes on to future generations, in that access to the greatest number of partners maximizes gene survival. Women, on the other hand, maximize the transmission of their genes to future generations by attracting males who will remain with them after insemination to care for the children. Baron and Straus (1989) added models based on social disorganization and on legitimate use of violence to other existing traditional models to advance an integrated model to explain rape. While their model effectively combines the elements of many of the traditional theories, it still treats rape as a single phenomenon in which a male intends to use force to obtain sex from an unwilling resisting female who sees herself as being raped.

The argument advanced in this chapter is that there are types or sets of related forms of forced sexual intercourse that are sufficiently different as to require separate explanatory models if the phenomena are to be understood and examined effectively. In rape, a man forces a women whom he does not know, or whom he does not know very well, to have sex with him. In spousal rape, a man who is in a fairly long-term sexual relationship with a woman forces her to have sex. In predatory rape, a man pretends to engage in a legitimate dating relationship with a woman in order to manipulate her into a position in which he can force her to have sex with him. In courtship and dating forced sexual intercourse, a man and a woman are developing a long-term relationship. In the process, one or both of the actors lose control and the man forces the woman to have sex.

An expanded model for forced sexual intercourse in dating or courtship has been developed that can be used to frame future research in this area. This model assumes that the process of establishing a relatively permanent or long-term relationship involves progressively more intimate interaction as the relationship matures, with sexual intercourse anticipated at some point in the relationship. The point at which sexual intercourse becomes a part of the relationship and the conditions that must be met before this level of commitment to the relationship is accepted are determined by the woman. As the relationship moves to increasingly intimate contact, the potential for loss of control and the use of force increases. In these cases, neither the man nor the woman is likely to define the behavior as rape.

This model will be refined and assessed through empirical examination. As the model develops, a more thorough and accurate understanding of the use of force in intimate relationships will emerge. As conceptualization of the phenomena becomes more thorough and accurate, more effective responses will be developed for the justice system, and more effective educational materials can be developed to reduce the victimization of women at the hands of those with whom they seek to develop long-term, relatively permanent relationships.

REFERENCES

ADAMEC, C. S., & ADAMEC, R. E. (1981). Aggression by men against women: Adaptation or aberration. *International Journal of Women's Studies, 1*, 1–21.

AMIR, M. (1971). *Patterns in forcible rape*. Chicago: University of Chicago Press.

ARCHER, D., & GARTNER, R. (1984). *Violence and crime in cross-national perspective*. New Haven, CT: Yale University Press.

BANDURA, A. (1973). *Aggression: A social learning analysis*. Englewood Cliffs, NJ: Prentice Hall.

BARON, L., & STRAUS, M. A. (1984). Sexual stratification, pornography, and rape in the United States. In M. N. Malamuth & E. Donnerstein (Eds.), *Pornography and sexual aggression* (pp. 185–209). Orlando, FL: Academic Press.

BARON, L., & STRAUS, M. A. (1989). *Four theories of rape in American society: A state level analysis*. New Haven, CT: Yale University Press.

BARRY, K. (1979). *Female sexual slavery*. Englewood Cliffs, NJ: Prentice Hall.

BATEMAN, A. J. (1948). Introsexual selection in drosophila. *Heredity, 2*, 349–368.

BENDERLY, B. L. (1982). Rape free or rape prone. *Science, 82*(3), 40–43.

BLUMER, H. (1937). Social organization and individual disorganization. *American Journal of Sociology, 42*, 871–877.

BROWN, E. (1995). Changing the marital rape exception: I am chattel; hear me roar. *American Journal of Trial Advocacy, 18*(3), 657–671.

BROWNMILLER, S. (1975). *Against our will: Men, women, and rape*. New York: Simon and Schuster.

BRYDEN, D., & LENGNICK, S. (1997). Rape in the criminal justice system. *Journal of Criminal Law and Criminology, 87,* 1194–1384.

BULLOUGH, V. L. (1974). *The subordinate sex: a history of attitudes toward women.* Baltimore: Penguin Books.

BURT, M. R. (1980). Cultural myths and supports for rape. *Journal of Personality and Social Psychology, 38,* 217–234.

CHAMOVE, A., HARLOW, H. F., & MITCHELL, G. D. (1967). Sex differences in the infant directed behavior of preadolescent rhesus monkeys. *Child Development, 38,* 329–355.

CHECK, J. V. P., & MALAMUTH, N. M. (1983a). Sex-role stereotyping and reactions to stranger vs. acquaintance rape. *Journal of Personality and Social Psychology, 45,* 344–356.

CHECK, J. V. P., & MALAMUTH, N. M. (1983b) Can participation in pornography experiments have positive effects? *Journal of Sex Research, 20,* 14–31.

CHERRY, F. (1983). Gender roles and sexual violence. In E. R. Allgeier & N. B. McCormick (Eds.), *Changing boundaries: Gender roles and sexual behavior* (pp. 245–260). Palo Alto, CA: Mayfield Publishing.

CURTIS, L. A. (1975). *Violence, Race, and Culture.* Lexington, MA: Lexington Press.

DAILEY, A. (1986). To have and to hold: The marital rape exemption and the Fourteenth Amendment. *Harvard Law Review, 99,* 1255 passim.

DALY, M., & WILSON, M. (1978). *Sex, evolution, and behavior.* North Scituate, MA: Duxbury Press.

DAWKINS, R. (1976). *The selfish gene.* New York: Oxford University Press.

DEUTSCH, H. (1944). *The psychology of women: Vol. 1. Girlhood.* New York: Bantam Books.

DOBASH, R. E., & DOBASH, R. (1979). *Violence against wives: A case against the patriarchy.* New York: The Free Press.

DONNERSTEIN, E., LINZ, D., & PENROD, S. (1987). *The question of pornography.* New York: Free Press.

DOYLE, D. P., & BURFEIND, J. W. (1994). *The University of Montana sexual victimization survey executive summary.* Missoula, MT: Authors.

DURDEN-SMITH, J., & DESIMONE, D. (1983). *Sex and the brain.* New York: Warner Publishing.

ELLIS, L. (1989). *Theories of rape: Inquiries into the causes of sexual aggression.* New York: Hemisphere Publishing.

ESKOW, L. (1996). The ultimate weapon? Demythologizing spousal rape and reconceptualizing its prosecution. *Stanford Law Review, 48,* 677–709.

FELSON, R. B. (1992). *Motives for sexual coercion.* Paper presented at the annual meeting of the American Society of Criminology, Tucson, AZ.

FRIEDAN, B. (1963). *The feminine mystique.* New York: W. W. Norton.

GAGNON, J. H., & SIMON, W. (1973). Sexual contact: The sources of sexuality. Chicago: Adeline Press.

GASTIL, R. D. (1971). Homicide and a regional culture of violence. *American Sociological Review, 36,* 412–427.

GIBSON, L., LINDEN, R., & JOHNSON, S. (1980). A situational theory of rape. *Canadian Journal of Criminology, 22,* 51–63.

GOTH, A. N. (1979). *Men who rape: The psychology of the offender.* New York: Plenum Press.

HACKNEY, S. (1969). Southern violence. *American Historical Review, 74,* 906–925.

HAGEN, R. (1979). *The bio-social factor.* Garden City, NJ: Doubleday.

HOLDSTROM, L. L., & BURGESS, A. W. (1980). Sexual behavior of assailants during reported rapes. *Archives of Sexual Behavior, 9,* 427–439.

HUESMAN, L. R., & MALAMUTH, N. M. (1986). Media violence and antisocial behavior: An overview. *Journal of Social Issues, 42,* 1–6.

HUGGINS, M. D., & STRAUS, M. A. (1980). Violence and the social structure as reflected in children's books from 1850 to 1970. In M. A. Strauss & G. T. Hotaling (Eds.), *The social causes of husband wife violence* (pp. 51–67). Minneapolis, MN: University of Minnesota Press.

JOHNSON, D. G., PALILEO, G. J., & GRAY, N. B. (1992). Date rape on a southern campus: Reports from 1991. *Sociology and Social Research, 76*(2), 37–41.

JOHNSON, I. M., & SIGLER, R. T. (1998). Examining courtship, dating, and forced sexual intercourse: A preliminary model. *Free Inquiry in Creative Sociology, 26*(1), 99–110.

KOSS, M. P., DINERO, T. E., SEIBEL, C. A., & COX S. (1988). Stranger and acquaintance rape: Are there differences in the victim's experience? *Psychology of Women Quarterly, 12*, 1–24.

KUTCHINSKI, B. (1988). Towards an exploration of the decrease in registered sex cimes in Copenhagen. *Technical report of the Commission on Obscenity and Pornography* (Vol. 7). Washington, DC: Government Printing Office.

LAFAVE, W. R., & SCOTT, A. W. (1972). *Handbook on criminal law.* St. Paul, MN: West Publishing.

LAMBERT, W. W., TRIANDIS, L. M., & WOLF, M. (1959). Some correlates of beliefs in the malevolence and benevolence of supernatural beings: A cross cultural study. *Journal of Abnormal and Social Psychology, 58*, 162–169.

LESHNER, A. L. (1978). *An introduction to behavioral endocrinology.* New York: Oxford University Press.

MALAMUTH, N. M. (1981). Rape proclivity among males. *Journal of Social Issues, 37*(4), 138–157.

MALAMUTH, N. M. (1984). Aggression against women. In N. A. Malamuth & E. Donnerstein (Eds.), *Pornography and Sexual Aggression.* Orlando, FL: Academic Press.

MALAMUTH, N. M. (1986). Predictors of naturalistic sexual aggression. *Journal of Personality and Social Psychology, 50*, 953–962.

MALAMUTH, N. M. (1988). Predicting laboratory aggression against female and male targets: Implications for sexual violence. *Journal of Research Personality, 22*, 47–495.

MALAMUTH, N., BRIERE, J., & CHECK, J. V. P. (1986). Sexual arousal in response to aggression: Ideology, aggressive, and sexual correlates. *Journal of Personality and Social Psychology, 50*, 330–340.

MALAMUTH, N., FESBACK, S., & JAFFE, Y. (1977). Sexual arousal and aggression: Recent experiments and theoretical issues. *Journal of Social Issues, 33*, 110–133.

MARTINDALE, D. (1957). Social disorganization: The conflict of normative and empirical approaches. In H. Becker & A. Boskoff (Eds.), *Modern sociological theory in continuity and change* (pp. 340–367). New York: Holt, Rinehart & Winston.

MCCONNELL, J. (1992). Beyond metaphor: Battered women, involuntary servitude and the Thirteenth Amendment. *Yale Law Review, 4*, 207–249.

MELLEN, S. L. (1981). *The evolution of love.* San Francisco: W. H. Freeman.

MESSNER, S. F. (1983). Regional and racial effects on the urban homicide rate: The subculture of violence revisited. *American Journal of Sociology, 88*, 997–1007.

MOWER, E. R. (1941). Methodological problems in social disorganization. *American Sociological Review, 6*, 639–649.

NELSON, E. (1982) Pornography and sexual aggression. In M. Yaffee & E. Nelson (Eds.), *The influence of pornography on behavior.* London: Academic Press.

PALMER, S. (1997). Rape in marriage and the European Convention on Human Rights. *Feminist Legal Studies, 5*, 91–97.

PERSELL, C. H. (1984). *Understanding Society.* New York: Harper & Row.

QUINSEY, V. L. (1984). Sexual aggression: Studies of offenders against women. In D. Weisstub (Ed.), *Law and mental health: International perspectives* (Vol. 1). Elmsford, NY: Pergamon Press.

RICHARD, A. F., & SCHULMAN, S. R. (1982). Sociobiology: Primate field studies. *Annual Review in Anthropology, 11*, 231–255.

RIGER, S., & GORDON, M. T. (1981). The fear of rape: A study in social control. *Journal of Social Issues, 37*(4), 71–92.

RUSSELL, D. E. (1975). *The politics of rape: The victim's perspective*. New York: Stein & Day.

RUSSELL, D. E. H. (1984). *Sexual exploitation: Rape, child sexual abuse, and workplace harassment*. Beverly Hills, CA: Sage Publications.

SANDAY, P. R. (1981). The socio-cultural context of rape: A cross-cultural study. *The Journal of Social Issues, 37*, 5–27.

SCARPITTI, F., & SCARPITTI, E. (1977). Victims of rape. *Transaction, 14*, 29–32.

SCHWENDINGER, J., & SCHWENDINGER, H. (1985). Homo economics as the rapist in sociobiology. In S. R. Sanday & E. Toch (Eds.), *Violence Against Women*, (pp. 85–114). New York: Gordian Press.

SCULLY, D., & MAROLLA, J. (1984). Convicted rapists' vocabulary of motives: Excuses and justifications. *Social Problems, 32*, 530–544.

SCULLY, D., & MAROLLA, J. (1985). Riding the bull at Gilly's: Convicted rapists describe the rewards of rape. *Social Problems, 32*, 251–262.

SHIELDS, W. M., & SHIELDS, L. M. (1983). Forcible rape: An evolutionary perspective. *Ethnology and Sociobiology, 4*, 115–136.

SHOTLAND, R. L. (1992). A theory of the causes of courtship rape. *Journal of Social Issues, 48*, 127–144.

SIGELMAN, C. K., BERRY, C. J., & WILES, K. A. (1984). Violence in college students' dating relationships. *Journal of Applied Social Psychology, 14*, 530–548.

SITTON, J. (1993). Old wine in new bottles: The "marital" rape allowance. *North Carolina Law Review, 72*(1), 261–289.

SMITH, J. M. (1978). *The evolution of sex*. New York: Cambridge University Press.

SUNDAY, S. R., & TOBACH, E. (1985). *Violence against women: A critique of the sociobiology of rape*. New York: Gordian Press.

SYMONS, D. (1979). *The evolution of human sexuality*. New York: Oxford University Press.

THOMAS, W. I., & ZANIECKI, F. (1927). *The Polish peasant in Europe and America*. New York: Knopf.

THOMPSON, W. W. E., & BUTTELL, A. J. (1984). Sexual deviance in America. *Emporia State Research Studies, 33*, 6–47.

THORNHILL, R. (1980). Rape in Panorpa scorpionflies and a general rape hypothesis. *Animal Behavior, 28*, 55–59.

THORNHILL, R., & THORNHILL, N. W. (1983). Human rape: An evolutionary analysis. *Ethnology and Sociobiology, 4*, 137–173.

TRIVERS, R. (1972), Parental investment and sexual selection. In B. Campbell (Ed.), *Sexual selection and the descent of man* (pp. 136–179). Chicago: Aldine Publishing.

WALKER, P. A., & MEYER, W. J. (1981). Medroxyprogesterone acetate treatment for paraphiliac sex offenders. In J. R. Hays (Ed.), *Violence and the violent individual*. New York: Spectrum.

WEIS, K., & BORGES, S. S. (1977). Victimology and rape: The case of the legitimate victim. In D. R. Nass (Ed.), *The rape victim* (pp. 35–75), Dubuque, IO: Kendall/Hunt.

WEST, R. (1990). Equality theory, marital rape and the promise of the Fourteenth Amendment. *Florida Law Review, 42*, 45 passim.

WILDER, R. (1982, July). Are sexual standards inherited? *Science Digest*, p. 69.

WILLIAMS, G. C. (1975). *Sex and evolution*. Princeton, NJ: Princeton University Press.

WILLIAMS, J. E. (1979). Sex role stereotypes, women's liberation, and rape: A cross-cultural analysis of attitudes. *Sociological Symposium, 5*(1), 61–97.

WILSON, E. O. (1975). *Sociobiology: The new synthesis*. Cambridge, MA: Belknap Press of Harvard University.

WIRTH, L. (1940). Ideological aspects of social disorganization. *American Sociological Review, 5*, 472–482.

WOLFGANG, M., & FERRACUTI, F. (1967). *The subculture of violence*. London: Tavistock.

YEGIDIS, B. L. (1986). Date rape and forced sexual encounters among college students. *Journal of Sex Education and Therapy, 12*, 51–54.

CASES

Merton v. State, 500 so. 2d 1301-05 (Ala. Crim. App.) (1986)

People v. Liberta, 474 N.E.2d 567, 576 (1984)

Reed v. Reed, 404 U.S. 71, 92 S. Ct. 251, 30 L.Ed.2d 255 (1971)

Trammell v. United States, 445 U.S. 40, 52 (1980)

Abortion: A Right to Privacy

When the U.S. Supreme Court legalized abortion in 1973 with the decision in *Roe v. Wade*, many thought that this controversial subject would become marginalized. They appear to have been in error. Although the majority of Americans appear to support abortion rights, the ground is shifting. In 1995, 31 percent of Americans supported abortion; that figure dropped to 23 percent as of 1998. (http://www.dr-boehm.com/AbortionRightsShift.htm). Due to the partial-birth abortion controversy, some Americans are rethinking the entire abortion issue in 1999. Is the freedom for women to decide when and under what conditions they become mothers the most precious of all freedoms? Is abortion an issue that affects only women? Is it an issue of privacy? Can states intrude into the affairs and personal decisions of their citizens?

The issue is abortion and the readiness of the legal system to uphold others' rights to tell pregnant women what they may or may not do with their bodies is discussed in this section. Can women terminate their pregnancies? *Roe* says "yes," at least in the first trimester. Is this an egregious assault on women's sense of self and bodily integrity? Are the courts doing serious damage to a woman's mental health in an attempt to protect the fetus? The ability to protect one's bodily integrity may lead to helplessness and an acute sense of powerlessness.

In her chapter "Abortion: Is It a Right to Privacy or Compulsory Childbearing?" Roslyn Muraskin reviews the arguments as set forth in the *Roe v. Wade*. The Court did not accept the argument that a woman has a constitutional right to have an abortion whenever she wants one. Does the state have the right to interfere with the decision of childbearing? What the Court did in *Roe* was to establish a sliding scale that balanced the right of the woman against the right of the state at various times during her pregnancy.

What are the issues that the Court deals with regarding abortion? There are significant constitutional issues at stake in the judicial bias against women. The first issue deals with privacy, the other with the Fourteenth Amendment rights to due process and equal treatment. Is this a question of a woman's right to autonomy over her body, or does the issue go further? What compelling reason is there for the Supreme Court to continue to listen to arguments regarding a woman's right to privacy? A review of all cases since *Roe* is included. The decision may be in the hands of the courts and the legislators, but does a woman have the right to choose?

Joan C. Chrislers, in "Whose Body Is It Anyway? Psychological Effects of Fetal-Protection Policies," favors safer workplaces for women, widely available prenatal care, and better drug and alcohol abuse prevention and treatment programs. She examines the possible effects of fetal-protection policies on the mental health of women. It has been over seventy years since Margaret Sanger claimed that science would make woman the owner, the mistress of her self. Battles already won are still being fought.

23

Abortion

Is It a Right to Privacy or Compulsory Childbearing?

Roslyn Muraskin

When the first edition of this book was published in 1993, there was controversy over the rights of a woman to obtain an abortion. The issue of a woman's control over her own body is still with us. The Supreme Court has faced cases that further restrict the rights of women to have abortions. There continues to be public debate in state courts and legislatures as well as in the Supreme Court regarding women's rights to privacy. In this chapter the cases, the issues, and the holdings are reviewed. Not much has changed over the last years except a drive to stop abortions from occurring. We have yet to hear the end of this issue. Reproductive rights are the focus for recognition of the constitutional right to privacy; or better, is there a constitutional right to privacy? The cases that are evidenced today are good examples of the court's ability to "protect" the rights of women. Viewed from a different perspective, is the unborn fetus a person, and a person with rights? So far, in not determining when life begins, the Supreme Court indicates that a fetus is not a person and therefore not entitled to rights as protected under the constitution. It is pointed out that although the case of *Roe v. Wade* did not give to women the right to abortion at all times, it applied a sliding scale.

Reproductive freedom has been joined with such accepted rights as freedom of speech or assembly. There exist those who have come to the conclusion out of simple personal concern that if women do not control their bodies from within, they can never control their lives from the skin out. There are those who feel that women's role as the most basic means of production will remain the source of their second-class status if outside forces continue to either restrict or compel that production. Remember the words of Justice Miller in *Bradwell v. State of Illinois* (1872), where he stated that "[t]he paramount destiny and mission of woman are to fulfill the noble and benign offices of wife and mother. This is the law of the Creator."

The freedom for women to decide when to become a mother and under what conditions is an issue that remains of great concern. Is abortion an issue that affects women only, and is it an example of sex discrimination? Are we to think primarily of the fetus and thus conclude that abortion is murder, thereby involving the criminal courts? Is abortion to be viewed from a religious perspective, thinking of how the legal codes of Western religions treat the subject? Is abortion a question of privacy? Should states be prevented from intruding into the affairs and personal decisions of their citizens? Does there exist under *Reed v. Reed* (1971) a compelling state interest to interfere with a woman's right to choose? If a woman is a victim of rape or sexual abuse, is she entitled to an abortion without interference from the state? Is it an issue of discrimination against the poor, who may need the state to subsidize abortions, or even racial discrimination because of the high proportion of minorities who choose to abort? The question that comes to mind is not "How can we justify abortion?" but "Can we justify compulsory childbearing?" Is there a compelling interest on the part of the state to protect what the courts have refused to define as a person?

What are the issues that the courts have faced when we discuss the issue of abortion? There are two significant constitutional issues at stake in judicial bias against women. The first issue has to do with the right to privacy, implied by our Constitution in the Fourth Amendment. The other issue concerns the Fourteenth Amendment's right to due process and equal treatment. Is the issue simply one of female autonomy over her body? The conflict continues. It is an issue that comes back repeatedly to haunt the courts and legislators. When can a woman have a partial abortion? Whose rights are we protecting? The Supreme Court held that laws prohibiting abortion are unconstitutional. In *Roe v. Wade* (1973) the Court held that "no state shall impose criminal penalties on the obtaining of a safe abortion in the first trimester of pregnancy." Women cannot be charged criminally with obtaining an abortion, but there are administrative regulations and legal penalties that prevent her from doing so.

Abortion is an emotional, legal, religious, and highly volatile issue. In December 1971, the Supreme Court heard a case (*Roe v. Wade*) brought to it by an unmarried pregnant woman from Texas who complained that the Texas statute permitting abortions only when necessary to save the life of the mother was unconstitutional. (This person has since indicated that women should not be given the option of abortions, that all life is precious, and therefore, if pregnant, a woman should not have the right to choose.)

What was held in *Roe* was that a state may not, during the first trimester of pregnancy, interfere with or regulate the decision of a woman and her doctor to terminate the pregnancy by abortion; that from the end of the first trimester until the fetus became viable (usually about twenty-four to twenty-eight weeks), a state may regulate abortions only to the extent that the regulation relates to the protection of the mother's health; and that only after the point of viability may a state prohibit abortion, except when necessary to save the mother's life. The Court further permitted the state to prohibit anyone but a licensed physician from performing an abortion.

The Court did not accept the argument that a woman has a constitutional right to have an abortion whenever she wants one and that the state has no business at all interfering with her decision. Rather, the Court established a sliding scale that balanced the right of the woman against the right of the state to interfere with the decision; it would have to prove that it had a compelling interest in doing so. During the first three months of pregnancy, when continuing the pregnancy is more dangerous than ending it, the Court found that no such compelling state interest existed for overriding the *private* decision of a woman and her doctor. When abortion becomes a more serious procedure, the Court found that the state's interest in the matter increases enough to justify its imposition of regulations necessary to ensure that the mother's health will be safeguarded. In the last trimester of the pregnancy, the Court found that the state's interest in the health and well-being of the mother as well as in the potential life of the fetus is sufficient to outweigh the mother's right of privacy except where her life is at stake.

In the language of the Court:

> This right of privacy…is broad enough to encompass a woman's decision whether or not to terminate her pregnancy. The detriment that the State would impose upon the pregnant women is apparent. Specific and direct harm medically diagnosable even in early pregnancy may be involved. Maternity, or additional offspring, may force upon the woman a distressful life and future. Psychological harm may be imminent. Mental and physical health may be taxed by child care. There is also the distress, for all concerned, associated with the unwanted child, and there is the problem of bringing a child into a family already unable, psychologically and otherwise to care for it. In other cases as in this one, the additional difficulties and continuing stigma of unwed motherhood may be involved. All these are factors the woman and her responsible physician will consider in consultation.

The Court continued by indicating in *Roe* that the right to terminate her pregnancy at whatever time was not acceptable by the Court. They indicated further that the right to privacy was not absolute.

With regard to the argument presented that the fetus is a person, the Court went on to comment:

> [I]n nearly all…instances [in which the word "person" is used in the Constitution] the use of the word is such that it has application only postnatally. None indicates, with any assurance, that it has any possible prenatal application. All this together with our observation…that through the major portion of the nineteenth century prevailing legal practices were far freer than they are today, persuades us that the word *person* as used in the fourteenth amendment, does *not* include the unborn.…

In answering the question when life begins, the Court further stated:

> It should be sufficient to note…the wide divergence of thinking on this most sensitive and difficult question.
>
> In areas other than criminal abortion, the law has been reluctant to endorse any theory that life as we recognize it, begins before live birth or to accord legal rights to the unborn except in narrowly defined situations and except when the rights are contingent upon live birth. In short the unborn have never been recognized in the law as persons in the whole sense.
>
> We repeat…that the State does have an important and legitimate interest in preserving and protecting the health of the pregnant woman.…And that it has still another important and legitimate interest in protecting the potentiality of human life.

The Court had decided to allow the mother to abort at the end of the first trimester and then to allow her physician to decide medically if the patient's pregnancy was to be terminated after this period. The judgment was to be effectuated by a decision free from the interference of the state.

At the same time that the Supreme Court had decided the *Roe* case, it decided a second case—that of *Doe v. Bolton* (1973), which involved a Georgia abortion statute that set forth several conditions that were to be fulfilled prior to a woman obtaining an abortion. These included a statement by the attending physician that an abortion was justified with the concurrence of at least two other Georgia licensed physicians; the abortion was to be performed in a hospital licensed by the state board of health as well as accredited by the Joint Commission on Accreditation of Hospitals; there was to be advance approval by an abortion committee of not less than three members of the hospital staff; and the woman had to reside in the state of Georgia.

The Court then held that these provisions were overly restrictive, thereby treating abortion differently from comparable medical procedures and therefore violating the constitutional rights of a woman to have an abortion. Since *Roe*, several states had passed laws that require the husband of a pregnant woman or the parents of a single mother to give their consent prior to having an abortion. Both of these requirements were struck down by the Supreme Court (*Planned Parenthood of Central Missouri v. Danforth*, 1976).

What, then, is to happen when husband and wife cannot agree? Who is to prevail? The courts have argued that the woman should. Since it is the woman who bears the child physically and who is affected more directly and immediately by the pregnancy, the balance would seem to weigh in her favor.

Until this point the state did not appear to have the constitutional authority to give a third party an absolute and possibly arbitrary veto over the decision of the physician and his or her patient. There has developed the question of the authority that a parent has over a child. It has been well understood that constitutional rights do not mature and come into being magically when one attains the state-defined age of majority. Minors as well as adults are protected by the Constitution and possess constitutional rights.

There does exist a suggested interest in the safeguarding of the family unit and of parental authority. The idea of providing a parent with absolute power over a child and its physical well-being is not likely to strengthen the family unit. Neither is it likely that such veto power will enhance parental authority or control where the minor and the noncon-senting parent are so fundamentally in conflict that the very existence of the pregnancy already has fractured the family structure. The Court continues to review cases whereby the parent of the female will make the decision for her regardless of her wishes.

Two other important issues bearing on the ability of women to obtain abortions are the right of hospitals to refuse to perform abortions and the right of Medicaid to refuse to pay for nontherapeutic abortions. In the case of *Nyberg v. City of Virginia* (1983), a federal court of appeals concluded that a public hospital may not refuse to perform abortions: "It would be a nonsequitur to say that the abortion decision is an election to be made by the physician and his patient without interference by the State and then allow the State, through its public hospitals, to effectively bar the physician from using State facilities to perform the operation." Theoretically, private hospitals may refuse to perform abortions, but it is not always easy to determine when a hospital is private. One needs to review whether it leases its facilities from the local government, whether it is extensively regulated by the state, whether it has received tax advantages, whether it has received public monies for hospital construction, and whether it is part of a general state plan for providing hospital services. Litigation and debate continues.

Under the decision in *Roe v. Norton* (1973), the Court concluded that federal Medicaid provisions prohibit federal reimbursement for abortion expenses unless a determination has been made that the abortion was medically necessary. The Court held that the government is not required by the Constitution to pay for any medical service, but once it does decide to do so, it must not unduly disadvantage those who exercise a constitutional right. Of late, laws have been passed that no birth control clinic that receives funding from the federal government may give information dealing with abortion. Of course, that has not stopped those who are against abortion from using whatever tactics are necessary to prevent such information from being disseminated, including that of bombing abortion clinics.

Those who are against abortion state that when a woman chooses to have sex, she must be willing to accept all consequences. Those who are against abortion will defend the rights of the fetus to develop, to be given life, and to grow, regardless of the wishes of the mother. Those who are against abortion state that whatever the costs, even to those who are victims of rape and incest, there is a life growing, and it is murder to do anything but carry it to full term. Better that any number of women should ruin their health or even die than one woman should get away with not having a child merely because she does not want one.

There have been cases—in the state of Idaho, for example—that have attempted to make physicians criminally liable for performing abortions rather than lay the responsibility on the mother. Under the Idaho proposal, a man who had committed *date rape*, a term describing sexual assault by an acquaintance (although rape is still defined as rape), could conceivably force the woman to carry the child.

Further decisions have been made affecting the woman's right to choose. For example, in the case of *Bellotti v. Baird* (1979), the Court had voted by a majority vote of 8–1 that a state may require a pregnant unmarried minor to obtain parental consent for an abortion if it also offers an alternative procedure. In the case of *Harris v. McRae* (1980), the Court upheld by a margin of 5–4 the Hyde amendment, which denies federal reimbursement for Medicaid abortions. And in the case of *City of Akron v. Akron Center for Reproductive Health, Inc.* (1983), the Court voted 6–3 that states cannot mandate what doctors tell abortion patients or require that abortions for women more than three months pregnant be performed in a hospital. In *Thornburgh v. American College of Obstetricians and Gynecologists* (1986), the Court voted 5–4 that states may not require doctors to tell women about risks of abortion and possible alternatives or dictate procedures to third-trimester abortions.

In the case of Ohio upholding a law that required a minor to notify one parent before obtaining an abortion, Justice Kennedy wrote that "it is both rational and fair for the State to conclude that, in most instances, the family will strive to give a lonely or even terrified minor advice that is both compassionate and mature." However, Justice Blackmun, who was the senior author of *Roe*, wrote in what has been described as a stinging dissent that Kennedy and his adherents were guilty of "selective blindness" to the reality that "not all children in our country are fortunate enough to be members of loving families. For too many young pregnant women parental involvement in this intimate decision threatens harm, rather than promises of comfort." He ended by stating that "…a minor needs no statute to seek the support of loving parents…If that compassionate support is lacking, an unwanted pregnancy is a poor way to generate it." And in *Webster v. Reproductive Health Services* (1989), the Court upheld 5–4 Missouri's law barring the use of public facilities or public employees in performing abortions, and requiring physicians to test for the viability of any fetus believed to be more than twenty weeks old.

Debate over these and other issues has spawned extensive litigation and put the Court in the position of reviewing medical and operational practices beyond its competence. We therefore believe that the time has come for the court to abandon its efforts to impose a comprehensive solution to the abortion question. Under the constitution, legislative bodies cannot impose irrational constraints on a women's procreative choice. But, within those broad confines, the appropriate scope of abortion regulation "should be left with the people and to the political processes the people have devised to govern their affairs."

The Court stated that Missouri had placed no obstacles in the path of those women seeking abortions. Rather, the state simply chose not to encourage or assist abortions in any respect.

Abortion remains as newsworthy and important a subject today, as we begin the twenty-first century, as it was when *Roe* was decided in 1973. Perceptions of the abortion law differ. For the courts, it has become a constitutional issue. Others consider it an act of murder and believe that it should be turned over to the criminal courts. And indeed, there are those states who have at one time or other defined abortion as homicide. The focus is on the Fourteenth Amendment and whether a woman who is denied an abortion is denied due process. The issue is difficult because most people do not see it as a clear issue of law. Is the issue one that concerns woman's right to privacy? Is it a case of sexual discrimination? Or are we to look at the issue from the view of the fetus and then view it as an issue of murder? Should abortion be viewed from a religious perspective, thinking of how the legal codes of Western religions treat the subject? Is it simply an issue of privacy and telling the states that they cannot intrude into the private affairs of its citizens? Or do we view abortion as a matter of health, of preventing injuries and death to women who undergo abortions? The answer lies in the fact that there are no easy answers and no easy solutions. Abortion is an issue that explodes in the courts, in legislators and in the minds of citizens.

In the case of *Rust v. Sullivan* (1991), the Court upheld by 5–4 the federal government's ban on abortion counseling in federally funded family-planning clinics. In the case of *Planned Parenthood of Southeastern Pennsylvania v. Casey* (1992), the Court decided against the constitutionality of a law passed in Pennsylvania:

Informed Consent:

At least 24 hours before the abortion, except in emergencies, the physician must tell the woman:

- The nature of the proposed procedure or treatment and the risks and alternatives.
- The probable gestational age of the unborn child.
- The medical risks associated with carrying her child to term.
- That government materials are available that list agencies offering alternatives to abortion.
- That medical assistant benefits may be available for prenatal care, childbirth and neonatal care.

Parental Consent:

If the woman is under 18 and not supporting herself, her parents must be informed of the impending procedure. If both parents or guardians refuse to consent, or if the woman elects not to seek the consent, judicial authorities where the applicant resides or where the abortion is sought shall…authorize…the abortion if the court determines that the pregnant woman is mature and capable of giving informed consent.

Spousal Notice:

No physician shall perform an abortion of a married woman…without a signed statement…that the woman has notified her spouse.

Exceptions:

- Her spouse is not the father of the child.
- Her spouse, after diligent effort, could not be located.
- The pregnancy is the result of spousal sexual assault…that has been reported to a law enforcement agency.
- The woman has reason to believe that notifying her spouse is likely to result in bodily injury.

Reporting:

Each abortion must be reported to the state on forms that do not identify the woman but do include, among other items:

- The number of the woman's prior pregnancies and prior abortions.
- Whether the abortion was performed upon a married woman and if her spouse was notified.

The Constitution has been interpreted in many cases to protect the woman from arbitrary, gender-based discrimination by the government, yet the struggle continues. Cases continue to be heard by the courts. In no instance is reference made to women's rights. Rather, the cases are based on the constitutional theory of the right to privacy, which is subject to interpretation, there being no exclusive right of privacy mentioned in the constitution. Of the Supreme Court justices, Justice John Paul Stevens has supported abortion rights; Justice Antonin Scalia looks to overturn the decision in *Roe* but has yet to do so; Justice Sandra Day O'Connor has signaled her unhappiness with *Roe* but has yet to see it completely overturned; Justice David Souter has voted to uphold the ban on abortion counseling. Justice O'Connor has taken the "middle ground," as articulated in her dissenting opinion in *Akron v. Akron* and more recently in her concurring opinion in *Hodgson v. Minnesota* (1990), where she stated that the right to an abortion is a "limited fundamental right" that may not be "unduly burdened" absent a compelling government interest, but may be burdened less severely upon a rational basis (947 F. 2d. at 689-91).

What becomes noteworthy about cases dealing with the issue of abortion is that the motivation of a woman becomes entirely "irrelevant" to a determination of whether such a right is "fundamental." The Supreme Court has refused to overrule the *Roe v. Wade* decision, although erosion has taken place. The Court in their "wisdom" has upheld state restraints on a woman's right to choose an abortion freely, as supported in their decision in *Planned Parenthood of Southeastern Pennsylvania v. Casey* (1992) by a 5–4 decision, but the courts have yet to turn the clocks back to 1973, a time when states could make abortion a crime and punish both a woman and her physician. The Court in the case of *Planned Parenthood* does allow states to impose conditions on women seeking an abortion—an "informed consent" provision that includes a lecture to women in an effort to "educate" them about alternative choices to abortion, as well as a twenty-four-hour waiting period to "think it over."

The decisions of the Court has given the states considerable leeway that can make abortions costlier and more difficult to obtain. Such requirements by the state certainly continue to prove difficult for the poor woman who lives and works far from abortion clinics. Even a waiting period as short as twenty-four hours will force some women who cannot afford to stay overnight to make two trips to the clinic. The issue of whether such a procedure will pose an undue unconstitutional burden to choose remains open.

In the summer of 1992, Congress received a bill forforbidding states to restrict a woman's right to choose before the fetus was viable, or even later if the operation was needed to protect the life or health of the woman. The theory behind such legislation was that "Congress has a right to make secure the liberties protected by the Fourteenth Amendment, and that Congress has the duty to regulate interstate commerce, which would be burdened if women had to travel from state to state in search of safe abortions" (Clymer, 1992, p. A-11). No such bill was passed.

There are those that argue that abortion is counter to the interests of feminists; that abortion is sexist in nature (Bailey, 1995). The argument goes that a new movement of pro-life feminists argue that abortion is an act of desperation. The argument goes that when women "murder" their own children, society has done a great disservice to women. There arises the question of whether the act of abortion is "an offensive and sexist notion that women must deny their unique ability to conceive and bear children in order to be treated equally" (Smolin, 1990).

According to Ellen Chesler (1992), "[I]t has been seventy years since Margaret Sanger claimed that science would make women 'the owner, the mistress of her self.'" The spirit of her words lives on. The struggles of women and their right to choose and not to be punished in criminal courts continue. The final decision is not yet in. But for those who enjoy a safe bet, it is that women will be limited in years to come to choose for themselves whether to have an abortion. That battles were fought and won in prior years does not mean that these decisions will remain. Battles won will still be fought.

REFERENCES

BAILEY, J. T. (1995). Feminism 101: A primer for prolife persons. In R. McNair (Ed.), *Prolife feminism: Yesterday and today* (pp. 160, 163).

CHESLER, E. (1992, August 2). RU-486; We need prudence, not politics. *New York Times,* op ed. page.

CLYMER, A. (1992, July 31). Lawmakers fear amendments on abortion rights. *New York Times,* p. A11.

SMOLIN, D. (1990). The jurisprudence of privacy in a splintered Supreme Court. *Marquette Law Review, 75,* 975, 995–1001.

CASES

Bellotti v. Baird, 443 U.S. 622, 99 S. Ct. 3035, 61 L. Ed. 2d 797 (1979)

Bradwell v. State of Illinois, 83 U.S. 130 (1872)

City of Akron v. Akron Center for Reproductive Health, Inc., 462 U.S. 416, 103 S. Ct. 2481, 76 L. Ed. 2d 687 (1983)

Doe v. Bolton, 410 U.S. 179, 93 S. Ct. 739, 35 L. Ed. 2d 201 (1973)

Harris v. McRae, 448 U.S. 297, 100 S. Ct. 2671, 65 L. Ed. 2d 784 (1980)

Hodgson v. Minnesota, 110 S. Ct. 2926 (1990)

Nyberg v. City of Virginia, 667 F.2d 754 (CA 8 1982), dsmmd 462 U.S. 1125 (1983)

Planned Parenthood of Southeastern Pennsylvania v. Casey, 505 U.S. 833 (1992)

Planned Parenthood of Central Missouri v. Danforth, 428 U.S. 52 (1976)

Reed v. Reed, 404 U.S. 71 (1971)

Roe v. Norton, 408 F. Supp. 660 (1973)

Roe v. Wade, 410 U.S. 113, 93 S. Ct. 705, 35 L. Ed. 2d 147 (1973)

Rust v. Sullivan, 114 L. Ed. 2d 233 (1991)

Thornburgh v. American College of Obstetricians and Gynecologists, 476 U.S. 747, 106 S. Ct. 2169, 90 L. Ed. 2d 779 (1986)

Webster v. Reproductive Health Services, 492 U.S. 490, 109 S. Ct. 3040, 106 L. Ed. 2d 410 (1989)

24

Whose Body Is It Anyway?

Psychological Effects of Fetal-Protection Policies

Joan C. Chrisler

The possible effects of fetal-protection policies on women's mental health are examined in this chapter. Research on personal control, learned helplessness, and self-esteem/self-worth is reviewed and findings applied to pregnant women who are threatened by fetal-protection policies.

To consider pregnancy a conflict of maternal and fetal rights is even more negative and detrimental to women than to consider it a disease (Hubbard, 1990). Yet there is an alarming trend in the U.S. legal system to do just that. In recent years, pregnant women have been ordered to undergo Caesarean sections, have been barred from high-paying blue-collar jobs, have been temporarily prevented from having abortions (Gallagher, 1984), and have been arrested for drinking alcohol (Stellman & Bertin, 1990) and taking drugs (Roberts 1990). Although the physicians, employers, police officers, attorneys, and judges involved in these cases would argue that they were only trying to do what was best for the health of the woman and her fetus, these policies are a form of social control; the end result is the clear suggestion that "a pregnant woman is not a competent person" (Hubbard, 1990, p. 174).

Psychological research has shown that people need a sense of personal control—that is, the feeling that they can make decisions and take actions that result in desirable consequences (Rodin, 1986). Adler (cited in Rodin, 1986, p. 140) has argued that the need to exercise control is "a basic feature of human behavior." Those who have a strong sense of personal control are able to reduce the negative impact of stressors and thus tend to have better physical and mental health than those with a weak sense of personal control (Elliot, Trief, & Stein, 1986; Matheny & Cupp, 1983; Suls & Mullen, 1981).

The sense of personal control develops over the course of life and fluctuates in response to environmental events as one experiences stressors, success and failure, and how much control one actually has in different situations (Rodin, 1986). Thus the sense of personal control emerges as people develop theories of physical and social causality (Rodin, 1986) and estimate their own levels of competence in effecting change. It is not surprising that poor women of color would have fewer opportunities to experience the kind of personal control and success that leads to self-efficacy. These are also the women who make up the majority (about 70 percent) of the defendants charged with "prenatal crimes" (Roberts, 1990).

One's self-concept is multidetermined, but the sense of mastery, of being in control of one's environment, especially one's own body, is considered crucial (Ashurst & Hall, 1989). Everyone fears "being out of control" and "losing control" (Ashurst & Hall, 1989; Chrisler, 1991), and people have been known to take extraordinary measures to regain a sense of control over themselves, including self-destructive behaviors such as anorexia nervosa and suicide. "Stress can be reduced through five basic types of control (Sarafino, 1990): (1) behavioral control—the ability to take action; (2) cognitive control—the ability to think of possible strategies; (3) decisional control—the ability to choose between alternative responses; (4) informational control—the ability to obtain knowledge about events; and (5) retrospective control—the ability to understand the causes of events that have already occurred." The readiness of the legal system to uphold others' right to tell pregnant women what they may or may not ingest, where they may or may not work, whether they may or may not terminate their pregnancies, and how they may or may not give birth is an egregious assault on women's sense of self and bodily integrity. It strips women's ability to exercise behavioral, cognitive, and decisional control. It happens most often to women who lack informational control and often leaves women without retrospective control. In an attempt to protect the health of the woman and her fetus, the courts may be doing serious damage to the woman's mental health.

"According to learned helplessness theory, depression occurs when few rewarding, pleasurable experiences are available and/or people lack the ability to reduce or avoid unpleasant stressful experiences." Walker (1979) suggested that learned helplessness explains why battered wives stay with their husbands. These women have become depressed because every attempt they have made to avoid battering or escape from the situation has met with failure. Lack of personal and financial resources, the shortage of shelters, and well-meaning relatives and friends who urge them to give him another chance or to be a better wife have contributed to a sense of helplessness and to their resignation to an inescapable fate, which traps them in a cycle of violence.

Imagine a drug-addicted woman who discovers that she is pregnant. Her pregnancy is probably unplanned, perhaps a result of contraceptive failure, rape, exchange of sex for drugs, or drug-induced lack of motivation to use the contraceptives regularly or properly. Perhaps she cannot afford contraceptives or is uninformed about where to obtain them. Because some drugs (e.g., heroin and methadone) disrupt the normal menstrual cycle, addicted women are accustomed to irregular cycles and missed periods (Al-Issa 1980). She may not realize that she is pregnant until several months have passed. An abortion may not be possible because of cost, availability, religious values, or pregnancy stage. Drug treatment programs have long waiting lists, few emergency beds available for pregnant women, and poor reputations for meeting the needs of women addicts (Cuskey, Berger, & Densen-Gerber, 1981). If she has heard about women who have been arrested for fetal abuse, she may be afraid to seek prenatal care, for fear of being arrested. She will undoubtedly feel anxious, frightened, depressed, and helpless—a poor prognosis for both the woman and her fetus.

Self-esteem and perceptions of self-worth are crucial components in the etiology, maintenance, and remission of depression (Kuiper & Olinger, 1989). Fetal-protection policies contribute to women's low self-esteem and low self-worth in several ways. First, they affect women's judgments of their own virtue. The very fact that the policies exist suggest that women have inadequate morals and ethics or are incapable of living up to social standards. Left to their own devices, women will be neglectful, "bad" mothers who willingly subject their future children to toxic or unsafe conditions or frivolously obtain abortions for "convenience."

Second, these policies affect women's evaluation of their acceptance. It is difficult to maintain a sense of self-worth while knowing that society values a fetus more than a woman and while running the risk of being labeled a child abuser because one is addicted or attempting to earn a living by working in a dangerous environment. Society has extremely negative attitudes toward women alcoholics and drug users. The stigma of addiction is unquestionably greater for women than for men, particularly if those women are mothers, and leads to social rejection (Gomberg, 1979).

Third, these policies suggest that a pregnant woman cannot be a competent person (Hubbard, 1990). Denying women the right to control their own bodies and make decisions about their health and occupational status promotes an external locus of control. The inability to protect one's bodily integrity leads to helplessness and an acute sense of powerlessness.

Low self-esteem and self-worth are components of many psychological problems, including depression, addiction, eating disorders, and social anxieties and contribute to the continued oppression of women (Sanford & Donovan, 1984). It is ironic that policies intended to discourage women from taking health risks may actually have the effect of promoting that same risky behavior.

CONCLUSIONS

The very existence of fetal-protection policies leads to anxiety in women of childbearing age, affects the development of self-esteem and personal control in girls who grow up knowing that their ability to control their own bodies and make decisions about their own health is limited, and causes depression, helplessness, and powerlessness in women charged with fetal abuse. Commenting on the effects of these policies, Stellman and Bertin (1990) wrote that at best, women "will suffer the anxiety that even moderate normal activity can damage their real or potential offspring. At worst, women will be treated as walking wombs, perpetually pregnant until proven otherwise, with pregnancy police peeping in at every door and restricting every activity" (p. A23).

Making poor women into criminals is obviously easier than revamping the health care system (Roberts, 1990) to better serve everyone's needs. However, if government agencies, health care providers, and legislators are serious about improving the physical and mental health of women and children, they will do the following:

- Increase funding for research and training aimed at improving women's health
- Expand drug and alcohol treatment programs and make them more sensitive to the particular needs of women

- Develop and publicize health education and drug-abuse prevention programs
- Increase family planning services, which must be allowed to provide abortion information and referrals
- Make prenatal care available to all women and ensure the confidentiality of physician–patient communication
- Make certain that prenatal screening and fetal monitoring are available (but not mandated)
- Develop occupational health and safety standards to make the workplace safer for everyone and impose stiff penalties on employers who violate those standards
- Enact legislation to protect women against unnecessary surgery, including Caesarean section, hysterectomy, and tubal ligation.

The best way to improve women's mental health is to empower women to make their own decisions and to take control of their lives and to provide them with the resources they need to do so. When this occurs, there will be no further need for "pregnancy police" and fetal-protection policies.

REFERENCES

AL-ISSA, I. (1980). *The psychopathology of women*. Englewood Cliffs, NJ: Prentice-Hall.

ASHURST, P., & HALL, Z. (1989). *Understanding women in distress*. London: Tavistock/Routledge.

CHRISLER, J. C. (1991). Out of control and eating disordered. In N. Van Den Bergh (Ed.), *Feminist perspectives on the treatment of addictions* (pp. 139–149). New York: Springer.

CUSKEY, W. R., BERGER, L. H., & DENSEN-GERBER, J. (1981). Issues in the treatment of female addiction: A review and critique of the literature. In E. Howell & M. Bayen (Eds.), *Women and mental health* (pp. 269–295). New York: Basic Books.

ELLIOTT, D. J., TRIEF, P. M., & STEIN, N. (1986). Mastery, stress, and coping in marriage among chronic pain patients. *Journal of Behavioral Medicine, 9,* 549–558.

GALLAGHER, J. (1984, September). The fetus and the law: Whose life is it anyway? *Ms., 13,* 62–66, 134–135.

GOMBERG, E. S. (1979). Problems with alcohol and other drugs. In E. S. Gomberg & V. Franks (Eds.), *Gender and disordered behavior: Sex differences in psychopathology* (pp. 204–240). New York: Brunner/Mazel.

HUBBARD, R. (1990). *The politics of women's biology*. New Brunswick, NJ: Rutgers University Press.

KUIPER, N. A., & OLINGER, L. J. (1989). Stress and cognitive vulnerability for depression: A self-worth contingency model. In R. W. Neufeld (Ed.), *Advances in the investigation of psychological stress* (pp. 367–391). New York: Wiley.

MATHENY, R. B., & CUPP, P. (1983). Control, desirability, and anticipation as moderating variables between life changes and illness. *Journal of Human Stress, 9,* 14–23.

ROBERTS, D. (1990, August 11). The bias in drug arrests of pregnant women. *New York Times,* p. A25.

RODIN, J. (1986). Health, control, and aging. In M. M. Baltes & P. B. Baltes (Eds.), *The psychology of control and aging* (pp. 139–165). Hillsdale, NJ: Erlbaum.

SANFORD, L. T., & DONOVAN, M. E. (1984). *Women and self-esteem*. New York: Penguin.

SARAFINO, E. P. (1990). *Health psychology: Biopsychosocial interactions*. New York: Wiley.

STELLMAN, J. M., & BERTIN, J. E. (1990, June 4). Science's anti-female bias. *New York Times,* p. A23.

SULS, J., & MULLEN, B. (1981). Life changes and psychological distress: The role of perceived control and desirability. *Journal of Applied Social Psychology, 11,* 379–389.

WALKER, L. E. (1979). *The battered woman*. New York: Harper & Row.

SECTION VII

Women in Policing

Police work, probably better than any other social role, serves as an aspect of social life in which traditionally, men have predominated. The work of the police, especially patrol activities, has long been a bastion of male dominance. Power, assertiveness, force, and authority are central elements of the job. Additionally, patrol activities take place in the public arena. Police officers are expected to demand respect, establish control, and enforce rules under adverse and even hostile conditions. A central topic of this section is how well women perform those duties that were once considered to be the exclusive domain of men.

Until the extension in 1972 of Title VI of the Civil Rights Act of 1964, women in American policing were restricted to nonpatrol assignments—primarily those involving clerical work, crime prevention, and work with juveniles. The number of problems that women have faced in policing is astounding. Women have found themselves to be the subject of ridicule and mockery. Gaining the confidence of "fellow" police officers is half the battle. Can women perform as well as men in the full range of police activities? That question is answered in the affirmative in this section.

The number of problems that women have faced in policing is astounding. Women have found themselves to be the subject of ridicule and mockery. Gaining the confidence of their fellow officers is only one of the many hurdles that women police officers face. Can women do the job? The answer is that women can and do perform as well as men in the full range of activities.

The chapter "The Past, Present, and Future of Women in Policing" by Sean A. Grennan reviews the history of women in policing. Legal decision problems in the workplace are analyzed and a theoretical perspective is provided concerning women who enter in what has been considered a male domain. Women are as capable as their fellow officers of handling their assignments, if not more capable.

25

The Past, Present, and Future of Women in Policing

Sean A. Grennan

The sexual revolution has brought with it a long overdue increase in the number of women actively employed as sworn officers by law enforcement agencies in the United States. Today, females represent over 13 percent of the total law enforcement workforce, but this proportion is still well below the actual percentage of women within both our workforce and society. Recent research findings indicate that the ratio of females in policing has increased somewhat but that the total outlook for women in policing is still far from encouraging (Martin, 1989; National Center for Women and Policing, 1997).

Female participation in patrol work has been minimal until recently, even though the first female officer in the United States was appointed in 1910. Historically, female officers were assigned to low-visibility positions in most police departments; for the most part, they were used as matrons, traffic enforcement officers, clerical personnel, or juvenile officers until the Equal Employment Opportunity Act (Title VII) was passed in 1972 amending the Civil Rights Act of 1964. The 1972 amendments made it mandatory for all state and local governments to follow the same guidelines as the federal government in relation to discriminatory practices in employment. Henceforth, state and local governments could no longer use race, creed, color, or gender as a condition of employment. Since the enactment of Title VII, twenty-four female officers have been killed in the line of duty. The first female officer was killed by a robbery suspect in Washington, DC in 1974, and many of the others, like their male counterparts, were killed without any warning that they were in any type of imminent danger. Six of these female officers were assassinated and one was shot and killed by a sniper (Bell, 1982; Horne, 1980; Keefe, 1981; Milton, 1972; U.S. Department of Justice, 1997).

The view of most police executives in the United States is that women, for the most part, do not belong on patrol because of their lack of physical strength and their inability to maintain an imposing presence in the face of challenges to police authority. This opinion is supported by most males in a biased society, dominated by men, that views any upward mobility by women as a personal challenge to them. Yet it has been strongly indicated through prior research conducted by Bloch and Anderson (1994), Grennan (1987), Grennan and Munoz (1996), Martin (1980) and Sichel, Friedman, Quint, and Smith (1978) that women are more than capable of handling any type of police work on the same scale as their male counterparts.

HISTORY OF WOMEN IN POLICING

Women have been employed as police matrons since 1880 in order to satisfy the legal requirements related to the confinement of female offenders. The 1890s brought about the appointment of Marie Owen, the widow of a Chicago Police officer, as an assistant to Chicago investigators handling cases involving women or children. This appointment, made directly by Chicago's mayor, was probably a way of taking care of police widows rather than a change in police philosophy toward women in policing. Early in the nineteenth century women's responsibilities increased to include social work, juvenile work, and clerical work. In 1905, the city of Portland, Oregon, gave Lola Baldwin police powers to cope with the problems created by the large influx of workers arriving during the Lewis and Clark Expedition. In 1910, Alice Stebbins Wells, who was a social worker, petitioned and addressed the Los Angeles City Council and the Police Commissioner on the problems the city was facing with women and children and the need for female personnel to handle these problems. Wells was convincing and was appointed to the Los Angeles Police Department to work with women and children but was not permitted to perform field work outside police facilities. This created opportunities for women to be hired by police departments throughout the United States. One other major breakthrough took place in 1914, when the city of Milford, Ohio, appointed Mrs. Dolly Spencer as the first female police chief in the United States. The total number of women appointed remained small, however, and women's impact on the male-dominated profession was at best minimal. Whatever gains women made in the early years of this century were dissipated with the reduction in police personnel caused by the depression of 1929 (Buwalda, 1945; Connolly, 1975; Crites, 1973; Horne, 1980; Linn & Price, 1985; Milton, 1972; Perlstein, 1971).

At the end of World War II, poor police working conditions and low wages created significant personnel shortages in many Southern police departments. Lacking sufficient men, departments hired women to perform the tasks of traffic control and parking enforcement. The solution was so successful that it led to the employment of women by departments in many other jurisdictions throughout the United States. Although the job the women were hired to perform was basically traffic duty, it provided movement in the right direction for those women wanting to enter law enforcement (Horne, 1980; Milton, 1972).

Gradually, the social worker role of women disappeared and during the 1960s vanished entirely as females started to become actively engaged in more typical police field work. In 1968, women were officially assigned to perform patrol duties in Indianapolis, Indiana. Much more instrumental than the Indianapolis experiment in putting substantial numbers of females on police forces was the Equal Rights Amendment of 1972, expanding the Civil Rights Act of 1964 (Title VII) to include public employees. The *Griggs v. Duke Power Co.* (1971) case established the principle that a plaintiff in a job discrimination case need not prove discriminatory intent. Instead, the Supreme Court held, once it is evident that job qualifications appear out of proportion in relation to a group of class of people, the employer must prove that the said requirement is a bona fide occupational qualification (BFOQ) that is directly related to the occupation and that no other standards could reasonably replace this criterion. Sex could not be proven as a BFOQ simply because many police departments had never hired females and thus had no way of comparing the performances of men and women. For just about every standard—height, weight, age, etc.—*Griggs* made a winner of most actions by plaintiffs against police. In *Reed v. Reed* (1971) the Supreme Court banned discrimination on the basis of a person's gender. Taken together, legislation and court rulings have had more of an impact in opening employment to women than have isolated experiments by police departments (Horne, 1980; Keefe, 1981; Martin, 1980; Milton, 1972; Remmington, 1981).

Prior to 1970, very few large police departments placed women into significant positions in policing. In the 1970s women started to be integrated into the patrol ranks in most major police departments in the United States. In St. Louis County, Missouri, women were appointed to the police department and trained for one-person patrol units in 1975. One restrictive hiring practice, a height requirement, was abolished by many of the large urban police departments in the 1970s. This was a significant step for women officers, who were frequently eliminated from hiring considerations because they did not pass the height requirement. The elimination of the height requirement in New York City led to the hiring of more female officers, and ultimately, the placing of more women on patrol in 1973. Once the precedent was set by the New York City Police Department, many other large departments arranged similar guidelines to place women on patrol (Colgrove, 1983; Horne, 1980; Sichel et al., 1978).

Gaining appointment to police departments has not been the only problem that women have faced in their efforts to pursue careers in law enforcement. Having passed written, physical, and medical examinations, they were still placed in menial positions within most departments and denied the right to compete for promotion. In 1961, Felicia Shpritzer, a member of the New York City Police Department (NYPD), took her case to court. She had previously been denied the right to take the sergeant's examination. By 1963 she had won several court decisions, but the police department still refused to let her take the promotional exam. Finally, in 1964, the police department followed the court decision in *Shpritzer v. Lang* (1963) that gave women an equal opportunity to take promotional tests. Shpritzer was permitted to take the exam and was subsequently promoted to sergeant (Keefe, 1981; Milton, 1972).

In 1967, Shpritzer and Gertrude Schimmel both passed the lieutenant's test and were the first females in New York City promoted to that rank. In 1971, Schimmel was the first woman to attain the rank of captain. In 1972 the police department assigned fifteen female officers to patrol duties under a pilot project established by Police Commissioner Patrick F. Murphy. On January 1, 1973 the Commissioner changed the designation of "police-woman" to "police officer." Further progress was evident when the Policewoman's Bureau was abolished in 1973. This was significant because women were to be assigned throughout the department and were placed in the same category as their male counterparts on patrol.

Another court decision (*Anne Powers et al. v. Abraham D. Beame et al.* (1991) actually cited a specific number of discriminatory practices deployed by the NYPD to decrease the number of women employed by this agency. Women were prohibited from doing radio motor vehicle patrol, refused any type of continuous duties, and denied positions in high-profile positions in both plain clothes and other elite units. Until 1974, separate examinations were given according to the gender of the applicant for the position of police officer. Individualized by gender, examinations assisted this agency in limiting the number of women appointed to this agency to about 1 to 2 percent. This lawsuit, settled in 1991, was instituted by Sergeant Anne Powers, who managed to gain the support of 123 other female officers, all who suffered over a number of years, being at the whim of an almost totally biased police organization that improperly deployed women officers (Grennan & Munoz, 1996).

The major problem faced by female officers during this period was the lack of acceptance they received from male officers. An additional setback occurred in 1975 when a city fiscal crisis resulted in the layoff of 3000 police officers. At that time there were approximately 500 female officers. With the city's fiscal crisis in 1975, most of the newly appointed officers, male and female, were dismissed because of an inverse seniority rule under the New York State Civil Service Law requiring that the last person hired be the first person laid off. The state law also contained a ruling on veteran's preference giving a person thirty months seniority provided that person had served in the U.S. Armed Forces and had one year of police service. This ruling obviously favored the male officers. The numerical gains that female officers had attained saw many of them out of work until the city was able to get back on its feet financially (Acerra, 1978; Keefe, 1981; Linn & Price, 1985). The female officers had fallen victim to the last-hired/first-fired rule.

Since 1979 the New York City Police Department has more than tripled the total number of female members. In 1997 the figures for the NYPD show a total of 5655 females, compared to a total of approximately 600 female members in the department in 1979 (NYCPD, 1997). The recruitment and hiring of women suggests that this police department, as well as many others, does not accept the questionable view that only male officers can handle the vigorous and dangerous work of policing. Grennan's 1987 study, *The Role of Officer Gender during Violent Confrontations with Citizens,* clearly indicates that there is no difference between the way the male or female officer confronts the daily violence that is equally distributed throughout police work. All of this research was conducted on the actions taken and reported by members of the NYPD on a report known as the Firearms Discharges/Assault on Officer Report (FDAR). This form must be filled out in all cases where an NYPD officer's firearm is discharged or an officer is assaulted on or off duty. A total of 3360 assault cases were analyzed, and absolutely no variances were found in the way that male or female officers handled these cases because the number of incidents and the injury rates were equally distributed along gender lines. In 341 other cases involving the use of deadly physical force or firearms discharge that were investigated a significant statistical difference was discovered between the use of deadly force and office gender. These findings are significant because for the first time research has indicated that male officers are far more likely than their female counterparts in policing to fire their weapons (Grennan, 1987).

Chi-squared testing used in Table 1 signifies that female officers account for a very small percentage of all firearm discharges or uses of deadly force. The female shooting rate (3.5 percent), although smaller than the female population in the NYPD, refutes the

TABLE 1   Population of NYPD by Gender, NYPD-OEEO, 1983 ($n = 341$)

Officer Gender	Percent	Actual Number	Percent	Expected Number
Male	92.7	329	96.5	316
Female	7.3	12	3.5	25
	100.00	341	100.00	341
	Chi-squared = 7.30	$r = 0.146$	1 diff.	$p < 0.01$

argument by male officers and the public that because of stature difference, women officers are more likely to use deadly force during violent confrontations with citizens. This finding also contradicts the 1981 Remmington study of the Atlanta police, which indicated that male officers take command of all police–citizen confrontational situations. The real significance of this research is that it reveals for the first time that female officers are less likely to use deadly force than would be anticipated by their representation in policing (Grennan, 1987).

When police gender and the use of deadly force is discussed, a review of where or at whom shots were fired deserves a review. Table 2 indicates that of 341 shooting incidents analyzed, a total of 74 have to be considered pure firearms discharge incidents while the other 267 shooting incidents are considered confrontational. Included in a pure firearms discharge incidents are shootings characterized as accidental (18), shootings of dogs (27), suicides (3), other shoots (8), and shooting at citizens (18) (this can include wife, brother, or acquaintance) (Grennan, 1987).

The figures in Table 2 indicate that female officers seldom fire their guns during pure firearms discharge situations. The results indicated in Table 2 leave this researcher with a number of unanswered questions. Why don't female officers fire their guns in pure firearms discharge situations? Can it be that female officers do not respond to these types of calls? Does the male officer take charge in pure firearms discharge situations? Is the female officer more stable than her male counterpart? The theory of thinking before you act appears feasible. Do these results reflect a difference in the way police training is interpreted?

More women are entering police work than ever before, but most other police agencies are failing to address the question of promoting females in proportion to their representation within the police population. Table 3 indicates the disproportionate number of females in supervisory positions within 106 police agencies throughout the United States.

TABLE 2   Pure Firearms Discharge Incidents and Officer Gender, 1983 ($n = 74$)

Gender	Accidental	Other	Dog	Suspect	Suicide	Total
Male	18	7	27	16	2	72
Female	0	0	0	1	1	2
	18	7	27	17	3	74

Source: Grennan (1987).

TABLE 3   Law Enforcement Agency Ranking from Largest to Smallest Percentage of Sworn Women Officers, 1997

	Agency	Total Sworn Officers	Total Sworn Women Officers	Percent Sworn Women Officers	Percent Women Top Command	Percent Women Supervisory[a]	Percent Women Line Operations[a]
1	Pittsburgh Police	1,140	285	25.0	37.5	25.6	24.7
2	Washington Metropolitan Police	3,628	898	24.8	11.5	23.1	25.4
3	Detroit Police	4,018	869	21.6	19.7	22.0	21.6
4	Philadelphia Police	6,748	1,456	21.6	4.6	9.8	24.3
5	Miami-Dade Police	2,920	611	20.9	N/A	N/A	N/A
6	Toledo Police	731	146	20.0	10.5	12.1	22.1
7	Chicago Police	13,271	2,545	19.2	3.0	13.1	20.0
8	Buffalo Police	928	171	18.4	N/A	N/A	N/A
9	Hillsborough County Sheriff	1,740	317	18.2	7.4	11.4	19.1
10	Montgomery County Police	954	173	18.1	6.3	10.1	19.7
11	Birmingham Police	913	161	17.6	20.0	19.5	17.4
12	Miami Police	979	172	17.6	0.0	14.8	18.4
13	Orlando Police	612	107	17.5	0.0	18.0	17.9
14	Pinellas County Sheriff	1,425	248	17.4	4.8	14.3	18.3
15	Cincinnati Police	978	170	17.4	10.0	8.1	19.6
16	Los Angeles Police	9,392	1,626	17.3	3.3	10.2	18.5
17	Sacramento County Sheriff	1,216	207	17.0	5.0	9.1	16.7
18	Memphis Police	1,553	260	16.7	14.3	10.2	17.8
19	San Diego County Sheriff	1,802	300	16.6	15.4	15.9	16.8
20	Franklin County Sheriff	547	91	16.6	14.3	5.6	19.8
21	Cleveland Police	1,784	296	16.6	9.5	14.9	17.1
22	Tampa Police	1,032	169	16.4	19.0	18.9	16.2
23	Riverside County Sheriff	1,661	272	16.4	N/A	N/A	N/A
24	Orange County Sheriff-Coroner	1,127	182	16.1	10.7	13.6	21.5
25	Portland Police	938	150	16.0	5.9	16.0	16.2
26	Indianapolis Police	970	153	15.8	7.7	12.3	17.2
27	Dallas Police	2,815	444	15.8	20.7	14.1	26.9
28	Louisville Police	654	102	15.6	11.8	7.1	17.3
29	Fort Worth Police	1,201	187	15.6	11.8	8.5	16.8
30	Milwaukee Police	2,150	323	15.0	8.6	8.2	16.1
31	New York City Police	37,745	5,655	15.0	3.6	8.8	16.3
32	San Francisco Police	1,997	299	15.0	12.5	12.4	15.6
33	Tulsa Police	795	117	14.7	9.1	4.1	17.8
34	Tucson Police	813	119	14.6	14.3	13.0	14.9
35	Minneapolis Police	925	135	14.6	16.7	17.0	13.5
36	Atlanta Police	1,447	210	14.5	23.3	8.0	14.4

TABLE 3 (cont'd)

Agency	Total Sworn Officers	Total Sworn Women Officers	Percent Sworn Women Officers	Percent Women Top Command	Percent Women Supervisory[a]	Percent Women Line Operations[a]
37 Harris County Sheriff	2,482	359	14.5	9.7	9.0	15.1
38 Baltimore Police	3,081	433	14.1	5.6	7.8	15.3
39 St. Paul Police	548	77	14.1	0.0	8.2	17.1
40 San Diego Police	1,965	276	14.0	21.7	11.7	14.4
41 Prince George's County Police	1264	174	13.8	8.3	8.6	14.9
42 Los Angeles County Sheriff	7,481	1,025	13.7	12.7	10.4	14.5
43 Seattle Police	1,232	168	13.6	20.0	11.2	14.2
44 Baton Rouge Police	592	80	13.5	7.7	16.7	12.6
45 Kansas City Police	1,172	158	13.5	18.3	11.8	13.5
46 Columbus Police	1,736	229	13.2	4.3	7.8	14.2
47 East Baton Rouge Parish	545	71	13.0	N/A	N/A	N/A
48 St. Louis Police	1,600	202	12.6	N/A	N/A	N/A
49 Alameda County Sheriff	784	98	12.5	7.7	3.2	12.7
50 San Bernardino County Sheriff	1,184	143	12.1	2.8	3.7	14.0
51 Houston Police	5,307	632	11.9	4.3	7.6	13.1
52 Austin Police	952	113	11.9	N/A	N/A	N/A
53 Baltimore County Police	1,561	184	11.8	5.3	6.4	13.4
54 Albuquerque Police	874	102	11.7	7.7	11.7	11.5
55 Michigan State Police	2,139	248	11.6	0.0	7.5	13.8
56 Phoenix Police	2,353	270	11.5	10.7	8.6	12.0
57 Las Vegas Metropolitan Police	1,728	194	11.2	8.3	8.9	11.7
58 New Orleans Police	1,237	137	11.1	2.9	11.2	11.4
59 Yonkers Police	534	59	11.0	0.0	3.2	13.3
60 Virginia Beach Police	706	77	10.9	7.1	5.7	11.7
61 Richmond City Police	654	71	10.9	5.9	25.4	20.7
62 Long Beach Police	841	90	10.7	0.0	6.7	12.5
63 Denver Police	1,409	150	10.5	10.7	11.5	10.4
64 Fairfax County Police	1,049	103	9.8	10.7	8.0	10.2
65 Anne Arundel County Police	597	88	9.7	0.0	9.1	13.1
66 Cook County Police	853	81	9.5	11.1	2.9	10.1
67 Oakland Police	599	56	9.3	15.7	6.9	10.0
68 Nashville Police	1,229	113	9.2	18.5	9.3	9.5

TABLE 3   (cont'd)

Agency	Total Sworn Officers	Total Sworn Women Officers	Percent Sworn Women Officers	Percent Women Top Command	Percent Women Supervisory[a]	Percent Women Line Operations[a]
69 California Highway Patrol	5,478	583	9.0	4.7	6.6	9.2
70 Jacksonville Sheriff	1,424	128	9.0	20.0	3.4	9.9
71 Nassau County Police	2,935	260	8.9	4.2	3.9	9.8
72 Oklahoma City Police	953	84	8.8	2.2	9.5	7.6
73 El Paso Police	1,013	89	8.8	0.0	6.9	9.3
74 Jefferson Parish Sheriff	706	62	8.8	5.8	10.5	8.5
75 Rochester Police	675	58	8.5	0.0	7.3	9.2
76 Illinois State Police	1,982	169	8.5	8.5	7.5	9.2
77 Ohio State Highway Patrol	1,359	115	8.5	0.0	3.8	10.7
78 San Jose Police	1,312	110	8.4	6.3	3.3	9.8
79 Honolulu Police	1,716	142	8.3	3.8	5.4	10.4
80 Massachusetts State Police	2,896	223	8.3	2.9	5.3	12.5
81 Newark Police	1,077	89	8.3	0.0	4.6	9.3
82 Maryland State Police	1,556	126	8.1	3.2	8.2	8.2
83 New York State Police	3,990	321	8.0	4.2	5.9	8.5
84 Arizona Department of Public Safety	963	55	6.9	0.0	14.2	7.1
85 Connecticut State Police	945	63	6.7	6.7	5.2	7.0
86 San Antonio Police	1,886	114	6.0	8.0	6.5	5.9
87 Port Authority of NY-NJ	1,289	77	6.0	5.0	6.2	5.9
88 Oregon State Police	757	45	5.9	0.0	1.3	7.5
89 Iowa State Police	643	38	5.6	3.1	2.7	6.2
90 Jersey City Police	873	46	5.3	0.0	1.3	6.3
91 Indiana State Police	1,229	60	4.9	2.8	5.4	4.7
92 Tennessee Department of Safety	603	29	4.8	0.0	1.1	6.6
93 Washington State Patrol	939	43	4.6	5.6	3.5	4.8
94 Texas Department of Public Safety	2,765	128	4.6	N/A	N/A	N/A
95 Colorado State Patrol	625	25	4.0	2.7	4.1	4.1
96 Georgia State Police	857	33	3.9	0.0	3.3	4.2
97 Pennsylvania State Police	4,083	155	3.8	6.6	4.3	3.6
98 Virginia State Police	1,620	51	3.8	0.0	2.7	4.0

TABLE 3 (cont'd)

Agency	Total Sworn Officers	Total Sworn Women Officers	Percent Sworn Women Officers	Percent Women Top Command	Percent Women Supervisory[a]	Percent Women Line Operations[a]
99 Missouri State Highway Patrol	1,115	38	3.2	0.0	1.3	5.4
100 Louisiana State Police	933	28	3.0	0.0	2.4	3.4
101 New Jersey State Police	2,554	74	2.9	N/A	N/A	N/A
102 Kentucky State Police	1,000	27	2.7	2.6	1.8	2.9
103 South Carolina Highway Patrol	924	24	2.6	0.0	0.0	3.1
104 Alabama Department of Public Safety	694	15	2.2	2.5	2.9	2.0
105 Oklahoma Highway Patrol	699	10	1.4	0.0	0.0	1.8
106 North Carolina State Highway	1,380	11	0.8	0.0	0.7	0.8

Source: National Center for Women and Policing (1998).

[a]N/A, not applicable.

THEORETICAL CONSIDERATIONS

The entry of women into police work in more substantial numbers than ever before has caused considerable controversy in the law enforcement community. Studies have been conducted on the ability of females to perform in the patrol environment. Most of these studies indicate that women can function properly within that environment but that women may have problems when handling violent confrontations with citizens.

In discussing the evolution of the American image of the female role, Epstein theorizes that its roots are in European literature and the arts. Despite the fact that women of the lower classes have always worked inside or outside the home, the ideal feminine attributes were the ones "glorified by the urban middle or upper class role ideas, in which the expectation of what women should be and do was linked with the man's desire for beauty and pleasure and his demand for order and relaxation after work" (Epstein, 1970, p. 21).

Epstein notes that many of the so-called "feminine traits," such as passivity, non-aggression, and practicality, are found in all humans but have come to be "sexualized and are assumed, asserted, or expected to correlate with sexual differences" (p. 22). For the woman entering the work world, conflict is inevitable, as the traits most necessary to a successful career (such as competitiveness, aggressiveness, active persistence, emotional detachment) are considered to be masculine (Epstein, 1970).

A result of the process of socialization and consequent polariation of the sexes are the limitations placed on women entering the work field. She is limited not only by society pressures but by real external barriers (such as discriminatory policies, sex typing or particular jobs, etc.) in certain occupations, as well as her own internalized barrier, a limiting view of herself (Lipman-Blumen & Tickamyer, 1975). Thus for the woman entering a male-dominated occupation, conflict is not only inevitable, it is highly stressful. Epstein (1970) characterizes this stress as: "sociological ambivalence…the social state in which a person, in any of his statuses (as wife, husband, or lawyer, for example), faces contradictory normative expectations of attitudes, beliefs, and behavior which specify how any of these statuses should be defined" (p. 19).

Traditional family role research divided family functions into instrumental and expressive roles for male and female, retrospectively. At its worst, this division "reinforces sex role stereotyping. At its best, this instrumental expressive dichotomy fails to perceive the dysfunctional aspects of the traditional order into which men and women are socialized" (Lipman-Blumen & Tickamyer, 1975, p. 306). Thus the traditional role-casting of the male and female has failed to provide modern women with the prescriptive behavior and role models necessary for her successful entry into a male-dominated society.

Studies have concurred that for the most part, men and men's needs take precedence in a marriage. The husband's time, interests, and career are dominant over those of the wife. While the wife's professional status does not seem to have much effect on the family, her income does if it is greater than her husband's (Lipman-Blumen & Tickamyer, 1975). Certainly, it raises the family's standard of living but, in addition:

> The attitudes of social scientists have lent considerable legitimization to the popular suspicion that women who seek an independent identity outside the home are women with problems and that women who do not feel a strong drive to establish a family first and foremost should wonder what is wrong with them. Women who chose careers react to the cultural expectations of femininity by trying to prove themselves in all spheres. They attack all the role expectations attached to their female status, feeling that to lack any is to deny they are feminine. (Epstein, 1970, p. 31)

A woman entering a typically male profession may be subject to status inconsistency. She would also encounter a problem of dominance. Males tend to have the dominant gender status, and for many purposes, gender tends to be the most salient determinant of status: In many contexts, female executives are accorded less status than male secretaries.

Further, the public may look to a male police officer for confirmation of a female sergeant's orders, or a female sergeant's orders may be questioned by a male subordinate. Thus gender is often a principal factor in establishing status. Gender and racial status are among those statuses that are "central in controlling the choices of most individuals" (Epstein, 1970, p. 35).

ORGANIZATIONAL THEORY AND THE FEMALE ROLE

Social theory gives us reason to anticipate gender-related differences in police–citizen encounters. The police are, after all, in the business of getting people to defer to their authority (Muir, 1977), and we should expect that by virtue of the traditionally higher social status and authority accorded them, males might do this more easily than females. Martin (1980) analyzed the role of officers' gender on their general behavior as police officers and found that gender influences the exchange of deference when police officers interact with citizens. When by virtue of their higher status, male police officers interact with female citizens, citizen deference is likely. Conversely, the expectation of deference to the male can work to the disadvantage of female officers when encountering male citizens. Thus even though police officers possess a unique status separate and apart from their gender, the norms that operate in any encounter between police and citizens call for citizen deference to the police. These norms may or may not operate for women police officers and have been the topic of this study.

Prior research reports two broad types of behavior styles on the part of female police officers. The first is an aggressive posture usually interpreted as an effort to compensate for their relatively weak physical stature. Aggressiveness is used in an effort to "outmacho" male peers, and within the police world it is commonly assumed that female officers who adopt this proactive style of policing will be quicker than their male counterparts to use deadly force (Martin, 1980). To date, no evidence supports this belief. The second behavioral pattern, in which female officers perform their work, according to Martin, is a stereotypical and exaggerated feminine manner, which is an excessively passive style—more passive, in fact, than the average woman's behavior seen in work environments that do not require the exercise of authority. Thus Martin (1980) and Remmington (1981) suggest that there are female officers who exhibit a passive style of policing and may fail to take any action when a citizen does not comply with directions or otherwise resists. When such passive female officers work with male partners, they tend to rely on the male officer to gain citizen compliance and to maintain control (Martin, 1980; Remmington, 1981).

Kanter points out that management is a male category; those women who hold managerial positions tend to be concentrated in the lower-paying positions, in certain fields, and in less powerful organizations. Office work, on the other hand, is a predominantly female function: "women are to clerical labor as men are to management" (Millman & Kanter, 1976, p. 39). A "masculine ethic" early on became associated with the ideology of the managerial idea. It incorporated supposedly masculine qualities such as a hard-line approach to solving problems, analytical planning abilities, an ability to set aside the personal, emotional point of view in dealing with a task, and the intellectual approach to problem solving and decision making. This ethic defined a place for women in management in the people-handling staff functions where the intuitive-emotional approach was appropriate; thus the feminine stereotyping became operative (Kanter, 1977).

A woman entering a male-dominated profession encounters several problems related to tokenism. She may be categorized into one of the four stereotyped roles, which Kanter has given the self-explanatory labels of *mother, sex object or seducers, pet, or iron maiden.* She may also be treated as average or stereotypical, as when a female executive is assumed to be a secretary. The result is that the woman may be less likely to behave competently, and she may have a longer or more difficult time establishing her competence, due to the pressures of the role-defined situation (Kanter, 1977).

"Cultures demand that one must do masculine work to be considered a man, and not do it to be a feminine woman" (Epstein, 1970, p. 154). Women entering a masculine profession thus are seen as deviant and subject to social group sanctions. The salient status may be an irrelevant one, e.g., a female lawyer may be perceived as a woman first, a lawyer second, whereas a male lawyer is seen first as a lawyer. The male lawyer thus has the advantage, as his professional mode is not diffused by the intrusion of gender-role status (Epstein,

1970). For the woman, each new professional encounter usually begins with the focus on gender status: She is first received as a female, with the appropriate surprise and accompanying uncertainty of a favorable reception. Attention and energy are leeched away from the professional role, as "the working environment is always transmitting messages that she is unique, and she anticipates them" (Epstein, 1970, p. 23).

Women respond to gender-role typing and the correspondent status discrepancies by unobtrusive behavior, attracting as little attention as possible, and by over-achievement. One professional woman expressed the conflict: "[I]f you're a woman, you have to make less mistakes…a woman must put greater effort into her work…because if you make a fool of yourself, you're a damn fool woman instead of just a damn fool" (Epstein, 1970, pp. 191–192).

FEMALES IN THE POLICE ORGANIZATION

Women entering police organizations find the same kinds of obstacles to advancement found in other occupations. Martin notes that in this transitional period, many women still lack the seniority to be eligible for upper-level positions:

> [A] low promotion rate for women is likely to continue, however, since in most departments, promotion is based on both written examinations and ratings by one's supervisors; the criteria on which officers are evaluated are often unclear; and sponsorship by a [male] supervisor is, in fact, a necessity—few female officers are likely to gain such support. (Martin, 1980, p. 48)

Price and Gavin point out that the police management hierarchy is rigid and very narrow at the top, with a limited number of middle management and administrative positions. This pyramid structure and the emphasis on crime fighting and a good arrest record as the best means to promotion serve to "perpetuate the attitudes about policing being man's work" (Price & Gavin, 1981, p. 406).

In answer to the question of why women aren't fully accepted in the police organization, Price and Gavin (1981) theorize that there are two major sources of resistance: "(1) the social change process and the critical role that attitudes play in it; and (2) the impact of police attitudes shaped by the organizational structure, and in turn, reinforcing its social structure" (pp. 404–405). An important aspect of police officers' attitudes and feelings about their work is the deep-rooted conviction that it is men's work, requiring physical strength and bravery. Historically, the police task was defined as "maintaining order by intimidation." Those officers who are performing according to the old criteria are responsible for propagating this traditional attitude rather than acknowledging the fact that 80 to 85 percent of police work today is in service-related tasks, of which women have proven themselves to be equally capable (Price and Gavin, 1981).

Studies have shown that traditionally, policemen come primarily from working-class and lower-middle-class backgrounds (Neiderhoffer, 1969; Westley, 1970). Even those who don't

> tend to adopt a working-class perspective toward the meaning of masculinity as a result of the recruitment process, the nature of their work and the frequent interaction with working and lower-class citizens—the primary users of police services and the targets of patrol efforts….The police share with such males an emphasis on toughness, and seek to be smarter and tougher than the "street dudes" whose values and postures they often mirror. (Martin, 1980, p. 90)

Remmington's Atlanta study evidenced perhaps the most stereotypical attitudes and corresponding behaviors in male officers. "Women do not belong on the streets" was a frequent remark made in the presence of female officers and in conversations among male officers. Male officers expressed and demonstrated a lack of confidence in female peers. A male officer was present at every violent call during the year of observation and took charge in nearly every case. Females, on the other hand, seemed to fall into a stereotypical mode as well. When asked whether they would prefer a male or female partner, every female chose a male partner. "Most of the women expressed greater trust in the policing capabilities of the males" (Remmington, 1981, p. 167). Male officers complained extensively of the need for extra protection for female peers.

Males tended to take the initiative and tended to take a protective role with a female partner. On the other hand, a strong female partner tended to threaten the male:

> The men are caught in a bind: they want a partner who will be "tough" and fight, and back them up and whom, in turn, they are willing to back up. But women are not supposed to fight, be tough or protect a man. The more a female partner acts like a police officer the less she behaves like a woman. On the other hand, the more she is as a partner—although such behavior preserves the man's sense of masculinity. (Martin, 1980, pp. 93–94)

Policemen's status insecurity, due to the status ambiguity of the police role, is intensified by the appointment of female officers: "Traditionally, male occupations that seek out women recruits frequently suffer a decline in prestige, while traditionally female occupations become more prestigious following the entry of males" (Martin, 1980, p. 100). A female patrol partner is also in a double bind: As a strong partner she is a threat to the male partner's ego; as a weak partner, she is a threat to his safety and well-being. Male officers have also expressed the fear that because female officers lack virility and authority, they will weaken the police image with the public and potentially endanger the male during a stand-off with a criminal (Martin, 1980). Personal experience in policing indicates that female officers "think before they act," whereas male officers "act before they think." This knowledge comes from thirty-one years' experience working with and observing thousands of police officers performing their daily routines (Grennan, 1996). If anything, this would seem to be some type of indicator as to why male officers have more problems dealing with citizens than do female officers. One major indicator of the "act before think" theory is the fact that male officers receive civilian complaints at a much higher rate than do their female counterparts. Considering that females make up 15 percent of the NYPD, they receive on average only 4 to 5 percent of the total number of civilian complaints filed against members of the NYPD on a yearly basis (NYCPD, 1997).

For the female police officer, the additional stresses of role ambiguity, the conflicting demands of home and job, and other factors, such as male hostility and nonacceptance on the job, take their toll. Police officers have a unique background and position in the community.

FEMALE ON PATROL: PHYSICAL STRENGTH CONSIDERATIONS

A number of studies have examined the issues arising out of women's entrance into the police profession. Milton (1972) examined problems women faced when dealing with male officers, who for the most part, felt that females were incapable of performing police work. Men cited the physical strength factor as a reason for the perceived unsuitability for women for police work, but the men also noted that women may possess superior psychological skills. The results of the studies indicated that females may approach and handle situations differently from males, but males and females obtained the same results. Bloch and Anderson (1974) concluded that women were more than capable of performing patrol duties.

SUMMARY

The percent of females in policing has increased considerably in the past ten years; at the same time, police administrators in city after city have assigned women to patrol duties. Since their inclusion in the patrol force, researchers have taken an interest in their performance and in the responses of citizens to women police officers. Research demonstrates that female officers behave similarly to male officers in the handling of violent confrontations. No differences have been found in the injury rate of either male or female officers during violent confrontations with citizens. Research further indicates that in the use of deadly physical force, the male officer is more likely than the female officer to use a firearm. Female officers, whether with a partner or alone, are more willing to get involved in violent confrontations without fear of injury or death. These results indicate that female officers are just as capable as males in handling violent disputes and confrontations (Grennan, 1987). Positive changes have been noted in the status of female police officers. The total number of females in policing has increased dramatically since the early 1980s. Yet the opportunities for females in some police agencies are lacking and there is still a considerable need for improvement. This is especially prevalent in the areas of promotion and turnover rate. As far as promotional policy is concerned, most police departments have made few, if any, efforts to promote according to the proportional rate of females in their departments. A study by Grennan and Munoz (1996) shows that advancement in rank for female officers is proportionately lower than that of male officers, and therefore female officers are finding it difficult to attain leadership positions in many police agencies.

There seems to be a conspiracy on the part of male police executives to stifle the promotions of high-profile female police executives. This male police administrative strategem has been utilized over the past several years by the NYPD. It seems that NYPD administrators find it beneficial to their egos to remove highly successful female police executives from high-profile positions and put them in low-profile assignments somewhere in headquarters. This reassignment will, ultimately, force this officer to retire because she knows that once this takes place, there is no opportunity for upward mobility and promotion.

Martin (1989) states that "...women have a higher turnover rate than men, and thus more women are needed to enter policing even to maintain current sex ratios" (p. 7). This statement is a result of research conducted by the Police Foundation in 1989. A good portion of these turnovers can be eliminated if police departments take the time to create a professional and affirmative work environment for both male and female officers. A professional and positive work atmosphere would help remove a major portion of the animosity and offensiveness that is directed toward female officers in most police settings.

There have been some optimistic signs for women in policing in the past decade, but there is still a need for extensive reforms pertaining to the work environment and promotional policy. It is hopeful that a sizable portion of these improvements will reduce some of the problems encountered by women in policing. There is still a great deal to be accomplished to bolster and promote females in policing. It is true to say that women have come a long way, but there is much more that has to be accomplished in the future.

REFERENCES

ACERRA, L. (1978). From matron to commanding officer: Woman's changing role in law enforcement. In R. A. Scanlon (Ed.), *Law enforcement bible* (pp. 131–140). South Hackensack, NJ: Stoeger Publishing.

BELL, D. J. (1982). Policewomen: Myths and reality. *Journal of Police Science and Administration, 10*, 112–120.

BLOCH, P. B., & ANDERSON, D. (1974). *Policewomen on patrol: Final report*, Washington, DC: Police Foundation.

BUWALDA, I. W. (1945). The policewomen: Yesterday, today and tomorrow. *Journal of Social Hygiene, 31*, 290–293.

COLGROVE, S. B. (1983). Personality and demographic characteristics as predictors of burnout in female police officers. Doctoral dissertation, University of California at Berkeley. *Dissertation Abstracts International.*

CONNOLLY, H. A. (1975). Policewomen as patrol officers: A study in role adaptation. Doctoral dissertation, City University of New York. *Dissertation Abstracts International.*

CRITES, L. (1973). Women in law enforcement. *Management Information System, 5*, 1–16.

EPSTEIN, C. (1970). *A Woman's Place.* Berkeley, CA: University of California Press.

GRENNAN, S. A. (1987). The role of officer gender during violent confrontations with citizens. Doctoral dissertation, City of University of New York. *Dissertation Abstracts International.*

GRENNAN, S. A., & MUNOZ, R. (1996). Women as police supervisors in the twenty-first century: A decade of promotional practices by gender in three major police departments. In R. Muraskin & A. R. Roberts (Eds.), *Visions for change* (pp. 340–354). Upper Saddle River, NJ: Prentice Hall.

HORNE, P. (1980). *Women in law enforcement.* Springfield, IL: Charles C Thomas.

KANTER, R. M. (1977). *Men and women of the corporation.* New York: Basic Books.

KEEFE, M. L. (1981). *Overview of equal opportunity in policing for women.* Washington, DC: National Institute of Justice.

LINN, E., & PRICE, B. R. (1985). The evolving role of women in American policing. In A. S. Blumberg & A. Neiderhoffer (Eds.), *The ambivalent force* (pp. 69–78). New York: Holt, Rinehart & Winston.

LIPMAN-BLUMEN, J., & TICKAMYER, A. R. (1975). Sex roles in transition: A ten year perspective. *Annual Review of Sociology, 1*, 297–337.

MARTIN, S. E. (1980). *Breaking and entering: Policewomen on patrol.* Berkeley, CA: Sage Publications.

MARTIN, S. E. (1989). *Women on the move: A report on the status of women in policing.* Washington, DC: Police Foundation.

MILLMAN, M., & KANTER, R. M. (EDS.). (1976). *Another voice.* New York: Octagon Books.

MILTON, C. (1972). *Women in policing.* Washington, DC: Police Foundation.

MUIR, W. K., JR. (1977). *Police: Street corner politicians.* Chicago: University of Chicago Press.

NATIONAL CENTER FOR WOMEN IN POLICING. (1998). *The status of women in policing, 1997.* Los Angeles: NCWP.

NEIDERHOFFER, A. (1969). *Behind the shield: The police in urban society.* Garden City, NY: Doubleday, Anchor Books.

NEW YORK CITY POLICE DEPARTMENT. (1997). *Civilian complaint review board statistics for 1997.* New York: NYCPD.

PERLSTEIN, G. R. (1971). *An exploratory analysis of certain characteristics of policewomen.* Doctoral dissertation, Florida State University. *Dissertations Abstracts International.*

PRICE, B. R., & GAVIN, S. (1981). A century of women in policing. In D. O. Schultz (Ed.), *Modern police administration* (pp. 109–122), Houston, TX: Gulf Publishing.

REMMINGTON, P. W. (1981). *Policing: The occupation and the introduction of female officers.* Washington, DC: University Press of America.

SICHEL, J. L., FRIEDMAN, L. M., QUINT, J. C., & SMITH, M. E. (1978). *Women on patrol: A pilot study of police performances in New York City.* Washington, DC: Police Foundation.

WESTLEY, W. A. (1970). *Violence and the police: A sociological study of law, custom and morality.* Cambridge, MA: MIT Press.

CASES

Ann Powers et al. v. Abraham D. Beame, et al., 341 N.Y.S. 2d 437 (1991).
Griggs v. Duke Power Co., 91 S. Ct. 849 (1971).
Reed v. Reed, 92 S. Ct. 251 (1971).
Shpritzer v. Lang, 234 N.Y.S. 2d 285 (1963).

SECTION VIII

Women and Crime

"Female criminality in the 1990s [and heading into the twenty-first century] is, in some respects, as misunderstood as it was in the 1970s. The typical female offender is not a corporate or computer criminal, a terrorist, a burglar or a murder....she is likely to engage in theft, fraud, drug offenses, forgery, embezzlement, and prostitution" (Merlo, 1995, p.119). In this section we review published materials about ten different organized criminal groups as we examine the role of women not simply in crime but in organized crime. Studies indicate that women's involvement in organized crime is limited by their use as sexual commodities and by patriarchal gender expectations. Sue Mahan's work, "Women's Training for Organized Crime: Sex and Sexuality," demonstrates the barriers to female involvement in organized crime. In today's world, although we view women as participants in crime, women face interesting barriers to the opportunity to participate in organized crime because of the expectations for their gender in both the legitimate and criminal worlds.

Laura J. Moriarity and Kimberly L. Freiberger in their chapter, "Classifying Female Serial Killers: Application of Prominent Typologies," look at several typologies created to categorize serial murderers. They examine a population of sixty female serial killers who have killed three or more people over time. The authors conclude that while the crime of serial killing is a rare event, it is much more so for females. However, because both male and female serial murders occur at comparable rates, both need to be the focus of scholarly pursuits.

This section is not a comment on women's ability to commit crimes, such as property crimes rather than violent crimes, but rather, to demonstrate how, when given the opportunity, women do in fact act "like men."

REFERENCE

MERLO, A. V., & POLLOCK, J. M. (1995). *Women, law and social control.* Boston: Allyn & Bacon.

26

Women's Training for Organized Crime

Sex and Sexuality

Sue Mahan

An explanation of gang membership has to be based on the overwhelming impact of racism, sexism, poverty and limited opportunity structures.

Chesney-Lind & Shelden (1998, p. 50).

A collection of published materials about organized criminal groups was the basis for an examination of the participation of females. Not confined to U.S. groups, this comparative approach examined ten groups other than the U.S. mafia. Criminal groups from other cultures and other historical periods in the Americas were considered. From this broad perspective, available information suggested that the current role of women in organized crime is less significant than at other times. Investigation showed that women's involvement in organized crime is limited by gender expectations as well as by their use as sexual commodities. Important questions were raised about opportunities for women in organized crime, which are also related to those in legitimate enterprise.

Throughout history, in studies of organized crime (OC) the idea of opportunity appears as an important explanatory factor. As with other kinds of careers, opportunities to be a gangster are not equally distributed. Some people have many opportunities to get involved; others have few or no opportunities to join a criminal gang. It is significant to examine situations that provide more or fewer opportunities, and to study the ways that OC opportunities are structured (Cloward & Ohlin, 1960). In this chapter we examine the ways in which opportunities in OC are structured by history, ethnicity, and poverty as each

401

relates to women. It is a review of published materials about ten different OC groups with regard to gender and sex.

Issues of poverty and racism limit both legitimate and illegitimate opportunities for men and women. But from this review it was noted that there are sex and gender issues that are additional barriers to female involvement in OC. First, strong sexual double standards limit expectations for females. Second, women are involved as commodities, not traders, in the sex market. This survey points out the ways in which gender roles and sexual exploitation limit opportunities for women.

WHAT IS OC?

OC is a crime of enterprise. That basic assumption follows from the work of Chambliss and Block and others who do not believe that OC is run and controlled by a national syndicate. "It is a mistake to look for a godfather in every crime network" (Chambliss, 1988, p. 9). OC consists of a coalition of politicians, law-enforcement personnel, businessmen, labor leaders, and (in some ways least important of all) gangsters. The tendency to engage in systematic criminal behavior exists because criminal behavior is good business, makes sense, and is by far the most efficient and profitable way to organize the operations of political offices, businesses, law enforcement agencies, and trade unions in a capitalist democracy.

Block and Chambliss (1981) described OC as the sum of innumerable conspiracies, most often local in scope, which are part of the social and political fabric of everyday life. Crime enterprises pose a threat not to the political structure of society, but on a more subtle level to basic values and morals (Van Duyne, 1996). Traditional studies of OC in the United States have examined the ethnic families originating in New York and Chicago who gained national power from crime during the era of Prohibition. For a new perspective, the present study did not include the American Mafia but focused on other U.S. and international OC groups.

Most writers would agree with Levey (1990), who described OC as synonymous with corruption, murder, extortion, error, manipulation, and guile involved in conscious, willful, and long-term illegal activities. In addition, it is generally assumed that OC practices a division of labor and has as its aim the realization of large financial profits as quickly as possible.

Beyond this general level of agreement, though, there are differences in definitions of what is and what is not OC. Although debating the definitions of OC preoccupies many scholars, contradictions and controversy make agreement unlikely. To avoid conflict or ambiguity, in this review the term *organized crime* is used for a criminal group with the following characteristics, supplied by Abadinsky (1994, p. 6):

- *Nonideological.* The primary motivating force for OC is profit.
- *Hierarchical.* There is a pyramid organization with a few elites and many operatives.
- *Limited Membership.* The group must maintain secrecy and ensure loyalty.
- *Perpetuates Itself.* There must be recruitment and training.
- *Violence and Corruption.* Corruption is essential and violence is a resource.
- *Specialization.* OC groups form "task forces" to achieve organizational goals.

- *Monopolistic.* Maximizing profits means minimizing competition.
- *Explicit rules and regulations.* Members of OC groups have codes of honor.

Of course, having their own rules does not mean that gangsters always follow them. A code of behavior is also not to be confused with an ideology. Pursuit of profit is considered a driving force rather than a world view.

LITERATURE REVIEW

An extensive literature review was carried out for ten different OC groups.[1] The reference section includes the bibliographic information for the review with numerous sources about each of the ten groups. These groups were chosen because they were exemplars of different forms of OC, with a body of literature describing them. For each, there was a fascinating account that brought the group to life. These intimate accounts for each of the ten groups are included as an Appendix. There may be an unlimited number of OC groups that would be useful for studies regarding sex and gender. This work may inspire more investigation—not just literature reviews, but social scientific research of all types.

Table 1 lists the OC groups that were included. It indicates whether roles of women have been reported, if there are legendary women members, and if women's roles have been the subject of research. The table shows graphically how little is known about women's roles in OC.

The following examination of the ten exemplar groups focuses on three issues that are significant to OC and opportunities: poverty and economics, ethnicity and racism, and violence and sexism. Two groups, street gangs and outlaw motorcycle gangs, have been best described by social scientists. These descriptions provide pertinent information concerning the barriers to opportunities for women developed from gender roles and sexism.

TABLE 1   The Place of Women in Ten OC Groups

	Mentioned in Description of Decisions or Control	Legendary Women	Research
1. Pirates	Yes	Yes	
2. Moonshiners	Yes	Yes	
3. Corporate crime	No	No	
4. Russian Organizatsiya	No	No	
5. Chinese triads	No	Yes	
6. Japanese Yakuza	No	No	
7. Medellin cartel	No	No	
8. Street gangs	Yes	Yes	Yes
9. Prison gangs	No	No	
10. Outlaw motorcycle gangs	Yes	No	Yes

Historical Opportunities

It is likely that women's roles in OC have diminished with the contemporary trend toward rationality and internationality. Historical analysis provides more examples than contemporary studies do of female ringleaders and gangsters. Block (1980, 1981) studied the role of women in big-city OC at the turn of the century and found women in control of brothels, saloons, and other OC enterprises. These women were members of crime families and had opportunities in OC because of their connections. Potter and Gaines (1992) also described the significant roles of women in gambling and brothels run by organized gangs in southern U.S. river ports during the nineteenth century.

1. Pirates.   Piracy flourishes where elites promote smuggled traffic in plunder and stolen goods (Kenney & Finkenauer, 1995). In the early eighteenth century there were famous pirates who were women. They were known for their eagerness to plunder and their zeal in battle. The saga of female pirate Anne Bonney suggests that like other pirates operating off the east coast of the United States, she had friends in high places in Charleston, South Carolina, in 1720. In the pamphlets and journals of their day, Anne Bonney and her sometime companion, Mary Read, took on heroic grandeur. Together they plundered the seas, and together they were eventually captured by an armed sloop belonging to the governor of Jamaica. When Mary Read was sentenced to hang, she reportedly told the court: "[A]s to hanging, I think it no great hardship, for, were it not for that, every cowardly fellow would turn pyrate and so infest the seas, that men of courage must starve" (Browning & Gerassi, 1980, p. 60).

2. Moonshiners.   In moonshining organizations, women's roles were more diversified, as the operation was usually located at or near the home, and the entire family was likely to be involved in production and marketing. Women in the mountain South in the latter part of the nineteenth century aided and protected the men in the moonshine business. They had the important task of lookout, who delayed revenue officers with warrants to search for stills. They gave wholly unreliable information in answer to officers's questions and reportedly even pummeled officers with fists and occasionally fired at them. For example, Mollie Miller of Tennessee was first noticed during a raid on her father's still in which three revenuers were killed and the rest retreated under heavy fire. She went on to become a leader of Polk County moonshiners, credited with the deaths of three revenuers and four or five informers. Another Tennessee moonshiner named Bettie Smith wrote a book about her life: *The Blue Headed Sapsucker, or the Rock Where the Juice Ran Out.* Her testimony at a trial in which she was asked to explain how and to whom she sold her whisky, is part of moonshine lore. "A hunting party of gentlemen came out my way, and got out of whiskey, but found it difficult to buy any. After a while I told a man if he would put his jug down on a dollar and go away, he might when he came back, find the jug full of whiskey." The judge asked: "Would you know the man?" "Oh yes, sir," she responded, " I recognized him in a moment. You are the man, judge" (Miller, 1991, pp. 37, 38). Potter and others described a leadership role for women in rural OC that continues because of its roots in agriculture and home production (Potter & Gaines, 1992).

Modern Crimes of Enterprise

3. Corporate Crime.   In the study of enterprise it is noteworthy that women are very seldom active in the highest levels of sophisticated corporate crime (Albanese, 1993). Although Heidi Fleiss may have organized Hollywood prostitution at a corporate level, and Leona Helmsley was convicted for criminal international hotel deals, these female-headed criminal corporations involved smaller capital and less impact than the multinational-level corporate corruption that has been responsible for the rape of the third world (Clinard, 1990; Lyman and Potter, 1997). For example, compare a female's responsibility for crimes of enterprise with the chairman of Union Carbide Corporation, Warren Anderson's, responsibility for the world's worst industrial accident in Bhopal, India, in 1984. More than 3000 people died and 200,000 were injured. Union Carbide is the third-largest chemical producer in the United States and one of the fifty largest industrial corporations. It operates more than 700 facilities in more than thirty-five countries. Five years after it happened, Union Carbide paid a settlement of $470 million to the Indian government for the accident at Bhopal (Clinard, 1990, p. 139).

In transnational crime, women's involvement has been called "pink collar," as women involved in corporate crime are seen at clerical or administrative levels rather than making decisions or taking control (Daly, 1989). Just as women find that traditional institutions exclude them from the top levels, careers in crime for women at the top are also exceptional. Some writers see increasingly more participation by women in upper world crime. They assume that female participation in highly lucrative OC is a demand to be respected and acknowledged (Taylor, 1993, p. 198). Despite such assumptions, OC opportunities for women seldom afford them respect. The importance of females to crimes of enterprise has almost never been acknowledged. Steffensmeier (1983) pointed out that crime, in its more organized and lucrative dimensions, is virtually a male phenomenon. OC usually operates in ways that emphasize secrecy, trust, reliability, sophistication, and muscle. Compared to their male counterparts, potential female offenders are at a disadvantage in selection and recruitment into secret criminal groups. They are less likely to have access to crime skills and relationships of tutelage. OC as a career path is closed to most females, and the huge profits from illicit enterprise do not usually go to women. Where the stakes are high and the risk is great, OC is highly sexually segregated. The greater the profit, planning, monopoly, and stability of a criminal organization, the less likely are women to be in positions of power within it (Steffensmeir, 1983, p. 1026).

4. Russian Organizatsiya.   The Russian criminal Organizatsiya comes from a white-collar background. Its members have been linked to credit-card, IRS, and utilities frauds in the United States. The first known criminal enterprise of the Organizatsiya was a very large scale fuel tax scam that made millions in the northeastern United States during the 1980s (Kleinknecht, 1996). As with other rational, sophisticated criminal organizations, no women are known to be involved in the Mafiya.

Racism and Ethnicity

Connections between the issues of poverty and racism and the development of OC have been discussed widely. Some authors have presumed that OC develops because of ethnic or racial characteristics that facilitate it. However, efforts to show the causal links between OC and particular groups or social classes have proved fruitless. OC is not isolated to ethnic enclaves or caused by desperate poverty (Albanese, 1989). Outside the law, demands of secrecy and loyalty, needs for recruitment, and long-term associations are related to neighborhoods and communities and ties of kinship and culture (MacKenzie, 1967). For this reason, ethnicity cannot be ignored, even though it cannot be considered causal. In this regard, women are confronted by the same barriers of racism and poverty that men face. But females also face a barrier to the secrecy, recruitment, and associations that provide OC opportunities for males in their community.

5. Chinese Triads.   Women in positions of power in Chinese triads are almost unheard of. One woman known as "Big Sister Ping" was said to be the queen of "Snakeheads" or smugglers of Chinese immigrants (Kerry, 1997). But in the international drugs and arms trade, as in most other sectors of Chinese-directed OC, women are excluded. Women are asked to leave when men begin to discuss gang business.

Young women become associated with Chinese gangs through male gang members with whom they attend school. Some young women find hanging out with gang members fun; others become affiliated with gang members because they like the protection that gangs provide. Fun, excitement, and power are associated with hanging around with gang members, but so is sexual exploitation. Only those with steady boyfriends who are gang leaders are immune from rape by gang members. Gang leaders may assign females who are considered promiscuous to work in Chinatown massage parlors owned by the gang (Chin, 1996).

6. Japanese Yakuza.   In the Japanese Yakuza, there is no known woman ringleader or crime boss. Japanese gangsters are involved in the sex trade, and women are sexual commodities rather than decision makers. The trade is greatest in adolescents from Thailand and the Philippines, but there are also hundreds of young women in the United States who have been victimized by the Yakuza. They sometimes use agents who place ads for singers and dancers in entertainment presses and publications. The women who are selected are expected to act as hostesses and prostitutes in Japan, although they auditioned for a singing or dancing job. No matter what the duties of the woman, she will either not be paid or be paid far less than she was promised. Escape from Japan, and even escape from the employer, becomes nearly impossible. Women who return from what is often a hellish experience in the Yakuza clubs often seek revenge but usually get little satisfaction. Few of the agents can be located, and the victims have little in the way of legal recourse (Kaplan & Dubro, 1986, p. 251).

7. Medellin Cartel.   Contrary to the report by de Lama (1988), according to the literature, women were related to Medellin cartel membership only as romantic involvements or idolized and romanticized mother figures. According to a member of a gang of assassins on the fringes of the cartel, breaking a promise to a woman is worse than death. The assassins bring their money from murder contracts home to their mothers. The gangster becomes the provider, the surrogate father. His mother accepts his life as a sicario and, with a certain banality, she talks matter of factly about the violence. "That boy was killed by a very nice-looking kid," a mother would comment (Duzan, 1994, p. 213).

No other reports of women's involvement at the level of power or control have surfaced. Rather, reports about the cartel mention the victimization of women in both harassment and domestic violence and in political assassinations. According to one observer, "The woman's role has disintegrated into: keeping an eye on their men's weapons, serving as connections and for sexual satisfaction. Jealousy is a motive for murder. You love your girlfriend and give her a lot of presents. If she betrays you, you kill her" (Duzan, 1994, p. 214).

Poverty

8. Street Gangs. Patterns of women members of street gangs have been studied for more than a decade in the United States and there is a significant body of criminological literature devoted to women's participation (Maher & Curtis, 1995; Moore, 1985, 1991). Current media focus has settled on girls' commission of violent crimes in youth gangs, portraying girls as "meaner now than girls in earlier generations." The gender realities of street gangs are complicated. Although the media stereotype is clear and intensely male, every so often the media discovers that there are girls in gangs and that girls can also be violent. But the notion of gang as a social concern is pretty much all male. Perhaps if the public image of gang included girls as well as boys, it would humanize it too much. The reality is that up to one-third of those involved in street gangs are likely to be females (Moore, 1991).

Women, like men, find that gangs fill a growing void created by the continued presence of homelessness and unemployment. In many inner-city neighborhoods, 80 percent of the African-American families living below the poverty level are headed by single women. The dismantling of social service programs has devastated some urban-dwelling families. The ugly reality of mothers with children moving in and out of shelters has resulted in women forming alliances to survive. According to Taylor (1993): "The difference between females and males is their method of survival. Women are more involved in the less dangerous crime; they tend to try and trick people out of their money" (p. 195).

Girls in gangs challenge the conservative view of women as "wife and mother" which is promoted in patriarchal OC groups. They are viewed as having moved outside the realm of traditional values. Being marginal, girl gangsters may substitute strong ties to other outlaws for weak ties to their conventional families. Toughness, meanness, and aggression are highly valued for all gang members. Respect means a lot to both boys and girls. The streets may be dominated by young men, but girls and young women do not necessarily avoid the streets. They are involved in "hanging out," "partying," and the occasional fight. During the 1990s, research on girl gangs moved beyond simple, stereotypical notions about these groups as auxiliaries of male gangs to a more careful assessment of girls' lives (Chesney-Lind & Shelden, 1998).

According to Campbell's (1984) examination of the roles for females in street gangs, there are some essential patterns in girls' gang membership. It was clear that the girls' heterosexuality is crucial to their membership because it perpetuates male control. "Dykes" are scorned and abused. The separate nature of men and women is an explicit part of gang philosophy. Women's sexuality can be controlled by being labeled "cheap" and receiving abuse if they dispense sexual favors too freely. Reproductive functions also are a matter of male decision but women's responsibility. An important female role is that of the mother figure, offering advice and counsel on personal matters. The mother figure plays the role of social and emotional leader. A woman is afforded respect as a maternal figure. There are also aggressive girls in gangs who try to succeed on male terms. They are accepted with the same indulgence accorded to junior males. "The tomboy will grow out of it, have children, and a decent male will provide for her, keep her at home, and save her from the streets," according to the fundamentally conservative philosophy of gangs (Campbell, 1984, p. 246).

Males control gangs and continue to live out the male roles they grew up with, casting girls in all too recognizable complementary positions to themselves. In street gangs, girls find not a new sense of self, nor a new set of values, but the old ones disguised in a new way (Campbell, 1984, p. 257). For girl gangsters, as for their mothers, the most enduring bond in their lives is with their children. Children represent an escape from the abiding sense of isolation, the possibility of continuity and loyalty, and unconditional acceptance. Campbell provides the "new" woman's dream, the "new" agenda that she found among the gang girls she studied: "No more suffering or poverty. No more lonely, forced 'independence,' living alone on welfare in a shabby apartment. First, a good husband, strong but not violent, faithful but manly. Second, well-dressed children. Third, a beautiful suburban apartment. Later for the revolution" (p. 267).

9. Prison Gangs.   The links between street gangs and prison gangs in the United States have been well established (Jacobs, 1974; Moore, 1978). There is a growing body of research and literature on prison gangs. The authors depict a world that is strongly male dominated. Prison gangs may be the epitome of machismo; there are no "broads," according to Davidson (1974). Gang "ethics" prohibit feminine sexual practices. Prisoners who play the female sexual role are known as "punks." According to prison gangsters, "there is a certain weakness in 'punks'." As described in the literature about prison gangs, extreme negative treatment of punks implies negative feelings about women, for whom they are surrogates in this violent subculture (p. 83).

There are no studies of female prison gangs per se. Studies have examined cliques and pseudofamilies and have often focused on homosexuality or gender issues rather than on criminal organizations of incarcerated women (Pollock-Byrne, 1990). There is no real evidence to determine how female street gang members are involved when they are incarcerated (Davidson, 1974).

Sexism

10. Outlaw Motorcycle Gangs.   There have been several studies of outlaw bikers that examined the participation of women. It is the second pattern in OC about which there is substantial social sciences literature. In 1966, Hunter S. Thompson studied the Hell's Angels from a journalistic perspective. Although Thompson did not take into account views of the women involved, his description of degradation and sexual perversion was intensely personal. He carefully described one scene, which he labeled "somewhere between a friendly sex orgy and an all-out gang rape" (p. 247). Thompson explained the contradiction when he wrote: "So the Hell's Angels are working rapists…and in this downhill half of our 20th century, they are not so different from the rest of us as they sometimes seem. They are only more obvious" (p. 249). Thompson saw the relationship between OC patterns and roles and the patterns and roles in legitimate society.

The role of women in outlaw biker gangs is illustrative of the role of women in other OC enterprises (Hopper & Moore, 1990). Although women have a more or less active role in the various organizations, sexuality is a factor that separates and defines women's membership. The sex trade itself is often run by OC groups, including bikers. Since women may be commodities on the sex market, their care and control are important to the group's income. Control is a major factor if humans are to be sold and used as objects. The most effective form of control is voluntary. Outlaw bikers are able to control women to some extent based on a philosophy about appropriate male dominance and female submission. To some extent the control exerted on female gang participants is also based on fear. The threat of punishment and the arbitrary nature of rules for which punishments are attached leave women who are involved with outlaw bikers feeling insecure and powerless (Wolf, 1991).

The exclusion of women from formal participation and the pervasive attitude of chauvinism does not meant that females have no importance or influence. Women who participate in the outlaw subculture fall into one of three major categories: "broads," who drift in and out of the subculture in a casual and temporary status; "mamas," who maintain social–sexual interaction with the club as a whole on an informal or economic basis; and "ol' ladies," who have a long-standing personal relationship with a single member (Wolf, 1991, p. 133).

Many women who participate in the outlaw biker gang lifestyle had a history of involvement in prostitution and other sex-related services before they became part of the group (Quinn, 1987). For them, affiliation with outlaw bikers may offer social status and a sense of physical security from abuse by customers and pimps. Many veteran biker women see their male companions as somewhat interchangeable agents of status and protection.

Jackson and Wilson (1993) found that motorcycle gang members in Great Britain were all male, tough, aggressive, dogmatic, hedonistic, sensation seeking, impulsive, risk taking, irresponsible, and lacking in self-esteem and ambition. They were also significantly anxious and depressed. Despite these self-destructive tendencies, it appeared from other sources that outlaw bikers were taking increasing control of importation, distribution, and sales of illicit drugs, contraband alcohol, and the black-market tobacco trade throughout North America. The British Columbia Hell's Angels were regarded as one of the wealthiest outlaw motorcycle gangs in the world in 1996 (Criminal Intelligence Service Canada, 1996).

The outlaw biker gangs' public image contrasts with their private OC role. Their nature as hedonistic and thrill seeking on the one hand, and rational profit motivated on the other, puts women at a double disadvantage in these gangs. Female members' role as obedient followers and their status as objects have led women into roles increasingly defined by sexuality and made outlaw biker gangs extremely gender segregated. With opportunities for females structured by their value as sexual commodities, the status of women in OC is necessarily controlled by the men who run the market and who are the buyers.

DISCUSSION

From this review it is clear that knowledge about women's place in present-day OC is limited. Since there are more known historical OC figures who were women than there are modern women gangsters, it appears unlikely that today's women are becoming more important in the world of OC.

In the two OC groups about which there is a body of literature concerning female membership (street gangs and motorcycle gangs), two different patterns for women emerge. In street gangs, females participate at all levels, yet are still limited by the expectations for females held by the group. Very traditional gender roles were apparent in the expectations for female gangsters to be nurturing and supporting and in the girls' own desires to be provided for in a conventional family manner.

In outlaw motorcycle gangs, gender inequality was apparent in the expectations for female bikers to handle all domestic chores and to provide sexual favors on demand, as well as to remain silent and subservient. The double standard was made even more extreme by the sex trade carried on by outlaw motorcycle gangs. Their exploitation as commodities in the sex market presented barriers to decision-making levels of the gang. Sexual exploitation also determined the female's personal importance to the gang.

Two issues, gender and sexuality, stand between women and opportunities in OC. Historical literature about OC shows that gender roles and expectations can and do change with the passing of time. The literature also shows that in some contexts women have been able to take control of the market for sexual services. However, today in the structure of OC and the climate of violence in which it exists in the Americas, the sex trade has increasingly grown more oppressive and exploitative of women. It is an interesting parallel to the position for women and opportunities in legitimate enterprise. Women face barriers to opportunity because of expectations for females and exploitation for their sexuality in both the legitimate and criminal worlds.

NOTE

1. This review is part of a larger work entitled *Beyond the Mafia* by Sue Mahan (Newbury Park, CA: Sage Publications, 1998).

REFERENCES AND BIBLIOGRAPHY

ABADINSKY, H. (1994). *Organized crime* (4th ed.). Chicago: Nelson-Hall.

ALBANESE, J. (1989). *Organized crime in America* (2nd ed.). Cincinnati, OH: Anderson Publishing.

ALBANESE, J. (1993). Women and the newest profession: Females as white collar criminals. In C. Culliver (Ed.), *Female criminality: the state of the art*. New York: Garland Publishing.

ALBANESE, J. (1996). *Organized crime in America* (3rd ed.). Cincinnati, OH: Anderson Publishing Co.

ALLSOP, K. (1961). *The bootleggers and their era*. Garden City, NY: Doubleday.

BAKER, M. (1996). *Badguys*. New York: Simon & Schuster.

BARLEYCORN, M. (1975). *Moon-shiners manual*. Willits, CA: Oliver Press.

BLOCK, A. (1980). Searching for women in organized crime. In S. K. Datesman & F. R. Scarpitti (Eds.), *Women, crime and justice*. New York: Oxford University Press.

BLOCK, A. (1981). Aw! Your mother's in the Mafia: Women criminals in progressive New York. In L. H. Bowker (Ed.), *Women and crime in America*. New York: Macmillan.

BLOCK, A. (1994). *Space, time, and organized crime* (2nd ed.). New Brunswick, NJ: Transaction Books.

BLOCK, A., & CHAMBLISS, W. J. (1981). *Organizing crime*. New York: Elsevier/North-Holland.

BOOTH, M. (1990). *The triads: The growing global threat from the Chinese criminal societies*. New York: St. Martin's Press.

BOWKER, L. H. (ED.). (1981). *Women and crime in America*. New York: Macmillan Publishing.

BROOKHISER, R. (1965, June). Patriots, rebels and founding fathers: Analysis of the Shays' rebellion and the whiskey rebellion. *New York Times, 144*, 15–27.

BROWNING, F., & GERASSI, J. (1980). *The American way of crime*. New York: G.P. Putnam's Sons.

BUCKWALTER, J. R. (ED.). (1990). *International perspectives on organized crime*. Chicago: Office of International Criminal Justice, University of Illinois at Chicago.

BURNEY, J. (1912). *History of the buccaneers of America*. London: Allen & Unwin.

BUTTERFIELD, F. (1997, August 17). Study: Cohesion in community lowers violence. *Daytona Beach Sunday News Journal*, p. 3A.

CALIFORNIA DEPARTMENT OF JUSTICE, BUREAU OF INVESTIGATION. (1996). *Russian organized crime: California's newest threat*. Sacramento, CA: CDJ.

CAMPBELL, A. (1984). *The girls in the gang: A report from New York City*. New York: Blackwell.

CARSE, R. (1965). *The age of piracy*. New York: Grosset & Dunlap.

CHAMBLISS, W. (1988). *On the take: From petty crooks to presidents* (2nd ed.). Bloomington, IN: Indiana University Press.

CHAMBLISS, W. J. (1995). State organized crime: The American society of criminology. In N. Passas (Ed.), *Organized crime* (pp. 183–280). Aldershot, Hants, England: Dartmouth Publishing.

CHANG, D. H. (1995). A new form of international crime: The human organ trade. *International Journal of Comparative and Applied Criminal Justice, 19*(1), 1–18.

CHESNEY-LIND, M., & SHELDEN, R. G. (1998). *Girls, delinquency, and juvenile justice* (2nd ed.). Belmont, CA: Wadsworth Publishing.

CHIN, K. (1990). *Chinese subculture and criminality: Non-traditional crime groups in America*. Westport, CT: Greenwood Press.

CHIN, K. (1995). Triad societies in Hong Kong. *Transnational Organized Crime, 1*(1), 47–64.

CHIN, K. (1996). *Chinatown gangs: Extortion, enterprise, and ethnicity*. New York: Oxford University Press.

CHU, Y. (1996). Triad societies and the business community in Hong Kong. *International Journal of Risk, Security and Crime Prevention, 1*(1), 33–40.

CLINARD, M. B. (1990). *Corporate corruption: The abuse of power*. New York: Praeger.

CLOWARD, R., & OHLIN, L. (1960). *Delinquency and opportunity*. New York: Free Press.

COURTWRIGHT, D. T. (1986). *Violent land: Single men and social disorder from the frontier to the inner city*. Cambridge, MA: Harvard University Press.

CRESSY, D. R. (1995). Methodological problems in the study of organized crime as a social problem. In N. Passas (Ed.), *Organized crime* (pp. 3–14). Aldershot, Hants, England: Dartmouth Publishing.

CRIMINAL INTELLIGENCE SERVICE CANADA. (1996). *Annual report on organized crime in Canada* (Revised August 27).

CROWGEY, H. G. (1971). *Kentucky bourbon: The early years of whiskey making*. Lexington, KY: University Press of Kentucky.

CUMMINS, E. (1995). *California prison gang project* (final report). EDRS 387 616, CE 069 978. Chicago: Spencer Foundation.

DALY, K. (1989) Gender and varieties of white collar crime. *Criminology, 27*(4), 769–794.

DATESMAN, S. K., & SCARPITTI, F. R. (EDS.). (1980). *Women, crime, and justice*. New York: Oxford University Press.

DAVIDSON, R. T. (1974). *Chicano prisoners: The key to San Quentin*. Prospect Heights, IL: Waveland Press.

DAWLEY, D. (1992). *A nation of lords: The autobiography of the Vice Lords* (2nd ed.). Prospect Heights, IL: Waveland Press.

Debnam, B. (1997, August 19). The most famous pirate of all: Blackbeard the feared. *Daytona Beach News Journal*, p. 2C.

DE LAMA, G. (1988, November 20). Colombia becomes the Lebanon of Latin America. *Chicago Tribune*, p. 5.

DEMONT, J. (1996). Moonshine revival: History and hard times mean more illegal booze. *Maclean's, 109*(37), 18(1).

DOBNIK, V. (1997, January 25). Report: Chinese being paid slave wage. *Daytona Beach News Journal*, p. 12A.

DUZAN, M. J. (1994). *Death beat: A Colombian journalist's life inside the cocaine wars* (P. Eisner, Trans.). New York: HarperCollins. (Original work published 1992)

ESQUEMELING, J. *The buccaneers of America*. London: George Routledge & Sons. (Reprint of the manuscript originally produced in 1684–1685)

FENNELL, T. (1994). Risky business: Tax weary Canadians help support a boom in smuggled alcohol. *Maclean's, 107*(28), 14(3).

FONG, R. S., & BUENTELLO, S. (1991). The detection of prison gang development: An empirical assessment. *Federal Probation, 55*(1), 66–69.

FREEMANTLE, B. (1995). *The Octopus: Europe in the grip of organized crime*. London: Orion.

GIBBS, N. R. (1995, September 19). Yummy. *Time, 144*, 55–59.

GILBERT, J. N. (1996). Organized crime on the western frontier. *Journal of Criminal Organizations, 10*(2), 7–13.

GOODSON, R., & OLSON, W. (1995, January–February). International organized crime. *Society*, 18–29.

GRASSI, A. (1990). The role of the courts in combating international crime. In J. R. Buckwalter (Ed.), *International perspectives on organized crime* (pp. 37–47). Chicago: Office of International Criminal Justice, University of Illinois at Chicago.

HANDELMAN, S. (1994). The Russian mafya. *Foreign Affairs, 73*(2), 83–96.

HANDELMAN, S. (1995). *Comrade criminal: Russia's new mafya*. New Haven, CT: Yale University Press.

HOPPER, C., & MOORE, J. (1990). Women in outlaw motorcycle gangs. Journal of *Contemporary Ethnography, 18*(4).

HUEY, L. S., HURYSZ, J., & L. M. (1995). Victimization patterns of Asian gangs in the United States. *Journal of Gang Research, 3*(1), 41–49.

HUFF, C. R. (ED.). (1996). *Gangs in America* (2nd ed.). Thousand Oaks, CA: Sage Publications.

JACKSON, C., & WILSON, G. D. (1993). Mad, bad or sad? The personality of bikers. *Personality and Individual Differences, 14*(1), 241–242.

JACOBS, J. B. (1974). Street gangs behind bars. *Social Problems, 21*(3), 395–409.

JAMIESON, A. (1995). Transnational dimensions of Italian organized crime. *Transnational Organized Crime, 1*(2), 151–172.

JANKOWSKI, M. S. (1991). *Islands in the street: Gangs and American urban society*. Berkeley, CA: University of California Press.

JONES, L., & NEWMAN, L., WITH ISAY, D. (1997). *Our America: Life and death on the south side of Chicago*. New York: Scribner.

Kaplan, D. E., & Dubro, A. (1986). *Yakuza: The explosive account of Japan's criminal underworld*. Menlo Park, CA: Addison-Wesley.

KEISER, R. L. (1979). *The Vice Lords: Warriors of the streets* (Fieldwork Ed.). New York: Holt, Rinehart & Winston.

KELLNER, E. (1971). *Moonshine: Its history and folklore*. Indianapolis, IN: Bobbs-Merrill.

KENNEY, D. J., & FINCKENAUER, J. O. (1995). *Organized crime in America*. Belmont, CA: Wadsworth Publishing.

KERRY, J. (1997). *The new war*. New York: Simon & Schuster.

KINNEAR, K. L. (1996). *Gangs: A reference handbook*. Santa Barbara, CA: ABC-CLIO.

KLEINKNECHT, W. (1996). *The new ethnic mobs: The changing face of organized crime in America*. New York: Free Press.

KNOX, G. W. (1994a). *National gangs resource handbook: An encyclopedic reference*. Chicago: National Gang Crime Resource Center, Chicago State University. Wyndham Hall Press.

KNOX, G. W. (1994b). *An introduction to gangs* (New Rev. Ed.). Chicago, IL: Wyndham Hall Press.

KOTLOWITZ, A. (1991). *There are no children here*. New York: Doubleday, Anchor Books.

LAMOTT, K. (1963). *Chronicles of San Quentin: The biography of a prison*. London: John Long.

LANG, A. (1684). Adventures of buccaneers. In J. Esquemeling (Ed.), *The buccaneers of America* (pp. xiii–xix). New York: E.P. Dutton.

LAVEY, D. (1990). Interpol's role in combating organized crime. In J. R. Buckwalter (Ed.), *International perspectives on organized crime* (pp. 87–93). Chicago: Office of International Criminal Justice, University of Illinois at Chicago.

LEE, R. W., III. (1995). Columbia's cocaine syndicate. In N. Passas (Ed.), *Organized crime* (pp. 281–317). Aldershot, Hants, England: Dartmouth Publishing.

LICENSED BEVERAGE INDUSTRIES. (1974, January). *Moonshine: Formula for fraud and slow death*. New York: LBI.

LICENSED BEVERAGE INDUSTRIES. (1966, October). *Moonshine merchants: A study and report*. New York: LBI.

LOMBARDO, R. M. (1990). Asset forfeiture: Civil remedies against organized crime. In J. R. Buckwalter (Ed.), *International perspectives on organized crime* (pp. 49–62). Chicago: Office of International Criminal Justice, University of Illinois at Chicago.

LUPSHA, P. A. (1995). Individual choice, material culture and organized crime. In N. Passas (Ed.), *Organized crime* (pp. 105–125). Aldershot, Hants, England: Dartmouth Publishing.

LYMAN, M., & POTTER, G. W. (1997). *Organized crime*, Upper Saddle River, NJ: Prentice Hall.

MA, Y. (1995). Crime in China: Characteristics, causes and control strategies. *International Journal of Comparative and Applied Criminal Justice, 19*(2), 247–256.

MACDONALD, S. B. (1988). *Dancing on a volcano: The Latin American drug trade*. New York: Praeger.

MACKENZIE, N. (ED.). (1967). *Secret societies*. New York: Holt, Rinehart and Winston.

MAHER, L., & CURTIS, R. (1995). In search of the female urban gansta. In B. R. Price and N. J. Sokoloff (Eds.), *The criminal justice system and women* (2nd ed.). New York: McGraw-Hill.

MALTZ, M. D. (1990). *Measuring the effectiveness of organized crime control efforts* (Monograph 9). Chicago: Office of International Criminal Justice, University of Illinois at Chicago.

MARTENS, F. T. (1990). African-American organized crime. In J. R. Buckwalter (Ed.), *International perspectives on organized crime*. Chicago: Office of International Criminal Justice, University of Illinois at Chicago.

MARTIN J. M., & ROMANO, A. T. (1992). *Multinational crime: Terrorism, espionage, drugs and arms trafficking*. Menlo Park, CA: Sage Publications.

MARTINEZ, R., JR. (1996). Latinos and lethal violence: The impact of poverty and inequality. *Social Problems, 43*(2), 131–146.

MARX, G., & PARSONS, C. (1996, November 11). *Chicago Tribune*, pp. 1–8.

McCORMACK, R. J. (1996). *Organized crime: A north American perspective*. Trenton, NJ: College of New Jersey Department of Law and Justice.

McDONALD, W. F. (1995). The globalization of criminology: The new frontier is the frontier. *Transnational Organized Crime, 1*(1), 1–12.

McDONALD, W. F. (1997). Crime and illegal immigration: Emerging local, state, and federal partnerships. *National Institute of Justice Journal, 232*, 2–10.

MILLER, W. R. (1991). *Revenuers and Moonshiners*. Chapel Hill, NC: University of North Carolina Press.

MONTI, D. J. (1994). *Wannabe gangs in suburbs and schools*. Cambridge, MA: Blackwell.

MOORE, J. W. (1978). *Homeboys: Gangs, drugs, and prisons in the barrios of Los Angeles*. Philadelphia: Temple University Press.

MOORE, J. (1985). Isolation and stigmatization in the development of the underclass: The case of Chicano gangs in east Los Angeles. *Social Problems, 33*(1), 1–10.

MOORE, J. (1994). The chola life course: Chicana heroin users and the barrio gang. *International Journal of the Addictions, 29*(9), 1115–1126.

MOORE, J. W. (1991). *Going down to the barrio*. Philadelphia: Temple University Press.

MYERS, W. H., II. (1996). ORB weavers: The global webs, the structure and activities of transnational ethnic Chinese criminal groups. *Transnational Organized Crime, 1*(4), 1–36.

NAYLON, R. T. (1996). From underworld to underground enterprise crime, informal sector business and public policy response. *Crime, Law and Social Change, 24*(2), 79–150.

NEAPOLITAN, J. (1996). Cross national crime data: Some unaddressed problems. *Journal of Crime and Justice, 19*(1), 95–112.

NEW YORK STATE ORGANIZED CRIME TASK FORCE: NEW YORK STATE COMMISSION OF INVESTIGATIONS, NEW JERSEY COMMISSION, AND OTHERS. (1996). *An analysis of Russian-émigré crime in the tri-state region*. Albany, NY: Tri-state Joint Soviet-Émigré Organized Crime Project.

PACE, D. F. (1991). *Concepts of vice, narcotics, and organized crime* (3rd ed.). Englewood Cliffs, NJ: Prentice Hall.

PARIS-STEFFENS, S. (1990). The role of the United Nations in combating organized crime. In J. R. Buckwalter (Ed.), *International perspectives on organized crime* (pp. 13–17). Chicago: Office of International Criminal Justice, University of Illinois at Chicago.

PARSELS, E. (1996). Capitalism fosters gang behavior. In C. P. Cozic (Ed.), *Gangs: Opposing viewpoints*. San Diego, CA: Greenhaven Press.

PASSAS, N. (ED.). (1995). *Organized crime*. Philadelphia, PA: Temple University Press.

PATRICK, J. (1973). *A Glasgow gang observed*. London: Eyre Methuen.

POLLOCK-BYRNE, J. M. (1990). *Women, prison and crime*. Pacific Grove, CA: Brooks/Cole.

POSNER, G. L. (1988). *Warlords of crime: Chinese secret societies: The new Mafia*. New York: McGraw-Hill.

POTTER, G. W. (1994). *Criminal organizations: Vice, racketeering, and politics in an American city*. Prospect Heights, IL: Waveland Press.

POTTER, G. W., & GAINES, L. (1992). Country comfort: Vice and corruption in the rural south. *Journal of Contemporary Criminal Justice, 8*(1), 36–81.

QUINN, J. F. (1987). Sex roles and hedonism among members of outlaw motorcycle clubs. *Deviant Behavior, 8*(1), 47–63.

RANKIN, H. (1969). *The golden age of piracy*. New York: Holt, Rinehart & Winston.

RENARD, R. D. (1996). *The Burmese connection: Illegal drugs and the making of the golden triangle*. Boulder, CO: Lynne Rienner.

RHODES, R. P. (1984). *Organized crime: Crime control vs. civil liberties*. New York: Random House.

ROMO, R. (1983). *East Los Angeles: History of a barrio*. Austin, TX: University of Texas Press.

ROYAL CANADIAN MOUNTED POLICE TRAINING AND DEVELOPMENT BRANCH. (1994). Outlaw motorcycle gangs. *Royal Canadian Mounted Police Gazette, 56*(3–4), 1–39. Project Focus, Canada.

RUGGIERO, V. (1996). War markets: Corporate and organized criminals in Europe. *Social and Legal Studies, 5*(1), 5–20.

RUTH, D. E. (1996). *Inventing the public enemy: The gangster in American culture*. Chicago: University of Chicago Press.

RYAN, P. J. (1995). *Organized crime: A reference handbook*. Santa Barbara, CA: ABC-CLIO.

SAGA, J. (1991). *Confessions of a Yakuza: A life in Japan's underworld*. Tokyo: Kodansha.

SALE, R. T. (1971). *The Blackstone Rangers: A reporter's account of time spent with the street gang on Chicago's south side*. New York: Random House.

SALZANO, J. (1994). It's a dirty business: Organized crime in deep sludge. *Criminal Organizations, 8*(3–4), 17–20.

SANDERS, W. B. (1994). *Gangbangs and drive-bys: Grounded culture and juvenile gang violence*. Hawthorne, NY: Aldine de Gruyter.

SANZ, K., & SILVERMAN, I. (1996). The evolution and future direction of southeast Asian criminal organizations. *Journal of Contemporary Criminal Justice, 12*(4), 285–294.

SATO, I. (1991). *Kamikaze biker: Parody and anomy in affluent Japan*. Chicago: University of Chicago Press.

SCARPITTI, F. R., & BLOCK, A. A. (1987). America's toxic waste racket : Dimensions of the environmental crisis. In T. S. Bynum (Ed.), *Organized crime in America: Concepts and controversies*. Monsey, NY: Willow Tree Press.

SCHATZBERG, R., & KELLY, R. J. (1996). *African-American organized crime: A social history*. New York: Garland Publishing.

SEIBEL, G., & PINCOMB, R. A. (1994). From the Black P Stone Nation to the El Rukns. *Criminal Organizations, 8*(3–4), 3–9.

SEYMOUR, C. (1996). *Yakuza diary: Doing time in the Japanese underworld*. New York: Atlantic Monthly Press.

SHELLEY, L. I., SABERSCHINSKI, H., SINURAJA, T., ET AL. (1995). East meets west in crime. *European Journal on Criminal Policy and Research, 3*(4), 7–107.

SILBERMAN, M. (1995). *A world of violence*. Belmont, CA: Wadsworth Publishing.

SLAUGHTER, T. P. (1986). *The whiskey rebellion: Frontier epilogue to the American Revolution*. New York: Oxford University Press.

SMALL, G. (1995). *Ruthless: The global rise of the Yardies*. London: Warner.

STEFFENSMEIER, D. J. (1983). Organizational properties and sex segregation in the underworld: Building a sociological theory of sex differences in crime. *Social Forces, 61*(4), 1010–1032.

SUTHERLAND, E. H. (1949). *White collar crime*. New York: Holt, Rinehart & Winston.

TAYLOR, C. S. (1993). *Girls, gangs, women and drugs*. East Lansing, MI: Michigan State University Press.

THOMPSON, H. S. (1966). *Hell's Angels: A strange and terrible saga*. New York: Ballantine Books.

United States Code. Title 15. Criminal street gangs. Section 150001.

U.S. CONGRESS SENATE COMMITTEE ON GOVERNMENTAL AFFAIRS PERMANENT SUBCOMMITTEE ON INVESTIGATIONS. (1993). *The new international criminal and Asian organized crime: Report* (Report Item 1037-CMF). Washington, DC: U.S. Government Printing Office.

U.S. DEPARTMENT OF HEALTH AND HUMAN SERVICES. (1992). Elevated blood lead levels associated with illicitly distilled alcohol: Alabama, 1990–1991. *Morbidity and Mortality Weekly Report, 41*(17), 294(2).

U.S. DEPARTMENT OF JUSTICE. (1985). Prison gangs: Their extent, nature and impact on prisons (Grant 84-NI-AX-0001). Washington, DC: U.S. Government Printing Office.

U.S. GENERAL ACCOUNTING OFFICE. (1996). *Drug control: U.S. heroin program encounters many obstacles in southeast Asia* (Report to congressional requesters). Washington, DC: U.S. GAO.

VAKSBERG, A. (1991). *The Soviet Mafia* (J. & E. Roberts, Trans.). New York: St. Martin's Press.

VAN DUYNE, P. C. (1996). The phantom and threat of organized crime. *Crime, Law and Social Change, 24*(4), 341–377.

VARESE, F. (1994). Is Sicily the future of Russia? Private protection and the rise of the Russian Mafia. *Archives of European Sociology, 35*, 224–258.

VIGIL, J. D. (1994). *Barrio gangs: Street life and identity in southern California*. Arlington, TX: University of Texas Press.

VIGIL, J. D. (1997). *Learning from gangs: The Mexican American experience* (Report RC 020 943). Los Angeles, CA: University of California at Los Angeles. (ERIC Clearinghouse on Rural Education and Small Schools Temporary Accession RC 020 943)

VOLOBUEV, A. (1990). Combating organized crime in the U.S.S.R.: problems and perspectives. In J. R. Buckwalter (Ed.), *International perspectives on organized crime* (pp. 75–82). Chicago: Office of International Criminal Justice, University of Illinois at Chicago.

WALTHER, S. (1994). Forfeiture and money laundering laws in the United States. *Crime, Law and Social Change, 21*(1), 1–13.

WESSELL, N. H. (ED.). (1995). Special issues on crime in Russia. *Russian Politics and Law, 33*(4), 3–72.

WILKINSON, A. (1985). *Moonshine: A life in pursuit of white liquor*. New York: Alfred A. Knopf.

WILLIAMS, P., & SAVONA, E. (1995). The United Nations and transnational organized crime. *Transnational Organized Crime, 1*(3), 1–194.

WOLF, D. R. (1991). *The Rebels: A brotherhood of outlaw bikers*. Toronto, Ontario, Canada: University of Toronto Press.

WOODIWISS, M. (1988). *Crime, crusades and corruption: Prohibition in the United States, 1900–1987*. Totowa, NJ: Barnes & Noble Books.

ZHANG, S. X., & GAYLORD, M. S. (1996). Bound for the golden mountain: The social organization of Chinese alien smuggling. *Crime, Law and Social Change, 25*(1), 1–16.

APPENDIX: EXEMPLARS FOR TEN OC GROUPS

1. *Corporate corruption: The abuse of power*, by Marshall B. Clinard. New York: Praeger, 1980.

2. *The new ethnic mobs: The changing face of organized crime in America*, by W. Kleinknecht. The Organizatsiya (Chap.11). New York: Free Press, 1996.

3. *The American way of crime*, by Frank Browning and John Gerassi, Pirates and profiteers (Chap. 4). New York: G.P. Putnam's Sons, 1980.

4. *Revenuers and moonshiners: Enforcing federal liquor law in the mountain South, 1865–1900*, by Wilbur R. Miller. Chapel Hill, NC: University of North Carolina Press, 1991.

5. *Chinatown gangs: Extortion, enterprise and ethnicity*, by Ko-lin Chin. New York: Oxford University Press, 1996.

6. *Yakuza: The explosive account of Japan's criminal underworld*, by David E. Kaplan and Alex Dubro. Reading, MA: Addison-Wesley, 1986.

7. *Death beat: A Colombian journalist's life inside the cocaine wars*, by Maria Jimena Duzan (translated and edited by Peter Eisner). New York: HarperCollins, 1992.

8. *There are no children here*, by Alex Kotlowitz. New York: Doubleday, Anchor Books, 1991.

9. *Chicano prisoners: The key to San Quentin*, by R. Theodore Davidson. Prospect Heights, IL: Waveland Press, 1974.

10. *The rebels: A brotherhood of outlaw bikers*, by Daniel R. Wolf. Toronto, Ontario, Canada: University of Toronto Press, 1991.

27

Classifying Female Serial Killers

An Application of Prominent Typologies

Laura J. Moriarty and Kimberly L. Freiberger

Several typologies have been created to categorize serial murder, although none have been tested for their usefulness in classifying a sample of serial murders. The present study tests two typologies, one developed by Dietz (1986) and the other by Holmes and DeBurger (1985), to classify incidents of female serial murder. No other research has examined the utility of current typologies to classify female serial murder. The study hypothesis is that the current typologies will not accurately classify female serial killers. Using content analysis, three sources were examined to collect the data: *Women Serial and Mass Murderers: A Worldwide Reference, 1580 through 1990* (Segrave, 1992), *Hunting Humans: An Encyclopedia of Modern Serial Killers* (Newton, 1990), and *Serial Murderers and Their Victims* (Hickey, 1997). The population consists of sixty female serial killers who have killed three or more people over time. The results indicate moderate support for the hypothesis. While 65 percent of the cases can be classified when the typologies are combined, about 1 in 3 (35 percent) cannot be classified using the current schemes. For these cases, motive was found to include attention, jealousy, frustration, cult, and revenge. It is recommended that the current typologies be combined with the additional categories of motive to better explain female serial murder.

There is no universally accepted definition of serial murder; therefore, it is important to begin our chapter with a discussion of serial murder as distinguished from other types of multiple homicides. Rappaport (1988, p. 39) indicates the importance in clarifying mass murder, spree killing, and serial murder. He states that "differentiating the types of murder enables us to gain perspective on the overall phenomena, recognize how one type of offender compares with other types, and enables us to gain understanding and insight into the psychopathology of each type, since they differ so."

The most significant factor in defining categories of murder is the time frame between killings. Jenkins (1994, p. 21) concurs and defines *mass murder* as "murders committed in a brief period in one place" and *spree killing* as "those carried out over a few days or a week." Law enforcement defines *serial murder* as "the sexual attack and murder of young women, men and children by a male who follows a pattern, physical or psychological" (Hickey, 1991, p. 7). A problem with such a specific definition (i.e., sexual attack and male offender) is that many cases of serial murder will not be unclassified as such because a sexual attack may not be part of the crime and/or the offender may not be a male.

Academic researchers have proposed simple and elaborate definitions of serial murder. For example, Hickey defines a *serial killer* as "any offender who killed three or more victims over time (Hickey, 1991, p. 6). Keeney and Heide (1994) provide a more detailed definition of *serial murder* as "the premeditated murder of three or more victims, committed over time in separate incidents, in a civilian context, with the murder activity being chosen by the offender" (p. 384). Either of these approaches is valid, for our purposes, because both capture all offenders, whether male or female, who have killed over a period of time, whether or not a sexual act was part of the crime.

Contrary to popular belief, serial murder is not a recent or an exclusively male phenomenon (Egger, 1990; Leyton, 1986). A historical analysis of serial murder conducted by Eric Hickey refutes these beliefs. Hickey's research identified over 300 serial killers, with 117 dating back to the early nineteenth century and sixty-two being female.

Serial murder is believed to represent a relatively small proportion of all homicides in the United States (Hickey, 1997, p. 13); however, researchers have developed typologies to assist with classifying such behavior. These researchers typically focus on male offenders when developing such typologies. Historically, women who commit serial murder are labeled as "black widows" or "angels of death" and are summarily dismissed (Keeney & Heide, 1993, p. 4). Recent research, however, indicates that women are active in the crime of serial murder and should be part of academic discussions and research pursuits (Fox & Levin, 1993; Hickey, 1991, 1997; Keeney & Heide, 1994; Skrapec, 1994). U.S. homicide rates indicate that females account for roughly 12 to 15 percent of all murders. Ironically, women represent the same percentage of serial murderers (Hickey, 1991, 1997; Keeney & Heide, 1993, 1994; Skrapec, 1994). Conservative estimates attribute between 400 and 600 victims to female serial killers (Hickey, 1997, p. 205).

Dangerous females take the lives of innocent people every year. Segrave (1992, p. 6) lists twelve women who killed among them a total of seventy-one people, including eighteen husbands, twenty-nine of their own children, seven other children (e.g., stepchildren), four mothers, one father, four cousins, five in-laws, one brother, one aunt, and one uncle.

Serial killer Aileen Wuornos, the "Spiderwoman," is one of the most notorious female serial killers. Upon interrogation, Wuornos confessed to killing seven men by shooting each one multiple times. On January 30, 1992, a jury of five men and seven women took less than two hours to deliberate and return a guilty verdict, imposing the death penalty against Wuornos. During her trial in early 1992, television and newspaper accounts referred to her as "America's first female serial killer" and suggested that the presence of Aileen Wuornos marked the incipient stage of a trend toward growing numbers of women who commit serial murder (Fox & Levin, 1994, p. 259). Although Wuornos is often referred to as "America's first female serial killer," she is not the first, and undoubtedly will not be the last.

This raises the concern of how to study female serial killers. Can the same strategies used to understand serial killing in general be applied specifically to female serial killers? At present we do not know because there is a dearth of literature on female serial killers in comparison to males. In this chapter we explore the application of a useful tool, typologies, to the study of female serial murder.

TYPOLOGIES OF SERIAL MURDER

Typologies are a tool for organizing and classifying large amounts of data into mutually exclusive and mutually exhausting categories in order to better understand, predict, and prevent criminal behavior. Most serial murder typologies describe the act, the motive(s), or the personalities of the offenders and their mobility pattern. The FBI, for example, uses profiling techniques to identify characteristics of "organized" and "disorganized" murder crime scenes. Ressler, Burgess, and Douglas (1989) describe organized sexual murder offenders as more likely to plan the crime, use restraints, commit sexual acts with live victims, show or display control over the victim (e.g., manipulate or threaten victim), and use a vehicle in the commission of the crime. Disorganized offenders are more likely to leave a weapon at the scene, position the corpse, perform sexual acts on the corpse, keep the corpse, try to depersonalize the corpse, and are less likely to use a vehicle in the commission of the crime.

Holmes and DeBurger (1985) characterize serial murder by examining offender motive and propose four categories:

1. *Visionary*. The offender is psychotic, often hearing voices or seeing visions or both. In each incidence, the person believes that the voices or visions are instructing the offender to kill. In some cases the offender says "God" told him to kill; in other cases it is the "devil" or demons providing the instruction.

2. *Mission-oriented type*. The offender is attempting to correct a situation deemed inappropriate by the offender. His mission or purpose is to rectify the situation by getting rid of (killing) the undesirables or those unworthy to live with other humans. An example is a serial killer who kills only prostitutes.

3. *Hedonistic type*. The offender is motivated to kill for pure pleasure. The offender likes the way it feels when he kills. Holmes and DeBurger identify subcategories of the hedonistic type, offering the following reasons for such pleasure:

   a. *Lust-oriented*. Sexual gratification is derived from the killings.

   b. *Thrill-oriented*. Thrills or excitement are derived from the killings.

   c. *Comfort-oriented*. Enjoyment of life is derived from the killings.

4. *Power/control oriented*. The offender is driven primarily by the need to exert power or control over others. Gratification is achieved by total submission of the victim. The offender often has a self-inflated sense of importance and power.

Dietz (1986, as cited in Lester, 1995, p. 71) developed five categories of serial killers. His classifications are somewhat different than those of Holmes and DeBurger:

1. *Psychopathic sexual sadists.* These offenders have an antisocial (psychopathic) personality disorder and reflect sexually sadistic tendencies.

2. *Crime spree killers.* These offenders are motivated by the search for excitement, money, and valuables.

3. *Functionaries of organized criminal operations.* This category of offenders includes ethnic gangs, street gangs, members of organized crime, contract killers, illegal mercenaries, and terrorists.

4. *Custodial prisoners and asphyxiators.* These offenders include caretakers of the ill or of children and cases involving physicians and nurses.

5. *Supposed psychotics.* These offenders claim to be acting under the influence of hallucinatory voices or delusions.

Ronald Holmes (1989) developed a typology based on spatial mobility of an offender, which he labels as (1) geographically stable serial killers or (2) geographically transient serial killers. Those serial killers who live in one area and murder in that same area or nearby are labeled *geographically stable*, while those who travel about to kill are *geographically transient.*

Holmes, Hickey, and Holmes (1991) present a female serial killer typology based on behavioral patterns. They identify five categories:

1. *Visionary.* The offender is committing the crimes because of a break with reality. Their definition of visionary is very similar to that of Holmes and DeBurger's visionary and Dietz's supposed psychotics.

2. *Comfort.* The offender is motivated to kill for material gain, typically insurance benefits or acquisition of business interests or real estate.

3. *Hedonistic.* The offender is motivated to kill for the pure pleasure of it.

4. *Discipline.* The offender is under the influence of a charismatic leader. The motive to kill is psychological in that the woman desires acceptance by her "idol."

5. *Power.* The offender is motivated by power. She desires ultimate domination of her victims.

Although several typologies have been created to categorize serial murder, none have been tested for their usefulness in classifying a sample of serial killers. Further, no research has examined the utility of current typologies to classify female serial murder. Researchers have focused primarily on male offenders, resulting in a void in the literature. In the present chapter we examine female serial killers attempting to apply the male-dominate serial killer typologies to this group. Our purpose is to determine if these typologies explain female serial killing or if other typologies must be developed.

METHODOLOGY

The population studied is sixty female serial killers who have murdered three or more people over a period of time. The names of the sixty female serial killers studied are found in the

Appendix. Only these cases where the motive is clearly specified are included. Secondary data sources include Kerry Segrave's (1992) *Women Serial and Mass Murdererers: A Worldwide Reference, to 1580 through 1990,* Michael Newton's (1991) *Hunting Humans: An Encyclopedia of Modern Serial Killers,* and Eric Hickey's (1997) *Serial Murderers and their Victims.* These sources provided information on sixty-two female serial killers; however, motive could be discerned in sixty. Therefore, two cases were dropped from the analysis.

The population was divided into two groups: group 1, consisting of early or pre–World War II cases of serial murder ranging from 1800 to 1945; and group 2, consisting of recent or post–World War II cases ranging from 1946 to 1996. We compiled these two groups to manage the data better. Within these two groups, motive was examined using a combination of manifest and latent content analysis. Once motive was identified in each case, open coding was used to analyze and code the motive by reviewing each case for a specific and consistent set of variables.

Motive was conceptualized as the reasons or incidents causing one to act or the impulses behind the act to commit murder. Further, motive was operationalized according to the specific categories proposed by Dietz (1986) and Holmes and DeBurger (1985). Since all serial killings are not sexual murders, we exclude Ressler et al.'s organized and disorganized classification scheme. We also do not use Holmes, Hickey, and Holmes' female typology because this classification outline includes three of the same elements (visionary, hedonistic, power) found in the Holmes and DeBurger typology. We believe that the two typologies used in this research have the greatest potential for classifying female serial killers.

Therefore, using the Dietz typology, the attributes of motive are psychopathic sexual sadists, crime spree killers, functionaries of organized criminal activities, custodial prisoners and asphyxiators, supposed psychotics, unclassifiable, and mixed. Using the Holmes and DeBurger typology, the motive attributes are visionary, mission-oriented type, hedonistic type (including the subcategories of lust oriented, thrill oriented, and comfort oriented), power/control, unclassifiable, and mixed (see Figure 1 for the conceptualization of each attribute).

Our primary interest is to test whether the typologies described above are applicable to female serial killers. We do so by focusing on the following questions:

- Does the Dietz or Holmes and DeBurger typology best describe early cases (1800–1945) of female serial killing?
- Does the Dietz or Holmes and DeBurger typology best describe later cases (1946–1996) of female serial killing?
- When the cases are combined, which typology best describes all the cases?
- What percentage of all the cases cannot be classified using the Dietz and Holmes and DeBurger typologies?
- What percentage of all the cases are mixed or overlap categories found within the typologies?
- Do the typologies need to be expanded to include categories specific to female serial killers to better classify these offenders?

FIGURE 1   Conceptualization of the Attributes of Each Typology

Typology	Attribute	Operationalization
Dietz	Psychopathic sexual sadists	Antisocial personalities, sexually sadistic tendencies
	Crime spree killers	Excitement, money, and valuables are the motive for killing.
	Functionaries of organized criminal activities	Ethnic gangs, street gangs, members of organized crime, contract killers, illegal mercenaries, terrorists
	Custodial poisoners and asphyxiators	Caretakers who kill
	Supposed psychotics	Delusional killers
	Unclassifiable*	Motive is not represented by any category in the typology.
	Mixed*	Motive reflects two or more categories listed above.
Holmes & DeBurger	Visionary	Delusional killers
	Mission-oriented type	Motive to kill is to eliminate "undesirables."
	Hedonistic type, including subcategories of lust oriented, thrill oriented, and comfort oriented	Killing is pleasurable. Pleasure is derived from sexual gratification (lust), the thrill of killing (thrill), or enjoying life (comfort).
	Power/control	Motive is to have ultimate control over victims.
	Unclassifiable*	Motive is not represented by any category in the typology.
	Mixed*	Motive reflects two or more categories listed above.

*We added these categories to the original typologies.

RESULTS

Table 1 represents the percentage of cases conforming to Dietz's typology from the period 1800–1945. As indicated, twenty-five of the sixty cases examined occurred during this period. The percentages indicate that 16 percent are unable to be classified using this typology, 12 percent are mixed, and the remaining 72 percent can be classified into the specific categories of crime spree killer (64 percent), custodial prisoners and asphyxiators (4 percent), and supposed psychotics (4 percent). No cases are categorized as psychopathic sexual sadists or functionaries of organized crime.

TABLE 1   Percent of Cases Conforming to Dietz's Typology, 1800–1945

Type	Frequency	Percent
Psychopathic sexual sadists	0	0
Crime spree killers	16	64
Functionaries of organized crime	0	0
Custodial prisoners and asphyxiators	1	4
Supposed psychotics	1	4
Unable to classify	4	16
Mixed cases	3	12
	25	100

Table 2 reports the percentage of female serial killings conforming to Dietz's typology from 1946 to 1996. There are thirty-five such cases. As documented, 26 percent cannot be classified using Dietz's typology, 34 percent are mixed, and the remaining 40 percent classify into the specific categories of crime spree killers (31 percent), custodial prisoners and asphyxiators (6 percent), and supposed psychotics (3 percent). Again, no cases are categorized as psychopathic sexual sadists or functionaries of organized crime.

Table 3 provides the percentage of cases conforming to Holmes and DeBurger's typology from 1800 to 1945. Of the twenty-five cases, 16 percent are unable to be classified, 12 percent are mixed, and the remaining 72 percent are classified as hedonistic type (68 percent) and visionary type (4 percent). No cases are categorized as mission oriented or power/control oriented.

Table 4 displays the percentage of cases conforming to Holmes and DeBurger's typology from 1946 to 1996. Here 17 percent of the cases are unable to be classified, 40 percent are mixed, and the remaining 43 percent fall into the specific categories of hedonistic (34 percent), visionary (6 percent), and power/control oriented (3 percent). No cases are categorized as mission oriented.

TABLE 2   Percent of Cases Conforming to Dietz's Typology, 1945–1996

Type	Frequency	Percent
Psychopathic sexual sadists	0	0
Crime spree killers	11	31
Functionaries of organized crime	0	0
Custodial prisoners and asphyxiators	2	6
Supposed psychotics	1	3
Unable to classify	9	26
Mixed cases	12	34
	35	100

TABLE 3   Percent of Cases Conforming to Holmes and DeBurger's Typology, 1800–1945

Type	Frequency	Percent
Visionary type	1	4
Mission-oriented type	0	0
Hedonistic type	17	68
Power/control type	0	0
Not able to classify	4	16
Mixed cases	3	12
	25	100

Table 5 contains the percentage of cases conforming to Dietz's typology for the entire time period, 1800 to 1996. A high percentage (45 percent) is classified as crime spree killers, while a considerable number of cases are unable to be categorized (22 percent). An additional 25 percent are mixed. As mentioned previously, no cases are psychopathic sexual sadists or functionaries of organized crime.

Table 6 represents the percentage of cases conforming to Holmes and DeBurger's typology for the entire time frame. Here 17 percent of the cases are unable to be classified, 28 percent are mixed, 48 percent are hedonistic offenders, 5 percent are visionary, and 2 percent are power/control oriented. Again, none are mission oriented.

The hedonistic offender as proposed by Holmes and DeBurger contains three subcategories: thrill oriented, lust oriented, and comfort oriented. Table 7 represents the percentage of cases conforming to the subcategories of the hedonistic type of female serial offender. Twenty-nine cases are classified as hedonistic. The largest percentage (79 percent) is subclassified as comfort oriented, 14 percent thrill oriented, and 7 percent lust-oriented offenders.

There are twenty-one cases or 35 percent of the sample that cannot be classified when combining the Dietz and Holmes and DeBurger typologies. They were further

TABLE 4   Percent of Cases Conforming to Holmes and DeBurger's Typology, 1946–1996

Type	Frequency	Percent
Visionary type	2	6
Mission-oriented type	0	0
Hedonistic type	12	34
Power/control type	1	3
Not able to classify	6	17
Mixed cases	14	40
	35	100

TABLE 5   Percent of Cases Conforming to Dietz's Typology, 1800–1996

Type	Frequency	Percent
Psychopathic sexual sadists	0	0
Crime spree killers	27	45
Functionaries of organized crime	0	0
Custodial prisoners and asphyxiators	3	5
Supposed psychotics	2	3
Unable to classify	13	22
Mixed cases	15	25
	60	100

TABLE 6   Percent of Cases Conforming to Holmes and DeBurger's Typology for the Entire Time Frame, 1800–1996

Type	Frequency	Percent
Visionary type	3	5
Mission-oriented type	0	0
Hedonistic type	29	48
Power/control type	1	2
Not able to classify	10	17
Mixed cases	17	28
	60	100

TABLE 7   Percent of Cases Conforming to Holmes and DeBurger's Subcategories of Hedonistic Type, 1800–1996 ($n = 29$)

Type	Frequency	Percent
Thrill oriented	4	14
Lust oriented	2	7
Comfort oriented	23	79
	29	100

analyzed recording specific motive. The categories of motive not found in the Dietz or Holmes and DeBurger typologies but clearly the motive for some female serial killers include:

- *Attention.* Motive for the killing is to gain attention (i.e., notice).
- *Frustration.* Stressful situations compel the woman to kill as an alternative way to solve the situation.
- *Jealousy.* The woman kills because she feels she will be supplanted in a relationship by someone else. She is afraid she will lose the affection of a significant other.
- *Cult.* Killings are part of the cult's behavior. The female is part of a cult where obsessive devotion leads to murder.
- *Revenge.* Motive for the killing is to inflict pain in return for injury or insult. The woman retaliates.

Table 8 reports the distribution of cases into these new categories. Of the twenty-one cases, 33 percent are classified as attention killings, 29 percent as frustration killings, 19 percent as revenge killings, and 10 percent each as jealousy and cult killings.

DISCUSSION

Our findings are generally consistent with previous research regarding the motives of female serial killers. We found that by using the Dietz typology, 45 percent of the cases are classified as crime spree killings. When using the Holmes and DeBurger model, 48 percent are classified as hedonistic murders. Crime spree killers commit murder for the excitement of the act or monetary benefit, while hedonistic killers do so for the pure pleasure of the act. These findings are consistent with the literature in general. For example, Holmes and Holmes (1994) explain that female serial killers murder for "comfort" purposes, which include money, insurance benefits, or business interests. Lester (1995, p. 57) proposes that "the most common motive for female killers [is] monetary gain, closely followed by enjoyment." And Newton (1990, p. 2) indicates that 31 percent of female serial killers have murdered for gain, compared to 3 percent of their male counterparts.

TABLE 8   Percent of Cases (Not Classified Using the Dietz or Holmes and DeBurger Typologies) Conforming to the New Categories of Motive ($n = 21$)

Motive Type	Frequency	Percent
Attention	7	33
Jealousy	2	10
Frustration	6	29
Cult	2	10
Revenge	4	19
	21	100

Even though the present findings are consistent with the literature, the results are problematic. There are 21 or 35 percent of the cases that cannot be classified using the current typologies. This amounts to slightly more than one in three female serial killers not being classified when combining the Dietz and Holmes and DeBurger classification schemes. To classify female serial killers more accurately, we added specific categories to the typologies. We discovered that to better explain female serial killing, categories such as attention, jealousy, frustration, cult killings, and revenge must be incorporated into the typologies. Of the twenty-one cases not classified, 7 or 33 percent are determined to have attention as the motive for the killings.

CONCLUSIONS

Although the crime of serial killing is a relatively rare event, it is much more infrequent for the offender to be female. However, female murder and female serial murder occur at comparable rates. Therefore, both should be the focus of academic scholarly pursuits.

With most of the research on serial murder focusing on males, we were interested in finding out if the male serial murder typologies explained female serial murder. In the majority of these cases (65 percent), the typologies proposed by Dietz and Holmes and DeBurger explained the motive of the female serial killers.

A concern, however, is the realization that about one in three cases cannot be classified using these typologies. The motives for these cases are attention, jealousy, frustration, cult, and revenge and are not included in the typologies listed above. Therefore, to better comprehend female serial murder, we suggest adding the categories listed above to the two male serial murder typologies. The combination of the Dietz, Holmes, DeBurger and the current research findings will provide a more complete understanding of female serial murder.

REFERENCES

Dietz, P. E. (1986). Mass, serial and sensational homicides. *Bulletin of the New York Academy of Medicine, 62*, 447–491. As cited in Lester, D. (1995). *Serial killers: The insatiable passion.* Philadelphia: Charles Press.

Egger, S. (1990). *Serial murder: An elusive phenomenon.* New York: Praeger.

Fox, J. A., & Levin, J. (1994). *Overkill: Mass murder and serial killing exposed.* New York: Plenum Press.

Hickey, E. W. (1991). *Serial murderers and their victims.* Pacific Grove, CA: Brooks/Cole.

Hickey, E. W. (1997). *Serial murderers and their victims* (2nd ed.). Belmont, CA: Wadsworth Publishing.

Holmes, R. (1989). *Profiling violent crimes.* Newbury Park, CA: Sage Publications.

Holmes, R., & DeBurger, J. (1985). Profiles in terror: The serial murderer. *Federal Probation, 49*, 29–34.

Holmes, S., Hickey, E., & Holmes, R. (1991). Female serial murderesses: Constructing differentiating typologies. *Journal of Contemporary Criminal Justice, 7*, 245–256.

Holmes, R., & Holmes, S. (1994). *Murder in America.* Thousand Oaks, CA: Sage Publications.

Jenkins, P. (1994). *Using murder: The social construction of serial homicide.* New York: Aldine de Gruyter.

Keeney, B. T., & Heide, K. M. (1993). The latest on serial murderers. *Violence Update, 4*, 1–10.

KEENEY, B. T., & HEIDE, K. M. (1994). Gender differences in serial murder: A preliminary analysis. *Journal of Interpersonal Violence, 9*, 383–398.

LESTER, D. (1995). *Serial killers, The insatiable passion*. Philadelphia: Charles Press.

LEYTON, E. (1986). *Compulsive killers*. New York: University Press.

NEWTON, M. (1990). *Hunting humans: An encyclopedia of modern serial killers*. Port Townsend, WA: Loompanics Unlimited.

RAPPAPORT, R. (1988). The serial and mass murderer: Patterns, differentiation, pathology. *American Journal of Psychiatry, 146*(7), 887–891.

RESSLER, R., BURGESS, A., & DOUGLAS, J. (1988). *Sexual homicide: Patterns and motives*. Lexington, MA: D.C. Heath.

SEGRAVE, K. (1992). *Women serial and mass murderers: A worldwide reference 1580 through 1990*. Jefferson, NC: McFarland.

SKRAPEC, C. (1994). The female serial killer: An evolving criminality. In Birch, H. (Ed.), *Moving targets: Women, murder and representation* (pp. 241–268). Los Angeles, CA: University of California Press.

APPENDIX: CASES OF FEMALE SERIAL KILLERS USED IN THIS STUDY

Susan Atkins
Amy Archer-Gilligan
Margie Velma Barfield
Martha Beck
Kate Bender
Debra Denise Brown
Carol Bundy
Patty Cannon
Faye Copeland
Anna Cunningham
Nannie Hazel Doss
Ellen Etheridge
Christine Falling
Carino Favato
Tille Gburek
Janie Lou Gibbs
Amy Gillgan
Gwendolyn Graham
Belle Gunness
Anna Marie Hahn
Marie Hilley
Waneta Hoyt
Mary Jane Jackson
Dorothy Jean Jatajke
Martha A. Johnson
Genene Jones
Sharon Kinne
Tillie Klimek
Patricia Krevwinkle
Diana Lumbrera

Anjette Donovan Lyles
Rhonda Bell Martin
Blanche Taylor Moore
Robin Murphy
Judith Neeley
Ruby C. Padgett
Bonnie Parker
Lofie "Louise" Peete
Dorthea Montavo Puente
Jane Quinn
Terri Rachels
Mary Rose Robaczynski
Sarah Jane Robinson
Lydia Sherman
Sally Skull
Mary Eleanor Smith
Della Sorenson
Gloria Tannenbaum
Bobbie Sue Terrell
Marybeth Tinning
Jane Toppan
Lydia Trueblood
Leslie Van Houten
Louise Vermilyea
Annette Washington
Charlene Williams
Martha Hasel Wise
Catherine Wood
Martha Woods
Aileen Wuornos

SECTION IX

Girls and Delinquency

The majority of studies of delinquency and substance abuse usually focus on males, not females. What has been the failure of researchers is to adequately examine the impact of gender on theoretical development. In their chapter, "Gender Differences in Delinquency and Substance Use," Elizabeth P. Deschenes, Jill Rosenbaum, and Jeffrey Fagan examine patterns of delinquency and substance abuse. It appears from the results of their study that among females, substance use problems are more important than peer delinquency in explaining differences in rate of serious and general delinquency. The conclusions reached are that programs are needed as much for females as for young males to stop both from committing acts of delinquency. As measured by family and social integration, social bonding appears to be more important for females than males in explaining general and serious delinquency, even though family integration is a correlate of substance among males, but not among females.

There exist few topics that rival the research and policy attention bestowed on serious, violent, and chronic juvenile offenders. Kimberly Kempf-Leonard and P.E. Tracy focus on gender differences in offending across the "crime-prone" years of the 1958 Philadelphia cohort in "The Gender Effect among Serious, Violent, and Chronic Juvenile Offenders: A Difference of Degree Rather Than Kind." They demonstrate the importance of examining the gender effect in offending for policy formulation and theory development. Their findings indicate gender differences in degree of serious, violent, and chronic offending, but gender similarities in general career patterns of interest. Such findings lead the authors to conclude that status offenders need to be reintegrated as a feasible target of mainstream juvenile justice, while gender similarities in behavior, coupled with evidence of gender bias or differential processing, serve to remind us of the warning that criminal justice functions to maintain the modern patriarchy. There needs to be a balanced approach of prevention, early intervention, and graduated sanctions that provides for treatment just as it aims to strengthen the family.

28

Gender Differences in Delinquency and Substance Use[1]

Elizabeth Piper Deschenes, Jill Rosenbaum, and Jeffrey Fagan

The majority of studies of delinquency and substance use have traditionally focused on males and excluded females. Moreover, researchers have failed to adequately examine the impact of gender on theoretical development. The current study examined patterns of delinquency and substance use in random samples of 2356 high school students and snowball samples of dropouts drawn from six inner-city neighborhoods. Self-report surveys were conducted in 1983 and 1984. The study results provided clear evidence of a high correlation between substance use and delinquency. The different theoretical models tested showed that the confluence of delinquency and substance use was an important variable in explaining the frequency of these acts. However, peer delinquency remained the most significant correlate of adolescent delinquency, substance use, or dealing among males. For females, substance use problems were more important than peer delinquency in explaining differences in rates of serious and general delinquency. The results suggest that there is a serious need for delinquency and substance use prevention programs among females as well as males.

Historically, theories of crime and delinquency have focused on adolescent males. In addition, most research studies testing various theoretical models have used samples of males. The reason for this is simple. Official arrest records indicate that males commit greater proportions of crimes than females. Since 1970 there has been an increase in research on female delinquency, but the theoretical development has been lacking (Chesney-Lind, 1989) or inappropriate (Chesney-Lind & Shelden, 1992). All too often, researchers have just borrowed concepts that explain male delinquency and applied them to females. There has been almost no research on gender differences in delinquency that has tested distinct theoretical models for males and females.

431

Similarly, there has been a paucity of research examining gender differences in substance use. With the exception of some earlier studies of female heroin addicts (Anglin & Hser, 1987; M. Rosenbaum, 1981), most research and theory testing have focused on males. Again, males generally have higher prevalence rates of alcohol and drug use than females (Jessor, 1979; Kandel, 1980, 1982), but the trends have not been consistent over time (Elliott, Huizinga, & Menard, 1989).

There is evidence from several self-report studies of delinquency and substance use that similarities exist among males and females in the variety and substance but not in the frequency of those behaviors. For instance, in reanalysis of ten self-report data sets, Weis (1980) found that a large percentage of both males and females were involved in a wide variety of offenses. Hindelang (1971) reported that the females in this sample committed fewer crimes, yet their delinquent involvement paralleled the pattern of the males. Other studies showed similar patterns of delinquent behavior among the sexes (Canter, 1982; Cernkovich & Giordano, 1979) and few differences in the frequency of self-reported substance use (Johnson, O'Malley, & Bachman, 1985, 1993a, 1993b). Some studies have shown that the ratio of male to female crime was similar in both official and self-report data, yet the frequency of acts was greater for males than for females (Sarri, 1983). Using the National Youth Survey data, Triplett and Meyers (1995) found gender differences for both the prevalence and incidence of offending. Moreover, their research supported earlier findings of a larger gender difference for more serious offenses. Triplett and Meyers explained some of these differences in terms of the context of offending, but they did not examine the broader theoretical issues.

SOCIAL EXPLANATIONS OF DELINQUENCY AND SUBSTANCE USE

Studies of adolescent problem behaviors have consistently shown that a variety of social, psychological, and economic factors are associated with delinquency and substance use, and the overlap between these behaviors suggests common correlates and etiological paths (Elliott & Huizinga, 1984; Jessor & Jessor, 1977; Kandel, Simcha-Fagan, & Davies, 1986). Although there is extensive knowledge about each of these separate problems, relatively little is known about their joint distribution or whether these problems are causally related to one another. There are two possible approaches. A "spurious" explanatory framework suggests that the linkages between delinquency and substance use may be coincidental and occur as part of a common set of adolescent problem behaviors (Jessor & Jessor, 1977). A corollary proposition is that the behaviors are unrelated but are explained by a common set of factors. If the relationship between delinquency and substance use is "spurious," theoretical explanations should apply equally to the separate behaviors as well as their joint occurrence. Conversely, if the behavior patterns have different explanations, the relationship is not spurious, but the patterns have differential meanings and explanations. This study examined patterns of delinquency and substance use among students and dropouts and analyzed various theoretical factors to determine whether sets of common or different factors explain these behaviors among males and females.

Both social control and social learning theories were developed to explain delinquency on the part of males. Yet according to Box (1981, p. 144), "Control theory offers the best possibility for explaining both female delinquency and even more important, why it is less frequent than male delinquency." Social learning theories have also received some support as explanations of female behavior. Morris (1964) argued that at least in part, females committed fewer crimes than males because of the relative absence of subcultural support for delinquency. Furthermore, those youth, regardless of their gender, whose close friends had been picked up by the police were more likely to have police records themselves (Hindelang, 1971; J. Rosenbaum, 1987). Simons, Miller, and Aigner (1980) found that the gender differential in crime was a matter of having fewer delinquent friends; while Giordano (1978) traced the changes in female criminality to increased peer support for female involvement in crime. According to Weis and Hawkins' (1981) social development theory, the influence of peers should be more salient for girls than for boys and vary according to the type of delinquent behavior, while family influence should decrease more rapidly for boys than girls as they get older.

Many theories, including social control, social learning, and integrated theories, have been tested as they apply to both delinquency and substance use. For example, control theory has been tested under a variety of sampling and measurement conditions for delinquency (Hirschi, 1969; J. Rosenbaum, 1983; Wiatrowski, Griswold, & Roberts, 1981) and substance use (Kaplan, Smith, & Robins, 1984; White, Johnson, & Garrison, 1985). Social learning theory also has been tested for both delinquency (Burgess & Akers, 1966) and substance use (Jensen & Brownfield, 1983; Johnson, Marcos, & Bahr, 1987).

Integrated theories that combine social control and learning theories have been applied to delinquency (Elliott, Ageton, & Canter, 1979; Fagan, Hansen, & Jang, 1983; Weis & Hawkins, 1981), substance use (Johnson et al., 1987; Kandel, Simcha-Fagan, & Davies, 1986), and the joint behaviors (Elliott, Huizinga, & Ageton, 1985; White, Pandina, & LaBouvie, 1987). Although the studies using integrated theories disagree on the primacy of constructs from one theory or the other in explaining behavior, they agree that an integration of social learning and social control perspectives is superior to either in isolation (Johnson, et al., 1987).

Theoretical integrations specify both the domains of socialization and the temporal sequence of their influence. Weis and Hawkins (1981) suggested that the social bond develops incrementally in the milieu where the most salient socialization occurs: family, school, peer associations, and community. Johnson, et al. (1987) added religious influence as an early influence in social development. Fagan and Jones (1984) suggested that both positive and negative bonds could develop through socialization experiences in family or school, among peers, and in the community. For example, family supervision practices can shape conventional behaviors, while adolescents whose families use drugs or commit crimes are exposed to definitions and values conducive to deviant behaviors. The temporal sequence suggests that there is a cumulative effect of positive and negative bonding across domains. Thus positive socialization in the family influences bonding to school and, later, toward acceptance of law supporting attitudes and selection of peers. The causal paths hypothesized in an integrated model have recently been refined to include reciprocal effects—that is, delinquency may disrupt social bonds and lead to problems in the family or at school (Thornberry & Christenson, 1984). Therefore, bonding may alternatively be a predictor and an outcome of deviance, or have reciprocal effects of the bonding–behavior relationship (Thornberry, 1987). Other researchers have suggested that the locus and sequencing of bonds may be age-specific.

The current study used an integrated theoretical model to test for gender differences in delinquency and substance use. This integrated approach was used for several reasons.

First, sampling within inner-city neighborhoods provided a natural control for social structural and ecological effects. These effects may mediate the strength of theoretical relationships or confound them in studies across social areas. Second, empirical evidence from separate studies of delinquency and adolescent substance use consistently has identified common correlates of delinquency and substance use derived from these theories. For example, family attachments, peer associations, and educational attachments are constructs associated with control theory and the reinforcement processes of learning theory that also are correlates of both substance use and delinquency. The elements of the social bond are strengthened or weakened through socialization experiences in each domain, the family, school, peer groups, and the community. The elements of the bond are specified as positively related to nondeviant behavior. Third, the model included neighborhood influences on delinquency and substance use, which was a departure from earlier theoretical integrations that neglected the influence of youths' perceptions of neighborhood norms on illegal behavior.

The integration of control and learning theories provided a testable set of hypotheses to examine the relationship between delinquency and substance use. Since the lack of explanatory differentiation in integrated models based on social control and learning theories suggests that delinquency and substance use may be spuriously related (Fagan, Weis, & Cheng, 1990; White, et al., 1987), we hypothesized "spurious" relationships between them, suggesting a pattern of general deviance (Osgood, Johnston, O'Malley, & Bachman, 1988).

The current study focused on testing specific hypotheses about gender differences in delinquency and substance use among inner-city youths. First, we wanted to know if inner-city males and females would show similar patterns of prevalence and frequency of these behaviors or whether the gender differences would not be as great as in the general population. Second, was there a co-occurrence of delinquency and substance use among both males and females? If there were differences in the types of behaviors, what factors could be used to explain these differences? To examine this third question, we tested specific explanatory models—those factors related to social control theory, those related to social learning theory, and a combination of the two. Finally, we hypothesized that if we found significant gender differences in the prevalence and incidence of delinquency and substance use, the same model would not apply for both males and females.

METHODS

Samples and Data Collection

This study was part of a research and development program on violent juvenile crime in six inner-city neighborhoods (Bronx, New York; New Orleans, Louisiana; Dallas, Texas; Chicago, Illinois; Los Angeles, California; and San Diego, California).[2] Within each city, one sample of size 200 was drawn from high school students (grades 9 to 12) using a multistage cluster sampling technique, and another sample of fifty high school dropouts was drawn using the "snowball" technique (Biernacki & Waldorf, 1981).[3] Self-report surveys were administered in two iterations, once in the spring of 1985 and again in the fall of 1985.[4] Efforts were made to avoid repeat participants. Table 1 provides details on the sample characteristics for the present study. Respondents ranged in age from 13 to 20, were predominantly African-American and Hispanic, and included both males and females.

Measures and Constructs

Self-reported delinquency (SRD) and substance use items were derived from the National Youth Survey (Elliott, Knowles, & Canter, 1981) and included questions on delinquent behavior, alcohol and illicit substance use, and other "problem" behaviors.[5] Similar to the National Youth Survey, the recall period was twelve months, from "Christmas a year ago to this past Christmas" for spring surveys, and from "Labor Day a year ago until this past

TABLE 1   Background Characteristics (Percent)

	Male (*n* = 1226)	Female (*n* = 1199)
Age		
14	7.2	6.8
15	18.3	19.8
16	25.1	29.5
17	49.4	43.9
Race		
Anglo	2.1	1.8
African-American	72.5	76.2
Hispanic	21.4	19.0
Other	4.0	3.0
School grade		
8	10.8	10.0
9	14.8	9.8
10	23.2	25.5
11	24.5	26.6
12	26.8	28.0
Living with whom		
Both parents	27.6	26.4
Stepmother or father	11.1	8.3
Single parent	53.0	56.2
Other adult	8.3	9.1
Parents' employment		
None	15.8	15.8
Mother only	16.4	17.8
Father only	16.8	15.8
Both	51.0	50.6
Parents' education		
Less than high school	21.3	22.2
High school graduate	31.5	30.8
College graduate	47.2	47.0

Labor Day" for the fall surveys.[6] Responses were given using a categorical set of frequencies, ranging from "never" to "once a year to monthly" to "2 to 3 times a week." For the analysis, the responses were converted into annual incidence rates.[7] The items were then categorized into scales constructed from homogeneous crime types that are parallel with penal code definitions.[8]

An index of delinquent involvement was constructed, called INDEX. Similar to ordinal scales developed and validated by Dunford and Elliott (1984) and Fagan et al. (1990), this index included dimensions of both severity and frequency of delinquent acts over the previous twelve-month period. The index is a hierarchical typology that allows for less serious behaviors that have been committed by those in successively more serious categories of offenders. Specific alcohol use, drug use, or drug-selling behaviors and incidents of intoxication are not considered in the typology. The categories range from petty acts (e.g., going to school "high" or drunk) to index felonies.[9]

The questions and response sets for alcohol and drug use items followed the same format and response sets as the SRD items. Drug selling was included as an SRD item, as was "driving while drunk or high" and "attending school while drunk or high." Questions about personal use of substances were included in separate items. Questions were asked regarding alcohol (beer or wine; whiskey, gin, vodka, or other liquor) and illicit drug (marijuana, cocaine, heroin or opiates, hallucinogens, amphetamines or "speed," barbiturates or "downers," and inhalants or "glue-sniffing") use. The general format also asked: "How often in the past year, from [time anchor] a year ago until this past [time anchor] did you...?" Categorical response sets again were employed.

Drug-specific scales involved the frequency of use of each substance. These scales were not collapsed in estimating frequencies of particular drug use types; instead, the individual substances were retained to capture what ethnographic data suggest are distinct drug use patterns by youth network and locale (Feldman, Agar, & Beschner, 1979) as well as possible gender differences. An index of the severity of substance involvement was constructed as well, based on dimensions of the severity and frequency of substance use. For the scale DRUGTYPE, nonexperimental use (three or more times in the past year) of cocaine, opiates, or PCP is the most serious category. Experimental use (less than three times per year) is the next level, followed by chronic use of marijuana or alcohol (more than twelve times per year). Other trivial use of marijuana or alcohol is the least serious category of DRUGTYPE.

Explanatory variable sets were derived from the integrated theory described above. Sources of social development were hypothesized in three areas: social bonding to conventional norms and beliefs, social environments that influence the strength and direction of bonds and that may influence behavior directly, and psychosocial development of cognitive skills. The definitions of each scale are included in the Appendix.

Drug and alcohol problem scales were patterned after similar items in Jessor and Jessor (1977), Elliott and Huizinga (1984), and White et al. (1987). Self-reports of drug and alcohol problem behaviors were preferred to standardized scales or official records. Clinical records and official records have several weaknesses. The lack of standardized definitions, inconsistent quality control in record thoroughness and access, practical issues in privacy and access plus consistency with survey procedures, and lack of representativeness or validity all point to using self-reports (Jessor & Jessor, 1977). Moreover, they are direct reports, not clinical interpretations from clinicians or measurement tools, which raise validity and reliability questions for the inner-city youth sample.

These scales (drug problems, drinking problems) each included six items, reflecting negative social and personal consequences of alcohol or drug use. Each scale asked if the respondent "ever felt you had a drug [or alcohol] problem." Also, separate items asked whether in the past year "you have had a problem with your [family, friends, girlfriend or boyfriend, in school, with the police] because of your drug use [or drinking]." Additional items asked if the respondent had gotten into fights or been arrested "because of drinking [or drug use]." Finally, respondents were asked if he or she had sought treatment, been in treatment, or been told to seek treatment for drinking or drug use in the past year.

Overall, these measures have been shown to have strong explanatory power in both cross-sectional and longitudinal studies of serious delinquency, under a variety of sampling conditions. Fagan, Piper, and Moore (1986) validated these measures with samples of institutionalized and general population male adolescents from inner-city neighborhoods, while Fagan, Piper, and Cheng (1987) validated the items with both males and females in inner-city neighborhoods. Validity analyses specifically examined the relationship between the SRD and substance use scales and internal predictors. Validity was confirmed through selected bivariate correlations with theoretical variables whose independent relationships with substance use and delinquency also are well established. For example, involvement with delinquent peers is strongly associated with several deviant behaviors, under various sampling and measurement conditions (Hirschi, 1969; Wiatrowski et al., 1981). Accordingly, the Pearson correlation coefficients for peer delinquency and several SRD scales were compared, controlling for gender and school status. The correlation coefficients were all significant and in the directions predicted. Reliability analyses included calculation of consistency measures (Cronbach's alpha) for each scale and again for theoretically important subgroups: males and females, students and dropouts, and site-specific calculations. In general, reliabilities were at least adequate (alpha = 0.70) or excellent (alpha = 0.90) for the total sample and for four delinquent types.

RESULTS

Differences between males and females in the prevalence and frequency rates of self-reported delinquency are shown in Table 2. The severity and frequency of delinquent acts have been used to classify youths into the four different types of offenders described above as INDEX. Significant gender differences were found in both the types of offenses and the frequency rates of offending for all types of offenders. Over half of the youths interviewed, both males and females, reported they had engaged in no delinquent behavior or only minor offenses. This group, classified as petty offenders, averaged six to seven offenses in the past year. Males and females were almost equally engaged in minor offenses (13 percent versus 11 percent), but the frequency rates for property crimes and offenses in general were significantly higher for females than for males (fifteen property crimes per year for females compared to five per year for males). As expected, males were more likely than females to be serious and multiple offenders; few of the latter committed multiple index offenses (21 percent of males versus 8 percent of females). Yet those females who did commit multiple index crimes reported significantly higher rates of general delinquency and violent crime (a rate of forty-five per year versus thirty-six per year) than males. These findings suggest that once females are initiated into crime or delinquency, they become more hard core than males and commit delinquent acts with greater frequency.

TABLE 2   Prevalence and Frequency of Self-Reported Delinquency by Offender Type by Gender

	Male (n = 1226)		Female (n =1199)	
	Percent	Mean Number of Offenses	Percent	Mean Number of Offenses
Petty offenders				
General	52.0	7.29	71.2	6.39
Violent	0.0	0.00	0.0	0.00
Property	0.0	0.00	0.0	0.00
Minor offenders				
General	13.3	39.82	10.9	54.76
Violent	2.1	0.51	1.2	0.59
Property	6.8	4.85	6.8	15.07
Serious offenders				
General	13.9	66.95	9.7	72.88
Violent	5.9	1.51	2.8	0.82
Property	7.3	10.87	4.4	9.09
Multiple index offenders				
General	20.9	282.32	8.2	298.58
Violent	18.4	35.55	7.0	44.63
Property	17.5	49.21	6.3	49.07

Chi-squared $= 115.49$ $p = 0.000$

F-Tests	Gender	Offender Type	R^2
General	36.74*	888.17*	27.6
Violent	13.52*	416.81*	15.1
Property	17.13*	457.82*	16.4

*Significance < 0.0001.

As shown in Table 3, there were also significant gender differences in the type and frequency of substance use, described above as DRUGTYPE. A greater proportion of females than males was classified as nonusers (65% percent of females versus 58 percent of males). On the other hand, a greater proportion of males than females reported use of hard drugs (17 percent of males versus 12 percent of females). About the same proportion of males and females reported having used hard liquor or marijuana in the past year. But regardless of type of substance use or type of offense, males reported committing a higher number of delinquent acts than did females. There is also a clear association between hard

TABLE 3   Prevalence and Frequency of Self-Reported Delinquency by Type of
            Substance User by Gender

	Male (n = 1226)		Female (n = 1199)	
	Percent	Mean Number of Offenses	Percent	Mean Number of Offenses
Nonusers				
General	57.5	6.91	64.6	1.84
Violent	7.3	1.17	2.8	0.29
Property	7.8	1.43	4.3	0.42
Hard liquor or marijuana				
General	25.5	72.73	23.4	49.84
Violent	8.7	4.21	4.0	1.28
Property	11.0	9.45	7.3	7.68
Hard drugs				
General	17.0	322.84	12.0	242.86
Violent	10.4	35.11	4.2	27.53
Property	12.6	54.18	5.9	37.25

Chi-squared 16.48, $p = 0.0003$

F-Tests	Gender	Substance User	R^2
General delinquency	37.98*	999.37*	30.0
Violent	12.92	290.22*	11.1
Property	16.80*	403.25*	14.8

*Significance < 0.0001.

drug use and the frequency of serious crime. Within each sex, those who reported use of
hard drugs were much more serious offenders, reporting a greater frequency and severity
of offenses, than users of hard liquor or marijuana or nonusers. For example, males who
used hard drugs reported committing an average of thirty-five violent crimes and females
reported an average of twenty-eight crimes per year. Those males who reported use of hard
liquor or marijuana committed an average of nine violent acts, whereas females reported
a rate of four violent acts per year. These findings suggest that there may be gender differences in the relationship between substance use and rates and types of delinquency.

As shown in Table 4, the results of simple cross-classifications, conducted to further
examine gender differences in the relationship between delinquency and substance use, con-
firm the previous findings of a gender-specific association between hard drug use and serious
crimes. Among both males and females, nondrug users were more likely to be petty or minor
offenders (72 and 86 percent, respectively). However, a significantly lower proportion of

TABLE 4   Offender Type by Type of Substance User by Gender (Percent)

	Nonuser		Hard Liquor		Hard Drugs	
	Male	Female	Male	Female	Male	Female
Petty	71.8	85.7	33.5	48.6	12.5	37.5
Minor	11.3	7.1	18.2	22.1	12.5	9.7
Serious	10.1	5.3	24.6	20.0	10.6	13.2
Multiple	6.8	1.9	23.6	9.3	64.4	39.6
Chi-squared	48.1*		28.8*		34.2*	

*Significance < 0.00001.

female than male nondrug users were classified as serious or multiple-index offenders (7 percent of females in comparison to 17 percent of males). The same pattern was found among users of hard liquor or marijuana and among users of hard drugs—females were more likely to be petty or minor offenders than were males, and a lower proportion of females than males were serious or multiple-index offenders. For example, 40 percent of females who were hard drug users were also classified as multiple-index offenders compared to 64 percent of males.

Having found significant differences in both the prevalence and frequency of delinquency and substance use and the co-occurrence of delinquency and substance use, we wondered whether the same theoretical model, (e.g., the social development model) would explain these differences. Therefore, we ran a series of multivariate regression analyses to determine the contributions of the theoretical variables to the explanation of the prevalence of delinquent involvement and substance use. For each of the models we used the same three dependent variables: general delinquency,[10] serious delinquency,[11] and the combined rate of substance use and dealing.[12] Because the distributions of the variables were highly skewed, the dependent variable was transformed by taking the log of the mean. In each of the models we entered the same set of theoretical variables[13] in a stepwise regression, first entering demographic variables, then variables related to the environment, followed by conventional variables from delinquency theory and substance use theory. Finally, variables were entered that might explain the confluence of substance use and delinquency. These variables included INDEX or type of delinquent, DRUGTYPE or type of substance user, and the substance use problems scale described earlier.

The results of gender difference tests in the theoretical models are shown in Table 5. As indicated by the proportion of R^2 explained by the various sets of factors, the demographic variables explained little of the variance in the rates of delinquency and substance use, even though the beta weights for sex were significant for each model and age was a significant predictor in all the equations except general delinquency. In each of the models the sets of variables from delinquency theory and the variables related to the confluence of substance use and delinquency accounted for most of the variation, ranging from 12 to 18 percent of the variance, and the confluence variables accounted for a slightly higher proportion of variance than did the theoretical variables. For the two models of delinquency, the type of substance user and peer delinquency were the two strongest predictors. Similarly, for the model of substance use and dealing, the type of delinquent and peer delinquency were the strongest predictors. There were also interesting differences between the three models. The set of variables that was common to all three equations included gender, neighborhood violence, all of the delinquency variables, and victimization. School crime was a significant predictor of delinquency but not of serious delinquency or substance use and dealing. Being a school dropout was not a predictor of serious delinquency but was significant in the models of general delinquency and substance

TABLE 5 Contribution of Social Development Factors to Explaining the Incidence of Delinquency, Substance Use, and Dealing

	General Delinquency ($n = 2356$)			Serious Delinquency ($n = 2356$)			Substance Use/Dealing ($n = 2356$)		
	b	Beta	R^2	b	Beta	R^2	b	Beta	R^2
Demographic Characteristics			0.05*			0.04*			0.02*
Gender	0.60	0.08	*	0.47	0.07	*	-0.41	-0.05	*
Age	-0.12	-0.03		-0.15	-0.04	*	0.28	0.07	*
Hispanic	-0.37	-0.04		-0.15	-0.02		-0.37	-0.04	
African-American	-0.10	-0.01		0.11	0.01		-0.13	0.01	
Environment			0.02*			0.02*			0.02*
Neighborhood violence	0.30	0.06	*	0.19	0.06	*	0.37	0.09	*
School crime	0.23	0.05	*	0.17	0.05	*	0.02	—	
Delinquency theory			0.15*			0.14*			0.12*
Conventional values	-0.53	-0.09	*	-0.34	-0.10		-0.21	-0.05	*
Family integration	-0.24	-0.06	*	-0.16	-0.05		-0.20	-0.05	*
Peer delinquency	0.97	0.26	*	0.90	0.27		0.54	0.14	*
School integration	-0.16	-0.04	*	-0.07	-0.02		-0.21	-0.05	*
Substance use theory			0.03*			0.04*			0.04*
Social networks	-0.10	-0.03		-0.05	-0.06		-0.23	-0.06	*
Victimization	0.50	0.13	*	0.45	0.05	*	0.19	0.05	*
School dropout	-0.45	-0.04	*	0.02	0.09		0.88	0.08	*
Confluence			0.18*			0.15*			0.16*
Type of substance user	1.98	0.39	*	1.42	0.31	*	—	—	
Substance use problems	0.58	0.15	*	0.70	0.21	*	—	—	
Type of delinquent	—			—			1.60	0.46	*
Intercept	-0.92			-1.17			-6.96		
Adjusted R^2		0.43			0.39			0.36	
F-test		118.56			100.80			94.49	
Degrees of freedom		15			15			14	

*t-test significant at 0.05 level.

use and dealing. The social networks factor was a significant predictor of substance use and dealing but did not appear to be related to either general or serious delinquency.

Although gender was not a strong predictor of differences in the models of delinquency and substance use, it did appear to be related to all of the dependent variables and had the opposite effect for the delinquency models from the substance use/substance dealing model. Consequently, we tested each of the models separately for males and females, using the same stepwise regression techniques described earlier. Table 6 represents the results for the first models, with general delinquency as the dependent variable. There appear to be significant differences in the models for males and females, in both the

TABLE 6   Gender Differences in the Contribution of Social Development Factors to Explaining the Incidence of General Delinquency

	Male (n = 1186)			Female (n = 1169)		
	b	Beta	R^2	b	Beta	R^2
Demographic characteristics			0.001			0.02*
Age	-0.12	-0.03		-0.10	-0.03	
Hispanic	0.18	0.02		-0.94	-0.11	*
African-American	0.23	0.03		-0.35	-0.04	
Environment			0.02			0.02
Neighborhood violence	0.26	0.07	*	0.34	0.10	*
School crime	0.22	0.06	*	0.31	0.09	*
Delinquency theory			0.20*			0.11*
Conventional values	-0.26	-0.07	*	-0.37	-0.10	*
Family integration	-0.12	-0.03		-0.42	-0.12	*
Peer delinquency	1.09	0.31	*	0.71	0.18	*
School integration	-0.11	-0.03		-0.30	-0.09	*
Substance use theory			0.04*			0.07*
Social networks	-0.07	-0.02		-0.08	-0.02	
Victimization	0.46	0.13	*	0.47	0.12	*
School dropout	-0.27	-0.03		-0.57	-0.05	
Confluence			0.18*			0.18*
Type of substance user	2.16	0.42	*	1.69	0.35	*
Substance use problems	0.46	0.14	*	0.92	0.20	*
Intercept	-0.80			-0.72		
Adjusted R^2		0.44			0.36	
F-test		68.11			48.73	
Degrees of freedom		14			14	

*t-test significant at 0.05 level.

amount of variance explained by the different sets of variables and in the predictors. For both groups the type of substance user was the strongest predictor of general delinquency. For males, peer delinquency had a stronger effect than substance use problems, whereas for females, substance use problems were slightly more important. Being Hispanic entered into the equation for females but was not significant for males. In addition, two of the delinquency theory variables, family integration and school integration, were only significant predictors for females. As shown in Table 7, this same pattern of gender differences was found when serious delinquency was the dependent variable. Substance use problems was again the strongest predictor for females, but remained less important for males.

TABLE 7 Gender Differences in the Contribution of Social Development Factors to Explaining the Incidence of Serious Delinquency

	Male (n = 1186)			Female (n = 1169)		
	b	Beta	R^2	b	Beta	R^2
Demographic characteristics			-0.002			0.01*
Age	-0.14	-0.04		-0.14	-0.05	*
Hispanic	-0.11	-0.01		-0.15	-0.02	
African-American	0.12	0.01		0.23	0.03	
Environment			.02			.01
Neighborhood violence	0.19	0.05		0.18	0.06	*
School crime	0.15	0.04		0.27	0.09	*
Delinquency theory			0.17*			0.11*
Conventional values	-0.32	-0.09	*	-0.34	-0.11	*
Family integration	-0.08	-0.02		-0.30	-0.10	*
Peer delinquency	1.01	0.31	*	0.64	0.19	*
School integration	-0.05	-0.01		-0.16	-0.05	*
Substance use theory			0.05*			0.05*
Social networks	-0.04	-0.01		-0.02	—	
Victimization	0.40	0.12	*	0.45	0.14	*
School dropout	0.30	0.03		-0.29	-0.03	
Confluence			.15*			0.18*
Type of substance user	1.63	0.34	*	1.10	0.27	*
Substance use problems	0.55	0.18	*	1.06	0.28	*
Intercept	-0.98			-1.11		
Adjusted R^2		0.39			0.34	
F-test		55.54			43.20	
Degrees of freedom		14			14	

*t-test significant at 0.05 level.

The model for substance use and dealing shown in Table 8 also indicates gender differences in the explanatory variables. As in the previous models for the delinquency variables, the strongest predictors were the confluence and delinquency theory variables, more specifically the type of delinquent and peer delinquency, for both substance use and dealing, regardless of gender. These two variables, plus age, neighborhood violence, conventional values, and being a school dropout entered into the models of substance use and dealing for both males and females. However, there were gender differences for other variables. For example, school integration did not enter the model for males, yet was a predictor for females. Family integration, social networks, and victimization entered the model for males but were not significant for females.

TABLE 8   Gender Differences in the Contribution of Social Development Factors to Explaining the Incidence of Substance Use and Dealing

	Male (n = 1186)			Female (n = 1169)		
	b	Beta	R^2	b	Beta	R^2
Demographic characteristics			0.003			0.01*
Age	0.31	0.07	*	0.24	0.06	*
Hispanic	-0.35	-0.04		-0.35	-0.04	
African-American	-0.22	-0.02		0.01	—	
Environment			0.03*			0.02
Neighborhood violence	0.35	0.09	*	0.36	0.10	*
School crime	-0.03	—		0.09	0.02	
Delinquency theory			0.14*			0.10*
Conventional values	-0.22	-0.05	*	-0.19	-0.15	*
Family integration	-0.26	-0.06	*	-0.14	-0.04	
Peer delinquency	0.48	0.13		0.62	0.14	*
School integration	-0.11	-0.02		-0.35	-0.09	*
Substance use theory			0.05*			0.03*
Social networks	-0.34	-0.08	*	-0.08	-0.02	
Victimization	0.23	0.06	*	0.12	0.03	
School dropout	0.81	0.08	*	1.28	0.11	*
Confluence			0.16*			0.15*
Type of delinquent	1.57	0.47	*	1.66	0.43	*
Intercept	-7.77			-6.53		
Adjusted R^2		0.38			0.31	
F-test		57.31			41.57	
Degrees of freedom		13			13	

*t-test significant at 0.05 level.

CONCLUSIONS

The results of our study provide an interesting look at the prevalence and frequency of substance use and delinquency among inner-city youths and offer gender-specific explanations of the occurrence of these behaviors. These findings are limited in their generalizability since the data were collected in six urban areas in 1984, prior to the emergence of crack cocaine. The models we tested are further limited by the data because they did not contain some of the variables, such as peer substance use, which might explain additional variance in the frequency of substance use and dealing. Nonetheless, our results show significant gender differences in the correlates of serious delinquency and substance use/substance dealing, which have important policy implications.

As expected from both theory and research (Huizinga, Loeber, & Thornberry, 1991), gender differences were found in both the prevalence and frequency of delinquency and substance use, females being categorized as less serious than males. With three exceptions (property crime among minor offenders, general and violent crime among multiple-index offenders), the frequency of delinquency was lower among females than among males. There was clear evidence of a high correlation between substance use and delinquency, which supports findings from research with more recent interviews of youths (Huizinga et al., 1991). A smaller proportion of petty offenders and a greater proportion of more serious offenders were found among users of hard liquor or marijuana. Hard-drug users were the most likely to be involved in multiple-index crimes. These differences were exaggerated by gender differences, males who used hard drugs being the most hard-core offenders. The recent longitudinal studies conducted in Denver and Rochester (Huizinga et al., 1991) showed lower prevalence rates for girls but similar offense rates for both minor and serious offenses.

The different theoretical models tested in this study showed that whereas the confluence of delinquency and substance use was an important variable in explaining the frequency of these acts, peer delinquency remained the most significant correlate of adolescent delinquency, substance use, or dealing among males. For females, substance use problems were more important than peer delinquency in explaining differences in rates of serious and general delinquency. Peer influence may also be a factor in substance use problem behavior among females, but this variable was not measured for both students and dropouts in our sample and could not be used in the analysis. Using longitudinal data to further examine the roles of peers in delinquency causation, Thornberry, Lizotte, Krohn, Farnworth and Jang (1994) conclude that the delinquent behavior is part of a dynamic social process: "Although delinquency is influenced by peer associations and delinquent beliefs, it also influences those associations and beliefs to create behavioral trajectories toward increasing delinquency for some youths and toward increasing conformity for others" (p. 75). The authors suggest that an interactional framework be used for understanding delinquency.

As measured by family and social integration, social bonding appears to be more important for females than males in explaining general and serious delinquency, even though family integration is a correlate of substance use among males but not among females. The association between school involvement, delinquency, and substance use among females, noted by other researchers (Bjerregaard & Smith, 1993; J. Rosenbaum & Lasley, 1990; White, 1992), suggests that school-based delinquency and substance use prevention programs and school activities might be more successful with girls than with boys. However, as noted by others (Huizinga et al., 1991; Fagan & Pabon, 1991), these programs should be aimed at preadolescent youths since there is also an association between substance use and school dropout.

Victimization and neighborhood violence were significant correlates of both delinquency and substance use, as noted in earlier research (Fagan et al., 1986, 1987, 1990). Thus, as has been suggested by Greenwood (1992), the greatest need for prevention and intervention programs is among inner-city youth that are at risk for delinquency, substance use, and other problem behaviors. Even though there were few differences between the models for general delinquency and serious delinquency, our results support findings from other research on violent offending. For example, Elliott (1994) suggests that there is a common etiology for minor delinquency, alcohol use, and serious violence (e.g., peer normlessness, attitudes toward deviance, and delinquent peers are proximal predictors of onset). He further contends that minor delinquency precedes both index crime and substance use. White (1992) also states that delinquent behavior predicts later substance use among both males and females. However, she finds that violence is not part of a "problem behavior syndrome" among females. The findings from our research contradict those of White (1992) since substance use problems were a significant correlate of serious delinquency, and dropping out of school was associated with substance use and dealing. The confluence of substance use problems and serious violence in the females interviewed in our sample is supported by a recent retrospective study of violent females by Baskin and Sommers (1993). Similar to our cross-sectional analyses, they found that the early onset of violent offending among females was correlated with neighborhood violence, victimization, school crime, and substance use. However, Baskin and Sommers also found that violent behavior usually preceded substance use. Our findings in conjunction with those of other colleagues indicate a serious need for delinquency and substance use prevention programs among females as well as males. Even though the prevalence rates were significantly lower for females in comparison to males, those females who were classified as multiple-index offenders had higher frequency rates of violent crime. Thus, among females there also appears to be "a violent few" that need attention, just as been found among males (Hamparian, Schuster, Dinitz, & Conrad, 1978; Piper 1983; Wolfgang 1983; Wolfgang, Figlio, & Sellin, 1972). The lack of research on females and on gender differences in delinquency and substance use has contributed to our paucity of knowledge about effective programming for female delinquents and substance users, noted by Chesney-Lind & Shelden (1992) and others. It is time to focus on these gender differences and find ways to reduce the prevalence and frequency of violent crime among females as well as males.

NOTES

1. This research was supported in part by Grant 85-JN-AX-C001 to the URSA Institute from the National Institute for Juvenile Justice and Delinquency Prevention. The opinions are those of the author. (An earlier version of this paper was presented at the 1990 annual meeting of the American Society of Criminology.)

2. The Violent Juvenile Offender Research and Development Program was initiated in 1980 to develop prevention programs for violent delinquency in high-crime urban neighborhoods and treatment methods for chronically violent juvenile offenders. Both components utilized variants

on integrated theory as described by Elliott, Ageton, and Canter (1979) and Hawkins and Weis (1985). for a complete description of the program origins and design, see Office of Juvenile Justice and Delinquency Prevention (1981).

3. High school student samples were chosen from classrooms randomly selected from all classes in the school that served youths from the target neighborhoods. To determine whether controls were needed for inter-city differences in explanatory or dependent measures, regression analyses were conducted for each of the six city samples. The analyses compared models for two alternative dependent measures with a subset of six predictor variables chosen based on their known correlations with delinquency and their validity in other research (Fagan, Piper, & Moore, 1986; Elliott, Huizinga, & Ageton, 1985). The results revealed little variation in the overall explanatory power of the models across sites, the predictor variables entered each of the equations, and the same three variables had the highest standardized coefficients in each model. Accordingly, survey data from the six cities were aggregated for analyses.

Ethnographic samples of school dropouts were recruited from chain referral methods ("snowball") samples within known dropout groups. The dropout sampling parameter, 25 percent, reflected a consensus of the high school principals in the six inner-city neighborhoods, although the reported rates varied from 15 to 45 percent across the cities. This strategy was used since systematic sampling of dropouts was not feasible. None of the school districts kept accurate or comprehensive records of dropouts to allow specific sampling of individuals or even to develop sampling parameters to inform the construction of dropout samples (Hammack, 1987). The strategy was flexible in targeting, locating, and reaching all known dropout groups within and across communities. Because so little is known about the nature and prevalence of dropouts, this strategy ensured that no known or emerging dropout strata was either over- or underrepresented.

Chains were initiated through local social service agencies or community-based organizations to recruit dropouts from among known dropout populations: pregnant teens, working-class youth, non-English-speaking or foreign-born youth, and "official" (labeled) delinquents. Once chains were initiated in each city, two recruitment processes were used. First, dropout respondents were asked to refer others they knew. Recruitment often involved referrals within chains, where the respondents were encouraged to refer or bring with them "people just like you." At the conclusion of their participation, respondents were asked to refer anyone "that also is a school dropout, comes from the same neighborhood, and is the same age and sex as you." A short screening interview determined eligibility. Second, referrals were sought from social agencies that dealt routinely with dropouts. Advertisements were distributed through channels likely to reach them. For example, notices were posted and distributed in family planning clinics to teenage females who had sought services or advice. Similar outreach occurred through unions (for working youth), community-based counseling or drop-in centers for substance use prevention, alternative schools, and other agencies or locales where dropouts are likely to gather. The chains were monitored to ensure that none of these groups was overrepresented among the dropouts and to incorporate any new (unanticipated dropout groups) that were discovered.

4. A random schoolday was selected within a two-month period for survey administration. Both student and dropout respondents received a stipend for their participation in the form of either coupons from local record stores or T-shirts. These nominal stipends were both incentives and compensation for their time and participation. The surveys were described as voluntary and anonymous. Neither names nor identifiers were requested anywhere on the survey forms.

Student surveys were conducted in classrooms, or alternatively, after school hours. In three of the six high schools, surveys were held during regular study periods. Students were convened in an auditorium or large classroom that was capable of seating 200 students. In the other schools, scheduling problems required that surveys be conducted immediately after school hours in the same facilities. This procedure risked several sources of bias, from exclusion of working youths to self-selection of participants with different motivations and interests. To estimate biases between the two survey conditions, analyses compared relationships between explanatory and behavioral variables for the in- and after-school samples (see the section "Measures and Contructs"). Multiple regression analyses of delinquent involvement and substance use showed that the explained variance, univariate F-tests, and order of entry of explanatory variables were comparable for the two survey procedures.

Dropout surveys were conducted in small groups of ten to fifteen youth in neighborhood facilities, with several scheduled time slots to accommodate youths with other commitments. To avoid repeats, proctors from the community groups, familiar with neighborhood youth, monitored attendance and selected out repeaters. Together with members of the research staff, they kept informal logs of the number of each type (i.e., chain membership) of participant. The research staff in consultation with the intermediary organizations made decisions on management of the chains.

The survey schedule included demographic items, self-reported delinquency and substance use/sales measures, victimization items, and measures tapping social learning and control variables. In addition, dropouts were asked about their reasons for dropping out, their school experiences (e.g., suspensions and expulsions, attendance, problems in school), and the pressures and supports they received from family and community during the process of dropping out. For both student and dropout surveys, items were read aloud by research staff while respondents followed along on the survey form. The researchers also held up large displays of the response sets for sequences of items (e.g., self-reported delinquency items). In addition, four or five proctors per session from local neighborhood organizations walked through the classrooms or facilities to answer respondents' questions, provide other assistance, and randomly spot check for such errors as out-of-range codes.

5. The original forty-seven-item scales were modified in two ways. First, since the surveys were designed for adolescents in inner-city neighborhoods with high crime rates, adjustments were necessary to eliminate trivial offenses. Many behaviors in inner-city areas are law violations, which neither evoke official action nor are perceived by local youth as illegal (Anderson & Rodriquez, 1984). The items modified and retained were those that measure "high consensus" deviance (Thio, 1983) and included only acts that harm, or do damage. Second, at the request of school officials, certain items in the original scales were eliminated, modified, or collapsed.

6. Such anchoring techniques are consistent with other studies attempting to reconstruct behaviors for even trivial offenses (Anglin & Speckart, 1988).

7. Rates were calculated based on the median frequency within each value. Although information is lost in the truncated categories, other analysts using similar procedures report high correlations between categorical responses and open-ended frequency estimates (Elliott & Huizinga, 1984). These procedures are particularly important for high-rate offenders, due to the psychometric properties of open-ended versus categorical response sets, making them particularly well suited for theoretical tests.

8. Two sets of scales were constructed to measure homogeneous behavior groupings and to distinguish serious and trivial behavior. For SRD items, offense-specific scales, such as robbery or felony theft, were constructed for narrow homogeneous crime types parallel with UCR categories, patterned after Elliott and Huizinga (1984). The scale measures were derived by summing the reported incidence scores for nonoverlapping items within the scale. Second, offense-summary scales were constructed to measure broader categories of behavior. These scales increased the range of seriousness of each domain while preserving homogeneity of behavior. These general scales, such as violence or property, capture broader behavioral

trends while retaining validity with respect to type of behavior. General scales were constructed as summary scales for all types of delinquent behavior. See Fagan, Piper, & Moore (1986), or Fagan, Piper, & Cheng (1987) for item and scale construction.

9. The categories include:
    - *Multiple-index offenders*: those reporting at least three index offenses (felony assault, robbery, or felony theft) within the past year.
    - *Serious delinquents*: those reporting one or two index offenses (felony assault, robbery, or felony theft) in the past year; or three or more incidents in the past year of extortion or weapon offenses.
    - *Minor delinquents*: those reporting no index offenses and one or two incidents in the past year of extortion of weapon offenses; or four or more incidents in the past year of minor theft, minor assault, vandalism, or illegal activities (buying or selling stolen goods, selling drugs).
    - *Petty delinquents*: those reporting no index offenses and three or fewer incidents in the past year of minor theft, minor assault, vandalism, or illegal activities (buying or selling stolen goods, selling drugs).

    Obviously, definitions and criteria of "severity" of behavior contribute significantly to perceptions of the concentration of minor and serious juvenile crime within a sample. The use of this scheme is not intended to reify these categories. Rather, it is intended as a heuristic to illustrate empirically the relationship between substance use and delinquent behaviors.

10. General delinquency includes felony and minor assault, robbery, felony and minor theft, property damage, drug use, drinking, drug sales, extortion, weapon use, and illegal services.

11. Serious delinquency includes felony and minor assault, robbery, felony theft, extortion, and weapon use.

12. Substance use and dealing also includes drinking. Separate models were run for drug use and drinking, apart from dealing, but there were too few differences to report both models.

13. Definitions of the independent variables appear in the Appendix.

REFERENCES

ANDERSON, N., & RODRIGUEZ, O. (1984). Conceptual issues in the study of Hispanic delinquency. *Research Bulletin* (Hispanic Research Center, Fordham University), 7, 2–5.

ANGLIN, M. D., & HSER, Y. (1987). Addicted women and crime. *Criminology, 25*, 359–397.

ANGLIN, M. D., & SPECKART, G. (1988). Narcotics use and crime: A multisample, multimethod analysis. *Criminology 26*(2), 197–234.

BASKIN, D., & SOMMERS, I. (1993). Females' initiation into violent street crime. *Justice Quarterly, 10*(4), 559–584.

BIERNACKI, P., & WALDORF, O. (1981). Snowball sampling: Problems and techniques of chain referral sampling. *Sociological Methods and Research, 10*, 131–163.

BJERREGAARD, B., & SMITH, C. (1993). Gender differences in gang participation, delinquency, and substance use. *Journal of Quantitative Criminology, 9*(4), 329–355.

BOX, S. (1981). *Deviance, Reality and Society*. London: Holt, Rinehart & Winston.

BURGESS, R., & AKERS, R. (1966). A differential association-reinforcement theory of criminal behavior. *Social Problems, 14*, 128–147.

CANTER, R. J. (1982). Sex differences in self-reported delinquency. *Criminology, 20*, 373–394.

CERNKOVICH, S., & GIORDANO, P. (1979). Delinquency, opportunity and gender. *Journal of Criminal Law and Criminology, 70*, 145–151.

CHESNEY-LIND, M. (1989). Girls' crime and woman's place: Toward a feminist model of female delinquency. *Crime and Delinquency, 35*, 5–29.

CHESNEY-LIND, M., & SHELDEN, R. (1992). *Girls, delinquency and juvenile justice*. Pacific Grove, CA: Brooks/Cole.

DUNFORD, F., & ELLIOTT, D. (1984). Identifying career offenders using self-reported data. *Journal of Research in Crime and Delinquency, 21*, 57–86.

ELLIOTT, D. (1994). Serious violent offenders: Onset, developmental course, and termination. *Criminology, 32*(1), 1–21.

ELLIOTT, D., AGETON, S., & CANTER, R. (1979). An integrated perspective on delinquent behavior. *Journal of Research in Crime and Delinquency, 16*, 3–27.

ELLIOTT, D., AND HUIZINGA, D. (1984). *The relationship between delinquent behavior and ADM problems*. National Youth Survey Report 28. Boulder, CO: Behavioral Research Institute.

ELLIOTT, D., HUIZINGA, D., & AGETON, S. (1985). *Explaining delinquency and drug use*. Newbury Park, CA: Sage Publications.

ELLIOTT, D., HUIZINGA, D., & MENARD, S. (1989). *Multiple problem youth: Delinquency, substance use, and mental health problems*, New York: Springer-Verlag.

ELLIOTT, D., KNOWLES, B., & CANTER, R. (1981). *The epidemiology of delinquent behavior and drug use among American adolescents*. National Youth Survey Report 14, Boulder, CO: Behavioral Research Institute.

FAGAN, J., HANSEN, K., & JANG, M. (1983). Profile of chronically violent delinquents: An empirical test of an integrated theory of violent delinquency. In J. Kleugel (Ed.), *Evaluating juvenile justice*, Newbury Park, CA: Sage Publications.

FAGAN, J., & JONES, S. J. (1984). Toward a theoretical model for intervention with violent juvenile offenders. In R. Mathias, P. DeMuro, & R. Allinson (Eds.), *Violent juvenile offenders: An anthology*, San Francisco, CA: National Council on Crime and Delinquency.

FAGAN, J., & PABON, E. (1991). Contributions of delinquency and substance use to school dropout. *Youth and Society, 21*, 306–354.

FAGAN, J., PIPER, E., & MOORE, M. (1986). Violent delinquents and urban youth. *Criminology, 24*, 439–466.

FAGAN, J., PIPER, E., & CHENG, Y. (1987). Contributions of victimization to delinquency in inner cities. *Journal of Criminal Law and Criminology, 78*, 586–613.

FAGAN, J., WEIS, J., & CHENG, Y. (1990). Delinquency and substance abuse among inner-city students. *Journal of Drug Issues, 20*(3), 351–402.

FELDMAN, H., AGAR, M., & BESCHNER, G. (EDS.). (1979). *Angel dust: An ethnographic study of PCP users*. Lexington, MA: D.C. Heath.

GIORDANO, P. (1978). Research note: Girls, guys and gangs: The changing social context of female delinquency. *Journal of Criminal Law and Criminology, 69*(1), 126.

GREENWOOD, P. (1992). Substance abuse problems among high-risk youth and potential interventions. *Crime and Delinquency, 38*(4), 444–458.

HAMMACK, F. (1987). Large school systems' dropout reports: An analysis of definitions, procedures, and findings. In G. Natriello (Ed.), *School dropouts: Patterns and policies* (pp. 20–37), New York: Columbia University Teachers College Press.

HAMPARIAN, D., SCHUSTER, R., DINITZ, S., & CONRAD J. (1978). *The violent few: A study of dangerous juvenile offenders*. Lexington, MA: Lexington Books.

HAWKINS, J., & WEIS, J. (1985). The social development model: An integrated approach to delinquency prevention. *Journal of Primary Prevention, 6*(2), 73–97.

HINDELANG, M. (1971). Age, sex, and the versatility of delinquent involvement. *Social Problems, 18*(14), 522–535.

HIRSCHI, T. (1969). *Causes of Delinquency*. Berkeley: University of California Press.

Huizinga, D., Loeber, R., & Thornberry, T. (Eds.). (1991). *Urban delinquency and substance abuse*. Final Report to the Office of Juvenile Justice and Delinquency Prevention. Washington, DC: U.S. Department of Justice.

Jensen, G., & Eve, R. (1976). Sex differences in delinquency. *Criminology, 13,* 427–448.

Jessor, R. (1979). Marihuana: A review of recent psychological research. In R. L. Dupont, A. Goldstein, & J. O'Donnell (Eds.), *Handbook on drug abuse* (pp. 337–355). Washington, DC: U.S. Government Printing Office,.

Jessor, R., & Jessor, S. (1977). *Problem behavior and psychosocial development: A longitudinal study of youth*. New York: Academic Press.

Johnson, R., Marcos, A., & Bahr, S. (1987). The role of peers in the complex etiology of adolescent drug use. *Criminology, 25,* 323–340.

Johnston, L., O'Malley, P., & Bachman, J. (1985). *Use of licit and illicit drugs by American high school students: 1975–1984*. Washington, DC: National Institute on Drug Abuse.

Johnston, L., O'Malley, P., & Bachman, J. (1993a). *National survey results on drug use from the Monitoring the Future study, 1975–1992: Vol. I. Secondary school students*. Rockville, MD: National Institute on Drug Abuse.

Johnston, L., O'Malley, P., & Bachman, J. (1993b). *National survey results on drug use from the Monitoring the Future study, 1975–1992: Vol. II. College students and young adults*. Rockville, MD: National Institute on Drug Abuse.

Kandel, D. (1980). Drug and drinking behavior among youth. *Annual Review of Sociology, 6,* 235–285.

Kandel, D. (1982). Epidemiological and psychosocial perspectives on adolescent drug use. *Journal of the Academy of Child Psychiatry, 21,* 328–347.

Kandel, D., Simcha-Fagan, O., & Davies, M. (1986). Risk factors for delinquency and illicit drug use among adolescents to young adulthood. *Journal of Drug Issues, 16,* 270–289.

Kaplan, H., Smith, S., & Robins, C. (1984). Pathways to adolescent drug use: Self derogation, peer influences, weakening of social controls, and early substance use. *Journal of Health and Social Behavior, 25,* 270–289.

Morris, R. (1964). Female delinquents and relational problems. *Social Forces, 43,* 82–89.

Office of Juvenile Justice and Delinquency Prevention. (1981). *Background paper for the Violent Juvenile Offender Research and Development Program* (Parts I and II). Washington, DC: OJJDP.

Osgood, D. W., Johnston, L. O., O'Malley, P. M., & Bachman, J. G. (1988). The generality of deviance. *American Sociological Review, 53,* 81–93.

Piper, E. (1983). *Patterns of violent juvenile recidivism*. Unpublished dissertation. University of Pennsylvania.

Rosenbaum, J. (1983). *Sex differences in delinquent behavior: A control theory explanation*. Unpublished dissertation. State University of New York–Albany.

Rosenbaum, J. (1987). Social control, gender, and delinquency: An analysis of drug, property, and violent offenders. *Justice Quarterly, 4*(1), 117–132.

Rosenbaum, J., & Lasley, J. (1990). School, community context, and delinquency, rethinking the gender gap. *Justice Quarterly, 7*(3), 493–513.

Rosenbaum, M. (1981). *Women on heroin*. New Brunswick, NJ: Rutgers University Press.

Sarri, R. (1983). Gender issues in juvenile justice. *Crime and Delinquency, 29,* 381–97.

Simons, R. L., Miller, M., & Aigner, S. (1980). Contemporary theories of deviance and female delinquency: An empirical test. *Journal of Research on Crime and Delinquency, 17*(1), 42–53.

Thio, A. (1983). *Deviant Behavior* (2nd ed.). Boston: Houghton-Mifflin.

Thornberry, T. (1987). Toward an interactional theory of delinquency. *Criminology, 25,* 863–892.

Thornberry, T., & Christenson, R. (1984). Unemployment and criminal involvement: An investigation of reciprocal causal structures. *American Sociological Review, 49,* 398–411.

THORNBERRY, T., LIZOTTE, A., KROHN, M., FARNWORTH, M., & JANG, S. (1994). Delinquent peers, beliefs, and delinquent behavior: A longitudinal test of interactional theory. *Criminology, 32*(1), 47–84.

TRIPLETT, R., & MEYERS, L. B. (1995). Evaluating contextual patterns of delinquency: Gender-based differences. *Justice Quarterly, 12*(1), 59–84.

WEIS, J. (1980). Sex differences: Study data publication. Seattle Center for Law and Justice.

WEIS, J., & HAWKINS, J. D. (1981). *Preventing delinquency: The social development approach.* Washington, DC: U.S. Government Printing Office.

WHITE, H. (1992). Early problem behaviors and later drug problems. *Journal of Research in Crime and Delinquency, 29*(4), 412–429.

WHITE, H., JOHNSON, V., & GARRISON, C. (1985). The drug-crime nexus among adolescents and their peers. *Deviant Behavior, 6*, 183–204.

WHITE, H., PANDINA, R., & LABOUVIE, E. (1987). Longitudinal predictors of serious substance use and delinquency. *Criminology, 25*, 715–740.

WIATROWSKI, M., GRISWOLD, D., & ROBERTS, M. (1981). Social control theory and delinquency. *American Sociological Review, 46*, 525–541.

WOLFGANG, M. (1983). Violent juvenile: A Philadelphia profile. In K. Feinberg (Ed.), *Violent Crime in America* (pp. 17–24). Washington, DC: National Policy Exchange.

WOLFGANG, M., FIGLIO, R., & SELLIN, T. (1972). *Delinquency in a birth cohort.* Chicago: University of Chicago Press.

APPENDIX: DEFINITIONS OF CONSTRUCTS AND MEASURES

Social Environment

neighborhood violence Violence within neighborhood families on the same residential block or the same neighborhood.

school crime Crimes in school by other students—percentage of students who commit specific criminal acts within schools.

Delinquency Theory

conventional values An index of conformity based on the personal importance of attainment of social status and material goods.

family integration The strength of the respondents' attachment to family.

peer delinquency Crimes by peers—percentage of peers outside school who commit specific criminal acts.

school integration Participation in school activities, achievement and performance in school, relationships with teachers and other students.

Substance Use Theory

school dropout Dichotomous measure indicating whether the person was part of the student sample or dropout sample.

social networks The strength of respondents' immersion in a peer group and personal involvement with his or her peers.

victimization A scale of respondents' reports of their own victimization in the past year for each of three types of violent or property crimes.

29

The Gender Effect among Serious, Violent, and Chronic Juvenile Offenders

A Difference of Degree Rather than Kind

Kimberly Kempf-Leonard and Paul E. Tracy

Gender differences in offending across the "crime-prone" years of the 1958 Philadelphia birth cohort are described in this chapter. Official records mark the offense careers from early onset as juveniles through age 26 for 27,160 persons, including 14,000 females. This large database is unique in its ability to support analysis of gender differences in offense prevalence, incidence, and type, as well as significant dimensions across criminal careers, such as serious, violent, and chronic offending. The importance of examining the gender effect in offending for policy formulation and theory development is demonstrated.

There are few topics that rival the research and policy attention currently bestowed on serious, violent, and chronic juvenile offenders. Major efforts are under way to identify these threatening offenders, develop effective intervention strategies to stop their criminality, and initiate prevention programs that will assure that subsequent youth do not follow in such delinquency career paths. Unfortunately, little attention has been devoted to females in this important quest. In this chapter we examine gender differences in serious, violent, and chronic offending among the 1958 Philadelphia birth cohort. With a large number of subjects and extensive history information through age 26, these data enable us to make gender comparisons across delinquent and criminal careers that are available only for males in many other investigations. Based on our findings, we offer suggestions on how knowledge about gender differences might affect future research and policy efforts.

PRIOR RESEARCH

Serious, violent, chronic juvenile offenders first gained notice in the 1970s with the publication of *Delinquency in a Birth Cohort* (Wolfgang, Figlio, & Sellin, 1972), *The Violent Few* (Hamparian, Schuster, Dinitz, & Conrad, 1978), and Shannon's (1978, 1980) research on three cohorts in Racine, Wisconsin. These studies identified a very small proportion of juvenile offenders as responsible for the majority of juvenile crime, including the most serious acts of delinquency. More recently, Tracy, Wolfgang, and Figlio (1990) reported an even higher prevalence of chronic offenders in the 1958 Philadelphia birth cohort and Tracy and Kempf-Leonard (1996) extended the research on the 1958 cohort to include the transition from delinquent career to adult crime. The significance of these descriptive studies, and *Delinquency in a Birth Cohort* in particular, led Samuel Walker (1985) to cite it as "the single most important piece of criminal justice research in the last 25 years and a major influence on crime control thinking" (p. 39).

The widespread interest in the topic of career criminals and criminal careers led the National Academy of Sciences to convene a Panel on Research on Criminal Careers in 1983 to assess the evidence and recommend directions for future research. According to panel chairperson Al Blumstein, "members were in general agreement about the findings and conclusions of the scientific evidence on criminal careers, but there were divergent views on the ethics of how such information should be used in dealing with offenders" (Blumstein, Cohen, Roth, & Visher, 1986, p. x). Views among panelists ranged from objections to any criminal justice action based on anticipated future offending to a desire to see weak results put to use as quickly as possible (Blumstein et al., 1986, p. x). A better understanding of the ethical issues associated with measurement difficulties and various intervention ideas may be the major legacy of the panel's two published volumes.

Of relevance here is the fact that females were included in fewer studies reviewed by the panel. Based on those studies and concerning gender differences in criminal careers, it was reported that "[i]n general, patterns of participation among females parallel those among males: higher estimates for broad crime domains and low thresholds of involvement. The most consistent pattern with respect to gender is the extent to which male criminal participation in serious crimes at any age greatly exceeds that of females, regardless of source of data, crime type, level of involvement, or measure of participation" (Blumstein et al., 1986, p. 40). There was reportedly "substantial debate" over causes of the strong empirical associations between demographic variables and aggregate arrest rates, but "the panel did not attempt to resolve those theoretical debates" (Blumstein et al., 1986, p. 26). Concluding comments about gender differences included: "much ambiguity surrounds the underlying theoretical meaning of differences," and "these differentials reflect relationships with other variables that are not yet well understood" (Blumstein et al., 1986, pp. 24–25).

Most recently, the Office of Juvenile Justice and Delinquency Prevention initiated a Comprehensive Strategy for Serious, Violent, and Chronic Juvenile Offenders (Howell, 1995; Wilson & Howell, 1993), and established a study group on serious and violent juvenile offenders. In a volume published in 1998, this study group reviewed knowledge about serious, violent, and chronic juvenile offenders and the types of interventions that can reduce their level of offending (Loeber & Farrington, 1998).

Perceptions of gender differences in offending are clearly evident among members of the study group. One chapter begins with the contention that "in any birth cohort, the incidence and prevalence of violent and serious delinquency are more frequent among males than females" (Lipsey & Derzon, 1998, p. 86). The only chapter devoted to demographic descriptions of serious juvenile offenders is based on data for which information on females are available, regrettably it includes discussion only on issues pertaining to race and ethnic differences in offending. In a footnote, the authors comment that gender differences are beyond the scope of their paper and refer to a study based only on young black women (Hawkins, Laub, & Lauritsen, 1998, p. 46).

A few descriptive findings of similar gender patterns are reported. For example, among the 524 females and 580 males in the Denver Youth Study, problem use of both alcohol and marijuana was higher among both male and female serious offenders than among other delinquents (Huizinga & Jakob-Chien, 1998, pp. 50–51). The finding of higher rates of violence among male adolescents with histories of abuse and neglect compared to other males in the Rochester Youth Study also held for females (Smith & Thornberry, 1995). Prevalence of serious offending across multiple years for females in the National Youth Survey data was 3.8 percent for late-onset females versus 15.4 percent for early-onset females and 2.5 percent for late-onset males versus 12.7 percent for early-onset males (Tolan & Gorman-Smith, 1998, p. 76).

Among efforts to identify different pathways of development, a primary focus of the study group, findings based on females have either not been reported or have been discounted. For example, Loeber and Hay (1994) reported that their conceptual model of three pathways based on 1500 males in the Pittsburgh Youth Study can account for most delinquency career patterns. There has been, however, only one subsequent test of this model using data from the National Youth Survey and 1102 boys in the Chicago Youth Development Study, and no gender comparisons were made (Tolan & Gorman-Smith, 1998, pp. 80–84).

In reporting on relationships between predictor variables and outcome measures for serious or violent offending among the prospective longitudinal studies in their meta-analysis, Lipsey and Derzon identify that most of the studies include samples that are primarily male (1998, p. 89). It is interesting that they still identify gender as a significant predictor of subsequent violent and/or serious delinquency, more so than any other personal characteristics examined (Lipsey & Derzon, 1998, pp. 96–98). In their assessment of potential targets for preventive intervention, they note that although gender and race are not "malleable," the prediction models suggest that male gender is "not a feasible target" among the 6–11 and 12–14 age groups (Lipsey & Derzon, 1998, p. 100).

The link between early aggression and conviction and subsequent behavior is cited as "among the most stable characteristics, when measured for populations" (Tolan & Gorman-Smith, 1998, p. 73). The correlations for this relationship, however, are identified as "0.25 to 0.40 for males and lower for females" in two studies (i.e., Cairns, Cairns, Neckerman, Gest, Gariepy, 1988; Coie & Dodge, 1983) and as "nonsignificant for females" in one other (i.e., Huesmann, Eron, Lefkowitz, & Walder, 1984; Tolan & Gorman-Smith, 1998, p. 73). Violence at age 15 predicted violence in later years among the 205 males but less consistently and strongly among the 219 females in the Rutgers Health and Human Development Project (White, 1992). Similar findings from the Seattle Social Development Project show that gender is significantly able to predict self-reported violent behavior at age 18, with the likelihood of violence among males double that of females (Hawkins, Herenkohl, Farrington, Brewer, Catalano, & Harachi, 1998, p. 144).

Other gender differences also were reported for the Seattle Social Development Project. Inverse relationships between violent behavior and both parent–child communication and school bonding were weak for females but strong for males (Williams, 1994, pp. 136, 138). The influence of delinquent siblings, however, was stronger for girls than boys (p. 140).

Among other findings reviewed by the study group, Deborah Denno (1990) reported an inverse relationship between academic achievement and subsequent violent offending for both males and females, and the relationship was strongest for females. For both males and females, leaving home before age 16 was linked to increased levels of violence in McCord and Ensminger's Woodlawn Study of African American Children in Chicago (Hawkins et al., 1998, pp. 137–138). Finally, in the only report on gender differences among factors associated with gang membership, Terence Thornberry (1998) provided the following account for the 250 females and 750 males in the Rochester Youth Study:

> On the one hand, school variables, access to and values about drugs, and prior delinquency operate in generally similar ways for males and females. On the other hand, neighborhood characteristics appear to be much more important in increasing the likelihood of gang membership for the females than for the males. In contrast, family, peer, and psychological states (depression, stress, and self-esteem) are more potent predictors of gang membership for the males than the females. (p. 156)

Apart from the relatively small number of comparisons identified here, no other gender-based predictions of behavior are reported in the OJJDP study group volume. We do not posit that gender bias is responsible for the omission of gender differences in this research, as measurement difficulties associated with observing the low-base-rate phenomena of serious, violent, and chronic juvenile offenders in general, and for females in particular, are clearly noted. For example, Huizinga & Jakob-Chien (1998) contend that "because statistical significance is dependent on sample sizes, some differences that appear to be substantively significant are not statistically different, especially for girls" (p. 53). It also is reported that "estimates for females are less stable," but there is some suggestion of (1) a lower proportion of high aggression but (2) a higher proportion of serious criminal behavior among the more aggressive" (Tolan & Gorman-Smith, 1998, p. 74). These authors conclude that because most studies have focused on males, there are substantial limitations in applying a knowledge base developed only on males, and much of what can be concluded about serious, violent, and chronic juvenile offenders may only apply to males (p. 70).

The notable exception to research based on small numbers of subjects is analysis of 151,209 juvenile court careers by Howard Snyder. He provides interesting evidence that the large majority of youths handled by the juvenile court were referred only once. Most of the delinquents were never charged with a serious offense. Delinquents born later were not more frequent, more serious, or more violent than their earlier counterparts. Most chronic offenders did not commit violence, although most violent delinquents were also chronic offenders. Further, the majority of chronic and violent offenders also were involved in serious but nonviolent offending. In these findings, Snyder (1998) finds "comfort in the fact that the juvenile justice system is largely achieving its goal of successfully intervening in the lives of delinquent youth" (p. 442). He also contends, however, that "the juvenile justice system may be spreading its net wider, bringing in more juveniles, not more serious juvenile offenders because much of the recent growth in referrals was due to nonserious offenses" (p. 443). Regrettably absent in this interesting work is an indication of gender differences, although females presumably are included among the large number of cases spread across fifteen cohorts that Snyder examined.

Of course, it is nothing new to ignore gender differences. Omission of how males and females differ actually is more the routine than the exception (Bergsmann, 1989; Chesney-Lind, 1997, pp. 17–21). A recent reminder of this situation appears in an aptly named book *The Invisible Woman*, in which Joanne Belknap (1996) comments: "[I] found it frustrating to search through mainstream journals (and some books) to find out if women and/or girls were included in the research questions or samples. For example, studies with male-only samples rarely identified this in the title, while studies with female-only or female and male samples almost consistently reflected this in their titles. If women were excluded from the study, then most authors perceived no need to include 'male' in the title" (p. 4).

Although seldom questioned, the justification usually offered for the absence of gender-specific analysis is that too few females are available for observation. Indeed, plenty of convincing evidence exists that both male prevalence and incidence of offending far exceed that of females. But beyond these two parameters of offending, we know very little about the nature of other gender differences and about female offending in particular. The irony, and perhaps the greatest shame, in ignoring gender differences in offending is that this demographic factor actually may have the best ability to distinguish crime, at least better than age, race, or social class, which are far more common in scientific inquiries about offending (Hagan, Gillis, & Simpson, 1985; Leonard, 1982).

Another problem with the lack of attention paid to female offending is that considerable unfounded speculation exists in place of accumulated research. Both historically and today, there is a tendency to view female offenders and offending as aberrations, abnormal even among society's deviants, and certainly not feminine. For example, Lombroso's beliefs in the late nineteenth century that females are less developed on the evolutionary scale and that female criminals exhibit male characteristics are no longer appreciated, but support for his contention that female delinquency is linked to biological traits can certainly still be found today. Similarly, Pollack's contention in 1950 that the onset of menstruation, pregnancy, and menopause are linked to criminality has been widely cast aside but his idea that females use their sexuality to obtain deferential treatment reappears today as the "chivalry hypothesis" in some explanations of differential treatment. Freud's concept of penis envy has been strongly questioned, but the influence of his views is evident in psychological theories that trace gender differences in personality, development and adaptations.

The influence of these early theorists is evident among the criminal career panel debates on explanations based on "biological differences, differences in moral training, differences in socialization experiences, and fewer criminal opportunities for girls because they are more closely supervised" (Blumstein et al., 1986, p. 25). Although there is no consensus on the relative influence of "nature" or "nurture," and most explanations integrate popular elements, prevailing theories include themes that gender differences in offending can be explained by corresponding gender differences in socialization, cognitive abilities, personality adaptations, neurological functioning, and hormonal and biochemical composition (Weisheit & Mahan, 1988). The most common diminished views of female offending continue to relegate it to a symptom of moral, emotional, or family problems and not "real" [male] delinquency and crime (Caine, 1989; Chesney-Lind, 1997; Naffine, 1987).

More important than presumptions about the inherent causes of crime, however, is the lack of attention and the misguided responses that females receive from criminal justice agencies. The range of behavior generally considered acceptable is narrower for females (Chesney-Lind, 1973, 1995; Dembo, Williams, & Schmeidler, 1993; Kempf-Leonard & Sample, 1998) and different factors appear to affect how females are processed (Chesney-Lind & Shelden, 1992; Gelsthorpe, 1989; Krohn, Curry, & Nelson-Kilger, 1983; Rosenbaum & Chesney-Lind, 1994; Visher, 1983). Females may receive more restrictive, harsher, and longer interventions than comparable males from police (Visher, 1983), courts, and correctional facilities (Bishop & Frazer, 1992; Chesney-Lind, 1973; Krisberg, Schwartz, Fishman, Eisikovits, & Guttman, 1986; Rhodes & Fischer, 1993). Females are also sent for treatment to mental hospitals in lieu of traditional juvenile justice facilities more often than males (Chesney-Lind, 1995; Miller, 1994; Weithorn, 1988). Further, some female-specific treatment programs dictate stereotypical feminine behavior (Chesney-Lind & Shelden, 1992; Gelsthorpe, 1989; Kersten, 1989), and even new reform efforts in this area may be problematic (Kempf-Leonard & Sample, 1998).

Some of these situations no doubt exist because inadequate resources are allocated and too few programs attend to the prevention and treatment of girls and women who offend (Chesney-Lind, 1997, p. 90; Lipsey, 1992, p. 106; Valentine Foundation, 1990, p. 5). Even among those criminal justice agencies that do try to respond to females, there are many inappropriate services, interventions, and sanctions. According to Meda Chesney-Lind (1997), "there have been major changes in the way that the United States has handled girls' and women's crime in recent decades that do not necessarily bode well for the girls and women who enter the criminal justice system" (p. 3). In placing blame, Chesney-Lind says, "[the silence about females] has hidden key information from public view and allowed major shifts in the treatment of women and girls—many on the economic margins—to occur without discussion and debate" (p. 3).

The "forgotten few" female offenders (Bergsmann, 1989) may be small in number, but their ability to help us understand wider behaviors should not be discounted. Even differential treatment by juvenile and criminal justice has been attributed to paternalism prevalent in general society (Chesney-Lind, 1995; Odem, 1995; Price & Sokoloff, 1995), which itself merits better understanding. Indeed, our understanding of crime and criminal justice would be much less, and criminology might not have become the large and growing field it now has, if its "parent disciplines" had forestalled attention to deviants among investigations of routine behaviors. It is for these reasons that we now examine gender differences among serious, violent, and chronic juvenile offenders.

DATA

This study uses the data files from the 1958 Philadelphia Birth Cohort Study. Records from all public and private schools in Philadelphia were used to identify the population of 27,160 males and females born in 1958 who resided in Philadelphia at least from ages 10 through 17. Together with the criminal history data that were collected for the cohort through age 26, these data are superior to those on which many previous investigations have been based. The present data permit the systematic structuring of the longitudinal sequence of police contacts and thereby help to facilitate the identification of youths, both delinquents and nondelinquents, who are most likely to proceed to adult crime.

The 1958 Philadelphia birth cohort comprises a population and, as such, is not vulnerable to the usual threats of external validity posed by sampling procedures because every available subject is included regardless of their delinquency or adult crime status. This cohort of 13,160 males and 14,000 females is the largest of its kind and includes detailed information drawn from several sources able to identify characteristics of its members.

The requirement of Philadelphia residence between ages 10 and 18 for defining the cohort provides a uniform time frame and setting within which cohort members were at risk for offending. Sample mortality is not problematic in this longitudinal investigation because the retrospective data collection involved unobtrusive archival examination of records that are maintained routinely by the Philadelphia Police Department and area schools.

Police rap sheets and investigation reports were provided by the Juvenile Aid Division of the Philadelphia Police Department to characterize police encounters that the cohort experienced before age 18. In addition to official arrests, the rap sheet data also contain "police contact" information. The police maintain records of these contacts that result in "remedial," or informal, handling of the youth by an officer whereby youth are generally remanded to the custody of their parents. Thus the juvenile delinquency data contain both official arrests and informal contacts that did not result in an arrest thereby representing a total record of official delinquency, and further, representing a much better record of delinquency than data that are based solely on arrest information. The police investigation reports were used to supplement information provided in the rap sheets with detailed descriptions of the criminal event in which the subject was involved.

The Municipal and Court of Common Pleas of Philadelphia served as data sources for offenses committed by the cohort after reaching the legislatively imposed adult status of age 18. Adult criminal history data are available through December 31, 1984, or through age 26 for all cohort members. The 1958 Philadelphia Birth Cohort Study is rich in the criminal history and offense data available to assess important criminological issues. Further description of the 1958 Philadelphia Birth Cohort Study data collection procedures and the results of a comparison study of the juvenile delinquency careers for males in the 1958 and 1945 Philadelphia cohorts may be found in Tracy and Kempf-Leonard (1996) and Tracy et al (1985, 1990).

It is important to note that an assumption was made that the residential status of subjects remained stable after age 17. FBI rap sheets on adult offending were obtained to capture even migratory adult crime, but those data were not used because it was too difficult to identify subjects accurately. Married females with new surnames were lost because the distinct federal numbering system necessitated identification based on the subject's name.

RESULTS

Female subjects ($n = 14,000$) comprise 51.5 percent of the 27,160 persons in the 1958 Philadelphia birth cohort. Yet they comprise just 14.1 percent of the 6287 delinquents and 14.9 percent of the cohort members who committed offenses as adults. Collectively, these females were responsible for 3897 juvenile offenses and 909 adult crimes. In this chapter we investigate gender differences and similarities in the nature and distribution of these offenders and offenses. We first examine the prevalence of delinquency, which refers to the proportion of a subject group that has officially been recorded as delinquent.

Table 1 shows 4315 males and 1972 females officially recorded as delinquent; thus the prevalence of delinquency is 32.8 percent for males and 14.1 percent for females in the 1958 cohort. Given the smaller number of females, a gender comparison based merely on frequencies or counts would be inappropriate—the males would predominate and comparisons would be misleading. However, the percentage of delinquents adjusts for the population size at risk. Thus, in calculating the ratio of males to females, we rely on the percentage rather than the frequency. The ratio of the percentage of male delinquents to that of female delinquents indicates that for each female delinquent, there were about 2.3 male delinquents. As would be expected from prior research, males are much more likely than their female peers to become officially involved with the juvenile justice system.

Gender differences in the frequency, or incidence, of delinquency are show in Table 2. We first provide data for all officially recorded delinquent acts, followed by only those delinquent acts that were law violations or crimes (i.e., status offenses were excluded). The largest proportion of both male delinquents (41.8 percent) and female delinquents (59.9 percent) had only one officially recorded delinquent offense of any kind. Roughly one-third each of the males and females exhibited moderate recidivism and had from two to four delinquent offenses. High recidivism, five through nine offenses, was observed for 15.2 percent of the males and 6.2 percent of the females. The smallest proportion of both males (7.6 percent) and females (1.2 percent) had very high recidivism and accumulated ten or more official contacts with police.

The male/female ratios for these percentages indicate a distinct gender effect. That is, as delinquency becomes more frequent, or more chronic, each female offender has a much higher percentage of male counterparts. The ratios start at 0.69:1 at the level of one-time offender, then increase consistently as we move to two to four offenses (1.09:1), and then five to nine offenses (2.45:1). Among the group responsible for the highest incidence of delinquency—ten or more offenses—there were 6.3 male delinquents for each female.

When delinquents who committed only status offenses are excluded and only criminal law violations are considered, the pattern shown above becomes even more pronounced. The group with no law violations, or status offenders only, includes just 11.7

TABLE 1 Frequency and Percentage of Delinquents by Gender

	Males		Females		M/F
	n	%	*n*	%	% Ratio
Nondelinquents	8,845	67.2	12,028	85.9	0.78:1
Delinquents	4,315	32.8	1,972	14.1	2.33:1
	13,160	100.0	14,000	100.00	

TABLE 2   Number and Percentage of Delinquent Offense Groups by Gender

		Males		Females		M/F
		n	%	*n*	%	% Ratio
All offenses (including status)						
	1	1804	41.8	1182	59.9	0.69:1
	2–4	1529	35.4	643	32.6	1.09:1
	5–9	654	15.2	123	6.2	2.45:1
	10+	328	7.6	24	1.2	6.33:1
		4315	100.0	1972	99.9	
Criminal law violations						
	0	504	11.7	876	44.7	0.26:1
	1	1697	39.3	794	40.3	0.98:1
	2–4	1383	32.1	274	13.9	2.31:1
	5–9	515	11.9	24	1.2	9.92:1
	10+	216	5.0	4	0.2	25.0:1
		4315	100.0	1972	100.3	

percent of the male delinquents as compared to 44.7 percent of the female delinquents. Similarly, the offender group with but one single crime encounter includes 40.3 percent of the females and 39.3 percent of the males. Thus, taken together, a substantial proportion of females, 85 percent, committed either no crimes or at most one crime in their delinquency career as compared to 51 percent of male delinquents.

When we examine recidivists, we see that at the level of two through four criminal law violations, only 13.9 percent of the females as compared to 32.1 percent of the males were so classified. At the level of high criminal violations, five through nine offenses, this group included 11.9 percent of the males but only 1.2 percent of the females. Finally, at the highest recidivism level of criminal violations, ten or more offenses, we find 5 percent of the male delinquents but less than 1 percent of the females (0.2 percent).

The ratio of these percentages shows about four female delinquents for each male delinquent with no law violation and approximately 1:1 among the group with a single crime. However, there were 2.3 males per female with two to four offenses, 9.9 males per female for five to nine offenses, and 25 males per female for 10 or more offenses. These ratios clearly indicate that as the levels of crime-related delinquency increase, fewer and fewer females are found compared to males.

In Table 3 we turn to data concerning gender differences in the probabilities of recidivism at each offense rank in the delinquency career, from the first to the *n*th offense. The probability estimate for male delinquents making the transition from a single offense to a second one is 0.58 compared to 0.40 for female delinquents, or looked at another way, about

TABLE 3   Juvenile Recidivism Probabilities: All Delinquent Acts

Offense Rank	Males, Any Offense			Females, Any Offense		
	Career Frequency	Total Frequency	Probability	Career Frequency	Total Frequency	Probability
1	1804	4315	1.0000	1182	1972	1.0000
2	705	2511	0.5819	379	790	0.4006
3	502	1806	0.7192	163	411	0.5203
4	322	1304	0.7220	101	248	0.6034
5	212	982	0.7531	51	147	0.5927
6	174	770	0.7841	32	96	0.6531
7	119	596	0.7740	18	64	0.6667
8	74	477	0.8003	13	46	0.7188
9	75	403	0.8449	9	33	0.7174
10	56	328	0.8139	6	24	0.7273
11	46	272	0.8293	6	18	0.7500
12	40	226	0.8309	3	12	0.6667
13	37	186	0.8230	2	9	0.7500
14	25	149	0.8011	2	7	0.7778
15	16	124	0.8322	1	5	0.7143
16	10	108	0.8710	1	4	0.8000
17	12	98	0.9074	1	3	0.7500
18	13	86	0.8776	1	2	0.6667
19	16	73	0.8488		1	0.5000
20	11	57	0.7808		1	1.0000
21	8	46	0.8070		1	1.0000
22	2	38	0.8261		1	1.0000
23	2	36	0.9474		1	1.0000
24	6	34	0.9444	1	1	1.0000
25	3	28	0.8235			
26	4	25	0.8929			
27	1	21	0.8400			
28	2	20	0.9524			
29	3	18	0.9000			
30	3	15	0.8333			
31	1	12	0.8000			
32	2	11	0.9167			
33		9	0.8182			

TABLE 3   Juvenile Recidivism Probabilities: All Delinquent Acts (cont'd)

Offense Rank	Males, Any Offense			Females, Any Offense		
	Career Frequency	Total Frequency	Probability	Career Frequency	Total Frequency	Probability
34	3	9	1.0000			
35		6	0.6667			
36		6	1.0000			
37	1	6	1.0000			
38		5	0.8333			
39	1	5	1.0000			
40		4	0.8000			
41	2	4	1.0000			
42		2	0.5000			
43		2	1.0000			
44		2	1.0000			
45		2	1.0000			
46		2	1.0000			
47		2	1.0000			
48	1	2	1.0000			
49		1	0.5000			
50		1	1.0000			
51		1	1.0000			
52		1	1.0000			
53	1	1	1.0000			

42 percent of males compared to 60 percent of females commit only one delinquent offense. Male delinquents have a higher probability of recidivism than do female delinquents at each offense rank. The exception to this pattern occurs for the transition between nineteen and twenty offenses, for which the probability for females stays at 1.0 until the twenty-fourth offense. But these higher scores are unreliable, as they are based on only one female delinquent.

Although Table 3 confirms the greater involvement of males in delinquent recidivism and that the distribution of career totals is smaller and more constrained for the females, these results also indicate that female recidivists, like males, exhibit a pattern of escalating recidivism probabilities as offense rank increases. That is, while far fewer female delinquents recidivate at each offense rank, the pattern of such recidivism follows a probabilistic process that is very similar to that for males, thus suggesting a difference of degree rather than of kind.

Of the 19,145 officially recorded offenses, male delinquents were responsible for 15,248 (79.6 percent) and female delinquents for 3,897 (20.4 percent). The distribution of these offenses across specific offense categories is shown in Table 4. The most common

TABLE 4   Number, Percent, and Rate (per 1000) of All Delinquent Acts by Gender

	Male			Female			M/F
	n	%	Rate	*n*	%	Rate	% Rate
Index Offenses							
Homicide	55	0.4	4.18	5	0.1	0.36	11.61:1
Rape	101	0.7	7.67	2	0.1	0.14	54.79:1
Robbery	1290	8.5	98.02	43	1.1	3.07	31.93:1
Aggrivated assault	561	3.7	42.63	107	2.7	7.64	5.58:1
Burglary	1673	11.0	127.13	52	1.3	3.71	34.27:1
Theft	1671	11.0	126.98	500	12.8	35.71	3.56:1
Vehicle theft	640	4.2	48.63	18	0.5	1.29	37.70:1
Nonindex Offenses							
Males predominate							
Simple assault	698	4.6	53.04	209	5.4	14.93	3.55:1
Arson	42	0.3	3.19	7	0.2	0.50	6.38:1
Receive stolen							
goods	69	0.5	5.24	7	0.2	0.50	10.48:1
Weapons	457	3.0	34.73	23	0.6	1.64	21.18:1
Vandalism	813	5.3	61.78	63	1.6	4.50	13.73:1
Drugs	714	4.7	54.26	100	2.6	7.14	7.60:1
Drunk driving	40	0.3	3.04	1	0.0	0.07	43.43:1
Liquor laws	211	1.4	16.03	43	1.1	3.07	5.22:1
Truancy	1987	13.0	150.99	347	8.9	24.79	6.09:1
Disorderly	1837	12.0	139.59	319	8.2	22.79	6.13:1
Trespass	603	4.0	45.82	93	2.4	6.64	6.90:1
City ordinance	534	3.5	40.58	82	2.1	5.86	6.92:1
Sex offenses	66	0.4	5.02	9	0.2	0.64	7.84:1
Gambling	8	0.1	0.61	1	0.0	0.07	8.71:1
Vagrancy	35	0.2	2.66	4	0.1	0.29	9.17:1
Drunkenness	166	1.1	12.61	17	0.4	1.21	10.42:1
Prostitution	11	0.1	0.84	1	0.0	0.07	12.00:1
Escape	205	1.3	15.58	14	0.4	1.00	15.58:1
Conspiracy	31	0.2	2.36	2	0.1	0.14	16.86:1
Incorrigible	6	0.0	0.46	4	0.1	0.29	1.59:1
Explosives	8	0.1	0.61	n/a			
Disturbance	5	0.0	0.38	n/a			
Fraud	6	0.0	0.46	6	0.2	0.43	1.07:1
Females predominate							
Runaway	467	3.1	35.49	1518	39.0	108.43	0.33:1
Invest. person	235	1.5	17.86	296	7.6	21.14	0.84:1
Forgery	3	0.0	0.23	4	0.1	0.29	0.79:1
	15,248	100	1158.66	3897	100.0	278.36	4.16:1

offense categories among male delinquents were truancy (13 percent), disorderly conduct (12 percent), burglary (11 percent), theft (11 percent), drugs (5 percent), and simple assault (5 percent). By comparison, female delinquents were most actively involved in runaway (39 percent), theft (13 percent), truancy (9 percent), disorderly conduct (8 percent), and simple assault (5 percent). As would be expected from prior research, males predominate significantly among index crimes for which the male/female ratios are quite substantial. Further, the gender ratios show similarities for the offenses of runaway, forgery, fraud, investigation of person, and incorrigibility, while the biggest differences occur for rape, drunk driving, auto theft, burglary, robbery, and weapon offenses for which the male/female ratios are substantial.

The overall estimate for male/female percent ratio based on total number of offenses indicates that over four male delinquents were apprehended for every female delinquent. Similarly, the offense rate for males, 1158.66, is about four times higher (4.16) than the rate, 278.36, for females. Clearly, these offense data demonstrate, as expected, that delinquency of males far exceeds that of females when frequency of violations is the operative measure.

In Table 5 we examine gender differences among delinquents who could be classified as serious, violent, and/or chronic offenders. Violent offenders had delinquency records that included homicide, rape, robbery, aggravated assault, or aggravated sexual intercourse. These violent delinquents included 1128 males, or 26 percent of the 4315 male delinquents, and 140 females, or 7.1 percent of the 1972 female delinquents. Thus for every violent female delinquent there were nearly four males who could be classified as violent.

The serious offenders include all violent offenders, plus those with burglary, theft, automobile theft, arson, and vandalism in excess of $500. In this category, there were 2182 males (50.6 percent) and 326 females (16.5 percent). The male/female ratio is about 3:1. Serious crime specialists committed over half of their total career offenses in that category. There were 112 male specialists in serious crime (2.6 percent) but only 3 females, for a male to female ratio of 13:1.

The familiar classification of chronic offenders is those with a career total of five or more offenses. There were 982 chronic male delinquents (22.8 percent) and 147 chronic female delinquents (7.5 percent), for a male/female ratio of 3:1.

The intersection among serious, violent, and chronic juvenile offenders and the proportion of each that subsequently became adult offenders are depicted in Tables 6 and 7 and in Figure 1. In Table 6 we note that there were 895 males who were classified as both serious and chronic offenders. Although comprising only one-fifth of all male delinquents,

TABLE 5 Number and Percentage of Offenders by Delinquency Career Type

	Males		Females		M/F
	n	%	*n*	%	% Ratio
Violent offender	1128	26.1	140	7.1	3.68:1
Serious offender	2182	50.6	326	16.5	3.07:1
Serious specialist	112	2.6	3	0.2	13.0:1
Chronic offender	982	22.8	147	7.5	3.04:1

TABLE 6   Number and Percent of Career Types by Gender[a]

| | Males | | Females | | |
| | | % of | | % of | M/F |
Career Type	n	Delinquents	n	Delinquents	% Ratio
Total delinquents	4315	100.0	1972	100.0	n/a
Serious delinquents	2182	50.6	326	16.5	3.07:1
Violent delinquents	1128	26.1	140	7.1	3.68:1
Chronic delinquents	982	22.8	147	7.5	3.04:1
Serious and chronic	895	20.7	69	3.5	5.91:1
% of serious		41.0		21.2	1.93:1
% of chronic		91.1		46.9	1.94:1
Violent and chronic	612	14.2	39	2.0	7.10:1
% of violent		54.2		27.9	1.94:1
% of chronic		62.3		26.5	2.35:1
Not delinquents	8845	67.2[b]	12,028	85.9[b]	0.78:1

[a]There is no consensus on the optimal cutoff to define chronic offenders, or whether the same definition should apply to males and females. One argument offered against a gender-neutral definition is that it is likely to capture a much smaller proportion of female offenders than male offenders, who also would "probably represent a more extreme group" (Blumstein et al, 1986; Loeber, Farrington, & Waschbusch, 1998, pp. 15–16). Having already addressed high incidence separately, however, the traditional definition of five or more offenses is adopted here.

[b]Rather than all delinquents, this percentage is based on the population total of 13,160 males and 14,000 females.

TABLE 7   Number and Percentage of Career Types by Gender

	Total	Males			Females			
	No. of	No. of	No. of		No. of	No. of		
	Delin-	Delin-	Adult	Percent	Delin-	Adult	Percent	M/F
Career Type	quents	quents	Offenders	of Row	quents	Offenders	of Row	% Ratio
Total delinquents	6287	4315	1805	41.8	1972	236	12.0	3.48:1
Serious delinquents	2508	2182	1123	51.5	326	81	24.8	2.08:1
Violent delinquents	1268	1128	634	56.2	140	36	25.7	2.19:1
Chronic delinquents	1129	982	619	63.0	147	42	28.5	2.21:1
Serious and chronic	964	895	571	63.8	69	30	43.5	1.47:1
Violent and chronic	651	612	394	64.4	39	17	43.6	1.48:1
Not delinquents	20,873	8845	1273	14.4	12,028	304	2.5	5.76:1

this group represents 91.1 percent of the total chronic subset and 41.0 percent of the serious male delinquents. In contrast, the 69 serious and chronic female delinquents comprised less than 4 percent of the total, 46.9 percent of the chronic group, and 21.2 percent of the serious female delinquents. For each such female delinquent, there were approximately two male delinquents.

Delinquents who were both violent and chronic offenders included 612 males, or 14 percent, and 39 females, or 2 percent. This career type represented two-thirds of the male chronic offenders, one-fourth of the female chronic offenders, just over half of the violent males, and just over one-fourth of violent females. The male/female percent ratio was again 2:1.

The prevalence of subsequent adult offending through age 26 is shown in Table 7 separately by gender for each delinquency career type. Among both males and females, adult offending was least prevalent among nondelinquents (14 percent males, 3 percent females) and most prevalent among chronic offenders who also had records of either violent or serious crimes (64 percent males, 44 percent females). Although parallel patterns of adult prevalence exist among the delinquency career types for males and females, the lower prevalence among females is very clearly evident. The male/female ratio of nearly 6:1 suggests the most variation among virgin adult offenders, those with no juvenile record. The ratio for overall delinquents is 3.5:1, and for each of the serious, violent, and chronic delinquency careers, the adult offending ratios identify males to females as 2:1.

Figure 1 provides a useful display of the information from Tables 6 and 7, using Venn diagrams with intersecting circles to represent the proportion of delinquents in each of the significant delinquency career types. All delinquents are encompassed within the outer circle. Those delinquents who had no record of any serious offense and fewer than five encounters with the police are included in the proportion of the large circle outside the other circles. Overlapping areas between the circles represent delinquency careers with attributes from two or more subgroups. The shaded portion of each circle represents the percentage of each delinquency career subgroup that also committed adult crime.

In comparison to Snyder's analysis of multiple court cohorts, we use a more conservative definition of chronic offending, the traditional five or more police contact, whereas he relied on a cutoff of four or more delinquency referrals to court (Snyder, 1998, p. 437). We had no cases of kidnapping and include rape as a violent offense. We also include vandalism of property in excess of $500 as a serious offense, which Snyder does not, and he includes drug trafficking and weapons as serious nonviolent offenses (Snyder, 1998, p. 429). Despite these differences, there is value in comparing our findings of the intersecting career paths of delinquents.

Snyder reports the percentages of the various career paths for the 151,209 court careers of the fifteen Maricopa County cohorts as follows: 33.6 percent serious delinquents, 14.5 percent chronic, 12.1 percent serious and chronic, and 4.2 percent violent and chronic. Our data cover a single urban cohort as compared to the mix of urban, suburban, and semi-rural areas encompassed by Maricopa County, and thus, the compositional dissimilarity between the two counties may produce a greater proportion of serious career paths for Philadelphia. However, we use a more conservative definition of career path eligibility that may counterbalance the compositional differences. Snyder reported 33.6 percent serious delinquents, while we found 39.9 percent of the 1958 cohort had serious delinquency (50.8% for males; 16.5% for females). The Maricopa County data showed 14.5 percent chronic careers, while Philadelphia had 17.9 percent (22.8% for males; 7.5%

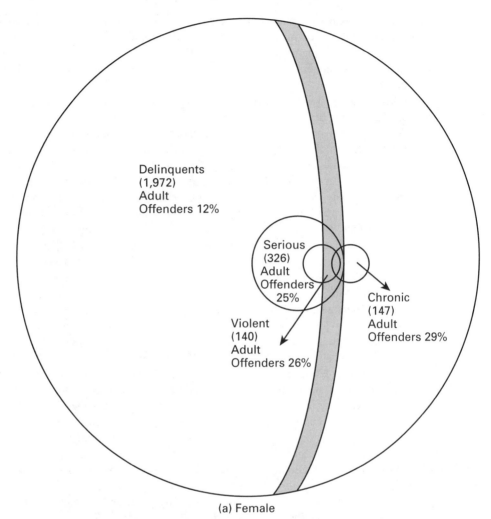

Delinquents
(1,972)
Adult
Offenders 12%

Serious
(326)
Adult
Offenders
25%

Chronic
(147)
Adult
Offenders 29%

Violent
(140)
Adult
Offenders 26%

(a) Female

FIGURE 1 Venn diagram showing intersection between delinquency career types: (a) female; (b) male.

for females). Snyder found that 8.1 percent of the careers were violent, while we found that 20.2 percent (26.1% for males; 7.1% for females) of the 1958 delinquency careers involved violence. With respect to serious and chronic careers, Snyder found 12.1 percent, while the Philadelphia cohort had 15.3 percent (20.7% for males, 3.5% for females). Finally, 4.2 percent of the Maricopa County cohorts were both violent and chronic, while the Philadelphia cohort showed 10.4 percent (14.2% for males; 2.0% for females).

Variation in delinquent behavior across different geographic areas of the country or different birth years may yield explanations of differences in career paths. Regardless, the 1958 cohort produces higher percentages for each of the designated career paths compared to the results reported by Snyder. More important, we have disaggregated by gender to

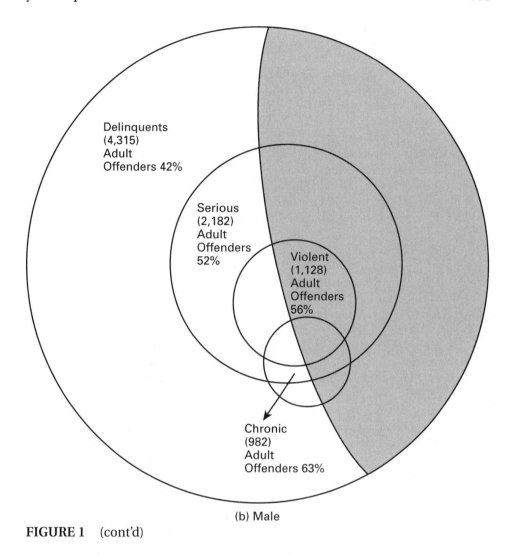

(b) Male

FIGURE 1   (cont'd)

sharpen the relevance of our findings. In particular, our ability to assess adult offending parameters illustrates further the extent to which attention to gender differences is important.

SUMMARY AND IMPLICATIONS

We have investigated a number of topics surrounding gender differences in delinquency. The following summarizes the major findings with respect to the topic areas of interest: prevalence, incidence, and juvenile delinquent subgroups. The prevalence data clearly indicated that the phenomenon of delinquency is very different among girls than among boys. Of the 14,000 girls in the 1958 cohort, 1972, or about 14 percent, had at least one delinquent offense before reaching age 18. The boys were almost two and one-half times more likely to be delinquent as their female counterparts. When prevalence was broken down by level of delinquency status, the gender differences were pronounced. Among females, 60 percent of the delinquents were one-time offenders, whereas only 7 percent where chronic recidivists. Thus the girls were about one and one-half times more likely to be delinquents with but one delinquent offense, while boys were about three times more likely to have been chronic offenders with five or more offenses.

In particular, therefore, chronic delinquency was a very different phenomenon among girls than among boys in the 1958 cohort. Of the 1972 female delinquents, 147 were classified as chronic offenders. These chronic females represented just 1.4 percent of the girls at risk, 7.5 percent of the delinquent subset, and 18.5 percent of the recidivists. The proportion of male chronics exceeded that of females by factors of 7.5:1 among subjects, 3:1 among delinquents, and 2:1 among recidivists.

The 1972 female delinquents were responsible for a total of 3897 delinquent acts. The offense rate (per 1000 cohort members) was 278.36. Seven hundred and twenty-seven, or 18 percent, of the female offenses were UCR Index offenses with a rate of 52.0 per 1000 cohort girls. One hundred and fifty-seven of the female offenses were violent index offenses (4 percent of the total delinquent acts and 22 percent of the index crimes) with a rate of 11 per 1000 girls in the cohort.

The gender effects shown among these data were quite pronounced. The offense rate for boys was four times greater than that for girls. The gender disparity increased to a factor of almost 9:1 for UCR Index offenses. The male/female ratio increased even further to 14:1 for violent offenses. The most glaring differences occurred for the following serious offenses: 14:1 for homicide, 33:1 for robbery, 10:1 for aggravated assault, 34:1 for burglary, and 37:1 for vehicle theft.

We also examined the intersection among various classifications of delinquency to determine the extent to which the categories of the serious offender, the violent offender, and the chronic offender were capturing the same group of delinquents. We found that males were much more likely than females to be serious and chronic (about six times more likely), and violent and chronic (about seven times more likely).

Finally, we examined the prevalence of adult crime in association with the various offender classifications in order to detect the extent to which a history of a particular type and/or frequency of juvenile delinquency was predictive of adult crime status. We found first that females had comparatively low adult crime status compared to males. That is, 236 (12 percent) of the 1972 female delinquents and 304 (2.5 percent) of the other females went on to commit a crime as an adult. These findings were overshadowed by the male results, which showed that 1,805 (41.8 percent) of the 4315 male delinquents and 1273 (14.4 percent) of the other males had records of adult crime. However, we also found that when we examined the intersection of the offender classifications and their association with adult crime, the gender disparity diminished. That is, male delinquents were about 3.4 times as likely as female delinquents, and other males were 5.76 times as likely as other females to go on to adult crime, but the results for serious, violent, and chronic offenders were generally in the range of twice as likely. More interestingly, when we examined the intersections we found that the male predominance declined even further, to about 1.5:1 for both the serious and chronic and violent and chronic intersections. Clearly, these findings indicate that a combined history of frequent and serious, or frequent and violent, places a female at substantial risk of adult crime that is closer to that of her male counterpart than when such combined traits are missing from the juvenile career. Thus a female who uncharacteristically has a delinquency career that is similar to that of her male counterpart rather than her female peers who generally have a limited involvement in delinquency— exhibits a substantially higher risk of continuing the offense career as she becomes an adult, just like her chronic male counterpart.

Overall, our results produce the finding that males are far more involved in offending than are females. When analysis of recidivism and seriousness of offending is extended to females, however, the findings show that females are indeed found among the small group of offenders present at the limited end of the continuum of those who behave most badly.

Our findings have highlighted many differences; still others remain to be examined. For gender differences to be understood, research must attend to offending over the criminal career, or life course, and focus on crime-specific modeling. For example, a better under-standing of the links between crime and responses to victimization, including how juvenile justice processing serves to label the responses of female victims as offenses, would help illuminate the criminal career pathways that flow from such victimization. Important contextual differences across age, race, social class, and geographic location also merit a lot more attention (Chesney-Lind, 1997; Simpson, 1991). We must examine gender similarities to better understand the differences. We urge other researchers to take seriously Meda Chesney-Lind's (1997) contention that "[g]irls' pathways into crime, even into violence, are affected by the gendered nature of their environments and particularly their experiences as marginalized girls in communities racked by poverty" (p. 176).

While Feld (1997, p. 132) argues that juvenile courts go to great lengths to evade the unpleasant topic of punishment and its "disagreeable qualities," it is the connection of Chesney-Lind (1997) that such feelings of avoidance and discomfort are even more acutely directed at females. Meanwhile, disproportionate media accounts of serious juvenile crime approaching epidemic proportions (Blumstein, 1995; DiIullio, 1996; Fox, 1996) have given rise to the notion of the "superpredator" (DiIullio, 1996), including the liberated 'female gansta' (Chesney-Lind, 1997, pp. 34–37; Maher & Curtis, 1995). Such media portrayals have affected public perception of juvenile offenders and the corresponding "feeding frenzy" of policy responses (Howell, 1997; see also Doi, 1998; Zimring, 1996, 1998).

Issues about the social construction of childhood and adolescence have been raised (Bernard, 1992; Feld, 1997). It also has been argued that teenagers, in general, tend to be demonized in contemporary U.S. society and that serious, violent, and chronic juvenile offenders exist because society has not acted responsibly toward youth in other important arenas (Males, 1996). Concerning females criticism has been advanced that "those who tout these 'crime waves' use a crude form of equity feminism to explain the trends observed and, in the process, contribute to a 'backlash' against the women's movement (Faludi, 1991)" (Chesney-Lind, 1997, p. 56).

The policy debate and legislative action has resulted in harsher, more restrictive codes and procedures for processing juvenile offenders, and especially serious, violent, and chronic delinquents, in nearly every state (Torbet et al., 1996; Walker, 1995). Some policy initiatives aim to limit discretion, standardize court decisions, and classify offenders for correctional supervision and treatment (Weibush, Baird, Krisberg, & Onek, 1995; Wilson & Howell, 1993). Other changes couple juvenile justice with criminal justice, typically through greater use of juvenile transfer to criminal court (Fagan, 1995; Howell,

1996; Singer, 1996; Tracy & Kempf-Leonard, 1998). Accountability is a recurrent theme, with changes aimed at holding juvenile offenders—and sometimes also their parents—responsible for their actions (Albert, 1998). In some areas, the accountability objective links with treatment (Bazemore & Day, 1996; Bazemore & Umbreit, 1995; Wilson & Howell, 1993), but more often the focus is on punishment and retribution (Feld, 1997). According to Feld:

> These recent changes signal a fundamental inversion in juvenile court jurisprudence from treatment to punishment, from rehabilitation to retribution, from immature child to responsible criminal....The common over-arching legislative strategy reflects a jurisprudential shift from the *principle of individualized justice* to the *principle of offense*, from rehabilitation to retribution, and an emphasis on the seriousness of the offenses rather than judges' clinical assessments of offenders' "amenability to treatment." (p. 79)

Feld subsequently advocates abolition of the juvenile court in favor of a single explicitly punitive criminal justice process in which culpability and sanctions are discounted for youth (Feld, 1997). Although Feld might appear the lone advocate of this position, it is clearly implicit in much of the public and policy debate.

In terms of effectiveness, it is important to note that a purely punitive response to serious juvenile offenders discounts advances made in the area of treatment. According to Lipsey (1992), "[i]t is no longer constructive for researchers, practitioners, and policy makers to argue about whether delinquency treatment and related rehabilitative approaches work. As a generality, treatment clearly works. We must get on with the business of developing and identifying the treatment models that will be most effective and providing them to the juveniles that will benefit" (p. 85). In their review of programs, Lipsey and Wilson (1998) identify reductions in recidivism as high as 40 percent among the best programs for serious juvenile offenders, a larger effect than shown for delinquents in general. They conclude, "If anything, then, it would appear that the typical intervention in these studies is *more* effective with serious offenders than with less serious offenders" (Lipsey & Wilson, 1998, p. 332). Characteristics of the most effective treatment programs were intensive services, more contact hours, longer stays, multiple services, consistent implementation, and external evaluation terms. Most important, not only has treatment been found far more effective in reducing recidivism than punishment (Gendreau, 1996), but it is also clearly more cost-effective (Greenwood, Model, Rydell, & Chiesa, 1996).

We know that effective treatment can be administered by the juvenile courts. Rates of recidivism tend to be lower in juvenile courts than in criminal courts (Howell, 1996). Moreover, our own research shows that early routine probation intervention is effective even for serious chronic juvenile delinquents, whereas the same may not be true of routine commitment to correctional facilities (Tracy & Kempf-Leonard, 1996, pp. 109–142). Similarly, Dean, Brame, and Piquero (1996) attributed lower recidivism to early probation intervention among several hundred North Carolina youths they followed for six years. Howell (1996) also reports on a twelve-month follow-up evaluation in which reductions as high as 50 percent in arrests, court petitions, probation violations, and new facility commitments were attributed to an early intervention program in a California probation department.

Of course, as might be expected, attention to females is noticeably absent among the policy discussion and most of the policy initiatives. Two notable exceptions appear under provisions of the JJDP Act of 1974, as reauthorized in 1992:

1. To be eligible for federal funding, each state must provide "an analysis of gender-specific services for the prevention and treatment of juvenile delinquency, including the types of such services available and the need for such services for females and a plan for providing the needed gender-specific services" [Public Law 102-586, 106 Stat. 4982 (1992)].

2. As part of the challenge grant program for state advisory groups, additional funds are available to examine policies for gender bias and to develop female-specific programs. Based on the number of responses from states, the gender area has been the most popular among those available in the challenging grant program (Girls Inc., 1996, p. 26). In the larger policy arena, however, these two initiatives barely make a mark.

In light of our observations that policy responses to serious, violent, and chronic juvenile offenders have not attended to gender differences even though our research findings suggest that they should, we offer four recommendations. First, most policy reforms are predicated on notions of individual responsibility and accountability, which should require that we know more about the high incidence of delinquency that involve adolescents' miscalculation of risk (Bernard, 1992; Feld, 1997; Matza, 1964). Zimring (1996, p. 90–99) equates the "self-autonomy" of adolescence with a "learner's permit" that provides youth with the opportunity to make choices and learn responsibility, yet "preserves the life chances for those who make serious mistakes." Although gender is not mentioned, Feld (1997, p. 121) acknowledges that "youthful development is highly variable." It is age which explains his view that "the ability to make responsible choices is learned behavior, and the dependent status of youth systematically deprives them of chances to learn to be responsible" (p. 114). Given prevailing arguments that girls are more sheltered and closely supervised than boys, although their prevalence also is lower, gender differences in responses to independence and in learning responsibility could prove very valuable in the policy arena. Fortunately, many scholars research gender differences in development (e.g., Bem, 1993; Chesney-Lind & Shelden, 1992; Messerschmidt, 1993; Orenstein, 1994; Osgood, Wilson, O'Malley, Bachman & Johnson, 1996; Sadker & Sadker, 1994), and their contributions need to be appropriately targeted and included in the policy responses to juvenile offenders.

Second, Feld (1997) relies on knowledge gleaned from delinquency career research that desistance, maturation, or "aging out" typically occur—which he interprets as a natural phenomenon—to justify the feasibility of his system as follows: "Unlike a rehabilitative system inclined to extend its benevolent reach, an explicitly punitive process would opt to introduce fewer and more criminally 'deserving' youths into the system….In allocating scarce resources, [this system] would use seriousness of the offense to rationalize charging decisions and 'divert' or 'decriminalize' most of the 'kids' stuff' that provides the grist of the juvenile court mill until it became chronic or escalated in severity" (pp. 128–129). This stance in favor of ignoring problem juvenile behavior until it reaches an intolerable level, however, also ignores research findings showing success associated with early intervention. Further, it creates a system in which the needs of economically and culturally outcast populations are conveniently ignored. Not only does this omission seem contrary to Feld's own concern for social justice (1997, pp. 72, 132–136), but it is likely adversely to affect females who are disproportionately represented among the socially marginalized populations (Chesney-Lind, 1997, p. 115). Thus, we recommend rejection of Field's abolition idea.

Third, although we strongly advocate a better understanding and more awareness of gender similarities and differences in delivering services, we currently find ourselves in opposition to gender-specific policy developments. Because justice should equate to equity, female-specific services seem likely to perpetuate stereotype and diminished aid to girls and women (Chesney-Lind, 1997, p. 162). In this area, we agree with Feld (1997, p. 121) that fairness and the objectivity of law are sacrificed when dispositions reflect subjective explanations of behavior and personal responsibility. Indications to this effect in the form of well-intentioned but premature or poorly conceived programming efforts already exist among the new policy initiatives (Kempf-Leonard & Sample, 1998).

Our findings indicate gender differences in degree of serious, violent, and chronic offending, but gender similarities in general career patterns of interest. These findings lend support to suggestions that status offenders should be reintegrated as a feasible target of mainstream juvenile justice (Krisberg & Austin, 1993). Gender similarities in behavior, coupled with evidence of gender bias or differential processing, serve to remind us of the warning that criminal justice functions to maintain the modern patriarchy (Chesney-Lind, 1997, p. 4). How this occurs would be the important first step in helping to abolish it. Of course, obstacles to equity presented by the greater social stratification of rights and privileges remain (Simpson, 1991). Fortunately, the progressive ideas found within the new strategy for a comprehensive juvenile justice system are consistent with our findings and with other research on gender differences, and on male serious, violent, and chronic juvenile offenders (Howell, 1995, 1997; Wilson & Howell, 1993). Thus we support a balanced approach of prevention, early intervention, and graduated sanctions that provides for treatment, just as it aims to strengthen the family, support core institutions in their supporting roles of youth development, and identify and control the small group of serious, violent, and chronic juvenile offenders.

REFERENCES

ALBERT, R. L. (1998). *Juvenile accountability incentive block grants program.* OJJDP Fact Sheet 76. Washington, DC: Office of Juvenile Justice and Delinquency Prevention.

BAZEMORE, G., & DAY, S. E. (1996). Restoring the balance: Juvenile and community justice. *Juvenile Justice,* 3–14.

BAZEMORE, G., & UMBREIT, M. (1995). Rethinking the sanctioning function in juvenile court: Retributive or restorative responses to youth crime. *Crime and Delinquency, 49,* 296–316.

BELKNAP, J. (1996). *The invisible woman.* Belmont, CA: Wadsworth Publishing.

BEM, S. (1993). *The lenses of gender.* New Haven, CT: Yale University Press.

BERGSMANN, I. (1989, March 1). The forgotten few: Juvenile female offenders. *Federal Probation, 53,* 73–78.

BERNARD, T. J. (1992). *The cycle of juvenile justice.* New York: Oxford University Press.

BISHOP, D., & FRAZER, C. (1992). Gender bias in the juvenile justice system: Implications of the JJDP Act. *Journal of Criminal Law and Criminology, 82*(4), 1162–1186.

BLUMSTEIN, A. (1995, August). Violence by young people: Why the deadly nexus? *NIJ Journal,* pp. 1–9.

BLUMSTEIN, A., COHEN, J., ROTH, J. A., & VISHER, C. A. (1986). *Criminal careers and "career criminals."* Washington, DC: National Academy Press.

CAINE, M. (ED.). (1989). *Growing up good: Policing the behavior of girls in Europe.* Newbury Park, CA: Sage Publications.

CAIRNS, R. B., CAIRNS, B. D., NECKERMAN, H. J., GEST, S. D., & GARIEPY, J. L. (1988). Social networks and aggressive behavior: Peer support or peer rejection? *Developmental Psychology, 24,* 815–823.

CHESNEY-LIND, M. (1973). Judicial enforcement of the female sex role. *Issues in Criminology, 8,* 51–71.

CHESNEY-LIND, M. (1995). Girls, delinquency, and juvenile justice: Toward a feminist theory of young women's crime. In B. R. Price & N. J. Sokoloff (Eds.), *The criminal justice system and women* (2nd ed., pp. 71–88). New York: McGraw-Hill.

CHESNEY-LIND, M. (1997). *The female offender: Girls, women, and crime.* Thousand Oaks, CA: Sage Publications.

CHESNEY-LIND, M., & SHELDEN, R. (1992). *Girls, delinquency and juvenile justice.* Pacific Grove, CA: Brooks/Cole.

COIE, J. D., & DODGE, K. A. (1983). Communities and changes in children's socioeconomic status: A five-year longitudinal study. *Merrill-Palmer Quarterly, 29,* 261–282.

DEAN, C. W., BRAME, R. & PIQUERO, A. R. (1996). Criminal propensities, discrete groups of offenders, and persistence in crime. *Criminology, 34,* 547–574.

DEMBO, R., WILLIAMS, L., & SCHMEIDLER, J. (1993). Gender differences in mental health service needs among youths entering a juvenile detention center. *Journal of Prison and Jail Health, 12,* 73–101.

DENNO, D. (1990). *Biology and violence: From birth to adulthood.* Cambridge, UK: Cambridge University Press.

DIIULLIO, J. J. (1996, Spring). They're coming: Florida's youth crime bomb. *Impact,* pp. 25–27.

DOI, D. J. (1998, April). The MYTH of teen violence. *State Government News,* pp. 17–19.

FAGAN, J. (1995). Separating the men from the boys. In R. Howell, R. Hawkins, B. Krisberg, & J. Wilson (Eds.). *Sourcebook on serious violent juvenile offenders* (pp. 238–257). Thousand Oaks, CA: Sage Publications.

FALUDI, S. (1991). *Backlash: The undeclared war against American women.* New York: Anchor Books.

FELD, B. C. (1997). Abolish the juvenile court: Youthfulness, criminal responsibility, and sentencing policy. *Journal of Criminal Law and Criminology, 88*(1), 68–136.

FOX, J. A. (1996). *Trends in juvenile violence: A report to the U.S. attorney general on current and future rates of juvenile offending.* Technical report. Boston: Northeastern University.

GELSTHORPE, L. (1989). *Sexism and the female offenders: An organizational analysis.* Aldershot, Hants, England: Gower.

GENDREAU, P. (1996). The principles of effective interventions with offenders. In A.T. Harland (Ed.), *Choosing correctional options that work* (pp. 117–130). Thousand Oaks, CA: Sage Publications.

GIRLS, INC. (1996). *Prevention and parity: Girls in juvenile justice.* Indianapolis, IN: Girls Incorporated National Resource Center.

GREENWOOD, P. W., MODEL, K. E., RYDELL, C. P., & CHIESA, J. (1996). *Diverting children from a life of crime: Measuring costs and benefits.* Santa Monica, CA: RAND Corporation.

HAGAN, J., GILLIS, A. R., & SIMPSON, J. (1985). The class structure of gender and delinquency: Toward a power-control theory of common delinquency behavior. *American Journal of Sociology, 90,* 1151–1178.

HAMPARIAN, D. M., SCHUSTER, R., DINITZ, S., & CONRAD, J. (1978). *The violent few.* Lexington, MA: Lexington Books.

HAWKINS, D. F., LAUB, J. H., & LAURITSEN, J. L. (1998). Race, ethnicity, and serious juvenile offending. In R. Loeber & D. P. Farrington (Eds.), *Serious and violent juvenile offenders* (pp. 30–46). Thousand Oaks, CA: Sage Publications.

HAWKINS, J. D., HERRENKOHL, T., FARRINGTON, D. P., BREWER, D., CATALANO, R. F., & HARACHI, T. W. (1998). A review of predictors of youth violence. In R. Loeber & D. P. Farrington (Eds.), *Serious and violent juvenile offenders* (pp. 106–146). Thousand Oaks, CA: Sage Publications.

HOWELL, J. C. (ED.). (1995). *Guide for implementing the comprehensive strategy for serious, violent, and chronic juvenile offenders*. Washington, DC: Office of Juvenile Justice and Delinquency Prevention.

HOWELL, J. C. (1996). Juvenile transfers to the criminal justice system: State-of-the-art. *Law and Policy*, 18, 17–60.

HOWELL, J. C. (1998, February). *Juvenile justice and youth violence*. Thousand Oaks, CA: Sage Publications.

HUESMANN, L. R., ERON, L. D., LEFKOWITZ, M. M., & WALDER, L. O. (1984). Stability of aggression over time and generations. *Developmental Psychology, 20*, 1120–1134.

HUIZINGA, D., & JAKOB-CHIEN, C. (1998). The contemporaneous co-occurrence of serious and violent juvenile offending and other problem behaviors. In R. Loeber & D.P. Farrington (eds.), *Serious and violent juvenile offenders* (pp. 47–67). Thousand Oaks, CA: Sage Publications.

KEMPF-LEONARD, K., & SAMPLE, L. (1998). *Disparity based on sex: Is gender-specific treatment warranted?* Paper presented at the annual meeting of the Academy of Criminal Justice Sciences.

KERSTEN, J. (1989). The institutional control of girls and boys: An attempt at a gender-specific approach. In M. Caine (Ed.). *Growing up good: Policing the behavior of girls in Europe* (pp. 129–144). Newbury Park, CA: Sage Publications.

KRISBERG, B., & AUSTIN, J. F. (1993). *Reinventing juvenile justice*. Newbury Park, CA: Sage Publications.

KRISBERG, B., SCHWARTZ, I. M., FISHMAN, G., EISIKOVITS, Z., & GUTTMAN, E. (1986). *The incarceration of minority youth*. Minneapolis, MN: Hubert Humphrey Institute of Public Affairs.

KROHN, M., CURRY, J., & NELSON-KILGER, S. (1983). Is chivalry dead? *Criminology, 21*, 417–439.

LEONARD, E. (1982). *Women, crime, and society*. New York: Longman.

LIPSEY, M. (1992). Juvenile delinquency treatment: A meta-analytic inquiry in the variability of effects. In T. A. Cook, H. Cooper, D. S. Cordray, H. Hartmann, L. V. Hedges, R. J. Light, T. A. Louis, & F. Mosleller (Eds.), *Meta-analysis for explanation: A casebook* (pp. 83–126). New York: Russell Sage.

LIPSEY, M., & DERZON, J. H. (1998). Predictors of violent or serious delinquency in adolescence and early adulthood: A synthesis of longitudinal research. In R. Loeber & D.P. Farrington (eds.), *Serious and violent juvenile offenders* (pp. 86–105). Thousand Oaks, CA: Sage Publications.

LIPSEY, M. W., & WILSON, D. B. (1998). Effective intervention for serious juvenile offenders: A synthesis of research. In R. Loeber & D. P. Farrington (Eds.) *Serious and violent juvenile offenders* (pp. 315–345). Thousand Oaks, CA: Sage Publications.

LOEBER, R., & FARRINGTON, D. P. (EDS.). (1998). *Serious and violent juvenile offenders* (pp. 106–146). Thousand Oaks, CA: Sage Publications.

LOEBER, R., FARRINGTON, D. P., & WASCHBUSCH, D. A. (1998). Serious and violent juvenile offenders. In R. Loeber & D. P. Farrington (Eds.), *Serious and violent juvenile offenders* (pp. 13–29). Thousand Oaks, CA: Sage Publications.

LOEBER, R., & HAY, D. F. (1994). Developmental approaches to aggression and conduct problems. In M. Rutter & D. F. Hay (Eds.), *Development through life: A handbook for clinicians* (pp. 488–515). Oxford: Blackwell Scientific.

MAHER, L., & CURTIS, R. (1995). In search of the female urban "gansta": Change, culture, and crack cocaine. In B. R. Price & N. J. Sokoloff (Eds.), *The criminal justice system and women* (2nd ed., pp. 148–166). New York: McGraw-Hill.

MALES, M. A. (1996). *The scapegoat generation: America's war on adolescents*. Monroe, ME: Common Courage Press.

MATZA, D. (1964). *Delinquency and drift*. New York: Wiley.

MESSERSCHMIDT, J. (1993). *Masculinities and crime: Critique and reconceptualtization*. Lanham, MD: Rowman & Littlefield.

MILLER, J. (1994). Race, gender and juvenile justice: An examination of disposition decision-making for delinquent girls. In M. D. Schwartz & D. Milovanovic (Eds.), *The intersection of race, gender and class in criminology* (pp. 219–246). New York: Garland Publishing.

NAFFINE, N. (1987). *Female crime: The construction of women in criminology.* Sydney, Australia: Allen & Unwin.

ODEM, M. E. (1995). *Delinquent daughters.* Chapel Hill, NC: University of North Carolina Press.

ORENSTEIN, P. (1994). *School girls.* New York: Doubleday.

OSGOOD, W., WILSON, J., O'MALLEY, P., BACHMAN, G., & JOHNSON, L. (1996). Routine activities and individual deviant behavior. *American Sociological Review, 61*(4), 635–655.

PRICE, B. R., & SOKOLOFF, N. J. (EDS.). (1995). *The criminal justice system and women* (2nd ed.). New York: McGraw-Hill.

RHODES, J., & FISCHER, K. (1993). Spanning the gender gap: Gender differences in delinquency among inner city adolescents. *Adolescence, 28,* pp. 880–889.

ROSENBAUM, J., & CHESNEY-LIND, M. (1994). Appearance and delinquency: A research note. *Crime and Delinquency, 40,* 250–261.

SADKER, M., & SADKER, D. (1994). *Failing at fairness: How America's schools cheat girls.* New York: Charles Scribner's Sons.

SHANNON, L. (1978). A longitudinal study of delinquency and crime. In C. Wellford (Ed.), *Qualitative studies in criminology.* Beverly Hills, CA: Sage Publications.

SHANNON, L. (1980). *Assessing the relationship of adult criminal careers to juvenile careers.* Washington, DC: U.S. Government Printing Office.

SIMPSON, S. (1991). Caste, class, and violent crime: Explaining differences in female offending. *Criminology, 29*(1), 115–135.

SINGER, S. (1996). *Recriminalizing delinquency.* Cambridge: University of Cambridge Press.

SMITH, C., & THORNBERRY, T. P. (1995). The relationship between childhood maltreatment and adolescent involvement in delinquency. *Criminology, 33,* 451–481.

SNYDER, H. N. (1998). Serious, violent, and chronic juvenile offenders: An assessment of the extent of and trends in officially recognized serious criminal behavior in a delinquent population. In R. Loeber & D. P. Farrington (Eds.), *Serious and violent juvenile offenders* (pp. 428–444). Thousand Oaks, CA: Sage Publications.

THORNBERRY, T. (1998). Membership in youth gangs and involvement in serious and violent offending. In R. Loeber & D. P. Farrington (Eds.), *Serious and violent juvenile offenders* (pp. 147–166). Thousand Oaks, CA: Sage Publications.

TOLAN, P. H., & GORMAN-SMITH, D. (1998). Development of serious and violent offending careers. In R. Loeber & D. P. Farrington (Eds.), *Serious and violent juvenile offenders* (pp. 68–85). Thousand Oaks, CA: Sage Publications.

TORBET, P., GABLE, R., HURST, H., MONTGOMERY, I., SZYMANSKI, L., & THOMAS, D. (1996). *State responses to serious and violent juvenile crime.* Washington, DC: Office of Juvenile Justice and Delinquency Prevention.

TRACY, P. E., & KEMPF-LEONARD, K. (1996). *Continuity and discontinuity in criminal careers.* New York: Plenum Press.

TRACY, P. E., & KEMPF-LEONARD, K. (1998). Sanctioning serious juvenile offenders: A review of alternative models. *Advances in Criminological Theory, 8,* 135–171.

TRACY, P. E., WOLFGANG, M. E., & FIGLIO, R. M. (1985). Delinquency in two birth cohorts, executive summary. Washington, DC: Government Printing Office.

TRACY, P. E., WOLFGANG, M. E., & FIGLIO, R. M. (1990). *Delinquency careers in two birth cohorts.* New York: Plenum Press.

VALENTINE FOUNDATION. (1990). *A conversation about girls.* Bryn Mawr, PA: Valentine Foundation.

VISHER, C. (1983). Gender, police arrest decisions, and notions of chivalry. *Criminology, 21,* 5–28.

WALKER, S. (1985). *Sense and nonsense about crime: A policy guide.* Monterey, CA: Brooks/Cole.

WALKER, S. (1995). *Sense and nonsense about crime: A policy guide* (2nd ed.). Monterey, CA: Brooks/Cole.

WEIBUSH, R. G., BAIRD, C., KRISBERG, B., & ONEK, D. (1995). Risk assessment and classification for serious, violent, and chronic juvenile offenders. In J. C. Howell, B. Krisberg, J. D. Hawkins, & J. J. Wilson (Eds.), *A sourcebook: Serious, violent, and chronic juvenile offenders* (pp. 171–212). Thousand Oaks, CA: Sage Publications.

WEISHEIT, R., & MAHAN, S. (1988). *Women, crime and criminal justice*. Cincinnati, OH: Anderson Publishing.

WEITHORN, L. A. (1988). Mental hospitalization of troublesome youth: An analysis of skyrocketing admission rates. *Stanford Law Review, 40*, 773–838.

WHITE, H. R. (1992). Early problem behavior and later drug problems. *Journal of Research in Crime and Delinquency, 29*, 412–429.

WILLIAMS, J. H. (1994). *Understanding substance use, delinquency involvement, and juvenile justice system involvement among African-American and European-American adolescents*. Unpublished dissertation, University of Washington, Seattle.

WILSON, J. J., & HOWELL, J. C. (1993). *A comprehensive strategy for serious, violent, and chronic juvenile offenders*. Washington, D.C.: Office of Juvenile Justice and Delinquency Prevention.

WOLFGANG, M. E., FIGLIO, R. M., & SELLIN, T. (1972). *Delinquency in a birth cohort*. Chicago: University of Chicago Press.

ZIMRING, F. E. (1996, August 19). Crying wolf over teen demons. *Los Angeles Times*, p. B5.

ZIMRING, F. E. (1998). American youth violence. New York: Oxford University Press.

SECTION X

Conclusions

Roslyn Muraskin

In the words of Justice Ruth Bader Ginsburg, "[t]he classification man/dependent woman is the prototypical sex line in the law and has all the earmarks of self-fulfilling prophecy." That discrimination against women is of a long tradition is an understatement. Have we remembered the ladies?

> Words are more than a collective art: they are simultaneously a collective cage. Unconscious and unquestioned obedience to established meanings binds humankind with steel bands to both the good and the bad of yesterday. Law is called upon to serve goals other than predictability and certainty, which logic being what it is, walk backwards. The paramount obligation of law is to secure, to make safe, equal rights and justice under law. This is the daunting task of the remarkably few words which comprise the United States Constitution. (Thomas, 1991, p. xx)

We have come a long way since the days of Jean-Jacques Rousseau (1906) when he wrote that

> [t]he whole education of woman ought to be relative to men. To please them, to be useful to them, to make themselves loved and honored by them, to educate them when young, to care for them when grown, to counsel them, to console them, and to make his life sweet and agreeable to them—these are the duties at all times, and what should be taught them from their infancy.

As we have learned through these many chapters, women have had to struggle to be considered persons under the law and to be afforded the same opportunities as men before the law. The struggle is not yet over. Man may have been thought of as women's protector, but in the world in which we live today, every woman and man must be given the same chances to succeed. History has taught us that women have suffered as much and perhaps more than men. As pointed out in the Declaration of Seneca Falls in 1848: "[T]he history of mankind is a history of repeated injuries and usurpations on the part of man toward woman, having in direct object the establishment of an absolute tyranny over her."

The Fourteenth Amendment to the Constitution of the United States states that "no state…shall…deny to any person within its jurisdiction the equal protection of the laws." That amendment is to be applied equally to woman and man. Hopefully in today's world, we no longer adhere to the tenets of the words of Justice Brenner as he delivered the majority opinion in the case of *Muller v. Oregon* (1908):

> That woman's physical structure and the performance of maternal functions place her at a disadvantage in the struggle for subsistence is obvious. This is especially true when the burdens of motherhood are upon her…
>
> [H]istory discloses the fact that woman has always been dependent upon man. He established his control at the outset by superior physical strength, and the control in various forms …She is properly placed in a class by herself, and legislation designed for her protection may be sustained, even when like legislation is not necessary for men, and could not be sustained.

Admittedly, laws can discriminate, but such discrimination becomes unconstitutional when it is judged to be arbitrary and serves no legitimate purpose. *Frontiero v. Richardson* (1973) needed one more vote to declare that *sex was a suspect classification*, although it did concede that the differential treatment accorded men and women serves no purpose. Women and men are equal before the law—that is sound judicial practice. Today, the attitude of the criminal justice system has changed. We recognize that women are victims of crime and that they too perpetuate crimes. We recognize that equal treatment is demanded and is an absolute necessity. Having moved from traditional homebound social roles into positions of power and influence, women have become more assertive and aggressive while being capable to compete with men in all realms of life. As noted, litigation, changes in laws, and constitutional amendments have held our criminal justice system to task in demanding that women are properly defined as people and are deserving of all the rights and privileges of men. To do otherwise would make our system of law a public disgrace.

After the impeachment trial of President Clinton where he was acquitted on all charges, it was suggested that sexual matters are now so central to modern life that the courts cannot avoid getting more deeply involved in such issues. Others, including some feminist's reaction to the impeachment trial, felt that the concentration on sexual interaction was hurtful to women, having diverting attention from women's rights. Two schools have emerged: expand the definition of rape to include other forms of intimidation beyond violence, like the coercion of women to have sex with men who have power over them, like professors, therapists, or lawyers, with others arguing that there is too much preoccupation with sexual matters. Regardless of the impact of this historical case, women's rights and privacy have once again become a focal point for discussion.

But although litigation provides an opportunity for all persons to have a role in altering their conditions of life, a judicial opinion requiring such comprehensive change does not necessarily bring about such change. We have found that litigation is but a catalyst for change rather than an automatic mechanism for ending wrongs found. We know that within the criminal law, litigation indicates that disparate treatment of any kind is not permissible absent meaningful and objective justification. From Lombroso to the present, "criminological thought has been wrought with the sexism, inherent in assuming that there exists two distinct classes of women—those on pedestals and those in the gutter" (Muraskin, 1989). Throughout history we have lived with a double standard. Disparate treatment can no longer exist, for it is all about women and men, justice and fairness. And we must never forget the ladies, for then *it will be a crime*.

REFERENCES

MURASKIN, R. (1989). *Disparity of correctional treatment: Development of a measurement instrument*. Unpublished doctoral dissertation, City University of New York.
ROUSSEAU, J.J. (1906). *Émile, or A treatise on education* (Payne, W. H. ed.). New York and London.
THOMAS, C. S. (1991). *Sex discrimination in a nutshell*, (2nd ed.). St. Paul, MN: West.

CASES

Frontiero v. Richardson, 411 U.S. 677 (1973).
Muller v. Oregon, 208 U.S. 412 (1908).

Biography of Editor/Author

--- ❖ ---

Roslyn Muraskin, Ph.D., is Professor of Criminal Justice at the C.W. Post Campus of Long Island University. She has served in the capacity of Associate Dean of the College of Management (1990–1996) as well as Associate Dean of the School of Public Service. She currently serves as the Director of the Long Island Women's Institute of the College of Management as well as the Director of Alumni Development for the College of Management. Dr. Muraskin serves as Vice President of Health and Education for the Long Island Women's Agenda, an umbrella organization servicing all women's organizations on Long Island. She served as President of the Northeastern Association of the Academy of Criminal Justice Sciences (1995–1996) as well as Vice-President of Region V for the Criminal Justice Educators of New York State (CJEANYS).

She is the Editor of *The Justice Professional*, a refereed journal published quarterly by Gordon and Breach Publishers, as well as the editor of the series "Women and Law" for Gordon and Breach. The first edition was titled "Women and Justice: Development of International Policy." Future editions will include "The African-American Woman and Criminal Justice," "Sexual Harassment: an International Prospective," and "Women Abusing Drugs." She is the coeditor/author of *Visions for Change: Crime and Justice in the Twenty-First Century* (Prentice Hall, 1999), as well as the author of numerous articles, including "Police Work and Juveniles," in *Juvenile Justice Policies, Programs, and Services* (Roberts, Nelson Hall, 1997). Other articles include "Measuring Disparity in the Correctional Institutions," "Mothers and Fetuses: Enter the Fetal Police," and "Directions for the Future." The first edition of this work, *It's a Crime: Women and Justice*, was published by Prentice Hall in 1993.

She received her doctorate in criminal justice from the Graduate Center at the City University of New York, and her Master's degree at New York University. She received her bachelor's degree from Queens College.

Dr. Muraskin's main interests are those of gender disparities within the criminal justice system. She is a frequent lecturer on issues of gender.

Biographies of Contributors

Michele C. Bafuma is currently a doctoral candidate in criminology at Indiana University of Pennsylvania. Her research interests include female criminality and gender issues within the criminal justice system.

Kate Bagley is Professor of Sociology in the Department of Sociology and Social Work at Westfield State College. Previously, she was the Coordinator of the Women's Studies Program at Westfield State College and Chair of the Department of Sociology and Social Work. Professor Bagley's research interests are in sociology of gender, sociology of law, sociology of education, and women and religion.

Barbara Bloom, Ph.D., is a criminal justice consultant and researcher with over 20 years of experience working with local, state, and national criminal justice agencies. She specializes in the development and evaluation of programs serving women and girls under criminal justice supervision and their families. Her publications include: *Why Punish the Children? A Reappraisal of the Children of Incarcerated Mothers in America* and *Female Offenders in the Community: An Analysis of Innovative Strategies and Programs.*

Meda Chesney-Lind, Ph.D., is Professor of Women's Studies at the University of Hawaii at Manoa. She has served as Vice President of the American Society of Criminology and President of the Western Society of Criminology. Nationally recognized for her work on women and crime, her books include *Girls, Delinquency and Juvenile Justice* which was awarded the American Society of Criminology's Michael J. Hindelang Award for the "outstanding contribution to criminology, 1992" and *The Female Offender: Girls, Women and Crime*, published by Sage in 1998.

Joan C. Chrisler, Ph.D., is an Assistant Professor of Psychology at Connecticut College. Her research has focused on various aspects of both women's physical and mental health. She coedited *New Directions in Feminist Psychology: Practice and Research.*

Mona J. E. Danner is Assistant Professor of Sociology and Criminal Justice at Old Dominion University. She earned her Ph.D. in sociology and justice from American University. Her interests are in social control, inequalities (gender, race/ethnicity, class, and nation), and women globally. She is currently engaged in research on gender and the process of negotiating the academic contract in the cross-national investigation of the relationship between gender inequality and criminalization mechanisms in the social control of women. Dr. Danner received the New Scholar Award in 1997 from the Division on Women and Crime of the American Society of Criminology.

Elizabeth Piper Deschenes, Ph.D., is a Professor in the Department of Criminal Justice at California State University, Long Beach. Her research areas include evaluations of juvenile and adult correctional and treatment programs and longitudinal studies of drug addicts, gang members, and violent juveniles. Dr. Dechenes' recent publications include "Alternative Placements for Juvenile Offenders: Results from the Evaluation of the Nokomis Challenge Program" in the *Journal of Research in Crime and Delinquency.* Recently, Dr. Deschenes has been collaborating with Drs. Barbara Bloom, Barbara Owen and Jill Rosenbaum on a study of gender specific studies and needs in juvenile justice in the state of California for the Office of Criminal Justice Planning.

Jeffrey Fagan, Ph.D., is Director for the Center for Violence Research and Prevention at the Columbia School of Public Health and Visiting Professor at the Columbia Law School. His research analyzes the causes, consequences, and control of interpersonal violence. His current research examines the jurisprudence of adolescent crimes, social contagion of violence, situational contexts of adolescent violence, and the deterrence of domestic violence. His recent publications include "Declining Homicide in New York City," in the *Journal of Criminal Law and Criminology*, "Guns, Youth Violence, and Social Identity," in *Crime and Justice: A Review of Research*, and "The Comparative Impacts of Juvenile and Criminal Court Sanctions for Adolescent Felony Offenders, in *Law and Policy*. He is past Editor of the *Journal of Research in Crime and Delinquency.*

Lynette Feder received her Ph.D. from the School of Criminal Justice at State University of New York at Albany in 1989. She has conducted research in the areas of mentally disturbed offenders, discretion and discrimination in the criminal justice system, juvenile delinquency, and domestic violence. She is presently completing a federally funded experiment that tests the efficacy of court-mandated counseling for convicted misdemeanor domestic violence offenders.

Laura T. Fishman, Ph.D., is an Associate Professor of Sociology at the University of Vermont. Her research activities have culminated in the acquisition of streetwise familiarity with crime, drug distribution, and the administration of justice. Her major research interests include the criminalization of African-Americans, drugs, and American society. She has published numerous articles and a book, *Women at the Wall: A Study of Prisoners' Wives Doing Time on the Outside*. Currently, she is working on a manuscript that addresses the reactions of African-American and Latino convicted offenders and their significant women to AIDS, imprisonment, and reentry.

James R. Franz earned his bachelor's degree in psychology at Ohio University and is currently working toward his doctorate in clinical psychology at Wright State University School of Professional Psychology. His clinical interests include the postpartum syndromes and the portrayal of psychologists in popular literature.

Kimberly L. Freiberger received her Master's degree in criminal justice from Virginia Commonwealth University in 1997. She currently is employed as an investigator in the Enforcement Division of the Department of Professional and Occupational Regulation. Her future academic plans include pursuing a Ph.D. in criminal justice.

Evelyn Gilbert is a Visiting Professor in the Criminal Justice Program at the University of North Florida. Her research interests include race and crime, criminal justice education, and homicide.

Sean A. Grennan, Ph.D., is an Associate Professor of Criminal Justice at the C.W. Post Campus of Long Island University, New York. His major areas of research are women in policing, police use of deadly force, and organized crime. Dr. Grennan is a twenty-year veteran of the NYPD and retired with the rank of detective.

Thomas E. Guild, J.D., is a Professor of Business Law at the University of Central Oklahoma. He has taught and conducted research in the areas of constitutional law, privacy rights, sexual harassment, employment law, and the Americans with Disabilities Act. He was recently named the Outstanding Researcher in the University of Central Oklahoma's College of Business Administration.

Zelma Weston Henriques, Ph.D., is a Professor in the Department of Law and Police Science at the John Jay College of Criminal Justice, City University of New York. Her major research interests are: imprisoned mothers and their children; race, class, and gender issues: cross-cultural studies of crime and human rights. She is the author of *Imprisoned Mothers and Their Children: A Descriptive and Analytical Study* published by the University Press of America. Henriques holds a doctorate from Columbia University and was a Rockefeller Research Fellow in Human Rights at Columbia University.

Drew Humpries, Ph.D., is an Associate Professor in the Department of Sociology, Anthropology, and Criminal Justice at Rutgers University. Her book, *Crack Mothers: Pregnancy, Drugs and the Media*, published by Ohio State University Press, addresses maternal drug use in the context of the war on drugs. She has recently coedited "The Media, Crime and Women," a special issue of *Violence against Women*.

Ida M. Johnson, Ph.D., is an Associate Professor in the Department of Criminal Justice at the University of Alabama. She has conducted research studies in the areas of domestic violence, date rape, and female criminality. Her most recent publication is *Forced Sexual Intercourse in Intimate Relationships*.

Ciuinal Jones serves on the staff of Illinois Treatment Alternatives for Safe Communities as well as being the organization's manager for health program services at the Cook County Sheriff's Womens' Furlough Program. She has extensive experience with HIV education and program development.

Janice Joseph, Ph.D., is a Professor of Criminal Justice at the Richard Stockton College of New Jersey. Her research interests include violence against women, women and criminal justice, youth violence, juvenile delinquency, gangs, and minorities and criminal justice. Her major publications include *Black Youths, Delinquency and Juvenile Justice*.

Kimberly Kempf-Leonard, Ph.D., is an Associate Professor of Criminology and Criminal Justice and Research Fellow at the Public Policy Research Centers of the University of Missouri–St. Louis. Her research focuses on measurement of criminal careers, and juvenile and criminal justice policy, particularly on effective and equitable processing. Her coedited volume, *Minorities in Juvenile Justice*, won the 1997 Gustavus Myer's Award for Human Rights in North America.

Arthur J. Lurigio, Ph.D., a social psychologist, is a Professor of Criminal Justice and a member of the Graduate Faculty at Loyola University. He serves as Chairperson of the Department of Criminal Justice at Loyola and is a Research Associate at TASC. Dr. Lurigio was an Assistant Professor of Psychology and Urban Affairs at Northwestern University and a Research Associate at the Center of Urban Affairs and Policy Research. He has spent more than seventeen years working in the probation and court systems in Cook County.

Joan Luxenburg, Ed.D., LCSW, is Professor and Chair of the Sociology and Criminal Justice Department at the University of Central Oklahoma. She has been certified by the Oklahoma State Department of Health as an AIDS Education and HIV Test Site Counselor. She is the former chair of the Sexual Behavior Division of the Society for the Study of Social Problems, as well as an author in the areas of prostitution, HIV assaults on corrections officers, and Oklahoma's gay liberation movement.

Sue Mahan, Ph.D., is the Coordinator of the Criminal Justice Program at the University of Central Florida–Daytona Beach. The chapter included in this work was adapted from "Beyond the Mafia: Organized Crime in the Americas," which she edited for Sage Publishers in 1998. She is the author of three books: *Unfit Mothers, Women, Crime and Criminal Justice* (with Ralph Weisheit), and *Crack, Cocaine, Crime and Women*. She has been a Kellogg International Fellow (1991–1993) and a Fulbright Distinguished Lecturer (1996).

Zina T. McGee, Ph.D., is an Assistant Professor at Hampton University. In 1994 she was awarded a two-year grant to examine patterns of victimization among 200 inner-city high school students in the state of Virginia. In the summer of 1997, Dr. McGee was awarded a grant from the National Institute of Mental Health to examine patterns of victimization, personality dimensions, and coping strategies among African-American adolescents in the state of Virginia. This project is part of the Hampton University Faculty Development Program designed to encourage behavioral science research among faculty at minority institutions. She has five research publications examining violence among youth.

Michelle L. Meloy is a doctoral student at the University of Delaware in the Department of Sociology and Criminal Justice. She received her M.A. degree in sociology from Northern Illinois University. Her research interests include deviance, social control and moral panics, and gender and crime. She has worked as a probation officer supervising both juvenile and adult ofenders and specializing in sex offender supervision.

Alida V. Merlo, Ph.D., is an Associate Professor of Criminology at Indiana University of Pennsylvania. She coedited *Women, Law and Social Control* (1995) with Joycelyn M.

Pollock and *Dilemmas and Directions in Corrections* (1992) with Peter J. Benekos. She served as the First Vice President of the Academy of Criminal Justice Sciences and serves as President as of March 1999.

Cheryl L. Meyer received her Ph.D. in psychology from Miami University (Ohio) and her J.D. from DePaul University. Dr. Meyer is currently on faculty at Wright State University in the School of Professional Psychology. In 1997, she published a book through New York University Press, *The Wandering Uterus: Politics and Reproductive Rights of Women*. Her current research interests include forensic psychology, feminist jurisprudence, and program evaluation.

Susan L. Miller, Ph.D., is an Associate Professor of Sociology and Criminal Justice at the University of Delaware. She has published extensively on gender, crime, and social control issues. Her recent edited book, *Crime Control and Women: Feminist Implications of Criminal Justice Policies*, examines the gender/race/crime nexus and related policy implications. She is currently completing a book that explores the gendered nature of community policing practices.

Etta F. Morgan, M.A., M.S., is currently completing a doctorate degree in interdisciplinary studies with concentrations in criminal justice and women's studies at the University of Alabama. Her research interests include female criminality, gender and racial disparities in the criminal justice system, sentencing reforms, juvenile justice, and capital punishment.

Laura J. Moriarty, Ph.D., is an Associate Professor, Department of Criminal Justice and Assistant Dean, College of Humanities and Sciences at Virginia Commonwealth University. Her primary research interests include victimology, fear of crime, and violence crime. She is the coauthor of the victimology textbook, *Victims of Crime* (with Robert A. Jerin, Nelson-Hall, 1998). In addition, she is the author or coauthor of over 25 research articles and scholarly book chapters.

Tara C. Proano is a doctoral student in clinical psychology at the Wright State University, School of Professional Psychology. She received a bachelor's degree from the University of Michigan.

Christine E. Rasche, Ph.D., is Associate Professor of Criminal Justice and Sociology at the University of North Florida, Jacksonville, Florida, where she also serves as the Director of the Graduate Program in Criminal Justice. She is the immediate Past Chairperson of the Division on Women and Crime, American Society of Criminology. She specializes in the study of women and homicide, women and domestic violence, and women in prison. Among her publications, she has authored a training curriculum for correctional officers on "The Special Needs of the Female Offender," and has served as a consultant to the National Institute of Corrections and several states on developing specialized training in this area.

Jill Leslie Rosenbaum is Professor of Criminal Justice at California State University, Fullerton. Her research interests include gender differences in adolescent behavior, women and crime, and juvenile justice. She has been working with the California Office of Criminal Justice Planning to transition their Sexual Assault and Domestic Violence Programs to Outcomes-Based Accountability.

Inger Sagatun-Edwards, Ph.D., is a Professor and Chair of the Administration of Justice Department at San Jose State University, California. She has served on the board of the Women and Crime section of the American Society of Criminology and the Western Society of Criminology. She is the coauthor with Leonard P. Edwards of *Child Abuse and the Legal System*, and the author of many journal articles and research reports. She has been the Project Director and Co-Director on several large research grants supported by the Office of Juvenile Justice and Delinquency Prevention. She is currently the Project Director for a three-year Collaborative Model Agency Intervention Grant for Substance Abusing Mothers and Their Children. She was awarded a Senior Scholar Fulbright grant to Norway in 1999 to study Norwegian law and court practices in the area of child and fetal abuse.

Robert T. Sigler, Ph.D., is a Professor in the Department of Criminal Justice at the University of Alabama. His research interests include domestic violence, courtship and dating violence, stress in criminal justice employees, and constitutional issues in corrections.

James A. Swartz, Ph.D., received his doctorate in clinical psychology from the Medical School at Northwestern University and holds a Master's degree in behavioral research from Loyola University, Chicago. For the past ten years he has conducted both evaluation studies of drug treatment programs and large-scale surveys of drug treatment programs and large-scale surveys of criminal justice clients. He is presently the Director of Research and Information Services at Illinois Treatment Alternatives for Safe Communities.

Paul E. Tracy is Professor of Sociology and Political Economy at the University of Texas–Dallas and served as former Director of Graduate Studies at the Sellin Center for Studies in Criminology and Criminal Law at the Wharton School of the University of Pennsylvania and at the Graduate School of Criminal Justice at Northeastern University. He coauthored with Dr. Kempf-Leonard, *Continuity and Discontinuity in Criminal Careers: The Transition from Juvenile Delinquency to Adult Crime*.

Nanci Koser Wilson, Ph.D., is Professor of Criminology at Indiana University of Pennsylvania, where she is also a member of the Women's Studies Faculty. She pioneered the study of Women and Crime, teaching one of the first courses in this area at Southern Illinois University. She is the cofounder of the Division on Women and Crime, American Society of Criminology. She has published on women as victims, as offenders, and as workers in the criminal justice system, as well as the teaching of Feminist Criminology.

TEXAS A&M UNIVERSITY LIBRARY